CRITICAL SURVEY OF
MYTHOLOGY AND FOLKLORE

World Mythology

CRITICAL SURVEY OF
MYTHOLOGY AND FOLKLORE

World Mythology

SALEM PRESS
A Division of EBSCO Information Services
Ipswich, Massachusetts

GREY HOUSE PUBLISHING

Publisher's Cataloging-In-Publication Data
(Prepared by The Donohue Group, Inc.)

Critical survey of mythology and folklore. World mythology / [edited by
  Salem Press]. -- [1st ed.].

    p. : ill., maps ; cm. -- (Critical survey of mythology and folklore ; [3])

  A collection of 213 essays on traditional literature from a broad range of regions and cultures in the world.
  Includes bibliographical references and index.
  ISBN: 978-1-61925-182-3

  1. Mythology. I. Salem Press. II. Title: World mythology III. Series: Critical survey of mythology and folklore ; [3].

BL312 .C75 2013
398.2

ebook ISBN: 978-1-61925-187-8

CONTENTS

ASIA

EUROPE

◆

APPENDIXES

INDEXES

PUBLISHER'S NOTE

Critical Survey of World Mythology and Folklore: World Mythology, by Salem Press, covers traditional literature from a broad range of regions and cultures in the world. This volume is distinguished by contemporary perspectives on the cultural contexts from which mythology and folklore originate, as well as by a balance between familiar and, for many readers, rarely read literature. In a period where cross-cultural understanding is particularly resonant, our aim is to provide students and their teachers with an advanced analysis of stories that continue to hold rich cultural meaning for peoples around the world.

This volume contains many kinds of texts that represent myth, fairy tales, folklore, oral tales, and a hybrid of genres in traditional literature. Rather than simply categories of myth and folklore, this collection offers an in-depth exploration of the diversity of storytelling that encompasses a broad realm of human experience, cultural belief, and religion. Readers will note common subjects in tales from widely divergent regions in the world. Creation, love and loss, adventure and bravery, and cultural heroes, readers will find, are important motifs in tales across cultures and periods.

The aim of this collection is to further the study of traditional literature in cultural and literary analysis. Designed for advanced high school and college students, essays emphasize the major approaches to analyzing mythology and folklore, including such commonly studied topics as gender, cross-cultural meaning, and religion, among other areas of contemporary interest. New readings of major authors in mythology and folklore are represented, from Homer and Ovid to the Brothers Grimm and Andrew Lang. In addition, tales from American Indian, African, Oceanic, and East Asian traditions, among other world cultures, are included. The editors' goal was to provide an inclusive collection that would serve as an authoritative introduction to traditional world literature.

ESSAY AND VOLUME FORMAT

The collection includes 213 essays, covering more than ten world regions and twenty-five cultures. The top matter of each essay includes reference information on the author (when available), the country or culture of origin, the period in which the myth or tale originates, and the genre. Following a standard format, critical essays provide a condensed version of the story, introducing principle characters and actions, developed from authoritative sources. These condensed myths and tales will prepare readers to go on to read the primary sources in their entirety. Following the overview is an in-depth analysis grounded in the leading scholarship in the field. Each essay, of approximately one thousand to fifteen hundred words, offers a bibliography of additional readings for further research.

SUPPLEMENTAL FEATURES

- "Maps and Mythological Figures" presents twelve maps and charts detailing the cultural or geographic placement of many of the deities, authors, and tales in the volume.
- "Mythology in the Classroom" explains major approaches to studying mythology and fairy tales.
- A sample lesson plan, on creation stories, accompanies the essay on teaching mythology in the classroom. The aim is to provide one model for comparative analysis.
- A time line lists major authors, publications, and events related to mythology and traditional literature.
- A chronological index of titles and a culture and country index offer supplemental information on the overall coverage of the volume.

CONTRIBUTORS

Salem Press would like to extend its appreciation to all involved in the development and production of this work. The essays are written and signed by scholars and writers in a variety of disciplines in the humanities. Without these expert contributions, a project of this nature would not be possible. A full list of contributor's names and affiliations appears in the front matter of this volume.

INTRODUCTION

The word *myth* is derived from the Greek work *mythos*, meaning "speech" and "discourse," and then evolved to mean "legend" or "fable." Myth's closest relation is "fairy tale," a more literary derivation of the storytelling tradition established by seventeenth-century French luminaries such as Charles Perrault and Marie-Catherine d'Aulnoy. Myths and fairy tales mark a fine line between the dream, legend, and religion. Gods, spirits, and fantastical creatures characterize every cultural tradition, from Greek to Maya, Norse to American Indian. For contemporary readers, these tales inhabit a territory of the unbelievable, beyond everyday sense and meaning that may be outside our belief systems today, but nonetheless provide a line of meaning between the past and the present that is as culturally rich as the great literature of our period.

This collection surveys a broad range of traditional literature from major regions in the world, drawing from the great myths of the Western tradition, while revisiting tales from cultures that remain underrepresented in collections of this kind. The design is meant to emphasize a universal story told by myth and folklore, represented by four great narratives that encompass all geographies and periods: cosmic myths, hero tales, quest stories, and narratives of death and the underworld. So many of these tales capture each of these realms, human beginnings woven with a hero's story and the mystery of death. Cosmic myths explore the beginnings of the human and natural world. Every culture recounts the story of the hero, who holds the extraordinary vision and bravery required to combat the mysterious forces of the cosmic and natural world. Closely related to these stories, then, is a quest journey in search of either an object or a place. The quest may also be a story of spiritual and psychic transformation. If the cosmic mythis concerned with the celestial world, its opposite holds as important a place in ancient storytelling. The descent into the underworld is often in search of a loved one (a story of resurrection) or knowledge of what lies beyond the rational and living.

The term *mythology* also represents an area of academic study, a field that is concerned with cultural understanding based on storytelling, ritual, and religious tradition. In the study of cross-cultural meaning—inquiry into the belief system of another culture, particularly in relation to one's own values and beliefs—metaphor is as important as the facts of a given culture. We hope that this collection, as a whole, will emphasize the rich history of storytelling while offering insight into the significance of cultural traditions in the world. To be sure, the geographical organization of tales may belie the heterogeneity of the subject matter in each chapter. Within the geography of the Americas, for example, the grouping of Mesoamerican and South American myths represents as broad a juxtaposition as Egyptian mythology and Yoruba folklore in Africa. Nonetheless, readers will appreciate how each region, while not defined by any one cultural tradition, reveals a great mythic history.

Who are the sources for these myths? Or, who first told them? The question regarding the origin of myth is as complex as the diversity of cultures and periods from which they emerged. We understand that oral tradition, which is often joined with ceremony and performance, is based upon storytelling. These cultures explored the mysteries of the world—such as how to explain the stars, the change in the seasons, or the nature of death. Told by shamans or priests, these stories, songs, and ceremonies, retold and performed over generations, established a communal mind, a collective authorship by the community. The transmission of stories to readers reveals a far more complicated journey, often through the work of many hands inside and outside of the communities of origin. In the American Indian oral tradition, for example, the spiritual and mythological storytelling of a community served as a way of knowing a culture in the work of the anthropologist, who documented these stories in written form beginning as early as the seventeenth century. The authority of myth and folklore may serve as a rich source of truth about a community, while the questions of origin remain steeped in a complicated history of translation.

Poems from Sumerian mythology are well known, yet authorship represents an alternative history. The *Epic of Gilgameš*, the most well known of Sumerian myths, tells of the historical king of Uruk, whose story is compiled on multiple clay tablets. The closest we know of authorship is the work of an ancient editor, Sîn-Leqi-Unninni, believed to have compiled the poem sometime in the seventh century BCE. Although the *Prose Edda*, one of the major published collections of Old Norse mythology, was first transmitted through oral tradition, its authorship is attributed to a thirteenth-century historian by the name of Snorri Sturluson. The great Greek poets were among the earliest and most widely read chroniclers of mythology to be attributed authorship. The poet Homer is nearly as mythic as his iconic heroes Odysseus and Achilles. While Homer may be the most famous of classical storytellers, uncertainly continues to surround the authorship of the *Odyssey* and the *Iliad*. Ovid, in his *Metamorphosis*, follows Homer in the upper realm of the great Western poets, as his "retellings" of Greek mythology represent one of the major literatures of the genre. Homer and Ovid are recognized as the first great mythmakers to mine the cultural history of their eras.

A broad collection of this kind is necessarily based on subjective choices of tales, themes, and national literatures. American Indian folklore comprises hundreds of tribal cultures and traditions. The same can be said of the heterogeneity of literature in Eastern Europe, East Asia, Africa, and Oceania. This book does not pretend to present a comprehensive coverage of world mythology and folklore. Nor is the distinction between myth and folklore strictly defined within any given chapter. At best, offering more than two hundred tales, this volume attempts to be inclusive of the mythological character of many major regions across the world.

CONTRIBUTORS

Michael P. Auerbach, MA
Marblehead, Massachusetts

Adam Berger, PhD
New York, New York

Haley Blum, MA
University of Massachusetts, Amherst

Pegge Bochynski, MA
Beverly, Massachusetts

Patrick G. Cooper
Orlando, Florida

Sally Driscoll, MLS
State College, Pennsylvania

Jack Ewing
Boise, Idaho

T. Fleischmann, MFA
Dowelltown, Tennessee

Ashleigh Imus, PhD
Ithaca, New York

Micah Issitt
Philadelphia, Pennsylvania

Judy Johnson, MLS, MTS
Clark State Community College

Mark S. Joy, PhD
Jamestown College

R. C. Lutz, PhD
Bucharest, Romania

G. Matthews, MA
Washington State University, Pullman

John Pritchard
Burlington, Vermont

Theresa L. Stowell, PhD
Siena Heights University

MAPS AND MYTHOLOGICAL FIGURES

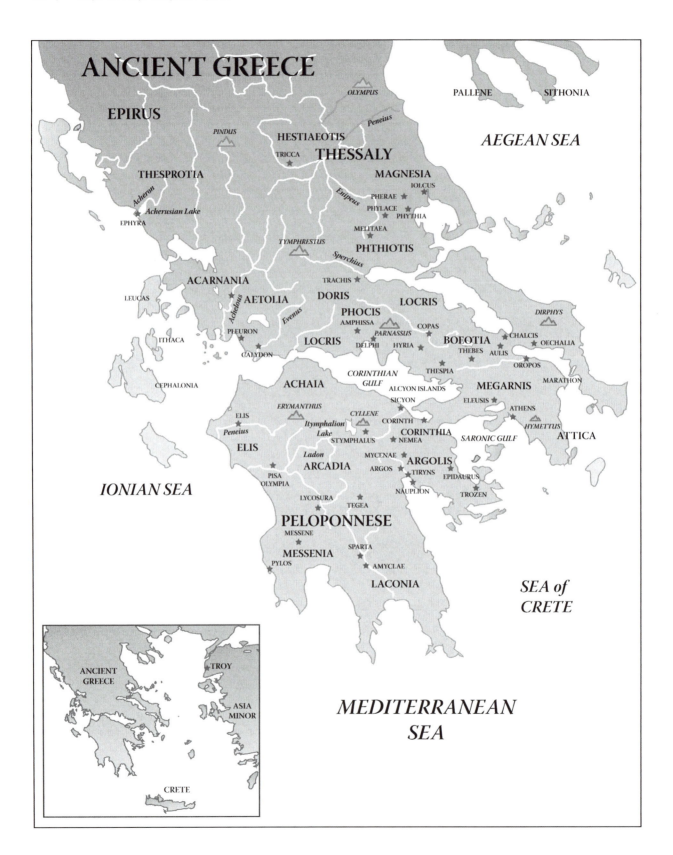

ANCIENT GREECE

EPIRUS

OLYMPUS

PALLENE   SITHONIA

PINDUS

Peneius

HESTIAEOTIS

AEGEAN SEA

THESPROTIA

TRICCA

THESSALY

MAGNESIA

Acheron

IOLCUS

Acherusian Lake

PHERAE

EPHYRA

Enipeus

PHYLACE

PHYTHIA

MELITAEA

TYMPHRESTUS

PHTHIOTIS

Sperchius

ACARNANIA

TRACHIS

LEUCAS

DORIS

LOCRIS

DIRPHYS

AETOLIA

Achelous

Evenus

PHOCIS

AMPHISSA

PARNASSUS

COPAS

CHALCIS

OECHALIA

ITHACA

PLEURON

LOCRIS

DELPHI

HYRIA

BOEOTIA

THEBES

AULIS

CALYDON

THESPIA

OROPOS

CEPHALONIA

CORINTHIAN
GULF

ACHAIA

ALCYON ISLANDS

MEGARNIS

MARATHON

ERYMANTHUS

SICYON

ELEUSIS

ELIS

CYLLENE

CORINTH

ATHENS

Peneius

Itymphalion
Lake

STYMPHALUS

CORINTHIA

HYMETTUS

ELIS

Ladon

NEMEA

SARONIC GULF

ATTICA

ARCADIA

MYCENAE

ARGOLIS

PISA

ARGOS

TIRYNS

EPIDAURUS

OLYMPIA

LYCOSURA

NAUPLION

TROZEN

TEGEA

IONIAN SEA

PELOPONNESE

MESSENE

MESSENIA

SPARTA

PYLOS

AMYCLAE

LACONIA

SEA of
CRETE

ANCIENT
GREECE

TROY

ASIA
MINOR

MEDITERRANEAN
SEA

CRETE

GREEK MYTHOLOGICAL FIGURES

The Major Titans	Cult of the Twelve Olympians	Bestiary of Ancient Greece
Koios (Coeus) Northern cosmic pillar holding heaven and earth apart **Krios (Crius)** Southern cosmic pillar **Kronos (Cronus)** God of time and the ages **Hyperion** Eastern cosmic pillar **Iapetos (Iapetus)** Western cosmic pillar and titan of mortal life **Mnemosyne** Goddess of memory, words, and language **Okeanos (Oceanus)** A primeval deity of the earth-encircling river **Phoibe (Phoebe)** Goddess of intellect **Rhea** Goddess of female fertility **Tethys** Mother of the rivers and springs **Theia** Mother of sun, moon, and dawn **Themis** Goddess of natural order and divine law	**Aphroditê (Aphrodite)** Goddess of beauty, love, procreation **Apollôn (Apollo)** God of prophecy and oracles, music, and healing **Arês (Ares)** God of war, battle, and manly courage **Artemis** Goddess of hunting, wilderness, and animals **Athênê (Athena)** Goddess of wise counsel, war, and heroism **Dêmêtêr (Demeter)** Goddess of agriculture, grain, and bread **Dionysos (Dionysus)** God of wine, vegetation, and pleasure **Hêphaistos (Hephaestus)** God of fire, metalworking, and sculpture **Hêrê (Hera)** Goddess of women and marriage **Hermês (Hermes)** God of animal husbandry, travel, language, and writing **Poseidôn (Poseidon)** God of the sea, rivers, flood, and drought **Zeus** God of sky and weather, justice, and fate	**Khimaira (Chimera)** A fire-breathing monster slain by Bellerophon astride the winged horse Pegasus **Drakôn Kolkhikos (Colchian Dragon)** Guard of the Golden Fleece; slain by Jason **Kêtos Aithiopios (Ethiopian Cetus)** A sea monster slain by Perseus **Grypes (Griffins)** Lions with the head and wings of eagles **Harpyia (Harpies)** Directed by Zeus to steal away people from earth **Hydra Lernaia (Lernaea)** A nine-headed water serpent slain by Hercules **Drakôn Ismenios (Ismenian Dragon)** A giant serpent slain by Cadmus **Drakôn Ladôn (Ladon)** A hundred-headed dragon slain by Heracles **Drakôn Pterôtoi (Winged Dragons)** Two winged serpents used by Medea to escape Corinth **Pythôn (Python)** A giant serpent slain by Apollo **Seirênes (Sirens)** Three sea nymphs who sang to lure sailors to drown

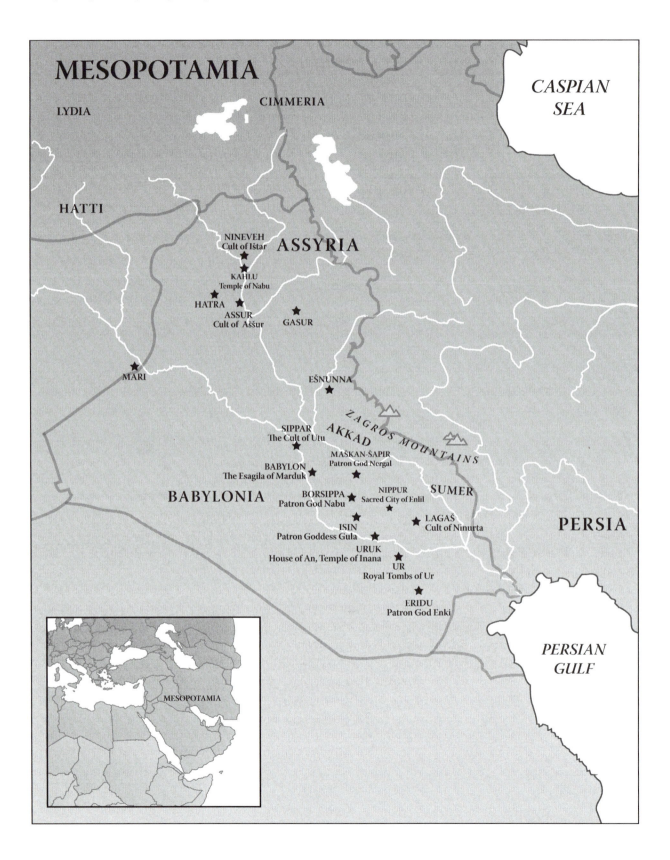

MESOPOTAMIAN MYTHOLOGICAL FIGURES

Sumerian ca. 3500 BCE–2000 BCE The settlement of temple towns in honor of the gods and goddesses; the height of Sumerian civilization	Babylonian and Assyrian Babylonian (ca. 2000 BCE–500 BCE) and Assyrian (ca. 2400 BCE–600 BCE) periods	Demigods, Heroes, and Kings
An Sun and heaven god	**Adad** God of storms	**Alulim** First king of Eridu
Ašnan (Ashnan) Goddess of grain fields	**Anšar (Anshar) and Kišar (Kishar)** Primordial gods	**Apkallu** Seven sages
Dumuzid Food and vegetation god	**Anu** God of the sky	**Ašur (Ashur)** God of all Assyria
Enki Water, creation, and fertility god	**Apsû** God of the underworld	**Atra-hasīs** Boat builder of Great Flood myth
Enlil Rain, wind, and air god	**Aruru** Mother goddess	**Bel** Sage of the gods
Ereškigala (Ereshkigal) Goddess of the underworld	**Dagan** God of grain and fertility	**Dumuzid** Shepherd king; fertility god
Inana Goddess of sexuality, fertility, and warfare	**Ea** God of wisdom, waters, crafts, and magic	**Enkidu** Natural man, lord of the forests and wildlife
Ki Earth goddess; consort of An	**Ellil** God of earth and wind	**Ĝeštinana (Geshtinanna)** Goddess of wine; sister of Dumuzid
Lahar Goddess of cattle	**Ereškigala (Ereshkigal) and Nergal** Goddess and god of the underworld	**Gilgameš (Gilgamesh)** Demigod; King of Uruk
Namma Primeval sea; birth to An and Ki	**Gula** Goddess of healing	**Gudgalanna (Gugalanna)** The bull of heaven
Nanna or Nanna-Suen God of the moon	**Ištar (Ishtar)** Goddess of love, procreation, and war	**Huwawa** God of the cedar forest
Ninĝišzida (Ningishzida) God of vegetation, underworld, and innkeepers	**Mammu** God of mist and craft	**Lamaštu (Lamashtu)** Demoness; slayer of infants and children
Ninhursaĝa (Ninhursag) Mother goddess	**Marduk** God of magic	**Lugalbanda** Father of Gilgameš; warrior king
Ninlil Healing and mother goddess; consort of Enlil	**Nabû** God of wisdom and writing	**Namtar** God of death
Ninurta God of war and agriculture	**Nintinuga** Goddess of healing	**Ninsun** Goddess and mother to Gilgameš
Sumugan God of the plains	**Nuska** God of light and fire	**Pazuzu** King of the demons of the wind
Utu God of the sun	**Šamaš (Shamash)** Sun god	
	Sîn God of moon; son of Enlil	
	Tammuz Demigod of vegetation	
	Tiāmat Primeval sea	
	Zaltu Goddess of strife	

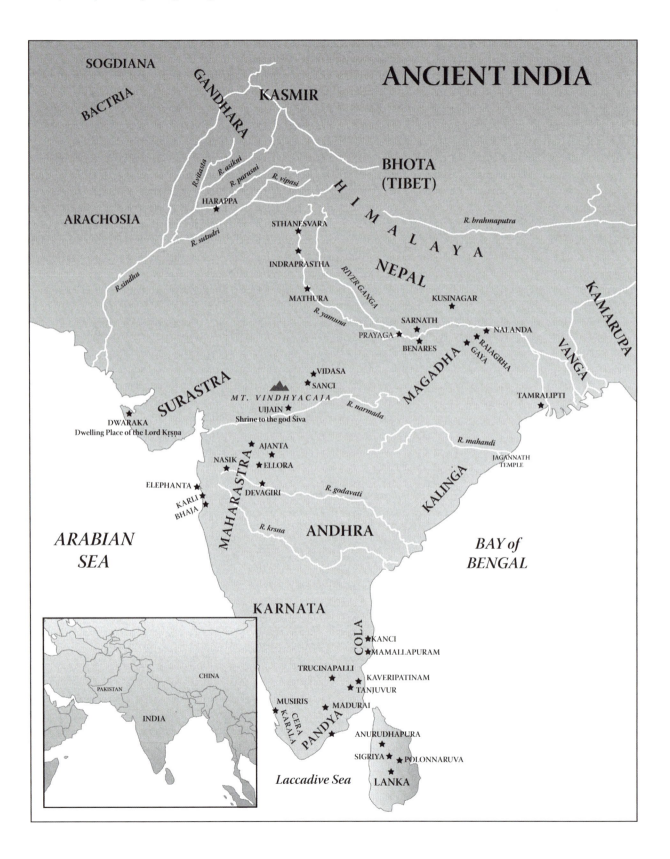

HINDU MYTHOLOGICAL FIGURES

Vedic Deities ca. 1500 BCE–300 BCE The *Rig Veda, Sāma Veda, Yajur Veda,* and *Atharva Veda*	Puranic Deities ca. 300 BCE–1000 CE Brahmā, Viṣṇu, and Śiva texts	Avatars of Viṣṇu (Vishnu) The divine descent of Viṣṇu, in order of incarnation
Aditi Mother of many of the gods	**Brahmā** Supreme being or creator	**Matsya** The great fish
Agni God of earth	**Durgā** Warrior goddess	**Kurma** The tortoise
Brahmā The creator, preserver (Viṣṇu), and destroyer (Śiva)	**Gaṇeśa (Ganesh)** God of prudence and policy; the elephant-headed god	**Varāha** The wild boar
Dyauṣ pitā God of the sky	**Lakṣmī (Lakshmi)** Goddess of love, beauty, and prosperity	**Narasimha** The man-lion
Indra God of the air	**Kālī** Goddess of time and change; the black one	**Vāmana** The dwarf
Karṇa God of love and desire	**Kāma or Kāmadeva** God of love and desire	**Paraśurāma (Parashurama)** Rāma with axe
Pṛthvī (Prithivi) Goddess of earth	**Kārttikeya** God of war	**Rāma** Hero of the Rāmāyaṇa
Pūṣaṇ (Pushan) God of meeting	**Hanumān** The monkey god	**Kṛṣṇa (Krishna)** The adorable one
Mitra and Varuṇa Rulers of day and night	**Pārvatī** Consort of Śiva; reincarnation of Satī	**Buddha** The enlightened one
Sarasvatī Goddess of the river	**Sarasvatī** Goddess of wisdom and science; mother of the Vedas	**Kalki** Destroyer of time; avatar yet to come
Skanda or Kārttikeya God of war	**Satī** Consort of Śiva; reincarnated as Pārvatī	
Soma God of intoxicating juice (soma plant); god of the moon	**Śiva (Shiva)** The destroyer	
Sūrya God of the sun	**Tvaṣṭr (Tvastar)** God of a thousand arts	
Uṣas (Ushas) Goddess of the dawn	**Varuṇa** God of the ocean	
Vāyu God of the winds	**Viṣṇu (Vishnu)** The preserver of cosmic order	
Viśvakarmā (Vishvakarma) Architect and workman of the gods	**Yama** Judge of men; king of the unseen world	
Yama God of the infernal regions		

WESTERN EUROPE

NORWAY
Peter Christen Asbjørnsen
Jørgen Engebretsen Moe

SWEDEN

DENMARK
Hans Christian Andersen

NORTH SEA

IRELAND
Samuel Lover
Patrick Kennedy

POLAND

ENGLAND
Andrew Lang
Edgar Taylor
Joseph Jacob

NETHERLANDS

GERMANY
Johann Karl August Musaus
Jacob and Wilhelm Grimm
Benedikte Naubert

BELGIUM

English Channel

LUXEMBOURG

CZECH
REPUBLIC

FRANCE
Charles Perrault
Catherine Bernard
Madame Le Prince de Beaumont
Madame d'Aulnoy

AUSTRIA

SWITZERLAND

BAY of
BISCAY

SLOVENIA

ITALY
Giuseppe Pitrè
Laura Gonzenbach
Domenico Comparetti

Adriatic
Sea

Mediterranean
Sea

THE GREAT FOLKLORISTS OF EUROPE

The term *fairy tale,* first coined by Marie-Catherine d'Aulnoy in France in 1697, describes a genre of traditional literature that emerged in various cultures throughout the world. This list presents a selection of major authors and publications of fairy tales in Western Europe that have shaped the cultural imagination of authors and readers for generations.

Charles Perrault (1628–1703; France)
- *Histoires ou contes du temps passé* (*Stories or Tales from Times Past*, 1697)
- First publication of "Le petit chaperon rouge" ("Little Red Riding Hood")

Marie-Catherine d'Aulnoy (1650–1705; France)
- *"L'île de la félicité"* ("The Isle of Happiness," 1690)
- Introduces the term *conte de fées*, or "fairy tale," in 1697

Catherine Bernard (1662–1712; France)
- *Inès de Cordoue* (*Inez of Cordoue*, 1696)

Gabrielle-Suzanne de Villeneuve (ca. 1695–1755; France)
- First publication of "La belle et la bête" ("Beauty and the Beast," 1740)

Jeanne-Marie Le Prince de Beaumont (1711–1780; France)
- "La belle et la bête" ("Beauty and the Beast," 1756)

Johann Karl August Musäus (1735–1787; Germany)
- *Volksmärchen der Deutschen* (*Fairy Tales of the Germans*, 1782–1786)

Benedikte Naubert (1752–1819; Germany)
- *Neue Volksmärchen der Deutschen* (*New Fairy Tales of the Germans*, 1789)

Karoline Stahl (1776–1837; Germany)
- *Fabeln, Mährchen und Erzählungen für Kinder* (*Fables, Tales and Stories for Children*, 1818)

Jacob Grimm (1785–1863; Germany) and **Wilhelm Grimm** (1786–1859; Germany)
- *Kinder- und Hausmärchen* (*Children's and House-hold Tales*, 1812)
- *Deutsche Mythologie* (*German Mythology*, 1835)

Edgar Taylor (1793–1839; England)
- *German Popular Tales* (1823), first English translation of Brothers Grimm

Thomas Crofton Croker (1798–1854; England)
- *Fairy Legends and Traditions of the South of Ireland* (1825)

Hans Christian Andersen (1805–1875; Denmark)
- *Eventyr fortalte for børn* (*Fairy Tales Told for Children*, 1835)

Samuel Lover (1797–1868; Ireland)
- *Legends and Stories of Ireland* (1837)

Peter Christen Asbjørnsen (1812–1885; Norway) and **Jørgen Engebretsen Moe** (1813–1882; Norway)
- *Norske folkeeventyr* (*Norwegian Folktales*, 1842)

Svend Hersleb Grundtvig (1824–1883; Denmark)
- *Gamle danske minder i folkmunde* (*Danish Popular Tales*, 1854)

Laura Gonzenbach (1842–1878; Italy)
- *Sicilianische Märchen* (*Sicilian Fairy Tales*, 1870)

Patrick Kennedy (1801–1873; Ireland)
- *Fireside Stories of Ireland* (1870)

Giuseppe Pitrè (1841–1916; Italy)
- *Biblioteca delle tradizioni popolari siciliane* (*Library of Sicilian Popular Traditions*, 1871)
- *Fiabe, novelle e racconti popolari siciliani* (*Sicilian Fairy Tales, Stories, and Folktales*, 1875)

Domenico Comparetti (1835–1927; Italy)
- *Novelline popolari italiene* (*Italian Popular Tales*, 1875)

Charles Deulin (1827–1877; France)
- *Les contes de ma Mère l'Oye avant Perrault* (*The Tales of Mother Goose from Before Perrault*, 1879)

Andrew Lang (1844–1912; Scotland)
- English translation of "Beauty and the Beast" (1889)

George McDonald (1824–1905; Scotland)
- *Dealings with the Fairies* (1867)

Joseph Jacobs (1854–1916; England)
- *English Fairy Tales* (1890)
- Revision of "Beauty and the Beast" (1916)

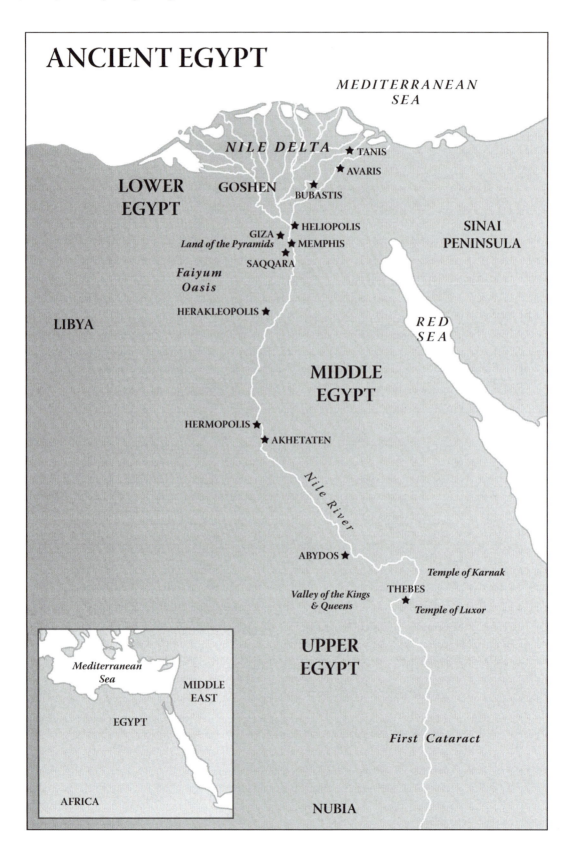

ANCIENT EGYPT

MEDITERRANEAN SEA

NILE DELTA

★ TANIS

★ AVARIS

LOWER EGYPT

GOSHEN

★ BUBASTIS

★ HELIOPOLIS

GIZA ★

Land of the Pyramids

★ MEMPHIS

★ SAQQARA

Faiyum Oasis

HERAKLEOPOLIS ★

LIBYA

SINAI PENINSULA

RED SEA

MIDDLE EGYPT

HERMOPOLIS ★

★ AKHETATEN

Nile River

ABYDOS ★

Temple of Karnak

Valley of the Kings & Queens

THEBES ★

Temple of Luxor

UPPER EGYPT

First Cataract

Mediterranean Sea

MIDDLE EAST

EGYPT

AFRICA

NUBIA

EGYPTIAN MYTHOLOGICAL FIGURES

Aker
God of the earth; protector of the eastern and western horizons

Amen (Amun or Amon)
Supreme god of all gods; primeval deity

Amen-Ra (Amun-Ra or Amon-Ra)
Chief among the gods

Anubis
God of funerals and embalming, depicted with a hound's head; anointer of the dead

Aten (Aton)
Solar creator deity worshipped monotheistically under Amenhotep IV (Akhenaten); represented by a disk

Atum (Tem)
God of the sun and creator of the universe; father of twins Shu and Tefnut

Bastet (Bast)
Goddess of cats, pregnant women, music, dance, and prosperity; depicted as a cat-headed woman

Geb and Nut
God of the earth and goddess of the sky; sibling spouses who bear Isis, Osiris, Nephthys, and Set

Hapi
God of the Nile, flooding, and fertility

Hathor
Goddess of sexual love, dancing and music, and destruction; depicted as a cow; a symbolic mother of the pharaoh

Horus
God of the sky; depicted as a falcon-headed man; son of Osiris and Isis

Isis
Goddess of motherhood and great magic; sister-wife of Osiris; a symbolic mother of the pharaoh

Khonsu
God of the moon; sometimes depicted with head of a hawk

Mut
Goddess of Thebes; wife of Amen; a symbolic mother of the pharaoh

Nephthys
Funerary goddess; sister-wife of Set

Nun
Primeval waters from which Atum emerged

Osiris
God of the dead and ruler of the underworld; brother-husband of Isis; depicted as a mummy with white crown

Ra (Re)
God of the sun and lord of all gods; depicted with the head of a falcon

Set (Seth)
God of chaos and violence; brother-husband of Nephthys

Shu
Primeval god of sunlight and dry air

Sobek
God of pharaonic power; depicted as a crocodile or part-crocodile

Tefnut
Primeval goddess of moisture; sister and consort of Shu

Thoth
God of knowledge and writing, magic, and the moon; provider of mathematics, medicine, and astronomy

EAST ASIAN MYTHOLOGICAL FIGURES

Ba Xian (Pa Hsien): The Eight Immortals of Daoism (Taoism)	Major Shintō Spirits
Cao Guojiu (Ts'ao Kuo-chiu) Associated with a tablet of admission to the court of the Song dynasty **Han Xiang (Han Hsiang-tzu)** Associated with the peaches of immortality; said to make flowers grow and bloom at will **He Xiangu (Ho Hsien-ku)** A beautiful maiden depicted with the magic lotus blossom in hand; patron of unmarried women **Lan Caihe (Lan Ts'ai-ho)** The wandering singer associated with the flute and cymbals; patron of the poor **Li Tieguai (Li T'ieh-kuai)** Associated with the crutch and medicine gourd; patron of pharmacies **Lu Dongbin (Lü Tung-pin)** Possesses a magic sword; able to fly and walk on clouds; associated with the elixir of life **Zhang Guolao (Chang Kuo-lao)** An old man usually astride a white mule and associated with matrimonial happiness **Zhongli Quan (Chung-li Ch'üan)** Associated with a fan of feathers or palm fronds; the messenger of heaven	**Amaterasu** Kami of sun; ruler of heaven **Ame no Uzume** Dancing goddess of the dawn and laughter; patron of drama and performance **Fūjin** Kami of wind **Hachiman** God of war and peace, culture, and divination; protector of children **Inari/Inara** Kami of rice, prosperity, and fertility; associated with foxes; shown as both male (Inari) and female (Inara) **Izanagi and Izanami** Primordial sibling spouses who created the earth **Kaze no Kami** Kami of wind **Ninigi** Kami of rice and plenty **Raijin** Kami of thunder **Ryūjin (Ryūō)** Sea kami or dragon king who lives in Ryugu and controls the tides with tide jewels **Suijin** A water spirit **Susanoo (Susano-Wo)** Kami of storms who captures the eight-headed, eight-tailed dragon Koshi **Tenjin** Kami of learning and calligraphy who aids those learning difficult lessons **Toyotamabime** Daughter of the sea kami Ryūjin (or Wata-tsumi) who becomes a sea monster **Tsukuyomi (Tsuki-Yomi)** Kami of the moon and night

CENTRAL AND SOUTH AMERICA

Gulf of Mexico

CHICHÉN ITZÁ

TENOCHTITLÁN

ATLANTIC OCEAN

CENTRAL AMERICA

Caribbean Sea

PACIFIC OCEAN

Amazon River

SOUTH AMERICA

MACHU PICCHU
CUZCO

CIVILIZATIONS

1   TOLTEC 900–1200 CE AND AZTEC 1325–1521 CE

2   TEOTIHUACÁN 100 BCE–750 CE

3   OLMEC 1200–100 BCE

4   MAYA 100–1542 CE

5   ZAPOTEC AND MIXTEC 300–1524 CE

6   CHIBCHA 1200–1538 CE

7   MOCHICA 100–1000 CE AND CHIMÚ 1000–1471 CE

8   CHAVÍN 1000–500 BCE

9   TIAHUANACO 600–1000 CE

10   INCA 1200–1535 CE

CENTRAL AND SOUTH AMERICAN MYTHOLOGICAL FIGURES

Aztec Gods	Maya Gods	Inca Gods
Chalchihuitlicue (Chalchiuhtlicue) Goddess of freshwater and storms; protector of infants and women giving birth **Chicomecóatl** Goddess of mature corn **Coatlicue** Goddess of the earth; mother of Huitzilopochtli **Huitzilopochtli (Uitzilopochtli)** God of sun and war; depicted as a bird **Mictlantecuhtli** God of the dead and ruler of the underworld **Quetzalcóatl** God of Venus, the sky, wind, agriculture and fertility, and writing; patron god of priests and rulers; depicted as a feathered serpent **Tezcatlipoca** Supreme god of sun and darkness, north and cold, war and death, fortune and misfortune; sees the future with his smoking mirror; brother of Quetzalcóatl **Tlaloc** God of rain, mountains, and fertility; depicted with huge fangs **Xipe Totec** God of the springtime, vegetation, and regeneration; patron of metalworkers **Xolotl** God of bad luck, illness, lightning, and twins; protector of the night; depicted as a deformed dog	**Ah Puch (or Hun Came and Vucub Came)** Ruler of the lowest underworld realm; depicted as a skeleton or decaying body **Bacabs** Four gods who support the skies at the four points of the compass **Chac (Chaac)** God of rain, thunder, and lightning and of fertility; discoverer and provider of corn **Itzámna** God of the sky and sun; granter of writing, religion, and medicine **Kinich Ahau** God of sun and fire by day; jaguar ruler of Xibalba, the underworld, by night **Pauahtun** Four-part god who holds up the sky at the four points of the compass; god of thunder and lightning	**Apo (Apu)** God of the mountains **Illapa (Ilyap'a)** God of storms, thunder, and lightning **Inti (or Apu-punchau)** God of the sun, vegetation, and growth; face depicted with emanating golden disks and rays **Mama Cocha (Mama Qoca)** Sea mother goddess **Mama Quilla (Mama Kilya)** Goddess of the moon; sister-consort of Inti; face depicted as a silver disk **Pachamama** Earth mother goddess **Viracocha (Huiracocha or Wiraqoca)** Creator of sun, moon, earth, sky, stars, and human beings; father of Inti and Mama Quilla

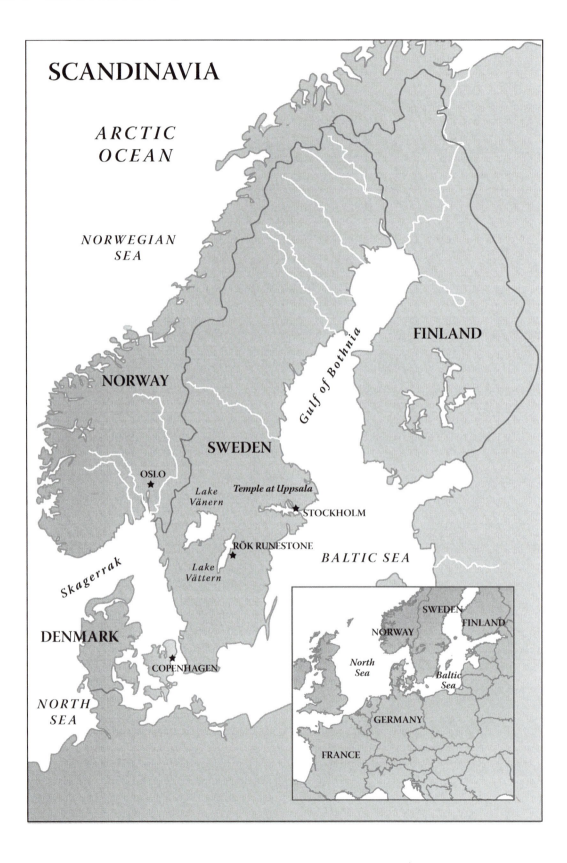

SCANDINAVIA

ARCTIC OCEAN

NORWEGIAN SEA

NORWEGIAN SEA

NORWAY

SWEDEN

FINLAND

Gulf of Bothnia

OSLO ★

Lake Vänern

Temple at Uppsala

★ STOCKHOLM

RÖK RUNESTONE ★

Lake Vättern

BALTIC SEA

Skagerrak

DENMARK

★ COPENHAGEN

NORTH SEA

SWEDEN

NORWAY

FINLAND

North Sea

Baltic Sea

GERMANY

FRANCE

NORSE MYTHOLOGICAL FIGURES

Major Norse Gods and Goddesses	Other Female Figures in Norse Mythology
Balder Beloved of the gods; son of Odin and Frigg	**Norns** Three maidens who decide the fates of all living creatures
Bragi God of poetry and music	**Valkyries** Warrior maidens who gather fallen heroes to Valhalla, the palace of Odin
Frey God of fertility, harvest, peace, and prosperity	
Freya Goddess of fertility	
Frigg Goddess of the earth and of marriage; wife of Odin	
Heimdall Watchman of the domain of the gods	
Idun Goddess of eternal youth; wife of Bragi	
Loki Deceiver and rescuer of the gods	
Njörd Sea god; father of twins Frey and Freya	
Odin Father god; god of the sky, knowledge, poetry, war, and death	
Thor Thunder god; son of Odin and Frigg	
Tyr Bravest of the gods, known for his justness	

AFRICAN MYTHOLOGICAL FIGURES

Asante (Ashanti)
Asase Ya
Earth goddess

Kwaku Anansi (Ananse)
Spider god

Nyame
Supreme creator god; sky god

Baganda
Nagadya
Goddess of rain

Nagawonyi
Goddess of hunger

Kibuka and Nende
War gods

Mbale
God of female fertility

Mukasa
Chief god

Berber
Bonchor
Creator god

Djinns
Shape-shifting spirits

Dinka
Nhialic (Nyalich)
Supreme god

Macardit
Divinity of ill-fortune

Deng (Denka)
God of rain and fertility

Fon
Aido-Hweli
Cosmic serpent; Mawu-Lisa's servant

Da Zodji
Chief earth god

Mawu-Lisa
Creator deity

Sagbata
First earth god

Tovodu
Spirits of the ancestors

Sogbo(or Hevioso)
Deity of thunder, lightning, and fire

Mami Wata
Water goddess

Igbo
Amadi-Oha
God of lightning

Chuku
Supreme god

Ala
Earth goddess

Isoko
Cghene
Creator and supreme god

Oyise
Intermediary of Cghene

Kamba
Ngai (Engai)
Supreme creator god

Aimu
Intermediary spirits

Khoekhoe and San
Kaggen (Cagn)
Supreme creator god; trickster

Heitsi-Eibib (or Kabip)
Culture hero; god of hunt

Aigamuxa
Man-eating dune monsters

Eland antelope
Master animal

Lugbara
Adro-Adroa
Creator and sky god

Adroanzi
Spirits of the dead

Ori
Spirits of important ancestors

Malagasy
Ataokoloinona
Messenger spirit

Zanahary
Creator gods

Vazimba
Spirits of the dead

Masai (Maasai)
En-kai (Ngai)
Supreme god; storm-fertility god

Kintu
First man

Neiterogob
Earth goddess

Nenaunir
Malevolent storm god

Tumbuka
Chiuta
Supreme god

Yoruba
Eshu
God of chance; messenger and trickster

Jakuta
Thunder god

Olorun
Supreme deity

Orisa-nla
First deity

Yemaja
Mother of many gods

Zulu
Unkulunkulu
Creator; first human

Mamlambo
Goddess of rivers

Inkosanzana
Goddess of agriculture

Mbaba Mwana Waresa
Goddess of rain and harvest

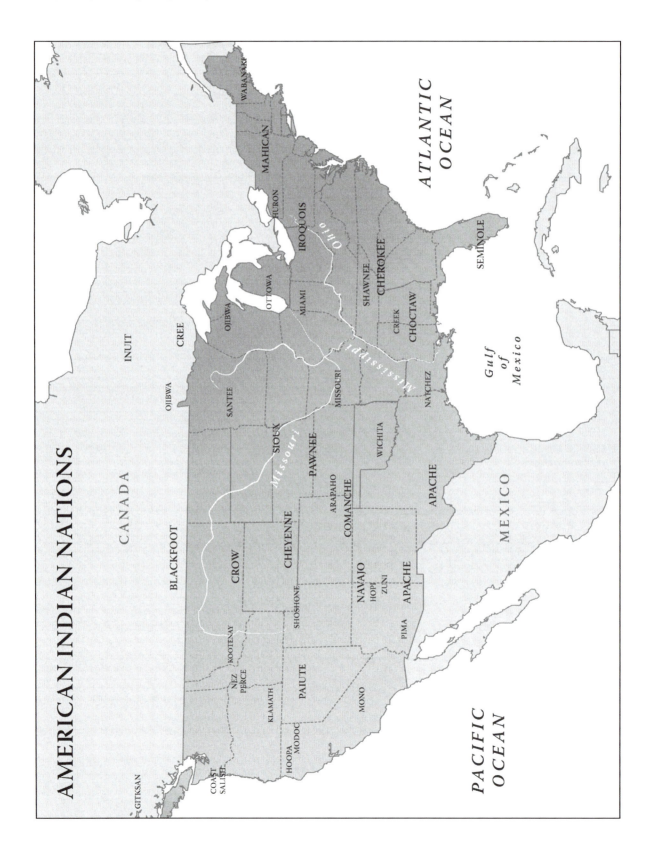

AMERICAN INDIAN NATIONS

AMERICAN INDIAN MYTHOLOGICAL FIGURES

Apache
Assanutlije
Creator of the Milky Way

Killer-of-Enemies and Child-of-Water
Twin culture heroes

Blackfoot
Apistotoke
Creator

Sta-au
Ghosts of the wicked

Komorkis
Moon goddess

Natos
Sun god

Cherokee
Asgaya Gigagei
Lightning and thunder deity

Oonawieh Unggi
Wind spirit

Tsul 'Kalu
Giant lord of the hunt

Cheyenne
Aktunowihio
Earth spirit

Heammawihio
Creator and sky spirit

Coast Salish
Amotken
Creator god

Hoopa
Kihunai
First beings

Yimantuwingyai
Culture hero who established
world order

Yinukatsisdai
God of vegetation

Hopi
Taiowa
Creator god

Huruing Wuhti
Deity who created humankind

Huron
Aatentsic (Ataentsic)
Sky Woman

Heng
God of thunder and fertility

Ioskeha (Yoskeha)
Creator of the first humans; grandson
of Sky Woman

Ketqskwaye
Creator of the Hurons

Tawiscara (Tawiskaron)
Evil twin of Ioskeha

Inuit
Torngasoau
Supreme deity

Sedna (or Nuliajuk)
Goddess of the sea

Sila
Storm deity

Lakota
Wakan Tanka
Creator

Iktomi
Spider trickster

Capa
Beaver spirit

Lenni Lenape (Delaware)
Kitanitowit
Creator

Menominee
Anamaqkiu
Evil spirit responsible for the Deluge

Navajo
Niltshi
Wind spirit

Thonenli
Water spirit

*Ahsonnutli and Yolaikaiason
(Yolkai Estsan)*
Creators of heaven and earth,
or first people

Hastsezini
God of fire

Ojibwa (Ojibwe)
Gitche Manitou
Creator and supreme being

Wunzh
Father of corn

Paiute
Tobats
Creator and supreme god

Cunawabi
Trickster god associated with night,
sickness, and gambling

Pawnee
Tirawa
Creator and sky god

Uti Hiata
Corn mother

Basket Woman
Mother of the moon and stars

Seneca
Dagwanoenyent
Whirlwind spirits

Deohako
The spirits of the three sisters
(bean, corn, squash)

Hawenniyo
Supreme spirit

Wabanaki
Glooskap (Gluskap)
Trickster and culture hero

Zuni
Apoyan Tachi
Sky father

Awitelin Tsta (Tsita)
Earth mother

Awonawilona
Creator and supreme spirit

THE CELTIC WORLD

OUTER HEBRIDES

SCOTLAND

Iona

Giant's Causway

ULSTER

N. IRELAND

Croagh Patrick

Glasgow

EDINBURGH

Lindisfarne

BELFAST

Dun Aengus

IRELAND

Hill of Tara

Irish Sea

Clonmacnoise

DUBLIN

Glendalough

Caernarfon

ENGLAND

Aberystwyth

WALES

Coed Llathen

CARDIFF

CELTIC SEA

Glastonbury

LONDON

ATLANTIC OCEAN

Carn Euny

English Channel

Landévennec

FRANCE

BRITTANY

PARIS

Bay of Biscay

CELTIC MYTHOLOGICAL FIGURES

Aonghus Óg (Aengus)
Irish and Scottish god of youth, beauty, and poetry

Áine (Enya)
Irish sun goddess or fairy queen

Andraste
Gaulish and British war goddess

Annwn (Annwyn)
The Welsh Netherworld

Arawn
King of Annwn

Arianrhod (Arianrod)
Welsh goddess of the moon, dawn, or land

Badb
Irish goddess of war and fury

Banba (Banbha)
Irish goddess of earth

Belisana
Gaulish goddess of healing

Bile
Irish god of the underworld; father of the Milesians

Blodeuwedd
Welsh flower-maiden goddess; wife of Llew Llaw Gyffes

Bran
The hunting hound of Irish hero Fionn mac Cumhaill

Brân
Welsh sea god or hero-king; giant brother of Branwen

Branwen
Welsh goddess who married an Irish king

Brigit (Brigid)
Pan-Celtic threefold goddess of poetry, healing, and smithies

Camulus (Camulos)
British god of war

Cernunnos
Pan-Celtic stag god of wealth, fertility, and life

Coventina
British goddess of healing, associated with water

Cúchulainn
Irish warrior hero

Dagda (Daghdha)
Irish god of fertility and plenty

Danu (Anu)
Irish earth goddess; mother of the Tuatha Dé Danann

Dian Cécht
Irish god of medicine

Epona
British and Gaulish horse goddess, associated with fertility and death

Étain (Aideen)
Irish goddess or fairy

Esus (Hesus)
Gaulish god of the woodlands, merchants, and warriors

Finnabair (Findabar)
Irish goddess-queen; daughter of Medb

Fionn mac Cumhaill
Leader of the Fianna, fierce Irish warriors

Flidais (Fliodhas)
Irish goddess of animals and forests

Formorians
Race of demonic giants; enemies of the Tuatha Dé Danann

Gwalchmei
Welsh hero synonymous with Arthurian Gawain

Gwydion
Welsh god of magic; brother of Arianrhod

Kerridwen (Cerridwen)
Welsh goddess of wisdom and poetry

Llew Llaw Gyffes
Welsh god; son of Arianrhod

Llyr
Welsh sea god; father of Brân and Branwen

Lugh
Irish god of the sun, harvest, and arts

Mabon
Welsh god of poetry and youth

Macha
Irish goddess of war

Manannán
Irish god of magic; shape-shifter; protector of the gods

Math
Welsh enchanter-king; uncle of Arianrhod

Medb
Irish warrior queen

Morrígan (Morrígu)
Irish goddess of battle, strife, and fertility

Myrddin (Merlin)
Early solar deity or Welsh prophet

Nemetona
Gaulish warrior goddess of the oaks

Nemain
Irish goddess of war

Nuada
Irish chief god of the Tuatha Dé Danann

Nwyvre
Welsh god of space

Ogma
Irish god of eloquence and poetry

Pwyll
Welsh hero-king

Sadb (Sadhbh)
Irish heroine who cursed to be a deer

Sirona
Gaulish goddess of healing, fertility, and rebirth

Taliesin
Welsh poet and seer

Taranis
Continental god of thunder

Tethra
Irish ruler of the Otherworld

Tuatha Dé Danann
Race of gods founded by the goddess Danu

Twrch Trwyth
Monstrous boar hunted by King Arthur

KING ARTHUR'S WORLD

N O R T H S E A

LOTHIAN
(SCOTLAND)

River Tweed

★
Drumelzier

NORTHUMBERLAND

ATLANTIC OCEAN

ISLE OF MAN

I R I S H S E A

ANGLESEY

CHESIRE

GWYNEDD

LOGRES
(ENGLAND)

WALES

DYFED

GWENT

CAERLEON
★

River Thames

London
★

Bristol Channel

GLASTONBURY
★

Stonehenge
★

Tintagel
★

SOMERSET

AMESBURY
★
WINCHESTER

Strait of Dover

DEVON

CORNWALL

English Channel

FRANCE

Lyonesse
★

THE WORLD OF KING ARTHUR AND THE KNIGHTS OF THE ROUND TABLE

ENGLAND	WALES
Cheshire Alderley Edge: One of about a dozen proposed locations for the enchanted cave in which Arthur and his Knights sleep for eternity **Cornwall** Bedegraine (Bedingran, Bredigan): Site of battle where King Arthur subdued the rebel subkings Camelford: Possible site of King Arthur's death following the Battle of Camlann against his enemy Mordred Cameliard (Carmelide): Home of Guinevere and her father, King Leodegrance, possibly in present-day Cornwall Dozmary Pool: Possible site where Caliburn (Excalibur) was cast away upon the waters St. Michael's Mount: Site of battle between Arthur and a giant, according to the anonymous poem *Morte Arthure* Tintagel Castle: Birthplace of King Arthur **Hampshire** Winchester Castle: Possible site of the Round Table, the gathering place for the order of King Arthur and his Knights **Northumberland** Bamburgh Castle: Possible site of Lancelot's castle, Joyous Guard (Garde) **Somerset** Cadbury Castle: Site most commonly associated with Camelot, the capital of Arthur's realm and of the Round Table Chalice Well: Sacred spring below Glastonbury Tor Glastonbury Abbey: According to local legend, the burial place of King Arthur Glastonbury Tor: A hill associated with the island of Avalon, where Arthur was brought to heal his mortal wounds **Wiltshire** Stonehenge: According to legend, constructed by Merlin; sometimes considered the burial place of Arthur's uncle Pendragon	**Dyfed** Bryn Myrddin: According to local legend, a cave set in a hill, where Merlin lives under enchantment St. Govan's Chapel: According to local legend, the hermitage of Sir Gawain after King Arthur's death **Gwent** Caerleon-upon-Usk: Arthur's chief city and coronation site, according to Geoffrey of Monmouth **Gwynedd** Dinas Emrys: The mountain fort where, according to both Nennius and the *Mabinogion,* Merlin prophesied the reign of King Arthur and defeated the magicians of the usurper Vortigern Llyn Barfog: According to local legend, lake where Arthur battled an Afanc monster, with the help of his horse

World Mythology

THE AMERICAS

MESOAMERICA

The Azteca

Author: Traditional Aztec
Time Period: 1001 CE–1500 CE
Country or Culture: Mesoamerica
Genre: Myth

PLOT SUMMARY

According to myth, the Azteca (Aztec people), originated in an ancestral land known as Aztlán—possibly meaning "white place" or "place of herons"—an idyllic world filled with sufficient bounty to nurture a large population. In Aztlán, the people learned to cultivate maize and the other principal crops of their culture and developed vast, floating gardens on the waters surrounding a central mountain. The land was filled with birds of white and green plumage, and flocks of ducks populated the waters. Huitzilopochtli, the god of war, convinced some of his people to leave Aztlán to explore the world that surrounded them. Outside of Aztlán, they encountered murderous jaguars, dangerous thorned plants, and other warring tribes. Over time, the immigrants conquered the new land, subdued the animals, and planted the crops they had grown in Aztlán and had carried from their floating gardens.

The Azteca divided time into sets of fifty-two years called "bundles" and celebrated the passage of a fifty-two-year period with a ceremony known as the Tying of the Years. At each ceremony, priests would analyze portents they believed would foretell future fortunes and dangers facing the empire. During one ceremony, which is attended by Montezuma, the king of the Aztecs, the omen reveals a pair of sandals found in the temple of Huitzilopochtli. Montezuma believes that the sandals are a message that Huitzilopochtli will never leave the Azteca. Messengers are dispatched to deliver the sandals to Coatlicue, Huitzilopochtli's mother, and to inform her that her son will never return to Aztlán because he will not leave the people who had proved to be such able conquerors.

The priests of Huitzilopochtli decipher the path to Aztlán, and Montezuma's messengers eventually find the ancestral land. Once there, they realize time does not pass at the same rate in Aztlán, with the residents living for hundreds of thousands of years. They also learn that the diet of the Azteca, consisting of meat and pulque (a fermented drink made from agave), makes them heavy, while the diet of the people in Aztlán is vegetarian and they only consume water, making them light and agile. The ambassadors deliver the sandals to Huitzilopochtli's mother, who is dressed in a garment made of serpents, and she is saddened that her son will not be returning to her.

Upon their return to the empire, the messengers learn that another fifty-two years have passed and that Montezuma has died, passing rule on to his son, Montezuma II. At a new Tying of the Years ceremony, a number of dread portents are revealed, including a shining stone found lodged in the skull of a bird caught by a fisherman. Montezuma II and the priests then see a vision of the king's deceased sister, who tells them she has seen great ships bearing men from beyond the Eastern Sea (the Atlantic Ocean), carrying weapons more deadly than any known to the Aztecs. This vision is believed to signal the end of the Aztec Empire.

SIGNIFICANCE

The term *Aztec* is derived from the Nahuatl language and translates as "people from Aztlán." The myth of the ancient exodus from Aztlán has appeared in many different forms and is one of the most important myths in Aztec culture. Historians speculate that Aztlán was called the "white place" because it was home to large populations of bird species with white feathers, such as herons and egrets, which feature prominently in many Aztec myths. Some historians believe that Aztlán refers to a portion of what is now central Mexico, which is believed to have been one of the birthplaces of the Nahuatl language.

The myth of the Aztec return to Aztlán may be considered part of a class of myths that display the evolution of humanity through environmental or self-inflicted actions that serve to remove humans from the path of their ancestors. While Aztlán is depicted as an idyllic, balanced, and largely perfected world, the outside world is portrayed as harsh and imperfect. In one sense, this myth explains that the hardships of the outside world result from the fact that humanity has not achieved perfection in the new kingdom, thus allowing room for improvement and growth.

This version of the myth of the Azteca was reformulated long after the fall of the Aztec Empire following the Spanish conquest of Mexico in the sixteenth century. Montezuma II, the last ruler of the Aztec Empire, lived from 1466 until June 30, 1520, when he was killed during the Spanish conquest under Hernán Cortés. Though some Spaniards used early muskets called harquebuses, it was the Spanish cavalry and their superior hand weapons, including swords and spears, that allowed the force of a few thousand Spaniards and their allies to defeat tens of thousands of Aztec warriors. In the wake of the collapse of the Aztec Empire, many of the myths were reworked to reflect the end of the empire in a way that suggested that the Aztec gods had known what would occur and even warned the people that their end was approaching.

Many of the myths of the Aztec Empire have been absorbed into modern Mexican culture. The god Huitzilopochtli is considered the patron of Mexico and features prominently in a number of myths that involve the differentiation of the Mexican people from their Aztec ancestors. The legend of Aztlán has also been embraced by modern sociocultural movements seeking to celebrate or recognize the pre-Columbian cultural legacy that was shared by the Olmecs, Toltecs, Maya, and Aztecs and is part of the important cultural ancestry of the modern Mexican people.

Micah Issitt

BIBLIOGRAPHY

Aguilar-Moreno, Manuel. *Handbook to Life in the Aztec World*. New York: FOF, 2006. Print.

Carrasco, Davíd, and Scott Sessions. *Daily Life of the Aztecs*. 2nd ed. Santa Barbara: ABC-Clio, 2011. Print.

Clendinnen, Inga. *Aztecs: An Interpretation*. Cambridge: Cambridge UP, 1991. Print

Dils, Lorna. "Aztec Mythology." *Yale-New Haven Teachers Institute*. Yale-New Haven Teachers Inst., 2013. Web. 29 Apr. 2013.

Herrera-Sobek, María. *Chicano Folklore: A Handbook*. Westport: Greenwood, 2006. Print.

León-Portilla, Miguel. *Aztec Thought and Culture: A Study of the Ancient Nahuatl Mind*. Trans. Jack Emory Davis. Norman: U of Oklahoma P, 1990. Print.

◆ The Aztec Creation Myth

Author: Traditional Aztec
Time Period: 1001 CE–1500 CE
Country or Culture: Mesoamerica
Genre: Myth

PLOT SUMMARY

Before the current version of the universe was created, the universe was created and destroyed on four separate occasions by disasters that included fires, winds, and floods. According to Aztec culture, this fifth universe will eventually be destroyed as well, in keeping with the natural cosmic balance of creation and obliteration.

The current universe begins with the sky father, Citlalatonac, and the earth mother, Citlalicue. Citlalicue gives birth to a flint knife, which falls to the ground and splinters into sixteen hundred earth gods. The earth gods are unhappy because they have to forage for their own food and petition the earth mother to create a race of individuals to serve them. Citlalicue tells the earth gods how to accomplish this task.

The earth god Xolotl (or, in other versions, the feathered serpent Quetzalcóatl) travels to the realm of the dead, Mictlampa (or Mictlan), and meets Mictlantecuhtli, the skull-headed lord of the underworld. Mictlantecuhtli tells Xolotl that a new race of giants could be created by mixing a bone from the ancient giants that once roamed the earth with a drop of blood from each of the earth gods. Xolotl knows that although Mictlantecuhtli purports to be helping the earth gods, he secretly plans to trap Xolotl in the underworld. Xolotl steals the bone fragment and attempts to flee but is injured by Mictlantecuhtli's owl guardians in the process, dropping the bone, which breaks into thousands of shards.

Once he escapes, Xolotl and the other earth gods follow Mictlantecuhtli's instructions and mix their blood with the fragments of bone. After four days, the mixture bubbles and produces a male infant. Four days later, the brew bubbles again and produces a female infant. The earth gods nurture the children, who eventually marry and give rise to the race of humans that now occupy the earth. Because Xolotl dropped the giant bone he stole from Mictlampa, the resulting fragments are of irregular sizes and shapes, thus giving rise to humans who are also of irregular sizes.

The world inhabited by the original humans does not have a sun, moon, or stars. It is determined that two of the earth gods must sacrifice themselves to be resurrected as luminaries. After a ceremony involving a traditional human sacrifice, two of the gods throw themselves into ceremonial fires and are destroyed, returning four days later in the form of the sun and the moon. At first, the sun and moon are of equal brightness, but one of the earth gods hurls a rabbit toward the moon, which dims the light from the moon and creates a pattern of shadows on its face. The sun and moon determine then that the rest of the earth gods must be sacrificed, and they conjure a great wind that destroys the remaining gods and transforms them into the stars. This same wind pushes the sun, causing it to move across the sky each day.

SIGNIFICANCE

The Aztecs envisioned the world as the result of ancient and ongoing struggles between powerful deities that represent the primal forces of nature and the universe. The role of humanity was ultimately to appease the gods, and thus to appease the primal forces that dominated their lives, including climatic patterns and the patterns of famine and bounty that affected their agricultural and hunting success.

The myth of the creation of men and women explains the diversity observed in humanity as an artifact of humanity's magical origins, with each person having originated from a fragment of bone. As was clearly observable to the Aztecs, who often fashioned items using bone, a shattered fragment would tend to produce pieces with unique characteristics in terms of size and shape. This is the phenomenon that was chosen to symbolize the differences between individuals. The myth also establishes humans as descendants of the earth gods, having been created through a combination of the blood of earth gods and the bone of an ancient earth race. In this way, the myth establishes a primary order of being and emphasizes that humans are the children of the earth gods and are therefore bound to the earth. This facet of Aztec mythology reflects an ancient ecological impulse within Aztec spirituality.

The origin of the sun, moon, and stars represents the belief that the sun and moon exist primarily to provide light to those living on the earth. This type of belief is common in cultures that consider the earth to be the central point in the celestial environment. The myth also explains the observed luminosity of the sun and the moon by relating the creation of these bodies to the ceremonial fires used to sacrifice the earth gods. To the Aztecs, whose only other source of light was fire, the light of the sun and moon were naturally seen as bearing a relationship to this primary element.

Interestingly, the Aztecs attributed the relative brightness of the moon and the patterns of shadows observed on its surface to the presence of a rabbit flung onto the surface of the moon. The Aztecs were not the only culture to envision the shape of a rabbit on the surface of the moon, and similar myths have been discovered in ancient East Asian and African folklore. While some cultures saw the shape of a rabbit on the moon, many other cultures envisioned the shape of a face among the craters, giving rise to the preponderance of myths about a man in the moon in various cultures. In many ancient cultures, it was common to explain complex visual features by relating them to more familiar shapes. A similar process motivated the invention of constellations from patterns of stars in the night sky.

Micah Issitt

BIBLIOGRAPHY

Aguilar-Moreno, Manuel. *Handbook to Life in the Aztec World*. New York: Oxford UP, 2006. Print.

Carrasco, David, and Scott Sessions. *Daily Life of the Aztecs*. 2nd ed. Santa Barbara: ABC-CLIO, 2011. Print.

Clendennin, Inga. *Aztecs: An Interpretation*. Cambridge: Cambridge UP, 1991. Print.

Colum, Pádraic. "The Gods of the Azteca." *Orpheus: Myths of the World*. New York: Macmillan, 1930. 302–5. Print.

Dils, Lorna. "Aztec Mythology." *Yale-New Haven Teachers Institute*. Yale U, 2013. Web. 29 May 2013.

León-Portilla, Miguel. *Aztec Thought and Culture: A Study of the Ancient Nahuatl Mind*. Trans. Jack Emory Davis. Norman: U of Oklahoma P, 1990. Print.

◆ The Birth of the War God

Author: Traditional Aztec
Time Period: 1001 CE–1500 CE
Country or Culture: Mesoamerica
Genre: Myth

PLOT SUMMARY

Coatlicue lives in Aztlán, the mythical home of the Azteca (Aztec people). She has two daughters, Coyolxauhqui and Malinalxochitl, and four hundred sons. One day, she finds a magical ball of feathers on the ground, and when she tucks it under her clothing, feeling inextricably drawn to it, she becomes pregnant. Coatlicue's children are furious, demanding to know the identity of the father and believing that their mother has dishonored the family. The baby inside Coatlicue speaks to her and tells her to flee to the top of a mountain. Coatlicue's children pursue, intending to kill her. However, Coatlicue's divine baby, Huitzilopochtli, is born full grown, wearing armor and brandishing weapons. He defends his mother's life, killing his sister Coyolxauhqui and flinging her head into the sky, where it remains as the moon. He also kills many of his brothers, scattering their bodies in the heavens as the stars.

The ancient Aztecs accept Huitzilopochtli as their god of war, and he tells the people that he will lead them forth to a new land, where they will conquer and unite the various people and establish great kingdoms. Huitzilopochtli and his followers depart one night while his surviving sister, Malinalxochitl, is sleeping. When she wakes up, she is furious at her brother and leads her own followers to the mountain Texcatepetl, where she gives birth to a son, Copil.

When the Azteca arrive in Techcatitlan (now Texcaltitlán), Huitzilopochtli is forced to battle with his nephew Copil, who by then has grown to become a great warrior. Huitzilopochtli defeats Copil and cuts out his heart; he gives the heart gives to a servant and tells him to throw it into the forest in a bed of reeds. At this point, Huitzilopochtli leaves the Azteca to attend to other concerns, but he continues to watch over them in spirit as they search for their new home.

For more than forty years, the Azteca wander the wilderness looking for the land foreseen by Huitzilopochtli, occasionally trying to settle in various areas they find along the way. While watching over them, Huitzilopochtli uses magic and trickery to prevent the Azteca from settling until they reach the chosen land. The Azteca eventually reach the borders of Lake Texcoco, where one of the priests receives a vision of Huitzilopochtli, who tells the Azteca to be on the lookout for an eagle perched on a *tenochtli*, or stone cactus, while holding a snake in its beak. This cactus has grown from the discarded heart of Copil, and the eagle is the physical manifestation of Huitzilopochtli. In a patch of grasses near a marsh, the people spot the eagle perched on the cactus, and it bows to them, signifying their arrival at their new home. It is here that the Azteca found their kingdom of Tenochtitlán, which would become the largest city of the Aztec Empire and remain the home of the Aztec people into the modern era.

SIGNIFICANCE

Historians have theorized that the mythical land of Aztlán may have referred to a real place where the ancestral Nahuatl-speaking people lived before establishing the Aztec Empire in central Mexico. The Aztec Empire formed through conquest, with the ancestral Aztecs invading and subduing a number of other societies in the process of building their empire. Huitzilopochtli is seen as having influenced this migration, using magic and trickery to prevent the migratory Azteca from settling in other locations before they reached the land he envisioned. While there are no historical records of this journey, in myth, the people continued moving because of floods, famines, and the hostility of other kingdoms. Some historians have suggested that these mythical events might be rooted in various actual experiences that the Azteca encountered during the migration.

The myth of the birth of Huitzilopochtli has also been utilized as part of the overall creation theory of the Aztecs, with parts of the story explaining the existence of the heavenly bodies, such as the birth of the moon and stars from the bodies of Huitzilopochtli's siblings. The cosmic genesis elements of the Huitzilopochtli myth were a late development in Aztec culture, occurring after the reformulation of their religion in the fifteenth century. It was during this renaissance period that the Aztecs elevated Huitzilopochtli to become one of their primary gods and reformulated many myths to focus on Huitzilopochtli as the primary character. Huitzilopochtli was also the god of war, and his acceptance as the patron of the fifteenth-century empire reflects the fact that warfare and conquest were a central part of this culture's values and history.

In many reformulated versions of the myth—changed after the Spanish conquest of the Aztec Empire in the sixteenth century—Huitzilopochtli tells the Aztec people that after they leave Aztlán they will no longer to be known as the Azteca and should instead call themselves the Mexica. Huitzilopochtli is still considered the patron of the Mexican people; the ancestral city of Tenochtitlán was rebuilt after the Spanish conquest and is now known as Mexico City.

Huitzilopochtli and the myth of the eagle perched on the cactus is also an important part of modern Mexican heritage and has been preserved in the Mexican coat of arms, which depicts a golden eagle perched on a prickly pear cactus and struggling with a rattlesnake. This emblem reflects the cultural history of Tenochtitlán and the continuity of modern Mexican culture and the Aztec Empire.

Micah Issitt

BIBLIOGRAPHY

Aguilar-Moreno, Manuel. *Handbook to Life in the Aztec World*. New York: Oxford UP, 2006. Print.

Carrasco, David. *Quetzalcoatl and the Irony of Empire*. Chicago: U of Chicago P, 1982. Print.

Carrasco, David, and Scott Sessions. *Daily Life of the Aztecs*. 2nd ed. Santa Barbara: ABC-Clio, 2011. Print.

Clendennin, Inga. *Aztecs: An Interpretation*. Cambridge: Cambridge UP, 1991. Print

Dils, Lorna. "Aztec Mythology." *Yale-New Haven Teachers Institute*. Yale-New Haven Teachers Inst. , 2013. Web. 29 Apr. 2013.

León-Portilla, Miguel. *Aztec Thought and Culture*. Norman: U of Oklahoma P, 1990. Print.

Spence, Lewis. *The Myths of Mexico and Peru*. New York: Cosimo, 2010. Print.

Webley, Kayla. "Huizilopochtli, Aztec God of Sun and War." *Time*. Time, 7 Feb. 2011. Web. 29 April 2013.

◆ Cihuacóatl as Warrior

Author: Traditional Aztec
Time Period: 1001 CE–1500 CE
Country or Culture: Mesoamerica
Genre: Myth

PLOT SUMMARY

The goddess Cihuacóatl has existed since the beginning of time and has taken many shapes, exhibited many characteristics—often contradictory—and been known by a variety of names in different places and eras. In ancient times, she is called Toci, Our Grandmother, or Tonatzin, Our Blessed Mother. In this form, she appears aged, sometimes with black spots on her face and sometimes with a skull head, signifying death and resurrection. She wears a headdress covered with spools of cotton to indicate her creative nature. A fertile earth mother, she carries a shield and a broom in clawlike hands to symbolize her dual nature: she is both a skilled warrior ready to kill and a domestic figure.

Among the tribes who migrate to the Valley of Mexico, she is called Yaocihuatl, Enemy Woman, or Itzpapalótl, Butterfly with Claws. In this guise, she is a ferocious warrior. She can appear in many shapes, especially as a beautiful woman who lures the unwary to death or as a skeleton with transparent butterfly wings tipped with claws or knives—an attractive but deadly creature.

Later, she is called Teteoinnan, Mother of the Gods, or Coatlicue, Serpent Skirt. In this form, she is credited with giving birth to fire, the stars, and four hundred other children, though she remains a virgin. As Coatlicue, she finds and pockets a ball of feathers while sweeping a temple, through which she becomes pregnant with Huitzilopochtli, a god of war who later becomes the sun. This pregnancy angers Coatlicue's daughter Coyolxauhqui and her many other offspring, who gather to kill and decapitate their mother. At the moment of her death, Huitzilopochtli is born fully formed; he soon avenges his mother's death by killing most of his siblings. He beheads Coyolxauhqui and flings her head into the sky, where it became the moon. From Coatlicue's headless corpse grow a pair of fearsome snakes, eager to devour. Around her neck hang human hands, hearts, and skulls to show her power over life and death. Her skirt is made of living snakes.

In yet another form, she is Tlazolteotl, Eater of Filth. She appears naked, squatting to give birth and to defecate simultaneously. A goddess of the purification derived through steam baths and of midwives who assist at births, Tlazolteotl both creates and forgives sins. A seductress who lures men into adultery, she allows them to make a one-time confession of their transgressions, which she swallows, absolving them.

Her best-known manifestation is Cihuacóatl, Serpent Woman, guardian of female warriors who died during the battle of childbirth. Linked with bellicose creation goddess Quilaztli, Cihuacóatl is a chief deity during the heyday of the Toltecs, the spiritual progenitors of the Mexica, later called Aztecs, who adopt the goddess as their own and adapt her for their own purposes. A patron deity across a broad swath of Central America, she protects Culhuacán and is closely associated with Lake Xochimilco. Both a creator and a destroyer, she holds a hoe and an ear of corn to demonstrate the cause and effect of her beneficence, yet in portraits she sometimes carries a spear, and her glyphic symbol is a mouth ringed with sharp, bloody teeth. She is alternately depicted with the head of a young woman, her face whitened in the manner of the nobility, or a bare skull. Cihuacóatl always wears pure white. Characterized as a mother who abandoned her son and afterward regretted it, she wanders the night weeping and searching for her lost child, an activity that was interpreted as a harbinger of approaching war and doom.

SIGNIFICANCE

Cihuacóatl is representative of the complicated, flexible, and incorporative nature of Mesoamerican myth and religion. Ancient Mexican beliefs often combined the qualities of similar gods old and new and modified theology as necessary to accommodate the rising or falling fortunes of various tribal groups. Cihuacóatl, one of the most important figures in Aztec mythology, was associated in some way with most major deities.

Initially conceived as a goddess of both fertility and war, Cihuacóatl developed conceptually during waves of pre-Columbian migrations of tribes. These migrations began with the Chichimeca, followed by a dozen groups of Nahuatl-speaking peoples and finally the Mexica. All the migrants supposedly traveled from Aztlán or Chicomoztoc, legendary lands somewhere to the north, to the Valley of Mexico. Depictions from this period of Cihuacóatl as a soldier carrying weapons probably reflected a common reality: women often fought alongside men in tribal warfare.

The first of the migrant groups arrived at their destination ca. 950 CE to find the area under the dominion of the Toltecs. By then, the deity representing Cihuacóatl had merged with numerous related goddesses, been elevated into the upper echelon of the Mesoamerican pantheon, and inherited attributes subtly indicative of an increasingly male-dominated civilization. She was still an earth mother and implement-inventing goddess, but she was relieved of soldiery and more strongly than ever identified with the type of warfare only women can appreciate: the life-or-death battle women undergo during childbirth. Women who died in childbirth were considered the equal of those killed on the battlefield and entitled to the same honorable afterlife.

Cihuacóatl was so popular among worshippers that when the Aztecs came into power in the thirteenth century, they built temples to her in their capital of Tenochtitlan; her name appeared more frequently than that of any other deity on city structures. The Aztecs also named an important governmental post in honor of the Serpent Woman. The *cihuacóatl* was second in command under the emperor during the last century of Aztec rule. A nobleman who for ceremonial occasions wore a snakelike skirt suggestive of the most recognizable feature of the goddess, the cihuacóatl served as supreme judge in criminal matters, as military campaign planner and organizer, and as head of state when the emperor was absent from the city.

Jack Ewing

BIBLIOGRAPHY

Bierhorst, John. *The Mythology of Mexico and Central America*. New York: Morrow, 1990. Print.

Carrasco, Davíd. *City of Sacrifice: The Aztec Empire*

and the Role of Violence in Civilization. Boston: Beacon, 1999. Print.

Littleton, C. Scott, ed. "Mesoamerica's Gods of Sun and Sacrifice." *Mythology: The Illustrated Anthology of World Myth and Storytelling*. San Diego: Thunder Bay, 2002. 526–81. Print.

MacKenzie, Donald A. *Pre-Columbian America: Myths and Legends*. London: Senate, 1996. Print.

Soustelle, Jacques. *Daily Life of the Aztecs: On the Eve of the Spanish Conquest*. Stanford: Stanford UP, 1970. Print.

◆ The Creation of Music

Author: Traditional Aztec
Time Period: 1001 CE–1500 CE
Country or Culture: Mesoamerica
Genre: Myth

PLOT SUMMARY

The modern earth, which is the fifth incarnation of the world, is considered the most beautiful and serene of all the manifestations. Humanity lives under the protection of Tezcatlipoca, who is one of the four sons of the first god, Ometeotl, and is associated with night winds, water, the earth, and the jaguar. Tezcatlipoca laments that though the earth is beautiful, it is too silent because it lacks the sounds of music. He believes that music alone has the power to bring happiness to the people and to delight the soul.

Tezcatlipoca knows that the Sun keeps musicians in his kingdom, where they play beautiful music throughout the celestial heavens. Tezcatlipoca asks Quetzalcóatl, god of wind and spirit, to travel to the house of the Sun and to return music to the earth. In some versions of this myth, Quetzalcóatl calls upon the winds from the four directions to create a forceful gale that propels him directly to the house of the Sun. In another version of the story, Quetzalcóatl relies on the aid of three of Tezcatlipoca's servants—Water Woman, Water Monster, and Cane-and-Conch—who unite their bodies to create a living bridge that Quetzalcoatl can follow to the Sun.

Once he arrives in the realm of the Sun, Quetzalcóatl sees musicians of many different varieties, each wearing a color that is associated with a musical specialty. Those who play lullabies wear white clothing, while wandering minstrels wear blue robes. Those who play flutes and spend their days in the sun wear yellow clothing, and those who concentrate on "musical stories" and love songs wear cherry-red clothing. In most versions of the myth, Quetzalcóatl notices that none of the musicians wear dark clothing, for no sad songs are played in the realm of the Sun.

The Sun realizes that Quetzalcóatl has come to take his musicians and orders them to be silent, so that Quetzalcóatl cannot find them. In some versions of the myth, the Sun uses his powers to transform the musicians to stone statues. Quetzalcóatl calls out to the musicians, telling them that their music is needed on earth, but the musicians do not make any sound, fearful of the Sun. Angered, Tezcatlipoca conjures lightning and thunder, while Quetzalcóatl calls forth strong winds. Frightened and realizing that the two gods can destroy them, the musicians flee to Quetzalcóatl, who gently cradles them in his feathers and brings them to the earth. Once there, the musicians from the Sun teach their music to the people and also to the other animals and elements of nature. This is why music can be heard in birdsong and also in the ocean's waves, the water of the sea, and the patterns of the wind.

SIGNIFICANCE

Music played an important role in Aztec culture and was seen as both an expression of happiness and hope and a symbol of the Aztec connection to nature and the gods. In part, this reflects the sociobiological theory that the inspiration for the first forms of music were likely derived from natural phenomena, such as the songs of birds and the noises heard from rushing water, thunder, and wind rustling through the trees. Among the most important types of Aztec music were songs that Western historians have termed sacred hymns, which generally pay homage to one or more of the Aztec gods. Often, the sacred hymns functioned to transmit mythological lessons by describing various deeds attributed to the gods, while the hymns were also sung to ask the gods for assistance. The Aztec *cantares*, sometimes called ghost songs, were sung to honor ancestors or historical events. Generally, only specially trained singers and musicians performed the *cantares*, and the songs were often sung only during specific ceremonies.

The myth of the creation of music also mentions a symbolic relationship between different types of music and different colors. In Aztec culture, each color was associated with a variety of physical, emotional, and spiritual entities, and these relationships were often reflected in stories, myths, and songs. For instance, the myth relates red to love and passion by stating that musicians who play love songs are clad in red. The color white, in contrast, is related to the serenity and calm of the lullaby, a color that was also associated with motherhood and peace. This part of the myth also communicates the roles of musicians in Aztec culture; some sang love songs or songs for children, some were traveling musicians, and others played music to celebrate the sun and the bounties of nature.

Another symbolic message contained within the myth can be found in the statement that there were no sad songs played in the realm of the Sun. Surveys of Aztec music show that sad songs, including songs of mourning, were common in Aztec music. The absence of sad songs in the Sun's dominion creates a dichotomy between the perfection of the heavenly realm and the suffering inherent to life on earth. Sadness is therefore a quality not inherent to music but inherent to humanity. One of the most famous *cantares*, known as the "Cuicapeuhcayotl," or the "Beginning of Songs," reflects this belief, describing the earth as essentially a place of unhappiness and reminding the people that music can only be found by maintaining a connection with the supernatural realm in which there is no suffering and where, therefore, the beauty of music can originate.

Micah Issitt

BIBLIOGRAPHY

Aquilar-Moreno, Manuel. *Handbook to Life in the Aztec World*. New York: Oxford UP, 2006. Print.

Carrasco, David, and Scott Sessions. *Daily Life of the Aztecs*. 2nd ed. Santa Barbara: ABC-CLIO, 2011. Print.

Clendinnen, Inga. *Aztecs: An Interpretation*. New York: Cambridge UP, 1991. Print

Dils, Lorna. "Aztec Mythology." *Yale-New Haven Teachers Institute Online Materials*. Yale U, 2013. Web. 29 Apr. 2013.

Herrera-Sobek, Maria. *Chicano Folklore: A Handbook*. Westport: Greenwood, 2006. Print.

Leon-Portilla, Miguel. *Aztec Thought and Culture*. Norman: U of Oklahoma P, 1990. Print.

Smith, Michael E. *The Aztecs*. 3rd ed. New York: Wiley-Blackwell, 2013. Print.

Stevenson, Robert. *Music in Aztec and Inca Territory*. Berkeley: U of California P, 1968. Print.

◆ Hunahpú and Xbalanqué

Author: Traditional Maya
Time Period: 999 BCE–1 BCE; 1 CE–500 CE
Country or Culture: Mesoamerica
Genre: Myth

PLOT SUMMARY

In a time before humans, before sun and moon exist, there live twin brothers, Hun-Hunahpú (One Hunter) and Vucub-Hunahpú (Seven Hunter). Hun-Hunahpú marries and fathers twin sons, Hunbatz (One Monkey) and Hunchouén (One Artisan). The adult twins, Hun-Hunahpú and Vucub-Hunahpú, do little but gamble and play ball. Their noisy sport disturbs the lords of the underworld, Xibalba, who send owl messengers to summon the twins to play on the ball court of their kingdom. The twins journey to Xibalba expecting to demonstrate their athleticism, but it is a deadly trap. The underworld lords trick the brothers and sacrifice them. The Lords of Xibalba decapitate Hun-Hunahpú and hang his head as a warning on a tree branch at the entrance of the underworld. Fruit immediately appears on the tree, and Hun-Hunahpú's head also takes the shape of the fruit. Amazed and troubled, the Lords of Xibalba forbid anyone to pluck fruit from the tree.

However, the daughter of a Xibalban lord, Xquic (Blood Woman), is drawn by curiosity to the wondrous tree. When she reaches for a fruit, the head of Hun-Hunahpú spits into her hand, and she instantly becomes pregnant. For disobeying the Lords, Xquic is ordered to be sacrificed. But through subterfuge, she escapes to the aboveground world and gives birth to Hunahpú and Xbalanqué, who become known as the Hero Twins.

Hunahpú and Xbalanqué, skilled blowgun hunters and ballplayers with cunning minds and a wealth of special abilities, perform many miracles. They transform their envious, lazy elder brothers, Hunbatz and Hunchouén, into monkeys. They interact with animals, shortening the tails of deer and rabbits and making the rat's tail hairless. Through trickery, they destroy the arrogant bird monster Vucub-Caquix (Seven Macaw) and his sons Zipacná (Giant) and Cabracán (Earthquake).

As with that of their father and uncle, the ball playing of Hunahpú and Xbalanqué disturbs the peace of the underworld lords. The Lords of Xibalba command the twins to appear in their realm. With the aid of a mosquito sent ahead to spy on the Xibalbans, the young twins successfully pass a series of tests that had undone their late father. Through cleverness, magic, exploitation of the special abilities of particular animals, and divine power, they survive all six Xibalba challenges: the houses of darkness, knives, cold, jaguars, fire, and bats. As a grand finale, Hunahpú and Xbalanqué repeatedly kill, dismember, and resurrect themselves. By this time severely intoxicated from fermented corn liquor and stupefied at the twins' performance, the Lords of Xibalba insist that they too want to experience death and revival. The twins agree and kill supreme lords Hun-Camé (One Death) and Vucub-Camé (Seven Death), whom they do not restore to life. The Xibalbans are thus robbed of leadership and power.

With their work done, Hunahpú and Xbalanqué ascend into the sky, where Hunahpú becomes Venus, the Morning Star, and Xbalanqué becomes the sun.

SIGNIFICANCE

Long before the stories were collected into the sixteenth-century written work the *Popol Vuh*, characters and incidents from Maya mythology were depicted in their art and architecture. The posthumous father of the Hero Twins, maize god Hun-Hunahpú, appeared as a stylized ear of corn—stripped from its stalk to symbolize his beheading—on temples during the early classic period of Maya history (ca. 250–562 CE). References to Hunahpú and Xbalanqué have been found on even earlier structures, such as on monuments of the late preclassic period (ca. 300 BCE–250 CE) at Izapa and Cerros in the lowlands of the Yucatán Peninsula, which indicates that the myth of the Hero Twins was well known and established some two thousand years before it was preserved in print. Tales were told and retold orally, and mnemonic reminders of myths, in the form of glyphs suggesting characteristics or events, were carved into stone, painted on pottery, and shaped into statuary across the history and territory of the Mayas. Vignettes pertaining to Xibalba and the exploits of Hunahpú and Xbalanqué have been found at sites from Chichén Itzá in the northeast to Palenque in the west and from Tikal in modern-day Guatemala to Copán in Honduras.

The Hero Twins constituted an elemental part of Maya mythology. They brought to life the fundamental religious principle of a tripartite universe: the heavens, earth, and underworld. They illuminated complex relationships among a multitude of deities and shaped complicated beliefs regarding death and the afterlife. They helped explain natural phenomena and laid a foundation for a whole culture by providing shining examples of leadership, determination, and creative thinking to which Maya leaders could aspire.

The independently developed twin motif, repeated throughout the myth of Hunahpú and Xbalanqué, was not unique to the Mayas. Twins or twin-like figures also appear in the mythology of the Sumerians and Babylonians (Gilgameš and Enkidu), Greeks and Romans (Heracles and Iphicles, Castor and Pollux, Romulus and Remus), and many other cultures worldwide. However, unlike such classical creations, often used to illustrate contrasts in nature, the Maya Hero Twins demonstrate the special, almost supernatural bond shared by siblings born at the same time.

The Hero Twins are also an amalgam akin to another figure common to the mythology of many other civilizations: the trickster. Like Loki in Norse mythology, and especially like Coyote or Raven in American Indian folklore, the Maya brothers use imaginative ruses to foil, confuse, and overcome foes such as the prank-loving Lords of Xibalba, who are defeated at their own game.

Jack Ewing

BIBLIOGRAPHY

Carrasco, Davíd. *Religions of Mesoamerica: Cosmovision and Ceremonial Centers.* Long Grove: Waveland, 1998. Print.

Chládek, Stanislav. *Exploring Maya Ritual Caves: Dark Secrets from the Maya Underworld.* Lanham: AltaMira, 2011. Print.

Colum, Pádraic. "The Twin Heroes and the Lords of Xibalba." *Orpheus: Myths of the World.* New York: Macmillan, 1930. 289–98. Print.

Freidal, David, Linda Schele, and Joy Parker. *Maya Cosmos: Three Thousand Years on the Shaman's Path.* New York: Morrow, 1995. Print.

Goetz, Delia, and Sylvanus G. Morley, trans. *Popol Vuh: The Sacred Book of the Ancient Quiché Maya.* Norman: U of Oklahoma P, 1978. Print.

McKay, John P., et al. *A History of World Societies.* Vol. 1. New York: Bedford/St. Martin's, 2011. Print.

McKillop, Heather. *The Ancient Maya: New Perspectives.* New York: Norton, 2006. Print.

Tiesler, Vera, and Andrea Cucina, eds. *New Perspectives on Human Sacrifice and Ritual Body Treatments in Ancient Maya Society.* Berlin: Springer, 2007. Print.

◆ Legend of the Fifth Sun

Author: Traditional Aztec
Time Period: 1001 CE–1500 CE
Country or Culture: Mesoamerica
Genre: Myth

PLOT SUMMARY

In the beginning, there is darkness. Out of the void springs Ometeotl, the god of duality (both male and female, light and dark, life and death, good and evil, and every other contrast). The substance of Ometeotl splits into male and female principles, Ometecuhtli and Omecihuatl, and the halves engage in perpetual intercourse. From their never-ending union, the primary gods are born.

Ometecuhtli and Omecihuatl produce quadruplets, all originally named Tezcatlipoca. Together, they form the cosmos in the shape of a voracious crocodile monster, Cipactli. Cipactli's head contains the thirteen layers of heaven, where the gods dwell. Its body is the water-surrounded earth disk. Its tail holds the nine levels of the underworld, home of the death demons. Each Tezcatlipoca rules a quarter of the earth. The west is ruled by White Tezcatlipoca, called Quetzalcóatl, who is the god of light and wind. Blue Tezcatlipoca, or Huitzilopochtli, the god of war and fire, governs the south. The east is ruled by Red Tezcatlipoca, or Xipe Totec, the god of agriculture. Black Tezcatlipoca, the god of night, rules the north. The gods destroy Cipactli and prepare earth for the advent of humans. They make four attempts to create life before succeeding.

Black Tezcatlipoca takes control of the first era, or First Sun, called Four Jaguar. During this time, a race of giant but weak vegetarian people is created. Tezcatlipoca, desiring glory, rises as the sun into heaven, but his envious brother Quetzalcóatl strikes him down. Tezcatlipoca falls from the sky, and the earth grows dark again. Tezcatlipoca in his anger assumes the form of a jaguar and eats the giants. Thus ends the First Sun.

During the Second Sun, called Four Wind, normal-sized, seed-eating humans are created under the reign of Quetzalcóatl, who controls both the sun and the wind. Tezcatlipoca, in revenge for his downfall during the previous age, mischievously turns humans into monkeys. He usurps Quetzalcóatl's wind-creating powers, blows his brother from the sky, and catapults the surviving monkeys into the jungle, where they dwell to this day.

During the Third Sun, called Four Rain, the newly created god of fertility and rain, Tlaloc, is given his chance. From on high, he commands the humans, who develop agriculture and grow grain. Then Tezcatlipoca kidnaps Tlaloc's wife, Xochiquetzal, and makes her his mate. Tlaloc, depressed, becomes uninvolved with humans. He refuses to make rain, and drought ruins all of the crops. Later, in a fit of pique, Tlaloc makes it rain fire. The sun is consumed, along with most people. The surviving humans become dogs, turkeys, and butterflies.

Tlaloc's second wife, Chalchihuitlicue, the goddess of still and running water, reigns during the Fourth Sun, called Four Water. During her rule, her husband frequently beats her, which makes Chalchihuitlicue cry blood for years, extinguishing the sun and drowning the maize-eating humans. The only people who survive are those who turn into fish.

With no people left, Quetzalcóatl (or, in some versions, the earth god Xolotl) has to travel into the underworld to retrieve the bones of human ancestors to create the next people. He grinds the bones into dust, mixes them into a paste with his and other gods' blood, and shapes them, and the humans of the Fifth Sun—the Sun of Motion—come to life. The Fifth Sun, it is predicted, will end with massive, destructive earthquakes.

SIGNIFICANCE

The Aztecs—who during their dominance between the mid-thirteenth and early sixteenth centuries CE called themselves Mexica, "the People of the Sun"—derived the legend of the Fifth Sun from existing Mesoamerican mythology. Meaningful aspects of cosmology were collected from oral or inscribed narratives of the Toltecs, the Mayas, and other regional tribal groups past or present, then adapted to fit current beliefs. The borrowing from other cultures and traditions, many related through the common language of Nahuatl, accounts for the complexity of Aztec mythology and theology, in which the gods have many names, changeable roles, and overlapping attributes. As with most early civilizations, the Aztec universe is divided into three parts—upper, middle, and lower worlds—and centered on four elemental forces: earth, air (wind), fire, and water.

The primary written sources of the legend of the Fifth Sun are two post-conquest documents that an enlightened Spanish priest, Bernardino de Sahagún (ca. 1500–1590), commissioned. The decades-long research project gathered information about native beliefs and customs, resulting in the *Codex Florentine* and the *Codex Chimalpopoca*. Other works on pre-conquest Aztec life that survived Spanish book-burnings—intended to wipe out native idolatry—provide additional details about the numerous deities and fragmentary accounts of the legend. Many variations of the legend of the Fifth Sun exist in which cause and effect, and the order of serial creations and destructions, differ. Perhaps the ultimate authority on the proper organization of the legend's successive ages is the massive twenty-five-ton, ten-foot-wide Sun Stone unearthed at Tenochtitlán near modern-day Mexico City, on which the Suns are arranged in counterclockwise order: First (Jaguar), Second (Wind), Third (Rain), and Fourth (Water).

The Aztecs made a major contribution to the established myth of multiple cycles of death and rebirth of the sun. This is their explanation—and justification for—the shedding of blood through human sacrifice and self-mutilation, practices that horrified the invading Spaniards but that were vital to Aztec belief.

At the beginning of the fifth age, the deities gather at Teotihuacán, the abode of the gods and the ceremonial center of the Aztec capital of Tenochtitlán, to discuss how to reanimate the sun and begin life anew. It is decided that sacrifice is necessary to persuade the sun to rise, and two gods are chosen to immolate themselves by walking into a bonfire. The offering succeeds, and the sun rises but becomes stationary in the sky. Only regular tribute, infusions of life-giving blood—drawn from the hearts of willing victims or from the lips, tongues, or penises of god-kings—could fuel the sun's energy and keep it moving across the heavens.

Jack Ewing

BIBLIOGRAPHY

Bierhorst, John, trans. *History and Mythology of the Aztecs: The Codex Chimalpopoca.* Tucson: U of Arizona P, 1998. Print.

---. *The Mythology of Mexico and Central America.* New York: Morrow, 1990. Print.

Carrasco, Davíd. *City of Sacrifice: The Aztec Empire and the Role of Violence in Civilization.* Boston: Beacon, 1999. Print.

Caso, Alfonso. *The Aztecs: People of the Sun.* Norman: U of Oklahoma P, 1959. Print.

Littleton, C. Scott, ed. "The Five Suns." *Mythology: The Illustrated Anthology of World Myth and Storytelling.* San Diego: Thunder Bay, 2002. 546–49. Print.

Miller, Mary Ellen, and Karl A. Taube. *The Gods and Symbols of Ancient Mexico and the Maya.* New York: Thames, 1993. Print.

Phillips, Charles. *The Lost History of Aztec and Maya.* Leicester: Hermes, 2005. Print.

Pierce, Donna, ed. *Exploring New World Imagery: Spanish Colonial Papers from the 2002 Mayer Center Symposium.* Denver: Denver Art Museum, 2005. Print.

Read, Kay Almere, and Jason J. González. *Mesoamerican Mythology.* New York: Oxford UP, 2000. Print.

◆ The Lords of Xibalba

Author: Traditional Maya
Time Period: 999 BCE–1 BCE; 1 CE–500 CE
Country or Culture: Mesoamerica
Genre: Myth

PLOT SUMMARY

The journey to Xibalba (the "place of fear") is long and hazardous. Unlucky travelers undertaking the trek voluntarily or by command from inhabitants of Xibalba do so knowing they may never again see their families and might never return alive.

The footpath to Xibalba, the deepest level of the underworld, descends steep steps leading to a fast-flowing river. There are many obstacles to be overcome along the way, including toxic rivers of blood and sewage. If passage across such killing barriers is successful, the path continues to a crossroad where four roads intersect: red, yellow, white, and black. The black road leads down beneath the earth to a cavern of unknown dimensions. This cavern is the kingdom of the lords of Xibalba.

The dwellers of Xibalba are evil, death-dealing spirits—malicious and mischievous tricksters, hobgoblins, and imps—who are responsible for all of humankind's pain and suffering. Supreme devil lords of the empire are Hun Camé (One Death) and Vucub Camé (Seven Death), once worthy of receiving sacrifices, still commemorated as two of twenty days on the Maya calendar. They have many subordinates, each with specific duties while working as teammates. Ahalmez (Filth Maker) and Ahaltocob (Wound Maker) leap from dust piles to stab humans to death. Ahalpuh (Pus Maker) and Ahalgana (Dropsy or Jaundice Causer) give people sores, make them swollen, and infect them with jaundice. Chamiabac (Bone Staff) and Chamiaholom (Skull Staff) make people waste away, die, and become skeletons. Quicxic (Bloody Wing), Quicrixcac (Bloody Claw), and Quicré (Bloody Teeth) cause assorted ills that weaken humans through loss of blood. Xic (Hawk) and Patán (Tumpline) squeeze the throats and hearts of people until they burst and bleed out. Xiquiripat (Flying Scab) and Cuchumaquic (Gathered Blood) cause blood diseases in humans.

The lords of Xibalba's gloomy realm resembles an aboveground city with houses and gardens. Xibalba even boasts a court where ritual ball games take place. These games are sports contests in which players use their hips, heads, and forearms to propel a rubber ball through a stone hoop, with human sacrifice a possible consequence of losing. But the amenities are deceptive, designed to fool, trap, humiliate, and overcome unwary humans, and in Xibalba, the ball is made not of rubber but of sharp bone.

Xibalba contains six houses to challenge the wiles of visitors. The House of Darkness presents guests with a challenge: they must light the interior and smoke tobacco without consuming the pine-pitch torch and cigar they are given. The House of Cold dares entrants to survive the bone-chilling climate; the House of Fire is an all-consuming conflagration; the House of Knives is a thicket of flesh-cutting obsidian blades; the House of Bats is filled with gigantic, bloodthirsty bats; and in the House of Jaguars, carnivorous jungle cats prowl restlessly, waiting for fresh meat. Failure to solve the puzzle of how to survive in any house means death for unfortunate guests.

From the beginning of time, the lords of Xibalba have reigned supreme in their underworld, carrying out their dastardly work. They are only undone with the coming of the hero twins, Hunahpú and Xbalanqué, who subdue the demons and take away most of their powers.

SIGNIFICANCE

As a people, the Mayas flourished in southeastern Mexico and Central America longer than the Roman Empire, for some fifteen hundred years (ca. 300 BCE–ca. 1200 CE). When Spanish conquistadors arrived in the New World in the late fifteenth century, most Maya centers of population had been long deserted. Possible reasons for abandonment—disease, tribal warfare, drought, or overexploitation—are still hotly debated among scholars.

Though millions of Maya descendants still live throughout territories they once dominated, most of what is known about the ancient civilization and its mythology has been obtained from translations of hieroglyphs inscribed on temples, monuments, and stelae erected as early as two thousand years ago. However, the primary source for current study of Mayan myths is the *Popol Vuh*, meaning "book of counsel" or "book of the community." A postconquest work, probably written between 1554 and 1558 and translated into Spanish by Father Francisco Ximénez in the early eighteenth century, the *Popol Vuh* is the record of oral recitations memorized and passed along from generation to generation.

According to the *Popol Vuh*, the Mayas, like many ancient cultures, divided the universe into three parts: the heavens, the earth, and the underground world. Similar to other civilizations, Mesoamericans based theological concepts on an elaborate mythology keyed to familiar flora, fauna, objects, landmarks, and events.

To the Mayas, the structure of the cosmos was illustrated through the example of the ceiba, a towering, thorny, fruit-bearing tropical tree. The ceiba is the national tree of modern Guatemala, where two of the last surviving Maya nations, the K'iche' (Quiché) and Cakchiquel, ruled before the Spanish defeated them in the 1520s. The trunk of the ceiba, which the Mayas symbolized in glyphs and architecture with a cruciform shape, represents the physical middle earth, the domain of humans. The leafy canopy reaching for the sky illustrates the thirteen levels of the upper world, where gods lived in ascending order of importance. Spreading buttress roots plunging deep into the soil represent the nine layers of the underworld. The lords of Xibalba, the most potent of subterranean deities, with the power of life and death in human affairs, ruled in the lowest compartment.

The Mayas envisioned Xibalba as an actual physical location. The entrance to the place of fear was thought to lie among the vast network of limestone caves, some of which collapsed to form natural wells called "cenotes," and freshwater rivers beneath the Yucatán and other parts of Central America. Explorations of such underground systems have uncovered considerable archaeological evidence, such as incense burners, statuettes of gods, pottery, skulls, and bones, that the Mayas used caves to worship many different deities, including gods of the underworld, in religious rituals that culminated in human sacrifice.

Jack Ewing

BIBLIOGRAPHY

Carrasco, Davíd. *Religions of Mesoamerica: Cosmovision and Ceremonial Centers*. San Francisco: Harper, 1990. Print.

Chládek, Stanislav. *Exploring Maya Ritual Caves: Dark Secrets from the Maya Underworld*. Lanham: AltaMira, 2011. Print.

Colum, Pádraic. "The Twin Heroes and the Lords of Xibalba." *Orpheus: Myths of the World*. New York: Macmillan, 1930. 289–98. Print.

Freidel, David, Linda Schele, and Joy Parker. *Maya Cosmos: Three Thousand Years on the Shaman's Path*. New York: Morrow, 1993. Print.

Goetz, Delia, Sylvanus G. Morley, and Adrián Recinos, trans. *Popol Vuh: The Sacred Book of the Ancient Quiché Maya*. Norman: U of Oklahoma P, 1950. Print.

McKay, John P., et al. *A History of World Societies, Volume 1: To 1600*. Boston: Bedford-St. Martin's, 2011. Print.

McKillop, Heather. *The Ancient Maya: New Perspectives*. Santa Barbara: ABC-CLIO, 2004. Print.

Mercer, Henry C. *The Hill-Caves of Yucatan: A Search for Evidence of Man's Antiquity in the Caverns of Central America*. Norman: U of Oklahoma P, 1975. Print.

Mott, William Michael. *Caverns, Cauldrons, and Concealed Creatures: A Study of Subterranean Mysteries in History, Folklore, and Myth*. 3rd rev. ed. Nashville: Grave Distractions, 2011. Print.

Tiesler, Vera, and Andrea Cucina, eds. *New Perspectives on Human Sacrifice and Ritual Body Treatments in Ancient Maya Society*. New York: Springer, 2007. Print.

◆ The Maya Creation Myth

Author: Traditional Maya
Time Period: 999 BCE–1 BCE; 1 CE–500 CE
Country or Culture: Mesoamerica
Genre: Myth

PLOT SUMMARY

At first, the creator gods Tepeu, the god of the sky, and Gucumatz (Plumed Serpent), god of the seas, are all alone in the universe; there is nothing but the sky above and the ocean below. The gods live in the depths of the ocean, sheltered by green and blue feathers. When they grow tired of living in a featureless existence, they bring the world into being with the help of Hurakan, the god of the wind and the storm. When they see it, they are very happy. However, it soon occurs to them that the world is much too quiet, so they create animals and birds and command them to live in their distinctive ways and make their distinctive cries.

Although the world is now filled with sounds, the creator gods are not wholly satisfied. They wish for creatures to worship them, not merely make unintelligent noises. They decide to create humans to do just this. At first, they make people out of mud, but these people are blind, unintelligent, and unable to stand up properly, and they fall apart when it rains. The creator gods destroy the mud people and start again.

The next people are made from sticks. These are better, as they can stand, move around, and reproduce. However, they have no real intelligence or emotions, do not know how to cook, and are cruel to their pets. The gods flood the stick people's domain with sap and allow the dogs they have mistreated to attack them. Some escape by climbing trees, and these become monkeys.

Frustrated by their failures, the creator gods are determined to find a way to make human beings who can worship them correctly. At this point, they are visited by a coyote, a crow, a mountain lion, and a parrot, who tell them of a new food called corn that is growing at the Broken Place. This site has been identified by present-day Maya descendants as Paxal, in the western highlands of Guatemala, near the Mexican border. The gods are excited by this information and go there at once.

The gods ask coyote and crow to gather yellow and white corn (maize). They grind and mix the corn together with the blood of the tapir and serpent. Xpiyacoc and Xmucane, the father and mother of the gods, make nine broths and mix them with the corn mixture, using it to form four perfect human specimens, known as the men of maize, four fathers of humanity: Balam-Quitzé (Smiling Jaguar), Balam-Agag (Nighttime Jaguar), Mahucutan (Famous Name), and Iqui-Balam (Moon Jaguar). The four fathers then drink corn broth, which gives them strength and intelligence. They are very grateful and are able to understand everything.

In time, however, Tepeu, Gucumatz, and Hurakan realize the four fathers are too perfect and may grow to rival the gods themselves. They blow mist into the eyes of the fathers, partially fogging their sight and understanding so that they are still fairly intelligent but not perfect. Pleased with this state of affairs, the gods make women to keep the four fathers company and allow them to fill the world with their children. The four mothers are: Caha-Paluma (Falling Water), wife of Balam-Quitzé;

Choimha (Beautiful Water), wife of Balam-Agag; Tzununiha (House of the Water), wife of Mahucutan; and Cakixa (Water of Parrots), wife of Iqui-Balam. The gods also give the people fire, although they do not allow them to make it for themselves.

The four fathers, however, wish to see the dawn, for the world remains in darkness. They decide to travel to the place where the sun rises. They come to the seashore, and using a magic staff given to them by the gods, part the sea to continue their journey. They eventually arrive at the magnificent land where the sun rises for the first time. The first animals, when they stand in the sunlight, turn to stone, as do the gods who were to watch over the men of maize. The four fathers realize that they cannot return home and live among their descendants, so they ascend the mountain Hacavitz, never to be seen again.

SIGNIFICANCE

Traditional Maya culture flourished from around 1500 BCE until the early sixteenth century CE, when it was nearly obliterated by Spanish invaders. In that vast span of time, Maya civilization consisted of a series of interrelated but largely independent city-states. These were scattered throughout what is now southern Mexico, Guatemala, Belize, western Honduras, and northern El Salvador.

The precolonial Mayas were skilled artists, creating magnificent statuary, pottery, and jewelry. Uniquely among the peoples of the Americas, they are known to have been prolific writers, producing books from perishable material such as deer hide and tree bark as well as more permanent glyphic accounts in stone. However, modern understanding of Maya culture is limited, largely because the conquering Spanish systematically destroyed Maya books and suppressed traditional beliefs, which they considered to be inspired by devil worship.

During this period of Spanish suppression of Maya beliefs, elite members of the Quiché band living in the western Guatemalan highlands secretly authored the *Popol Vuh*, meaning "council book" or "book of counsel," among other possible interpretations. This vast poetic work is a quasi-historical account of the Maya people. The *Popol Vuh* describes a complex mythological system that revered many divinities, including gods of the sky, the earth, various natural phenomena, and human economic activities. Although it is undated, internal evidence suggests that it was penned in the mid-1550s, three decades after the Spanish invaders began their conquest of the Maya homeland.

The authors of the *Popol Vuh* claim that the content of the work came from an earlier book, still in their possession at the time that they were writing. It is known from contemporary accounts from Spanish officials, many of whom were intent on seeking out and destroying such works, that there was a fair amount of Maya religious literature written on specially prepared deer hides and folded-bark books. The original source referred to by the Quiché authors was likely made of such perishable material.

It is difficult to determine the degree to which the myths in the *Popol Vuh* can be taken as representative of ancient Maya beliefs. The Maya pantheon of gods was wide and complex, and specific modes of worship varied between city-states and within different ruling families. Moreover, non-Maya influences had probably led to cultural changes in the centuries before the *Popol Vuh* was written. Specifically, the central Mexican Nahuatl language, the mother tongue of the Aztec and Toltec people, had become a common language for elites throughout Mesoamerica, including among the Mayas. It is likely that this newly adopted language brought about some changes in mythological beliefs.

Adam Berger, PhD
Michael P. Auerbach, MA

BIBLIOGRAPHY

Christenson, Allen J., trans. *Popol Vuh: The Sacred Book of the Maya*. Norman: U of Oklahoma P, 2007. Print.

Foster, Lynn V. *A Brief History of Central America*. 2nd ed. New York: Checkmark, 2007. Print.

Rubalcaba, Jill. *Empires of the Maya*. New York: Chelsea, 2010. Print.

Sharer, Robert J. *Daily Life in Maya Civilization*. 2nd ed. Westport: Greenwood, 2009. Print.

Tedlock, Dennis, trans. *Popol Vuh: The Definitive Edition of the Mayan Book of the Dawn of Life and the Glories of Gods and Kings*. Rev. ed. New York: Simon, 1996. Print.

Young, Peter A. *Secrets of the Maya*. New York: Hatherleigh, 2004. Print.

NORTH AMERICA

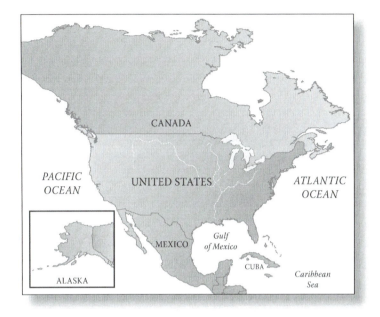

The Fight with the Water Monster

Author: Traditional Wabanaki
Time Period: 1001 CE–1500 CE
Country or Culture: North America
Genre: Folktale

PLOT SUMMARY

The Wabanaki man-god Glooskap is a powerful immortal hero who protects the world from evil. Considered a spirit and a man of medicine, he is also responsible for making the animals that roam the earth today. For example, when Glooskap first came to the earth, he noticed that squirrels and beavers were far too large to live in the world without causing untold damage to it. He therefore shrank them to their present sizes. Glooskap is benevolent and willing to help humanity—he created a village, teaching the people who lived there how to hunt, fish, and happily live harmony with another—but occasionally tires of his many responsibilities and paddles away to rest in what is now Nova Scotia.

The village only has one water source, a spring containing fresh and clean water. One day, however, the spring ceases to flow, so a man from the village travels upstream to see what has happened. He comes across a tribe of amphibious people, who live along a lake of stinking, slime-covered water. The lake is the spring, dammed up in this area. The people tell the villager that they cannot give him any water because their chief wants all of the water for himself. The man asks to meet the chief and is brought before him, only to discover that the chief is in fact a gigantic water monster. When the man asks him to release the water downstream, the monster simply laughs and threatens to kill him. Unsuccessful in restoring the flow of water, the man returns to his village and reports that the situation is hopeless.

The man-god Glooskap, however, becomes aware of the situation and tells the people not to despair, saying that he will visit the monster. When Glooskap finds the monster, the giant bullfrog laughs at his request and threatens to swallow Glooskap whole. The hero becomes enraged, making himself into a giant, towering above the monster. He gets ready for war and removes a mountaintop, which he forges into a very sharp spear tip. The monster attempts to eat Glooskap, and a thunderous battle ensues. Glooskap uses the flint spear he has created to split wide open the beast's stomach and all of the water the monster consumed flows downstream again in a great river. Glooskap takes the shrunken water monster in his hand and squeezes the water from it with great force—which is why frogs came to have bumps and wrinkles on their backs—eventually throwing the former monster into a swamp.

Glooskap returns to the village victorious. The people in the village, however, become rebellious, and Glooskap decides not to live among them anymore. He returns to the river in his canoe, leaving the village behind, as the loons and other water birds cry mournfully at his departure to the end of the world.

SIGNIFICANCE

The story of Glooskap's fight with the water monster is demonstrative of this figure's many abilities and characteristics. Glooskap is both a man and a god, capable of doing anything. He brings happiness and guidance to humanity and is capable of making people laugh and love one another. He is also a fierce warrior, imbued with great powers that he uses to defend the world against evil. Although he occasionally grows tired of his tasks, he never loses his love or dedication to the good inhabitants of the earth. In light of these many otherworldly abilities, Glooskap is similar to many legendary heroes of ancient Greece (such as Oedipus), Egypt (including Horus), and even the folklore of early Christianity (such as St. George, who slays a dragon to protect townspeople and convert them).

However, Glooskap is also a creator. He regulates the size of all animals, ensuring that they will live in harmony with humans. According to a continuation of this story (a version told by the Passamaquoddy and Micmac tribes), after Glooskap vanquishes the water monster, he returns to find the people of the village so joyful at life in the water that they wish to live in it. He therefore helps them become fish, crabs, leeches, and other water creatures, living in the river that he created by his battle.

This story of Glooskap was revealed to the rest of the world by Silas Tertius Rand, a Nova Scotian missionary traveling into Wabanaki territory (in a large portion along the Atlantic seaboard) during the late nineteenth century. Glooskap is said to have formed many of the region's geographic features in addition to reducing the size of the animals there. This story provides examples of both actions. During his battle with the water monster,

Glooskap levels a mountain peak to create a spear; when he vanquishes his enemy, he creates a slash a mile wide across the frog's stomach, creating a mighty river that leads to the sea. Meanwhile, he squeezes the frog down to its unique size and appearance.

In addition to providing explanations for elements of the natural world, the story also invites people to follow Glooskap's example. He is a benevolent figure but tires of the people when they become insolent or self-centered. When ordinary people fail to adhere to his teachings, Glooskap takes his leave of them and returns to his home. Although it is implied that he will never truly leave humanity, Glooskap's departure at the end of this story leaves the people and animals mournful.

Michael P. Auerbach, MA

BIBLIOGRAPHY

Bastian, Dawn Elaine, and Judy K. Mitchell. *Handbook of Native American Mythology*. Goleta: ABC-CLIO, 2004. Print.

"Glooskap Fights the Water Monster." *First People— The Legends*. First People, 2013. Web. 28 Apr. 2013.

Leeming, David, and Jake Page. *Myths, Legends, and Folktales of America: An Anthology*. Oxford: Oxford UP, 1999. Print.

Leland, Charles G. "How Glooskap Conquered the Great Bull-Frog, and in what Manner All the Pollywogs, Crabs, Leeches, and Other Water Creatures Were Created." *The Algonquin Legends of New England*. Boston: Houghton, 1884. 114–19. Print.

Mathis, Andy, and Marion Wood. *North American Civilizations.* New York: Rosen, 2004. Print.

Rand, Silas Tertius. *Legends of the Micmacs*. Whitefish: Kessinger, 2006. Print.

◆ George Washington: I Cannot Tell a Lie

Author: Mason Locke Weems
Time Period: 1701 CE–1850 CE
Country or Culture: North America
Genre: Legend

PLOT SUMMARY

Mason Locke Weems's famous tale of George Washington and the cherry tree appears in chapter 2 of his narrative *The Life of Washington*. After briefly introducing

Washington's childhood, Weems presents truth as a theme in the boy's history. He praises at length the boy's honesty, as testified by his father, who delivers a speech in which he praises honesty and then declaims its opposite. He describes truth as the best quality of youth and swears that he would ride fifty miles to see a boy who is so honest that every word he speaks is dependable. Everyone loves such a boy: parents and relatives exalt him endlessly and beg his peers to follow his angelic example. In contrast, a dishonest boy has no credibility and is actively shunned by other parents.

Mr. Washington assures the young George of his affection but declares, "Gladly would I assist to nail you up in your little coffin, and follow you to your grave" rather than know that his son is a liar (Weems 9). To this, George asks whether he has ever told lies. The father replies with great relief that George is impeccably honest, and he condemns parents who inadvertently encourage lying by beating their children for the offense, which then encourages further lying to avoid additional abuse. He urges young George that when he errs, he should come to his father "like a little man" (9) and confess the deed, and he promises to honor rather than punish the boy.

As evidence of George's honesty and his father's sound parenting, Weems then offers the famous anecdote. At six years old, George receives a hatchet as a gift. "Like most little boys," Weems notes, George is "immoderately fond" of the tool, so he proceeds to chop "every thing that came in his way" (9–10). In the family garden, where he is accustomed to cutting his mother's pea stalks, he turns his hatchet on an English cherry tree. When his father discovers that one of his favorite trees has been irreparably damaged, he enters the house to determine who is responsible.

At first, no one comes forward with information about the deed, but then George presents himself, and his father asks him directly whether he knows who has destroyed the tree. George does not answer immediately as he struggles with the question, but then he looks squarely at his father and admits, "I can't tell a lie, Pa; you know I can't tell a lie. I did cut it with my hatchet" (10). The father's elation at his son's honesty is immediate and unequivocal. "Such an act of heroism in my son," he proclaims, "is more worth than a thousand trees though blossomed with silver, and their fruits of purest gold" (10).

SIGNIFICANCE

The tone of Weems's language in the story of Washington and the cherry tree is exultant and, along with other elements of the tale, serves to mythologize the first US president as a man of flawless virtue from the time of his boyhood. The intent to mythologize evolved over several years; Weems's 1806 work *The Life of Washington the Great*, in which the tale first appeared, was the fifth edition of an earlier, modestly successful biography that he had first published in 1800. The earlier edition was less enticingly titled *The Life and Memorable Actions of George Washington* and did not feature the legend of the cherry tree. This late addition is one sign that Weems invented the cherry tree anecdote. However, Robert G. Miner explains in his preface to the work that Weems sought to exalt and mythologize George Washington just as other nations had done with their national heroes. Weems saw an opportunity to create in Washington a virtuous hero specifically for young people to emulate. Miner describes Weems's objective clearly: "Weems was not concerned with reality. His 'mishandling' of the facts of Washington's early life is a *myth*-handling, a journey beyond mere history to the collective unconscious of the nation" (ix).

Interestingly, Weems constructs Washington's heroism by underscoring the meaning of his virtue not in public but in private terms, which he claims have special meaning, particularly for his target audience of children. In chapter 1, Weems forcefully makes the argument that it is not the public life of military exploits and statesmanship that matter but private life, because "private life is always real life" (4). His biography is necessary, he claims, because nothing has been written of the private roles that Washington played: "the dutiful son; the affectionate brother; the cheerful school-boy; the diligent surveyor; the neat draftsman; the laborious farmer; the widow's husband; the orphan's father . . . and poor man's friend" (4). He argues that these private virtues are important because they form the basis of strong character and all the achievements that stem from it. Moreover, Washington's private virtues are relevant to children because they generally care most about character, and although the vast majority of young people cannot hope to aspire to Washington's great deeds, they can aspire to match his personal virtue. This claim to represent Washington's private virtue via true childhood anecdotes reveals Weems's rhetorical effectiveness and explains some historians' objections to the semifictional nature of this biography.

Ashleigh Imus, PhD

BIBLIOGRAPHY

Cornog, Evan. *The Power and the Story: How the Crafted Presidential Narrative Has Determined Political Success from George Washington to George W. Bush.* New York: Penguin, 2004. Print.

Leary, Lewis. *The Book-Peddling Parson: An Account of the Life and Works of Mason Locke Weems Patriot, Pitchman, Author and Purveyor of Morality to the Citizenry.* Chapel Hill: Algonquin, 1984. Print.

Levy, Philip. *Where the Cherry Tree Grew: The Story of Ferry Farm, George Washington's Boyhood Home.* New York: St. Martin's, 2013. Print.

Lewis, Thomas A. *For King and Country: The Maturing of George Washington, 1748–1760.* New York: HarperCollins, 1993. Print.

Miner, Robert G. Preface. *The Life of Washington the Great.* By Mason L. Weems. New York: Garland, 1977. iii–x. Print.

Rejai, Mostafa. *The Young George Washington in Psychobiographical Perspective.* Lewiston: Mellen, 2000. Print.

Weems, Mason L. *The Life of Washington.* 1800. Introd. Peter S. Onuf. Armonk: Sharpe, 1996. Print.

◆ The Girl Who Married a Gnome

Author: Traditional Inuit
Time Period: 1001 CE–1500 CE
Country or Culture: North America
Genre: Folktale

PLOT SUMMARY

A young woman named Arouk lives with her parents in a sealskin tent near a beautiful fjord. Arouk desperately wants to marry, but her father has yet to meet a man who is good enough for her. One day an unfamiliar man appears in his kayak and calls out to Arouk by name. When she peeks through the tent flap, her father yells at the man to go away. Instead of leaving, the young man starts to walk right up to the tent, which angers the father and incites a shoving match. After the father is pushed to the ground by the stranger, he throws a rock at the young man's head and knocks him unconscious.

Fearing for his life, Arouk's father then orders his wife and daughter to pack their belongings. Just as the young man regains consciousness, they paddle safely away from the fjord, though they cannot ignore the man's menacing voice threatening them, vowing that Arouk will never marry and her family will never be fed if they are starving. After paddling all day, the family reaches an island where there is an abandoned house. They live there happily for a long time and make the island their home.

One day, much to her parents' surprise, Arouk announces that she is married, although when her father first sees his son-in-law he thinks he is hallucinating, for the man is a tiny atliarusek, or gnome. When Arouk confesses to the marriage, the father is quite happy, especially when the gnome hunts food for them.

One day the gnome says that he must leave Arouk temporarily to visit his family. Arouk and her parents insist upon following his kayak in their umiak. As they travel toward the fjord, other gnomes join them. At one point, the gnomes travel under the water so they cannot be seen, but they eventually resurface. Finally, the caravan reaches the Valley of the Caribou, where Arouk and her family stay all summer and fill their umiak with meat and furs.

Upon arriving home, Arouk's father hears that the families in their old village are starving to death. After some consideration, he decides to bundle up some meat and hides and return to the village. When he arrives, rather than being greeted by grateful friends and neighbors, he is spoken to harshly, especially by the young man who had threatened him years earlier. He is ridiculed for lying about his hunting prowess and for claiming to have procured all that meat without a son-in-law.

The father leaves the food behind in anger and returns home furious about their lack of appreciation. When he expresses his feelings, his son-in-law suggests that he invite the villagers to their home for a feast. The father immediately warms to the idea. Soon the old neighbors appear in their kayaks, including all of the young men whom he had rejected for his daughter, and they begin to feast on dishes made from seal and caribou. Meanwhile, the father takes advantage of their presence and proceeds to speak to them about their insensitivity, especially regarding the treatment he received from his daughter's belligerent suitor. Most of the guests express remorse and shame. When he is finished, he has made peace with the villagers, and they with him.

SIGNIFICANCE

Unlike Irish leprechauns or Norse elves, the venerated "little people" in European mythology and literature, gnomes do not feature as prominently in Inuit culture. The story of the girl who married a gnome was first collected by Dr. Hinrich Johannes Rink and published in *Tales and Traditions of the Eskimo* (1875). In Greenland, gnomes were called *atliaruseks* or *ingnersuaks* and were believed to live within rocks along the shores where they interacted with humans as they fished and hunted from their kayaks and umiaks. They were mostly benevolent creatures and were considered guardians of humans, although they were capable of inflicting harm or creating unwanted mischief.

This folktale conveys much about Inuit family life, marriage, and social values and the challenges to Inuit survival. In Inuit society, men were the hunters and were thus responsible for feeding their families. Hunting, then, was more than a desirable skill in a husband; it was crucial for survival.

When seal, whale, fish, and other sea life were plentiful, families would congregate together near the coastline. During the summers, hunters also chased reindeer inland to places such as the Valley of the Caribou. The sharing of meat and skins between villagers—many of whom were related—was commonplace, and community-wide feasts often marked successful hunts. During famines, the sharing of food between neighbors and relatives became especially crucial. Both the Inuit father and his gnome son-in-law in the tale, then, demonstrate a strong sense of conscience toward their fellow villagers when they share their food not just once but twice. The tale also serves to provide a means to teach societal and familial values from generation to generation.

Sally Driscoll, MLS

BIBLIOGRAPHY

Bierhorst, John. *The Deetkatoo: Native American Stories about Little People*. New York: Morrow, 1998. Print.

Campisi, Jack. "Legends from Greenland: Or, What Became of the Norse?" *Pequot Museum*. Mashantucket Pequot Museum and Research Center, 2002. Web. 31 May 2013.

"Canada's First Peoples: The Inuit." *First Peoples of Canada*. Goldi Productions, 2007. Web. 30 May 2013.

Rink, Henry. *Tales and Traditions of the Eskimo: With a Sketch of Their Habits, Religion, Language, and Other Peculiarities*. 1875. Mineola: Dover, 1997. Print.

Wolfson, Evelyn. *Inuit Mythology*. Berkeley Height: Enslow, 2001. Print.

How Jack O'Lanterns Came to Be

Author: Zora Neale Hurston
Time Period: 1851 CE–1900 CE; 1901 CE–1950 CE
Country or Culture: North America
Genre: Folktale

PLOT SUMMARY

During the time of slavery, there is an incredibly strong and large slave named Big Sixteen, so called because of his shoe size. Big Sixteen's slave master recognizes how powerful he is and assigns him the most arduous tasks around the plantation. One day, the slave master tells him to go retrieve heavy twelve-by-twelve sills that have been left in a swamp. This seems like an impossible task for one man, but Big Sixteen brings all of the sills back to the slave master's house and stacks them himself.

After the chore with the sills is complete, the slave master instructs Big Sixteen to go and retrieve some mules that are out in the pasture. The mules are stubborn and uncooperative when Big Sixteen tries to lead them along by their bridles. The bridles snap, so he picks a mule up under each arm and brings them back to the slave master that way.

Surprised by Big Sixteen's astonishing strength, the slave master says that if he is strong enough to carry mules under his arms, then he must be strong enough to catch the Devil. Big Sixteen agrees to the task, as long as he is supplied with a nine-pound hammer, a pick, and a shovel. The slave master gives Big Sixteen these tools, and the slave goes to work digging his way down to Hell. It takes him nearly a month of digging to reach the Devil's house. Upon arriving, Big Sixteen knocks on the door. When the Devil pokes his head out, Big Sixteen smashes him over the head with the hammer, killing him. He carries the Devil back up to the slave master, who is shocked that Big Sixteen was actually able to catch him. Repulsed by the sight of the corpse, the slave master tells Big Sixteen to throw the Devil back down to Hell, which he does.

Big Sixteen lives for many years after this event. When he does die, Big Sixteen goes up to Heaven. Saint Peter looks at him and sees that he is too powerful to reside there. Fearing that Big Sixteen might cause trouble, Saint Peter tells him to leave. With nowhere else to go, Big Sixteen goes down to Hell.

The Devil's children are playing near the gates of Hell when they spot Big Sixteen. They recognize him as the man who killed their father and begin to call for their mother. The Devil's wife yells for the children to run inside the house. When Big Sixteen gets to the door, the wife says he is not allowed in Hell. She hands him a flaming hot coal and tells him to go start a hell of his own.

People who see a jack o'lantern in the woods at night know that it is Big Sixteen wandering around with his coal, looking for a place to rest for eternity.

SIGNIFICANCE

When enslaved Africans were brought over to the Americas, they brought their long tradition of storytelling with them. Since slaves were prohibited from learning how to read and write, it became essential for them to pass on their histories, morals, and folklore orally to preserve their cultural heritages. Generations of storytellers passed on traditional songs, legends, folktales, proverbs, and other orally transmitted traditions. This strong oral tradition helped enslaved Africans hold onto their cultural identity and values while adapting to their harsh new environment in America.

Many African American folktales provided exaggerated and sometimes humorous explanations for the creation of certain things. For example, there are stories about how snakes became poisonous and how possums lost the hair on their tail. These folktales are also colloquially referred to as "lies" and are similar to American tall tales. Other types of African American folktales include fables centered on animals and stories of trickster slaves who outsmart their masters. The tricksters in these stories are often named John or Jack. Oftentimes, perhaps because of their situation, many folktales created by slaves are concerned with escape and fantasy.

The folk hero of Big Sixteen is one such fantasy, as he possesses superhuman strength and stature. He is strong enough to kill the Devil, in fact. He can be compared to American tall-tale characters such as Paul Bunyan and John Henry, who is possibly the best-known African American tall-tale hero. Since any sign of verbal defiance or strength might be seen as a threat to the slave master, tall tales of superhuman characters such as Big Sixteen were rare in African American folklore until after emancipation.

"How Jack O'Lanterns Came to Be" is an example of an exaggeration story. The story explains the origins of jack o'lanterns, which, besides being a contemporary Halloween tradition, are prevalent in folktales around the globe. This African American version is similar in its conclusion to many of the other stories, particularly the Irish folktale "Stingy Jack." In this tale, a man named Jack manages to trap the Devil. He later frees him under the condition that when he dies, the Devil will not claim Jack's soul in Hell. The Devil agrees, but when Jack dies, he is refused entrance into Heaven. The Devil insultingly gives Jack a hot coal to light his way as he wanders the earth. Jack carves out a turnip, into which he puts the burning coal, and is thereafter known as Jack of the Lantern or Jack O'Lantern.

It is commonly believed that jack o'lantern stories evolved from will-o'-the-wisp stories, which can also be found in folk traditions around the globe. The will-o'-the-wisps refer to ghostly lights or orbs that have frequently been seen at night, typically around swamps and marshes. In many folktales, these lights draw travelers off their path. "How Jack O'Lanterns Came to Be" can be read as the African American version of these various tales.

Patrick G. Cooper

BIBLIOGRAPHY

Abrahams, Roger. *African American Folk Tales: Stories from Black Traditions in the New World*. New York: Pantheon, 1999. Print.

Andrews, William L. "How Jack O'Lanterns Came to Be." *African American Literature: Voices in a Tradition*. Austin: Holt, 1992. 182–84. Print.

Brownlee, Catherine Thornton. *Recurring Themes of African American Folktales*. Philadelphia: Teachers Inst. of Philadelphia, U of Pennsylvania, 5 July 2004. PDF file.

Courlander, Harold. *A Treasury of Afro-American Folklore: The Oral Literature, Traditions, Recollections, Legends, Tales, Songs, Religious Beliefs, Customs, Sayings and Humor of Peoples of African American Descent in the Americas*. Boston: De Capo, 2002. Print.

Hurston, Zora Neale. *Mules and Men*. New York: Harper, 2008. Print.

"The Legend of Stingy Jack." *History of the Jack O'Lantern*. History.com, 2013. Web. 28 May 2013.

Roberts, John. *From Trickster to Badman: The Black Folk Hero in Slavery and Freedom*. Philadelphia: U of Pennsylvania P, 1990. Print.

Iroquois Creation Story

Author: Traditional Iroquois
Time Period: 1001 CE–1500 CE
Country or Culture: North America
Genre: Myth

PLOT SUMMARY

In the beginning, the Great Spirit rules over other superior beings in the otherworld beyond the clouds. One day, his daughter (called Sky Woman in most versions) becomes pregnant illegitimately. In a rage, the Great Spirit reaches down, yanks out a great tree, and pushes her through the newly opened hole. She falls through the sky onto Great Turtle, whose shell oozes with mud, and together they form the earth.

Sky Woman gives birth to the first child on earth, a daughter. When the young woman reaches the age of maturity, various spirits disguised as humans make offers of marriage, but her mother rejects all until a certain middle-aged hunter appears. She invites him into the house to spend the night with her daughter. As she spies on them from the other side of the hearth, she notices that the hunter does not lie down beside her daughter but rather pulls two bows from his quiver and mysteriously sets them beside her. At dawn, he removes the bows and disappears.

The young woman becomes miraculously pregnant and gives birth to twins who are polar opposites, Teharonghyawago ("Holder of Heaven") and Tawiskaron ("Flinty Rock," named for the covering on his skin). The younger, Tawiskaron, insists upon using his flint-like skin to cut through his mother's side, creating a slit that kills her as he enters the world.

While the twins grow up under the guardianship of their grandmother, they spend most of their time apart. Teharonghyawago resents Tawiskaron for killing their mother and for doing evil. Upset over his inability to stop the evil doings, Teharonghyawago seeks solace in the woods. There, he meets his father, Great Turtle, who gives him the first ear of corn to plant. In addition to ushering in agriculture, Teharonghyawago also bears responsibility for peopling the earth and seeing to it that clans are happy.

Tawiskaron, who spends most of his time hunting, has begun to capture elk and other gentle animals and imprison them in a cave for his own use, a practice that defies the relationship between humans and animals as set forth by the Great Spirit. Teharonghyawago spies on Tawiskaron from a tree and frees the captured beasts when Tawiskaron is away from the cave. Angered by this, Tawiskaron retaliates by antagonizing the people Teharonghyawago nurtures.

Eventually, the brothers fight each other in a prolonged contest, with battles taking place over the region that would later become the land of the Iroquois Confederacy. Teharonghyawago is victorious, killing Tawiskaron. The story ends by linking the sites of the widespread battles with the evolution of different languages spoken by the different tribes of the confederacy.

SIGNIFICANCE

This version of the Iroquois creation story was recorded in 1816 by John Norton, who was of mixed Cherokee and Scottish descent and had been adopted by Joseph Brant, chief of the Mohawks and a Christian missionary. The purpose of the story is to account for the creation of North America (or the earth), called Turtle Island by the Iroquois Confederacy (or Haudenosaunee League), as well as its people, plants, and animals. It also explains the origin of good and evil. At the time Norton collected the story, the Iroquois Confederacy had grown into the Six Nations (the Cayugas, Mohawks, Oneidas, Onondagas, Senecas, and Tuscaroras, whose territory originally stretched across the woodlands of what is now central New York and southern Ontario and Quebec). While they relied heavily on hunting for survival, the Iroquois were also known for their agricultural expertise, having developed maize, beans, and squash crops. Each tribe spoke a different language, although they shared some similarities, and each tribe was divided into matriarchal clans, with the mother at the center of the clan.

While Norton's version is representative of the confederacy's belief in the Great Turtle as a major force in creation, the Iroquois creation story varies in the details of key events, the names of spiritual beings, and other elements from tribe to tribe. In most cases, Sky Woman is identified as the bearer of medicinal plants into the world, the originator of plant and human life on earth, the moon (which controls the seas and menstruation), and the feminine force that presides over all of humanity and nature. In some versions, her daughter becomes a corn mother after her body fertilizes the ground and yields the first corn, beans, and squash plants. She is often considered the mother earth. Sky Woman and her daughter's roles as major deities or spirits reflect the matrilineal society and respect for the feminine.

Norton's version, however, seems to subordinate the role of the feminine while crediting most of creation to male deities or spirits. The female beings are unnamed, simply referred to as the young woman, the old woman, the daughter, the mother, or the grandmother. In most versions, Sky Woman is either in an equal relationship with the Great Spirit or married to another supernatural being, instead of being depicted as a pregnant daughter. The illicit nature of the pregnancy is a common motif, however; in some variants, Sky Woman is accused of adultery. Some say she creates the hole through which she accidentally falls, and many say the birds in the sky call upon Great Turtle to rescue her, as opposed to the angry Great Spirit pushing his disparaged daughter through the hole that he created and, seemingly as an afterthought, commanding Great Turtle to save her.

Related to this alteration are the Christian influences seen throughout the Norton narrative: the apparent virgin birth; the attention given to the Great Spirit as a supreme deity; and the focus on the twin brothers, who are in some ways reminiscent of the biblical first brothers, Cain and Abel. Therefore, while Norton's version remains an important account, its authenticity as a traditional American Indian narrative is questionable.

Sally Driscoll, MLS

BIBLIOGRAPHY

Bierhorst, John. *The Woman Who Fell from the Sky: The Iroquois Story of Creation*. New York: Morrow, 1993. Print.

Doxstater, Elizabeth. "Creation Story." *Iroquois Museum*. Iroquois Indian Museum, n.d. Web. 28 May 2013.

Elm, Demus, and Harvey Antone. *The Oneida Creation Story*. Lincoln: U of Nebraska P, 2000. Print.

Hewitt, John N. *Iroquoian Cosmology*. New York: AMS P, 2004. Print.

Olan, Kay. "Creation Story." *Iroquois Museum*. Iroquois Indian Museum, n.d. Web. 28 May 2013.

Norton, John. "Iroquois Creation Myth, 1816." *The Journal of Major John Norton, 1816*. Ed. Carl F. Klinck

and James J. Talman. Toronto: Champlain Soc., 1970. 88–91. Print.

Vecsey, Christopher. "The Story and Structure of the Iroquois Confederacy." *Journal of the American Academy of Religion* 54.1 (1986): 79–106. Print.

◆ John Henry: The Steel Driving Man

Author: S. E. Schlosser
Time Period: 1851 CE–1900 CE
Country or Culture: North America
Genre: Legend

PLOT SUMMARY

The legend of John Henry takes place during the Reconstruction era, the period following the American Civil War, as emancipated African American slaves found work in labor and industry; Henry is assumed to have been a freed slave in real life. In the tale, Henry is a big and brawny man—exaggerated to the height of eight feet—who takes a job driving steel for the Chesapeake & Ohio Railroad. In 1869, when construction of the railroad reaches the formidable Great Bend Mountain near Talcott, West Virginia, it becomes apparent that the only way to reach the other side is to blast through the mile of hard Appalachian mountainside.

On the railroad, Henry's job is to drill the long holes needed for inserting and lighting dynamite. Using a whopping fourteen-pound sledgehammer, he manually pounds a steel drill into rock by delivering one mighty blow after another for twelve hours a day. Another man, known as a shaker, turns the drill after each blow. The work is exhausting, hot, and sweaty, and the hazardous dust is just one of many factors that make the working conditions deplorable. During the course of the three-year project, hundreds of men die and many are buried in makeshift graves near the tunnel. John Henry's longevity and perseverance, however, earn him quite a reputation.

One day, a salesman brings a newfangled steam-powered drill that threatens to put Henry and other steel-drivers out of work. Henry rises to the challenge of testing his might against the machine in a one-day competition. Using two twenty-pound hammers, one in each hand, he begins drilling. The other men whoop and cheer him on as the dust and noise overpower the tunnel. By the end of the first thirty-five minutes, he succeeds in drilling two seven-foot holes compared to the meager nine-foot hole drilled by the steam engine. Exhausted, Henry raises his hammers above his head to claim victory but then falls to the ground as a blood vessel bursts in his brain. Although he takes his last breath that day, John Henry lives on in the memory of the men who continue to toil on the railroad. As the verse in the popular ballad states, "you could hear John Henry's hammer ring" forever.

SIGNIFICANCE

As a folktale as well as a popular musical ballad, the legend of John Henry has permeated American and African American culture. The many versions represent the diverse human creative spirit, as well as the varied nature of oral transmission. This narrative version can be found in the storyteller S. E. Schlosser's *Spooky South: Tales of Hauntings, Strange Happenings, and other Local Lore* (2004). The musical ballad, which begins with John Henry as a baby with a hammer in his hand, born to fulfill his legendary feat, represents one of the most recorded traditional songs in the world, with versions by Pete Seeger, Johnny Cash, Mississippi John Hurt, and many other musicians from the folk, country, blues, and rock genres.

The legend of John Henry can be appreciated from several different perspectives. As a historical narrative, John Henry attests to the period of Reconstruction and westward expansion, when the railroad linked the Carolinas, Virginias, and other eastern states with the frontier and helped bridged the divisiveness between the racially torn north and south. It speaks to the contributions and sacrifices made by African Americans to the growth of the country after emancipation, when racial discrimination continued to set boundaries between laborers and their white bosses. It also attests to the oppressive, often capricious working conditions and the sacrifice of laborers prior to modern government health and safety regulations and the rise of labor unions.

As John Henry came to serve as an icon of the labor movement, his work ethic—a blend of hard work, long hours, and unusual fortitude—also became representative of the American way to success, especially during the industrial era. Despite a shift in modern times toward a more relaxed, balanced approach to work and leisure, Americans still share this story of human success achieved from hard work and physical stamina, especially when challenged by a machine. The theme of man versus machine, common especially in science fiction, confronts the human fears and the challenges of being dominated by technology. Thus, Henry's victory represents hope for continued control of humanity by humans.

As the cultural equivalent of Paul Bunyan or Johnny Appleseed, Henry is an African American superhero who provides a collective sense of both literary history and cultural pride, while people throughout the world also relate to the upbeat themes in this powerful tale.

Sally Driscoll, MLS

BIBLIOGRAPHY

Hunn, Vanessa Lynn, and Carlton David Craig. "Depression, Sociocultural Factors, and African American Women." *Journal of Multicultural Counseling & Development* 37. 2 (2009): 83–93. Print.

"John Henry." *Black History Now*. Black Heritage Commemorative Soc., 9 June 2011. Web. 1 May 2013.

Laliberte, Richard. "The John Henry Syndrome." *Men's Health* 7.2 (1992): 86–87. Print.

Nelson, Scott Reynolds. *Steel Drivin' Man: John Henry, the Untold Story of an American Legend*. New York: Oxford UP, 2006. Print.

Nikola-Lisa, W. "John Henry: Then and Now." *African American Review* 32.1 (1998): 51–57. Print.

Whitehead, Colson. *John Henry Days: A Novel*. New York: Anchor, 2001. Print.

◈ La Llorona, Omen of Death

Author: Traditional Mexican American
Time Period: 1851 CE–1900 CE
Country or Culture: North America
Genre: Folktale

PLOT SUMMARY

María is a beautiful young girl from a small rural village. She takes great pride in her beauty, determining that she will not settle for any men of the village but will instead marry a handsome man from an upper-class family. One day, she meets a handsome young ranchero from a prominent, wealthy family. The young ranchero notices María's beauty and courts her. Though she is interested, she feigns disinterest to encourage his desire, turning away when she sees him, refusing his many attempts to give her gifts, and ignoring him when he serenades her with his guitar. The ranchero falls for María's deception and becomes obsessed with her.

When María realizes her ploy has been successful, she relents to the ranchero and allows him to court her. Eventually they marry, and María gives birth to two children. Before long, the ranchero seems to lose interest in María and returns to his wandering ways, traveling the plains and capturing wild horses. The ranchero disappears for months at a time and only returns to visit his children. Rumors around the village tell María that her husband has even considered marrying a wealthy woman of his own class and leaving María behind.

One night when María is walking with her children on a shadowy path near a river, her husband rides by in a carriage, with an elegant female passenger next to him. He stops and speaks to his children but ignores María. After being spurned, María becomes furious and directs her anger at her children, seizing them and throwing them into the river. Realizing what she has done, María chases after her children as they float downstream, moaning in pain with her arms outstretched; but she is unable to catch up with them, and the children die. The next morning, the villagers find María dead by the river. They dress her in white funerary garments and bury her body near the spot where she was found.

That night, the villagers hear moaning coming from the banks of the river, and some of the villagers see María's ghostly image walking along the river calling for her children. Night after night, the villagers hear and see the ghost of María, wandering near the river dressed in her white funerary garments and calling out, "Where are my children?" After some time, the villagers no longer call her María and begin calling her *la Llorona* (the "weeping woman"). From that time on, the people of the village warn their children against going out unattended at night, lest la Llorona steal them, thinking that they are her children.

SIGNIFICANCE

The folktale of la Llorona is known primarily from versions told among the Mexican American population of California and the American Southwest. Similar versions of the myth exist elsewhere in Mexico and throughout Central and South America. La Llorona can be considered an example of a broad category of folktales and myths that are used culturally to threaten children into avoiding "bad behavior." Children in communities where la Llorona was a popular folktale were often warned that la Llorona steals children who are out after dark or who misbehave in other ways. Folktales of this type reinforce parental discipline by providing an additional, supernatural incentive to avoid violating parental rules.

In addition, the story of la Llorona transmits a moral lesson to women by displaying how María's pride in her beauty and obsession with her lover causes her to doom her soul to unrest when she turns her frustration on her children. In the male-dominant culture of post-Columbian Mexico and Central America, excessive pride in one's appearance was especially frowned upon in women, who, it was believed, should remain modest. This story, like many local customs in this culture, promotes these qualities among women and warns of hardships and suffering that will befall women who become too proud or vain.

Some scholars have noted connections between the pre-Columbian Aztec goddesses Coatlicue and Cihuacóatl and later representations of women in Mexican culture, including the folktale of la Llorona. In the colonial era, stories of both Cihuacóatl and la Llorona were common and portray both women as dangerous and destructive figures. This depiction deviates from the traditional Aztec portrayals of the serpent woman Cihuacóatl as the patroness of midwives and a goddess of fertility. Historians believe that the patriarchal Spanish culture absorbed and adjusted the female figures of Aztec mythology to produce characters that fit the male-dominated mold of Spanish Catholic culture. In this way, stories in which Coatlicue appears to the Aztecs crying for the loss of her child became a story of a vain woman who destroys her own children and then threatens others because of her grief.

Despite the somewhat misogynistic depiction of women in Mexican folktales, some modern writers have resurrected la Llorona as a feminist symbol. La Llorona has been utilized in essays and novels as a symbol of the female struggle against male domination, both in the colonial era and in the modern struggle against domestic violence and spousal abuse. In reframing the myth of la Llorona from a feminist perspective, the ranchero becomes the symbolic villain, as he callously discards the mother of his children to pursue his own desires. While the ranchero's behavior would once have been seen as typical of any man, the feminist embrace of la

Llorona indicates the way that gender norms and values have changed in the modern world.

Micah Issitt

BIBLIOGRAPHY

Carbonell, Ana Maria. "From Llorona to Gritona: Coatlicue in Feminist Tales by Viramontes and Cisneros." *Melus* 24.2 (1999): 53–74. Print.

Castro, Raphael. *Chicano Folklore: A Guide to the Folktales, Traditions, Rituals, and Religious Practices of Mexican Americans*. New York: Oxford UP, 2001. Print.

Madsen, Deborah L. *Understanding Contemporary Chicana Literature*. Columbia: U of South Carolina P, 2000. Print.

Romero, Rolando, and Amanda Nolacea Harris, eds. *Feminism, Nation and Myth: La Malinche*. Houston: Arte Público, 2005. Print.

◆ The Legend of Joaquín Murrieta

Author: Traditional Mexican American
Time Period: 1851 CE–1900 CE
Country or Culture: North America
Genre: Legend

PLOT SUMMARY

Joaquín Carillo Murrieta is thought to have descended from a noble Basque family that relocated from Spain to Mexico early in the nineteenth century. Joaquín was born in 1830 in the northwestern Mexican state of Sonora, possibly near Alamos, a mining center. Those who claim to know him describe Joaquín as a handsome, well-spoken youth with flowing hair, flashing eyes, and impeccable manners. Joaquín falls in love with a young woman in a neighboring village, Rosa "Rosita" Féliz, and the couple run off together.

After the discovery of gold in California in early 1848, Rosa's three brothers travel north, joining half a million others in the rush for treasure. Joaquín, his paramour, and his half brother, Jesús, also trek to California to seek their fortunes.

The Murrieta-Féliz party begins mining a potentially rich claim in the Mother Lode Country of the Sierra Nevada. To supplement their income, they round up wild mustangs to sell. In the lawless boomtown climate of the gold rush, the new immigrants soon run afoul of Anglo miners hostile to foreign intrusions. After falsely accusing Joaquín and his half brother of stealing a mule, they lynch Jesús, bind Joaquín to a tree and whip him, and force him to witness the brutal gang rape of his beloved Rosa. The incident transforms honest, hardworking Joaquín into a bloodthirsty criminal bent on taking revenge against white settlers, particularly those who humiliated him and dishonored his woman.

Joaquín and his brother-in-law Claudio Féliz, accused of horse stealing, form a band of like-minded Mexican outlaws. The gang becomes known as the Five Joaquíns for Murrieta and his companions, four of whom—surnamed Botellier, Carrillo, Ocomorenia, and Valenzuela—are also supposedly called Joaquín. The bandits embark on a campaign of terror, ruthlessly robbing other miners, holding up stagecoaches, raiding ranches to rustle livestock, and indiscriminately killing anyone who opposes them. The men involved in the rape of Rosa are tracked down, savagely knifed or dragged to their deaths, and horribly mutilated.

By 1853, Murrieta and his felonious companions have murdered forty people and committed scores of crimes throughout California. That year, the state government authorizes the creation of the California Rangers and charges a twenty-man salaried posse, under the leadership of former Texas Ranger Harry Love, to hunt down and end the depredations of the Five Joaquíns.

In July 1853, the Rangers encounter a band of Mexicans in the mountains. Harsh words are traded, leading to an exchange of gunfire. In the aftermath, several Mexicans lie dead. One, a man with a mustache, is identified as Joaquín Murrieta. Another corpse with a missing digit is thought to be a bandit called Three-Fingered Jack. The Rangers decapitate the mustachioed man, lop off the disfigured hand, and preserve the relics in brandy for transport. They collect their pay and disband. Murrieta's head and Jack's hand are widely exhibited before being permanently displayed in San Francisco.

To this day, it is said that on foggy nights in California's central valleys, the ghost of Joaquín Murrieta can still occasionally be glimpsed, galloping in search of his missing head.

SIGNIFICANCE

Like all legends worthy of the designation, the story of Joaquín Murrieta is long on supposition and short on facts. The individual most responsible for establishing the legend was John Rollin Ridge (also known as Cheesquatalawny or Yellow Bird), who, in 1854, published a romanticized, highly fictionalized account, *The Life and Adventures of Joaquín Murieta*. The half-Cherokee Ridge slanted the story to make the hero not a mere bandit but a noble patriot, a righter of racial wrongs.

There undoubtedly were, and are, people named Joaquín Murrieta (or Murieta or Murrietta) in both Mexico and California. Allegedly, according to church records, a boy named Joaquín Murrieta was indeed born in Sonora in 1830. Additionally, there is some historical evidence that a Joaquín Murrieta was part of a band of outlaws led by Claudio Féliz, and it is true that a head purported to belong to Murrieta was exhibited in San Francisco after 1853. However, there is no evidence that Murrieta's wife was raped or that his brother was murdered, as the legend claims. It is far more likely that if Murrieta the bandit did exist, he was motivated simply by greed. The nineteenth-century discovery of precious minerals in the American West—in California, Idaho, Montana, Colorado, South Dakota, and elsewhere—lured starry-eyed and greedy people from around the world. Hastily built gold-rush communities were hotbeds of criminal behavior and transient violence.

California's gold rush had an added element. Before the Treaty of Guadalupe Hidalgo ended the Mexican-American War (1846–48), the territory had belonged to Mexico, and tensions ran high between whites newly in control and Mexicans suddenly relegated to the status of second-class citizens. An anti-immigrant state legislature exacerbated conditions by imposing special fees on foreign miners. Nativist masters likewise blamed rampant crime on the most convenient scapegoats. Robberies and murders simultaneously committed hundreds of miles apart were all blamed on Mexican banditos and on Joaquín Murrieta in particular.

There is no question that such gangs roamed the California hills: Claudio Féliz confessed to numerous crimes before he was imprisoned, escaped, and then shot to death. There is also no doubt that the California Rangers later killed and beheaded a Mexican man. Afterward, more than a dozen people came forward to identify the dead man's head as that of Joaquín Murrieta. However, others who knew Joaquín intimately claimed the head was not his. Some swore they had seen him alive years after his presumed death. The head is said to have been destroyed during the great San Francisco earthquake and subsequent fire of 1906.

Dead or alive, bandit or hero, the legend of Joaquín Murrieta, known as the Robin Hood of El Dorado, has provided material for countless songs, poems, plays, novels, stories, nonfiction books, articles, movies, and television shows. Murrieta's alleged exploits may have inspired the fictional character of Zorro, and they have certainly raised Mexican American awareness and helped give impetus to the modern Chicano movement.

Jack Ewing

BIBLIOGRAPHY

Boessenecker, John. *Gold Dust & Gunsmoke: Tales of Gold Rush Outlaws, Gunfighters, Lawmen, and Vigilantes*. New York: Wiley, 1999. Print.

Crutchfield, James A., Bill O'Neal, and Dale L. Walker. *Legends of the Wild West*. Lincolnwood: Publications International, 1995. Print.

Johnson, Susan Lee. *Roaring Camp: The Social World of the California Gold Rush*. New York: Norton, 2000. Print.

Latta, Frank F. *Joaquín Murrieta and His Horse Gangs*. Exeter: Bear State, 1980. Print.

Paz, Ireneo. *Life and Adventures of the Celebrated Bandit Joaquin Murrieta: His Exploits in the State of California*. Trans. Francis P. Belle. Introd. Luis Leal. Houston: Arte Público, 2001. Print.

Ridge, John Rollin. "From *The Life and Adventures of Joaquín Murieta*." *Gold Rush: A Literary Exploration*. Ed. Michael Kowalewski. Berkeley: Heyday, 1997. 222–27. Print.

Sherman, William T. "The California Gold Rush." *Warriors and Pioneers*. Ed. T. J. Stiles. New York: Perigee, 1996. 28–40. Print.

Thorton, Bruce S. *Searching for Joaquín: Myth, Murieta, and History in California*. San Francisco: Encounter, 2003. Print.

Wilson, Lori Lee. *The Joaquín Band: The History behind the Legend*. Lincoln: U of Nebraska P, 2011. Print.

◆ Legend of the Buffalo Dance

Author: Traditional Blackfoot
Time Period: 1001 CE–1500 CE
Country or Culture: North America
Genre: Folktale

PLOT SUMMARY

The legend of the Buffalo Dance tells the story of how the buffalo befriended the Blackfeet (or Blackfoot) people. Like most Great Plains people, the buffalo was central to the lifestyle of the Blackfeet tribe and considered an animal with great spiritual powers. Before they acquired horses from tribes further to the south, Plains tribes hunted the buffalo by using a buffalo jump. Hunters would try to stampede the herds of buffalo toward a high hill with a sharp cliff or drop-off, and many buffalo would be killed as they plunged over this edge. The legend of the Buffalo Dance tells of a time when the buffalo would not go over the cliff, thus leaving the people hungry and in great need.

A young woman goes out early one morning to fetch water from a source below the cliff. She sees a herd of buffalo grazing and cries out to them, promising to marry one of them if they will jump over the cliff. To her surprise, the buffalo begin running over the jump, and her people are supplied with meat, hides, and other resources from the buffalo in plenty. But a large bull buffalo requires that she fulfill her promise and marry him.

Later, the young woman's father misses her from their camp and begins to search for her. He asks a magpie to help search for her. The magpie finds the young woman, but she warns her father that he will be killed if he tries to rescue her. As she fears, the buffalo tramples her father to death. But when the buffalo who had married the young woman sees her sorrow, he takes pity on her and tells her that if she can bring her father back to life, then she and her father can safely return to her people. She asks the magpie for help, and the bird finds a joint from her father's backbone. Through spiritual songs, she restores the body of her father and, through further singing, brings him back to life. The buffalo-husband admits that strange things have taken place and notes, "The people's holy power is strong" (Campbell 285). The buffalo then teaches the woman and her father the dance and song of the buffalo, and when they return to the tribe, they teach these to a select group of young men who perform the dance to assure that the buffalo will continue to come back to life after being killed for the needs of the people.

SIGNIFICANCE

The Blackfeet people live in central and eastern Montana and northward into the western Plains region of Canada. Today, there are three Blackfeet reserves in the Canadian province of Alberta and one reservation in Montana, but not all tribal members live on these reservations.

Like most of the tribes that inhabited the North American Great Plains, the Blackfeet depended on the vast herds of buffalo that roamed their homelands. The buffalo was the principal source of food, but the hides, bones, sinew, hair, and horns were all used for a variety of purposes. Buffalo were considered animals with great spiritual power as well, and significant beliefs and rituals associated with the buffalo are found among virtually all Plains peoples. A common spiritual theme among many hunting tribes is an account of how the hunted animal has, sometime in the past, given the people *permission* to kill it, if good use is made of the food and other resources the animal represents and if proper ritual and respect is demonstrated. In the story of the Buffalo Dance, the young woman represents a human who is willing to make a sacrifice for the good of her people—if the buffalo will go over the cliff to provide food for her people, she will marry one of the buffalo. The magpie, who helps the father find his daughter and then finds the piece of bone that allows the young woman to reconstitute her father's body and then bring it to life, represents an intermediary figure, a creature that can connect the world of humans with the spirit world that surrounds him. Thus, the magpie may represent the role of the shaman in Blackfoot life. Shamans, whom early European observers often called "medicine men," were men or women who had the ability to contact the spirit world directly in order to find guidance and power for their people. After the young woman's spiritual songs resurrect her father, the buffalo-husband recognizes the great spiritual power of the humans and agrees to teach the woman and her father the song and dance that will allow them to bring the buffalo back to life after they have been killed to provide for the needs of the people. Thus, the people can make use of the resources the buffalo provide but still have a confident hope that the buffalo will continue to exist for the future needs of the people. As the young woman had sacrificed herself, the buffalo are willing to give themselves for the benefit of the Blackfeet people.

Mark S. Joy, PhD

BIBLIOGRAPHY

Bullchild, Percy, and Woody Kipp. *The Sun Came Down: The History of the World as My Blackfoot Elders Told It.* Lincoln: U of Nebraska P, 2005. Print.

Campbell, Joseph. *The Masks of God: Primitive Mythology*. 1959. New York: Penguin, 1976. 282–86. Print.

Grinnell, George Bird. "Origin of the I-kun-uh'-kah-tsi: The Bull Band." *Blackfoot Lodge Tales: The Story of a Prairie People*. New York: Scribner's, 1915. 104–7. Print.

Hefner, Alan G. "Legend of the Buffalo Dance." *Encyclopedia Mythica*. Encyc. Mythica, 2005. Web. 18 June 2013.

Hungry Wolf, Beverly. *The Ways of My Grandmothers*. New York: Morrow, 1998. Print.

McClintock, Walter. *The Old North Trail; or, Life, Legends, and Religion of the Blackfeet Indians*. 1910. Lincoln: U of Nebraska P, 1993. Print.

Wissler, Clark, and David C. Duvall, comp. and trans. *Mythology of the Blackfoot Indians*. Norman: U of Oklahoma P, 1995. Print.

◆ Ottawa Creation Story

Author: Traditional Ottawa
Time Period: 1001 CE–1500 CE
Country or Culture: North America
Genre: Myth

PLOT SUMMARY

In Nicolas Perrot's account of the Ottawa (Odawa) creation story, after the earth is created, each species of animal lives in the environment most suited to its needs and abilities. After some of these first animals die, a spiritual power known as the Great Hare creates humans out of the corpses of these dead animals. Perrot notes that many Ottawa people believe they are descended from those people who were created from various animals, the names of those animals or birds having become attached to certain clans and villages among the tribe. He also notes that the Ottawas, when they first encountered Europeans, believed these strange people must have been created by a different deity or spiritual power, since the Europeans' culture and technology was so different from their own.

The account goes on to describe how some of the basic aspects of the Ottawa culture developed. "Inspired by the Great Hare with an intuitive idea" (Perrot 38), they learn to make bows and arrows, which they can use to hunt animals for food. When they cannot eat this meat raw, they learn to make fire and use it to cook the meat. They also learn to make clothing out of the hides or furs of the animals they have killed. Since deep snows make hunting difficult in the winter, they learn to make what Perrot calls "a sort of racket" (snowshoes), and they build canoes for navigating the nearby rivers (39).

SIGNIFICANCE

The Ottawas are a tribe who originally lived in the Eastern Woodland cultural area of North America. Their language is a part of the Algonquian language family, which is typical of the tribes of eastern North America. They were closely related to the Ojibwas (also known as the Ojibways, Ojibwes, Anishinaabeg, or Chippewas) and the Potawatomis. The three tribes together were sometimes referred to as the Council (or People) of Three Fires and represented a powerful confederation that sometimes balanced or countered the power of the Iroquois in the region. When they first encountered Europeans, the Ottawas were living on Manitoulin Island in Lake Huron and in parts of present-day Ontario along the lake. Later, many of the Ottawas moved into the Lower Peninsula region of what is now Michigan. The Ottawas, like other Eastern Woodland peoples, lived by hunting, fishing, trading, collecting wild foods, and some farming in semipermanent settlements.

This version of the Ottawa creation story was recorded by a French fur trader, Nicolas Perrot, around 1720. Although Perrot's recounting of the story betrays a Eurocentric bias that places little confidence in the reliability of the account, it does preserve some traditional teachings of the Ottawas. In this brief story, the Ottawas sum up the creation of humans, the origins of their own clans, and the beginnings of the ways of life that were important to the Ottawa culture. Like most Indian cultures, the Ottawas traditionally believed a host of spiritual powers, called "manitous," inhabit the natural world and are closely connected to the lives of human beings. In the Ottawa account of creation, the manitou known as the Great Hare creates both the land and the first humans. The concept that those first humans are brought forth from the corpses of dead animals shows the intimate connection between humans and the natural world around them. The Ottawas also traditionally believed that their different clans, which each had a totem representing an animal or bird, traced back to those animals from whom the first people were created. The spirits of each of these animals were thought to have special significance to members of that particular clan.

The close connection between the spiritual world and human life is also shown in the way that the Great Hare shows the early humans how to make the weapons they would need for hunting for the animals and birds they would need for food. Because the Great Hare endows humans with minds and intuition, they also learn to develop other things needed for their lives, such as the use of fire for cooking, making garments from the hides and furs of animals, and making snowshoes for travel in the deep snows of winter. Many of the handicrafts that were necessary for creating the material culture of the Ottawa people are thus attributed to direction and providence of the Great Hare, the original creator.

Mark S. Joy, PhD

BIBLIOGRAPHY

Cash, Joseph H., and Gerald W. Wolff. *The Ottawa People.* Phoenix: Indian Tribal Series, 1978. Print.

Feest, Johanna E., and Christian F. Feest. "Ottawa." *Northeast.* Vol. 15 of *Handbook of North American Indians.* Ed. William C. Sturtevant. Washington: Smithsonian Inst., 1978. 772–86. Print.

Frazer, James George. "Totemism among Other Algonkin Tribes of the Great Lakes." *Marriage and Worship in the Early Societies.* Vol. 3. Delhi: Mittal, 1986. 64–68. Print.

Kinietz, W. Vernon. *The Indians of the Western Great Lakes, 1615–1760.* Ann Arbor: U of Michigan P, 1940. Print.

Leavalle, Tracy Neal. "Histories: Origins and Experience." *The Catholic Calumet: Colonial Conversions in French and Indian North America.* Philadelphia: U of Pennsylvania P, 2012. 19–46. Print.

Perrot, Nicolas. "Belief of the Savages Regarding the Creation of Man." *The Indian Tribes of the Upper Mississippi Valley and the Region of the Great Lakes.* Vol. 1. Trans. Emma Helen Blair. Ed. Blair. Cleveland: Clark, 1911. 37–40. Print.

Petrik, Paula. "Native American Creation Stories." *Exploring US History.* Roy Rosenzweig Center for History and New Media, George Mason U, Apr. 2004. Web. 18 June 2013.

◆ Paíyatuma and the Maidens of the Corn

Author: Traditional Zuni
Time Period: 1001 CE–1500 CE
Country or Culture: North America
Genre: Folktale

PLOT SUMMARY

In a time long ago, the sky father and the first mother set about creating the heavens and the earth. The sky father spreads out his hand, throwing out seeds that land in the soil and grow into corn that would nourish the people and animals living on earth. Paíyatuma, the god of the dew and the dawn (as well as the inventor of the flute and the beautiful music it creates), soon arrives and plants seven plants of corn. To help the plants grow, Paíyatuma brings forth seven maidens, dressed in white. Each virgin maiden dances around the corn, magically creating colorful and fiery light as the plants grow. The people rejoice at the corn maidens' dance, celebrating Paíyatuma's gift. Paíyatuma reminds the people to hold these maidens sacred and not to violate their purity, for their flesh would enrich the corn.

Over time, however, the people become aware of a new music, coming from the mountains. They determine that it is again Paíyatuma, who this time is playing intoxicating music accompanied by the dancing of maidens of the dew. The maidens of the mist perform their own captivating dance, creating rainbows and ethereal light as they follow Paíyatuma's flute music. When their dance is over, the maidens of the corn return to perform their own dance. However, the men and women who had previously celebrated the corn maidens' dance are not as captivated as they once were. The dance of the maidens of the mist now holds their attention. In response, the maidens of the corn lay down their magic wands and white robes and disappear.

The people attempt to call forth the maidens of the corn, but the maidens do not appear. The men and women soon realize that the maidens are gone. They looked to Eagle, who can see everything in the world, but Eagle cannot find the maidens. The people then turn to Falcon, who flies much closer to the ground than Eagle. Despite this different perspective, Falcon cannot find the maidens either. The people next look to Raven, who is known to dig his beak into the dirt. They offer him food and tobacco to find the maidens. He agrees and begins searching along the ground, digging in mounds of dirt and trash heaps. Although Raven cannot find them, he does have a suggestion: Paíyatuma can find the maidens.

The priests find Paíyatuma, but the god is in his daytime form, that of a human with a rude, clownish attitude. The priests beseech him to help them, but Paíyatuma scolds the priests and the people alike for their sins. The priests purify themselves, and Paíyatuma transforms into his sacred form—the god of the dew and the dawn. The priests bring forth four boys who have not sinned. Paíyatuma takes the boys and begins searching for the maidens. While Paíyatuma plays his flute, the butterflies and birds begin to gather around the maidens, who are hiding in Summerland.

The maidens of the corn return to the village. They are received with great rejoicing. However, as each maiden embraces her respective corn plant, she becomes one with the plant and disappears. Paíyatuma solemnly explains to the people that because they did not hold the maidens sacred, the flesh of the corn maidens will join the corn and the maidens will never be seen again. Still, because of this merger between the maidens and the corn, the village will be nourished. He adds that although the maidens will not return, the people should forever hold sacred the use of corn as a seed.

SIGNIFICANCE

The story of Paíyatuma and the maidens of the corn reflects two major themes in the tradition of the Zunis, who today are located largely in New Mexico. The first of these themes is the presence of Paíyatuma. Like the Greek god Apollo, Paíyatuma is associated with music, which is used for the benefit of the natural world. In the story, Paíyatuma creates the maidens of the corn, whose magical dance (accompanied by the god's flute music) helps the people's crops grow. Paíyatuma is also associated with the morning and the dew. When he is not in his god form, Paíyatuma is described as a clown who does not wish to be bothered by the villagers. Only when the village priests ingratiate themselves to Paíyatuma does he return to his celestial form and help the people find the maidens.

The second major theme of the story is the corn. Paíyatuma instructs the village to hold the maidens in the highest regard, as their relationship with the corn is essential to feeding the people. When the maidens join with the corn, their flesh helps it grow. Furthermore, Paíyatuma

instructs the villagers to show the same reverence they were to show the maidens to the corn itself. Each kernel of corn, when planted, is to be seen as sacred—when buried in the ground, this burial should not be unlike burying a loved one. After all, Paíyatuma reminds the people, the corn contains the spirits of not just Paíyatuma and the corn maidens. Since corn grows annually under certain conditions, it contains the spirits of the god of the seasons and time, Tenatsali, and the god of heat, Kwelele, as well. For this reason, the people are advised in this story to give deference to all aspects of corn, a tradition that continues to the present day.

Michael P. Auerbach, MA

BIBLIOGRAPHY

Colum, Pádraic. "Paíyatuma and the Maidens of the Corn." *Orpheus: Myths of the World*. New York: Macmillan, 1930. 311–18. Print.

Cushing, Frank H. *Outlines of Zuni Creation Myths*. Whitefish: Kessinger, 2006. Print.

Hewitt, Edgar Lee. *Ancient Life in the American Southwest*. New York: Biblo, 1968. Print.

Judson, Katharine Berry, comp. and ed. "The Corn Maidens." *The Myths and Legends of California and the Old Southwest*. Chicago: McClurg, 1912. Print.

Miller, Joseph. *New Mexico: A Guide to the Colorful State*. New Mexico: Native American Book Distributors, 1953. Print.

◆ Raven Steals Daylight from the Sky

Author: Traditional Inuit
Time Period: 1001 CE–1500 CE
Country or Culture: North America
Genre: Folktale

PLOT SUMMARY

In the beginning, it is so dark that the Animal People cannot fish or mind their children. To keep track of each other, they must chatter constantly. Only on clear, star-filled nights can the Frog Fishermen see what they are spearfishing, and then they have to expend energy to prevent Raven from stealing the fish from their spears. To fool Raven they splash the water at one end of the boat, and while he follows the sound they hide their fish at the other end.

Raven finally gets tired of being the victim of the Frog Fishermen's games. He decides to return to the sky and steal the box that contains light so that everyone will be able to see what they are doing. Raven flies through a hole in the sky and finds his way to Sky Chief's house. There, he waits at the spring for Sky Chief's daughter to fetch water. When he sees her approaching, he quickly transforms himself into a small cedar leaf and floats in the spring. The young woman drinks the water without noticing the leaf and becomes mysteriously pregnant. She gives birth to a boy with a long and pointy nose, dark and piercing eyes, and skin marked with feathers.

While strikingly beautiful, the baby is fussy and grows into a miserable little boy. His mother and grandparents try everything they can think of to stop his crying spells, giving him more food and changing his clothing more frequently. Sky Chief finally resorts to bringing in the tribal elders to see if they have any suggestions. While most of them end up stuffing their ears with cotton to muffle the boy's annoying cries, one of them notices astutely that the boy wants a box that is hanging in the corner. The box is called the *mä*, and inside is daylight. Reluctantly, the grandfather removes the box and gives it to the boy. Delighted, the boy stops his crying and proceeds to play with the box, cooing in contentment. The adults watch him closely at first, but when it appears that the boy can be trusted with the box they go about their normal routines.

Each day, the boy plays with the box closer and closer to the door. One day when the adults are preoccupied, he sneaks outside and runs away with the box. Sky Chief tries to catch him, but he flies through the hole in the sky as if he is a bird. Indeed, the boy shifts back to Raven while in the sky. When he arrives back on earth, he finds the Frog People fishing and tries to exchange the box of daylight for a bite to eat. The Frog People neither believe he has daylight nor feel like putting up with his lazy ways. He threatens to punish them for their indifference, but still they ignore him. Finally, he drops the box onto the shore, and daylight spreads out through the valleys and over the mountains. The North Wind then mysteriously begins to blow, sweeping the Frog People out to sea. Their canoes eventually crash into the side of a cliff, and the North Wind freezes them in place when they attempt to climb the rocks.

SIGNIFICANCE

The story in which Raven steals the box of light and gives it to the people is indigenous to the Alaskan Tlingits and other Inuit groups across the Arctic region and even into Siberia, as well as the Haidas, Tsimshians, and other American Indians of the Pacific Northwest; it is one of the most widespread and well-known folktales of North America. This particular version is attributed to the Tlingits. Variations exist within their society, however, as well as across the geographic region. One common variation features Raven stealing a bouncing ball of light.

As a shape-shifter who can change back and forth between bird and human and inhabit both the spiritual and the earthly worlds, Raven serves as a revered cultural and spiritual figure. Although he can exhibit many undesirable qualities, such as laziness and selfishness, he is valued and even worshipped for the generous and good deeds he does for humans. In addition to bringing light to the people, some Inuit groups have credited Raven with bringing fire, creating the oceans and rivers, and putting salmon in the water, while some have considered him the creator of all life or the spirit who made order in the universe out of the original chaos. He has also been valued for his intelligence, ingenuity, and sense of humor, qualities that make him more appealing to humans. To many individuals, Raven symbolizes hope and direction in life by offering a path out of the darkness and into the light.

For his ability to transform and get into mischief, Raven is known as a trickster, a label that some American Indians attribute to Christian missionaries who attempted to associate animal deities with the devil. Thus, Raven's negative qualities were magnified, and he evolved to be a more malevolent and feared, or simply trivial and ineffective, folk character.

Along with Bear, Wolf, and other animals from American Indian spirituality, Raven was often chosen for a family or clan's crest and featured on totem poles in the Pacific Northwest region. When portrayed on masks, which were typically made from red cedar, driftwood, or animal skins, Raven usually required a mask within a mask to represent his ability to shape-shift into a human form. Raven has also featured prominently in other art forms, dance, and music.

Sally Driscoll, MLS

BIBLIOGRAPHY

Erdoes, Richard, and Alfonso Ortiz, eds. *American Indian Trickster Tales*. New York: Penguin, 1999. Print.

Hall, Edwin S., Jr. *The Eskimo Storyteller: Folktales from Noatak, Alaska*. Knoxville: U of Tennessee P, 1975. Print.

McDermott, Gerald. *Raven: A Trickster Tale from the Pacific Northwest*. San Diego: Harcourt, 1993. Print.

Miller, Jay. *Tsimshian Culture: A Light through the Ages*. Lincoln: U of Nebraska P, 1997. Print.

Reid, Bill, and Robert Bringhurst. *The Raven Steals the Light*. Seattle: U of Washington P, 1984. Print.

Tagaban, Gene. "The Box of Daylight." *Native Peoples Magazine* 25.6 (2012): 38–39. Print.

◆ Sedna, Goddess of the Sea

Author: Traditional Inuit
Time Period: 1001 CE–1500 CE
Country or Culture: North America
Genre: Myth

PLOT SUMMARY

In a sealskin tent along the coast of Baffin Island lives a young girl, Sedna, and her father, Kinuk. When Sedna reaches a marriageable age, she cannot find a man who matches her intelligence and beauty. One day, a handsome and charismatic young stranger arrives in his kayak. Wearing a unique black-and-white-striped anorak and carrying a spear made of ivory, he is clearly a man of wealth and distinction. While Sedna and her father remain inside the tent, the stranger professes his love for her and promises many splendid things, including beautiful animal skins, feasts, a warm home surrounded by other large houses, and an endless supply of oil for her lamp. Thus captivated, Sedna steps out of the tent to get a better look and is greeted with further amorous promises until she is thoroughly wooed. She gathers her sewing needles and bids farewell to her father, who is sad at the thought of her leaving him but happy that she has found a suitable mate.

The man sets Sedna in his kayak, and away they paddle into the sea. They journey until evening, when they reach a rocky coastline that the man calls home. Rather than the large houses and fattened animals she was promised, Sedna sees only hundreds of loons. When she turns around to complain, in her husband's place is a black-and-white loon; her husband is a spirit-bird. She cries and cries at the thought of marrying a loon and living among all those noisy, waddling birds. She begs him to take her back home, offering to give him her pouch of sewing needles or any other possession he might desire, yet he ignores her pleas

and continues to fluff up their nest and feed her fresh fish.

In time, Sedna's father becomes worried, as the newlyweds have yet to visit. He paddles around the islands in search of Sedna until he finally finds her in a nest, crying her heart out. She gladly accompanies him back to the kayak, and he begins to paddle home in all haste, only to find his son-in-law following in hot pursuit. When Sedna's husband catches up, he demands to see her, as she is hiding under some skins. When her father refuses, her husband angrily transforms into a loon and commands a storm that sends powerful waves crashing into the kayak. The tossing and turning makes Sedna's father fearful of capsizing, and he knows the only way he can survive is to placate the spirit-bird by tossing his daughter overboard.

As poor Sedna frantically grips the kayak, her father cuts off her fingers. From her joints are born seals, whales, and walruses. From that day forward, Sedna rules over the animals of the sea as a one-eyed goddess—she lost the other to the stormy sea—with a long mass of black hair. As for Sedna's father, who is sad beyond belief, he returns to his tent only to be swept into the sea by another violent storm. As punishment, his soul is now imprisoned at the bottom of the sea, in the land ruled by his daughter, the sea goddess.

SIGNIFICANCE

This version of the myth of Sedna is based on the tale recounted in Evelyn Wolfson's anthology *Inuit Mythology*. There are many other versions told by the indigenous people of the Arctic region. In some cases, Sedna is not a beautiful and proud young woman but a grotesque, cannibalistic figure born of the original creator-giants or a maltreated orphan who is pushed into the sea by other children. Other stories say that she marries a dog rather than a bird or that the bird she marries is not a loon but a fulmar. In many accounts, Sedna's father kills the spirit-husband and they are pursued by his angry relatives. Sedna is sometimes referred to as Taleelayuk, Nuliajuk, or Uinigumasuittuq, among other names.

Regardless of the variations, the sea goddess is among the most important spirits or deities in Inuit culture, as she oversees the seals, whales, walruses, and other animals of the sea upon which the people depend for their survival and livelihood. Regardless how mean-spirited or benevolent she can be, she always has two sides, as do most Inuit spirits, and thus commands deep respect. Indeed, dualism pervades traditional Inuit cosmology and society.

To honor Sedna, the Inuits traditionally held annual feasts during which they shared meat, exchanged gifts, and made offerings to the sea goddess. They also drank from a special vessel of water to honor her water home. Such feasts were especially important during periods of famine. Humans had to observe taboos and rituals to appease Sedna, lest she be displeased and bring pestilence, tempest, or famine. To plead for more animals for hunters during a famine, the people would call upon a shaman to use his powers to communicate with Sedna. Typically, the shaman would also offer to comb and braid her hair, as she cannot do so herself without fingers. Alternatively, the shaman might have to grapple with and overcome the goddess.

Sedna takes many forms in Inuit sculpture, paintings, and other artwork. She is sometimes depicted as half human and half seal or whale. She has been alternately portrayed as a classically beautiful goddess with long, flowing hair and dreamy eyes or as a capricious and assertive goddess with staring or anguished eyes and a mass of untamed hair. Her fingerless hands usually feature prominently in artwork.

In 2004, Sedna was honored by American astronomers who named a newly discovered object in the solar system for the goddess. This celestial Sedna has yet to be officially classified, although some believe it to be a dwarf planet smaller than Pluto.

Sally Driscoll, MLS

BIBLIOGRAPHY

Laugrand, Frédéric B., and Jarich G. Oosgten. *Inuit Shamanism and Christianity: Transitions and Transformations in the Twentieth Century*. Montreal: McGill-Queens UP, 2010. Print.

---. *The Sea Woman: Sedna in Inuit Shamanism and Art in the Eastern Arctic*. Fairbanks: U of Alaska P, 2008. Print.

Rudinger, Joel. *Sedna: Goddess of the Sea*. Huron: Cambric, 2006. Print.

San Souci, Robert D. *Song of Sedna*. Garden City: Doubleday, 1981. Print.

Tchana, Katrin Hyman. "Sedna, Woman of the Sea: Supreme Deity of the Inuit People." *Changing Woman and Her Sisters: Stories of Goddesses from around the World*. New York: Holiday, 2006. 22–29. Print.

Wight, Darlene Coward. "The Inuit Sea Goddess." *Canada's Changing North*. Ed. William C. Wonders. Rev. ed. Montreal: McGill-Queens UP, 2003. 94–95. Print.

Wolfson, Evelyn. "Sedna, Goddess of the Sea: Baffinland Inuit of Nunavut, Canada." *Inuit Mythology*. Berkeley Heights: Enslow, 2001. 67–77. Print.

◆ Shaman Isaac Tens

Author: Traditional Gitksan
Time Period: 1901 CE–1950 CE
Country or Culture: North America
Genre: Folktale

PLOT SUMMARY

When Isaac Tens is thirty years old, he has two experiences that prove he will be a shaman for his community. In the first experience, Tens is up gathering firewood in the hills one evening when an owl swoops down on him. It catches his face with its claws and tries to lift him up. Tens loses consciousness. When he comes to, he notices that he has fallen into snow. His head is covered with ice, and blood is trickling from his mouth.

As Tens makes his way down the hill, still carrying some firewood, he feels the trees are sneaking up on him like snakes. He reaches his father's house, where two shamans try to restore his health. Tens feels as if flies cover his face and he is adrift in a large whirlpool.

Tens's second uncanny experience occurs while he is out trapping animals. He catches two otters, kills them, and removes their pelts. Looking for a bear's den, he sees an owl in a tall cedar. He shoots it and sees it falling into bushes. When he looks for it there, it has disappeared.

Tens walks down, crosses the river, and enters the village of Gitanmaax (Gitenmaks). When he reaches the fishing station, he hears a crowd of people who are apparently pursuing him. Tens runs away from them. Yet when he looks back, there is nobody there but the trees. Again, he loses consciousness and falls down.

Tens regains consciousness with his head covered by a bank of snow. As he walks home, he meets his father. At home, Tens heart beats rapidly and his body trembles. His skin is hot and he hears strange noises. Suddenly, he involuntarily begins to sing chants. He says that he has learned the songs by heart by repeating them.

Tens's first song is about the death of a salmon that is linked to his own death. Yet the death of the salmon gives life to his people. He and a female robin fly over their village in the sky.

The second song mentions a grizzly hiding in the sky. The bear circles, and the door to Tens's house swings shut. As fires burn beneath the house, the crowd watches.

In the third song, Tens is up to his knees in the mud of a lake. Shellfish hold him down, cutting his ankles as he dies.

In the fourth song, Tens and a stranger glide along in a canoe. Their boat floats past trees and water to enter a whirlpool.

Tens's fifth song describes his vision of being stung by beehives, which might be ghosts of bees. Giants and an old woman work him until he swells and listens within the old woman's dreams.

SIGNIFICANCE

In December 1914, Canadian anthropologist and folklorist Marius Barbeau (1883–1969) began to collect myths, legends, and folktales of the First Nations in the Canadian province of British Columbia. He was supported in this by interpreter William Benyon (1888–1958). Benyon, who was of Welsh and Nisga'a (Nishga) descent, was a hereditary chief of the Gitlaan tribe of the Tsimshian people and fluent in their language, which is closely related to that of the Gitksan (Gitxsan). From 1923 to 1924, Barbeau and Benyon visited the Gitksan people on the upper reaches of the Skeena River. There, they collected indigenous folktales and songs. Gitksan shaman Isaac Tens's songs, revealed to him during a trance state, form part of their collection.

In 1958, Barbeau published Tens's songs, together with his account of how he became a shaman. Since then, they have been included in anthologies such as anthropologist David Leeming's *Mythology: Voyage of the Hero* (1978) and poet Jerome Rothenberg's *Technicians of the Sacred* (1985).

Tens's songs reverberate with cultural significance for his community. They reveal the shaman's role as a bridge—not only between the real world and the supernatural, the living and the dead, but also between the past and the present, someone who gives expression to their collective experience through the sharing of songs, stories, and oral traditions. Full of survival tips, the shaman's tales help preserve the people's history and culture as well as the people themselves.

The first song establishes the essential connection between the people and the salmon of the Skeena River. The song implies that salmon die to provide food, and thus life, to the people. While Tens identifies with the salmon, he soars along in the sky with a female robin.

From there, he surveys the life of his people below. The second song celebrates survival of the people against natural enemies. Dangerous animals such as grizzlies are kept at bay by sturdy dwellings and smart use of fire. In the vision expressed in the third song, the shaman describes a lake's shellfish, both a food source and a hazard. The fourth song celebrates communal life along the river while also warning of its sudden dangers.

The fifth song reflects on the personal plight of the shaman. By accessing the mind of an elder woman, full of the community's lore, he proves himself a worthy successor. His task is to keep up the tradition of safeguarding the community's collective memory.

R. C. Lutz, PhD

BIBLIOGRAPHY

Barbeau, Marius. *Medicine-Men of the North Pacific Coast*. Ottawa: Dept. of Northern Affairs and National Resources, 1958. Print.

Fee, Margery. "Rewriting Anthropology and Identifications on the North Pacific Coast: The Work of George Hunt, William Benyon, Franz Boas, and Marius Barbeau." *Australian Literary Studies* 25.4 (2010): 14–32. Print.

Hunt, Norman Bancroft. *Shamanism in North America*. Richmond Hill: Firefly, 2003. Print.

Leeming, David Adams. "Isaac Tens." *Mythology: The Voyage of the Hero*. 3rd ed. Oxford: Oxford UP, 1998. 79–81. Print.

Rothenberg, Jerome. *Technicians of the Sacred*. 2nd ed. Berkeley: U of California P, 1985. Print.

Tedlock, Dennis, and Barbara Tedlock. *Teachings of the American Earth: Indian Religion and Philosophy*. 1975. New York: Liveright, 1992. Print.

Temkin, Owsei. *The Falling Sickness. A History of Epilepsy from the Greeks to the Beginning of Modern Neurology*. Baltimore: John Hopkins UP, 1994. Print.

◆ Sioux Creation Story

Author: Traditional Sioux
Time Period: 1001 CE–1500 CE
Country or Culture: North America
Genre: Myth

PLOT SUMMARY

In the creation account told by modern-day Brulé Sioux spiritual leader Leonard Crow Dog, other worlds existed before the present world. Displeased with the people of the world before the current one, the Creating Power decides to begin the world anew. That world is destroyed by flood, much as the first world had been destroyed by fire.

The Creating Power floats on the floodwaters that cover the earth, floating on the bag that held the sacred pipe, an important ritual object to many of the Sioux people. The flood destroys all human and animal life, except for the crow, Kangi. Kangi flies above the waters and begs the Creating Power to make dry earth so that the crow can land and rest. The Creating Power then takes four animals, each in turn, out of the sacred pipe bag. Each is an animal known for being able to stay underwater a long time, and each is told to dive under the water and find some mud. First, a loon is sent, then an otter, and then a beaver. But none can dive deep enough to find mud. Lastly, the Creating Power sends the turtle.

Crow Dog narrates how important the turtle is to the Sioux people—it symbolizes long life and the ability to endure. The turtle dives and remains under water so long that the other animals believe it has died, but it finally returns to the surface with mud. From this mud, the Creating Power makes dry land, and the crow is able to land and rest. The Creating Power uses two large eagle feathers to spread the land over everything, and soon all the water is covered by earth. Knowing that life needs both the land and the water, the Creating Power soon weeps until the tears create oceans, streams, and lakes.

Then, the Creating Power takes all kinds of animals and plants out of the pipe bag. The various races of humanity are made from different colors of earth and are given the power of speech and understanding. The rainbow is created to show the people that there will never again be a Great Flood to destroy the world. But the Creating Power also reminds the human race that the previous worlds were destroyed because the people did not know how to behave. Now, if the people can live in peace with each other and with the rest of the living things on the earth, all will be well. Otherwise, this world will be destroyed as well.

SIGNIFICANCE

The Sioux people of the American Great Plains region are made up of three large, culturally related subgroups that are each further subdivided into various tribal units. The larger groupings are named for the dialect

the people speak. The westernmost and ultimately largest group is known as the Lakotas. A middle group, the Nakotas, historically lived in the valleys of the James River and the Big Sioux River in the area that is now North and South Dakota, Iowa, and Minnesota. The eastern bands are called the Dakotas. This creation story comes from the Brulé Sioux—or Kul Wicasa and Heyate Wicasa, as they call themselves—who are part of the Lakotas. There are two Brulé reservations in South Dakota today, the Lower Brulé and Rosebud Reservations, but many Brulé Sioux also live off the reservation or on one of the other Sioux reservations in the region. Many versions of the creation story exist among the various Sioux subgroups.

This creation story shares many similarities with accounts from other cultures worldwide, including some that originated in the ancient world. In the Judeo-Christian tradition, there is an account of a worldwide flood that destroyed most of humanity in the book of Genesis in the Hebrew Bible, and in the Gilgameš (Gilgamesh) epic from ancient Mesopotamia, there is also an account of a great flood. The rainbow being seen as a sign that there will never again be a flood to destroy the world is also reflected in the Genesis account. Many other North American native peoples also have accounts of a great flood that had destroyed a previous world. Elements of the Brulé Sioux myth suggest the influence of Christianity on the myth's development; however, the extent of that influence is unclear.

Two creatures that are important in this story are also significant in many other native cultures. Kangi, the crow, is the only surviving animal before the Creating Power brings forth all kinds of animals again. Many native peoples considered the crow to be a wise, resourceful creature. The turtle brings mud up from below the deep waters so that the earth can be re-created. The turtle was very important to many native tribes. Some referred to North America as a "turtle continent," and some believed that the entire earth rests of the back of a giant turtle. This creation account shows a close relationship between humans and the natural world, which is typical of many American Indian cultures.

Mark S. Joy, PhD

BIBLIOGRAPHY

Crow Dog, Leonard. "Remaking the World." *American Indian Myths and Legends*. Ed. Richard Erdoes and Alfonso Ortiz. New York: Random, 1984. 496–99. Print.

Crow Dog, Leonard, and Richard Erdoes. *Crow Dog: Four Generations of Sioux Medicine Men*. New York: HarperCollins, 1995. Print.

Hassrick, Royal B. "The Universe and the Controllers." *The Sioux: Life and Customs of a Warrior Society*. Norman: U of Oklahoma P, 1964. 245–65. Print.

Petrik, Paula. "Native American Creation Stories." *Exploring US History*. Roy Rosenzweig Center for History and New Media, George Mason U, 2004. Web. 20 June 2013.

Rice, Julian. *Before the Great Spirit: The Many Faces of Sioux Spirituality*. Albuquerque: U of New Mexico P, 1998. Print.

◆ Talk Concerning the First Beginning

Author: Traditional Zuni
Time Period: 1001 CE–1500 CE
Country or Culture: North America
Genre: Myth

PLOT SUMMARY

At the beginning of time, Earth's surface is empty. The Sun rises and sets every day, without prayers or homage from any person or living thing. Sun is lonely. He calls upon his children to go deep into the layers of Earth, where they would bring forth people, including priests and others who would immediately pay their respects to Sun. Using his rainbow bow, Sun shoots an arrow of lightning into the ground, creating an opening for his sons to enter Earth's many wombs to find humanity.

When they reach the fourth womb, the sons of Sun encounter a person hidden in the dark. They speak with him, revealing to him that they are from the surface. They light a fire to see the man better, but he is revealed to be a slimy creature with a horn and webbed hands. They put out the fire, for it blinded the reptilian man. As they continue their travels westward in the dark, they find more people, huddled alongside the road.

When the sons of Sun reveal their identities, the people pay respect to them in the manner that they were taught by the priest of the north. The two sons visit the priest, who greets them warmly. The lifestyle of these people, it is revealed, is a wretched one. They trample one another in the dark, stepping into the waste of the others. They welcome the opportunity to travel into the world of Sun, the priest says. However, his younger brother, the priest of the west, must be the one to authorize such a migration.

The two sons travel along many different roads, gathering more people and their priests. When the people are all assembled, it is time to venture out of the wombs and into Sun's light. However, they cannot find the road out that would take them this way. They consult with the eagle priest, along with other bird priests, but none can find the way out of the depths. They also look to the locust, whose spirit is strong. The locust travels through three worlds but does not have the strength to continue his journey. The Reed Youth is also asked to go forth, and he does, but he does not return.

While the brothers and their companions wait, they construct ladders from different trees. The ladders take them into new wombs, where the group rests and sings songs. Each level is different; some smell of sulfur while others have plant life. Finally, the group emerges into the fog. They finally arise from the wombs and onto the surface. When they arrive, Sun greets them, opening their dark eyes.

Over time, as they explore Earth's surface, the people learn how to wash themselves and grow crops. The people change from the slimy creatures found in the dark of the fourth womb, taking the appearance they have today. As they continue to travel, however, many become tired from the journey and are transformed into different animals, such as turtles, squirrels, and other creatures. These creatures vie for Sun's light. Meanwhile, the people themselves form different tribes and clans, sometimes fighting with one another. Despite their differences, however, they all seek the center of the universe, Itiwana. The water bug, stretching out his arms, shows them all the way to this spot. All of the people, their priests, and the grandchildren of Sun, settle in Itiwana.

SIGNIFICANCE

This story of creation comes from the Zuni tribe, which today lives predominantly in western New Mexico. The tale is significant for two major reasons. First, it underscores the natural roots of humanity and other living organisms. For example, unlike in the Judeo-Christian tradition, in which men and women are considered to have been created by God, the Zuni myth emphasizes that men and women were born from the womb of Earth. Indeed, the world described in this story is hollow, with many different wombs in which early humans were conceived. Once on the surface, the people evolve into the men and women seen today, while others transform into animals. Still, these creatures retain the sentience of humans, and humans are considered to be equal in status to animals and even plants, holding no position of lordship or governance over the natural world.

The second significant point demonstrated in this story is that of society and order. When the people are first found inside the fourth womb, they are described as stumbling over and befouling one another in the dark. When they emerge onto the surface, however, they are taught how to divide themselves into societies and, within those societies, families. Central to both their spirituality and social order is the priest, who helps the people find their way out of the darkness and across the world. Social order is an important element of Zuni culture. With such order, the different responsibilities within society are effectively distributed.

Michael P. Auerbach, MA

BIBLIOGRAPHY

Bunzel, Ruth L. *Zuni Origin Myths*. Washington: GPO, 1932. Print.

Cushing, Frank H. *Outlines of Zuni Creation Myths*. New York: AMS, 1976. Print.

Gill, Sam D. *Mother Earth: An American Story*. Chicago: U of Chicago P, 1991. Print.

Kroeber, Karl, et al., eds. *Traditional Literatures of the American Indian: Texts and Interpretations*. Lincoln: U of Nebraska P, 1981. Print.

 # Wunzh

Author: Traditional Ojibwa
Time Period: 1001 CE–1500 CE
Country or Culture: North America
Genre: Folktale

PLOT SUMMARY

A kindhearted boy named Wunzh is born to poor, but benevolent and spiritually devout parents. When Wunzh comes of age, his father builds a small lodge some distance from their home so the young man can undergo the *keiguishimowin* ceremony, or vision quest. This rite of passage requires a week of fasting in a solitary setting, and is undertaken to encourage men to find meaning and direction in life with the help of spiritual guides. As Wunzh begins his vision quest, he spends the first few days walking through the woods and over the mountains, where he examines the plants, berries, and flowers. He yearns for a better understanding of what makes plants nutritious or succulent, while others are poisonous or have beneficial medicinal properties. He wonders why the Great Spirit has not provided more edible plants instead of requiring humans to hunt and fish for their food.

As Wunzh fasts, he becomes weaker and soon confined to his bed. While lying there, he envisions a man dressed in varying shades of green and yellow with a plume of feathers on his head that wave in the breeze. The man speaks about being sent by the Great Spirit to teach Wunzh how to fulfill his desire to help humans. He then tests Wunzh's commitment to bettering humanity by challenging him to wrestle. Although a little weak, Wunzh accepts the challenge and wrestles until he is spent. The next day, when he is even weaker, the spirit-man returns and Wunzh repeats the challenge, using his mind to overcome his physical adversity. Impressed, the man warns that he will be back one more day and that Wunzh must again win the wrestling challenge in order to succeed at his quest. The next day, Wunzh proves himself by conquering the spirit-man one more time. The man then rewards Wunzh with additional instructions to follow over the course of the next few months.

The next day, the seventh day of the fast, Wunzh's father brings him a light meal; however, Wunzh declines to eat it until sundown, per the spirit-man's instructions. Later that day, the man appears and Wunzh draws upon all his inner courage and physical will to conquer him in a wrestling match. With supernatural strength, he throws the man on the ground and removes his yellow and green clothing and feathers. When he is sure the man is dead, he buries him, as instructed.

After Wunzh returns to the lodge, he eats some of his father's meal, careful not to gorge himself lest he become sick. In the days that follow, he secretly returns to the grave to watch for any plant growth. Soon he notices shoots poking through the ground. Over the course of the next few months, he keeps the plot weeded of grass and wildflowers. By the end of summer, the plants have grown tall with silky hair and golden husks growing from the sides. Just as the spirit-man had predicted, it is Mondawmin, the corn plant, Wunzh's "friend of all mankind" (Leeming 84).

Wunzh brings his father to the site and shares the details of his vision quest while pulling off the husks to reveal the ears of corn inside, just as he had pulled off the spirit-man's clothing while wrestling. He tells his father how they are to cook the corn over a fire, and then the family feasts. And that is how corn came into the world.

SIGNIFICANCE

Narratives that explain the origin of corn are endemic to many American Indian mythologies. This folktale comes from the Ojibwas (also known as Ojibwes, Anishinaabeg, Ojibways, or Chippewas) of the Great Lakes and Plains regions of the United States, and is included in David Adams Leeming's *Mythology: The Voyage of the Hero* (1998). What sets this apart from the others is the focus on the Ojibwa vision quest as a path to enlightenment and to the betterment of humankind. A ritual undertaken by boys as a passage to adulthood, the vision quest has historically relied upon the altered state of consciousness made possible by the separation of the individual from people, food, and other comforts of life. It represents the American Indians' strong faith in drawing upon spirits to help guide people to purposeful lives. Living an inspiring, moral life has long been an important component of Ojibwa society. If the vision quest is not successful the first time around, adults are encouraged to continue undertaking them until they do find the right vocation for which they are intended or to receive guidance in another realm of life. The vision quest has also historically been a test of physical stamina that tended to separate the boys from the men, with death from starvation or other causes sometimes being one of the unfortunate consequences.

For his highly successful vision quest, Wunzh became known as the Father of Corn and has served as a legendary, heroic role model and spiritual guide to American Indians ever since. His story became more widespread during the mid-nineteenth century, when Henry Wadsworth Longfellow (1807–82) based his poem *The Song of Hiawatha* (1855) on Wunzh. Longfellow dedicated chapter 5, "Hiawatha's Fasting," to detailing the spiritual quest. Here he describes Hiawatha's initial meeting with Mondamin, another youth in the poem:

> And he saw a youth approaching,
> Dressed in garments green and yellow,
> Coming through the purple twilight,
> Through the splendor of the sunset;
> Plumes of green bent o'er his forehead,
> And his hair was soft and golden. (lines 63–68)

The chapter ends with Mondamin giving forth "this new gift to the nations, / Which should be their food forever" (279–80).

Sally Driscoll, MLS

BIBLIOGRAPHY

Johnson, Basil. *The Manitous: The Spiritual World of the Ojibway*. New York: Harper, 1995. Print.

Leeming, David Adams. "Wunzh." *Mythology: The Voyage of the Hero*. New York: Oxford UP, 1998. 82–84. Print.

Leeming, David Adams, and Jake Page. *God: Myths of the Male Divine*. New York: Oxford UP, 1996. Print.

Longfellow, Henry Wadsworth. *Hiawatha: A Poem*. 1855. Chicago: Reilly, 1909. Print.

Mathews, Cornelius. *The Enchanted Moccasins: And Other Legends of the American Indians*. 1877. New York: AMS, 1970. Print.

SOUTH AMERICA

◆ Amalivaca

Author: Traditional Tamanac
Time Period: 1001 CE–1500 CE; 1701 CE–1850 CE
Country or Culture: South America
Genre: Myth

PLOT SUMMARY

Amalivaca is a mythical young explorer who settles near the mouth of the Essesquibo River. The legend casts Amalivaca as a patriarch who appears after concluding a lengthy journey on which he has surveyed the remains of the earth in the aftermath of a massive deluge that has flooded the entire planet. Amalivaca illustrates people, animals, and shapes, describing what he has encountered on his travels in *timehri*, carvings etched with a giant diamond on numerous rocks and rock formations in and around the Essesquibo's banks.

When Amalivaca encounters a contingent of tribesmen utilizing the land to harvest cane reeds with which to make weapons, specifically arrow shafts, he disparages their violent intentions, insisting that the earth is intended to harvest mutual prosperity among all people. Impressed by both his wisdom and the quality construction of Amalivaca's fire-hollowed canoe, the farmers invite the mysterious young traveler to settle with their tribe so that he may offer them instruction in both farming and shipbuilding. He agrees, showcasing both his knowledge of industry and several magical powers.

Before his departure from the tribe, Amalivaca insists that the purpose of the wisdom he has bestowed on their tribe is communal and that the true intention of knowledge is for it to be shared among all people. As a testament of gratitude and admiration, the tribe shares their new skills throughout the region. Amalivaca's travels continue while legend of his teachings and powers continues to grow.

Eventually known throughout the land for his wisdom and wizardry, Amalivaca encounters another group and its members urge him to make the Essesquibo's current travel in both directions. The tribe describes the difficulty it has paddling against the strong current, believing that two directions of travel on the river would make the waterway easier to use in travel and trade. Though he is unable to use his powers to make the river travel in both directions simultaneously, Amalivaca is successful in creating ocean tides, which force the currents at the river's mouth to alternate directions during different times of the day, an alteration for which the people express profound gratitude.

After several more years of travel and instruction, Amalivaca retires to the Maita Plains, where legend has it that he carved out a giant rock formation for use as a drum and that Amalivaca's stone drum is still visible to this day. The legend concludes with a regional farewell to Amalivaca on the banks of the Essesquibo, where the traveler, now an old man, takes to the Atlantic Ocean by canoe to spread his wisdom throughout the world.

SIGNIFICANCE

Amalivaca is a creation myth that, in similar fashion to creation myths from throughout history, casts the Carib-speaking Tamanac people of the Orinoco River basin as the root of all humankind. It is one of the region's earliest to illustrate the transposition of a natural world to the commune of humankind. Many creation myths introduce humanity at the end of several years of chaos—in this case a great flood—in the natural world.

There is scholarly agreement on the likelihood that the legend has root in the indigenous Guyanese discovery of and intended explanation of *timehri*, primitive rock carvings are still visible today near the mouth of the Essequibo River.

In other iterations, extensions, and adaptations of the Amalivaca legend, Amalivaca is additionally credited with the creation of the world's first music and the first musical instrument, the rattle, which would play a key part in indigenous ceremonies. The legend also exhibits the importance of drums and other percussion instruments in the lives of indigenous tribes. Some versions even credit the floodwaters abating to Amalivaca's drumming.

Amalivaca presents an uncommon exception from many of the creation myths of several other cultures and epochs. The variant recounted by Odeen Ishmael is particularly in its optimistic supposition that shared knowledge is intended to be one of the mainstays of a peaceful existence among humankind. Amalivaca's inability to wholly convert the river's flow into two different currents is also a rare instance of fallibility in a godlike creator character. According to a version recorded by Alexander von Humbolt around 1800, Amalivaca was aided in this endeavor to by a brother named Vochi but neither demigod was successful.

Another key variance of the Tamanac legend of Amalivaca as compared to other creation myths is that its creator-protagonist is not an invisible divine being, the worship of whom rises from an attempt to describe the origins of nature and society, but a personification of humanity's potential for industry, technical aptitude, and communal prosperity.

Von Humbolt's version also alludes to the formation and ordering of society; in it, Amalivaca's daughters are filled with wanderlust, so he breaks their legs to force them to populate the immediate area, producing the Tamanac people Anthropologist Claude Lévi-Strauss postulates that this bizarre episode, along with the river current episode, represents a regulation of women's sexual activity and the establishment of tribal marriage rules to prevent both incest and distant liaisons.

The existence of stories related to Amalivaca throughout the Orinoco River basin and even as far as the Caribbean was a testament to the myth's power—particularly in its personification and explanation of common events in the natural world and its basis in the belief that its authoring people had distant, if not specifically divine, instructions and purpose for prosperity and survival.

John Pritchard

BIBLIOGRAPHY

De Goeje, C. H. "The Loss of Everlasting Life." *Philosophy, Initiation and Myths of the Indians of Guiana and Adjacent Countries*. Leiden: Brill, 1943. 116–17. Print.

Ishmael, Odeen. "Amalivaca." *Guyana Legends: Folk Tales of the Indigenous Amerindians*. Bloomington: Xlibris, 2011. 200–204. Print.

Lévi-Strauss, Claude. "M415. Tamanac. 'The Girls Who Were Forced to Marry.'" *The Origin of Table Manners*. Trans. John Weightman and Doreen Weightman. Chicago: U of Chicago P, 1990. 159–61. Print. Mythologiques 3.

Rowbotham, J. F. "Musical Myths." *Chambers's Journal of Popular Literature, Science and Art* 3.394 ser. 5 (1891): 449–51.

Von Humbolt, Alexander, and Aimé Bonpland. "Native Legends of a Deluge." *Personal Narrative of Travels to the Equinoctial Regions of America, during the Years 1799–1804*. Vol. 2. Trans. and ed. Thomasina Ross. London: Bell, 1889. 473. Print.

The Boy Who Rose to the Sky

Author: Traditional Inca
Time Period: 1001 CE–1500 CE
Country or Culture: South America
Genre: Myth

PLOT SUMMARY

There lives a poor couple in a modest, remote house with their only child, a son. The family grows excellent potatoes in a field far from their house, and they are the only people to have the prized potato seeds.

Someone begins stealing the potatoes out of the field at night. The parents tell their son to stand guard. The boy tries to stay awake to catch the thieves, but he falls asleep at daybreak. He goes home and tells his parents, and they forgive him.

The next night, he again tries to stay alert, but he blinks at midnight and the thieves again steal the potatoes. When he tells his parents what has happened, they beat and scold him and accuse him of being out with girls instead of standing guard.

Once more, his parents implore the boy to stay alert. As he forces himself to stay awake, his eyelids shake, and he sees a swarm of gorgeous maidens with flowery faces, silver dresses, and golden hair. They rapidly dig up potatoes. Although he does not know it, they are stars from the sky.

The boy falls in love with the star maidens. He manages to catch one, but the rest slip back up to the sky. The maiden is frightened and begs him to let her go. She offers to give back all the potatoes, but the boy is in love and means to make her his wife.

The maiden warns him not to let his parents see her. He tells her not to worry and lies to her saying he had his own house. Eventually, his parents see the maiden and are astounded by her beauty. They care for her but never let her out into the world lest anyone else see her. She becomes pregnant, but the child dies. The star maiden eventually escapes while the boy is away, and she returns to the sky.

When the boy returns home and finds her gone, he is inconsolable. He wanders like a crazy person and eventually encounters a condor that offers to fly him to his bride in exchange for two llamas—one to eat before departing and one to eat in transit. The boy gets them from his parents, the condor eats one, and they fly on their way.

The condor tells the boy to keep his eyes closed and to put a piece of meat in its beak whenever it asks or the condor would drop the boy from its back. As they fly, the llama meat eventually runs out, and the frightened boy cuts off flesh from his own leg to feed the bird.

After a year, the bird and the boy come to a plateau with a lake. They look at their reflections and see they have grown old, but their youth is restored when they bathe in the lake's water. The condor tells the boy that maidens will come from the temple of the sun and the moon by the side of the lake and that he will only be able to tell his wife from the others because she will be the last to emerge and will brush against him. It tells the youth to grab onto her and not let go.

When the boy catches his bride, she leads him to a house and hides him from her parents, the sun and moon. She gives him some quinoa grain and tells him to make a soup. When he does, the quinoa keeps expanding, and she helps him get rid of it so her parents will not see it. For a year, the boy lives in the house, and the star maiden visits him with food. Eventually, she grows bored and neglects him.

Having grown old in appearance once more, the boy and the condor bathe in the lake. Their youth restored, they take the yearlong flight back to his home. The youth pays two more llamas for the condor's help. At home, the boy tells his now elderly parents that he cannot remarry. He lives in sadness for the rest of his days.

SIGNIFICANCE

"The Boy Who Rose to the Sky" is considered by some scholars to be similar to the better-known Inca myth of Coniraya and Cahuillaca. Both are stories of thwarted love, where the romantic connection between the male and female protagonists ends in tragedy. In both myths, the male character is eager to marry, but his female counterpart escapes his advances, which prevents the relationship from maturing into a fully developed marriage.

Unlike the story of Coniraya and Cahuaillaca, which is about the love between two gods, "The Boy Who Rose to the Sky" describes a failed attempt at love between different beings from different spheres of existence. The celestial nymphs come down from the heavens at night in order to steal potatoes, which are portrayed in this myth as a very rare and precious commodity. Charged with the task of keeping watch over his family's valuable crop, the boy witnesses the beautiful thieves, and he manages to hold onto one, preventing her from floating back up to the sky. With the assistance of his parents, who view her as a suitable wife for their son, the boy keeps the nymph as a prisoner in his family's home. She conceives a child by him, but the child dies. Not long after, she escapes back to the stars. Both of these events point to the futility of an earthly being trying to maintain a relationship with one from the heavenly realm.

In a fit of desperation after being spurned the first time by his would-be heavenly wife, the young man wanders around the earth like a madman. He then meets a condor. For the Inca people, the choice of this bird as the vessel for connection between the earth and heaven would be a natural fit, as condors were considered masters of the upper world who soared far into the heavens. For a price to be paid in flesh, the condor agrees to give the boy a ride to the palace of the sun and the moon.

Ultimately, the boy pays this price both with the llama meat they initially agreed upon and with flesh from his own body. The impossible journey, which takes a year to complete, robs both the bird and the boy of their youthful looks. After bathing in a magical pool, they are rendered young again.

As she emerges from a temple, the boy grabs onto his would-be bride, just as he did in the potato field, and refuses to let her go until she agrees to hide him in a house and live as his wife. Here, she gives him quinoa, which along with potatoes, was a staple starch for the people of medieval Peru. The sharing of quinoa, like potatoes, initiates a kind of de facto marriage. However, the quinoa keeps expanding when the boy tries to make a soup from it, which in turn symbolizes his inability to control and maintain a mature relationship, and the girl becomes worried that her parents, the sun and moon, will find out about her secret marriage and punish her.

In the end, both the boy and his lover refuse to take on the serious responsibility of marriage and ultimately choose to continue to live with their parents. In that way, they both remain children, preserving their youthful existences indefinitely and failing to fulfill the human life cycle, which the Inca held as a sacred duty.

Adam Berger, PhD

BIBLIOGRAPHY

Baur, Brian. *Ancient Cuzco: Heartland of the Inca*. Austin: U of Texas P, 2004. Print.

Bierhorst, John. *Black Rainbow: Legends of the Incas and Myths of Ancient Peru*. New York: Farrar, 1976. Print.

Brundage, Burr Cartwright. *Empire of the Inca*. Norman: U of Oklahoma P, 1985. Print.

Cobo, Bernabe. *Inca Religion and Customs*. Austin: U of Texas P, 1990. Print.

D'Altroy, Terence. *The Incas*. Malden: Blackwell, 2009. Print.

Jones, David. *The Myths & Religion of the Incas*. London: Southwater, 2008. Print.

Julien, Catherine. *Reading Inca History*. Iowa City: U of Iowa P, 2002. Print.

Malpass, Michael. *Daily Life in the Inca Empire*. 2nd ed. Westport: Greenwood, 2009. Print

Markham, Clements. *The Incas of Peru*. 1910. New York: AMS, 1969. Print.

Moseley, Michael. *The Incas and their Ancestors: The Archaeology of Peru*. Rev. ed. London: Thames, 2008. Print.

◆ How Evils Befell Mankind

Author: Traditional Carib
Time Period: 1001 CE–1500 CE
Country or Culture: South America
Genre: Myth

PLOT SUMMARY

"How Evils Befell Mankind" begins in a world of perfect harmony, where harvests are constant and plentiful and the entire animal kingdom lives at peace with itself and humankind. A man named Maconaura, a young hunter, discovers that a caiman, or crocodile, has been tampering with his fishing nets. Maconaura enlists a cuckoo bird to warn him when the caiman returns, and when he does, Maconaura shoots an arrow through the caiman's head.

When he returns to the site a third time, Maconaura finds a beautiful young girl named Anuanaitu weeping at the site of the caiman's murder. Maconaura insists the girl tell him her name and from which tribe she hails, but she refuses; Maconaura takes the girl back to his village to live with him and his mother.

After the girl becomes a young woman, Maconaura proposes, and she reluctantly accepts. After some time, Anuanaitu is overcome with a desire to see her mother. Maconaura agrees to let her return home to visit, but he insists that he accompany her because he never formally asked for permission to marry her. Anuanaitu insists that such a meeting would result in misfortune for both the couple and Maconaura's mother, but Maconaura insists and accompanies his new bride to her original home.

Maconaura successfully passes a series of tests put forth by his bride's father, a mysterious tribal elder whose head is constantly cloaked, and he is accepted as her husband by the tribe. After living an extensive period of time with Anuanaitu's tribe, he longs to return to his mother and his tribe. Maconaura insists his wife accompany him on the return journey, but her father, Kaikoutji, forbid her to go. Maconaura returns home alone.

Maconaura spends a period of time with his own tribe, recounting his travels and adventures; he eventually decides to return to his wife, despite his mother's misgivings. When he returns to Anuanaitu's village, she warns him that Kaikoutji is enraged in the wake of recent news he has received. Determined to discover the source of Kaikoutji's rage, Maconaura goes to visit his father-in-law. When Maconaura arrives at Kaikoutji's dwelling, the old man kills him by shooting an arrow through his head.

Maconaura's fellow tribesmen attack Anuanaitu's village in revenge for his death, sparing no one. It is revealed that Kaikoutji's head is constantly hidden because he has the head of a caiman. The caiman killed by Maconaura at the beginning of the story was Kaikoutji's son.

Anuanaitu becomes possessed with rage for the slaying of her own people and her husband, becoming a personification of vengefulness and sorrow combined. She insists that all would be forgiven had her mother been spared in her village's destruction. Anuanaitu's cries of rage transform the animal kingdom and the natural world from that of peacefulness to one of conflict and aggression. The world's newfound evils become permanent when Anuanaitu joins her husband in death by plummeting into a waterfall.

SIGNIFICANCE

"How Evils Befell Mankind" is a myth from the Carib people, the ancient civilization from which the Caribbean Islands get their name. The Caribs, also known as the Kalinagos, are believed to have populated the islands of South America around the twelfth century CE. The myth describes the corruption of a utopian world after violence and revenge interrupt the marriage of a man and his wife.

Scholars have lauded the dramatic vividness of the myth of Maconaura and Anuanaitu and praised the story for offering invaluable insight into the social ideas and cultural customs of the Carib people. Though the tale describes a domestic struggle, it does so by interweaving many intricate aspects of Carib life—hunting strategies, sacred rituals, and the culture's interaction with the natural world.

It is also important to note that the Caribs considered Maconaura and Anuanaitu to be the father and mother of all humankind. This point is potentially illustrative of their firm belief in humankind's intrinsic capabilities for potent passion and love and, conversely, for violence and revenge.

The crude justice depicted in "How Evils Befell Mankind" places the liberation of the world of evil on the female sex. Furthermore, Anuanaitu's revenge is based in the murder of a half beast, half man whose motivation for eating out of the traps of the hunter Maconaura is never fully made clear. The caiman-man may have been the Caribs' way of illustrating humankind's permanent connection to the primal self and the natural world.

John Pritchard

BIBLIOGRAPHY

Alexander, Hartley Burr. *The Mythology of All Races: Latin-American*. Vol. 11. London: Jones, 1920. 261–68. Print.

Bingham, Ann, and Jeremy Roberts. *South and Meso-American Mythology A to Z*. New York: Chelsea, 2010. Print.

Crask, Paul. Dominica: *The Bradt Travel Guide*. Guilford: Globe Pequot, 2007. Print.

Monaghan, Patricia. *Encyclopedia of Goddesses and Heroines*. Santa Barbara: Greenwood, 2010. Print.

---. *Women in Myth and Legend*. London: Junction, 1981. Print.

◆ How the Jaguar Lost His Fire

Author: Traditional Mapuche
Time Period: 1001 CE–1500 CE
Country or Culture: South America
Genre: Myth

PLOT SUMMARY

One day while hunting birds with his older brother, a boy named Botoque discovers a large macaw nest perched atop a cliff edge. Botoque climbs a pole and discovers two macaw eggs in the nest. However, when he tosses the eggs to his brother on the ground, they turn to stones and break his brother's hands. Enraged, the older brother removes the pole and leaves Botoque stranded atop the cliff.

Botoque is stranded on the cliff for two days without food or water until he is discovered by a jaguar, who is armed with a bow and arrow and carries a large basket of newly killed prey. The jaguar replaces the pole, and Botoque reluctantly climbs down.

The jaguar invites Botoque to his home for a meal of cooked meat. The boy is shocked by the sight and warmth of the open flame and by the wonderful taste of the jaguar's cooked boar meat, as neither fire nor cooked meals are known to the people of his native village. The jaguar teaches Botoque his methods for hunting and killing prey with a bow and arrow and shows him how to prepare the meat by creating a fire. However, Botoque soon draws the ire of the jaguar's wife, who is jealous of the attention he is receiving and lashes out at the boy at every opportunity.

Homesick for his village and no longer capable of enduring the harsh treatment by the jaguar's wife, Botoque eventually leaves his jaguar mentor to return home. Prior to Botoque's departure, the jaguar gives the boy a basket of cooked meat and tells him not to let his tribe know about fire. Upon his return home, however, Botoque's tribe is so intrigued by the basket of cooked meat that the boy breaks his promise and tells his fellow villagers about fire.

When Botoque returns to the jaguar's home with two tribesmen, they steal the logs from the hearth. Enraged at Botoque's betrayal, the jaguar becomes a wild animal who abandons his bow and arrow to hunt with his claws and teeth and eat meat raw. Botoque, in turn, is forever lauded as a hero for granting his tribe supremacy over the animal kingdom and for bestowing on them the knowledge of fire.

SIGNIFICANCE

The myth of how the jaguar lost his fire has parallels to many other indigenous myths found throughout world history. The most notable similarity is the tale's notion that humans have—through some trial or tribulation—achieved superiority over the animal kingdom and the ability to harness the planet's natural resources.

The myth is particularly interesting because the South American tribes among which the myth originated did not kill large carnivores, such as the jaguar, for food. Nevertheless, the tribes' admiration of the animal's aggressive qualities made jaguars an important cultural influence, particularly because the animals possessed many qualities that the tribes sought in their men, such as courage and strength.

This myth has also been identified by scholars as offering a crucial insight into father-son relationships. This is demonstrated by the jaguar's fatherlike role to Botoque, the social and cultural progress the boy is able to make upon his departure from the cliff, and his acceptance of and respect for the jaguar's teachings.

Scholars have also noted the duality of the jaguar character. The animal is mythologized as a forbearer of knowledge regarding the natural world yet simultaneously viewed with caution and respect, given the constant danger it presents to humans as a potential predator. Prominent mythological scholars such as Claude Lévi-Strauss have investigated the character of the jaguar's wife to examine what reflection she may have, if any, on the cultural role and societal significance of women in indigenous South American culture. While several South American populations offer variations on the myth that depict the jaguar's wife as a human woman, in the best-known rendition of the tale, which originated among the Kayapo tribe, the jaguar's wife is, in fact, actually a jaguar. This fact renders any in-depth interpretation of the jaguar's wife as a reflection on women in Kayapo culture unlikely.

The story of the jaguar and his fire is also somewhat contradictory in that while it trumpets the necessity of respect and reverence one must have for fatherlike figures, it offers little explanation for its repeated illustration of disrespect among family members. This notion is prominently illustrated by both Botoque's callous abandonment by his brother and the jaguar's wife blatant, although never explicit, disdain for her houseguest.

John Pritchard

BIBLIOGRAPHY

Leeming, David. *The Oxford Companion to World Mythology*. New York: Oxford UP, 2009. Print.

Parker, Janet, and Julie Stanton, eds. *Mythology: Myths, Legends and Fantasies*. Cape Town: Struik: 2006. Print.

Penner, Hans. *Teaching Lévi-Strauss*. Oxford: Oxford UP, 1998. Print.

Rosenberg, Donna. *Folklore, Myths, and Legends: A World Perspective*. Chicago: NTC, 1997. Print.

Urton, Gary. *Animal Myths and Metaphors in South America*. Salt Lake City: U of Utah P, 1985. Print.

The Men from the Sea

Author: Traditional Ecuadorian
Time Period: 1001 CE–1500 CE
Country or Culture: South America
Genre: Myth

PLOT SUMMARY

As presented in English, "The Men from the Sea" comprises three thematically linked myths. They tell of seaborne foreign invasions of Ecuador in ancient, pre-Columbian times. The first myth describes how, one day, male giants arrive at what is contemporary Santa Elena Peninsula in Ecuador in big boats made of reeds. They are either dressed in animal skins or remain naked, and ordinary humans reach up only to the knees of the giants.

The giants build a village on the coast. They dig out very deep wells from the rocks, lining them with masonry to endure for a long time. The giants forage for meat in the countryside and catch fish from the sea because they require fifty times the food of a regular person. The giants sexually assault and even kill the local people, causing the locals to pray to their god for deliverance. In response, a fire comes down from the heavens, and an angelic figure kills the giants with a shining sword as fire consumes their fallen bodies. All that is left of them are the bones by which people can remember their punishment.

The second myth tells of humans coming ashore. As calculated by the Spanish later on, this happens about six to seven centuries after the giants were destroyed at the beginning of the Common Era. The new "Men from the Sea" call themselves the Caras. The Caras arrive on balsas—boats that are made of logs bound together to form a hull and topped by a platform on which masts for sails are erected. After their successful invasion from the sea, the Caras expand their territory by war and conquest. By around 980 CE, the Caras establish their stronghold near Quito, the contemporary capital of Ecuador. They call their king Scyri and rule until the fifteenth century until they are defeated by the Incas. The Caras worship the sun and moon and build them temples. They worship the sea as well. To their war god Tumbal, they offer prisoners as human sacrifices.

The third myth tells of "The Men from the Sea" led by the chief Naymlap. Naymlap, his wife Ceterni, their court officials, and their common people arrive from the north with a fleet of balsas. They land just south of Ecuador's Santa Elena Peninsula. A court officer called

Fongasigde spreads shell dust before the feet of Naymlap as he lands. The seaborne invaders build a temple called Chot. They place an idol in the temple called Llampallec, or "figure of Naymlap." Naymlap reigns for many years until he flies away on wings he has grown.

Naymlap's successor, Cium, bricks himself up in an underground cave. There, he starves himself to death so that his people outside may think he remains immortal, never to reappear. The tenth king after Cium, Tempellec, lets himself by seduced by a demon that looks like a beautiful woman. As result, it rains for an unprecedented thirty days. A year of famine follows. The priests tie up Tempellec and throw him into the sea before changing the kingdom to a republic.

SIGNIFICANCE

After the Spanish conquered the region of contemporary Ecuador from the Incas by 1534, they collected the myths of the local people. Before the Spanish, the Incas had just conquered this region from 1462 to 1500. Local myths of the region far predate the Inca conquest. They originate with South American Indian tribes like the Caras mentioned in "The Men from the Sea," or others no longer known.

In 1920, American philosopher Hartley Burr Alexander presented "The Men from the Sea" in English in his collection of myths from Latin America. Burr bases his rendition on Spanish texts. For the myth of the giants, Burr used the account of sixteenth-century Spanish conquistador Pedro de Cieza de León. The myth of the coming of the Caras is told by eighteenth-century Ecuadorian priest and historian Juan de Velasco. The myth of Naymlap's arrival was recorded by sixteenth century Spanish priest Miguel Cabello de Balboa. Today, only Cieza de León's text is available in English.

Significantly, the three myths of "The Men from the Sea" tell of seaborne invasions of Ecuador. The balance between their purely mythological elements and elements affixed to historical and material evidence varies considerably from myth to myth. However, at least two myths can be traced to historical events.

For the myth of the invasion by the giants, an American archaeological expedition to Ecuador from 1906 to 1908 revealed the existence of deep stone-lined wells just as described in the myth. The archeologists found many stone seats carved with images of animals and humans. These stone seats resemble those found in the Antilles and as far north of Ecuador as across the Isthmus of Panama. This indicates archaeological evidence for the arrival of a foreign people in Ecuador bringing along these artifacts as a material source of the myth.

The origin myth of the Caras describes the arrival in Ecuador of an American Indian tribe that still exists there. There is historical evidence that the Caras arrived on the Santa Elena Peninsula. From there, they traveled inland along the Esmeraldas River. They defeated the people of the local Quitu culture and established a kingdom centered on contemporary Quito by the tenth century CE. They were conquered by the Incas by 1470. The ancient name for the Caras kings mentioned in the myth, Scyri, has even been adopted by the contemporary Ecuadorian navy.

So far, no archeological or other evidence has been found to identify the people led by Naymlap in "The Men from the Sea." However, scholars are convinced of the authenticity of the myth by its narrative detail, suggesting that it belonged to a South American Indian tribe that is no longer known.

R. C. Lutz, PhD

BIBLIOGRAPHY

Alexander, Hartley Burr. "The Men from the Sea." *The Mythology of All Races: Latin-America*. Vol. 11. Boston: Jones, 1920. 204–9. Print.

Cieza de León, Pedro de. *The Travels of Pedro de Cieza de León, AD 1532–50, Contained in the First Part of His Chronicle of Peru*. Trans. Clements Markham. 1883. Cambridge: Cambridge UP, 2010. Print.

Klein, David, and Ivan Cruz Cevallos, eds. *Ecuador: The Secret Art of Precolumbian Ecuador*. New York: 5continents, 2007. Print.

Lauderbaugh, George. *The History of Ecuador*. Santa Barbara: Greenwood, 2012. Print.

Saville, Marshall Howard. *The Antiquities of Manabi, Ecuador*. New York: Irving, 1907. Print.

◆ The Monkey's Exploit

Author: Traditional Acawoios
Time Period: 1001 CE–1500 CE
Country or Culture: South America
Genre: Myth

PLOT SUMMARY

The myth of "The Monkey's Exploit" begins with a description of how the first tree is found by the animal known as the *ahkoo*, or the agouti, a small rodent. The animals help the first humans—represented by the master—to plant trees across the landscape, except for Iwarreka, the brown monkey, who refuses to work and instead torments the other animals as they attempt to complete their jobs. The master tells Iwarreka to go off and work on his own, fetching water from a stream.

After cutting down a large tree, the master notices swirling water within, containing a wealth of fish. These fish are later used to populate the rivers and streams of the world. The master then learns, after speaking to the well he has discovered, that the waters within are swelling and will soon cover the land in a flood. To protect the people, the master fashions a basket over the mouth of the well to prevent the swelling waters from enveloping the land.

Iwarreka comes upon the basket while he is again shirking his work and believes that the master has hidden fruits under the basket. When Iwarreka removes the basket to fetch the fruit, the monkey is swept away by a torrent of water and mud, and the land is flooded. The master leads the animals of the forest to a tall hill topped by cocorite trees, and he tells all the animals that can climb or fly to seek haven in the trees while the other animals take shelter in a nearby cave, located high on the hill. The birds are the first to reach safety, followed by the opossum and the coati, which have excellent climbing abilities. Next, the monkeys surround the master and attempt to reach the safety of the trees. The spider monkey, the squirrel monkey Sakuwinki, the red howler monkey Arowata, and the marmosets all reach the trees and are saved.

The fierce storm lasts for several days and is far more violent than any storm experienced by humans before or since. The master remains calm and patiently waits, dropping the seeds of the cocorite tree to judge the depth of the water by the sound of the falling seeds. When he determines that the water has receded, the master and the animals return to the ground and feast on the fruits of the breadfruit tree.

SIGNIFICANCE

"The Monkey's Exploit" is one of several Acawoios myths relating to the formation of the world, and attempts to explain the physical characteristics of common landscape features, including the distribution of fruit trees and the presence of freshwater fish in the rivers and streams. Humankind is portrayed through a figure known as the master, who was the leader of a group of animals cooperating to build the world. The benefits of cooperation and adherence to assigned tasks, as imposed by a just and wise leader, are portrayed as the driving force behind the successful development of the landscape; this model is one of the primary functions of the myth. Creation myths of this type are often believed to have had a role in the transmission of essential values, such as the value of hard work and the benefits of following the example of those who have been chosen to lead.

While the other species in the story are content to follow the master's leadership, Iwarreka shirks his responsibilities and torments the other animals. Iwarreka is utilized in the myth as a symbol of negative qualities that may be observed in humans, including laziness and selfishness. Iwarreka's laziness causes him to avoid work, while his selfish desire to entertain himself makes the situation worse by urging him to interrupt the work of others. This depiction of Iwarreka may have been meant partially as a lesson to children, whose own desire to play and to avoid work sometimes causes them to interrupt the work of their parents or peers.

The result of Iwarreka's selfishness is revealed when he attempts to steal fruit from the master and unwittingly releases the flood over the landscape. The full consequence of Iwarreka's actions are not explained until the next part of the myth—called "mishaps"—which explains the physical and behavioral features of some of the common animals through their experiences during and after the flood. For instance, the *marūdi*, a kind of wild foul found in the bush, accidentally swallows a burning coal while foraging for ants; the marūdi has a red throat is attributed to his haste to feed and accidental ingestion of hot coals.

The brown monkeys, Iwarreka's kin, were doomed to remain in a permanent state of fear, like that experienced by Iwarreka when he first released the flood. Iwarreka's ancestors also shared with their progenitor the tendency to be curious, to the point of becoming a nuisance, and to steal unguarded food when they are able. The story of Iwarreka therefore provides a mythical explanation of some of the monkey's core behavioral characteristics, including their opportunistic tendency to scavenge food and their nervous behavior as they try to avoid their numerous potential predators.

Like many myths involving wildlife, "The Monkey's Exploit" utilizes the behaviors of the monkeys observed in the environment to tell a story that transmits core social values, while simultaneously recording the tribal knowledge of animal behavior in the form of oral myths about the period of creation. Many human cultures that shared their environment with monkey species were fascinated by the behavior of monkeys and integrated the animals into their mythology. "The Monkey's Exploit" mirrors stories about the mischievous monkey god Sun Wukong in Chinese mythology and the Hindu monkey god Hanumān, both of whom were also portrayed as curious and mischievous figures. The popularity of monkeys in human myths may also be related to the similarities between humans and other primates, making monkeys of all kinds a source of fascination in many human societies.

Micah Issitt

BIBLIOGRAPHY

Brett, William Henry. "The Monkey's Exploit." *Legends and Myths of the Aboriginal Indians of British Guiana.* 2nd ed. London: Gardner, 1880. 127–30. Print.

---. "Mythology and Legendary Tales." *The Indian Tribes of Guiana.* London: Bell, 1868. 373–403. Print.

Forbes, Jack D. *Africans and Native Americans: The Language of Race and the Evolution of Red-Black Peoples.* Champaign: U of Illinois P, 1993. Print.

Kelsen, Hans. *Society and Nature: A Sociological Inquiry.* Clark: Lawbook Exchange, 2010. Print.

Lewis, Ioan M. *Social and Cultural Anthropology in Perspective.* New Brunswick: Transaction, 2003. Print.

◆ Origin of Living Creatures

Author: Traditional Arawak
Time Period: 1001 CE–1500 CE
Country or Culture: South America
Genre: Myth

PLOT SUMMARY

Beneath the sacred ceiba (or silk cotton) tree, wise old men tell a story of how the moon, sun, earth, sky, and sea all stand before the high god, the Mighty One. The Mighty One looks at them with pride, having created them. While all of the natural wonders he brought into the world are beautiful and tranquil—evidenced by the sound of waves gently breaking on the beach and the light, gentle breezes overhead—the Mighty One feels that there is something missing. There is no life, he observes, while sitting atop the *komaka* (ceiba tree). There is no movement in the bushes. There are no bird songs. The Mighty One decides to bring life into the world.

Still sitting in a throne atop the ceiba, he causes the tree to grow. It grows so high it reaches upward into the clouds. Spread out all around the foot of the ceiba are the earth, sea, and sky. The great god waves his hand, and bark and twigs begin to fall from the tree, falling all over the air and land around it. Wherever the pieces fall— on the land, the water, and in the air—new life starts to appear. In the waters, fish begin to swim around where the twigs have come to rest. In the air, the debris makes colorful birds. On the solid ground, different beasts and reptiles begin to appear. The earliest humans also appear from this falling bark and tree debris. However, the Mighty One, using his great hand, helps the people rise and stand upright. This special act makes people distinct from the other animals that were created from the sacred ceiba tree.

In this new world, humans do not hunt the other animals, nor do the animals inflict any harm upon the people. The early humans eat the fruit from the trees and drink only water. The beasts and the birds play with human children, as the people do not take the animals' lives for food. However, over time, a new human, the first of the Arawaks, comes into the world. Wadili, as he is known, encounters the women living in this new world. Falling in love with them, Wadili takes them as his brides, thus siring the entire Arawak people. He also teaches his fellow humans how to hunt, fish, and domesticate the animals. With the arrival of Wadili, the Arawaks begin to multiply and take a dominant role in the new world created by the Mighty One and his sacred ceiba.

SIGNIFICANCE

The legend of the ceiba tree is part of the tradition of the Arawak tribes, indigenous peoples who occupied much of the West Indies, including what is now Haiti and Guiana. The Arawaks were among the tribes that Christopher Columbus and his crew encountered during their voyages to the New World. Much of the Arawak population was eradicated—both by conflict with rival tribes, such as the Caribs, and under the rule of Spanish colonizers. Because most Arawaks were wiped out, it has proven difficult for experts to piece together their religious traditions and mythologies. However, many stone artifacts have been unearthed in the region, and

Arawak legends and myths were handed down via oral tradition.

This story describes the actions of the Awaraks' highest god, who sits atop a ceiba tree and creates all living things. As is the case with many of the traditions of other indigenous tribes of Latin America, this god—the Mighty One—possesses great power over the natural world. However, he does not demonstrate any characteristics that distinguish him from other gods, known as *zemi*. In this story, the focus is not on the Mighty One but on what he creates from the debris of the ceiba tree.

The ceiba tree is held sacred by many Latin American tribes. The Mayas believed that a great ceiba tree stood at the center of the earth, connecting the terrestrial world and the heavenly world of the spirits.

Although it varies in size and appearance from species to species, the ceiba is frequently a tall tree and has wide-reaching branches. Its distinctive appearance features prominently in many indigenous mythologies. In another Arawak myth, for example, this tree is broken open by a hero named Suko. The rupture releases an enormous flood that covers the world. One of the distinguishing characteristics of the Arawaks (who, on the island of Hispaniola, were also known as Taino) was the fact that they used the wood of the ceiba tree for the construction of their canoes, which they used to travel throughout the West Indies and to the mainland.

The story's focus on the father of the Arawaks, Wadili, is also significant. This individual gives the humans that were created by the falling ceiba debris a distinctive set of characteristics. Following his arrival, the humans with whom he interacts evolve to become hunters and begin to dominate the other living creatures of the earth.

Michael P. Auerbach, MA

BIBLIOGRAPHY

Brett, William Henry, comp. and ed. "Origin of Living Creatures (Legend of the Ceiba Tree)." *Legends and Myths of the Aboriginal Indian of British Guiana.* London: Gardner, 1880. 7–8. Print.

Corbett, Bob. "Arawak/Taino Native Americans." *Pre-Columbian Hispaniola.* Webster U, Feb. 2009. Web. 26 May 2013.

Lankford, George E. *Native American Legends of the Southeast.* Tuscaloosa: U of Alabama P, 2011. Print.

Roth, Walter E. "Creation of Man, Plants, and Animals." *An Inquiry into the Animism and Folk-Lore of the*

Guiana Indians. Washington: GPO, 1915. 141–48. Print.

---. "No Evidence of Belief in a Supreme Being." *An Inquiry into the Animism and Folk-Lore of the Guiana Indians*. Washington: GPO, 1915. 117–18. Print.

Woodward, Catherine L. "The Ceiba Tree." *Ceiba.org*. Ceiba Foundation for Tropical Preservation, 2010. Web. 12 July 2013.

The Rod of Gold

Author: Traditional Inca
Time Period: 1001 CE–1500 CE
Country or Culture: South America
Genre: Myth

PLOT SUMMARY

In a time before the Inca Empire, the people live as beasts in the wild. They do not wear clothes but are clad in fur or bark or go nude. They do not have houses but live in caves and crags where they can find temporary shelter. They do not know of marriage, instead mating opportunistically like other animals. They do not live in towns but are scattered about the land in groups of two or three. They have no knowledge of agriculture or animal husbandry, instead foraging for food. Some even practice cannibalism.

The sun god, known as Inti by the Incas, takes pity on the savage human beings. He wants them to live in a civilized manner and worship him correctly. He sends his two children, Manco Cápac and Mama Ocllo, who are also husband and wife, to emerge from an island (in some versions, from a boat) in Lake Titicaca. He tells the pair to rule justly and be warm and benevolent to all people, just as he is. Their mission is to civilize the people, teaching them to practice agriculture and making subjects of them. Inti gives his children a golden rod half the length of a person's arm and two fingers thick to use to test the ground as they journey north. Where the rod goes in all the way with a single thrust, Inti tells them, they should establish the seat of their empire.

Manco Cápac and Mama Ocllo plant the rod in many places, to no avail. Then they rest at a sheltered place called Pacaritambo ("the House of Dawn"). From there they go into the untamed wilderness that is destined to be the city of Cuzco. They stop at an overlook called Huanacauri ("Rainbow") and successfully plant the golden rod in the ground, realizing that this is the place to build their capital city.

Manco Cápac goes north, and Mama Ocllo goes south, telling all the people they meet that a new era is upon them. They say that the sun has sent them to be the people's new rulers. The people are mightily impressed by the fine clothes the two wear, as well as their stretched-out earlobes, and willingly join their cause.

Manco Cápac and Mama Ocllo teach the people to built proper houses, and they thereby construct upper and lower Cuzco. Manco Cápac shows the men how to grow crops such as corn and quinoa, to herd llamas, and to make shoes. Mama Ocllo instructs the women in the textile arts, and they are soon weaving cotton and wool into clothing.

Manco Cápac and Mama Ocllo's reputation for benevolent leadership soon causes many people to join their cohort. Within seven years, the children of the sun have enough followers to form a formidable army. Manco Cápac teaches his followers to fight with bows and arrows, spears, and clubs. They are able to defend themselves against external aggression and rapidly expand their empire through conquest.

Once their empire is well established, Manco Cápac and Mama Ocllo choose to leave. They tell their followers that the sun will adopt all of them as his children. The people are overjoyed to be accepted by this supernatural power. The Incas build holy shrines to Inti, the sun, and dedicate many maidens to their upkeep.

SIGNIFICANCE

"The Rod of Gold" is one of the best-known myths from precolonial Peru. Though it is the main origin myth that survives from the Inca culture, it does not describe the beginning of the Inca people as an ethnic identity, as is typical of origin myths from other cultures. Rather, it provides a legendary account of how the Incas forged an empire in the fifteenth century CE. Although this form of origin myth is somewhat unusual, it is not unprecedented, and the Aztec Empire left behind a similar tale.

There are two main versions of the myth. The one rendered here, in which the main protagonists are Manco Cápac and his sister and wife, Mama Ocllo, is typically ascribed to Garcilaso de la Vega (1539–1616), who was the son of a Spanish conquistador and an Inca noblewoman. In the other version, Manco Cápac and Mama Ocllo are joined by three other sibling-spouse pairs, often called the Ayar siblings. These are Ayar Cachi and

Mama Cora, Ayar Auca and Mama Huaco, and Ayar Uchu and Mama Rahua. In this myth, the four pairs originate from Pacaritambo. This variant describes Ayar Cachi as very prone to violence and states that he has a slingshot that he uses to destroy mountains. The other siblings are afraid of Ayar Cachi, so they trick him into going back into a cave, supposedly to retrieve a golden trinket they accidentally left behind, and trap him there by collapsing the cave's entrance. When the remaining siblings reach Huanacauri, Ayar Uchu is turned to stone. The siblings first glimpse Cuzco from Huanacauri, where Ayar Uchu is to dwell for eternity. When they reach the site of the settlement, Ayar Auca also turns to stone, leaving Manco Cápac and the sisters to found the city. This version is more widely attested than de la Vega's version and was first recorded in slightly different forms by Pedro Cieza de León (ca. 1520–54), a conquistador, and Juan de Betanzos (ca. 1510–76), who was married to the former wife of the Inca leader Atahualpa (1497–1533).

To fully appreciate the historical and cultural significance of "The Rod of Gold," it is necessary to know that the supremely powerful creator god in the Inca pantheon is not the sun but a being called Viracocha. Although there is a small canon of stories in which Viracocha takes the form of a beggar or herder to inspect his creation, he was typically considered to be without form and was removed from the affairs of the world. Viracocha first created a world that was wholly dark. To bring light to his creation, he formed the sun and the moon. At first, these two celestial bodies were equally bright, but the sun became jealous and threw soot in the moon's face.

Scholars believe that sun worship was widespread among the ancient peoples of Peru, particularly in the highland region. Sun worship was also a traditional part of Inca religion, and they certainly revered the solar god Inti since before their imperial period. However, Inti worship became much more important as the Inca Empire expanded and engulfed neighboring cultures.

The Inca sphere of influence was dramatically expanded by the great leader Pachacuti Inca Yupanqui (ca. 1438–71). He began an ongoing war of conquest that resulted in the Incas defeating tribal rivals and becoming the undisputed lords of the region. In building this empire, Pachacuti Inca Yupanqui and his successors had to rely on complicated diplomatic relationships to hold onto a large and diverse body of more than ten million subjects.

Many scholars contend that "The Rod of Gold" was a form of mythical propaganda, a religious justification of their right to rule. By repeating the story that they were the direct descendents of Manco Cápac and Mama Ocllo, these Inca rulers could claim to have divine status themselves. This assertion was especially likely to have helped them gain acceptance from the non-Inca peoples living in the area of Lake Titicaca, who traditionally worshipped the sun as their most important god.

Clearly, Inti worship became the central state cult during the imperial era. Beginning during Pachacuti Inca Yupanqui's reign, the Incas established several important temples to Inti, including ones on the so-called Island of the Sun in Lake Titicaca and the Coricancha (Golden Enclosure) in Cuzco. These temples were staffed by hundreds of maidens consecrated to Inti's glory. The temple-building activity is mentioned in the myth as taking place when the children of the sun left the world, but it actually started generations after the legendary rule of Manco Cápac, as the Inca Empire was expanding under Pachacuti Inca Yupanqui.

Further evidence that the myth emerged during Pachacuti Inca Yupanqui's reign comes from a contemporaneous shift in marriage patterns. At this point, brother-sister marriages became the preferred form of marriage within the Inca royal family, a way of asserting that the Inca nobility were categorically different from other, more common people. It bolstered the belief that they were descended from the sun via the sibling-spouses Manco Cápac and Mama Ocllo and that they therefore must take measures to ensure the purity of their divine bloodline.

Adam Berger, PhD

BIBLIOGRAPHY

Baur, Brian. *Ancient Cuzco*. Austin: U of Texas P, 2004. Print.

Bierhorst, John. *Black Rainbow: Legends of the Incas and Myths of Ancient Peru*. New York: Farrar, 1976. Print.

Brundage, Burr Cartwright. *Empire of the Inca*. Norman: U of Oklahoma P, 1963. Print.

Cobo, Bernabé. *Inca Religion and Customs*. Trans. Roland Hamilton. Austin: U of Texas P, 1990. Print.

D'Altroy, Terence. *The Incas*. Oxford: Blackwell, 2002. Print.

Jones, David. *The Myths and Religion of the Incas*. London: Anness, 2008. Print.

Julien, Catherine. *Reading Inca History*. Iowa City: U of Iowa P, 2000. Print.

Keatinge, Richard W. *Peruvian Prehistory*. Cambridge: Cambridge UP, 1988. Print.

Malpass, Michael. *Daily Life in the Inca Empire*. Westport: Greenwood, 1996. Print.

Markham, Clements. *The Incas of Peru*. New York: Dutton, 1910. Print.

Moseley, Michael. *The Incas and Their Ancestors*. Rev. ed. New York: Thames, 2001. Print.

Urton, Gary. *The History of a Myth*. Austin: U of Texas P, 1990. Print.

Uitoto Creation Story

Author: Traditional Uitoto
Time Period: 1001 CE–1500 CE
Country or Culture: South America
Genre: Myth

PLOT SUMMARY

In the beginning, the creating entity comes about through a word. This creator is variously named Naimuena, meaning "father of illusion," or Buinaima, which has several meanings, including "father of creation." Naimuena is an illusion, and illusion is all that is. He has a vaguely defined dream of existence, which he concentrates on at length.

The creator then attaches the illusion, which is all that exists, to the thread of his dream. Grasping it like a piece of cotton, he stomps on it with his feet, and then rests on his dreamed earth. He then spits, and from his saliva, the forests of the earth come forth. He lies down and creates the heavens and the sky. A being called Rafuema, the storyteller, sits in the sky to pass along the account of how he has created existence to those who will come to populate the world.

SIGNIFICANCE

The Uitoto (often spelled Witoto or Huitoto) people are an indigenous group in the northwestern Amazon region. They inhabit southeastern Colombia and northern Peru, primarily dwelling along rivers, including the Putumayo and Caquetá. Before the twentieth century, they were the largest group in the Putumayo region, with an estimated population of fifty thousand. The rubber boom that began in the early twentieth century had a

deep impact on the Uitotos and their way of life. The incoming rubber tappers pressed many Uitoto people into forced labor, and grueling conditions and ensuing waves of disease decimated their population. Many of the Uitoto people who survived fled the region, losing their cultural identities. As of 2013, the total Uitoto population is fewer than eight thousand.

The Uitoto creation myth was first recorded by a German ethnologist named Konrad Theodor Preuss sometime between 1912 and 1914. It was told to him by a Uitoto shaman named Rigasedyue. Significantly, there have been a number of very different creation accounts recorded among the Uitotos. For instance, the one told to Fernando Urbina by Uitoto Octavio Garcia in 1982 bears little resemblance to the one Preuss published. Other social scientists, including the American William Farabee, who were working with the Uitotos at the beginning of the twentieth century claim that the Uitotos actually do not have a creation account.

There is a compelling explanation for why there are different takes on the Uitoto creation myth. Although their current population is rather small, the Uitotos were once a large group. They traditionally lived in relatively insular communal villages that were often at war with one another. As such, significant cultural and linguistic differences developed among the different bands of Uitoto people, and this heterodoxy remains to this day. Moreover, myths are traditionally passed down from fathers to sons within families, rather than as entire villages, meaning that each family essentially has its own folkloric customs.

Despite this profound cultural diversity, the version of the Uitoto myth recorded by Preuss has been the most repeated in academic circles, and indeed has become one of the best known myths of the entire Amazon region. It is an example of an ex nihilo account of the origin of the universe. While it is intellectually puzzling to contemplate existence coming from nothing, this form of creation story is common among world cultures.

The name *Uitoto*, which members of the group use today, is actually a word meaning "enemy" from the Carijona tribe. The Uitotos and Carijonas are known to have been bitter enemies at least as far back as the Spanish conquest. One significant reason for the constant animosity was Uitoto belief that death comes not from natural causes, but from sorcery. Shamanic healers intoxicate themselves and sick patients with tobacco paste, coca, and a hallucinogenic snuff. In the dreamlike state induced by these drugs, the shamans try to determine who sent the evil spirit responsible for illness and to reattach the afflicted person's soul to his or her body.

There are clearly deep symbolic connections between these ritual practices and the Uitoto creation myth. The practitioner of a healing ritual is often called Buinaima, just as the creator god often is. The myth begins by stating that the creator was born of a word, and indeed, the idea of manifesting reality through saying the proper words in chants is an important part of Uitoto belief. The concept is referred to as *rafue*, meaning "the power of turning words into objects or outcomes." Likewise, just as the creator god generated the forests through saliva, the shaman, aided by the ingestion of intoxicants, drools during the ceremony. It is while chanting the correct words and drooling that the healer attempts to reattach the sick person's body and soul. The healing ritual is fundamentally an act of linking the illusory to the physical to form a unity of complementary opposites, which is a refrain often heard in Uitoto myths, including the famous version of the creation story.

Adam Berger, PhD

BIBLIOGRAPHY

Bierhorst, John. *The Mythology of South America*. New York: Oxford UP, 2002. Print.

Candre, Hipólito. *Cool Tobacco, Sweet Coca: Teachings of an Indian Sage from the Columbian Amazon*. Trans. Juan Alvaro Echeverri. Totnes: Themis, 1996. Print.

De Osa, Verónica. *The Troubled Waters of the Amazon: The Plight of the Colombian Indians in Amazonia*. London: Hale, 1990. Print.

Echeverri, Juan Alvaro. "The People of the Center of the World: A Study in Culture, History, and Orality in the Colombian Amazon." Diss. New School for Social Research, 1997. Print.

Farabee, William Curtis. *Indian Tribes of Eastern Peru*. 1922. New York: Krauss, 1977. Print.

Kline, Harvey. *Historical Dictionary of Colombia*. Lanham: Scarecrow, 2012. Print.

Olson, James S. *The Indians of Central and South America*. Westport: Greenwood, 1991. Print.

Sanders, Thomas E., and William Peek. *Literature of the American Indian*. Beverly Hills: Glencoe, 1976. 28. Print.

Seward, Julian Haynes. *Handbook of South American Indians*. New York: Cooper Square, 1963. Print. Smithsonian Institution Bureau of American Ethnology Bulletin 143.

Whiffen, Thomas. *The North-West Amazons: Notes of Some Months Spent among Cannibal Tribes*. 1915. Cambridge: Cambridge UP, 2009. Print.

Wilbert, Johannes. *Encyclopedia of World Cultures*. Vol. 7. Boston: Hall, 1994. Print.

◆ Viracocha

Author: Traditional Peruvian
Time Period: 1001 CE–1500 CE
Country or Culture: South America
Genre: Myth

PLOT SUMMARY

The myth of Viracocha begins by explaining that while the civilized Incas revere the sun, there are some who recall that it too is a product of creation. The being that made the sun and the moon and gave life to people and all other beings, they say, is named Viracocha. They remember that the sun and the moon were once equally bright, but the sun grew jealous and threw ashes into the moon's face to dim it.

Viracocha, the creator of all things, decides to adopt a disguise in order to survey his creation. Dressed as a dirty beggar, he goes to see how the gods are behaving. The disguise is convincing, and none of them knows his real identity.

During his sojourn, Viracocha happens upon a beautiful goddess named Cavillaca. She sits under a fruit-bearing lucma tree, surrounded by llama lambs and weaving white wool. Viracocha forms his semen into a ripe fruit and put it next to her. Cavillaca eats the fruit and becomes pregnant, but she has no idea who the father is. When her son is born, her family admonishes her to find out who has gotten her pregnant. Cavillaca invites all gods living nearby to gather at the tree and lets the baby crawl amongst them, as the baby will know its father. When the baby picks out the dirty beggar, Cavillaca is horrified. Viracocha reveals himself as the great god, but it is too late; Cavillaca has already fled with her son.

Viracocha chases after the mother of his child. Along his way, he encounters a condor and asks where Cavillaca has gone. The condor tells him she is not far, and the great god blessed the condor. Then Viracocha meets a fox and asks where Cavillaca can be found. The fox says he will never find Cavillaca, so Viracocha curses the fox. This pattern continues: he meets a puma, who tells Viracocha she is near, and he blesses it; he encounters parrots, who say she is far, and he curses them. Finally, Viracocha meets a falcon, which guides him to the sea, so he blesses it.

Just as Viracocha catches up to Cavillaca, she plunges into the sea with her son, and they turn to rocks. Viracocha is inconsolable for a time, but then he discovers that there are two virgin daughters of the fish goddess Urpihuachac living nearby. He uses his powers to subdue a giant snake that is guarding them. One daughter turns into a bird and flies away, but the other stays with Viracocha. She shows him the pond where her mother stores all existing fish, and Viracocha smashes its walls, allowing fish into the bodies of water of the world.

Viracocha continues to live among men and teaches them agriculture. Finally, he puts a giant cross on the top of a tall mountain, and when the dawn's first rays of sunlight light it up, he leaves the world of people and walks west across the sea. The people who have known him remember his greatness and praise him.

SIGNIFICANCE

The story of Viracocha and Cavillaca appears in several forms. The form related by Pádraic Colum in his book *Orpheus: Myths of the World* (1930), summarized above, begins with a synopsis of another myth, that of the origins of the Inca Empire. It describes how there was a time when people were uncivilized, so after Viracocha creates the sun, it sends its son and daughter to earth at Lake Titicaca. These two, named Manco Cápac and Mama Ocllo, have a golden rod that they use to probe the ground. When they find the place where it goes in, they found the city of Cuzco, the seat of the Inca Empire. They show their new followers how to live as proper human beings: growing crops, raising llamas, wearing clothes, and living in houses.

This version of Viracocha's story ends by incorporating another tale into its narrative. In it, Viracocha lives for a time in the highlands, showing people how to grow crops on the mountain face. It states that in the end, he builds a cross atop a mountain, and when dawn's first light hits the cross, the god departs the world of humans. He does so by walking west, right across the surface of the ocean.

In other versions of the story, Viracocha is called Coniraya Viracocha or simply Coniraya and is alternately described as Viracocha himself, a minor god or divine spirit who may be a descendant or reincarnation of Viracocha, or a different version of Viracocha who is both trickster and creator. In a retelling closely analyzed by John Bierhorst in *Black Rainbow* (1976), in which Coniraya falls into the latter category, he is said to wander secretly through the world to inspect his creation. He takes the form of a bird to spy on the beautiful virgin goddess Cavillaca, here spelled Cahuillaca. All of the gods want to marry her, so Coniraya puts his semen into a ripe fruit to trick her into conceiving his child.

The story as recounted by Bierhorst closely follows Colum's version until the end, which is quite different. The young virgins he encounters at the sea are the daughters of Urpihuachac and the lowland creator god Pachacamac. There is no giant snake protecting them for Coniraya to overcome, but Urpihuachac herself attempts to kill him in revenge for ravaging one of her virgin daughters and causing the other to turn to a dove and fly away. He pretends to have to urinate and runs off, living the rest of his life in upland villages as a prankster.

This variation is historically significant. In fifteenth-century Peru, as the Inca Empire was becoming the most powerful force in the region, there were indeed two main creator gods. The first, Viracocha, was associated with the highland region; the other, Pachacamac, was associated with the lowlands and the coastal area. The inclusion of Pachacamac in Bierhorst's version of the myth underscores this opposition, and the fact that Coniraya Viracocha flees to the highlands in the end solidifies his association with the upland mountains.

Whatever the differences between them, however, both versions of the myth are ultimately about the same thing: they speak to the failure of the couple to marry as proper adults. By fleeing Viracocha's advances after she bears his child, Cavillaca refuses to participate in the cycle of human maturation, which the Incas held as sacred. In the end, she is turned to stone for this transgression. For failing to be a proper husband, as is fitting for an adult, Viracocha lives in the highlands either in a sort of voluntary exile or as a prankster, the latter of which Bierhorst suggests is a form of perpetual childhood.

Adam Berger, PhD

BIBLIOGRAPHY

Bierhorst, John. *Black Rainbow: Legends of the Incas and Myths of Ancient Peru.* New York: Farrar, 1976. Print.

Brundage, Burr Cartwright. *Empire of the Inca*. Norman: U of Oklahoma P, 1963. Print.

Cobo, Bernabé. *Inca Religion and Customs*. Trans. and ed. Roland Hamilton. Austin: U of Texas P, 1990. Print.

Colum, Pádraic. "Viracocha." *Orpheus: Myths of the World*. New York: Macmillan, 1930. 275–79. Print.

D'Altroy, Terence. *The Incas*. Malden: Blackwell, 2002. Print.

Jones, David M. *The Myths & Religion of the Incas*. London: Southwater, 2008. Print.

Julien, Catherine. *Reading Inca History*. Iowa City: U of Iowa P, 2000. Print.

Malpass, Michael A. *Daily Life in the Inca Empire*. Westport: Greenwood, 1996. Print.

Markham, Clements. *The Incas of Peru*. New York: Dutton, 1910. Print.

Moseley, Michael E. *The Incas and Their Ancestors: The Archaeology of Peru*. Rev. ed. New York: Thames, 2001. Print.

◆ A Young Man and the Star

Author: Traditional Brazilian
Time Period: 1001 CE– 1500 CE
Country or Culture: South America
Genre: Myth

PLOT SUMMARY

The Xerente star myth tells the story of a young man who is drawn to the vast beauty of the night sky. He laments that he cannot have a star of his own to admire at any time. He awakes in the middle of the night to find a star beside him, personified as a young woman. The man greatly admires her beauty. The star-girl asks the young man to gather a cluster of fruit from a tree for her. As the young man ascends the tree, the star-girl strikes it with a magic wand, where it grows in height until it reaches the heavens, or sky world.

Once they enter the sky world, the young man is intrigued by the sounds of festivity and the dancing and songs he hears nearby. The star-girl forbids him to go and investigate the activity, but when she leaves him alone momentarily, he gives in to his curiosity. What he witnesses is the dance of the dead, a hideous gang of skeletons dancing amid an odor of rotting flesh.

The young man returns to the tree in fear, and it sinks back into the earth. As he does so, the star-girl calls after him, saying that even if he leaves, he will return to her soon. The myth does indeed end with the young man dying shortly after telling his people the story of his adventure. It can be assumed that, despite their reverence for things celestial, the divine fate of humankind was, to the Xerentes, essentially unknowable and even potentially dangerous to consider.

SIGNIFICANCE

The Xerentes (alternately spelled Cherentes or Sherentés) are one of several indigenous peoples of Brazil whose mythology survived through a tradition of oral storytelling passed down from one generation to another. While there is little scholarly writing on the Xerentes and their mythological canon, they—like other numerous indigenous cultures all across the world—adopted a divine reverence for the sky and the celestial bodies within it. The Xerentes held the sun as their supreme god and object of worship. The moon and the stars, conversely, took on an antagonistic role, often illustrated as cult-like figures closely associated with death.

Observers of Xerente festivals related to death noted the people's use of long poles, which symbolized an interaction between humans and each heavenly world. The poles can be directly correlated to the Xerente star myth above, which was extracted from the tribe's oral tradition and recorded by the nineteenth-century anthropologist José Feliciano de Oliveira, who studied the tribe at length and penned perhaps the quintessential text about the tribe. Oliveira regards the Xerente star myth as an assertion that the tribe held little belief in the notion that salvation or eternal happiness awaited them in the afterlife. Rather, the Xerente star myth paints celestial beings as desirable but ultimately malevolent harbingers of doom.

The Xerente star myth also adopts several narrative features that scholars have found to be common in the mythology of indigenous Brazilian tribes, most notably the illustration of the unification of heaven and earth by the rapid and wondrous growth of a tree or rock.

The death of the young man at the conclusion of the narrative also paints a rather grim picture with regard to the exploration of fate amongst the Xerentes, for it seems to imply that those curious about the afterlife or the heavens themselves do so at their own peril.

John Pritchard

BIBLIOGRAPHY

Alexander, Hartley Burr. *The Mythology of All Races: Latin-American.* Vol. 11. Boston: Jones, 1920. Print.

Bierhorst, John. *The Mythology of South America.* New York: Oxford UP, 2002. Print.

Bingham, Ann, and Jeremy Roberts. *South and Meso-American Mythology A to Z.* 2nd ed. New York: Chelsea, 2010. Print.

Gifford, Douglas, and John Sibbick. *Warriors, Gods and Spirits from Central & South American Mythology.* New York: Schocken, 1987. Print.

Oliveira, José Feliciano de. *The Cherentes of Central Brazil.* London: Congress of Americanists, 1913. Print.

THE PACIFIC

Oceania

OCEANIA

◆ Birth of Sea and Land Life

Author: Traditional
Time Period: 1001 CE–1500 CE; 1851 CE–1900 CE
Country or Culture: Hawaii
Genre: Myth

PLOT SUMMARY

The Hawaiian myth of the birth of sea and land life begins one night in spring. The earth grows hot, the heavens turn, and it is dark. Some primordial slime rises up from the sea and becomes the source of the earth. The first two people are born: "The night gave birth / Born was Kumulipo in the night, a male / Born was Po'ele in the night, a female" (Beckwith lines 12–14). After Kumulipo and Po'ele, sea and land life is created. This creation begins with humble forms of sea life, such as coral polyps, sea urchins, and oysters. For each new species created, the myth identifies another species or subspecies as its child, creating a genealogy of sea life: "Born was the conch shell, his child the small conch shell came forth" (31).

After describing the creation of the different sea creatures, the myth turns to land life, describing its creation in thirteen similarly constructed stanzas. Each stanza

begins with the reaffirmation of the birth of the first man and woman from water. Man comes from a narrow, forceful stream and woman from a broad, tranquil stream. Next, the creation of each new sea plant is paired with the creation of a corresponding land plant that is similar in name and nature. Thus, for example, the creation of the 'ekaha moss of the sea is followed by the creation of the 'ekahakaha fern on land. Earth and water sustain the land plants that have been newly created. The creation process of sea and land life is described as sacred, a realm into which "man can not enter" (39). This assertion is repeated throughout the myth.

When this period of creation is completed, a god with a water gourd enters. His water nourishes the vines on the land, and as a result of this water, lush plant life multiplies voraciously. The myth celebrates the growth and flourishing of vegetation. Soon, there is so much fruitful vegetation that it props up the earth and supports the sky.

Throughout this process of first creation, the myth asserts, it has been night. This early period at the dawn of creation is referred to as the "night of Kumulipo" after the first man (121). This is especially apt, for as American scholar Martha Beckwith explains in the introduction to her translation of the myth, Kumulipo literally means "beginning-(in)-deep-darkness" in Hawaiian (38).

SIGNIFICANCE

Originally an oral narrative, the Hawaiian myth of the birth of sea and land life was first transcribed in the mid-nineteenth century. In this extant form, the myth is used to open the genealogical chant known as the Kumulipo, which chronicles the creation of the world and the first humans and goes on to name the subsequent generations of noble men and women, ending with the birth of the eighteenth-century Hawaiian chief Ka-'I-i-mamao, to whom the chant was dedicated. This genealogical chant allowed the chief to trace his noble line back to the dawn of creation and served as confirmation of his ancestral claim to power.

The myth of the birth of sea and land life is much older than the Kumulipo. Scholarly comparison with other Polynesian creation myths indicates that the core of the narrative may have reached Hawaii during the thirteenth century CE, when Tahitians arrived on the islands. The myth's concluding idea that vegetation nourished by water from the god's gourd is "propping up earth, holding up the sky" (120) is echoed in a Tahitian creation chant, as Beckwith notes.

According to Hawaii's last queen, Lili'uokalani, the Kumulipo was composed in 1700 by the poet Keāulumoku. However, as Keāulumoku lived from 1716 to 1784, either the date of the composition or the authorship must be wrong. Beckwith suggests that either the name Keāulumoku was a court poet's title passed through generations or the Kumulipo was composed at a later time.

There are two historically documented occasions at which the Kumulipo, and thus the myth of the birth of sea and land life, was chanted publically. On one occasion, those reciting the chant welcomed British captain James Cook upon his first visit to Hawaii in 1779. The second occasion occurred in 1804 following the death of Ke'eaumoku, an uncle of Hawaiian king Kamehameha I, who founded Hawaii's last royal dynasty.

In 1889, a transcription of the Kumulipo was printed in Hawaiian, based on a manuscript owned by Hawaiian king Kalākaua. After her deposition in 1893, Kalākaua's sister and successor, Lili'uokalani, translated the Kumulipo into English. Her lines are deliberately poetic, as in her rendering of the beginning of creation: "At the time of the night of Makalii / Then began the slime which established the earth, / The source of deepest darkness" (5–8). In 1951, Beckwith translated the Kumulipo into

English and published what has become the authoritative version of the chant.

Following Beckwith, Hawaiian and international scholars have identified several different interpretations of this Hawaiian creation myth. The first is that it is a straightforward story of the creation of the people of Hawaii. Other scholars have noted that King Kalākau, in facilitating the print publication of the chant, may have used the creation myth and subsequent genealogy to emphasize the authority of his noble ancestors.

The myth of the birth of sea and land life could additionally be interpreted as symbolizing a Hawaiian chief's passage from infancy to adulthood. Another view sees the myth as alluding to conception and the growth of a human embryo in the womb. In this view, the myth's central themes of water and darkness allude to the fetus swimming in the amniotic fluid in the darkness of the womb. All of these interpretations may contribute to the overall significance of the myth, which not only chronicles the creation of the world in general but also sets in motion the development of Hawaii as a kingdom.

R. C. Lutz, PhD

BIBLIOGRAPHY

Beckwith, Martha Warren. *Hawaiian Mythology*. New Haven: Yale UP, 1940. Print.

---. *The Kumulipo: A Hawaiian Creation Chant*. Chicago: U of Chicago P, 1951. Print.

Fornander, Abraham. *Fornander's Ancient History of the Hawaiian People to the Times of Kamehameha I*. Honolulu: Mutual, 2005. Print.

Liliuokalani. *An Account of the Creation of the World according to Hawaiian Tradition*. Boston: Lee, 1897. Print.

Thompson, Vivian Laubach. *Hawaiian Myths of Earth, Sea, and Sky*. Honolulu: U of Hawaii P, 1988. Print.

◆ Borah of Byamee

Author: Traditional
Time Period: 999 BCE–1 BCE; 1 CE–500 CE
Country or Culture: Australia
Genre: Myth

PLOT SUMMARY

A large gathering of Aboriginal tribes is set to take place at Googoorewon, the place of trees. The elders of the tribes decide that the gathering would be the proper occasion for a *borah*, a revered ceremony in which boys transition into young men. Once a boy has been initiated through a borah, he is allowed to marry, consume emu meat, and train to be a warrior. A *wirreenum*, or elder, named Byamee (Baiame or Baayami) is part of the gathering and brings along his two sons, Ghindahindahmoee and Boomahoomahnowee.

Many tribes attend the gathering, including the Dummerh (pigeons), the Mahthi (dogs), and the Wahn (crows). During the day, the tribes engage in hunting, and at night, there is much feasting, dancing, and singing. With the blessing of the elders, the men exchange gifts and arrange marriages for many of the unmarried women. Following several days of revelry, the men decide it is time for the borah to begin. They construct a large circle in the brush, surrounded by an earthen dam, as well as a path through the brush leading to a larger clearing. The preparations for the borah are hidden from the women, who are prohibited from witnessing the ceremony.

Before the borah begins, Byamee displays his great power by putting a curse on the Mahthi tribe. The tribe had been disrespectful to the elders and the sacred borah rites throughout the gathering, and despite being warned several times, the tribe continues to laugh and play without any concern. Byamee punishes the tribe by cursing them to speak in barks and howls for all eternity. Other tribes are transformed during the gathering as well. For instance, the Dummerh tribe steals grinding stones from the women with the aid of ghosts and spirits. Afterward, the members of the tribe are cursed with the cooing voice of the spirits who aided them.

As the borah is about to begin, the women are concealed in ditches around the circle and covered with boughs. The men and boys pair up and prepare to leave the circle for their journey through the brush when a distressed widow named Millindooloonubbah enters the camp. She explains that she was left behind with her large family to travel alone to the camp while everyone else moved ahead. The tribes drank all of the watering holes dry along the way, which caused all of her children to die of thirst. Just before collapsing dead in front of the men, she curses them all. The tribes standing near the edge of the circle are transformed into trees. The other tribes are changed into animals: the Mahthi into barking dogs, the Wahn into shrieking crows, the Dummerh into cooing pigeons, and so on.

Byamee and other tribe members who had not yet reached the circle are spared this fate. Fearing that enemies had slain the other tribes and are now pursuing them, Byamee leads the remaining men far into the country. When they reach a spring in a place called Noondoo, Byamee's dog gives birth to a litter of deformed puppies with the heads of pigs and ferocious strength. Byamee will not go near this breed of dog, and he remains in the ridges and brush of Noondoo for all time.

SIGNIFICANCE

Australian Aboriginal mythology is predominantly associated with the landscape, animals, and geography of Australia. Aboriginal mythology features an animist creation narrative that contains a concept commonly referred to as the Dreaming or Dreamtime. This highly spiritual concept revolves around everlasting creating and formative creation. The concept is also used in reference to significant locations where creation spirits and symbolic ancestors are believed to reside.

The myth of the borah of Byamee is connected to a specific Dreaming location called Noondoo, a locality in the state of Queensland. It is there that, at the end of the story, Byamee chooses to reside for eternity. Byamee is a very significant god in the mythology of several Aboriginal groups of southeastern Australia, including the Kamilaroi, Eora, and Wiradjuri peoples. A creator god believed to have come down from the sky and created the landscape, he is also said to have given people their laws of life as well as their songs, culture, and traditions.

One such tradition is the borah detailed in this myth. The word *borah* refers to the initiation itself as well as to the location where it is performed. In the southeastern region of Australia, the ceremony involves boys walking along a path meant to represent their transition to manhood. In some regions, the ceremony begins in a public place, and the boys then travel with initiated men to a private location out in the brush to finish it. The Werrikimbe National Park in New South Wales contains borah rings made of individually placed stones.

In Aboriginal art, Byamee is often depicted in a humanlike form with a large head, limbs, and eyes. Wiradjuri paintings in a cave near Milbrodale in New South Wales feature a giant figure thought to be Byamee. This cave, known as the Baiame Cave, is listed on the Register of the National Estate, is considered a significant natural and cultural heritage sites in Australia.

Patrick G. Cooper

BIBLIOGRAPHY

Marett, Allan. *Songs, Dreamings, and Ghosts: The Wangga of North Australia*. Middletown: Wesleyan UP, 2005. Print.

Mills, Philo Loas. *Prehistoric Religion: A Study in Pre-Christian Antiquity*. Washington: Capital, 1918. Print.

Parker, Katie Langloh. "The Borah of Byamee." *Australian Legendary Tales*. London: Nutt, 1896. 94–105. Print.

---. *The Euahlayi Tribe: A Study of Aboriginal Life in Australia*. London: Constable, 1905. Print.

Wardrop, Martin. "Dreaming and the Dreamtime." *Aboriginal Art Online*. Aboriginal Art Online, 2000. Web. 24 May 2013.

◆ Bram-Bram-Bult

Author: Traditional
Time Period: 999 BCE–1 BCE; 1 CE–500 CE
Country or Culture: Australia
Genre: Myth

PLOT SUMMARY

One day, a mighty spirit named Doan, who has taken the body of a gliding possum, sets out to hunt a kangaroo. The kangaroo, named Purra, manages to elude Doan for some time. Just as Doan closes in on Purra, he crosses into the territory of an echidna spirit known as Wembulin, who attacks him. Doan manages to escape, but Wembulin soon catches up with him and kills him. Wembulin and his two daughters eat Doan and then begin to pursue Purra.

Shortly after Doan goes missing, his maternal uncles, Yuree and Wanjel, renowned warriors also known as the Bram-Bram-Bult, go in search of him. During their search, they come across ants carrying small bits of Doan's body back to their nest. Nearby they find the site where Wembulin killed Doan and discover the remainder of his body.

Realizing that the echidna had killed their nephew, the two men, who are also highly skilled trackers, set off in pursuit of Wembulin. After three days, Yuree and Wanjel find Wembulin and his daughters. Catching Wembulin by surprise, the two warriors slay him and marry his daughters.

As they return to their home, Yuree and Wanjel become suspicious of the daughters and begin to fear their anger over the death of their father. Worrying that their new wives will take revenge against them, the two warriors kill Wembulin's daughters. They then journey through the countryside, naming all of the plants, rock, rivers, and other aspects of the landscape they come across and thus bringing the surrounding world into being.

One day, Wanjel is bitten by a poisonous snake named Gertuk and dies. Yuree carves a wooden representation of his dead brother and magically gives it life. This revives Wanjel, and the two brothers continue their journey until finally settling in a cave. When the two die, they ascend to the sky and live on as stars.

SIGNIFICANCE

Like many stories in Australian Aboriginal mythology, the story of the Bram-Bram-Bult directly concerns the Australian landscape and its creation. The brothers Yuree and Wanjel name many aspects of the landscape, thereby creating them. When they die, the brothers become stars in another act of creation.

The sky, particularly the night sky, is crucial to Aboriginal mythology. In one tale of Yuree and Wanjel, the brothers defeat a savage emu that is attacking a man named Bunya, whom they then change into a possum. Some Aboriginal Australians believed that the four-star constellation known as the Southern Cross represents this myth; the four stars represent the emu, the possum, and the brothers' spears. In northwestern Australia, Aboriginal peoples saw the Southern Cross as a representation of the origin of fire.

As Philip Wilkinson notes in *Myths and Legends*, Yuree and Wanjel are just one of many pairs of siblings in Aboriginal mythology. Siblings, particularly brothers, are prevalent in the mythology of many Aboriginal peoples, although the relationships between the mythological siblings vary widely. While Yuree and Wanjel are said to be close brothers who fight and travel together, other siblings are said to clash with one another, at times with disastrous consequences. For instance, one Aboriginal myth concerns two brothers who argue over the rights to water. One brother wisely fills up a leather bag with the water he finds. When the other one becomes thirsty, he fights with his brother and spills the water in the bag, causing a large flood. Another sibling myth concerns the Iguana Men, who rescue a woman from an attack. Like Yuree and Wanjel, these brothers work together, and they ultimately ascend to the sky.

Many figures in Aboriginal mythology are eternal spirits that take the form of animals. Aboriginal Australians believed that their ancestors lived on as these spirits, which were given the physical traits of animals and human characteristics. In the myth of the Bram-Bram-Bult, a gliding possum chases a kangaroo in the hope of killing it. Of course, a typical possum cannot accomplish this, but in the story, he can because the possum is an ancestral spirit. Doan is unable to achieve his goal not because of his body's small size and limited hunting ability but because of the actions of Wembulin. The role of the kangaroo as prey in this myth is unique; in most Aboriginal myths, the kangaroo is a heroic ancestor spirit.

In the myth of the Bram-Bram-Bult, Yuree revives Wanjel by carving a figure of him out of wood. Such carved figures and totems representing animals and ancestral figures were an important part of Aboriginal Australian art. Many Aboriginal groups believed that living animals were their ancestors, so much of their art consists of carved, painted, or etched images of these animals. Regardless of the medium, nearly all Aboriginal art has some kind of mythological undertone concerning the spiritual concept of Dreaming or Dreamtime. This concept refers to the period of time when the world was created and the subsequent perpetual creating. Many Aboriginal ceremonies, such as the borah rite in which boys transition to manhood, involve the use of art to create a close connection with the spirit world.

Patrick G. Cooper

BIBLIOGRAPHY

Allen, Tony, et al. *Journeys through Dreamtime: Oceanian Myths*. Amsterdam: Time-Life, 1999. Print.

Lawlor, Robert. *Voices of the First Day: Awakening in the Aboriginal Dreamtime*. Rochester: Inner Traditions, 1991. Print.

Mudrooroo. *Aboriginal Mythology*. London: Aquarian, 1994. Print.

Sutton, Peter, ed. *Dreamings: The Art of Aboriginal Australia*. New York: Viking, 1989. Print.

Wilkinson, Philip. *Myths and Legends: An Illustrated Guide to Their Origins and Meanings*. New York: Penguin, 2009. Print.

◆ The Children of Heaven and Earth

Author: Traditional
Time Period: 1001 CE–1500 CE
Country or Culture: Polynesia
Genre: Myth

PLOT SUMMARY

Rangi (or Rangi-nui) and Papa (or Papa-tū-ā-nuku), heaven and earth, are the source from which all things in the universe originate. At the time of creation, only darkness exists. Rangi and Papa are joined together in embrace, which causes their children to live in perpetual darkness. The darkness begins to take a toll on the children. Tū-mata-uenga (or Tū), the strongest of the children, wishes to slay Rangi and Papa, but the others agree that it is better to rend them apart and let heaven stand above them while the earth stays below. All of Rangi and Papa's children agree their parents should be separated, except Tāwhiri-mātea, the father of winds and storms. He is saddened by the decision and fears that his kingdom will be overthrown.

It is decided that Rongo-mā-tāne, the god and father of the cultivated food of man, will be the one to rend apart Rangi and Papa. However, he is not strong enough to do so. Tangaroa, the god and father of fish and reptiles, makes a second attempt but also fails. Finally, Tāne-mahuta, the god and father of forests, accomplishes the task of breaking the embrace. Rangi and Papa both cry out as heaven is separated from the earth. Once they are rent apart, the human beings who have been concealed between them are revealed.

Tāwhiri-mātea, the son who had keep Rangi and Papa together, now desires to wage war against his brothers for separating them, so he follows his father to heaven to hide in the sky. There, he schemes against his brothers and sends his winds, squalls, hurricanes, whirlwinds, and clouds across the earth. These varying winds and storms smite the forests of Tāne-mahuta, snapping branches and trees. Then Tāwhiri-mātea focuses on Tangaroa, the god of the seas and father to all sea creatures. Tangaroa had begotten Ika-tere, the father of fish, and Tū-te-wehiwehi, the father of reptiles. When Tāwhiri-mātea begins ravaging the waters, Tangaroa flees to the seas. Ika-tere and his children also hide themselves in the sea while Tū-te-wehiwehi and his children hide ashore. Tangaroa is angry that some of his children have deserted him and wages war thereafter on Tāne-mahuta, who rules the forests where Tū-te-wehiwehi fled.

Tāne-mahuta therefore supplies his brother Tū-mata-uenga with fishing equipment so that they can eliminate the children of Tangaroa, while Tangaroa swallows the children of Tāne-mahuta with his waters. Tāwhiri-mātea then wishes to attack his brothers Rongo-mā-tāne and Haumia-tiketike, the gods of cultivated and uncultivated food, but Papa hides them away. Unable to find those two brothers, Tāwhiri-mātea wishes to test his strength against Tū-mata-uenga. But Tū-mata-uenga cannot be shaken, for he is the strongest of the brothers.

Tū-mata-uenga then reflects on how his brothers did not come to his aid when Tāwhiri-mātea attacked him. He sees them as cowardly and exacts revenge first on Tāne-mahuta, whose children are multiplying quickly. Then he takes revenge on the rest of his brothers until he has consumed them and taken on their attributes—all, that is, except Tāwhiri-mātea, whom he cannot consume. Tāwhiri-mātea thus becomes an enemy of humans, attacking humankind with storms and hurricanes. His rage causes the submergence of a great portion of the earth, leaving only a small amount of land above the waters. From then on, light increases on the earth and the children on Rangi and Papa continue to multiply.

SIGNIFICANCE

"The Children of Heaven and Earth" is a Māori Polynesian creation myth that recounts the origins of the human race. Rangi and Papa, a primal couple, represent the source of all things in the universe, including humans and other gods. They play an essential role in the mythology of the native Māori people of New Zealand. The myth implies that the Māori are direct descendants of Rangi and Papa, who were preceded by a great void of nothingness (Te Kore) that created the darkness (Te Po). It was out of this darkness that heaven and earth came into being.

The Māori have a strong spiritual and physical connection to the land of New Zealand and their creation myth contains many references to the landscape. Throughout their history, the Māori people lived on coastal lands and heavily dependent on the ocean and fishing for sustenance. They lived at the mercy of rain, wind, storms, and other harsh conditions. The story of Rangi, Papa, and their children provides an explanation for many weather phenomena.

As in many creation myths, "The Children of Heaven and Earth" features motifs of the children doing harm or causing unrest to their parents. One son desires to kill the parents, while all the children agree in the end that they should be rent apart. The theme of patricide is also present in the Greek and Babylonian creation myths. Other common creation myth motifs that appear in this story are polytheism, world development, and—possibly the most common—a mother and a father. The belief in multiple gods, or polytheism, was dominant in pre-Christian cultures, and these gods typically spawn more gods that participate in the development of the world. In this story, it is a seething sibling rivalry that creates the oceans and the force of evil in the world, in the form of Tāwhiri-mātea, who continues to exact revenge by making life difficult for the Māori fishermen through meteorological phenomena such as rainstorms and winds.

Sir George Grey compiled the best-known version of this myth in the 1840s and 1850s while he served as the British governor of New Zealand. Several Māori chiefs referred to their myths during their negotiations with Grey. In the effort to communicate more effectively with the chiefs, Grey translated and compiled their stories. His compilation, *Polynesian Mythology & Ancient Traditional History of the New Zealanders*, was published in England in 1855. Many scholars have argued that his handling of relations with the Māori people during the settlement of New Zealand by Europeans in the nineteenth century make him one of the most significant figures of the era.

Patrick G. Cooper

BIBLIOGRAPHY

Andersen, Johannes C. *Myths and Legends of the Polynesians*. Mineola: Dover, 2011. Print.

Grey, George. "The Children of Heaven and Earth." *Polynesian Mythology & Ancient Traditional History of the New Zealanders, as Furnished by Their Priests and Chiefs*. London: Murray, 1855. Print.

Reed, A. W. *Maori Myths & Legendary Tales*. London: New Holland, 1999. Print.

Shortland, Edward. *Maori Religion and Mythology: Illustrated by Translations of Traditions, Karakia, etc.* 1882. Cambridge: Cambridge UP, 2011. Print.

Sproul, Barbara C. *Primal Myths: Creation Myths around the World*. San Francisco: Harper, 2013. Print.

Dream of Haumaka

Author: Traditional
Time Period: 1001 CE–1500 CE
Country or Culture: Polynesian
Genre: Myth

PLOT SUMMARY

In the mythical Pacific Ocean nation of Hiva, on the island of Marae Renga, lives the priest and wise man Haumaka. One night, Haumaka has a prophetic dream. In this dream, his spirit is lifted into the sky over Hiva. From there, he begins a journey eastward across the sea. Above the ocean waters, Haumaka's spirit travels first over seven islands. These appear either completely desolate or remain hidden beneath dense fog. It is only at the eighth island that Haumaka's spirit sees promising features. All in all, Haumaka can discern and name twenty-eight distinct sites. The first three are the islets of Motu Nui, Motu Iti, and Motu Kao Kao, real islets at the southwestern tip of Rapa Nui (Easter Island). Other exciting, real geographical features foreseen in Haumaka's dream are the round crater hole of Rano Kau and the island's only sandy beach, Anakena, as well as its highest point, the extinct volcano Terevaka.

In his dream, Haumaka gives the island various names. One is Mata ki te rangi, meaning "eyes looking to the sky." Another name is Te pito o te kainga a Hau Maka ("little piece of land of Haumaka"). The third name Haumaka gives the island is Te pito o te henua, which can be translated either as the "navel of the world" or "land's end of the world."

Awakening from his dream, Haumaka asks six or seven youths to travel east by canoe to the island he saw in his dream. The young men do so and reach the island. There, they find everything as foretold by Haumaka. In the key version of the myth, they also encounter one original inhabitant of the island, called Nga Tavake. Nga tells them of the recent death of his sole companion.

When Haumaka and the young men return to Hiva from their successful exploration, they tell their chief, Hotu Matua, of their discovery, foretold in Haumaka's dream. Haumaka shares a special bond with Hotu Matua because he has tattooed him.

The news of discovery comes at a perfect moment for Hotu Matua. His father has just died, and Hotu lost three battles of succession against an opponent (depending on the version of the myth, either his evil rival Oroi or his own brother Ko Te Ira-ka-atea). In addition, the island nation of Hiva is doomed by rising ocean waters and is slowly sinking beneath the surface of the sea. For all these reasons, Hotu Matua leaves Hiva with his wife, Vakai-a-hiva, and loyal settlers. Hotu Matua succeeds in becoming the first chief, or king, of Rapa Nui.

SIGNIFICANCE

The story of the dream of Haumaka gives a mythological account for the Polynesian discovery of Rapa Nui. Most scholars agree that Rapa Nui was settled in a daring act of Polynesian seaborne discovery. If the original settlers came to Rapa Nui from the South Sea island of Mangareva, they traversed sixteen hundred miles in one- or two-hulled canoes or catamarans, across the open sea. If they came from another Polynesian island, such as the Marquesas, the distance would have been even farther at two thousand miles. Successfully completing such a feat would have provided material for a moving legend among the settlers' descendants.

The age of the myth depends on the date when scholars believe that Rapa Nui was first settled. Traditional scholars have presented archaeological, linguistic, and anthropological evidence for a settlement between the sixth century and ninth century CE. A second group uses radiocarbon dating of geologic layers at Anakena, the site of mythical Hotu Matua's first settlement, for its claim that the first settlement was about 1200 CE.

Most scholars believe that this myth quickly established itself as an orally transmitted legend among Rapa Nui people. The linguistic similarity of Chief Hotu Matua to the name of the Mangarevan god Atu Motua has led Steven Roger Fischer to believe that the myth was substantially altered by Mangarevan missionaries who came to Rapa Nui in 1860, creating a new hero as recipient of Haumaka's discovery. However, if the settlers to Rapa Nui came originally from Mangareva, they may have used a similar name of their old god for their new first noble ancestor.

Since the mid-1860s, various European visitors to Rapa Nui have heard and written down oral versions of the dream of Haumaka and the related Hotu Matua cycle. This means there are some inevitable variances in story details. Once Rapa Nui people began using a romanized version of their language in the late nineteenth century, variants of the myth were written down.

Among them, "Manuscript E" stands out. "Manuscript E" was written by Pua Ara Hoa A Rapu around 1920. In 1955, it was discovered by German scholar Thomas Barthel in a private family collection on Rapa Nui. Barthel eventually published and translated "Manuscript E." It is considered the most authoritative version of the myth.

One of the most significant aspect of the myth of the dream of Haumaka is that it survived the near-total destruction of the people of Rapa Nui. Most scholars agree that self-made ecological disasters began to destroy Rapa Nui's population before the arrival of the first Europeans in the eighteenth century. However, the 1862 enslavement and deportation of most surviving Rapa Nui people by Peruvian slave traders nearly wiped out the island's indigenous population. By 1877, before more of the indigenous inhabitants of Rapa Nui could return, their population had dwindled to 111 recorded people.

That "Dream of Haumaka" was saved into the period of gradual recovery of Rapa Nui's people during the twentieth century speaks to its power and persistence. Rapa Nui has become a popular, if still exotic and remote, tourist spot, and local people have taken pride in disseminating many different versions of the myth. At the core of all the versions remain one man's prophetic dream and his bold action of sending young men on a voyage of exploration to prove the veracity of his vision.

R. C. Lutz, PhD

BIBLIOGRAPHY

Barthel, Thomas. *The Eighth Land: The Polynesian Discovery and Settlement of Easter Island.* Trans. Anneliese Martin. Honolulu: UP of Hawaii, 1978. Print.

Diamond, Jared. *Collapse: How Societies Choose to Fail or Succeed.* Rev. ed. New York: Penguin, 2011. Print.

Fischer, Steven Roger. *Island at the End of the World.* London: Reaktion, 2006. Print.

Métraux, Albert. *Ethnology of Easter Island.* Rpt. Honolulu: Bishop Museum P, 1971. Print.

Routledge, Katherine. *The Mystery of Easter Island.* London: Sifton, 1919. Print.

◆ Kahalaopuna, Princess of Manoa

Author: Traditional
Time Period: 1001 CE–1500 CE
Country or Culture: Polynesia
Genre: Myth

PLOT SUMMARY

The Hawaiian mountain god Akaaka (who is represented by the mountain ridge overlooking Waikiki) marries the goddess Nalehuaakaaka (who is seen as the red lehua bushes along the mountain) and the two have twin children: the boy Kahaukani (the Manoa wind) and the girl Kauakuahine (the rain of the mountain ridge). When the twins are born, however, they are adopted separately by a chief, Kolowahi, and a female chief, Pohakukala.

When the two twins reach adulthood, their respective adoptive parents, unaware that they are in fact brother and sister, decide that the two should be married. The union of Kahaukani and Kauakuahine forever link the rain and the wind. The marriage also produces the most beautiful girl of her time, Kahalaopuna (also known as Kaha and Kahala). Stories of her exquisite beauty spread throughout the land. The red glow from her cheeks and face can be seen through the walls of her house (which are surrounded with fencing and signs that indicate that entry into that sacred building is forbidden). When she bathes, beams of rainbow colors radiate from and surround her.

When she is still an infant, Kaha is betrothed to the young chief Kauhi. Many would-be suitors express interest in her hand, but Kaha (well trained by her parents) remains committed to Kauhi. Two men of inferior rank, Keawaawakiihelei and Kumauna, fall so in love with her—despite never having seen her—that they devise a plan. They make and wear flower wreaths (leis) and other adornments, claiming that they were given to the men as love gifts from Kaha.

As the time of the wedding draws near, Kauhi arrives at Waikiki (near Kaha's home) to surf. He has heard stories about his betrothed and the two strange men, and becomes enraged at his fiancée's alleged infidelity. He travels to her house, and when she sees him at her door, she immediately knows who he is. She invites Kauhi into her home, but he instead invites her for a walk in the woods. There, he beats her to death and buries her. The owl god accompanying her, however, resurrects her. Kauhi kills her again, and the owl brings her back to life again, and this process is repeated several more times. Kauhi eventually kills her and buries her so deep under roots and brambles that the owl cannot unearth her. However, another man unearths her body and resurrects her.

The young man, Mahana, wants Kaha to become his bride, but she cannot as long as Kauhi lives. Mahana, through a game with Kauhi, is able to trick the latter into admitting his terrible deeds. King Akaaka becomes aware of Kauhi's actions as well (in addition to the boasts of Keawaawakiihelei and Kumauna) and has all three punished by baking them in *imus* (ovens). The remains of Kauhi are swept away in a tidal wave. However, a shark god who is related to Kauhi resurrects him as a shark. Meanwhile, Akaaka gives Mahana permission to marry his granddaughter. Two years later, Kaha is surfing (defying the wishes of her grandfather, who knows of Kauhi's transformation). Kauhi bites her in half, burying the lower half of her body at the bottom of the sea so she cannot be brought back to life. Upon learning of her death, her parents and grandparents give up their human forms and return to their natural forms.

SIGNIFICANCE

The Manoa Valley lies near Hawaii's capital and largest city of Honolulu. Overlooking the valley and Waikiki Beach is a range of steep mountains. The valley itself is very lush, the product of almost daily rainfall. Also a product of this weather are the frequent rainbows associated with the valley. The Polynesian tribes occupying Hawaii long before Westerners arrived paid tribute to the beauty of this region by telling stories of the gods, heroes, spirits, and villains who made the valley the natural wonder it is today. Such tales, which were handed down through oral tradition, were eventually documented and compiled into a collection by missionaries during the mid-nineteenth century.

The story of Kahalaopuna illustrates the relationship seen by the indigenous people of Hawaii between humans, the gods, and the natural world. One of the key figures in this story, for example, is Akaaka (translated as "laughter"), a god who exists as a large promontory on the mountains overlooking the valley. When Kaha is born, Akaaka, his wife, and their twin children (whose later marriage forever links the Manoa wind with its rain) all become a royal family of humans. Although they exert power over their subjects, this family does not demonstrate supernatural power until Kaha's death

takes place. When this event takes place, the family returns to their status as gods and as the natural features of the valley. Additionally, Kahalaopuna's beauty is seen as the source of the frequent rainbows and a beautiful red glow, both of which are indicators of her presence for the people (who were not allowed to see her while she was betrothed to Kauhi).

Also prominent in the story are spirits. Despite Kaha's multiple deaths at the hand of her fiancé, her spirit remains intact, returning to her body when it is uncovered by her companion. It is only when her body cannot be repaired that her spirit disperses into the valley. Hawaiian folklore thus attributes the rainbows and the red glow that sometimes appears with them to Kaha's spirit, revisiting her home near Waikiki.

Michael P. Auerbach, MA

BIBLIOGRAPHY

Beckwith, Martha. *Hawaiian Mythology*. New Haven: Yale UP, 1940. Print.

Kalakaua, David. *The Legends and Myths of Hawaii: The Fables and Folk-Lore of a Strange People*. 1888. Print.

Kawaharada, Dennis. Introduction. *Ancient Oʻahu: Stories from Fornander and Thrum*. Ed. Kawaharada. Honolulu: Kalamaku. 2001. Print.

Thrum, Thomas G. "Kahalaopuna, Princess of Manoa." *Hawaiian Folk Tales*. Chicago: McClurg, 1907. Print.

Westervelt, W. D. *Legends of Gods and Ghosts: Hawaiian Mythology*. Boston: Ellis, 1915. Print.

# Mataora's Visit to Hawaiki

Author: Traditional
Time Period: 1001 CE–1500 CE
Country or Culture: Polynesia
Genre: Myth

PLOT SUMMARY

The princess of the underworld, Niwareka, comes up from the underworld, Hawaiki, with a group of other *tūrehu* (fairies or spirits). When they arrive at the above world, they come across a young man named Mataora. Niwareka and the other women begin making fun of him, for his appearance is different from theirs. He then offers to bring them some food. While the women eat, Mataora spots Niwareka, who is the most beautiful among them. When the meal is finished, Mataora dances his ceremonial *haka* (dance) before them. Then the women dance, and Mataora asks for Niwareka's hand in marriage. The two wed and live a long time together.

One day, Mataora beats Niwareka in a jealous rage. She flees back to the underworld, where her father, the chieftain Uetonga, lives. Mataora pursues her and eventually comes to Pou-tere-rangi, the entrance of Hawaiki, where a guardian named Te Kūwatawata resides. His house has four doors from which the winds come forth before spreading over the sky father and earth mother. The dead return to one of these four particular doors every quarter of the year. After reaching this house, Mataora begins descending down into Hawaiki.

He reaches a shed in the village of Uetonga where many people were congregated. There, he finds Uetonga tattooing someone using a method very different from the one used in the above world. Mataora calls out to Uetonga, telling him that he is tattooing incorrectly. The chieftain explains that carving the skin is the customary way of tattooing in the underworld while aboveground they simply paint the skin. To prove himself, Uetonga rubs the tattoo off Mataora's face and the crowd bursts out with laughter. Ashamed, Mataora asks the chieftain to give him a proper tattoo. Uetonga agrees and calls for his artists to outline the pattern on Mataora's face. Uetonga takes his chisel and begins tattooing the young man, who starts to sing out to Niwareka when the pain becomes too great.

Ue-kuru, the younger sister of Niwareka, hears Mataora's song and flees to tell her sister. Niwareka is busy weaving a cloak called "Te Raupapanui" for her father. Ue-kuru tells Niwareka of the stranger singing her name, and the princess runs to see if it was her husband. When she sees that it is Mataora, she instructs her younger sister to lead him to the village. There, he finds Niwareka and her tūrehu in an areas spread with mats. He sits before her. At first, the tūrehu do not recognize him with the new face tattoos. The couple reunite and dwell in the underworld for some time.

One day, Mataora asks Niwareka if she would return with him to the world above. Niwareka and her family try to convince him to stay, believing the upperworld to be evil. After much debate, Uetonga consents for his daughter to go to the upperworld if the two promise to come back and adopt the ways of the underworld. So the couple returns to the world above, but as they pass through Te Kūwatawata's guardhouse, they do not give him a gift of one of Niwareka's cloaks. In response, Te

Kūwatawata tells them that the gates of the underworld are now closed to the living and ever after only souls would be allowed through. Since he is no longer allowed back in the underworld, Mataora uses his tattoos as a reminder that he should avoid the evils of the world above. This is how Mataora and Niwareka brought the art of tattooing and cloak weaving to the world.

SIGNIFICANCE

The Hades depicted in the mythology of the Māori people of Polynesia differs from the concept of the underworld found in other cultures. In Māori mythology, the underworld, known as Hawaiki, is considered the original home of the Māori. According to tradition, Māori Polynesians traveled the seas in open canoes from Hawaiki to the islands of the Pacific Ocean, including New Zealand. Hawaiki is of great importance to Māori tradition as it is considered the home of the gods, including the supreme being, Io, who created the entire world and its first people. The Māori believe that the where people are born in the underworld and that they return after death. In Māori culture, Hawaiki is a symbol of the life cycle.

"Mataora's Visit to Hades" tells of the origin of tattooing, called *toi moko* by the Māori. The Māori hold tattoos to be sacred art. Tattoos are used to tell a person's history and achievements. Because the Māori hold the head as the most sacred part of the body, facial tattoos are common. In the distant past, women were traditionally given tattoos on their chin, lips, and shoulders, while men's faces and buttocks were tattooed to signify rank. Tattoo art was also used to make warriors attractive to women. Commonly, the left side of the face was designated for the father's history and the right would tell the mother's history. High birth was sometimes required before a facial tattoo could be given.

Tattooing was also traditionally used as a rite of passage for adolescents entering adulthood. Due to the sacred nature of tattooing, the act was highly ritualized. Those soon receiving tattoos were prohibited from engaging in sexual intercourse and eating solid foods. Tattooing was done using a sharpened bone chisel and a sooty pigment typically made from Kauri gum or burnt caterpillars. These bone chisels have been found in archaeological sites of different ages in New Zealand, including some Eastern Polynesian sites.

The facial tattoo process was very time consuming and painful. Oftentimes, a tattoo artist would examine a person's bone structure before beginning. Since the person could not consume any solid foods and nothing could come in contact with the face while the tattoos were healing, liquid food and water was drained through a wooden funnel into the mouth.

Many contemporary Māori tattoo artists still practice the traditional art, while combining it with modern designs. While most Māori tattoo artists in New Zealand now use modern tattooing equipment and technology, some still practice with bone chisels out of admiration and respect for the traditional art.

Patrick G. Cooper

BIBLIOGRAPHY

Barlow, Cleve. *Tikanga Whakaaro: Key Concepts in Maori Culture*. Oxford: Oxford UP, 1991. Print.

Māori Dictionary. John C. Moorfield, 2013. Web. 17 July 2013.

Reed, A. W. *Maori Myths & Legendary Tales*. London: New Holland, 1999. Print.

"The Story of Niwareka and Mataora." *Te Ao Hou* Mar. 1965: 17–19. Print.

Te Awekotuku, Ngahuia. *Mau Moko: The World of Maori Tattoo*. New York: Penguin, 2011. Print.

Whatahoro, H. T. "Mataora's Visit to Hades: The Origin of Tattooing." *The Lore of Whare-Wānanga*. Trans. S. Percy Smith. New Plymouth: Avery, 1913. 182–93. Print.

Whitmore, Robbie. "The Tattoo (Ta Moko)." *The Maori. New Zealand in History*, 2008. Web. 17 July 2013.

◆ The Polynesian Creation Myth

Author: Traditional
Time Period: 1 CE–500 CE
Country or Culture: Polynesia
Genre: Myth

PLOT SUMMARY

In the beginning, there is only a giant shell. At the top of the shell is the sky—Rangi (or Rangi-nui)—and at the bottom is the earth—Papa (or Papa-tū-ā-nuku). There is no light, for Rangi simply presses down on Papa, allowing nothing to live. The only god who exists at this time is Tangaroa, god of the sea, who dwells between the two. Rangi and Papa love each other and give birth

to six sons, the gods. The gods, however, are forced to crawl about in the darkness under the pressure of the contact between Rangi and Papa.

The fiercest of Rangi and Papa's children, Tū-mata-uenga (or Tū), calls upon his siblings to help him slay their parents so that the gods will live in light and in greater space. The god of the forests, Tāne-mahuta (or Tāne), disagrees with his brother and suggests that they instead simply separate their parents, pushing their father, the sky, away from their nurturing mother earth. Most of the siblings agree with Tāne-mahuta. Only Tāwhiri-mātea, the god of winds and storms, refuses to go along with the actions Tāne-mahuta and his brothers choose to take. He believes such an action will kill their parents. The gods disregard his concerns and try to separate Rangi from Papa. Each one attempts to push open the shell. Their efforts are unsuccessful, however, as the sky and the earth remain joined.

Tāne-mahuta tries again but this time with a different approach. He positions himself in the place where his siblings stood when they attempted to push Rangi up and away from Papa. He then lies down in the middle of Papa and pushes his legs upward into Rangi. His approach yields success, as Rangi and Papa begin to separate with groans and cries. Rangi and Papa bleed what becomes red clay, but Tāne-mahuta continues to push unabated. As the two are separated, light is let into the shell, allowing the gods to grow flowers, plants, and fruit-bearing trees. Tāwhiri-mātea, still angry with his fellow gods, promises them that he will not act out against his siblings for splitting apart their parents. Instead, he decides to remain between Rangi and Papa, occasionally sending storms into the world as a reminder of his disapproval of their actions.

The gods are pleased to see this growth, which by now includes wildlife, and decide to create people as well. They form men and women from the red clay, and Tāne-mahuta breathes into their nostrils, giving them life. Humans are therefore related to Rangi and Papa, just like the gods.

With such an abundance of life now living in the space between Rangi and Papa, Tāne-mahuta pushes them farther apart to make more room. Rangi and Papa, seeing what their children have created by separating them, are eventually pleased. However, the two still long sadly for each other's touch. Today, Papa sighs for Rangi, creating the morning mist, which travels from the mountaintops into the sky. In turn, Rangi cries tears onto Papa's bosom. These tears are known as dewdrops.

SIGNIFICANCE

Demonstrative of the great diversity of the Polynesian region—which consists of over one thousand islands, from New Zealand in the southwest, to Hawaii in the north, to Easter Island in the east—the Polynesian myth of creation occasionally varies in terms of its plotline. In some versions, for example, Rangi and Papa have always been in existence, while other stories tell of a supreme god, Io (or Po), who creates the two. In some stories, it is not the gods who separate Rangi and Papa but a great spider that crawls inside the shell and then needs more room. While Rangi and Papa's six sons are often part of the story of their separation, many sources cite the couple as having seventy children or more.

Although there are different versions, the general theme of the myth is consistent throughout this vast region. The earth and sky are separated, letting in light. When light is introduced as the sky and earth are separated, life is produced from this material. The primordial material used to create and sustain all life on earth is always present, existing in the nothingness between Rangi and Papa. The origins of Rangi and Papa are not entirely clear, however. In the version told by the Māori, the indigenous Polynesian people of New Zealand, the Io is identified in the version as the supreme deity, but how he creates the world and his relationship with the rest of the gods after creating them, the earth, and the sky, are matters that are not given much exposition.

Another consistent theme is the relationship between Rangi and Papa. Until they are separated, the two are pressed against one another in a procreative manner. Their separation is both painful and initially unwelcome, as the two love each other deeply. They are, however, pleased with the life that emerges on earth because of their separation. Nevertheless, they are saddened by their separation, a fact that is underscored by the tears they shed, which become life-giving water. The earth and the sky remain separated but always present, with only the storms and the clouds—the product of the storm god's wrath for the act made against his parents—between them.

Still another important and consistent theme is the heritage shared between the gods and humanity. Men and women are forged from the soil, according to the story, and given life by the gods. There is therefore a direct link between the gods and humanity. According to at least one version of the myth, the incest of Papa and Rangi is done to strengthen the blood of the gods—to give them *mana*, or power. However, the story comes with a warning: any coupling of siblings beyond this first generation would dilute the bloodline. Thus, to keep the connection between gods and humans pure, incest becomes *tabu* (the origin of the word "taboo")—a nearly universal societal concept.

Michael P. Auerbach, MA

BIBLIOGRAPHY

Colum, Pádraic. "Polynesian: In the Beginning." *Orpheus: Myths of the World*. New York: Macmillan, 1930. Print.

Doherty, Brian. "Creation Myth—Maori." *Masterworks of World Literature*. University of Texas: College of Liberal Arts, n.d. Web. 21 May 2013.

Elliott, Daphne. "Oceana/Polynesia Creation Myths." *Encyclopedia Mythica*. Encyclopedia Mythica, 14 Nov. 2004. Web. 21 May 2013.

"Polynesian Creation Myth." *Education Scotland*. Crown, 1 Sept. 2012. Web. 21 May 2013.

"The Samoan Story of Creation – A 'Tala.'" *Journal of the Polynesian Society* 1.3 (1892): 164–89. Print.

Taonui, Rāwiri. "Polynesian Myths: Ranginui—The Sky." *Te Ara—The Encyclopedia of New Zealand*. New Zealand Government, 22 Sept. 2012. Web. 21 May 2013.

◆ The Samoan Story of Creation

Author: Traditional
Time Period: 1001 CE–1500 CE
Country or Culture: Polynesia
Genre: Myth

PLOT SUMMARY

In the beginning, there is no land or sea, only a vast expanse. The great god Tagaloa, who created the universe, eventually becomes tired from traveling in this expanse and decides to raise a rock on which to stand; this rock is called Manu'a-tele (greater Manu'a). Tagaloa splits the rock open to create different types of rock. He splits it open again, and out pours the sea, surrounding the rocks. He splits the rock again, and fresh water pours out. He splits the rock yet again, and the sky emerges, followed by Tui-te'e-langi, the god who holds aloft the sky. Next come Ilu (immensity) and Mamao (space). Ilu and Mamao give birth to Po (night) and Ao (day), who in turn create the sun and stars. These occupy the first heaven. Then, Ilu and Mamao give birth to Le-la-gi, the second heaven, and Le-lagi brings forth seven more heavens. In all, nine heavens are created, each one propped up by Tui-te'e-lagi. When Tui-te'e-lagi is unable to keep the sky from falling on his own, he uses two umbrella-shaped plants found on the islands to help him hold it up.

Tagaloa then returns to Manu'a-tele to create the various islands of the Pacific. First, he creates the eastern islands of Samoa, including the islands of Manu'a (Ta'u, Ofu, and Olosega). Then, he creates the islands of Fiji and Tonga. Finally, he returns to Samoa to create the western islands, including Savai'i and Upolu. He discovers that the distance between Savai'i and Manu'a is too great and creates another island between them, Tutuila.

After this, Tagaloa sets out making the islands hospitable for humans. He gives them water and clouds, as well as vegetation and other natural resources. He then plants a type of vine, called *fue*, throughout the islands. As the vine sits out in the sun, its leaves decay and fall away, and wormlike creatures come out of the juice of the leaves. Tagaloa gives these creatures heads, arms, legs and beating hearts, and they become people. Most importantly, Tagaloa gives the people spirit, heart, will, and thought. On each of the islands he creates, Tagaloa places a male and a female so that they will populate the earth.

Tagaloa decides that these people need to be governed by a chief. He chooses Manu'a, a son of Po and Ao, to serve this purpose. Today, because of the great reverence shown to Manu'a, people are expected to look to the island group that bears his name as the central authority of the island nation. This group is also considered the spiritual center of not only Samoa but all of Polynesia as well.

SIGNIFICANCE

There are a number of versions of the Samoan myth of creation, reflective of the geographical diversity in the Samoan archipelago. In some versions, the son of Tagaloa (also spelled Tangaloa), Tuli the plover, is the one who travels to and from the surface, returning to his father to ask for the creation of land, vegetation, and even

humanity. In others, Tagaloa himself comes down from the heavens. In some stories, Tagaloa makes the islands rise from the waters, while in others, he throws down from the heavens sacred rocks that form the islands when they land. These variations can be explained by the distance between Samoan islands as well as the diversity of cultures not just in this particular archipelago but in Polynesia as a whole.

Despite the various differences in these stories, there are common themes. One of the most important themes concerns Manu'a. According to the story, Tagaloa delivered Manu'a to the people to serve as their king. This figure, who was the brother of the sun and moon, governed the people and resided on the first islands that Tagaloa created, which today share his name. In honor of this original king of Samoa, the islands of Manu'a became the spiritual and cultural center of Samoa. Subsequent ruling chiefs of Manu'a were given the title Tui Manu'a and were said to be descended from Tagaloa himself. The title was retired following the cession of Manu'a to the United States in 1904 and the death of the last Tui Manu'a in 1909. Attempts to revive the position in 1924 were suppressed by the US government.

Also significant in this story is the role of rock. Before creating the sky, the earth, and all life on the planet, Tagaloa placed rocks in the ocean. These rocks split and transformed, providing the basis for all of the natural resources on which humans would rely. Rock therefore acts as the foundation of the earth and the life it would sustain.

Finally, the story provides an organic basis for humanity. The earliest humans, according to the myth, were worms that emerged from the decayed *fue*, a creeping vine native to Samoa. Although they were produced from natural elements, Tagaloa shaped them and, most importantly, imbued in them such critical elements as spirit and heart. Such supernatural gifts underscore the distinctiveness of humans from the other creatures in the world.

Michael P. Auerbach, MA

BIBLIOGRAPHY

Craig, Robert D. *Handbook of Polynesian Mythology.* Santa Barbara: ABC-CLIO, 2004. Print.

Fraser, John. "The Samoan Story of Creation: A 'Tala.'" *Journal of the Polynesian Society* 1.3 (1892): 164–89. Print.

Harding, Thomas G., and Ben J. Wallace, eds. *Cultures of the Pacific*. New York: Free, 1970. Print.

McLachlan, Craig, Brett Atkinson, and Celeste Brash. *Rarotonga, Samoa & Tonga*. 7th ed. Oakland: Lonely Planet, 2012. Print.

"The Samoan Creation Legend—National Park of American Samoa." *National Park Service*. US Dept. of Interior, n.d. Web. 25 June 2013.

◆ Seven Sisters

Author: Traditional
Time Period: 999 BCE–1 BCE; 1 CE–500 CE
Country or Culture: Australia
Genre: Myth

PLOT SUMMARY

When seven sisters reach adolescence, they decide that the only way for them to transcend into a higher state of being is to subject themselves to a series of grueling trials that will teach them to control the effects of hunger, pain, and fear. The sisters believe that upon completion of these trials, their bodies and their minds will be prepared to advance into higher beings. They consult the elders of the tribe for guidance through these trials. The elders warn the girls that the ordeals they wish to undergo will be extremely severe, but the sisters remain steadfast in their request to go through with them.

The first stage of the trials lasts for three years. During this time, the sisters are separated from their siblings. The elders feed the girls only a small portion of food at sunrise and at sunset. These two meager portions consist of fish or meat from an emu, kangaroo, or wombat. When the third year of this hunger trial is completed, the sisters have to travel on a journey through thick brush filled with thorns that tears at their flesh. They have to trek across plains and rivers during the day, enduring blazing heat along the way. At the end of the weeklong journey, the elders instruct them to fast for three days as they travel farther under the hot sun.

The sisters continue on despite their weakness from heat and hunger. At the end of the third day, the girls arrive at a campground where the elders prepare kangaroo and emu for them to eat. Each girl is given a flint knife and instructed to cut from one of the animals the amount of food they wish to eat. The elders are impressed when, after so many days of hunger, each girl takes only a normal-sized portion for themselves, rather than a large one. Afterward, the sisters pass several more grueling trials designed to control their appetites.

The purpose of the next stage of trials is for the sisters to overcome pain. The elders bring the girls to an area where sacred ceremonies are performed. Here, in front of other tribe members, the elders use axes and sticks to knock out a front tooth of each girl. Then a knife is drawn across their breasts and hot ashes are rubbed into the wounds, increasing the pain and healing them at the same time. After two days of recovery, the sisters are put through several more painful trials, including sleeping on a bed of ants, lying on hot cinders, and piercing their noses. The girls remain unfaltering throughout.

The final trial is for the sisters to control fear. For hours the elders tell the girls frightful stories about ghastly spirits and ghosts and then instruct them to camp out on a burial ground of their great-grandfathers. Despite several attempts during the night by the elders to scare the girls, they remain in their campground until daybreak. The next day, the elders and sisters rejoice. The girls have successfully passed all of their trials. The other girls of the tribe are so proud of the sisters that they consent to undergo the same trials.

The Great Spirit is also very pleased with the girls. He sends a great star to transport the sisters into the heavens where they can live on as celestial beings without pain or death. They become the constellation known as the Seven Sisters (the Pleiades). When people look up at the constellation, they are reminded of the difficult trials the girls endured.

SIGNIFICANCE

The story of the Seven Sisters is featured in the mythology of several Aboriginal groups. In one version, the girls are known as the Karatgurk who refuse to share their secret of fire. The girls possess live coals on the ends of sticks with which they used to dig up and cook yams. One day, the ancestral being Crow tricks the girls into losing their coals. He flies away to use the coals for himself. When others find out about the coals and harass Crow for them, he throws some of the coals to them, thus delivering fire to mankind. The Karatgurk sisters are then swept into the sky, where their fire sticks become the Pleiades star cluster.

Another depiction of the Seven Sisters and the Pleiades creation refers to the girls as the Napaltjarri sisters. In this story, a man named Jilbi Tjakamarra is chasing the sisters as he tries to use love magic on one of them. During the chase, spirits turn the sisters into stars and, while still in pursuit, Jilbi transforms himself into the Morning Star in Orion's belt.

Stars and constellations play an important role in Aboriginal mythology. They are used frequently as reminders of the moral lessons taught in their myths. When the Seven Sisters ascend to the sky, the myth says they become the Pleiades star cluster, located in the Taurus constellation. This star cluster appears in various mythologies from all over the world, including that of the Greeks, the Norse, and the Celts. In some parts of the world, the stars within the cluster are visible only on the eastern horizon right before sunrise. Many ancient peoples used this heliacal rising of Pleiades to mark important events on the calendar.

Contemporary Aboriginal artist Gabriella Possum Nungurrayi has frequently painted her depiction of the Seven Sisters myth. She states that her father gave her the story, which she inherited from her mother and grandmother. Many indigenous peoples of Australia pass on their mythological stories, also known as "dreaming" stories, to their children. Aboriginal art, both ancient and contemporary, frequently addresses the Aboriginal concepts of "dreaming" and "Dreamtime." Dreamtime refers to the period of time when the world was created, while "dreaming" is the subsequent perpetual creating.

Patrick G. Cooper

BIBLIOGRAPHY

Leeming, David Adams. "The Pleiades." *Mythology: The Voyage of the Hero*. 3rd ed. New York: Oxford UP, 1998. 85–88. Print.

Mudrooroo. *Aboriginal Mythology: An A–Z Spanning the History of the Australian Aboriginal People From the Earliest Legends to the Present Day*. London: Thorsons, 1994. Print.

Natale, Antonella Riem. "The Pleiades and the Dreamtime: An Aboriginal Women's Story and Other Ancient World Traditions." *Coolabah* 9 (2012): 113–27. Print.

Reed, Alexander Wyclif. *Myths and Legends of Australia*. Wellington: Reed, 1965. Print.

Smith, W. Ramsay. *Myths and Legends of the Australian Aborigines*. Mineola: Dover, 2003. Print.

Thomas, W. J. "The Story of the Seven Sisters and the Faithful Lovers." *Some Myths and Legends of the Australian Aborigines*. 1923. *Sacred Texts*. John Bruno Hare, 2010. Web. 20 May 2013.

◆ The Two Sorcerers

Author: Traditional
Time Period: 1001 CE–1500 CE
Country or Culture: Polynesia
Genre: Myth

PLOT SUMMARY

Upon the river Waikato there lives a revered and powerful sorcerer named Kiki. He is such a powerful sorcerer that he is not able to leave his house while the sun is out—if his shadow touches any plants, they wither and die. When strangers travel the river to call at his village, Kiki remains in his home and does not trouble himself to leave, but when he draws back the sliding door of his house, the strangers stiffen up and die. His magic is so strong that even as canoes paddle in from the upper parts of the river, Kiki just has to slide back his window shutter and the people onboard die.

Kiki's notoriety spreads throughout the tribes and all of New Zealand, including in Kawhia, where the chief Tamure becomes particularly interested in Kiki's magical powers. Tamure decides to go to Kiki's village and see who the more powerful sorcerer is. When the season is right to travel to Kiki's village, Tamure chooses two of his tribesmen to go with him as well as his young daughter. Together, Tamure's party travels in a canoe on the river Waikato to Kiki's village. Tamure is a cautious man, so as they paddle toward the village, he repeats an incantation called "Mata-tawhito" in order to protect himself and his party from Kiki's sorcery and to ward off evil spirits. Without being seen, the party makes it to the landing place, where they drag their canoe onto the beach.

Kiki welcomes the party to his village and invites them into the square in the center. Tamure and his party seat themselves on the ground as Kiki's people cook food for them. Kiki remains in his house, so Tamure takes the opportunity to repeat incantations over the house's entrance in order to cast a spell over the sorcerer when he exits. Kiki appears out of the house when the food is ready to be served. Tamure knows that the food is enchanted and that he will die if he eats it, so he has his young daughter eat while he repeats incantations to protect her. Seeing that no one else is eating the food, Kiki returns to his home. When he does, Tamure casts a spell on the threshold of the house so that Kiki will not be able to leave it.

Tamure and his party then leave Kiki's village, and when they depart, the sorcerer becomes sick. On their way home, the party passes a village where many good people are gathered on the riverbank. Tamure asks them to tell any canoe that pursues the party that they saw the canoe pass by a long time ago. Then Tamure and the party continue home in haste. Kiki quickly becomes very ill, and his people know that Tamure is to blame. A group of them chases after him in a canoe, and when they come to the good people on the riverbank, they are told that Tamure and his party passed by long ago. Hearing this, Kiki's people return to their village and the sorcerer dies shortly after.

It is said that both sorcerers have descendants. Both men passed down their incantations to the descendants, who are also skilled in magic.

SIGNIFICANCE

Sorcery is an integral part of traditional Māori culture, and during ancient times, rituals and rites were performed throughout all of the islands that make up Polynesia. Sorcerers were typically members of the priestly class and were highly revered (and often feared) by the community. In some Polynesian cultures, they were referred to as priests. With the assistance of spirits, sorcerers would tell the future, cause harm to others for revenge or other reasons, or influence the course of events. Some sorcerers harnessed their powers through small, humanlike statues called "fetchers." A sorcerer's fetcher would contain a spirit or a ghost. Many sorcerers owned several of these statues and cared for them like children.

Early Polynesians lived in fear of black magic, so they were careful not to let their personal belongings fall into the hands of an enemy, for personal items could be used in black magic rituals to cause their owner harm. If a member of a tribe thought he or she was a victim of black magic, he would consult a sorcerer, who could make a diagnosis. If the sorcerer determined the person was under a spell, he would require the person to offer up certain prayers and sacrifices to a specific god in the effort to stop the one who cast the black magic. For their services, sorcerers were highly paid. Highly successful sorcerers—the ones seen as the most powerful—garnered great reputations among the islands and were oftentimes hired by the various high chiefs.

It was not uncommon for Māori people to believe that these sorcerers possessed great supernatural powers. For instance, they believed that Kiki's shadow could wither plants. It was said that another Māori sorcerer named Papahurihia had the ability to transport himself from place to place. There were some recordings of this tradition of sorcery in modern times as well. One of the last Māori sorcerers was named Chief Te Heuheu. In the late nineteenth century, an Anglican bishop tried to convert the chief to Christianity, but Te Heuheu allegedly revived a dead leaf before the bishop's eyes and the bishop then left the chief alone.

The Waikato region where Kiki resided was densely populated with Māori people. Sir George Grey compiled this version of "The Two Sorcerers" in the 1840s and 1850s while he was serving as the British Governor of New Zealand. To communicate properly with the Māori chiefs, Grey had their myths translated and he compiled them in his work *Polynesian Mythology & Ancient Traditional History of the New Zealanders*, which was first published in 1855. It has since become an invaluable source for Polynesian mythological studies.

Patrick G. Cooper

BIBLIOGRAPHY

Craig, Robert D. *Handbook of Polynesian Mythology*. Santa Barbara: ABC-CLIO, 2004. Print.

Eason, Cassandra. "Maori Magick: Cassandra Eason on the History of Maori Magic." *Cassandra Eason*. Cassandra Eason, 2009. Web. 8 June 2013.

Edward, Tregear. *The Maori Race*. New York: Hard Press, 2013. Print.

Grey, George. "The Two Sorcerers." *Polynesian Mythology & Ancient Traditional History of the New Zealanders*. London: Murray, 1855. 273–79. Print.

Shortland, Edward. *Maori Religion and Mythology: Illustrated by Translations of Traditions, Karakia, etc.* Cambridge: Cambridge UP, 2011. Print.

◆ What Makes the Waves

Author: Traditional
Time Period: 999 BCE–1 BCE; 1 CE–500 CE
Country or Culture: Australia
Genre: Myth

PLOT SUMMARY

Arrilla is the brightest member of the Kamilaroi people. He spends much of his time roaming the coast and jungle areas of the land, examining flora and fauna. One day, while Arrilla is examining a lagoon, a dark figure is spotted on top of a tall mountain. The figure waves spears and shouts down at the Kamilaroi people. The stern king calls for a council of his people in order to find out who the dark figure is. Arrilla does not answer the call right away, so the determined king sends two strong men out to retrieve him.

When Arrilla is brought before the king, he explains that, while wandering earlier that day, he had seen an unfriendly spirit on top of the same mountain where the figure was spotted. He states that the dark figure was receiving courage from this wicked spirit. The only way to overcome the figure, Arrilla explains, is through cunning strategy, not brute force. The rest of the tribe acknowledges that Arrilla is the only one crafty enough to overcome the figure and the spirit, but the king is not convinced. He adjourns the council until nightfall, when he will decide what to do with Arrilla and the spirit.

Arrilla returns to his family's hut and, seeing that they are low on food, goes hunting until nightfall when the council will be called to meet once again. Fearing further disfavor from the king, Arrilla arrives promptly. The king then orders him to climb to where he had earlier seen the spirit and to ask it questions. Arrilla knows that he must obey, so he spends the rest of the night planning his travel to the high point.

He begins his arduous journey in the morning. Though it exhausts him, Arrilla manages to climb through many vines and other vegetation to reach the mountain peak. It is quiet at the top, and the sky is dark and cloudless. A shadow approaches him, and despite being afraid, Arrilla makes a signal in the Kamilaroi language. He is relieved to see that it is another Aborigine, one with a language similar to his own.

The Aborigine explains to Arrilla that he is traveling to the ocean because he has never seen it before. His people believe the ocean to be a sky that has fallen down and is gradually taking over the whole world. The Aborigine tells Arrilla the story of how a great ancestor left the earth and drove a hole right through the sky; when he tried to return, the hole had closed up so he beat upon the sky until it collapsed. The sky wanted to return to its home above, but when it tried to rise up, the ancestor continued to beat it back. The sky was only able to sink down and break itself upon the shores—the roar made by the waves is the voice of the ancestor refusing to give in to the sky. Despite being beaten, the sky is managing to spread and grow upon the shores, until one day it will consume the whole earth.

Arrilla is pleased with this story, for he had not known what made the waves. He asks the Aborigine to follow him back to his people and share the information from the spirit about the sky. The Aborigine is then given a wife from the Kamilaroi people and remains with them until his death.

SIGNIFICANCE

Australian author and compiler C. W. Peck suggests that Arrilla may have been a composite character developed by Aborigines in order to convey their traditions, rather than a representation of just one man. Peck's *Australian Legends* (1925) was the first noteworthy work concerned specifically with the Aboriginal folklore of eastern New South Wales. This version of "What Makes the Waves" is featured in that book.

The Kamilaroi people were indigenous Australians from New South Wales. They were nomadic hunters and gatherers who depended on a variety of fish for a good portion of their diet. Their mythology included a belief in a deity known as the All Father, who took the souls of dead Aborigines up to the sky. Kamilaroi people believed that each person has a soul, a dream spirit, and a shadow spirit. The dream spirit refers to the Aboriginal belief in the dreaming—the spiritual concept that creation is a perpetual cycle that helps various aspects of Aboriginal society. That is why their myths are frequently referred to as dreaming stories. Another aspect of the dreaming is Dreamtime, which is the sacred era before time, when their ancestors came to the earth and created the land, plants, animals, and humans. Aborigines used certain sacred rituals to recall the events of Dreamtime and to reenact the adventures of their ancestors.

Like other Aborigines, the Kamilaroi people's dreaming stories are heavily linked to the earth, plants, and animals. Similar to other ancient cultures, Aboriginal myths also provide accounts of how specific things came to be. For instance, this particular myth looks at why waves beat against the shores every day, while others explain how hills came to be or why possums do not have hair on their tails. Other Aboriginal tribes have similar myths in which the ocean falls from the sky. The Paakantji tribe of New South Wales had a story about the sky falling, and in South Australia, there is a story telling of the stars falling to the earth, creating lagoons along the coast.

Geographic evidence in New South Wales has led experts to believe that a tsunami once struck the southern coast. As the tsunami wave poured overhead, Aborigines may have believed that the sky was falling.

Patrick G. Cooper

BIBLIOGRAPHY

Cowan, James G. *Myths of the Dreaming: Interpreting Aboriginal Legends*. London: Prism, 1994. Print.

Masse, W. Bruce, and Luigi Piccardi, eds. *Myth and Geology*. Bath: Geological Soc., 2007. Print.

Parker, Katie Langloh. *The Euahlayi Tribe: A Study of Aboriginal Life in Australia*. London: Constable, 1905. Print.

Peck, C. W. *Australian Legends: Tales Handed Down from the Remotest Times by the Autocthonous Inhabitants of Our Land*. Sydney: Stafford, 1925. Print.

Wardrop, Martin. "Dreaming and the Dreamtime." *Aboriginal Art Online*. Aboriginal Art Online, 2000. Web. 1 May 2003.

AFRICA

SUB-SAHARA AFRICA

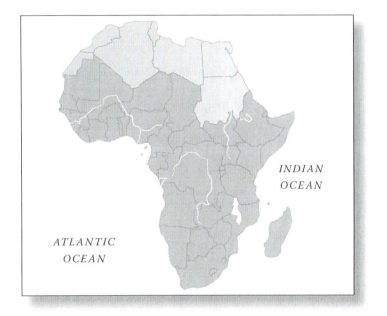

INDIAN OCEAN

ATLANTIC OCEAN

◆ The Daughter of Sun and Moon

Author: Traditional Mbundu
Time Period: 1001 CE–1500 CE
Country or Culture: Africa
Genre: Folktale

PLOT SUMMARY

The great Bantu chief Kimanaweze's son, Kimanuele, has finally reached the age of marriage. Finding a bride for the young man would normally be an easy task, as Kimanuele is extremely handsome and could have his pick of any of the women in the village. However, Kimanuele is set on a particular bride, the daughter of Sun and Moon, and refuses to consider any other women.

Although he is shocked by his son's choice, Kimanaweze does not try to dissuade Kimanuele from his decision. He suggests that the young man write a letter to both Sun and Moon, asking for their blessing. Kimanaweze next tries to find someone who is willing to deliver the letter. He approaches a rock rabbit, an antelope, a hawk, and a vulture, but all four animals refuse to deliver the letter to Sun and Moon. The situation seems hopeless until Minuti, a wise old frog, volunteers to deliver the message. Kimanuele doubts the frog's ability to do so, but with no other volunteers, he agrees to let Minuti take the letter.

Sun and Moon frequently allow their handmaidens to travel along a spider web to earth to draw water. Minuti places the letter in his mouth and hides in one of the handmaidens' buckets. The girls returns to heaven, and once there, Minuti secretly places the letter on a table. When Sun finds the letter, he is shocked by Kimanuele's boldness and his ability to deliver the letter to heaven, and he throws away the note. After returning to earth, Minuti reports that he delivered the letter as promised, but Kimanuele doubts the frog, as there has been no response. Kimanuele writes another letter to Sun and Moon and has Minuti carry it to heaven. This time, Sun responds, agreeing to Kimanuele's request. Minuti travels back and forth between heaven and earth as Sun and Moon and the young man negotiate the dowry.

When Sun and Moon finally agree to the terms of the marriage, another difficult task presents itself: delivering their daughter to Kimanuele. Although the chief's son is distraught at this obstacle, Minuti has yet another clever idea. He returns to heaven and places a strange slime over the young woman's eyes while she is sleeping. When she wakes and cannot see, Sun and Moon determine that Kimanuele must be responsible and decide to send their daughter to earth so that he can restore her sight. They have their spiders weave a tremendous web that can comfortably lower their daughter and the handmaidens to earth. Once they descend, the handmaidens leave the young woman near a secret pond, and Minuti removes the slime from her eyes. The young woman is overwhelmed by the natural beauty of the earth, and she happily marries Kimanuele. Because of Minuti's role in the betrothal, frogs become considered the wisest of all of Africa's creatures.

SIGNIFICANCE

The story of Kimanuele and the daughter of Sun and Moon is traditional to Bantu-speaking Mbundu (Kimbundu) people of Angola. The Bantu linguistic-cultural group also encompasses parts of Zambia, Namibia, and South Africa. Bantu folklore typically focuses on the relationship between humans and nature. In the story of the daughter of Sun and Moon, Kimanuele and his father are able to speak to and make requests of a wide range of animals. Meanwhile, the animals themselves take on human characteristics, as demonstrated by Minuti's wisdom and cleverness. In fact, the wise frog, because he develops a plan that surprises even the great Sun and Moon, is elevated in status among all other nonhuman creatures. This show of respect by humans toward all frogs, according to the story, is to continue for all time. Furthermore, the story's inclusion of spiders, on whose webs the handmaidens travel to and from earth, suggests that animals took part in the creation of the universe. When Sun and Moon's daughter is delivered to earth, the spider webs that carry her are snared on a number of celestial objects, forming the white streak in the sky known as the Milky Way.

The tale also brings to light humanity's relationship with the sun and moon. Scholars have long studied the view of the sun and moon in Bantu cosmology and attempted to determine whether the two bodies are viewed as deities or simply as part of the universe. Indeed, different versions of the story treat the celestial bodies in different ways; some refer to Sun and Moon as male and female, respectively, and others assign opposite genders. Regardless of these variations, the story of the daughter of Sun and Moon clearly calls attention to the significant respect that humankind has paid to the two celestial bodies over the centuries.

Michael P. Auerbach, MA

BIBLIOGRAPHY

Ferguson, Gary. *The World's Great Nature Myths*. Guilford: Globe Pequot, 2000. Print.

Knappert, Jan. *Bantu Myths and Other Tales*. Leiden: Brill, 1977. Print.

Schapera, I., ed. *The Bantu-Speaking Tribes of South Africa: An Ethnographical Survey*. London: Routledge, 1962. Print.

Werner, Alice. *Myths and Legends of the Bantu*. Philadelphia: Psychology, 1968. Print.

Willoughby, William Charles. *Nature Worship and Taboo: Further Studies in the Soul of the Bantu 1932*. Whitefish: Kessinger, 2004. Print.

◆ The Gods Descend from Heaven

Author: Traditional Yoruba
Time Period: 1001 CE–1500 CE
Country or Culture: Africa
Genre: Myth

PLOT SUMMARY

The chief priest of the Yoruba people, Arába, tells how the gods descended from heaven long ago. The supreme god, Arámfè, sent forth the gods from heaven to create the earth, along with Odudúwa, the father of the Yorubas. Odudúwa had earlier taken from heaven a bag filled with soil so that humanity could benefit once the world came into being. The gods, along with Odudúwa, were made to journey far across a barren desert before they could descend to the earth. They reached a high cliff, overlooking the dark depths of the sea far below, leaving behind them the vast wasteland. Odudúwa appealed to his uncle Orísha, the creator god, asking why Arámfè would make them take such a journey as though they were outcasts.

Orísha answered by reminding Odudúwa that he had stolen from the gods, including Orísha himself, to give gifts to humanity in order to win their favor. Orísha then said that he longed to use his talents to create humanity, especially since he and Odudúwa could not return to heaven without Arámfè's knowledge. Thus, Odudúwa set about his job, lowering a chain to the dark sea so that each god could be brought into position to perform his or her own task.

Odudúwa sent his priest, Ojúmu, to sprinkle the sand on the ocean and commanded a magical, five-clawed bird to build the earth, including the hills and the deep forests. As the land emerged from the sea, lagoons and bays appeared. However, the waters pounded the shores, threatening to undo the creation of the land. Odudúwa thus sent Olókun, the goddess of the sea, and Olóssa, the goddess of lagoons, to tend to the coastline and ensure that humanity, once introduced to the earth, would not suffer the wrath of the sea.

Odudúwa and the gods still lamented the mandate Arámfè placed on them—they did not wish to leave heaven and feared living in the cold, unfamiliar darkness of this strange new world. They were particularly saddened by the fact that they were leaving their sunlit world and living in a place where the dawn simply did not exist.

Odudúwa, through his messenger, Ífa, appealed to Arámfè to give them the light of the sun and moon. Arámfè was sympathetic to Odudúwa's request and sent the sun for the day—via the vulture, with the top of its head aflame—and the moon for the night. These gifts gave great joy to the gods and people alike, for they could now see the world. The sun and moon inspired the people to work hard in this land, known as Ilé-Ífè, and gave them the courage to build such things as wine vessels and iron tools. Over time, Ilé-Ífè began to resemble heaven in many ways. The celebratory sound of heaven's music played as Odudúwa began his reign over the new world.

SIGNIFICANCE

This tale comes from the Yoruba people, rooted predominantly in what is now Nigeria and Benin. The story shows the special status enjoyed by the legendary divine king Odudúwa. Odudúwa is traditionally identified as the father of the Yoruba people, as he is said to have conceived the first Yoruba children, all sixteen of whom became kings.

The supreme god asks Odudúwa and the gods to create the world under harsh conditions. They first undertake a long journey away from heaven and arrive at a cliff high above the vast, dark ocean. In a previous tale, Odudúwa had taken from the gods a bag of primordial sand after the god given charge of the bag drank too much and fell asleep. Odudúwa, ordered to leave the comforts of heaven and endure the hardships of the sunless, cold, and featureless world, is being punished for his misdeeds.

In this story, the land from which the creation of the world took place, Ilé-Ífè, is also presented. Ilé-Ífè is an ancient city in southwestern Nigeria, believed to have originated around 1300 CE (although it was likely initially populated earlier). According to Yoruba tradition, this region was originally the land at which the gods arrived to create the world. For this reason, many scholars refer to Ilé-Ífè as the Athens of Africa. Throughout Yoruba and African history, Ilé-Ífè has been viewed as an important cultural site.

Still, the creation of the earth presents the gods and Odudúwa alike with great opportunity. After all, theirs is a task that presents nearly limitless possibilities, as the gods and Odudúwa are given the chance to make the world as they desire. As each god is assigned his or her own tasks, Odudúwa becomes a king, giving life to an entire civilization, building the earth, and successfully asking Arámfè to give the world light. Although he is faced with hardship, Odudúwa endures it so that the world and its inhabitants may live and prosper.

Michael P. Auerbach, MA

BIBLIOGRAPHY

Abimbola, Kola. *Yoruba Culture: A Philosophical Account*. Birmingham: Iroko, 2006. Print.

Akintoye, S. Adebanji. *A History of the Yorùbá People*. Dakar: Amalion, 2010. Print.

Johnson, Kofi, and Raphael Tunde Oyinade. "Monotheism in Traditional Yoruba Religion." *Thinking about Religion*. North Carolina Religious Studies Assn., 22 May 2004. Web. 17 Jun. 2013.

Karade, Ifa. *The Handbook of Yoruba Religious Concepts*. York Beach: Weiser, 1994. Print.

Love, Velma E. *Divining the Self: A Study in Yoruba Myth and Human Consciousness*. University Park: Pennsylvania State UP, 2012. Print.

Wyndham, John. "The Descent." *Myths of Ífè*. Alexandria: Lib. of Alexandria, 1921. 20–26. Print.

How Beasts and Serpents First Came into the World

Author: Traditional Asante
Time Period: 1001 CE–1500 CE
Country or Culture: Africa
Genre: Folktale

PLOT SUMMARY

Kweku Tsin is the son of the man-spider Anansi. During a three-year famine, Kweku Tsin searches daily for food in the forest, finding little success. On one trip, however, he accidentally drops some nuts down a hole and, starving, decides to climb into the hole to retrieve them. He discovers that the hole is in fact the entrance to a strange, uninhabited village. While he explores the town, he meets an old woman, whom he tells of the famine in his own village.

The old woman agrees to help Kweku Tsin if he follows her strict instructions. He must go into her garden and pick the one yam that is not calling out to be picked. He digs out the yam and brings it to her. She then instructs Kweku Tsin to peel the yam, discard it, and boil the peeled rind. When he does, it becomes a yam. The two sit down to eat, and the woman asks that he not look at her while they eat. The obedient and polite Kweku Tsin grants her wish. Afterward, the woman tells Kweku Tsin to go back into the garden and select the drum that makes the sound "ding ding" when touched. When he brings it back to her, the woman tells him that he has but to tap on the drum and all the food he needs will appear.

Kweku Tsin returns to his village and calls his people into the assembly area. When they have gathered, Kweku Tsin beats the drum as he was taught by the old woman. An abundance of food appears, enough for the town to eat. Kweku Tsin is celebrated for providing food for the people. Meanwhile, Anansi becomes jealous and insists that Kweku Tsin tell him of the location of the mysterious town and its one resident.

Anansi seeks out the woman and impolitely asks her for the same gift she gave his son. She tells him to pick the yam that does not call out to be dug from the ground, but, suspecting that the woman is a witch with ill intentions, he instead picks a yam that does call for harvesting. He also refuses to discard the peeled yam and boil the rind, choosing to keep the peeled yam. When the yam turns to stone, he reluctantly agrees to boil the rind, and it turns into a yam. They sit down, and he again defies

her wish, looking upon her while he eats. She chooses not to eat her share of the yam. Finally, when the woman tells Anansi to pick a drum that goes "ding ding," he senses a trick and picks the one that goes "dong dong." He returns to his village without thanking the woman.

Anansi calls for his people to come to the village square to share the food he is about to make appear. When he sounds the drum, however, all manner of beasts and serpents, the likes of which had never before been seen on the earth, flood the land. Kweku Tsin and his family take shelter, but Anansi is caught in the rush he caused. The creatures spread out across the land and forests, where they will roam thereafter.

SIGNIFICANCE

The folktale telling how beasts and serpents first came into the world is one of the spider tales (also known as Nancy stories) focusing on the man-spider Anansi. The folktales of Anansi come from West Africa and are believed to have originated with the Asante (Ashanti) people of what is now Ghana. Anansi and his family are some of the most popular figures in folklore not only of West Africa but also of the African diaspora. The stories existed in oral traditions and were memorized by many Ashanti people as well as their West African neighbors. When the slave trade devastated those communities, many displaced people brought the Anansi stories with them to the Americas, where they survive in different forms through the present day.

According to this series of stories, Kweku Anansi is the son of the great sky god, Nyame, and his wife, Asase Ya, the earth goddess and the goddess of fertility. Anansi is occasionally benevolent (represented by his human side) and is therefore presented in many stories as a hero. On the other hand, as is the case in this fable, Anansi is often a trickster; in fact, his mischievous behavior leads his father to turn him into a man-spider. Although he means well, Anansi continues to act in a frequently greedy and self-serving manner. Still, in many stories his trickery and cunning bring success to him and others around him.

This fable is not just a story of the origin of the planet's countless animals. In fact, it is concerned more with the acceptable behavior of people toward others. Despite the fact that he is starving and desperate, Kweku Tsin is unwaveringly polite and obedient to the old woman, even when her requests are strange and seemingly contradictory (such as boiling the skin of a yam while discarding the rest). Kweku Tsin also makes a point of thanking the woman for her gracious gift. For his positive behavior, Kweku Tsin is rewarded with the gift of the magic drum, and his people are fed.

Additionally, Anansi becomes jealous of the accolades bestowed upon his son, who brings back the magic drum to feed his people. In order to gain glory for himself, he goes to the old woman as well. However, he calls the woman a witch, questions all of her requests, and openly defies the woman's commands. In the end, Anansi is embarrassed when his own drum produces not food but wild creatures. To be sure, these animals are ultimately of great benefit to the earth, but Anansi's rude and self-serving behavior is repaid with a great and fearsome stampede.

Michael P. Auerbach, MA
T. Fleischmann, MFA

BIBLIOGRAPHY

Abrahams, Roger D. *African Folktales: Traditional Stories of the Black World*. New York: Pantheon, 1983. Print.

Auld, Michael. "How Anansi Became a Spider." *Anansi Stories*. Anansi Stories, 2007. Web. 7 May 2013. Print.

Barker, William Henry, and Cecelia Sinclair, ed. "How Beasts and Serpents First Came into the World." *West African Folk-Tales*. Chapel Hill: Yesterday's Classics, 2007. 51–55. Print.

---. "Tit for Tat." *West African Folk-Tales*. Chapel Hill: Yesterday's Classics, 2007. 19–22. Print.

Sherlock, Philip Manderson. *Anansi, the Spider Man: Jamaican Folk Tales*. New York: Crowell, 1954. Print.

◆ The Sacrifice of Mórimi

Author: Traditional Yoruba
Time Period: 1001 CE–1500 CE
Country or Culture: Africa
Genre: Folktale

PLOT SUMMARY

During the rule of Odudúwa, the founder of the Yoruba nation, the beautiful and virtuous Mórimi is living in the country of Ilé-Ifè with her husband, Obálufon. Mórimi is unable to conceive a boy for her husband, although his lesser wives have succeeded in giving him a son. She has, however, given birth to a daughter, Adétoún, who is also beautiful. Nevertheless, Mórimi longs to be able to give a son to her loving husband.

Day after day and season after season, Mórimi is mired in great grief regarding her situation. She decides to consult a priest of the god Ífa. The priest uses a sacred charm, an Okpéllè, to determine the cause of Mórimi's plight. The divination of the Okpéllè reveals to the priest and Mórimi that the gods would have been willing to give her sons, but Éshu the Undoer (a god whose name is equated with the devil) is preventing such a conception. The priest explains that Éshu demands that Mórimi make a sacrifice to him in exchange for a son. The sacrifice must be her only daughter, Adétoún.

Mórimi is shocked by this revelation. Although she longs for a son, she refuses to give up her only child to make this happen. She becomes bitter at the gods who would manipulate her in such a way, and she returns home to avoid the action that "love command[s], and love condemn[s]" (Wyndham 38). However, the trickster god Édi approaches Mórimi to remind her of the gravity of the priest's words. Édi is known for his sly way with words, and he uses this quality to convince Mórimi to reconsider. Mórimi is defiant and questions the idea of using a person as currency and asks why her only daughter would be the only worthy sacrifice.

The priest, Édi tells her, is the messenger of Ífa, who is using the priest to convey the will of the gods. The word of Ífa, as relayed through his messengers, is just as important as it would be if Ífa spoke directly to Mórimi. Therefore, Édi says, Ífa's statement cannot be disregarded. Édi continues by telling Mórimi that her decision would be critical for her people. The gods spoke to Odudúwa and told him that he must father the Yoruba people. By sacrificing Adétoún, Mórimi would be creating a house of kings for Obálufon and the entire Yoruba nation.

Mórimi accepts Édi's comments as the truth, and Édi returns to the shadows while Mórimi sacrifices her daughter on the altar of Éshu. Her sacrifice brings her a son for Obálufon and helps strengthen the Yoruba people.

SIGNIFICANCE

Mórimi is considered one of the progenitors of the Yoruba nation. Mórimi was a member of the royal family of Odudúwa through her marriage with Obálufon. As such, Mórimi is considered larger than life, with each of her emotions powerful. Her grief for not conceiving a son, for example, is palpable since she experiences this pain year round, with every sight reminding her of the intense longing she feels. When Ífa, through the priest, tells her the reason she cannot bear a son for her husband, her grief is compounded by feelings of anger and even defiance. Such emotional strength illustrates Mórimi's personal power and distinction among the Yoruba people.

The story is also indicative of the relationship between mortals and the gods in Yoruba tradition. Although she is virtuous and loving, Mórimi is unable to conceive a son due to the demands of the gods. The god preventing her from achieving this goal is Éshu, described in many other African stories as the equivalent to the devil. Although Éshu is clearly not among the more benevolent gods (including Ífa), he is nonetheless powerful and autonomous. Mórimi, for example, cannot ask the other gods to intervene or even intercede with Éshu in order to meet her needs. Instead, she must sacrifice her beautiful daughter or live the rest of her life grieving.

Furthermore, Mórimi's experience underscores the enormous sacrifices that occurred in order to bring the Yoruba nation into being. Mórimi, although longing to provide a son for her husband and continue the bloodline of Odudúwa, nevertheless loves her daughter, Adétoún, too much to destroy her. Only after her third consultation with the messengers of the gods does she agree, but her acceptance comes after she is convinced to do so by Édi. This trickster god, speaking slyly and manipulatively, helps Mórimi come to understand that her sacrifice would benefit not only her immediate family, but the present and future generations of Yoruba people as well.

Mórimi's sacrifice of Adétoún would not be her last such action. In a later story, the son she later bears is also placed in jeopardy. In that tale, Mórimi helps her people defeat an invading nation (the Igbo) with the assistance of the gods. She allows herself to be captured and enslaved by the Igbo king, who, captivated by her beauty and strength, soon reveals his army's weaknesses. Mórimi escapes and shares this information with the Yorubas, who use it to defeat the Igbos. Mórimi attempts to thank the gods by making a number of offerings, but again, there is only one sacrifice they will accept: her only son. Mórimi reluctantly agrees, but when she commits the act, her son is brought back to life as a reward for Mórimi's willingness to do what is necessary for her people.

Michael P. Auerbach, MA

BIBLIOGRAPHY
Abrahams, Roger D., ed. *African Folktales.* New York: Pantheon, 1983. Print.

Dennett, Richard Edward. *Nigerian Studies; or; The Religious and Political System of the Yoruba.* London: MacMillan, 1910. Print.

"The Motherland—Moremi Ajasoro: Princess of the Yoruba." *Isikuro.* N.p., 18 Sept. 2013. Web. 19 June 2013.

Rosenberg, Donna, ed. *World Mythology: An Anthology of the Great Myths and Epics.* Lincolnwood: NTC, 1994. Print.

Wyndham, John. "The Sacrifice of Mórimi." *Myths of Ífè.* London: Erskine MacDonald, 1921. 35–39. Print.

◆ The Slave Called the World

Author: Traditional Hausa
Time Period: 1001 CE–1500 CE
Country or Culture: Africa
Genre: Folktale

PLOT SUMMARY

In R. Sutherland Rattray's translation of the Hausa folktale "The Story of the Slave by Name 'The World,'" a local chief owns a certain slave. The chief's community considers the wife of this slave to be promiscuous. However, the slave defends his wife's virtue. One day, on the suggestion of an old woman, the slave agrees to test his wife's morality. The slave saddles and mounts his horse and tells his wife that he is going to a remote village and will sleep there and return the next day.

The wife has three lovers. One is the local *galadima* (the son or brother of an emir, a high-ranking Muslim official), another is a vizier (a high-ranking minister or advisor), and the third is a foreign slave named the World. The wife sends notices to her lovers that her husband will be away all night. The galadima sends her a feast of meat and rice and arrives at night to share it with her. While feasting, he hears "the sound of the slippers of the vizier" and quickly hides under the bed. The vizier arrives and sits down for a meal.

Suddenly, the vizier hears slipper noises. Although they come from the World, the vizier thinks it is the wife's husband, so he hides under the bed. When he finds the galadima there, they agree to keep their visits a secret. When the World hears sounds of hooves approaching, he too flees under the bed. Upon discovering the other two men, they all agree to keep silent about the issue.

When the chief's slave returns, he is unaware of his wife's visitors. He asks for water to wash, enters his home, and sits down on his bed. He is astonished at how the community suspects his wife of infidelity when he can see no evidence of this. In puzzlement, he mutters repeatedly, "The World, the World." Under the bed, the World becomes angry because he believes the husband is accusing him only, so he curses the husband and yells that he is not the only one. The galadima and the vizier jump up and run away, leaving the husband to fight with the World. People rush in and separate the two.

The next morning, the slave brings the issue to the chief, and the chief's councilors laugh riotously at the matter. The chief inquires about the galadima and the vizier. He is informed that they are not present, and when he sends someone to look for them, they discover the men are not in their homes and that they have run away into the bush. The World is condemned to death as the chief issues his verdict, "Off with the rat's head."

SIGNIFICANCE

"The Story of the Slave by Name 'The World'" is a folktale of West Africa's Hausa people. By the early twenty-first century, Hausa people lived predominantly in northwestern Nigeria and southeastern Niger. There were Hausa communities in other West African nations as well. The vast majority of Hausa are Muslim, and Hausa is an important West African language.

In 1907, while serving in the British colonial administration of West Africa, the civil servant Robert Sutherland Rattray asked Shaihu, a local Hausa *maalam*, or learned scribe, to write down in Hausa a collection of Hausa folktales. For his sources, Shaihu primarily translated Hausa folktales that were already transcribed in Arabic. By 1911, Shaihu presented his manuscript to Rattray, who knew Hausa and translated Shaihu's texts into English. He published a bilingual edition of his work in 1913 as *Hausa Folk-Lore*. Because Rattray intended his anthology as a means for students to learn Hausa, his translation of the folktales is very literal, but there is one instance of censorship in this tale when Rattray refuses to translate the Hausa word by which the World addresses the husband of his lover.

As a foreigner, the slave is called the World, which is indicative of his status as an outsider and points to his coming from somewhere outside of the community. Additionally, the use of a general noun as a personal name, especially when building to the ironic climax of the tale, suggests that Hausa storytellers enjoyed playing with

language. When the husband states his amazement at the state of "the world" in misjudging his wife's virtue, the play on words leads to the surprising ending and humorous plot twist.

The folktale's self-stated moral is that leading citizens such as the galadima and the vizier should not indulge in shameful behavior. However, these men are able to escape punishment by running away. It is only the World who is beheaded, which may hint at the implied but significant message that only unimportant people such as slaves are punished for their transgressions. Those in higher classes may be hurt to some extent by their shameful actions, but they ultimately escape punishment.

R. C. Lutz, PhD

BIBLIOGRAPHY

Bivins, Mary Wren. *Telling Stories, Making Histories: Women, Words, and Islam in Nineteenth-Century Hausaland and the Sokoto Caliphate*. Portsmouth: Heinemann, 2007. Print.

Furniss, Graham. *Poetry, Prose and Popular Culture in Hausa*. Washington: Smithsonian Institution, 1996. Print.

Na'allah, Abdul Rasheed. *African Discourse in Islam, Oral Traditions, and Performance*. New York: Routledge, 2010. Print.

Ong, Walter S., and John Hartley. *Orality and Literacy: The Technologizing of the Word*. New York: Routledge, 2012. Print.

Rattray, R. Sutherland, trans. "The Story of the Slave by Name 'The World.'" *Hausa Folk-Lore: Customs, Proverbs, Etc*. 1913. *Internet Sacred Texts Archive*. Evinity, n.d. Web. 17 Sept. 2013.

Tremearne, A. J .N. *Hausa Folk Tales*. London: John Bale, 1914. Print.

◆ Thunder and Anansi

Author: Traditional Asante
Time Period: 1001 CE–1500 CE
Country or Culture: Africa
Genre: Folktale

PLOT SUMMARY

The man-spider Anansi, his family, and the entire village are faced with a famine. Desperate for food, Anansi sees an island far away in the distance. Upon the island is a single palm tree. He acquires an old boat and, after battling the waves on the shore, is finally able to put to sea toward the island on his seventh try. Once he gets to the island, he climbs the tree, seeking nuts for himself and his family. When he finds them, he drops them toward the boat, which is tied to the tree below. Each nut he throws downward, however, misses the boat and falls into the sea. Anansi, refusing to give up the food he is gathering, jumps in after the nuts and finds himself in front of a cottage on the seabed.

Living in the underwater house is Thunder. When he hears Anansi's story of the famine, Thunder gives the man-spider a magical pot that will provide enough food for all of Anansi's family and people. Anansi thanks Thunder and resurfaces. As he heads back to land, Anansi tests the pot's magic, calling upon it to produce food. It magically produces a large and satisfying meal for Anansi. He then decides that it would be better for him not to tell his family or neighbors about the pot, fearing that using it for so many people would wear out its magic. Anansi hides the magic cooking pot, using it only to feed himself. While his family and friends continue to starve, Anansi shows signs of weight gain.

Anansi's wife and his son Kweku Tsin grow suspicious of Anansi's resurgent health. Kweku Tsin turns into a fly and follows his father around the village. He witnesses his father's selfish acts and alerts his mother. Kweku Tsin and his mother use the magic pot to feed themselves and the entire village. However, Anansi's fears are confirmed, as the pot melts away due to overuse. Anansi is angry when he learns that his pot is missing and, believing his son and wife to be the culprits, seeks a way to punish them.

He goes back to the island and attempts to drop more nuts into the water so that he might visit Thunder again. This time, the nuts all fall into the boat. Anansi grows impatient and simply dives under the water. He finds Thunder again and tells him the story of the pot's theft. Thunder offers him a magic stick. Anansi goes back to the boat and heads for home. He calls upon the stick's magic, expecting it to produce more food. Instead, the stick comes alive and beats him severely. Anansi jumps overboard and swims home, battered, bruised, and remorseful for his selfish actions.

SIGNIFICANCE

The story of Anansi, Thunder, and the magic cooking pot is one of the so-called spider tales that originated among the Asante (Ashanti) people in what is now the West African country of Ghana. Stories of Anansi spread quickly throughout Africa and, by way of the slave trade, to Jamaica and other regions as well. As the stories expanded across Africa and the Atlantic Ocean, Anansi changed in form. For example, in the Bahamas, he is characterized as a tricky boy named Boy Nasty. Elsewhere, he appeared as a rabbit; in fact, this incarnation gave rise to the story of Br'er Rabbit in the United States.

According to the spider tales, Kweku Anansi is the son of the great sky god, Nyame, and his wife, Asase Yaa, the earth goddess and the goddess of fertility. Anansi is occasionally heroic and benevolent, represented by his human side. In other stories, however, Anansi is, like a spider, a trickster. According to the latter characterization, Anansi's mischievous behavior once led his father to turn him into a man-spider.

Anansi is not a malevolent being, however. His problem in many stories is that he frequently acts in a greedy and self-serving manner. In this folktale, for example, he strikes out to sea in search of food not only for himself but also for his family. He determines that the pot he eventually acquires will lose its magic if overused and therefore decides to use its power for his own needs. Still, in many of the stories of Anansi, the man-spider's trickery and cunning brings success to him and others around him, even if that success does not come as planned. In this case, Anansi's family and fellow villagers, when learning of the pot's magic, are saved from starvation.

When he is punished with the magic stick, Anansi immediately knows why and is remorseful. The ending of this tale is similar to others in the Anansi tradition. Anansi's trickery and selfishness provides a moral for the reader. Although he is characterized as someone whose powers exist somewhere between the divine and the earthbound realms and who frequently deceives others for personal gain, he is also frequently tricked and humbled by others—in humorous fashion—for his misdeeds. Additionally, in some cases, his missteps take place in the face of a far superior figure (such as Thunder), giving him a sort of heroic characteristic to which people can relate. In this story, for example, his selfishness is rewarded by the clearly magical Thunder with a stick that beats him in humiliating (but not brutal) fashion. Very popular among children, Anansi is typically a likeable character whose behavior teaches a lesson to others on the benefits of selflessness and community.

Michael P. Auerbach, MA

BIBLIOGRAPHY

Barker, William H., and Cecilia Sinclair. "Thunder and Anansi." *West African Folk-Tales*. 1917. Chapel Hill: Yesterday's Classics, 2007. 10–14. Print.

Brown, Marcia. *Anansi, the Spider Man: Jamaican Folk Tales*. Derrimut: Pan Macmillan Australia, 1956. Print.

Mazzucco, Roberta. "African Myths and What They Teach." *Yale-New Haven Teachers Institute*. Yale-New Haven Teachers Institute, 2013. Web. 27 June 2013.

Pelton, Robert D. *The Trickster in West Africa: A Study of Mythic Irony and Sacred Delight*. Berkeley: U of California P, 1980. Print.

Walker, Sheila S. *African Roots/American Cultures: Africa and the Creation of the Americas*. Lanham: Rowman, 2001. Print.

◆ The Thunder Bride

Author: Traditional Zulu
Time Period: 1001 CE–1500 CE
Country or Culture: Africa
Genre: Folktale

PLOT SUMMARY

The wife of Kwisaba is at home while her husband, a warrior, is away in battle over the course of many months. She takes very ill and, as a result, is too weak to build a fire in her hut. In her desperate state, she cries out, asking for someone to build a fire for her. She pleads that she would even welcome Thunder if he would help her split the wood and make a fire. After she makes this statement, a small cloud appears in the sky and quickly grows. She hears a rumble of thunder as a storm approaches. Suddenly, there is a flash of lightning, and Thunder, taking the form of a man, appears before the woman. He uses a small axe to split all of the woman's wood into kindling. Thereafter, he uses his hands as torches and lights a fire.

With the woman's needs met, Thunder tells her that he wishes to have her baby when it is born. She reluctantly agrees to his demand, and he vanishes. The woman eventually gives birth to a beautiful baby girl, whom she names Miseke. Kwisaba returns from battle and sees his newborn daughter and wife. Miseke tells him about her arrangement with Thunder. Kwisaba understands his wife's predicament and tells her that, as long as they do not let her play outside, they can hide Miseke and prevent her from being taken as Thunder's bride.

Thunder continues to give Miseke gifts during her childhood as a sign of his commitment to taking her as his wife. When Miseke laughs, bangles and other small gifts fall from her mouth. As Miseke reaches the age at which she may marry, her parents are increasingly concerned. They lock her in the house and forbid her from seeing anyone. Miseke's parents must leave their daughter alone when they are required to take a long trip away from their home. Miseke, defying her parents, leaves the house to be with her friends by the river. A dark cloud appears overhead. A clap of thunder and a lightning strike occur, and the cloud comes down to the ground. Thunder appears as a man and swallows Miseke into the cloud.

Miseke's parents are distraught, but Thunder treats Miseke very well. They have a number of children and live in an elegant palace in the heavens. However, Miseke begins to miss her parents. Thunder gives her permission to visit them, as long as she takes care to remain safe. Miseke, her children, and her servants arrive in the forest near her home village. Disoriented, they soon become lost and are suddenly attacked by an ogre. The ogre kills her servants and eats their supplies. Miseke tells her oldest son to follow the river to the village and find help. As she tries to protect her children from the ogre's attack, the villagers, led by her father, emerge from the forest and kill the ogre. The village shaman cuts off the monster's toe, and all of Miseke's belongings—including the people the ogre ate—are returned to her intact.

Miseke visits with her family and fellow villagers for one month. Then, a dark cloud appears and envelops Miseke, her children, her servants, and her belongings. She is never seen again. It is presumed that she lives happily ever after with her husband in the heavens.

SIGNIFICANCE

The nature of thunder is different in various African traditions. In some tribal traditions, thunder is a god of the sky. In others, thunder is like a god but also possesses human characteristics. In the story of the Thunder Bride, Thunder is equated with the Zulus' supreme god, Imana, who created the universe. In this story, his power is demonstrated in terms of thunder and lightning. His great estate in the heavens and his benevolence to Miseke and her family implies that he is indeed a great force with strong ties to the human race.

This tale is also an example of the traditional East African notion of Imana. Although he is the creator of the universe and the source of life, his is a remote existence. Imana is a father figure, commanding great respect from all other entities, mortal and immortal. In East African tradition, Imana is not the type of god to whom mortals must make daily sacrifices or offer constant prayers (such responsibilities are commanded by secondary deities). Rather, Imana makes his presence known to humans when they are in need of his help.

At the beginning of the story, Miseke's mother is so ill that she cannot make a fire. She is close to death. She prays to Thunder for his help, knowing that she has no other option. Thunder answers her prayer, using his power to build and light a lifesaving fire for her. Although Miseke's parents are frightened that Thunder will take away their only daughter, their fears are allayed when they see how Thunder treats Miseke as his wife. Furthermore, Thunder takes Miseke far away from earth and cannot allow her to return. This is illustrative of the spiritual distance between Thunder (or Imana) and the mortal world. Although the humans in the story are fearful of Thunder's power, he is consistently benevolent to the people of earth. The true villain in the story is the ogre, from whom Miseke is rescued.

Michael P. Auerbach, MA

BIBLIOGRAPHY

Husain, Shahrukh. *African Myths*. Ibadan: Evans Brothers, 2006. Print.

"Imana." *African Mythology A to Z*. Ed. Patricia Ann Lynch and Jeremy Roberts. 2nd ed. New York: Chelsea, 2010. 58–59. Print.

Kolini, Emmanuel M., and Peter R. Holmes. *Rethinking Life: What the Church Can Learn from Africa*. Colorado Springs: Biblica, 2009. Print.

Werner, Alice. "The Heaven Country and the Heaven People." *Myths and Legends of the Bantu*. 1933. Charleston: BiblioBazaar, 2007. 48–62. Print.

---. "Legends of the High Gods." *Myths and Legends of the Bantu*. 1933. Charleston: BiblioBazaar, 2007. 39–47. Print.

EGYPT

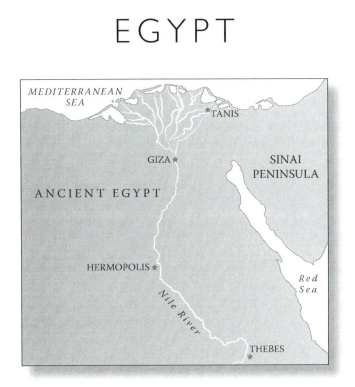

Amen-Ra, the God of Empire

Author: Traditional
Time Period: 5000 BCE–2500 BCE
Country or Culture: Egypt
Genre: Myth

PLOT SUMMARY

Amen (Amun or Amon) is a wind deity and a god of the Egyptian city of Thebes. He is also a deity of the moon and the son of the night goddess, Mut-Apet, the mother of all gods. While Amen is an important god in Thebes, in the city of Heliopolis, the people instead worship the sun god, Ra (Re).

Over the centuries, Thebes becomes the most important city in Egypt. During its rise to prominence, Amen also becomes more powerful, marrying his mother, Mut, and becoming both son and husband at once. Just as he fuses the entities of father and son in this marriage, so too he unites with Ra. Gaining Ra's solar characteristics and parting ways with his lunar association, he becomes

Amen-Ra, the great father of all the gods and the most powerful deity in Egypt. As Amen-Ra, he is a formidable, bearded man in an ornate headdress. The red, blue, and green of his outfit symbolize the flowing rivers of Egypt and the growth of the nation, and he sometimes wears powerful ram's horns on his head as well.

With Amen-Ra as their patron deity, the warriors and rulers of Thebes complete many successful military campaigns. They use the spoils of these wars to build huge temples in tribute to the god. It is in this tradition that Amenhotep I and his wife, Aahmes-Nefertari, rise to power. As pharaoh, Amenhotep unites many cities under the worship of Amen-Ra and orders the construction of a massive temple, located in Karnak, celebrating both the military victories of the rulers and the legend of the god. Nefertari even believes herself to be the wife of Amen-Ra, and as she sleeps in the temples dedicated to him, the people begin to believe that her children are the children of the god.

After Amenhotep and Nefertari die, the next ruler of Egypt, Thothmes I, likewise spends great wealth celebrating Amen-Ra, building massive pylons at the temple of Karnak. Thothmes prays to the god, asking that his daughter Hatshepsut become queen. Although Thothmes II and Thothmes III both briefly reign over Egypt, Hatshepsut gains the support of the priesthood of Amen-Ra and eventually seizes power with their assistance. For fourteen years, she rules alone, fetching rare animals and exotic trees to build the god one of the most beautiful gardens the people of Egypt have ever seen.

Hatshepsut, however, does not engage in military campaigns as previous rulers had, and so she does not increase the wealth and influence of Amen-Ra. Seeing this to be the case, the priests shift their support back to Thothmes III, who reclaims power and begins devastating military campaigns, conquering cities in the area now known as Syria, Lebanon, and Palestine.

Thothmes III is so successful that the priests of Amen-Ra compose a song for him. The hymn is sung from the voice of Amen-Ra, and in it, the god gives the pharaoh his blessing. "Like to a great young bull," he sings through the bodies of his priests, "I have made them behold thy power, Fearless and quick to strike, none is so bold to resist thee" (Mackenzie 292). With this blessing, Thothmes III rules for many years, expanding the influence of Egypt and the worship of his god, Amen-Ra.

SIGNIFICANCE

As can be seen in the story of Amen-Ra, the history of the gods of ancient Egypt is often inseparable from the political and military history of the nation. The priests of various temples held political power that, while not equal to that of the pharaohs, often granted them the influence to overthrow rulers and direct military campaigns; the temple of Karnak, built for Amen-Ra, even had its own navy. Likewise, for military and political leaders, promotion of the worship of a particular god was a powerful tool that assisted them in uniting cities and overthrowing rulers who supported less popular gods and goddesses.

The unification of Amen-Ra had particularly wide-ranging political consequences. While there were certainly similarities between the sun god Ra and the moon god Amen, the two were largely distinct for centuries, their respective worship in Heliopolis and Thebes comprising two distinguishable religions. This began to change in the sixteenth century BCE, when the rulers of the Eighteenth Dynasty claimed power in Egypt and expelled the previous rulers, the Hyksos, a West Asian people who had settled in Egypt two centuries before. The Eighteenth Dynasty's seat of power was in Thebes,

and so with their rise to power, the worship of Amen likewise became more prominent.

When the government of Thebes overtook the governments of different regions, one tactic used to secure power in the new cities was to merge Amen with whichever god was currently worshipped there. In taking over the African kingdom of Kush, for instance, the leaders of Thebes began to promote the belief that the horned ram god of the region was a manifestation of Amen himself. The people of Kush ultimately shifted their worship to the god of Thebes, while Amen absorbed that god's attributes (the ram's horns, for instance, as well as an association with fertility). The unification of Amen with Ra appears to have been a similarly advantageous political move: as Ra and his cult were extremely powerful in other parts of Egypt, the sun god was redefined as another aspect of Amen, allowing the political and religious power associated with his worship to remain in place as they were subsumed into the government of Thebes. This was particularly important because pharaohs had previously been considered descendants of Ra. In the new religion, they were incarnations of Amen-Ra himself.

Eventually, the worship of Amen-Ra became effectively monotheistic, with the Egyptian people roughly unified under a single god and a single political leadership. The worship itself took many different forms, and Amen-Ra appeared under different names and in different bodies. Nevertheless, the spread of Egyptian power throughout the ancient world came hand in hand with a united mythology and the joined traditions of Amen and Ra, the politics and religion of the kingdom so subtly intertwined that neither can be truly understood without the study of both.

T. Fleischmann, MFA

BIBLIOGRAPHY

Garry, Jane, and Hasan El-Shamy, eds. "Creation Myth: Cosmogony and Cosmology, Motifs A600–A899." *Archetypes and Motifs in Folklore and Literature: A Handbook*. Armonk: Sharp, 2005. 24–31. Print.

Lawler, Andrew. "Karnak." *Humanities* 31.1 (2010): 24. Print.

Mackenzie, Donald. *Egyptian Myth and Legend*. London: Gresham, 1907. Print.

Pinch, Geraldine. *Egyptian Mythology: A Guide to the Gods, Goddesses, and Traditions of Ancient Egypt*. New York: Oxford UP, 2004. Print.

Shaw, Ian. *The Oxford History of Ancient Egypt*. New York: Oxford UP, 2000. Print.

The Battle of Horus and Set

Author: Traditional
Time Period: 5000 BCE–2500 BCE
Country or Culture: Egypt
Genre: Myth

PLOT SUMMARY

For eighty years, Horus and his uncle Set (Seth) have squabbled about who should succeed the late Osiris to become the next god-king of Egypt. Finally, the matter is brought before the Ennead, the great council of gods, to be decided.

Horus, son of Osiris and Isis, maintains that he is rightful heir to the throne. Most members of the Ennead agree: the crown should pass from father to son. However, Ra-Atum, all-powerful sun god and Ennead figurehead, favors Horus's uncle Set, a mighty warrior and the accused murderer of Osiris.

In an effort to settle the issue, Thoth—god of writing and a stalwart supporter of Horus—writes to Neith, the ancient and wise goddess of war, to solicit her opinion. Neith suggests that Set be appeased with treasures and marriage to two of Ra-Atum's daughters and that Horus be made king. While the majority of the Ennead finds this solution agreeable, it does not sit well with Ra-Atum, who charges the two combatants to make their own case.

Set boasts of his superior strength and his important duty: he accompanies Ra-Atum on his daily boat voyage across the sky, fending off those who would interrupt the life-giving journey. Members of the Ennead agree this is true. Horus merely reiterates that he is son of Osiris, thus next in line for the throne.

Isis interrupts the proceedings with an emotional outburst, and the Ennead moves to a different venue where Isis is banned. She uses magic to change her appearance and gain access to the tribunal in the guise of a crone. She changes again into a young, beautiful woman and flirts with Set, manipulating him into admitting he is a usurper.

Ra-Atum is still not convinced, so Set proposes a contest: the rivals will change into hippopotamuses and remain submerged for three months. Whoever rises out of the water will reign. Worried about Set's superior strength, Isis creates a harpoon, and after accidentally jabbing Horus, she stabs Set. But Set reminds Isis that

they are brother and sister, so she relents and removes the barb. Her solicitude angers Horus, who decapitates his mother and runs away with her head.

Ra-Atum encourages the Ennead to pursue and punish Horus for his rash act. Set finds Horus, and the two rival claimants grapple. Set rips out Horus's eyes and buries them. But Hathor, goddess of love and motherhood, finds the blinded Horus and restores his sight.

Set, foiled in his plans, suggests a new contest: the rivals will build stone ships and race them. Whoever wins will be king. Horus cleverly builds a wooden ship and covers the exterior with plaster to make it appear stonelike. Set simply removes a mountain peak and carves it into a huge vessel. When the ships are launched, Horus's boat floats while Set's sinks. Set maliciously upends Horus's boat so neither can win.

With the issue still undecided, Thoth suggests they involve Osiris. In an exchange of letters, Osiris supports his son Horus. Osiris further reminds the assembled Ennead he is in charge of the underworld and, as such, is final arbiter of everyone's fate—gods, aristocrats, and commoners alike. This irrefutable fact convinces the Ennead, and they unanimously proclaim Horus king. In compensation, Ra-Atum takes in his favorite, Set, and gives him a new ability: "He shall thunder in the sky, and men shall fear him" (Mayer 179). With everyone happy, the council of the gods is adjourned.

SIGNIFICANCE

The story of the battle of Horus and Set is an abridged and greatly expurgated version of the original myth. The primary source of the tale is the Chester Beatty Papyrus I, a document from the Twentieth Dynasty of Egypt (ca. 1190–1070 BCE), transcribed in Thebes during the reign of Ramses V (ca. 1150–1145 BCE). First translated into English in 1931, the papyrus is now preserved in the Chester Beatty Library in Dublin, Ireland.

The Mayer-Prideaux 1938 retelling of the story, "The Contendings of Horus and Seth," was intended for the sensibilities of a general audience in the late 1930s. It presents the highlights of the plot but expunges the earthier elements of the myth. In the original, there are several interludes in which Set, to prove his superiority to the assembled Ennead, attempts—but fails—to dominate Horus in homosexual encounters. Isis, the magician and shape-shifter, employs not only clever words but also freely uses her sexuality with her brother Set and with Ra-Atum to aid the cause of her son.

Complete or bowdlerized, the battle of Horus and Set provides a final chapter to Egypt's most ancient, complex, and significant myth, a conflict over the line of succession for the throne. The story of Horus and Set has been interpreted as an allegory for the long conflict and eventual unification of Upper and Lower Egypt. With Set as a patron god of Upper Egypt and Horus as a patron god of Lower Egypt, the unification of the two regions required the mythology surrounding these rival gods to be revised and integrated. The Narmer Palette (ca. 3100 BCE), the earliest document commemorating the unification of Upper and Lower Egypt, depicts the pharaoh, King Narmer, dominating a conquered enemy. Above the kneeling enemy, facing the king, sits the falcon god Horus. This image connects Horus to the reigning king, thereby legitimizing his rule. Set, however, as the patron god of Upper Egypt, was still worshipped by many powerful supporters (represented in the myth by the sun god Ra-Atum). Several centuries later, in the Pyramid Texts (ca. 2400–2300 BCE), Horus and Set are shown to be ruling the sky together, essentially sharing their power. However, because the pharaoh was considered a manifestation of the falcon god on earth, Set and Horus's rival claims to the throne needed to be resolved.

The Osiris myth deals in part with the contendings of Set and the child god Horus. After Set murders his brother Osiris and dismembers his body, Isis reassembles the scattered body parts and conceives Horus with the reanimated corpse. Horus becomes Set's archrival at birth, and the two gods battle for eighty years over the line of succession for the kingship. Both gods have legitimate claims to rule and each claims many powerful supporters. Their battle culminates in the myth presented on the Chester Beatty Papyrus I, in which the line of succession is finally determined. With the council of gods supporting Horus's claim to the throne, the pharaoh, as a manifestation of Horus on earth, was seen to have been divinely ordained to rule.

Jack Ewing

BIBLIOGRAPHY

Assmann, Jan, and David Lorton. *The Search for God in Ancient Egypt*. Ithaca: Cornell UP, 2001. Print.

Babbitt, Frank Cole, trans. *Plutarch's* Moralia. Vol. 5. Cambridge: Loeb Classical Lib., 1936. Print.

Beatty, Alfred Chester, and Alan H. Gardiner. *The Library of A. Chester Beatty: Description of a Hieratic Papyrus with a Mythological Story, Love-Songs, and Other Miscellaneous Texts*. Oxford: Oxford UP, 1936. Print.

Budge, E. A. Wallis. *The Gods of the Egyptians*. 2 vols. New York: Dover, 1969. Print.

Clark, R. T. Rundle. *Myth and Symbol in Ancient Egypt*. New York: Thames, 1991. Print.

Frankfort, Henri. *Ancient Egyptian Religion: An Interpretation*. New York: Dover, 2011. Print.

Griffiths, John Gwyn. *The Conflict of Horus and Seth from Egyptian and Classical Sources: A Study in Ancient Mythology*. Liverpool: Liverpool UP, 1960. Print.

Loprieno, Antonio, ed. *Ancient Egyptian Literature: History and Forms*. Boston: Brill Academic, 1996. Print.

Mayer, Josephine, and Tom Prideaux. "The Contendings of Horus and Seth." *Never to Die: The Egyptians in Their Own Words*. New York: Viking, 1938. 173–79. Print.

Pinch, Geraldine. *Egyptian Mythology: A Guide to the Gods, Goddesses, and Traditions of Ancient Egypt*. New York: Oxford UP, 2004. Print.

◆ The Bentresh Stela

Author: Traditional
Time Period: 999 BCE–1 BCE
Country or Culture: Egypt
Genre: Myth

PLOT SUMMARY

The Bentresh stela is a stone monument that was discovered near the site of the temple of Khonsu in Karnak. It is carved with the myth of the princess and the demon. In this story, Ramses II travels to Mitanni, which the ancient Egyptians call "Naharin," to receive royal tribute. There, the prince of Bekhten presents him with many gifts, the greatest among them being his eldest daughter. The king, pleased with her beauty, gives her the name Neferure (Neferu-Ra), which means "the beauty of Ra (Re)," and the title of Great Royal Wife. Ramses then returns to Egypt.

Soon after his return, a messenger from the prince of Bekhten arrives. He informs Ramses that Neferure's younger sister, Bentresh (Bent-reshy), is very ill and beseeches the king to send a wise man to help her.

Ramses dispatches a learned man known as Tehuti-em-heb from the House of Life; however, upon arriving and seeing Bentresh, Tehuti-em-heb realizes that she is possessed by a hostile spirit and is far beyond his power to heal. He sends a message to the king that he needs the power of the god Khonsu, known as the Expeller of Demons.

Ramses heeds his words and goes to the temple of Khonsu in Thebes to perform a ritual. He and his courtiers take the statue known as Khonsu in Thebes Neferhotep, the leading manifestation of the god Khonsu, and set it in front of the statue known as Khonsu the Expeller of Demons (also called Khonsu the Plan Maker or Khonsu the Provider). Ramses instructs the statue of Khonsu in Thebes Neferhotep to send Khonsu the Expeller of Demons to Bekhten to assist Bentresh, and the statue nods twice in assent. Ramses asks Khonsu in Thebes Neferhotep to grant Khonsu the Expeller of Demons his protection, and again the statue nods twice. The king sends the statue of Khonsu the Expeller of Demons to Bekhten, accompanied by a royal retinue.

The statue of Khonsu arrives in Bekhten and is immediately taken to Bentresh. The statue performs a protection spell over her, and the demon that has been possessing Bentresh is cast out of her body. The demon acknowledges Khonsu as his master and tells Khonsu that he will bow to Khonsu's wishes and leave if the prince of Bekhten holds a holy day with a feast and sacrifice. Khonsu agrees, and the prince of Bekhten throws a lavish celebration in honor of the demon. The demon is satisfied and leaves.

The prince of Bekhten, however, is worried that the demon could return and that he may need Khonsu's impressive power again, so he keeps the statue rather than send it back to Khonsu's temple in Egypt, where it belongs. Over three years pass, until one night, the prince has a dream in which the god Khonsu emerges from his shrine in the form of a hawk and flies off in the direction of Egypt. The prince of Bekhten awakens and realizes that his dream was a sign that Khonsu wants the statue returned to Egypt. He swiftly sends the statue back, along with many gifts to appease the gods. Khonsu the Expeller of Demons returns to Thebes and gives Khonsu in Thebes Neferhotep all of the riches he acquired in Bekhten.

SIGNIFICANCE

This Egyptian myth is from a sandstone tablet known as the Bekhten stela, which was discovered in 1829. While the stela used in translations of the myth was likely carved around 300 BCE, traces of an earlier version have been unearthed in the courtyard of the Temple of Khonsu in Karnak. The king in this story has not been historically identified, but King Ramses in the myth is believed to be Ramses II, also called Ramesses the Great, who reigned as the third pharaoh of Egypt from 1279 BCE until 1213 BCE. The figure of Neferure is likely based on Ramses II's wife Maat-hor-neferure, a Hittite princess. There is also significant evidence that Egypt and its neighbors often exchanged physicians and healing statues; at one point, Maat-hor-neferure's father, Hattusili III, requested that Ramses II send him a physician, though it was in order to help the king's sister become pregnant rather than to free his daughter from a demon.

It is widely believed that the myth recorded on the Bentresh stela is a product of the priests of Khonsu, who devised this story as a means to increase the perceived influence of the god Khonsu and spread his worship. Khonsu was a god of the moon and was often considered the son of the god Amen (Amun) and the goddess Mut. Khonsu was associated with fertility, virility, and youth, and he was often depicted as a mummified youth. He was also known for bestowing prophecies and visions and was sometimes known as the Lord of Truth. A carving from the Bentresh tablet shows the two shrines of Khonsu facing each other as part of the ritual described in the myth. The statue of the god Khonsu the Expeller of Demons referred to in this myth was likely one of two alternative aspects of the main god, the other one being Khonsu Who Was a Child. In other sources, these aspects of Khonsu are depicted as baboons seated on either side of Khonsu in Thebes Neferhotep. Thus, the statue of Khonsu sent to Bekhten in this myth was likely one of the small baboon images that would have flanked Khonsu in Thebes Neferhotep in the original temple. Fragments of such a statue have been excavated from the temple's courtyard. These two aspects of Khonsu were also said to write books that told of a person's fate. As seen in this myth, he was also known for his power over evil spirits, and people afflicted with symptoms similar to those of Bentresh could pray to Khonsu for help.

The learned man mentioned in the myth, Tehuti-em-heb, was a scribe from the House of Life. The House of Life was a religious institution responsible for the creation and propagation of sacred texts. Scribes of the

House of Life were specifically trained in medicine and magic and frequently worked for the king, which explains why Ramses II would send such a man to help Bentresh.

The myth of Bentresh and the demon illustrates the importance of magic and ritual in ancient Egyptian religion. The myth provides repetitive elements throughout the story such as when the statues are turned to face each other, when the invocation is repeated twice, and when the statue nods twice each time. Repetition serves to help guarantee the efficacy of the ritual, and the myth stresses ancient Egyptians' belief in the importance of seeking direct divine intervention and in the power of the gods to help humans emerge from seemingly dire situations.

The fact that religion and medicine were so intertwined is also very important. The human body was considered sacred, and dissecting a dead body was considered a crime. Hence, Egyptian physicians were not skilled in identifying disease, and their treatments were often based on magic rather than anatomy or medicine.

Haley Blum, MA

BIBLIOGRAPHY

Bohleke, Briant. "An Oracular Amuletic Decree of Khonsu in the Cleveland Museum of Art." *Journal of Egyptian Archaeology* 83 (1997): 155–67. Print.

Budge, Ernest A. Wallis. *Egyptian Tales and Romances*. London: Butterworth, 1931. Print.

Gardiner, Alan H. "The House of Life." *Journal of Egyptian Archaeology* 24.2 (1938): 157–79. Print.

Hart, George. *The Routledge Dictionary of Egyptian Gods and Goddesses*. New York: Routledge, 2005. Print.

Ions, Veronica. *Egyptian Mythology*. Rev. ed. London: Chancellor, 1997. Print.

Murray, Margaret Alice. "The Princess and the Demon." *Ancient Egyptian Legends*. London: Murray, 1920. 11–19. Print.

Ritner, Robert K., trans. "The Bentresh Stela (Louvre C 284)." *The Literature of Ancient Egypt: An Anthology of Stories, Instructions, Stelae, Autobiographies, and Poetry*. Ed. William Kelly Simpson. 3rd ed. New Haven: Yale UP, 2003. 361–66. Print.

Wiedemann, Alfred. *Religion of the Ancient Egyptians*. New York: Putnam, 1897. Print.

◆ The Boat of Ra

Author: Traditional
Time Period: 5000 BCE–2500 BCE
Country or Culture: Egypt
Genre: Myth

PLOT SUMMARY

Every day, the sun god Ra (Re) undertakes a perilous but necessary twenty-four-hour journey. At daybreak, he begins sailing blissfully across the river of the sky, from east to west, in the decorative, luxurious Manzet boat. In the evening, Ra's boat transforms into the unadorned Mesektet boat and runs the dreaded gantlet from west to east along the meandering river of the Duat, the realm of the dead, where the god Osiris reigns supreme.

The Duat is divided into twelve countries, one for every hour of the night. Entrance and exit gates, which must be successfully traversed, close off the borders of each division. Every section has its own guardians, rules, and ceremonies and incantations that must be completed before the boat can pass. Ra's journey into the Duat begins in the diminished light of evening and grows progressively darker and gloomier until near the trip's end, when blackness lightens again toward dawn.

During the voyage, Ra assumes various guises, including that of a scarab, to meet various challenges and successfully pass through the regions of the underworld. To enter the kingdom of the dead at the start of the journey, Ra himself must take on a deathlike state. Ra's animate companions have specific roles, serving as pilot, oarsman, steersman, or warrior. Twelve goddesses of the hours in turn step forward to guide the sun god's boat through the hazards of each particular section of the Duat. Around every bend of the river wait awful adversaries, from fire-breathing serpents to voracious birds, that must be appeased or subdued.

At the center of the Duat is the realm of Osiris, god of the dead. It is here the judgment of human souls takes place. Each seeker's heart is weighed against a feather. The monster Ammut eats hearts that are too heavy, and the former owner of such a heart is doomed to destruction and eternal damnation. The light-hearted humans are permitted to dwell in a land of plenty with Osiris and enjoy all the pleasures of the living world until the end of time. Others must face the tortures of the damned, punishments for their misdeeds in life. As the unworthy are abandoned to their fates, their cries echo off the steep walls of the Duat.

After the kingdom of Osiris lies the greatest challenge of all. In the seventh division lurks Apep (also known as Apophis), the archenemy of Ra. A monstrous snake with an enormous maw, Apep tries to capsize the boat and plunge the world into never-ending darkness. Fortunately, the goddess Isis is aboard, and she uses her magic to incapacitate Apep long enough for the boat to pass beyond the serpent's grasp.

Finally, Ra's boat passes through the final gate and reenters the living world. The boat again becomes the plush Manzet barge, and the twenty-four-hour cycle begins anew.

SIGNIFICANCE

The sun has played a significant role in mythology and religion since the beginnings of human civilization. Because of the fiery orb's godlike ability to provide heat and light and its observable regular pattern of rising and setting, the sun assumed the position of supreme deity in the pantheons of many cultures. Represented in Egypt by the god Ra, the sun ruled over a plethora of gods representing birds, beasts, landmarks, and natural phenomena. Pioneering priests blended native lore and foreign mythology to devise a complex theology, elaborating on the attributes of the sun god and the many associated deities. The sun-based religion, focusing on easily understood symbolic contrasts of light and dark, life and death, and good and evil lent structure to everyday existence, promulgated standards of behavior, and gave believers purpose by presenting the possibility of an afterlife.

The orthodoxy of Ra worship was firmly in place by the Fifth Dynasty (ca. 2494–2345 BCE). Pyramids and burial chambers of pharaohs from that period onward were inscribed with detailed instructions, secret words to be spoken, and rites to be performed to ensure the safe passage of the dead king's soul through the obstacle course of the underworld. Many of ancient Egypt's myriad works of art, architecture, and literature were related in some way to the civilization's longstanding preoccupation with appeasing the gods in life and in the afterlife.

Over time, religious tenets changed to accommodate local deities, eliminate dogmatic difficulties, or paint a rosier picture of the hereafter; the blessed dead were no longer believed to reside with Osiris but instead thought to sail with Ra for eternity. In later dynasties, salvation was not limited only to rulers but extended to the nobility. By the Eighteenth Dynasty (ca. 1550–1295 BCE), even commoners who could afford

it were permitted their chance at immortality. From that point until the advent of monotheism, there was a brisk business in amulets, talismans, and personalized copies of the Book of the Dead, a manual buried with an individual's corpse that gave exact instructions for achieving life after death.

Jack Ewing

BIBLIOGRAPHY

Budge, E. A. Wallis. *The Egyptian Book of the Dead.* New York: Dover, 1967. Print.

Littleton, C. Scott, ed. *Mythology: The Illustrated Anthology of World Myth and Storytelling.* San Diego: Thunder Bay, 2002. Print.

Murray, M. A. "The Regions of Night and Thick Darkness." *Legends of Ancient Egypt.* New York: Dover, 2000. 86–107. Print.

Pinch, Geraldine. *Egyptian Mythology: A Guide to the Gods, Goddesses, and Traditions of Ancient Egypt.* New York: Oxford UP, 2004. Print.

Shaw, Ian, ed. *The Oxford History of Ancient Egypt.* New York: Oxford UP, 2004. Print.

◆ The Book of Thoth

Author: Traditional
Time Period: 5000 BCE–2500 BCE
Country or Culture: Egypt
Genre: Myth

PLOT SUMMARY

Nefer-ka-ptah is the prince of Egypt, husband of the beautiful Ahura and father to Merab. Although he has incredible riches available to him, he cares only about studying the ancient writings and wisdom of his ancestors. One day, Nefer-ka-ptah goes into his temple to worship. The walls of the temple are filled with engravings, and Nefer-ka-ptah soon forgets to pray, finding himself caught up in reading the old writing. When a priest sees him, he begins to laugh, telling Nefer-ka-ptah that he is wasting his time. Instead, the prince should seek out the Book of Thoth, the holy text written by the god of wisdom. The priest explains that this book allows one to communicate with the birds, enchant the sky, and come back from the dead. Nefer-ka-ptah is enthralled, and even though the priest warns that the book is buried in a chest at the bottom of a river and protected by magical snakes and scorpions, Nefer-ka-ptah insists that he will find it.

Nefer-ka-ptah runs to tell his wife of his plan. She foresees that his quest will bring him great sorrow but is unable to dissuade him from seeking the book. Accompanied by Ahura and Merab, Nefer-ka-ptah takes the royal barge and sails to Koptos (Coptos), where the chest is hidden. Once there, he consults with the priests of Isis, and together they make magical workers whom they task with searching for the box under the river. After three days, the workers uncover an iron box protected by a gigantic, immortal snake and countless smaller snakes and scorpions. Nefer-ka-ptah casts a spell that puts the smaller creatures to sleep, but he is forced to battle the larger snake. He slices it in half twice, but each time the head returns to the body and the snake goes on fighting. At last, he slices the snake in half and kicks sand between the two parts so that they cannot rejoin. With this done, the snake lies powerless on the ground, and Nefer-ka-ptah is able to retrieve the box.

Inside the box is the Book of Thoth, and indeed, as soon as Nefer-ka-ptah reads it, he receives great power. Ahura next reads the book and likewise learns the spells inside of it. As they rapidly gain this ancient knowledge, however, Thoth learns that his book is missing. Enraged, the god approaches the sun god, Ra. Ra understands Thoth's anger and grants him the permission and power necessary to take revenge.

As Nefer-ka-ptah sails his barge on the river, Thoth uses Ra's power to lure Merab to the edge of the barge and pull him into the water, where he drowns. Nefer-ka-ptah uses his magic to retrieve Merab's body and even to make the boy speak; Merab reports that Thoth seeks revenge for the theft of his knowledge. Nefer-ka-ptah and Ahura mourn the death of their son but also recognize that this is only the start of Thoth's vengeance. Soon, Ahura is also drawn into the water to drown. As with his son, Nefer-ka-ptah retrieves her body and makes her speak, hearing further of Thoth's anger. Only a short time passes before Nefer-ka-ptah himself is drawn to the water with an irresistible urge to drown.

Nefer-ka-ptah manages to tie the Book of Thoth to his body before succumbing to the god's power, and the book remains with him until his body is discovered. The king orders that Nefer-ka-ptah be buried with highest honors alongside his treasure. Although Thoth's vengeance costs Nefer-ka-ptah his life, the prince is never truly separated from the knowledge he so desperately craved.

SIGNIFICANCE

The Book of Thoth refers at once to the imagined text at the center of this myth and to a series of actual texts supposedly written by the god Thoth. Many temples in ancient Egypt contained small libraries (the rooms referenced at the start of the narrative of Nefer-ka-ptah), and as Thoth was a god of knowledge and learned wisdom, many of the texts in those libraries were attributed to him. While most of these books are lost to time, several survive in either complete or fragmentary forms.

Both the extant books attributed to the god and the mythological book sought in the narrative of Nefer-ka-ptah help to clarify the relationship between humans and magical knowledge in ancient Egypt. Nefer-ka-ptah himself is, in many ways, an ideal mortal. He has the blood of the king within him, which gives his life some divine properties from birth, and he devotes himself fully to the study and worship of the gods, taking time repeatedly throughout the myth to make sacrifices and visit temples. However, he is also improperly obsessed with obtaining the gods' sacred knowledge, an obsession that even distracts him from praying when he visits a temple early in the narrative.

The knowledge that Nefer-ka-ptah seeks, then, is knowledge that no mortal has the right to obtain. Thoth denies mortals this knowledge and protects his book with an immortal snake not out of selfishness but because the divide between the mortal realm and the divine knowledge of the gods is inherent to existence. This is further confirmed when Thoth seeks to punish Nefer-ka-ptah for overstepping his role and stealing the book. Thoth does not immediately attack the young prince, although he certainly has the power to do so, but instead consults with Ra, arguably the most powerful god in the Egyptian pantheon at that time. This consultation shows that the protection of divine knowledge is of significance to all the gods, and the support that Ra offers confirms that the theft of the book is an assault on the entire realm of the deities and not simply on Thoth himself.

Thoth plays an important role in ancient Egyptian mythology, representing the acquisition of knowledge and the development of the sciences. As much as the god champions learning and wisdom, however, myths such as the story of Nefer-ka-ptah and his search for the Book of Thoth serve as reminders that there are limits to human knowledge and that some aspects of the universe must stay unknown.

T. Fleischmann, MFA

BIBLIOGRAPHY

Brown, Brian. "The Story of the Book of Thoth." *The Wisdom of the Egyptians*. New York: Brentano, 1923. 279–91. Print.

David, Rosalie. *The Ancient Egyptians: Beliefs and Practices*. Portland: Sussex Academic, 1988. Print.

Pinch, Geraldine. *Egyptian Mythology: A Guide to the Gods, Goddesses, and Traditions of Ancient Egypt*. Oxford: Oxford UP, 2002. Print.

Shaw, Ian. *The Oxford History of Ancient Egypt*. New York: Oxford UP, 2000. Print.

"The Temple of Thoth at North Karnak." *Ancient Egypt Magazine* Apr. 2009: 9. Print.

◆ The Egyptian Creation Myth

Author: Traditional
Time Period: 5000 BCE–2500 BCE
Country or Culture: Egypt
Genre: Myth

PLOT SUMMARY

In the beginning, there is no sky or land, only the deep, dark waters of Nun. Contained in Nun are the building blocks of everything in the universe, but none of it has form or substance. From these waters, a serpentlike form of energy called Neb-er-tcher surfaces with the desire to create the world. In order to do so, he transforms himself into the god Khepri, also spelled Khepera. When Khepri emerges from the waters of Nun, he sees that there is nothing, not even a place on which to stand. Using the power of his words, Khepri creates that which he desires, such as land, the sky, and the sun and moon (which are seen as the eyes of Khepri).

Khepri takes three forms during a given day. In the morning he is Khepri, who takes the form of a scarab beetle; at midday he is Ra, a man with the head of a falcon; and in the evening he is Atum, usually a man, often elderly. He also creates the gods to rule over the elements. The first of these gods, Shu and Tefnut (the gods of air and liquid, respectively), are born directly from Khepri in a mystical form of self-fertilization: he "ha[s] union with [his] closed hand" (Budge 4-5) and uses his seed to produce Shu and Tefnut. The union of Shu and Tefnut produces two more gods, Geb (the earth god) and Nut (the sky god). While Khepri rests, his offspring continue to procreate, with Geb and Nut giving birth to the gods Osiris, Set, Nephthys, Horus, and Isis.

With the emergence of these gods comes the universe and those who dwell in it. At one point, Shu and Tefnut vanish back into Nun, so Khepri sends his eye (the sun) after them. In its absence, Khepri creates a second eye (the moon) to replace it. When Shu and Tefnut reemerge with his first eye, Khepri begins to weep, and his tears turn into human beings. However, his first eye is angry about being replaced, so he gives it greater power than the second one.

SIGNIFICANCE

This version of the ancient Egyptian myth of creation, known as the Heliopolis version, was found on a piece of papyrus in the early 1860s. It is similar to other Egyptian stories about the creation of the universe, although this version is significant for a number of reasons. For example, this version introduces Neb-er-tcher, whose name has been variously translated as "lord of time," "lord of the universe," "lord of the end," and "lord to the uttermost limit." This name suggests that Neb-er-tcher, not Ra or Atum, was considered the highest and eternal god (although other stories depict him as a form of the sun god, Ra, making Ra the creator of the universe). This deity does not just create the universe, including humanity and other living creatures; he also creates the gods. In fact, Neb-er-tcher wills himself into being, rising from the nothingness of Nun. In this light, the Heliopolis version of the myth of creation shows the entire process by which the universe was created.

When Neb-er-tcher takes shape, he becomes Khepri, which is both a name for the god and the mystical transformative action he uses to create everything. In order to create something, he simply utters the word he wishes. For example, to create the sky, he says "sky" and it comes into being, drawing its elements from the Nun. This is not the case for the gods, however. To create them, Khepri undergoes a magical reproductive process, and his children procreate and multiply, creating a family tree. Humans are also born from Khepri, though they alone are derived from the god's tears, giving them distinctiveness among all other nondeities in the universe.

Nun is also an important element of this story. Nun is a vast, black sea without shape or boundaries. However, Nun also contains the basic building blocks for the entire universe, according to descriptions found in the pyramids. Nun is like a dream world in which objects and beings are created simply by an act of will. That Nun is characterized as a vast ocean of black water is not coincidental, as the Nile River was an invaluable source of food, water, and life for the ancient Egyptians, as it is today. The people watched the river rise during rainy seasons, flooding to cover vast regions with dark water. When the waters of the Nile receded, the soil that was left behind was dark, rich, and fertile. In light of these facts, the Nile provided inspiration for those seeking to understand how the known universe came into being.

The Heliopolis version of the Egyptian story of creation may have inspired the ancient Hebrews as well. Both stories of creation emphasize the importance of water and nature as a whole. They also show the creation of the universe as a process, beginning with light, continuing with the sky and the earth, and ending with the earth's living inhabitants. Although the two faiths are decidedly different in structure, there are many similarities between their stories of how the universe came into being.

Michael P. Auerbach, MA

BIBLIOGRAPHY

Armour, Robert A. *Gods and Myths of Ancient Egypt*. 2nd rev. ed. Cairo: American U in Cairo P, 2006. Print.

Budge, E. A. Wallis. "The History of Creation¾A." *Legends of the Gods: The Egyptian Texts*. London: Paul, 1912. 2-7. Print.

Fadl, Ayman. "Egyptian Creation Myth: Heliopolis Version."*Ancient Egypt on a Comparative Method*. Fadl, 4 Dec. 2012. Web. 23 Sept. 2013.

Leeming, David A. "Egyptian." *Creation Myths of the World: An Encyclopedia*. 2nd ed. Vol. 1. Santa Barbara: ABC-CLIO, 2010. 102–6. Print.

Spence, Lewis. *Myths & Legends of Ancient Egypt*. Boston: Nickerson, 1915. Print.

◆ The Gods of Egypt

Author: Traditional
Time Period: 5000 BCE–2500 BCE
Country or Culture: Egypt
Genre: Myth

PLOT SUMMARY

The world is nothing but chaos, existence nothing but the swirling waters of disorder. From these waters comes Atum (or Tem), a god who contains within him all the gods and goddesses to come. Atum begins to give order to the universe by creating these deities, each one encompassing a different aspect of existence that had once been held within him. The gods include the Ennead, nine deities who represent nine of the most fundamental aspects of the cosmos. Among the Ennead are Geb, the god of the earth; Shu, who is the air; and Nut, who is the sky. As Geb and Nut are so close to one another, joined by the horizon, they quickly produce four children: Isis, Osiris, Nephthys, and Set (Seth).

In some Egyptian lands, particularly in Heliopolis, the people know Atum by the name of Ra (Re). Ra is the sun and the giver of life, and as such, he is the ruler of gods and men alike. While Ra is always a deity of great power, over time, his descendents come to rule, and so after many years, Osiris sits as the leader of Egypt, with the goddess Isis at his side as his wife and queen. Osiris is a force of *maat*, the necessary order and logic that governs the Egyptian world and keeps it safe from the chaos that preceded and surrounds civilization. Osiris happily protects maat and the Egyptian people until he is one day attacked by his brother, Set, who slays him. Set is a force of chaos and resents the leadership and order that Osiris represents.

After Osiris's murder, Isis enlists the aid of Thoth, god of magic, and Anubis, god of funerals and death, and resurrects her brother-husband. Isis can keep Osiris alive for only a brief period of time, during which she takes the form of a giant bird and conceives a child by him. That child is Horus, who bears the head of a bird and serves as a god of the sun.

With the birth of Horus, Osiris is sent to the Duat, the land of the dead. There, he governs as a powerful force, reigning in a land apart from the order of life and maat. In the land of the living, Horus begins a long battle with Set, with Horus defending the logic of the universe and Set constantly trying to bring back the chaos that preceded Egypt. While they battle, the god Ra continues his daily journey through the sky as the sun, entering the Duat every evening and clashing with Apep (Apophis), a serpent god who also champions chaos. Many other gods thrive and do battle in Egypt, and the struggles for power both in the realm of the living and in the Duat continue for ages. The gods associated with the Ennead, however, hold the strongest influence over the pharaohs, temples, and mortals of the land, and their ongoing struggles define the nature of the universe itself.

SIGNIFICANCE

Egyptian mythology was subject to constant change, the particulars of myths shifting significantly depending on the city and time period in which they were told. What survives to the modern day is a pantheon in constant evolution, with different deities being combined into one and with gods and goddesses as likely to turn against one another in combat as they are to join forces. Greatly influenced by the political change and historical struggles for power that defined ancient Egypt, Egyptian mythology can be understood as carefully reflecting the complex and nuanced worldview that permeated that culture and religion.

The mythology of ancient Egypt focuses on the tensions between order and chaos that define the universe. It also relies on metaphors of nonlinear time, the cycles of the seasons, and the types of changes that come about through repetition. The gods of Egypt, then, do not represent a consistent idea, such as Ra standing in for the sun and supreme leadership, but rather show core concepts of the culture magnified and made prismatic across a variety of stories: Ra is but one god of the sun, and his leadership extends to his heirs and to the pharaohs in such a way that he remains the ultimate king while allowing other figures to assume power. It is by this logic that Atum and Ra can be both independent deities and a single figure, Atum-Ra, while at the same time Ra can exist as Amen-Ra (Amun-Ra or Amon-Ra), another supreme ruler and composite of several mythological traditions.

For the ancient Egyptians, the stories of the gods seem to have fulfilled a distinct function. The Egyptian world was conceived of as a rare and tenuous order located within the swirling chaos of the cosmos and characterized by the annual flooding of the Nile River and the constant rise and fall of the sun. The gods, in their ongoing dramas, give life to that order. Chaos tries to intrude through the actions of Set and Apep; magic brightens and complicates the mundane world through the presence of Isis; and the core force of life, the sun, dies and is born again through the journey of Ra and his nightly meeting with Osiris. The complexity of Egyptian mythology is fitting. The greatest mysteries of the universe are not for humans to understand but for them to observe, always inventing new vocabularies and new stories in order to create some sense of order in a world perpetually on the edge of chaos.

T. Fleischmann, MFA

BIBLIOGRAPHY

Hart, George. *Egyptian Myths*. Austin: U of Texas P, 2004. Print.

Meeks, Dimitri, and Christine Favard-Meeks. *Daily Life of the Egyptian Gods*. Trans. G. M. Goshgarian. Ithaca: Cornell UP, 1996. Print.

Pinch, Geraldine. *Handbook of Egyptian Mythology*. Santa Barbara: ABC-CLIO, 2002. Print.

Troche, Julia. "Why Osiris?" *Calliope* 22.1 (2011): 18+. Print.

Tyldesley, Joyce. "Atum: Creating The World." *Ancient Egypt Magazine* Dec. 2011: 25–27. Print.

◆ Horus and the City of Pe

Author: Traditional
Time Period: 5000 BCE–2500 BCE
Country or Culture: Egypt
Genre: Myth

PLOT SUMMARY

Horus and Set (Seth) have been at war with one another for many years, and although Horus has the gods of the Egyptian pantheon supporting him, their battle has still not come to an end. Horus is the god of the sky and the patron deity of Lower Egypt, the fertile northern valley. Horus has the head of a falcon and is the son of the great gods Isis and Osiris. Set, in contrast, is the god of chaos, who comes from the vast desert of Upper Egypt. His head resembles an aardvark or a mule, and years ago, he slew Osiris, his brother.

Set is a wily god, capable of taking the form of any animal or human and of deceiving even other gods with his illusions. Horus, however, is an honest and just god, and so he does not rely on tricks as Set does. Instead, Horus has deep blue eyes that reflect the future back to anyone who gazes into them. One day, Set hears that the sun god Ra (Re) has planned to consult with Horus and gaze into his eyes. Set knows that this will be an ideal time to attack Horus, so he takes the form of a fierce black pig, larger than any normal pig and with tusks of incredible sharpness.

Ra arrives and gazes into the magical eyes of Horus, seeing reflected back to him gorgeous green waters with the light of the sun sparkling on their surface. He only stares at this pleasing image for a moment, however, before Set passes by in his pig form, startling Ra. With both gods distracted, Set blasts fire into Horus's open, vulnerable eye, causing Horus to cry out in pain.

Horus immediately realizes that the pig must have been Set, but by the time he recovers from the burn, Set has disappeared. Enraged, Ra curses the pig, saying that swine will from now on be an abomination to the god Horus. For this reason, pigs will be sacrificed to Horus every full moon, and those who raise swine will be forbidden from entering any temples and their children forbidden from marrying any person who worships the gods. Wishing also to compensate Horus for his injury, Ra gives him the city of Pe. This so pleases Horus that plants and flowers across the world begin to blossom and thunderclouds fade away.

SIGNIFICANCE

This minor fray between Horus and Set is one in a long history of conflicts between the two gods in Egyptian mythology. Horus is one of the oldest gods in ancient Egypt, and his personifications and histories evolve to such a great degree that many scholars consider the Horus of different eras to in fact be distinct (although directly related) deities. Set is likewise an ancient god, the brother and murderer of the god Osiris.

As Set and Horus battle through Egyptian mythology, their clashes are used to give meaning to a number of historical facts and natural occurrences. On a basic level, for instance, this narrative includes the maiming of Horus, whose left eye is permanently damaged by Set. Horus was often portrayed in falcon form, and the passing of the sun and the moon across the sky were explained as his two eyes shining as he traversed the earth. The fact that the moon is always dimmer than the sun is explained by this story, as the magical eye is no longer fully able to radiate its light after the injury.

Just as important, however, this myth deepens the long history of conflict and eventual unification between Upper and Lower Egypt (Upper Egypt being further south, as the Nile River runs south to north). Much of the political history, like much of the mythology, remains unclear after so many centuries; however, it seems likely that Horus was a sky god worshipped by people outside of the Nile region, whereas Set was a god worshipped by people indigenous to the area. As the worshippers of Horus invaded and conquered the Nile delta, Horus was incorporated into the greater Egyptian pantheon and Set's mythology was revised to make him an evil, hated deity. When Ra gives the city of Pe over to

Horus, then, one of the oldest and most powerful Egyptian gods is passing power on to another. Because Pe was an important cultural hub, this endorsement by Ra both legitimizes the Horus cult and shames the religious and political power associated with Set. It was later believed that the predynastic leaders who ruled Pe prior to the unification of Lower and Upper Egypt lived on as bird-headed, godlike beings. Called the Souls of Pe, their eternal role was to greet new pharaohs and offer protection over the region, strongly linking the mythology of Horus to the political stability of the delta. Despite the haziness around historical information, then, the story of Set maiming Horus provides a significant amount of depth to the understanding of the cultures that vied for power and influence in ancient Egypt.

T. Fleischmann, MFA

BIBLIOGRAPHY

Bunson, Margaret. *Encyclopedia of Ancient Egypt*. New York: Infobase, 2002. Print.

Cicarma, Elena Andra. "The Diversity and the Theriomorphism of Horus as the Exponent of Pharaonic Royalty: His Local Nomatic and Syncretic Henotheistic Hypostases." *Scientific Journal of Humanistic Studies* 5.8 (2013): 78–84. Print.

David, Rosalie. *The Ancient Egyptians: Beliefs and Practices*. Portland: Sussex Academic, 1988. Print.

Frankfort, Henri. *Kingship and the Gods*. Chicago: U of Chicago P, 1978. Print.

Murray, M. A. "The Black Pig." *Legends of Ancient Egypt*. Mineola: Dover, 2000. 56–58. Print.

◆ Instruction of Amenemhet

Author: Traditional
Time Period: 5000 BCE–2500 BCE
Coutnry or Culture: Egypt
Genre: Myth

PLOT SUMMARY

The poetic instructions of Amenemhet begin with a brief introduction of the author, King Amenemhet (Ammenemes) I, and intended recipient, his son Senusret (Sesotris or Senwosret). Amenemhet first wishes Senusret fortune in his reign and then advises him not to trust others. Amenemhet describes the various ways in which he showed kindness to others and how others betrayed him each time; he instructs his son not to become close to anyone and risk the same thing happening to him. Amenemhet gives his ultimate reason for this way of thinking: he himself was the victim of an assassination attempt.

Amenemhet describes the night of the assassination attempt. He had let his guard down and was dozing when he heard the sound of people fighting. At first he tried to stay out of sight, but when he finally joined the fray, he realized he was fighting with his own guards. Here, Amenemhet is apologetic, saying that had he risen to fight sooner, he might have been able to defeat his enemies; however, he lacked the courage to do so because he was alone and the hour was late.

Depending on the interpretation of his next words, Amenemhet either dies or is gravely wounded in this fight. His injury causes him to lament the fact that he has not made his joint rule with Senusret public and that his advisers are unaware that he wants to do so. He expresses shock that such an unexpected and violent thing has happened and denounces his disloyal servants for their betrayal.

In the final portion of the myth, Amenemhet defends his person and his reign by describing the various deeds he accomplished during his lifetime. These deeds included extensive traveling, fighting creatures such as lions and crocodiles, conquering various enemies, and making his realm prosperous through good relations with the local gods. He also accumulated enough wealth to decorate his lavish dwelling with gold, lapis lazuli, silver, and bronze. None of these accomplishments and riches, however, is as important to him as his son, and so he expresses his wish that Senusret will prosper. Amenemhet implies that Senusret's reign is what the gods wish and that he has prepared everything in order to ensure a smooth transition. Finally, he bids Senusret to continue to worship the gods, prepare well for his own death, remain an upstanding person, and continue the prosperous reign that Amenemhet began.

SIGNIFICANCE

Many copies of the instructions in this Egyptian myth have survived, indicating that this was likely considered a classic in ancient Egypt. Two major competing theories seek to explain the circumstances of its composition, stating that it was composed by Senusret I as propaganda or that it was written by Amenemhet himself an assertion of his joint rule with Senusret. What both schools agree upon is that these instructions are highly poetic

and offer a very bitter perspective; in them, Amenemhet advises his son to trust no one.

The theory that these instructions were written by Senusret assumes that Amenemhet was killed in the assassination attempt described in the story and that either Senusret or an individual named Khety, who is credited with recording the myth, intentionally set the story from Amenemhet's perspective to evoke sympathy in the reader. Amenemhet supposedly returns as a ghost to apprise Senusret of what happened and to advise him not to make the same mistakes. This interpretation also relies heavily on the brief sections in the beginning and end of the story that address Senusret directly and wish him success in his reign.

The competing theory argues that Amenemhet was not killed in the assassination attempt recorded in the story. There is no direct evidence in the story to suggest that he was killed, and the dates of his death do not line up with the timing of this tale. Rather than propaganda, this theory suggests that because this father-son pair formed Egypt's first coregency, this tale was actually written by Amenemhet to help legitimize the institution. When Amenemhet was targeted in the assassination attempt, he had not yet made any public proclamation of his intent that they should rule together. The event likely made him aware of the challenges they faced, and he may have written it to serve as a public declaration of their joint rule. Another interpretation is that Amenemhet wrote it in order to explain to his son the circumstances of the rebellion and to emphasize his lack of involvement in the event, casting himself as the victim. This helps explain the fact that the myth is very sympathetic to Amenemhet's character when it would seem to make more logical sense for it to be sympathetic to Senusret.

Finally, the content of this myth draws on ancient Egyptian mythology to assert the right of Amenemhet and Senusret to rule. The events described in the myth have been compared to the myths of the gods Osiris, Horus, and Set (Seth). In this interpretation, Amenemhet stands in for Osiris and Senusret for Horus, the father and son gods who ruled ancient Egypt. Those who rebelled against Amenemhet represent the traitorous and aggressive Set, god of chaos and violence. Over the course of the tale, the ancient Egyptian value of *maat* (meaning "truth" or "justice") is challenged; when father and son overcome the assassination attempt, they restore maat and thus prove their right to rule.

Haley Blum, MA

BIBLIOGRAPHY

Anthes, Rudolf. "The Legal Aspect of the Instruction of Amenemhet." *Journal of Near Eastern Studies* 16.3 (1957): 176–91. Print.

Foster, John L. *Ancient Egyptian Literature: An Anthology.* Austin: U of Texas P, 2001. Print.

Goedicke, Hans. "The Beginning of the Instruction of King Amenemhet." *Journal of the American Research Center in Egypt* 7 (1968): 15–21. Print.

Simpson, William Kelly, ed. *The Literature of Ancient Egypt: An Anthology of Stories, Instructions, and Poetry.* New Haven: Yale UP, 1972. Print.

Theriault, Carolyn A. "*The Instruction of Amenemhet* as Propaganda." *Journal of the American Research Center in Egypt* 30 (1993): 151–60. Print.

◆ Isis and the Seven Scorpions

Author: Traditional
Time Period: 5000 BCE–2500 BCE
Country or Culture: Egypt
Genre: Myth

PLOT SUMMARY

Isis is a powerful goddess and magician, capable of bringing gods back to life from the dead. She has a formidable enemy in her brother Set, an evil god who murdered her husband and brother, Osiris. One day, Isis receives an omen from the god Thoth, who urges her to flee her home. The omen suggests that Set might attempt to harm her again.

Isis gathers seven fearsome scorpions to travel with her and offer protection. Before she leaves, she instructs the scorpions not to attack any person that they pass. With the creatures flanking her, she roams throughout Egypt, passing through cities where they worship different gods and goddesses. Finally, she reaches the northern lands of swamps and marshes, and she and her scorpions gaze upon the green waters and the fields of papyrus.

In this land, Isis comes to the house of a woman named Glory. Isis is exhausted and weary from travel, and when she sees Glory at the door of her gorgeous home, she hopes to sit down and rest. However, Glory sees the scorpions that accompany Isis and shuts the door before the goddess can approach. Slightly farther, a poor woman of the marsh likewise sees Isis approaching. Rather than shut her door, she welcomes Isis and the scorpions inside, where they can finally rest.

Once inside, all of the creatures gather around the scorpion Tefen and touch their stingers to his, depositing some of their poison there. Tefen then creeps to the home of Glory, crawling through a crack beneath the door, and finds Glory's infant son. With the strength of all the scorpions' poisons inside of him, he lashes out and stings the baby. The poison is so strong that it not only kills the baby but also causes a fire to erupt inside of the home. Glory cries out to heaven, asking for mercy, but instead a storm gathers and begins to batter her home. She sobs and sobs, wishing she had not shut the door in the face of Isis, and eventually her moaning is so loud that Isis hears it.

Isis then goes to where Glory cries over her dead baby and begins an incantation. She announces her own name and calls on the god Horus, listing the great deeds of which she is capable. Speaking the name of each scorpion, she draws their poison out of the baby. Eventually, her great words are so powerful that the child comes back to life, the fire relents, and the storm passes. Glory is so thankful that she gathers up all of her riches and brings them to the poor marsh woman, who had known to show Isis compassion. The words of Isis are so powerful that for years people recite them over scorpion wounds, drawing out the poison and healing the injured.

SIGNIFICANCE

The goddess Isis is one of the most prevalent deities in ancient Egyptian mythology, and her extended conflicts and romances with Osiris and Set provide the backdrop for many myths. While her antagonistic relationship with Set lingers in the background of this story, however, the main narrative departs into the territory of another god.

Although never named here, this manifestation of Isis and her scorpions relies heavily on the mythology of the goddess Serket. Serket is a goddess of the scorpion, believed to heal the poisons inflicted by the creatures. As the scorpions that heavily populate Egypt are among the most lethal in the world, the treatment of their wounds has played a prominent role in Egyptian culture. Serket was originally a unique goddess associated with her own rituals and cults. She was believed to protect the bodies of those who have died, guarding them in their transition to the underworld, and to have power over the breath of the living (scorpion stings cause the throat to constrict, suffocating the victim). As the healing goddess Isis gained prominence in the Egyptian pantheon, however, the two were slowly combined, until many Egyptian belief systems taught that Serket was no more than Isis in an additional form. This was a common occurrence in the formation of Egyptian mythology—gods were brought together as cities gained power and spread the influence of their cults over smaller, localized belief systems.

In this particular myth, Isis stands as a unique deity, grounded in her conflict with Set and evoking the name of Horus, with whom she would come to be strongly associated. Serket's presence is brought about in the scorpions themselves, who can be understood as a manifestation of the goddess attending to and supporting Isis. The twofold nature of the goddesses provides an important duality: the invocation of the goddess Serket, who often appears either as a scorpion or with a scorpion upon her head, is meant to show respect and humility toward the deadly poison, while the invocation of Isis is a more direct call for healing and relief from the sting. For this reason, the narrative of Isis seeking shelter with her seven scorpions was often used in healing spells, spoken by countless people over the bodies of friends and relatives who had suffered the poison of a scorpion or a snake. As the myth of Isis spread in the Roman world, the narrative was sometimes acted out at festivals, with devotees of Isis handling live scorpions as a show of their devotion.

The myth of Isis and the scorpions highlights the importance of both the goddess's cult and the appreciation of the natural world that comes alongside it. It is a story of the power of Isis and of the scorpion, the ladies of the marsh demonstrating fear and humility to both at once. Over time, this power intensified rather than fading, with statues of Isis sometimes even appropriating the ominous scorpion head of Serket, the goddesses of healing and of poison brought together in one resonant image.

T. Fleischmann, MFA

BIBLIOGRAPHY

Capel, Anne K., and Glenn Markoe, eds. *Mistress of the House, Mistress of Heaven: Women in Ancient Egypt.* New York: Hudson Hills, 1996. Print.

Murray, M. A. "The Scorpions of Isis." *Ancient Egyptian Legends.* 1920. *Sacred Texts.* John Bruno Hare, 2009. Web. 4 June 2013.

Pinch, Geraldine. *Egyptian Mythology: A Guide to the Gods, Goddesses, and Traditions of Ancient Egypt.* Oxford: Oxford UP, 2002. Print.

---. *Magic in Ancient Egypt.* Austin: U of Texas P, 1994. Print.

Tyldesley, Joyce. "Isis: Great of Magic." *Ancient Egypt Magazine* 13.1 (2012): 50–53. Print.

◆ The Island of Enchantment

Author: Traditional
Time Period: 5000 BCE–2500 BCE
Country or Culture: Egypt
Genre: Myth

PLOT SUMMARY

A high-ranking Egyptian returns home after an unsuccessful mission to the south. He must now report to the pharaoh and is nervous about how his failure will be received. One of his comrades exhorts him to face the monarch with confidence and avoid stuttering; to encourage his companion further, the comrade tells the story of his own earlier voyage.

The unnamed companion once went on a mission bound for the pharaoh's mines to the south. He sailed with 120 brave crewmen aboard a ship 180 feet long and 60 feet wide. As they neared shore in the land of Punt, the vessel was overtaken by a violent storm, and waves smashed the ship against the rocks. The narrator managed to cling to a piece of wooden flotsam and was cast ashore on the island, the only survivor of the shipwreck. For three days, the castaway rested and foraged, finding abundant food. In gratitude for being spared from death, he built a fire drill, kindled a blaze, and made burnt offerings to the gods.

Suddenly, the marooned sailor heard a thunderous sound. The ground shook and the trees bent. It was not another storm, as he feared, but a gigantic serpent, with golden scales and blue eyes and a three-foot beard. Thinking himself in the presence of a god, the sailor prostrated himself. The snake spoke, asking the sailor three times what he was doing on the island. The snake threatened the sailor with destruction if he did not answer, boasting it could spit fire. But the sailor was so terrified he could barely speak. The snake gently picked up the sailor in his huge fanged mouth and took him to his lair without biting him. The serpent again asked three times who brought him to the island.

Gathering his wits, the sailor told the serpent he was sole survivor of a shipwreck. The snake, mollified, predicted the castaway would remain on the island for four months before he was rescued. The serpent then told his own tragic tale: his whole family, seventy-five children and other relatives in all, were wiped out, burned up when a star fell on the island. The bearded serpent alone survived.

The sailor—sorrowed by the fate of his benefactor's relatives, but relieved to learn his own destiny—promised to praise the serpent when he again reached civilization. He would have gifts brought and make burnt offerings to the serpent, as he would to any respected god. The serpent laughed, because he already had everything he needed. The snake told the man that, once he is rescued, he will never see the island again, saying that "it will become water" (Erman 34).

The unnamed companion tells the Egyptian missionary that everything the serpent foretold has come to pass. From a treetop, the marooned sailor spied a rescue ship. The serpent gave the man a wealth of parting gifts, including myrrh, kohl eye cosmetic, giraffes' tails, elephant tusks, greyhounds, monkeys, apes, and other valuables. The sailor boarded the ship and, after two months, reached the palace of the pharaoh to present the treasures the serpent had given him. The monarch rewarded him in kind, making him a royal assistant. After finishing his tale, the royal assistant reminds the anxious missionary that he can still succeed despite bad luck. The assistant gives the nobleman a final piece of advice: be humble.

SIGNIFICANCE

"The Island of Enchantment," variously known as "The Shipwrecked Sailor" and "The Sailor and the Serpent," among other similar names, is drawn from a Middle Kingdom (ca. 2133 BCE–1600 BCE) papyrus dating from the early twentieth century BCE. The first known example of the exotic adventure motifs involving a sole survivor cast away on an island—the progenitor of such stories as the *Odyssey*, *Robinson Crusoe*, and *Moby-Dick*—the tale probably originated much earlier. The scribe mentioned at the end of the papyrus, Ameny, son of Amenyaa, was likely commissioned during the reign of Twelfth Dynasty founder Amenemhet I (1991 BCE–1962 BCE) to adapt the tale as in allusion to that pharaoh's many profitable southern excursions. The scribe is said to have invented the literary framing device—an

introduction and conclusion—bracketing the story's main events.

Rumors about the mysterious land of Punt referred to in the papyrus had begun to circulate in Egypt by 3500 BCE. Egyptian expeditions to Punt were initiated by 2500 BCE and continued at least into the Eighteenth Dynasty (ca. 1550 BCE–ca. 1292 BCE). More than five thousand years after its first mention, scholars still debate the location of Punt. Because of the flora that produced fragrant oils, exotic fauna, desirable spices, and incense enumerated in the story, the most common modern candidates for Punt are the regions around the Horn of Africa or the heel of the Arabian Peninsula, though some speculate that Punt may have lain as far south as the island of Madagascar.

Besides providing a glimpse into ancient Egyptian commerce and trade, "The Island of Enchantment" also hints at courtly protocol, outlines contemporary religious rituals, and offers a few details of bygone maritime practices in its mentions of moorings and parts of ships.

Perhaps most interesting and relevant to modern readers, the tale demonstrates that, despite more than five millennia, certain aspects of human nature have not significantly changed. After the shipwrecked sailor has told his story, the fabulous serpent relates his own poignant tale of the destruction of his entire family and a human child when a star (likely a meteorite) fell and incinerated them. The serpent urges the sailor, when he returns home, to immediately "embrace thy children and kiss thy wife and see thine house—that is the best thing of all" (Erman 33). That is the moral of "The Island of Enchantment," as valid now as then: family is more precious than any treasure.

Jack Ewing

BIBLIOGRAPHY

Baroud, Mahmud. *The Shipwrecked Sailor in Arabic and Western Literature: Ibn Tufayl and his Influence on European Writers*. New York: Tauris Academic Studies, 2012. Print.

Erman, Adolf, ed. "The Story of the Shipwrecked Sailor." *The Ancient Egyptians: A Sourcebook of Their Writings*. New York: Harper, 1966. 29–35. Print.

Goedicke, Hans. *Studies in "The Instructions of King Amenemhet I for His Son."* San Antonio: Van Siclen, 1988. Print.

Robson, Eric. *In Search of Punt: Queen Hatshepsut's Land of Marvels*. Trenton: Red Sea, 2007. Print.

Shaw, Ian, ed. *The Oxford History of Ancient Egypt.* New York: Oxford UP, 2004. Print.

Weigall, Arthur. *A History of the Pharaohs Volume II: From the Accession of Amenemhet I of the Twelfth Dynasty to the Death of Thutkose III of the Eighteenth Dynasty, 211 to 1441 B.C.* Boston: Dutton, 1927. Print.

The Name of Ra

Author: Traditional
Time Period: 5000 BCE–2500 BCE
Country or Culture: Egypt
Genre: Myth

PLOT SUMMARY

The goddess Isis loves the gods and goddesses more than humans, and she wants to become as powerful as the god Ra (Re) and have control over the heavens and the earth. Isis decides that if she can learn the secret name of Ra, which grants him his powers, she will be able to achieve her goal. Ra travels through the sky every day, emerging from the eastern horizon in the morning and journeying across the sky until he exits below the western horizon every night. At this point, the god Ra has traveled this path so often that he has become old, and his spittle falls to the ground as he sits on his heavenly thrones each day. In order to trick him and learn his secret name, Isis collects this spittle and mixes it with earth, shaping it into a viper and placing it in the path that Ra walks every day. Because it contains the power of Ra, she does not need to rely on her magic to bring it to life.

Ra rises the next day and traverses this path accompanied by a host of other gods. As he passes the viper, it springs to life and strikes him with its fangs. His cry of pain is heard throughout the heavens, and one after another, the other gods ask him what is wrong. Ra is so weak from the poisonous bite that he is at first unable to answer them. When he finds the strength, he pleads with them to find someone with divine powers to heal him.

Among the gods and goddesses who come to his aid is Isis, who is well known for her prowess in healing. Ra describes his symptoms and Isis assures him that she can heal him as long as he tells her his name. He agrees and tells her all the various names humankind has given him based on the various powers he holds over the heavens and earth. He is not healed. Isis tells him that these names are not enough and that she cannot heal him without knowing his true name. Ra feels incredible pain from the viper's poison, and he finally agrees to tell her. He hides himself from all the other gods and causes his name to pass directly from his body into hers. He instructs her not to tell anyone his name except her son, Horus.

Isis tells Horus that she has obtained the secret name of Ra and that she will use this power to make Ra give up his eyes to Horus. Because of this, the eyes of Horus are the eyes of Ra; one is the moon, and the other is the sun. Once this is accomplished, Isis casts a spell and uses the eye of Horus to remove the poison from Ra's body.

This myth refers to Isis as the queen of the gods and instructs the reader to depend on her when trying to heal a person who has been poisoned. It includes a section saying that one should repeat the words of Isis's spell over images of Horus and Isis in order to help them heal.

SIGNIFICANCE

Isis is a very important goddess in Egyptian mythology. As described in the myth above, she was often viewed as the queen of the gods and was associated with healing and childbirth. She was sometimes called the Female Ra and was often considered Ra's equal. She was the wife of Osiris, the god of the dead and of the Nile River, and her son, Horus, is the traditional ruler of Egypt. This myth is particularly important because, in it, Isis overcomes an aged Ra and ultimately becoming just as powerful as the king of the gods. Here is an example of the strength of the goddesses of the Egyptian pantheon. This was perhaps a reflection of the power of Egyptian women, who were considered equal to men in the eyes of the law for much of ancient Egyptian history. Property was often passed from mother to daughter rather than from father to son, and if the pharaoh had no male heir, a woman could take the throne.

Isis is sometimes portrayed in art as having the head of a snake. The snake is traditionally an important symbol in Egyptian mythology. It can stand for the Eye of Ra, which is described as being a separate goddess who once punished humanity and then transformed into a snake when she returned to Ra. In a more general sense, it can be a symbol of any Egyptian goddess.

Another interesting aspect of this myth is the fact that Ra feels the effects of age. There is some debate over how time works in Egyptian myths. One theory is that myths about gods occur in one of two ways: for creation myths, they occur in an eternal present where the gods do not change, but in other myths, they are considered to exist in an actual historical time where they are subject to normal human problems and desires. Ra's age in this myth falls into the latter category; this explains why he can be portrayed as being frail and fallible and still be considered a powerful god.

In Egyptian mythology, various parts of one god or goddess can manifest as a separate god or goddess, such as the Eye of Ra mentioned above. Osiris, Isis's husband, is sometimes considered the soul or name of Ra, and there is some speculation that the secret name Isis learned was actually that of her husband.

Haley Blum, MA

BIBLIOGRAPHY

El-Aswad, el-Sayed. "Archaic Egyptian Cosmology." *Anthropos Institute* 92 (1997): 69–81. Print.

Budge, Ernest A. Wallis. *Egyptian Tales and Romances.* 1931. New York: Arno, 1980. Print.

Knapp, Bettina. "The Archetypal Woman Fulfilled: Isis, Harmony of Flesh/Spirit/Logos." *Symposium: A Quarterly Journal in Modern Literatures* 50.1 (1996): 28–39. Print.

Murray, M. A. "The Name of Ra." *Ancient Egyptian Legends.* London: Murray, 1920. 80–85. Print.

Pinch, Geraldine. *Egyptian Myth: A Very Short Introduction.* Oxford: Oxford UP, 2004. Print.

 **The Rise of Amen**

Author: Traditional
Time Period: 5000 BCE–2500 BCE
Country or Culture: Egypt
Genre: Myth

PLOT SUMMARY

When Egyptian civilization rises in the fourth millennium BCE, a complicated religious system is already well formed. A large and diverse pantheon of deities represents benevolent and destructive aspects of nature, with major gods taking on familiar physical forms, including those of snakes, falcons, crocodiles, lions, and hippopotamuses. Priesthoods supporting particular deities spring up in population centers to guide worshippers through ceremonies in propitiating the gods.

The head of the pantheon is the sun, a predominating force in Egypt, envisioned at different times and locations as a scarab beetle (Khepri), an elderly man (Atum), or a soaring falcon (Horus). Most often, the sun is known as Ra (or Re). This god's center of worship is in the northern community of Iunu, which Greek colonists later named Heliopolis. Other cities also support favorite deities, such as Neith in Saïs, Thoth in Hermopolis, Osiris in Busiris, Ptah in Memphis, and Sobek in Crocodilopolis.

In Waset, later known as Thebes, more than four hundred miles from the seat of power, the patron god is Amen (Amun or Amon). A lesser deity in predynastic times (before roughly 3000 BCE), Amen controls the wind. His name means "the hidden one" or "he who is concealed," possibly because the wind can be felt but not seen. At Thebes, Amen leads a triad that also includes his consort, Amaunet, and his son, moon god Khonsu, and heads an eight-member group of gods called the Ogdoad.

Amen languishes primarily as a local god while the national government gravitates south to Memphis, Herakleopolis, Hermopolis, and Abydos. In the Eleventh and Twelfth Dynasties (ca. 2055–1773 BCE), during the period known as the Middle Kingdom, the city of Thebes rises to political prominence, as does its patron deity. Dubbed Amen-Ra to incorporate solar power, he is now elevated to the status of a creator god. His position is improved when several pharaohs are named in his honor, beginning with Amenemhat I.

Thebes and Amen-Ra suffer setbacks at the end of the Middle Kingdom. The Hyksos, a people from western Asia, conquer much of Egypt in the mid-seventeenth century BCE and rule for a century from their northern capital of Avaris. In about 1550 BCE, Ahmose I (also known as Iahmose) ushers in the New Kingdom and the Eighteenth Dynasty by driving out the Hyksos and establishing Thebes as his capital. His success initiates a nearly five-hundred-year-long period of Theban dominance marked by military expansion, conquest, and wealth.

A multifaceted national deity and king of the gods, Amen-Ra becomes supreme during this period. Though usually portrayed as a man, he incorporates the attributes of other divine figures and thus is at times depicted with the head of an ape, lion, frog, snake, ram, bull, or sphinx. His rise to power spurs the pharaohs, as semidivine representatives of the deity, to build temples throughout Egypt, particularly at Luxor and Karnak. The priesthood that develops during this time will go on to play a pivotal role in the development of Egyptian religion, culture, and politics.

SIGNIFICANCE

Although Thebes prospered for centuries following the expulsion of the Hyksos and spread the worship of Amen-Ra through settlement and conquest, the patron god's period of dominance did not go uninterrupted. Two centuries after the restoration of Thebes as the controlling power and Amen-Ra as dominant god in Egypt, Amenhotep (or Amenophis) IV took the throne. Possibly dissatisfied with the prevailing authority of the priesthood, Amenhotep declared a new national religion centered on a single supreme and benevolent sun god, Aten (Aton), which featured personal communication between worshippers and the deity, without priests as intermediaries. To demonstrate his complete conversion to the faith, Amenhotep changed his name to Akhenaten in honor of the god. He also commanded that all signs of Amen-Ra—even the name of his own father, Amenhotep III—be chiseled off temples. Akhenaten further did away with the existing priesthood and the entire community that had grown up around the adoration of Amen-Ra. These actions were unpopular in Thebes, and Akhenaten eventually moved two hundred miles north with his family and followers, establishing his new capital at Amarna.

After Akhenaten's death, which left the kingdom in turmoil for a short period, his young son Tutankhaten succeeded him as pharaoh. He relocated to Thebes, abandoning Amarna to the desert, and hastily changed his name to Tutankhamen to signify the return of Amen as chief god. The priesthood was fully restored, and visible signs of Aten and Akhenaten were obliterated. Religion in Egypt resumed its pre-Akhenaten mode during its years of greatest glory in the Nineteenth Dynasty (ca. 1295–1186 BCE), and Karnak was expanded to become one of the largest religious complexes ever constructed. The worship of Amen-Ra spread throughout Egypt and into other lands, and the god would remain one of the most significant mythological figures in the region for many centuries.

Jack Ewing

BIBLIOGRAPHY

Breasted, James Henry. *A History of the Ancient Egyptians*. New York: Scribner's, 1908. Print.

Budge, E. A. Wallis. *The Egyptian Book of the Dead*. New York: Dover, 1967. Print.

Erman, Adolf, ed. "The Great Hymn to Amun." *The Ancient Egyptians: A Sourcebook of Their Writings*. New York: Harper, 1966. 283–88. Print.

Hart, George. *The Routledge Dictionary of Egyptian Gods and Goddesses*. London: Routledge, 2005. Print.

Mackenzie, Donald. *Egyptian Myth and Legend*. London: Gresham, 1907. Print.

Redford, Donald B., ed. "Amun and Amun-Re." *The Oxford Encyclopedia of Ancient Egypt*. Vol. 1. New York: Oxford UP, 2001. 82–85. Print.

Wilkinson, Richard H. *The Complete Gods and Goddesses of Ancient Egypt*. New York: Thames, 2003. Print.

Wilkinson, Toby. *The Rise and Fall of Ancient Egypt*. New York: Random, 2010. Print.

The Tale of Sinuhe

Author: Traditional
Time Period: 5000 BCE–2500 BCE
Country or Culture: Egypt
Genre: Myth

PLOT SUMMARY

Senusret (Sesostris or Senwosret), the son of King Amenemhet I (Ammenemes), is returning victorious from a war with the Tjehenu people when a messenger arrives with the news that his father has died. Sinuhe, a court official, overhears the messenger telling Senusret the news, and becomes fearful when he realizes that Senusret will become king. He flees, crossing the river in a rudderless boat and leaving Egypt. Sinuhe is taken in by the chief of Upper Retenu, who has heard of Sinuhe's intellect and character from other Egyptians crossing his lands. He asks Sinuhe why he left Egypt, but the only reason Sinuhe can give is that he felt compelled to leave, as if led to Retenu by a god. He emphasizes that he is not fearful of Senusret's rule; rather, he praises Senusret and lists the various reasons why he should be king. The chief is thus reassured and gives Sinuhe land and his eldest daughter for his wife.

Sinuhe spends many long years living well on the fertile land he has been given. He becomes a tribal leader. His wife bears children, and he watches them grow up and become tribal leaders themselves. Sinuhe becomes a rich and generous man, sheltering travelers and doing good deeds for others. One day, the strong man of Retenu, jealous of Sinuhe's wealth and favor, challenges Sinuhe to combat. Sinuhe is at first reluctant to fight, but then agrees and prepares his weapons.

During the battle, Sinuhe manages to fire an arrow into the strong man's neck and emerges victorious, to the delight of the chief of Retenu and his people. Sinuhe receives the strong man's wealth, and it is added to his own.

This prosperity is not enough for Sinuhe. As he grows older, he longs to return to Egypt once more before he dies. Finally, he sends a message to Senusret I asking that he be permitted to return. The king sends a message stating that Sinuhe has done nothing wrong, and thus is urged to return to Egypt, where he will be able to have the proper and stately burial an Egyptian courtier deserves. Upon receiving this reply, Sinuhe rejoices. He divides his wealth among his children and returns to the land of his birth.

Once inside the palace, Sinuhe has an audience with the king. The king is surprised at how much Sinuhe has changed since he has been gone and how much he has aged. The queen and her children enter the chamber, and the king must introduce Sinuhe to them because they do not recognize him. The children sing the praises of the king and ask him to turn Sinuhe over to them. The king agrees, and Sinuhe is taken to the home of one of the king's sons, where he is bathed, rubbed with oils, and dressed in fine linens. Afterward, Sinuhe is given his own estate and served meals brought from the palace itself. He is able to build a pyramid and supply it in preparation for the afterlife, and thus he passes the rest of his days enjoying the favor of the king.

SIGNIFICANCE

Among early Egyptian narratives, "The Tale of Sinuhe" from the early Twelfth Dynasty is one of the most frequently represented in existing copies and partial copies, demonstrating the popularity of the poem; in fact, scribes even copied this story for writing practice. "The Tale of Sinuhe" was important to early Egyptians because it emphasized the superiority of the Egyptian way of life and affirmed the importance of Egypt's king.

"The Tale of Sinuhe" is presented in the manner of an autobiography, which may have been done to lend credence to the tale. It is told in an *aba* format: *a* is Sinuhe's flight from Egypt, *b* is his prosperous life abroad, and the second *a* section is his return to Egypt, which closely parallels his initial flight and serves to restore his position in Egyptian society. This structure means that the main character does not have to change much over the course of the story, which implies that the myth's primary objective is not to focus on the importance of character or actions, but rather to assert the superiority of the Egyptian way of life, including the idea of proper social order. This notion of Egyptian cultural superiority is reinforced by the fact that Sinuhe is equally prosperous abroad as he is at home, yet he feels his life is lacking and keenly wishes to return home to Egypt to be buried as befits his station.

The king was the center of early Egypt in both a political and religious sense, and so it is no coincidence that he plays an important role in this myth. A king's death is what initially sends Sinuhe abroad in fear, and it is a king's grace that brings him back to Egypt at the end of the tale. Multiple lengthy sections of the text praise the king and list his virtues. Thus, one interpretation of this myth is that it was intended as propaganda in support of the king. However, this was not the king's only role; he was also viewed as a sacred being who held some authority with the gods. In the myth, when Sinuhe returns to Egypt to face King Senusret, he must leave behind his life with the desert tribes and be metaphorically reborn as an Egyptian. This parallels Egyptian creation myths: the king stands in for the creator god and the queen for Hathor, a goddess of birth and renewal. After this episode, Sinuhe becomes an Egyptian courtier once more, and when he dies, he is buried in the traditional Egyptian manner, which ultimately fulfills his proper social role.

Haley Blum, MA

BIBLIOGRAPHY

Baines, John. "Interpreting Sinuhe." *Journal of Egyptian Archaeology* 68 (1982): 31–44. Print.

Budge, Ernest A. Wallis. *Egyptian Tales and Romances*. 1931. New York: Arno, 1980. Print.

Mackenzie, Donald. "Tale of the Fugitive Prince." *Egyptian Myth and Legend*. London: Gresham, 1907. 207–20. Print.

Pinch, Geraldine. *Egyptian Myth: A Very Short Introduction*. Oxford: Oxford UP, 2004. Print.

Simpson, William Kelly, ed. *The Literature of Ancient Egypt: An Anthology of Stories, Instructions, and Poetry*. New Haven: Yale UP, 1972. Print.

The Two Brothers

Author: Traditional
Time Period: 5000 BCE–2500 BCE
Country or Culture: Egypt
Genre: Myth

PLOT SUMMARY

A pair of brothers lives in ancient Egypt. The elder, Anpu, has a wife and farm. Bata, the younger, lives with his brother as a farmhand. Strong and handsome, Bata has special powers, including the ability to communicate with animals.

One day, as Bata is retrieving a supply of seeds for planting, Anpu's wife attempts to seduce him. Bata spurns her advances and resumes his chores. When Anpu returns home, his wife, fearing Bata has revealed her lust, claims Bata tried to rape her. Enraged, Anpu lies in wait to kill his brother. A cow warns Bata of the ambush, and he runs away. Anpu pursues him. Bata prays to the gods, and his prayers are answered: a river full of crocodiles springs up between the brothers. From the far side of the reptile-infested waterway, Bata denies accusations of sexual assault and tells his brother what really happened. To prove his sincerity, Bata slices off his own genitals and flings them into the water, where fish eat them.

Bata vows to live in a far-off valley, where he will place his soul at the top of a tree. If anything happens to Bata's soul, Anpu will know: his beer will begin foaming. Bata then gives instructions for how to revive his soul, and leaves. Sad to lose his brother, Anpu returns home, kills his treacherous wife, and feeds her body to animals.

For a time, Bata lives and toils in a valley beside the sea. Sympathetic to his solitude, the gods create a beautiful but unscrupulous woman as mate for him. Bata loves her and tells her all his secrets, but emasculated, he cannot satisfy her sexually. While he works, she idles. As she is strolling by the sea, a wave surges and sweeps away a lock of her hair. The curl is carried to the shore of the pharaoh's lands. Enamored of the hair's alluring scent, the pharaoh sends soldiers to find the owner of the hair. They locate the woman and bring her back to the pharaoh, who falls in love and makes her a princess. To eliminate all traces of her former life, she soon demands that the tree where Bata's soul resides be cut down. The pharaoh so orders, and when the tree falls, Bata dies.

Meanwhile, back on the farm, Anpu's beer suddenly foams; he knows something dire has happened to his little brother. Anpu immediately leaves for his brother's home, finds Bata dead, and begins searching for his soul. Anpu finally finds the soul after three years of searching and, following Bata's earlier instructions, resurrects his brother. Bata transforms himself into a bull, and Anpu rides him to see the pharaoh.

Amazed at the talking bull, the pharaoh honors Bata with gifts. Bata's former wife, however, still wishes her husband dead, and persuades the pharaoh to kill the bull. The pharaoh does as the evil princess demands, and Bata is sacrificed. Drops of Bata's blood grow into huge trees by the pharaoh's palace, and the spirit of Bata speaks from them. The vicious princess then demands the trees be made into furniture. The smitten pharaoh cannot refuse the request and commands the tasks to be performed. While laborers chop down the trees, a chip bearing the essence of Bata flies into the mouth of the princess and impregnates her. Nine months later, a son is born. The joyous pharaoh makes him heir to the kingdom.

In time, the pharaoh dies, and his son, the reincarnated Bata, becomes ruler. He has the princess put to death, and makes Anpu heir. The new Bata rules for thirty years. When he dies, Anpu become pharaoh.

SIGNIFICANCE

One of the world's oldest written myths, "The Two Brothers," was recorded on a papyrus and a copy is kept in the British Museum in London, England. The papyrus dates from about 1200 BCE, during the reign of pharaoh Seti II (ca. 1200–1194) in the latter part of Egypt's Nineteenth Dynasty. However, it is believed that the story was composed many centuries earlier and transmitted orally over generations.

The principal characters of "The Two Brothers," Anpu and Bata, are both based on deities from the populous Egyptian pantheon. Anpu (whom the Greeks called Anubis) was originally a principal god from early Egyptian mythology. Jackal-headed Anubis was associated from the first dynasties throughout Egypt with the land of the dead, officiating at embalming ceremonies and guiding the deceased toward judgment in the underworld. Bata was likewise based on an earlier deity, one of the oldest in Egypt: Hathor, a cow-headed fertility goddess. Hathor originally represented the Egyptian concept of the universe, since the stars were symbolized as a splash of cow's milk, from which is derived the name of the Milky Way galaxy.

By the time the tale of the two brothers was transcribed in the Nineteenth Dynasty, the Egyptian gods, to become more accessible to believers, had lost some otherworldly aspects, though they retained certain divine characteristics. Anpu, in human guise, is still linked to death: he is solely responsible for bringing his deceased brother back to life. In the meantime, Bata has been transformed over time from a female cow to a male bull. His self-castration, however, renders him incapable of fatherhood by traditional means, and he must resort to magic to reproduce.

The women in the story—Anpu's unfaithful wife and Bata's vindictive, god-created mate—are never named, a fact that indicates the subservient role of females in ancient Egypt. While feminine deities were common in Egyptian mythology, in real life few women ruled throughout the country's long dynastic history; convention demanded they wear beards to conceal their gender. Though the female characters in "The Two Brothers" are anonymous, they are nonetheless memorable as prototypes of the malevolent seductress who uses sex to gain advantage. Directly or indirectly, the conniving women of the tale have inspired countless stories in world literature. Malevolent females are central to the accounts of Potiphar's wife and Salome in the Bible, the demon Lilith in Hebrew literature, the ancient Greek Siren Calypso, the mermaids of the medieval *Nibelungenlied* (ca. 1200; English translation, 1848), the banshees of Irish lore, and even more modern creations such as the femme fatale.

Jack Ewing

BIBLIOGRAPHY

Hollis, Susan Tower. *The Ancient Egyptian Tale of Two Brothers: A Mythological, Religious, Literary and Historico-Political Study*. Oakville: Bannerstone, 2008. Print.

Lichtheim, Miriam. *Ancient Egyptian Literature, Volume II: The New Kingdom*. Berkeley: U of California P, 2006. Print.

Loprieno, Antonio, ed. *Ancient Egyptian Literature: History and Forms*. Boston: Brill Academic, 1996. Print.

Maspero, Gaston, and Hasan M. El-Shamy, ed. *Popular Stories of Ancient Egypt*. New York: Oxford UP, 2004. Print.

Pinch, Geraldine. *Handbook of Egyptian Mythology*. Santa Barbara : ABC-CLIO, 2002. Print.

Shah, Indries. "Anpu and Bata." *World Tales: The Extraordinary Coincidence of Stories Told in All Times, in All Places*. New York: Harcourt, 1979. 86–92. Print.

Simpson, William Kelly, ed. *The Literature of Ancient Egypt: An Anthology of Stories, Instructions, Stelae, Autobiographies, and Poetry*. New Haven: Yale UP, 2003. Print.

◆ The Victory of Sinuhe

Author: Traditional
Time Period: 5000 BCE–2500 BCE
Country or Culture: Egypt
Genre: Myth

PLOT SUMMARY

An Egyptian courtier named Sinuhe (Senuhet) flees Egypt after the death of King Amenemhet I (Ammenemes) and travels through the desert lands. The chief of Retenu gives him shelter. He has heard of Senuhet's intelligence and is impressed when Senuhet praises Ammenemes's successor, Senusret (Sesostris or Senwosret). After a brief conversation, the chief of Retenu decides to give Sinuhe a parcel of land and his daughter's hand in marriage. Sinuhe becomes the leader of his own tribe, which provides food and other necessities for him. He is also placed in command of an army and enjoys many victories over Retenu's enemies. Sinuhe becomes prosperous and shares his good fortune by helping others.

Seeing this prosperity, a strong man of Retenu becomes jealous and challenges Sinuhe to a duel. Having conquered every opponent in Retenu, the strong man wants to defeat Sinuhe and claim his riches. Sinuhe speaks with the chief of Retenu and then takes up the challenge, believing his victory is assured. He spends the night preparing his various weapons, including his bow and his dagger.

The next morning, the strong man of Retenu arrives to face him. The people following the chief of Retenu and those on the side of the strong man all come to witness the fight. The strong man brings various heavy weapons to choose from, but Sinuhe decides to fight him with a bow and arrow, an Egyptian weapon with which he is skilled. The two face each other in battle, and Sinuhe turns aside his foe's weapons and then fires an arrow that lodges in the strong man's neck. The strong man falls, and Sinuhe finishes him with his dagger. Sinuhe is declared the winner, and the chief of Retenu joyfully embraces him. The strong man had been known as a troublemaker, and the chief and his people are overjoyed to see him defeated. Even the men who followed the strong man are pleased to be freed from his oppressive rule. Sinuhe takes the strong man's possessions, including a number of cattle, as his reward, just as the strong man had intended to do to Sinuhe. Even though he already has wealth of his own, it is increased by the spoils, and Sinuhe is able to live an even better life than before.

After his victory over the strong man, the aging Sinuhe grows dissatisfied with his life. Despite his success, he wants nothing more than to return to Egypt before he dies so that he can be buried properly in his homeland. He eventually petitions King Senusret and is allowed to return. All the riches Sinuhe accumulated in Retenu are passed down to his children, and he leaves everything behind in order to return to Egypt, where he lives out the rest of his days with peace and honor.

SIGNIFICANCE

The Egyptian myth of Sinuhe's battle with the strong man of Retenu is one episode from a larger myth about Sinuhe's flight from Egypt and eventual return. The myth is considered either a semifactual account of a historical Egyptian courtier or, more likely, a unique example of Egyptian fictional narrative written in an autobiographical style.

There are two important theories about the role this episode plays in the larger myth of Sinuhe. One interpretation is that this story was added later and possibly derived from a different source. The reasoning behind this is that the episode does not fit in with the parallel structure of the flight from Egypt and the return to Egypt, and some view Sinuhe's fight with the strong man to be tangential to the main plot. Confusion about the role of this episode is compounded by difficulties understanding the language of the original text.

However, Egyptologist Hans Goedicke has examined the language of this episode and determined that Sinuhe's victory is actually the myth's most important and telling scene. Even the choice of weapons reflects the myth's theme of the superiority of Egyptian ways over others. The strong man of Retenu brings many heavy weapons to the fight, but as the one who has been challenged, it is Sinuhe's right to choose which weapons will be used. Sinuhe thus chooses his Egyptian weapon, the bow and arrow. His skill with this weapon is remarked upon several times in the story, suggesting that proficiency with the bow and arrow was considered an important skill for an Egyptian courtier. The triumph of the Egyptian bow and arrow over the desert-dwelling strong man's heavy weapons thus becomes a metaphor for the myth's overarching theme.

Supporting this theory is the fact that Sinuhe, while prosperous in foreign lands, is in a precarious position politically. The episode with the strong man allows him to prove himself to the chief of Retenu and strengthen his position, establishing with certainty the idea that his status and quality of life are equal in both locations. This becomes important in the second half of the myth, when it is shown that between two equally prosperous lives, his life in Egypt is the one he prefers. In that respect, this episode can also be regarded as a turning point; this victory ought to have made Sinuhe happy, but on the contrary, it is after this victory that he begins to mourn for the life he left behind, eventually petitioning King Senusret to be allowed to return to Egypt.

Haley Blum, MA

BIBLIOGRAPHY

Baines, John. "Interpreting Sinuhe." *Journal of Egyptian Archaeology* 68 (1982): 31–44. Print.

Goedicke, Hans. "Sinuhe's Duel." *Journal of the American Research Center in Egypt* 21 (1984): 197–201. Print.

Mackenzie, Donald. "Tale of the Fugitive Prince." *Egyptian Myth and Legend*. London: Gresham, 1907. Print.

Pinch, Geraldine. *Egyptian Myth: A Very Short Introduction*. Oxford: Oxford UP, 2004. Print.

Simpson, William Kelly, ed. *The Literature of Ancient Egypt: An Anthology of Stories, Instructions, and Poetry*. New Haven: Yale UP, 1972. Print.

ASIA

West Asia

Mesopotamia

East Asia

India

WEST ASIA

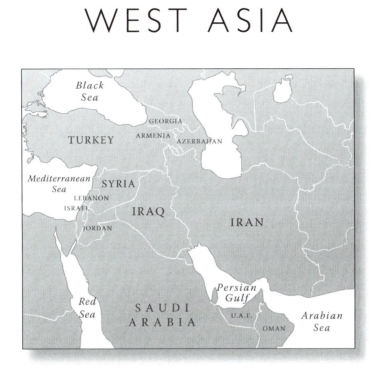

Ahura Mazda and the Battle between Good and Evil

Author: Traditional Persian
Time Period: 999 BCE–1 BCE
Country or Culture: Middle East
Genre: Myth

PLOT SUMMARY

Ahura Mazda is born of the first god in Zoroastrian lore, Zurvan. Existing alone in emptiness, Zurvan opts to create two sons. His first son, Ahura Mazda, is created to represent Zurvan's optimism, while his second son, Ahriman, symbolizes the great god's uncertainty. The core belief of Zoroastrianism is the notion that humankind will continue to evolve toward spiritual and moral perfection in the presence of the evil, illustrated in the faith's centuries-old myths by an eternal battle between the brothers.

Prior to his sons' creation, Zurvan predicts his firstborn will rule the world. Knowing this, Ahriman forces himself into the world before Ahura Mazda. However, Zurvan is keen to Ahriman's trick. Ahura Mazda takes his rightful place as ruler of the world, while his brother, Ahriman, is transformed into an evil being. Ahura Mazda and Ahriman are depicted in several relics from the period battling over a "ring of sovereignty" (Wilkinson 168) believed to represent control over the world.

Following his birth, Ahura Mazda creates the universe and all the celestial bodies within it: the sun, the moon, and the stars. He also creates six immortal beings to assist in overseeing his newly created universe. The six immortal children of Ahura Mazda are sacred beings, regarded as secondary in importance only to Ahura Mazda. The immortals oversee both divine and domestic realms, including many aspects of the natural world, leaving Ahura Mazda the ability to concentrate solely on humankind. Ahura Mazda additionally creates Gayomart, the first human man, who works under the auspices of the six immortals to perfect the world.

Vengeful about his place in the world and eager for revenge against his brother, Ahriman poisons Gayomart. Ahriman also gives birth to evil by bringing lust, pain, and death into the world, which defiles the earth. Aware that Gayomart is facing death, Ahura Mazda creates

Mashya and Mashyoi, the first human couple in the universe, whose children eventually ensure the survival of humanity. Ahura Mazda is ultimately unable to defeat Ahriman. Thus, humankind is granted the eternal choice of following either Ahura Mazda or Ahriman and their conflicting forces of good and evil.

SIGNIFICANCE

Ahura Mazda is the central figure in the ancient Iranian religion Zoroastrianism, founded in the seventh century BCE by the prophet Zoroaster. The faith is the first and oldest of all the world's monotheistic religions. Dualistic views at the basis of Zoroaster's teachings, illustrated at length in the myth of Ahura Mazda, are believed to have played an important role in the eventual development of Judaism and Christianity, both of which are predated by the foundation of Zoroastrianism.

Ahura Mazda was worshiped by the Persian king Darius I, whom ancient scholars regard as one of the greatest rules of the Achaemenid dynasty in the sixth century BCE. It is believed Ahura Mazda also played an important role in the political doctrine of Darius I, who was revered internationally for his strict adherence to the rule of law, his monetary system, and his military structure.

In fact, inscriptions on a cliff near the former site of the summer palace of Darius I indicate that Darius believed he received a divine right to rule from Ahura Mazda "When Ahuramazda saw this earth turbulent then he bestowed it on me," the inscription reads, "he made me king" (Hartz 45).

Zoroastrian worship was a common practice throughout the kingdom of Darius I, as noted by archeological evidence pointing to large-scale celebrations around open fires. But as outside cultural forces began to infiltrate the Iranian plain by the fifth century BCE, Zoroastrianism and widespread worship of Ahura Mazda began to wane.

Zoroastrianism is still practiced, though the faith's members are estimated at around only 100,000. Though few, the remaining practitioners represent evidence of the profound impact Ahura Mazda has played in humankind's cultural development of the world and of the Iranian region.

John Pritchard

BIBLIOGRAPHY

Briant, Pierre. *From Cyrus to Alexander: A History of the Persian Empire*. Winona Lake: Eisenbraun, 2002. Print.

Guzder, Deena. "The Last of the Zoroastrians." *Time*. Time, Inc., 9 Dec. 2008. Web. 10 July 2013.

Hartz, Paula R. *Zoroastrianism*. 3rd ed. New York: Chelsea, 2009. Print.

Ramakrishnan, Ram. *Many Paths, One Destination: Love, Peace, Compassion, Tolerance, and Understanding through World Religions*. Tucson: Wheatmark, 2009. Print.

Wilkinson, Philip. *Myths and Legends: An Illustrated Guide to Their Origins and Meanings*. London: Dorling Kindersley, 2009. Print.

◆ The Baal Myth from Ugarit

Author: Traditional Ugaritic
Time Period: 2499 BCE–1000 BCE
Country or Culture: Middle East
Genre: Myth

PLOT SUMMARY

The storm god Baal, known also as Ba'lu, Baal-Hadad (Haddu), or Baal Sapan, enjoys himself at a big banquet. Young deities offer him a giant goblet containing ten thousand pitchers' worth of wine. In the meantime Anat ('Anatu), Baal's sister and wife, slays humans along the coast. She attaches their severed heads to her chest and returns to the mansion of the gods, where she turns the furniture into warriors so that she can keep fighting. When she is finished, Anat washes herself with heavenly dew.

Baal sends messengers to Anat asking her to embrace peace, to oppose war, and to visit him so that he can give her a secret message. Worried, Anat puts on makeup of murex shells and visits Baal. He tells her that he still has no house of his own and must live in the mansion of Bull El (Bull Ilu), the father of the gods. Baal asks Anat to request his own home from Bull El. Anat agrees to ask Bull El, pledging to fight him if necessary.

Anat meets Bull El and finds out that he is afraid of the omen he has seen that shows Mot (Motu), the god of death, has called for Baal. When Bull El asks what Anat wants, she says that all gods must pay tribute to Baal. Bull El protests, along with the other gods. Bull El and his wife, Athirat (Athiratu), mother of the gods, entrust construction of Baal's palace to the famous craftsman Kothar-wa-Hasis (Kothar-wa-Khasis). During construction, Athirat denounces Baal to Bull El. Athirat persuades

Bull El to transfer power from Baal to his brother and enemy, Yamm (Yammu), the ruler of the sea.

At a banquet of the gods, Baal slays Yamm's messengers who demand his submission. Baal is temporarily arrested. Yamm ejects Baal from his throne on Mount Sapan (Sapanu). Yamm is promised a mansion in the sea by Bull El. Astartē, another sister of Baal, threatens Yamm with a variety of afflictions including impotence.

Kothar-wa-Hasis gives Baal a double-headed ax with which Baal strikes Yamm, but Yamm remains unharmed. Kothar-wa-Hasis gives Baal a second ax. With this, Baal hits Yamm between the eyes. Astarte shames Baal into letting Yamm live, albeit as a prisoner of war.

Despite his reservations, Bull El commands Kothar-wa-Hasis to build Baal a new house, along with a bribe for Athirat. Baal and Anat visit Athirat, who thinks they have come to assassinate her. Instead, he and Anat give Athirat gifts and hold a banquet. They ask Athirat to ask Bull El to speed the building of Baal's palace. At Bull El's residence, Athirat praises Bull El's wisdom and asks him to agree to Baal's rulership, and he accepts.

Finally, Baal's magnificent palace is ready. Baal celebrates and takes control over ninety human cities. His thunder makes the earth tremble.

Baal discovers invading messengers from Mot and invites Mot to a feast. Mot rejects angrily because he was not invited to Baal's victory banquet. Mot threatens to eat Baal alive and burns fruits of the earth with his breath.

Baal tells Mot that he will submit to him. Baal has sexual intercourse with a heifer that gives birth to his twin. Baal dresses his twin in his royal robes and sends him to Mot. Mot eats the twin, thinking he is Baal. The other gods mourn Baal's death.

Twice Anat meets Mot, who confesses that he ate Baal because he was hungry. Furious, Anat attacks Mot with a knife, a sieve, fire, and a grinding mill. She then asks Bull El to have a dream. Bull El dreams Baal is alive, and Anat is joyful, though she does not know where Baal is. A drought strikes the land. Appeased by a libation of wine from Anat, the sun goddess Shapshu looks for Baal.

Mot, remembering Anat's attacks, agrees to allow Baal to return if he gives one of his sons to Mot in exchange for his freedom. Again, Baal tricks Mot, sending him Mot's seven brothers. After a brief battle with Baal, Mot gives up and releases Baal.

Baal holds a feast with Anat and his friends. He sets out to battle sea monsters with Kothar-wa-Hasis.

SIGNIFICANCE

The Baal myth from Ugarit originates from an ancient people whose city of Ugarit was located in contemporary Syria. Ugarit may have been founded around 6000 BCE. The culture of Ugarit was at its height from about 1400 BCE until its total destruction in 1190 BCE. The Baal myth from Ugarit, known also as the Baal Cycle, was written down in the Ugaritic alphabet between 1400 and 1200 BCE. The surviving clay tablets containing the myth are from around 1250 BCE.

Ugarit was rediscovered by accident and excavated beginning in 1928 CE. Clay tablets containing the Baal myth were discovered in an ancient library at the site. Deciphering the Ugarit language enabled the Baal myth to be translated into English. By 2013, many scholarly translations of the myth existed. Among the foremost are the works of Johannes C. De Moor from 1987 and that of Mark Smith and Wayne Pitard from 2008.

The key significance of the Baal myth of Ugarit is the fact that the gods struggle ferociously among themselves and that this war deeply and negatively affects humanity. Baal, as storm god, irrigates the land with rain and thus functions as fertility god as well. He brings forth his doomed twin by copulating with a cow, indicating the vast extent of his powers of generation. His brother and archrival, Yamm, the god of the sea, threatens the land with floods. His second enemy, Mot, the god of death, brings death to humanity primarily through a prolonged drought. Baal's sister and wife, Anat, represents war.

In this savage strife of the Ugaritic gods and goddesses, scholars have seen a reflection of the geographical, social, and political challenges of the city of Ugarit. In the second millennium BCE, Ugarit was a fortified port city in the Northern Levant. It had a fertile agricultural area and sat along the trade route to Mesopotamia. The conflict between the forces of the sea—namely, seafarers and fishers symbolized by Yamm—and the agricultural community represented by Baal is central to the myth.

The power of Mot signifies the Ugaritic awe of the forces of death. Awareness of the horrors of war threatening Ugaritic civilization is illustrated by the graphic descriptions of Anat's slaughters. Anat's joy of killing uncannily foreshadows Ugarit's utter destruction in 1190 BCE, after which the city was abandoned forever.

Contemporary scholars have been very interested in tracing the spread of Baal across other ancient cultures of the Levant. Among the Phoenicians and the Canaanites, the word *baal* was used as a generic term for any powerful god. The Israelites came to violently oppose cults of Baal, who is often mentioned in the Old Testament, or Hebrew Bible. Discovery of the Baal myth from Ugarit in 1928 invigorated biblical scholarship. It appears that the myth of Baal survived the fall of Ugarit in 1190 BCE through his many incarnations in other ancient religions.

R. C. Lutz, PhD

BIBLIOGRAPHY

Caquot, André, and Maurice Sznycer. *Ugaritic Religion.* Leiden: Brill, 1980. Print.

De Moor, Johannes C. "Myth: Baal." *An Anthology of Religious Texts from Ugarit.* Leiden: Brill, 1987. 1–100. Print.

Gibson, John C., and Godfrey Rolles Driver. *Canaanite Myths and Legends.* Edinburgh: Clark, 2004. Print.

Smith, Mark S., and Wayne T. Pitard. *The Ugaritic Baal Cycle.* Vol. 2. Leiden: Brill, 2008. Print.

Tugendhaft, Aaron. "Politics and Time in the Baal Cycle." *Journal of Ancient Near Eastern Religions* 12.2 (2012): 145–57. Print.

Wyatt, Nick. *Religious Texts from Ugarit.* Sheffield: Sheffield Academic, 1998. Print.

◆ The Burning Bush

Author: Traditional Jewish; Southern Levant
Time Period: 2499 BCE–1000 BCE
Country or Culture: Middle East
Genre: Myth

PLOT SUMMARY

The book of Exodus, the second book of the Hebrew Bible (and of the Christian Old Testament), begins with the story of Moses. Several hundred years prior to his birth, the nascent Israelite people had gone to Egypt to escape famine. There Joseph, son of the patriarch Jacob and his wife Rachel, rises to second in command after the pharaoh and provides for his family of origin. They grow in number and power but are ultimately enslaved. Believing the growing population to be a threat, a new pharaoh commands that all Israelite boys be killed at birth; the Israelite midwives, however, disobey the order.

During this difficult time, the baby Moses is born. After being hidden for three months, he is placed in a basket of reeds and set adrift on the river. The pharaoh's daughter, coming to bathe, hears the baby's cries and adopts him as her own son, hiring his birth mother to nurse him. As a young man, Moses kills an Egyptian who is beating one of the Israelite slaves. He subsequently flees to Midian, where he marries a daughter of the priest Jethro and fathers two sons.

While tending his father-in-law's sheep, Moses sees a burning bush that is not consumed by the flames. Curious, he approaches the bush, only to have God (Yahweh) call to him from within it. Yahweh tells Moses to remove his sandals, for he is standing on holy ground. He then identifies himself: "I am the God of your father, the God of Abraham, the God of Isaac, and the God of Jacob" (Exod. 3:6). At this declaration, Moses hides his face out of fear of looking at God.

Yahweh tells Moses that he is aware of the suffering of his people and has come to deliver the Israelites from slavery through Moses, whom he will send to meet with the pharaoh. The would-be deliverer protests that he is unknown and ineloquent and that the people will not listen to him or know who sent him. Yahweh again identifies himself, this time stating, "I am who I am" (3:14). He also gives Moses power to perform miraculous deeds that will serve as signs, such as turning his shepherd's staff into a snake, making his hand appear to have leprosy, and turning water from the Nile River into blood.

When Moses continues to protest that he is not an eloquent speaker, Yahweh promises to send Moses's brother, Aaron, to be the speaker. Moses asks for and obtains permission from Jethro to return to Egypt, and he sets out with his wife and sons. Aaron meets Moses in the wilderness at Yahweh's command, and the two give the news of coming deliverance to the people, who worship Yahweh in gratitude.

SIGNIFICANCE

Traditionally, Moses has been named as the author of the Pentateuch or Torah, the first five books of the Hebrew Bible. Modern scholars, however, recognize the work of multiple, anonymous authors of these books, none of them Moses. The Pentateuch was likely solidified during the period of Israelite exile in Babylon in the sixth century BCE or in the subsequent early restoration period of Jewish history.

Scholar Bernard Robinson suggests that the Pentateuch was compiled by the time of the Second Temple (ca. 521 BCE) for liturgical use. Given that the five books would have been handwritten on multiple scrolls, copies for personal use would have been few, limited perhaps to royalty. The Mishnah, a text compiling Jewish oral traditions, relates that serial reading of the Torah took place on feast days and the Sabbath by about 200 CE, possibly earlier. Certainly there are instances within the Hebrew Bible of the texts being read aloud. Upon the return from Babylon, for example, the priest Ezra reads "the book of the law of Moses" to the assembled people (Neh. 8:1).

The story of the burning bush is a prototype for many subsequent "call" stories. Given a message to deliver, prophets often try to convince Yahweh of their inability or unworthiness to perform the task. The judge Gideon, for example, demands a sign of Yahweh before accepting the role of deliverer (Judg. 6). Jeremiah, like Moses, protests that he does not know how to speak and that he is too young for the task (Jer. 1).

As theologian Oliver Davies points out, the writer of the episode plays with the idea of seeing. In Exodus 2:25, God looks on the Israelites and takes note of them because of their cries. Two verses later, the pattern of speaking and looking is reversed. Moses looks around and notices a bush that is burning but not consumed. He then decides to take a closer look, and God calls to him from the bush. Davies posits that curiosity, a typical feature of wisdom literature, plays a role in Moses's call.

The notion of fire as a symbol of God appears in other texts within the Pentateuch. In Genesis 15, for example, a flaming torch passes between elements of sacrifice, sealing a covenant with Abraham. When the people leave Egypt in Exodus 13–14, a pillar of fire leads them by night. At the giving of the law on Mount Sinai, Yahweh descends in fire.

Robinson concludes that for exilic or postexilic Jews, this story offered comfort and reinforced the belief that God is in control of events and nature. The god they worshipped is not confined to a particular sacred space but able to make a sanctuary wherever he intervenes on their behalf. In this sense, the burning bush symbolizes the menorah, the seven-branched lamp made for the tabernacle and temple.

The burning bush has been interpreted by Jewish scholarship as a reference to the nation of Israel. This sign indicates that the fires of affliction will not consume the people, just as the flames do not consume the burning bush. As a tale of God's care for his people in distress, the story of the burning bush thus offers comfort during times of hardship.

Judy Johnson, MLS, MTS

BIBLIOGRAPHY

Davies, Oliver. "Reading the Burning Bush: Voice, World and Holiness." *Modern Theology* 22.3 (2006): 439–48. Print.

Garry, Jane. "Tabu: Looking, Motifs C300–C399." *Archetypes and Motifs in Folklore and Literature: A Handbook*. Ed. Garry and Hasan El-Shamy. Armonk: Sharpe, 2005. 308. Print.

The New Oxford Annotated Bible. Ed. Bruce M. Metzger and Roland E. Murphy. New York: Oxford UP, 1991. Print.

Paul, Shalom. "Burning Bush." *The Oxford Dictionary of the Jewish Religion*. Ed. Adele Berlin and Maxine Grossman. New York: Oxford UP, 2011. 151. Print.

Robinson, Bernard P. "Moses at the Burning Bush." *Journal for the Study of the Old Testament* 75 (1997): 107–22. Print.

◆ The Creation and Fall

Author: Traditional Jewish
Time Period: 2499 BCE–1000 BCE
Country or Culture: Middle East
Genre: Myth

PLOT SUMMARY

The first three chapters of Genesis, the first book of both the Hebrew Bible and the Christian Old Testament, relate the creation of the world and the fall of humanity. Chapters 1 and 2 offer two differing accounts of creation, although both ascribe the world's existence to God.

Genesis 1 is a stately litany of creative activity, with each of the first five days of creation beginning with the phrase, "And God said, 'Let there be . . . .'" Each day's activity concludes with some variant of the statement, "And God saw that it was good." Beginning with a formless void and the wind sweeping over the waters, God creates light; sky; earth and seas, with vegetation; sun and moon; and living creatures.

On the sixth day, the pattern changes. God says, "Let us make humankind in our image, according to our likeness; and let them have dominion over the fish of the sea, and over the birds of the air, and over the cattle, and over all the wild animals of the earth, and over every creeping thing that creeps upon earth" (Gen. 1:26). God creates man and woman, and following this sixth day of activity, he pronounces everything he has made "very good" (1:31). The seventh day is a day of rest, commonly called the Sabbath.

The second version of creation begins in chapter 2, which concentrates on the creation of humans. In this account, man is formed from the dust of the earth, and God breathes the breath of life into the creature, who becomes known as Adam. In this telling, God creates the Garden of Eden, in which grow the tree of life and the tree of the knowledge of good and evil. God tells Adam to care for the garden, prohibiting him from eating from the tree of the knowledge of good and evil. Eve, the first woman, is a second, separate creation, taken from Adam's rib as he sleeps and presented to Adam as a helpmeet. The text comments, "Therefore a man leaves his father and his mother and clings to his wife, and they become one flesh" (Gen. 2:24).

Trouble, in the form of a serpent, comes to the Garden of Eden in chapter 3. Approaching Eve, the serpent casts doubt on God's commandment not to eat from the tree of the knowledge of good and evil. Eve not only eats the tree's fruit but also gives some to Adam. The first piece of knowledge they receive is that of their nakedness; to cover themselves, they sew together fig leaves.

This disobedience is discovered when God enters the Garden of Eden and calls to Adam and Eve, who are hiding. When questioned, Adam places the blame on Eve, who shifts it to the serpent. God pronounces judgment on all those involved. The serpent will travel on its belly and experience enmity against the woman and her offspring. The woman will experience pangs in childbirth, and her husband will rule over her. The man will find caring for the earth burdensome, with thorns and thistles complicating the task. Finally, death is pronounced as a result of disobedience; Adam and Eve are driven from the Garden of Eden to prevent them from eating from the tree of life, which is guarded by an angel and a flaming sword.

SIGNIFICANCE

Scholars debate how the Hebrew Bible—particularly the first five books, called the Pentateuch—came together. Although the biblical prophet Moses has traditionally been held as the author of those books, modern source criticism posits four editors or compilers, based on the style and vocabulary of different passages. These editors worked with traditional stories that had been passed down in their communities, which became early Israel. According to the theory, the works of the Yahwist (J), Elohistic (E), Deuteronomic (D), and Priestly (P) writers were finally collated, probably after the exile to Babylon that occurred around 586 BCE. This final redactor seems to have been of the priestly class, which tended to focus on a majestic, distant God. Thus, the first chapter of Genesis reflects a Priestly sensibility. The redactor chose also to include a Yahwist story of creation, with its focus on a more personal God, one who forms humanity from clay rather than speaking the world into creation. For the Yahwists, God is anthropomorphized as one who is willing to get his hands dirty.

The theme of a fall from a pure state of innocence and grace is one of the major themes of the myth and one on which many writers and artists have focused. In the fifth century CE, Saint Augustine derived the idea of original sin, based on a mistranslation and misunderstanding of the writings of Saint Paul. In Romans 5, Paul creates an extended analogy of Christ's death controverting Adam's fall. Paul writes of death, not sin, coming upon all humanity. Both the Roman Catholic church and Protestant denominations adopted Augustine's faulty application of Paul's ideas.

The theology of reformer John Calvin, for example, included the concept known as total depravity. Original sin meant that babies were born in sin and condemned to hell if they had not been baptized. The Great Awakening in the United States during the eighteenth century, led by Jonathan Edwards and George Whitefield, stressed this doctrine. "Sinners in the Hands of an Angry God," one of Edwards's sermons, has been anthologized in generations of American literature and history textbooks, enshrining original sin in the curriculum.

Judy Johnson, MLS, MTS

BIBLIOGRAPHY

The Bible. Ed. Bruce M. Metzger and Roland E. Murphy. New York: Oxford UP, 1991. Print. The New Oxford Annotated Bible. Rev. Standard Vers.

Cunningham, Conor. "What Genesis Doesn't Say: Rethinking the Creation Story." *Christian Century* 127.23 (2010): 22–25. Print.

Kim, Yung-Suk. "A Lesson from Studies of Source Criticism: Contradicting Stories and Humble Diversity in Creation Stories (Gen 1–2)." *SBL Forum*. Society of Biblical Literature, 2007. Web. 11 June 2013.

Mühlberger, Richard. *The Bible in Art: The Old Testament*. New York: Portland House, 1991. Print.

◆ The Nursemaid of Rostam

Author: Abolqasem Ferdowsī
Time Period: 501 CE–1000 CE
Country or Culture: Middle East
Genre: Legend

PLOT SUMMARY

The ancient Persian hero Sam has an albino son called Zal. Frightened by the baby's white hair, Sam abandons him in the mountains. Zal is rescued by the Simurgh (Simorgh), a large bird similar to a phoenix, who flies him back to her nest and raises him. When he grows up and is ready to leave, the Simurgh gives him three of her feathers, telling him that whenever he burns one of her feathers, she will come to his aid.

In Kabul, Zal falls in love with the king's daughter, Rudabeh. Against considerable odds, their parents allow Zal and Rudabeh to marry. When Rudabeh is pregnant, her childbirth portends to be problematic. She feels that the baby she carries is as heavy as a bunch of stones or a lump of iron. Desperate, she tells Zal that although the baby is due, she cannot give birth to the burden within her. Later, she faints and causes panic in the palace.

In his agony over Rudabeh's pregnancy and his fears that she will die in childbirth, Zal remembers the Simurgh's promise. He burns part of one of her feathers. She appears to him immediately and, on seeing his tears, prophesies that the baby will be a great warrior. She then assumes the roles of midwife to the unborn child in Rudabeh's womb, giving Zal practical instructions to save mother and child: he must get a sharp knife and a sorcerer familiar with magic spells, and then give Rudabeh wine to alleviate her fear. He should turn away while the sorcerer intones his spells and cuts open her belly to deliver the baby. After this, Zal must sew up her belly and rub a specially prepared herbal mixture on the wound. Most importantly, Zal must swipe the Simurgh's feather over Rudabeh's belly. This will heal her completely. After giving him these instructions, the Simurgh encourages Zal not to be afraid. She plucks one of her wing feather for Zal to use to heal Rudabeh, and flies away.

Awestruck, Zal does exactly what the Simurgh has told him to do. A sorcerer performs the cesarean section on Rudabeh just as prescribed by the Simurgh. His successful delivery reveals that the baby, a boy, is very big. All who see the baby are in awe of him.

One day after the birth, Rudabeh awakens. She talks to her mother, Sindokht, as the people rejoice at the baby's birth and her recovery. Rudabeh exclaims that she escaped (*rastam*) the dangers of birth, and so the family names the boy Rostam.

Each day, the infant Rostam drinks all the milk provided by ten human wet nurses. As he grows up into a hero, the Simurgh will help Rostam twice more: once during his seven trials and again during his climactic battle with Prince Esfandyar, when she provides Rostam with the means to kill his opponent.

SIGNIFICANCE

The Persian poet and writer Abolqasem Ferdowsī (also known as Firdawsī or Abu al-Qasim Mansūr) was born in a village near Tus, Khurasan, a province in what is now Iran, in the mid-tenth century CE. In 1116 or 1117, a poet named Nezami-ye Aruzi visited Ferdowsī's grave and gathered stories about Ferdowsī that were still being told in his village and that remain the only trustworthy source of biographical information about him. Based on Nezami's account, Ferdowsī lived off income earned from the land he owned. Nezami does not specify the date of Ferdowsī's death, but he is believed to have died between 1020 and 1026 CE.

In 977, Ferdowsī began to write what would become the national epic of Iran, the *Shahnameh* (Book of kings). When he finally finished the *Shahnameh* in 1010, it was nearly sixty thousand couplets long. Ferdowsī presented the epic to Mahmūd, sultan of Ghazni. Though Ferdowsī drew on older source material, including an earlier prose version of the *Shahnameh*, for his epic, he gave it its poetic shape and therefore has been considered the legend's literary author by most scholars. The *Shahnameh* has been available in English translation since 1832.

The tales of the hero Rostam's many achievements and exploits over the course of a five-hundred-year-long life have been among the most popular sections of Ferdowsī's *Shahnameh*. Rostam's miraculous birth, as portrayed in "The Nursemaid of Rostam," represents a fitting beginning for a baby boy who will become an illustrious hero. Even while he was still in the womb, portents such as Rudabeh's symptoms and the apparent weight of the baby are harbingers of his superhuman qualities. The Simurgh, when summoned via her magic feather, also foretells the coming of a hero. In Ferdowsī's Persia, Rudabeh's survival of a cesarean section would have been highly unlikely, if not miraculous, and further marks Rostam's birth as exceptional, as does the Simurgh's participation as a supernatural midwife. Indeed, Rudabeh names Rostam after her sense of escape from a certain doom. Once Rostam is born, he displays a superhuman appetite, requiring the milk of ten wet nurses in order to appease his hunger.

R. C. Lutz, PhD

BIBLIOGRAPHY

Fee, Christopher. "The Persian Elephant-Bodied Hero." *Mythology in the Middle Ages*. Santa Barbara: Praeger, 2011. 194–95. Print.

Ferdowsī, Abolqasem. "The Birth of Rostam." *Rostam: Tales of Love and War from the* Shahnameh. Trans. Dick Davis. New York: Penguin, 2007. 53–60. Print.

Omidsalar, Mahmoud. *Poetics and Politics of Iran's National Epic, the* Shahnameh. New York: Palgrave, 2011. Print.

Rosenberg, Donna. "Rostam Has a Remarkable Birth and Youth." *Folklore, Myths and Legends: A World Perspective*. New York: McGraw Hill, 1997. 110. Print.

Sewell, Jane Eliot. *Cesarean Section—A Brief History*. US National Lib. of Medicine, 10 July 2012. Web. 18 July 2013.

Shahbāzī, 'A. Shāpūr. *Ferdowsī: A Critical Biography*. Cambridge: Harvard U, Center for Middle Eastern Studies, 1991. Print.

Pharaoh's Dreams

Author: Traditional Jewish
Time Period: 2499 BCE–1000 BCE
Country or Culture: Middle East
Genre: Myth

PLOT SUMMARY

When the pharaoh of Egypt wakes one morning, an ominous dream lingers with him. In the dream, he stood beside a river as seven healthy, plump cows rose out of it. A moment later, seven starving and hideous cows emerged from the water and began to feast on the healthy cows. The pharaoh tries to go back to sleep, but another dream comes to him in which seven healthy heads of grain rise on a single stalk, only to be eaten by seven thin and sickly heads of grain.

The dreams trouble the pharaoh, so he sends for all of his advisers and court magicians, hoping they will help him interpret the strange omens. Unfortunately, they are unable to offer guidance. The pharaoh's butler, however, has an idea. Years before, he was placed in jail, where he met a man named Joseph. The butler and the pharaoh's baker, who was also imprisoned, both had confusing dreams, which Joseph interpreted for them, claiming that the butler would be returned to freedom and the baker sentenced to death. When the butler tells the pharaoh that this did indeed come true, the pharaoh immediately sends for Joseph.

The pharaoh tells Joseph of his dreams and asks for an interpretation. Before he begins, Joseph reminds the pharaoh that it is not he who will provide the meaning, but rather God. After hearing the dreams, Joseph reveals that they both prophesy the same thing. Seven years of plentitude and fruitfulness will come to Egypt, during which the people will be able to feast throughout the seasons. This will be followed by seven years of famine and starvation. The pharaoh must save as much food as possible during the seven years of plentitude so that the people will have something to eat during the long famine. Joseph further suggests that the pharaoh should appoint a wise man to organize this effort and ensure that at least one-fifth of all the food grown gets put aside.

Knowing that Joseph is a wise man as well as a man of God, the pharaoh immediately appoints him to the position, placing a ring on Joseph's finger and clothing him with fine linen and gold. At once, Joseph becomes one of the most powerful men in Egypt and is given a beautiful wife as well as a chariot to ride throughout the land. With this power, Joseph does exactly as he suggested, putting aside food while he begins a family with his wife. When the famine does come, it spreads throughout the entire world, and while people in many lands suffer, in Egypt they come to Joseph, who provides for them and keeps them healthy. When the famine is over, Egypt's people are still alive, and the nation is rich from selling its extra grain.

SIGNIFICANCE

The story of Joseph's interpretation of the pharaoh's dreams comes from the book of Genesis, the first book in the Christian Old Testament and the Hebrew Bible, or Tanakh. Situated in these foundational texts, Joseph became a significant figure across a number of religious traditions; in addition to his roles in Christianity and Judaism, he is an Islamic prophet and a recurrent figure in the Bahá'í faith. In these traditions, Joseph's first meeting with the pharaoh comes after an already eventful life. Born to a rich family, Joseph has his own prophetic dream, which seems to suggest that his entire family will bow down to him one day. His brothers, jealous of this prophecy, capture him and sell him into slavery, which leads to his position in the pharaoh's prison.

The book of Genesis largely focuses on the promise given to the people of Israel by God and the salvation that they receive. In these religious traditions, by maintaining faith in their god, the people of Israel will receive redemption, even if they must go through a great many trials on the way. The story of Joseph offers these same themes on a smaller scale. On the individual level, Joseph is taken in a few short paragraphs from the prisons of Egypt to an exalted position as a ruler of the nation, blessed with riches and a growing family. He achieves this not because of his own abilities but because he constantly defers to God; it is even because he insists to the pharaoh that God, rather than Joseph himself, is responsible for the dream interpretations that the pharaoh selects him to lead Egypt through the famine. The entire nation of Egypt also goes through a similar process. Despite its usually fertile lands, Egypt suffered extensive famines during ancient times, so the prospect of the region failing to provide crops was a dangerous possibility. Through the dreams, both the famine and the time of plenty become attributed to God, and it is by abiding by the promises and prophecies given to them that the leaders of Egypt are able to prevent the prophesied disaster.

Joseph's transformation into one of the most powerful men in Egypt and the nation's increase in prosperity mirror the greater narratives of the book of Genesis. The sanctity of the Abrahamic god's blessing is reinforced alongside the role of humans in either accepting or denying that blessing. While the varying religious and spiritual traditions that include Joseph all interpret his narrative differently, the core idea remains consistent: he follows the promise of God and, through his faith, is able to endure great tragedy and feed not only his own people but also all the starving nations of the world.

T. Fleischmann, MFA

BIBLIOGRAPHY

Guzik, David. "Genesis 41: Joseph Interprets Pharaoh's Dream and Rises to Power." *Enduring Word Media*. Enduring Word Media Resource, n.d. Web. 28 May 2013.

Hamilton, Victor P. *The Book of Genesis: Chapters 18–50*. Grand Rapids: Eerdmans, 1995. Print. New Intl. Commentary on the Old Testament.

Kim, Hyun Chul Paul. "Reading the Joseph Story (Genesis 37–50) as a Diaspora Narrative." *Catholic Biblical Quarterly* 75.2 (2013): 219–38. Print.

Newman, Stephen. "Pharaoh's Dreams: An Extended Interpretation." *Jewish Bible Quarterly* 40.4 (2012): 253–54. Print.

Telushkin, Joseph. *Biblical Literacy: The Most Important People, Events, and Ideas of the Hebrew Bible*. New York: Morrow, 1997. Print.

◆ Samson the Judge

Author: Traditional Jewish
Time Period: 2499 BCE–1000 BCE
Country or Culture: Middle East
Genre: Myth

PLOT SUMMARY

The boy Samson is born during a time when the Israelites are facing harsh punishment from God, who has placed them at the mercy of their enemies, the Philistines. His mother, however, had been gifted with a divine apparition before her, who proclaimed that her child would free his people and stated that the boy must be raised as a Nazirite, promising never to cut his hair, drink alcohol, or come in contact with corpses. As long as Samson holds these restrictions as a holy pact with God, he will be granted incredible strength.

When he is older, Samson falls in love with a Philistine woman of Timnath. After telling his parents of his intended marriage, he and his parents travel to the woman's home. Before he arrives, however, Samson is attacked by a lion, which he quickly kills barehanded. After he arrives, the Philistine woman meets his approval, and it is agreed that they will wed. It is only a short while later, then, that he goes to Timnath once more for his own wedding. On the way, he passes the lion's carcass, in which bees have made a home, and eats the honey within it.

At the wedding, Samson challenges his thirty Philistine groomsmen to solve a riddle, wagering thirty fine linens and thirty outfits that they will fail. He then simply states, "Out of the eater came forth meat, and out of the strong came forth sweetness" (Judg. 14:14). The men cannot guess that Samson is referring to the lion, but under threat from them, his wife manages to pry the answer out of him and thus enable her family to win the bet. Furious and unable to pay the debt, Samson slaughters thirty Philistines and takes their wealth to provide the wagered goods. He then returns to his father's home.

The slaughter of the Philistine men begins a long stretch of violence between Samson and their people. When he returns to his wife's house, her father tries to give him her younger sister, saying that Samson's wife had been given to his friend. Samson is again enraged. Capturing three hundred foxes, he attaches torches to their tails and unleashes them in the nearby fields and vineyards, burning down crops. The other Philistines blame Samson for this and quickly slaughter his wife and her family. Samson, in turn, kills many more Philistines in retaliation, and the Philistines decide to avenge themselves upon the Israelites for the actions of this warrior. Several thousand men from the tribe of Judah then approach Samson, insisting on delivering him to the Philistines. They bind Samson and bring him to the Philistines, but he quickly breaks free, again slaughtering countless men. Samson then goes on to "judge Israel in the days of the Philistines twenty years" (Judg. 15:20).

One day Samson falls in love with a woman, Delilah. The Philistines approach Delilah and bribe her into learning the secret of Samson's strength. After repeated attempts to weaken and subdue him, she finally nags him into revealing his secret. One day, as Samson sleeps, Delilah cuts off his holy hair. The Philistines are then able to capture Samson, put out his eyes, and imprison him. When his hair has again grown long, the Philistines bring him into a temple, intending to sacrifice him to their god. With a last burst of strength, Samson tears the temple down, killing many men along with himself.

SIGNIFICANCE

The story of Samson is told in the book of Judges in the Hebrew Bible and Christian Old Testament. Although strikingly violent and cruel, the narrative is in line with the remainder of the book, which details a long period in which the Israelites face harsh punishments for betraying God, are led to salvation by a "judge" (Samson, in this case), and then fail God once more.

It is not entirely a coincidence that Samson resembles a vengeful god himself. The story is similar to many folktales from the region, which commonly feature superhuman heroes who are able to bring vast destruction on their enemies in order to avenge their communities. Perhaps most famously, the story of Samson reflects that of the Greek hero Heracles, a powerful demigod who completes a number of violent labors only to die in a sacrificial fire. As the ancient world was one of almost unimaginable violence and constant war, with ethnic groups and smaller cities in a state of constant vulnerability to larger powers, tales in which a single hero could defend a smaller population were understandably quite widespread. Samson feeds into this tradition, providing a mystical level of protection to the Israelites.

In the context of the Hebrew Bible and the Christian Old Testament, however, Samson plays an additional role. The period of the book of Judges is one of the most violent of the entire religious tradition, with God enacting harsh punishments with little apparent sense of forgiveness or compassion. Just as God throws the Israelites into subjugation under the Philistines for their lack of faith, Samson himself throws the Philistines into despair and bloodshed for seemingly inconsequential sins, such as winning a bet against him. These extremes can seem shocking to modern readers. However, they are treated in the text as essential to the covenant between God and his people. Faithfulness to God is of the utmost importance, trumping all else in life. This faith can lead to prosperity and dominance over other people or, if severed even by the simple infraction of cutting the hair that Samson had promised to grow, can result in further oppression. This cycle of failure and repentance, of violence and prosperity, defines much of the first books of the Bible, revealing as much about the foundations of the covenant itself as it does about the unimaginably precarious situation in which oppressed people of the ancient world often found themselves.

T. Fleischmann, MFA

BIBLIOGRAPHY

Doane, T. W. "Samson and His Exploits." *Bible Myths and Their Parallels in Other Religions*. 4th ed. New York: Bouton, 1882. 62–76. Print.

Gillmayr-Bucher, Susanne. "Framework and Discourse in the Book of Judges." *Journal of Biblical Literature* 128.4 (2009): 687–702. Print.

Harris, Rachel S. "Samson's Suicide: Death and the Hebrew Literary Canon." *Israel Studies* 17.3 (2012): 67–91. Print.

The Holy Bible. New York: American Bible Soc., 1999. Print. King James Vers.

Herzberg, Bruce. "Samson's Moment of Truth." *Biblical Interpretation* 18.3 (2010): 226–50. Print.

"Samson." *Merriam-Webster's Encyclopedia of Literature* (1995): n. pag. Web. 6 June 2013.

The Story of Job

Author: Traditional Jewish
Time Period: 2499 BCE–1000 BCE
Country or Culture: Middle East
Genre: Myth

PLOT SUMMARY

The book of Job is classified as one of the poetic books of the Hebrew Bible, which Christians sometimes call the Old Testament. It comprises mostly monologues, and most of its action is reported rather than depicted directly. The opening verses of the book introduce Job, a prosperous, God-fearing man and the father of seven sons and three daughters. His herds of cattle and sheep, which many servants tend, are extensive.

Yahweh, or God, portrayed as a Middle Eastern patriarch at court, points out Job to *Ha satan*, or Satan. *Ha satan* is a Hebrew term that means "the accuser." This is not the devil of later biblical thought, although most English translations capitalize the name. *Ha satan* is one of the heavenly beings, whose task appears to be patrolling the earth. Yahweh mentions the upright nature of Job, whom he calls his servant.

Satan first suggests that Job serves God only because God has blessed him. He is granted permission to destroy all of Job's possessions but not to touch his life. Soon a succession of Job's servants enter to report the utter destruction of his children and livestock. Job's response is to worship God, saying, "The Lord gave and the Lord has taken away; blessed be the name of the Lord" (Job 1:21).

Satan extends a second challenge, insinuating to God that Job would curse God if he did not have his health. God gives permission to this being to afflict Job, but not to take his life. Job is covered with boils, at which point he retires to an ash heap to scrape his sores. His wife seems to chide him for his faith, which Job maintains.

Three friends—Eliphaz, Bildad, and Zophar—arrive to commiserate with Job, keeping silence with him for seven days. At the end of this period, Job begins to lament his losses. For the bulk of the book, the men debate the reason for Job's affliction. Prevalent thinking of the time held that blessings were the result of God's favor; if this favor was withdrawn, sin must be the cause. A fourth man, Elihu, appears to castigate Job. However, Job maintains his innocence, ultimately demanding an answer from God.

God speaks to Job from a whirlwind. He does not explain the wager with Satan; instead, he poses a series of questions about creation, pointing out that Job does not make up the whole world. Job replies that he spoke of what he did not understand. Yahweh is angered by the wrong tack Job's friends have taken, but Job prays for them, and they offer animal sacrifices. In the end, Yahweh blesses Job with twice as much in material wealth as he had before, as well as seven sons and three daughters.

SIGNIFICANCE

The story of Job has deeply influenced theological thought and is well represented in the arts. Although scholars are not able to date conclusively when the book was written, it is clearly built on an older traditional story told within the early Jewish community. The anonymous writer took the tale of Job, a righteous suffering man, and split the story, adding dialogue that reflects popular understandings of suffering. The poetry of the opening and closing chapters brackets prose arguments.

Two major theological interpretations of Job's story exist. Many people view the book as a meditation on the meaning of suffering, an answer to the problem theologians refer to as a theodicy. In this interpretation, the book of Job explores the reason why, if God is all-powerful and loving, innocent people nonetheless suffer.

A more recent development in the understanding of Job comes from Latin American liberation theology, an outgrowth of Roman Catholicism formulated in the 1970s. Liberation theology posits that God demonstrates a "preferential option" for the poor. This can be seen in reading Jesus's words from the Sermon on the Mount, known as the Beatitudes, and also by examining the company Jesus kept—the poor, the outcasts of society, and women. Peruvian priest Gustavo Gutiérrez, considered the father of liberation theology, in his book *Hablar de Dios desde el sufrimiento del inocente* (1986; *On Job: God-Talk and the Suffering of the Innocent*, 1987) asks, "How are human beings to find a language applicable to God in the midst of innocent suffering?" He calls this the theme of Job, wondering, "How, then, is a human being to speak of God and to God in the situation that Job must endure?" (12). For him, these questions have special relevance for the very poor residents of Latin America. He concludes that God is love, offered and operating freely, not bound by human constraints of justice.

In literature, Archibald MacLeish, one-time US poet laureate, offers a modern retelling of Job. His 1958 Pulitzer Prize–winning drama, *J.B.*, portrays a man and wife who lose everything. MacLeish presents J. B. and his wife, Sarah, as typical New Englanders with everything in their favor. But then each of their five children perishes, and their town is bombed. In MacLeish's retelling, the contest is set in motion by Zuss (Zeus) and Nickels (Old Nick, a euphemistic title for the devil). The three comforters—a priest, a psychiatrist, and a communist—represent the major alternative understandings of suffering in the mid-twentieth-century United States. Like their biblical counterparts, however, they offer little real help. The play concludes with the reunion of Sarah, who had left, and J. B. Their reliance is on love, rather than on God's goodness.

Nineteenth-century poet and visual artist William Blake created several versions of a work titled *Satan Smiting Job with Sore Boils*. Naked and triumphant, wings outspread, a classically beautiful Satan dominates the center of the painting, standing atop a prone Job, who is covered with a loincloth. In his left hand Satan is holding a small vessel from which stream the boils. Job's head is tilted back, his mouth open in horror, and his hands posed in a gesture signifying halt. At the left, Job's wife sits hunched over, her head in her hands. Job's feet rest against her thighs. For theologians and artists alike, the book of Job has been a rich source of reflection and inspiration.

Judy Johnson, MLS, MTS

BIBLIOGRAPHY

The Bible. Ed. Bruce M. Metzger and Roland E. Murphy. New York: Oxford UP, 1991. Print. The New Oxford Annotated Bible. Rev. Standard Vers.

Ehrlich, Bernard. "The Book of Job as a Book of Morality." *Jewish Bible Quarterly* 34.1 (2006): 30–38. Print.

Gutiérrez, Gustavo. *On Job: God-Talk and the Suffering of the Innocent*. Maryknoll: Orbis, 1987. Print.

Wright, Susan. *The Bible in Art*. New York: Todtri, 1996. Print.

◆ The Tower of Babel

Author: Traditional Jewish
Time Period: 2499 BCE–1000 BCE
Country or Culture: Middle East
Genre: Myth

PLOT SUMMARY

The biblical story of the Tower of Babel begins in the context of a unified world, one that shares a single language. After journeying in the east, certain men settle in the plains of Shinar. Using bricks and mortar, the men decide to build a city, in which they build a tall tower to glorify themselves and their accomplishments. God descends to earth to observe the new city and its people. Examining the city, God realizes that because humanity shares but one language, its possible accomplishments are limitless. Therefore, God decides to scatter the people all over the earth, causing them to abandon the construction of their new city.

SIGNIFICANCE

The biblical account indicates that the city is called Babel "because the Lord there made a babble of the language of all the world" (Gen. 11:9). According to sources documented by T. W. Doane, the association of the name Babel with the transformation of language into "babble" is based on an error by the writer who inserted this story into the book of Genesis, the first book of the Hebrew Bible (Christian Old Testament). Doane reports that in Hebrew, Babel actually means "the gate of God," but the writer of the story confused this meaning by tracing Babel to the word *babal*, which means "to confuse" (34).

The writer's source for the story comes from a Chaldean story about the "confusion of tongues" (34). As related by Berosus, the Chaldean story offers more detail about the builders of the city and its whereabouts. In this account, the city is located in Babylon. The inhabitants are proud and disdainful of the gods, so they decide to build a tower that will touch the sky. Helped by the winds, the gods topple it and replace the inhabitants' single language with many different tongues. A Jewish historian named Josephus later elaborated this tale by adding an evil ringleader named Nimrod, and the motivation for building the tower became the desire for a safe haven in case God "should have a mind to drown the world again" (34); the people also wanted revenge against God for the destruction of their ancestors. In this case, God responds not by destroying the people (given that they failed to learn from the prior punishment) but by introducing many languages so that the people can no longer understand one another.

Interestingly, Doane gathers evidence of myths from around the world (including places such as Armenia, India, Africa, and Mexico) strikingly similar to the Tower of Babel story. Two versions from India and Mexico are particularly noteworthy. Doane relates a Hindu version called the "Confusion of Tongues" in which a "world tree," or "knowledge tree" (35–36) grows in the center of the earth and ascends almost to heaven. The tree says "in its heart: 'I shall hold my head in heaven, and spread my branches over all the earth, and gather all men together under my shadow, and protect them, and prevent them from separating" (36). The god Brahmā punishes the tree's pride by cutting off the branches and throwing them down to the earth, where they are reborn as *wata* trees that cause "differences of belief, and speech, and customs, to prevail on the earth, to disperse men over its surface" (36).

A version similar to the Genesis myth comes from Mexico. In this account, those who survived the flood sent to destroy humankind decide to build a lofty tower. Like the story elaborated by Josephus, the people built the tower for two reasons: to see what is happening in heaven and to have a place to hide if the gods send another flood. The wicked architect of this version is a giant named Xelhua, who orders bricks to be made and transferred hand to hand by a long line of men from a certain province to the city of Cholula, where the tower is to be built. Angered by Xelhua's audacity, the gods cast fire onto the tower and the men building it, and the families involved "received a language of their own, and the builders could not understand each other" (36).

A common theme emerges from these analogues: a desire to reach the heavens to attain some aspect of divine power. God or gods then punish those who seek this power by destroying the tower (and, in some cases, the people) and by introducing many languages to hinder the people's ability to communicate. These shared aspects point to a powerful etiological function of this story, showing how it serves to locate the origin of numerous languages in human transgression.

Doane also documents a historical reality that helps to explain the myth's survival: the existence of an actual tower in Babylonia. This tower was apparently built by a king and used to study astronomy. The structure had seven "stages" dedicated to the sun, the moon, and five planets. According to one source, the tower was neglected and eventually fell into ruins. Although this account includes no details related to the Tower of Babel myth, the historical presence of a ruined tower in Babylonia helps to explain how an architectural reality might have served to sustain the myth among ancient people.

Ashleigh Imus, PhD

BIBLIOGRAPHY

The Bible. Ed. Samuel Sandmel. New York: Oxford UP, 1976. Print. New English Bible with the Apocrypha, Oxford Study Ed.

Doane, T. W. *Bible Myths and Their Parallels in Other Religions*. New York: Commonwealth, 1882. Print.

Jacob of Serug. *Homily on the Tower of Babel*. Trans. Aaron Michael Butts. Piscataway: Gorgias, 2009. Print.

Kramer, Samuel Noah. "The 'Babel of Tongues': A Sumerian Version." *Journal of the American Oriental Society* 88.1 (1968): 108–11. Print.

Mengham, Rod. *On Language: Descent from the Tower of Babel*. Boston: Little, Brown, 1993. Print.

MESOPOTAMIA

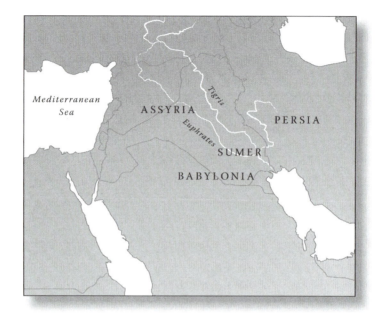

Before All Befores

Author: Traditional Sumerian
Time Period: 2499 BCE–1000 BCE
Country or Culture: Mesopotamia
Genre: Myth

PLOT SUMMARY

"Before All Befores" is a retelling of the Sumerian creation myths that relate the formation of the natural world. The myths take place before the existence of time, when Namma (Nammu), the primordial sea, is the only entity. Namma is regarded as the mother of the universe and of source of all primal matter.

In this account, Namma creates two beings, a daughter, Ki, and a son, An. They are dubbed creation's firstborn. Ki, the earth, is personified by a great mountain. An, her brother, is represented by the sky. Ki and An develop a divine spousal-sibling bond that results in the birth of Enlil, the infant lord of air, along with many other deities.

Enlil, however, struggles to grow while he seeks expansion; eventually, he breaks out of his parents embrace to encompass all of unconquered space. Oneness thus evolves into multiplicity. Enlil's quest sparks the "beginning of evolution, the never-ending adventure of being" ("Before All Befores").

Bearing witness to the alterations of her offspring, Namma decrees new fates for her children, Ki and An. She names An's dwelling place the Upperworld, and gifts him "knowledge, inspiration, dreams, and visions" to share. Ki's domain is henceforth known as Middle-world, "home of everything that grows and lives." In the wake of the creation of the new worlds, Namma also creates a third realm, Underworld, the "source of memories for what was."

Ki and An, though now separated, reaffirm their unity and vow to watch over each other for all eternity. Enlil, alone, feels bereft in his solitude. He asks to be reunited with his mother, Ki, the earth, so that they can construct eternity together as breath and form.

Namma and An then copulate, and as a result, divine twins are born, the first of the major Sumerian gods, Enki and Ereškigala (Ereshkigal). Namma charges the twins with an eternal quest for inner beauty amid the three worlds.

SIGNIFICANCE

The self-procreating deity Namma is regarding by many scholars of ancient mythology as the "oldest recorded name" of any deity (Alban 157). The Sumerian creation myths differ from those of other ancient cultures for one major reason: the source of all life and divinity is place in water, rather than the earth or the sky. This fact not only shows the great reverence the ancient Sumerians had for water as a life-giving force, but also the depths of their understanding surrounding its necessity as a provider of sustenance.

"Before All Befores" reflects significant themes in Sumerian mythology. The handful of myths upon which it relies lays the foundation for the entire canon of Sumerian and Babylonian literature that followed. The retelling is inclusive of several narrative strains that recur throughout Sumerian mythology, particularly the concept of deities brought to life to dwell in an environment created by and personified by their parents, as well as the notion that the planet's known natural elements were created as a fusion of one or more powerful gods.

It also interesting to note that while Namma is the first divine name in recorded history and regarded in Sumerian lore as the mother of all gods, she did not maintain such reverence in the mythological pantheon of the Tigris-Euphrates region, as scholars Samuel Noah Kramer and Betty Meador note. In fact, in later myths, Namma yields her rule over the life-giving waters to the male deity Enki, often described as her son, thus lending an air of somewhat greater legitimacy to this transfer of power. The potential reasons for this downgrade are entirely speculative, but it may be indicative of a cultural diminution of women in ancient Mesopotamian society. Although references to Namma as the creator of the universe eventually wane in Sumerian texts, she is mentioned again in the third millenium BCE at her rightful place as the divine creator, indicating that adoration for the goddess may have also remained intact and undercutting the idea that she had lost her importance.

The creation accounts not only lay the groundwork for ancient Sumeria's wildly diverse polytheistic pantheon, but also of the notion that the interaction between positive and negative forces in the universe is a major, if not the singular source, of all existence. Scholars also correlate the name Namma with Ur-Nammu (or Ur-Namma), founder of the Third Dynasty of Ur, although the exact connection is debated. The Third Dynasty marks a pivotal period in Mesopotamian law due to its establishment of the Code of Ur-Nammu, the oldest system of laws to have been recovered by archaeologists to date.

John Pritchard

BIBLIOGRAPHY

Alban, Gillian M. E. *Melusine the Serpent Goddess in A. S. Byatt's* Possession *and in Mythology*. Lanham: Lexington, 2003. Print.

"Before All Befores: How the Earth Mother and Queen Fell in Love with the Skyfather and King." *Gateways to Babylon*. N.p., n.d. Web. 18 June 2013.

Black, Jeremy Allen, and Anthony Green. "Creation." *Gods, Demons, and Symbols of Ancient Mesopotamia: An Illustrated Dictionary*. Austen: U of Texas P, 1992. 53–54. Print.

Kramer, Samuel Noah. "Creation: What the Gods Have Wrought and How." *From the Poetry of Sumer: Creation, Glorification, Adoration*. Berkeley: U of California P, 1979. 20–49. Print.

Leick, Gwendolyn. "The Cosmological Articulation of Sexuality." *Sex and Eroticism in Mesopotamian Literature*. London: Routledge, 1994. 11–20. Print.

Meador, Betty. "Light the Seven Fires, Seize the Seven Desires." *The Cultural Complex: Contemporary Jungian Perspectives on Psyche and Society*. Ed. Thomas Singer and Samuel L. Kimbles. New York: Brunner-Routledge, 2004. 171–84. Print.

◆ The Birth of the Great Gods and Goddesses

Author: Traditional Sumerian
Time Period: 2499 BCE–1000 BCE
Country or Culture: Mesopotamia
Genre: Myth

PLOT SUMMARY

At the beginning of the universe, the great sky god An (Anu in Babylonian) and his sister-wife, the earth goddess Ki, are joined. Their son, Enlil, the god of air, separates them, sending his father into the sky and away from his mother. Ki—sometimes called Ninhursaĝa (or Ninhursag, "Queen of the Holy Hill"), among other titles—is saddened at the loss of her partner, but she is buoyed by the fact that she is pregnant with more of

An's children. These children will be divine in nature, becoming great gods and goddesses themselves. In one retelling, An's voice is heard from the heavens, blessing his wife on this momentous occasion.

Ki calls upon Enlil to build a grand temple to accommodate her and his imminent siblings, as they will all need a home. The temple, she adds, will serve as an important reminder of the great bond between the earth and the heavens. The new gods will be called the Anunnaki (or Anuna), and the temple will be known as the Duku ("mound"). Enlil will serve as the steward over these gods. After Enlil has gathered stones for the temple, Ki sits down and gives birth to the Anunnaki.

SIGNIFICANCE

The Sumerian civilization is one of the world's oldest, dating as far back as 4000 BCE. Based in the valley between the Tigris and Euphrates Rivers (within a region known as the Fertile Crescent), the Sumerians were a major influence on subsequent cultures, including the Babylonians and others in the Middle Eastern region. Their religious traditions were also influential; the Sumerian stories of creation (including an account of a great flood) were similar to those found in the Hebrew Bible (and Christian Old Testament) and, in particular, the book of Genesis.

The story of the birth of the gods provides a foundation for religious tradition in this ancient civilization. Much of Sumerian religious tradition focused on the creation of life but did so in such a way that was relatable for humans. Although this story is focused on supernatural beings, the manner by which these beings are introduced is very humanlike: An impregnates his wife, Ki, through sexual contact, and their children arrive through a natural form of childbirth.

The fifty children of Ki—the Anunnaki—would each be charged with oversight of an aspect of life. Nabû, for example, would become the god of writing, while Ašnan (Ashnan) would be the goddess of grain. The Anunnaki would even influence later religions; several of these gods would be referenced in the Old Testament. Enlil, the oldest brother (who in some versions of the story is also Ninhursaĝa's husband or brother), would be responsible for managing the Anunnaki, ultimately acting as the supreme god. While the tale establishes the supernatural hierarchy, with Enlil at the apex, this story also reflects the great love between the primary gods—An, Ki-Ninhursaĝa, and Enlil—as the universe is created.

Michael P. Auerbach, MA

BIBLIOGRAPHY

Alford, Alan F. "Myth-Religion: Sumerian." *Eridu Books*. A. F. Alford, 2004. Web. 19 June 2013.

Black, Jeremy A., and Anthony Green. "Anuna (Anunnakkū)." *Gods, Demons, and Symbols of Ancient Mesopotamia*. Austin: U of Texas P, 1992. Print.

Lenhart, Gerry Anne. "First Prelude to Genesis: Antecedent Archetypes That Describe Basic Psychic Energy and the Four Functions." *A Developmental Hypothesis Based on the Order of Jung's Psychological Functions: The Genesis Model*. Diss. U of California, Berkeley, 1996. Print.

Kramer, Samuel Noah. *Sumerian Mythology*. New York: Harper, 1961. Print.

---. *The Sumerians*. Chicago: U of Chicago P, 1963. Print.

"Ninhursag's Children." *Gateways to Babylon*. N.p., n.d. Web. 26 June 2013.

Siren, Christopher. "Sumerian Mythology (FAQs)." *Stason.org*. Stas Bekman, 2013. Web. 26 June 2013.

Webster, Michael. "Sumerian Myth." *World Mythology*. Grand Valley State U, n.d. Web. 26 June 2013.

◆ The Creation of Enkidu

Author: Traditional Sumerian
Time Period: 2499 BCE–1000 BCE
Country or Culture: Mesopotamia
Genre: Myth

PLOT SUMMARY

In the ancient Sumerian city of Uruk (Erech), the people are unhappy with the wild ways of their king, Gilgameš (Gilgamesh). They implore the gods to find a way to temper him. The supreme sky god, Anu, responds. He instructs Aruru, the goddess of fertility who created humanity, to create a counterpart for Gilgameš to tame him. Aruru sets to her task. She creates Enkidu by molding clay in the wilderness.

Enkidu is created with a strong, hairy body. He does not know any other people. He spends his early life among gazelles. He eats grass like them and slakes his thirst at their watering hole. There, a trapper observes Enkidu. The trapper complains to his father that Enkidu has been freeing the animals from his snares and wreaking havoc with his traps. His father instructs the trapper to go to Uruk and ask Gilgameš for a temple prostitute.

The trapper should bring this woman to the watering hole. There, she will seduce Enkidu. Once Enkidu has been with her, his animals will flee from him.

The trapper does as instructed. From Uruk, he brings along a temple prostitute named Šamhat (Shamhat). They hide at the watering hole to catch Enkidu. On the third day of their vigil, Enkidu appears. The trapper tells Šamhat to disrobe and show her body to Enkidu. When Enkidu sees the naked Šamhat, he is aroused. He has sex with her for six days and seven nights. When he finally returns to his gazelles, they all flee from him, just as the trapper's father predicted would happen.

Šamhat suggests Enkidu should travel with her to Uruk to meet Gilgameš. Enkidu agrees, ready to challenge Gilgameš. Šamhat tells Enkidu that Gilgameš dreamed of their encounter already and that she loves Gilgameš, too. She tells Enkidu of Gilgameš's dream, then has sex with Enkidu again.

As they get ready to go to Uruk, Šamhat clothes Enkidu. She brings him to some shepherds, who are awed by Enkidu's physical prowess and his magnificent body. The shepherds offer Enkidu bread and beer, which is new food to him. Enkidu shaves his body hair and anoints himself, becoming increasingly civilized.

A messenger arrives and tells that Gilgameš will participate in a wedding at Uruk that night. Gilgameš will deflower the bride before she is given to her husband. Enkidu and Šamhat move into the city. There, Enkidu blocks Gilgameš's way into the bridal chamber. Enkidu and Gilgameš wrestle for a while, wreaking havoc on the place. Suddenly, they stop their fight. They kiss and become best friends.

SIGNIFICANCE

Enkidu is a mythological character originating with the ancient Sumerian people, who lived in what is present-day southern Iraq. The oldest surviving references to Enkidu, though they do not include the story of his creation, are found in Sumerian myths transcribed onto clay tablets dating from approximately 2100 BCE. The story of the creation of Enkidu is part of *The Epic of Gilgameš*, which was derived from these Sumerian sources and later combined into an epic poem in Akkadian. The epic has survived in two versions. The older one is from the eighteenth century BCE, and the other dates from the thirteenth to eleventh centuries BCE.

Parts of *The Epic of Gilgameš* were first translated into English in 1872 by the British Assyriologist George Smith. Since that time, many other English translations have been published. Maureen Kovacs's translation, which includes the story of Enkidu's creation, is both scholarly and accessible to contemporary readers.

The key significance of the Sumerian myth of the creation of Enkidu lies in its description of what it means to become fully human. Enkidu is purposefully created to provide a more human counterpart to Gilgameš. Part god and part human, Gilgameš is too overbearing because of his semidivine nature. It takes a fully human being like Enkidu to socialize Gilgameš to become a more suitable king of Uruk.

Enkidu's creation significantly relates to cultural ideas about the socialization of a human being. At first, Enkidu runs wild with herbivorous animals, eating grass and drinking plain water. It is only through love, represented by sexual intercourse with Šamhat, that Enkidu awakens to his humanity. Šamhat teaches Enkidu to behave like a human instead of an animal. She clothes him and introduces him to other people, who give him manmade foods, such as bread and beer.

The myths of divine creation of humans from clay, as occurs in the creation of Enkidu, appear to reflect the significance of pottery in early human civilizations. As humans learned to shape figures from clay, they appear to have ascribed to their deities the power to create humanity from animated clay figures. A counterpart to the story of the creation of Enkidu can be found in the Chinese myth of the goddess of Nüwa. As the Mesopotamian goddess Aruru does with Enkidu, Nüwa creates humans from clay. Since the late nineteenth century, many scholars have suggested that the biblical story of God creating Adam from dust was inspired by the Sumerian-Babylonian myth of the creation of Enkidu.

R. C. Lutz, PhD

BIBLIOGRAPHY

Gardener, John, and John Maier, trans. *Gilgamesh*. New York: Vintage, 1985. Print.

George, Andrew, trans. *The Epic of Gilgamesh*. London: Penguin, 2003. Print.

Jacobsen, Thorkild. *The Treasures of Darkness: A History of Mesopotamian Religion*. New Haven: Yale UP, 1976. Print.

Kovacs, Maureen Gallery, trans. *The Epic of Gilgamesh*. Stanford: Stanford UP, 1989. Print.

Leick, Gwendolyn. *Sex and Eroticism in Mesopotamian Literature*. London: Routledge, 1994. Print.

Thompson, Reginald Campbell, trans. *The Epic of Gilgamish*. London: Luzac, 1928. Print.

The Death of Enkidu

Author: Traditional Sumerian
Time Period: 2499 BCE–1000 BCE
Country or Culture: Mesopotamia
Genre: Myth

PLOT SUMMARY

The mighty warriors Enkidu and Gilgameš (Gilgamesh) rest in the city of Uruk (also known as Erech or Unug), having recently slaughtered the monster Huwawa (Humbaba) and the famed Bull of Heaven. Gilgameš is the king of Uruk and Enkidu his companion, a man brought out of the savage wilderness and civilized in part through the deep love he and the king share. It is as partners that the two complete their legendary deeds, battling ferocious monsters and spreading the fame of Uruk.

Enkidu succumbs to sleep and is visited by a horrible dream. In it, he sees a gathering of the gods Anu (An in Sumerian), Ellil (Enlil), and Šamaš (Shamash; also known as Utu). The gods discuss the deeds of Enkidu and Gilgameš and decide that as punishment for murdering the famed Bull of Heaven, one of the two warriors must die. While there is some debate, the gods quickly agree that Enkidu will lose his life for this great offense. When Enkidu wakes, the dream makes him tremble with fear, and he immediately begins to curse the gorgeous door that he had crafted to adorn the temple of Ellil, feeling betrayed by the god. Gilgameš tells Enkidu that he has begged the gods on behalf of his companion and even promises to build a giant golden statue to his friend in Uruk, but Enkidu only continues ranting, now even cursing the people who first brought him out of the wilderness and into civilization.

As Enkidu rages on and on, the god Šamaš calls out from the sky, reminding him that Gilgameš will bring great honor to his name and prophesying that Gilgameš's despair will consume him for the rest of his life. Šamaš also reminds Enkidu that had he never been brought into the city, he never would have known the great riches and greater friendship that he received there. The reminder of Gilgameš's love is enough to quiet Enkidu, and he quickly retracts his curse, thanking the gods for allowing him to be brought out of the wilderness and into Uruk. It is not long, however, before another deep and tortured sleep seizes Enkidu. He is haunted by visions of death, a land of dust in which people drink dirt and are terrorized by monstrous figures. The sheer horror of these visions does not fade but instead intensifies, with Enkidu taken by fevered dreams for days. At last, the illness overpowers him, and Enkidu takes his last breath, leaving Gilgameš alone to mourn the loss of his great companion.

SIGNIFICANCE

The death of Enkidu is a major turning point in the *Epic of Gilgameš*, set near the middle of the long narrative. Prior to his devastation at the hands of the gods, Enkidu is a powerful and feared man who rises from the wilderness to stand alongside Gilgameš as a leader of the civilized world, fights legendary creatures, and spreads glory throughout the land. When he dies, however, it becomes clear that he and Gilgameš are not unstoppable warriors but mortals subject to the whims and impulses of the gods.

The ancient Sumerian *Epic of Gilgameš* is one of the oldest works of literature to survive into the modern day. The narrative at its core explores the human struggle with mortality, focusing on Gilgameš and Enkidu's own search for immortality alongside the development of civilization. Prior to the gods' decision to kill Enkidu, the myth suggests that heroic acts on the battlefield and the expansion of civilization might in fact offer an escape from mortal death. Gilgameš and Enkidu are together able to slay monsters that others believe to be invincible, in a way overpowering death itself, while their legendary expansion of Uruk and protection of their civilization implies that their names will live on forever even if their bodies fail. Famed warriors accustomed to triumphing over all odds, Gilgameš and Enkidu suddenly find themselves confronted with the reality of their inevitable deaths.

That Enkidu's death comes so unexpectedly only heightens the irony of the myth. Among the deities debating who should be punished for slaughtering Huwawa and the Bull of Heaven is the god Šamaš, the same deity who initially encouraged Enkidu and Gilgameš to fight the beasts. Although they had the blessing of the gods at one point, the two warriors are now to be punished for their actions. Angered by this unfair judgment, Enkidu curses the gods and those who brought him into civilization, his rage emphasizing the way in which the myth examines the tension between the wills of mortals and the uncaring universe. This tension drives the remainder of the narrative and is never fully reconciled. Overcome by both the loss of his companion and the realization that he too will perish some day,

Gilgameš begins a long quest of despair, wandering the earth as he attempts to come to terms with the knowledge that he, like all mortal things, must one day cease to be.

T. Fleischmann, MFA

BIBLIOGRAPHY

"*The Epic of Gilgamesh*: Tablet VII." *Ancient Texts*. Timothy R. Carnahan, n.d. Web. 25 June 2013.

George, A. R., ed. *The Epic of Gilgamesh: The Babylonian Epic Poem and Other Texts in Akkadian*. New York: Penguin, 1999. Print.

"The Gilgamesh Epic." *Recommended Reading: 500 Classics Reviewed*. Pasadena: Salem, 1995. 80. Print.

Spatt, Hartley S. "The Gilgamesh Epic." *Masterplots*. Ed. Laurence W. Mazzeno. 4th ed. Vol. 4. Pasadena: Salem, 2010. 2265–68. Print.

Whitlark, James. "The Gilgamesh Epic." *Cyclopedia of Literary Places*. Ed. R. Kent Rasmussen. Vol. 1. Pasadena: Salem, 2003. 447–49. Print.

◆ The Death of Gilgameš

Author: Traditional Sumerian
Time Period: 2499 BCE–1000 BCE
Country or Culture: Mesopotamia
Genre: Myth

PLOT SUMMARY

The brave and powerful warrior Gilgameš (Gilgamesh), king of the city of Uruk (Erech), has accomplished much in his life. He has constructed great walls to protect his people, defeated mystical beasts in battle, and roamed the far edges of the world in search of immortality. Despite all these accomplishments, however, he lies down one day, weary and worn, and must at last face his inevitable death.

As Gilgameš starts to drift away, the gods gather in council to discuss him. They begin by listing his many accomplishments, which include retrieving rare cedar lumber from distant mountainsides in order to provide for his city. They also note that as a leader, he oversaw the construction of many temples that brought glory to the gods and likewise often obeyed the gods' decrees. In fact, Gilgameš is even part god himself, his father being a mortal king and his mother an immortal goddess. Because of this, some gods argue that it would be fitting to grant Gilgameš eternal life rather than allow him to slip into the land of death.

Despite these pleas on behalf of Gilgameš, the god Enki (Ea in Akkadian) reminds all of the deities that many years before, a tremendous flood had overtaken the earth. After the devastation of the flood, all the gods agreed that no human would be allowed to live forever; rather, a natural order would be put in place, with mortals all dying and new mortals rising to replace them. With this in mind, the gods bid Gilgameš to go on to the land of the dead. There, great gods and devoted priests wrapped in linen preside. Gilgameš's father, grandfather, and other ancestors wait for him there, as does his beloved and cherished companion, Enkidu. One day, the children of Gilgameš will meet their departed father there, and their descendents will follow.

When Gilgameš dies, the people of his city sound their loudest horns. They then open up their levies and, for days, divert the water of the mighty Euphrates River. When the bed of the river is dry, they build a large stone tomb and bury Gilgameš inside of it before allowing the water to return once more and flood over his final resting place. Although Gilgameš lamented his death and fought with all his power against his own mortality during his last days, his burial is completed with the greatest respect, his tomb both forever protected by the rushing waters and made a permanent part of the city itself. For all time, people will remember his deeds and honor the great accomplishments of the legendary king.

SIGNIFICANCE

The story of the death of Gilgameš is today considered a secondary tale to the main narrative of the *Epic of Gilgameš*. One of the oldest stories in world mythology, the tale of Gilgameš has survived for thousands of years, often retold and revised by new generations. Two existing sets of tablets, one written in the ancient language of Sumerian and the other in the somewhat later language of Akkadian, provide what is widely considered a comprehensive version of Gilgameš's mythology; scholars generally consider the latter set of writings to be the canonical version of the epic. Alongside these, however, are a large number of additional fragments and shattered tablets, some connecting with the primary narrative and some seeming to contradict it. A number of these fragmentary sources refer to the final days of Gilgameš, a time when the hero must at last face the truth of his own mortality.

The quests that Gilgameš undertakes during his life-time typically have one of two main objectives: to expand the glory and influence of the king's city, Uruk, or to achieve immortality for Gilgameš the man. In many ways, the story of Gilgameš is the tale of his slow acceptance of his own death and his realization that his fame as a leader and his contributions to civilization provide the closest alternative to true immortality. The story of his death highlights this realization, with the gods themselves listing his great deeds and acknowledging that he has done much for his city but ultimately concluding that he must meet the same end as all other mortals. However, they acknowledge the glory that comes along with a righteous mortal death, recognizing that in the afterlife, Gilgameš will take his rightful place alongside other legendary leaders. The narrative also stresses that the people of Uruk perform the magnificent feat of rerouting the Euphrates River in order to make his tomb a permanent part of the city and of the life-giving landscape of Mesopotamia, fueled as it was by that river.

Gilgameš himself does not entirely accept the generous nature of his fate, moaning and resisting his death until the last moment. The myth remains instructive for other humans, however, suggesting that they are of the greatest worth when they aid one another and sacrifice all they can for the glory of their civilization. The city of Uruk was one of the first major urban centers of the ancient world, and a real King Gilgameš seems to have existed there around 2500 BCE, overseeing the growth and security of his people alongside the fertile lands of the Euphrates River. Originating in an era when civilization was first developing and cities first rising to power, the myth surrounding this ancient ruler shows that the questions of mortality and the meaning of life that preoccupy modern humans were no less relevant in ancient times. An accomplished leader of legendary strength, Gilgameš must die in the flesh, even as the shattered tablets praising his many deeds extend his legacy across the centuries.

T. Fleischmann, MFA

BIBLIOGRAPHY

Black, Jeremy A., et al., eds."The Death of Gilgamesh." *Electronic Text Corpus of Sumerian Literature.* Faculty of Oriental Studies, U of Oxford, 2001. Web. 25 June 2013.

George, A. R., ed. *The Epic of Gilgamesh: The Babylonian Epic Poem and Other Texts in Akkadian.* New York: Penguin, 1999. Print.

"The Gilgamesh Epic." *Recommended Reading: 500 Classics Reviewed.* Pasadena: Salem, 1995. 80. Print.

Spar, Ira. "Gilgamesh." *Heilbrunn Timeline of Art History.* Metropolitan Museum of Art, Apr. 2009. Web. 25 June 2013.

Spatt, Hartley S. "The Gilgamesh Epic." *Masterplots.* Ed. Laurence W. Mazzeno. 4th ed. Vol. 4. Pasadena: Salem, 2010. 2265–68. Print.

Whitlark, James. "The Gilgamesh Epic." *Cyclopedia of Literary Places.* Ed. R. Kent Rasmussen. Vol. 1. Pasadena: Salem, 2003. 447–49. Print.

◆ Enki and Ninhursaĝa

Author: Traditional Sumerian
Time Period: 2499 BCE–1000 BCE
Country or Culture: Mesopotamia
Genre: Myth

PLOT SUMMARY

The myth of Enki and Ninhursaĝa (Ninhursag) is a complex Sumerian creation story that illustrates the creation of the earth. The myth surrounds two key Sumerian gods, Enki and Ninhursaĝa, and their offspring, each of whom enter into carnal relations with their father god Enki to give rise to another facet of the natural world.

Ninhursaĝa, a manifestation of the Sumerian earth mother goddess, resides in the land of Dilmun, the mythical land where the Sumerians believed creation occurred. When Enki, the god of freshwater, discovers Ninhursag in Dilmun, the two fall deeply in love. Ninhursaĝa asks Enki, the god of water, to provide water for her vast lands, a request that Enki fulfills. Enki summons Utu, the sun god, to assist. The ensuing carnal relationship between Ninhursaĝa and Enki results in the birth of Ninsar (or Ninnisig in some translations), the goddess of vegetation, nine days later. Ninsar covers the rocky landscape of Dilmun with grass, leaves, and flowerbeds.

Ninhursaĝa rejoices at the birth of her daughter but professes to both her and Enki that she must depart Dilmun in order to allow spring to return so that it can dismiss the winds of winter. For nine days, Ninsar further covers the land of Dilmun with vegetation before her mother, Ninhursaĝa, departs.

In the absence of his true love and wife, Enki lusts after his daughter, Ninsar, and seduces her. Ninsar gives birth to Ninkura (Ninkurra), the goddess of mountain meadows. Despite his love for Ninsar, Enki eventually realizes she is no replacement for Ninhursaĝa. As the myth unfolds, Enki seduces Ninkura as well, but similarly comes to the realization that she cannot replace his true love, Ninhursaĝa. Ninkura gives birth to Uttu, the goddess of weaving.

Ninhursaĝa returns to Dilmun engraged at Enki's unbridled lust. Ninhursaĝa warns Uttu to avoid Enki by staying away from the riverbanks of Dilmun. Not to be dissuaded, Enki lures Uttu with garden delicacies. Uttu falls deeply in love with Enki and vows to be bonded to him for all eternity, but like all the goddesses before, Enki eventually abandons her. Ninhursaĝa removes Enki's semen from Uttu and deposits it into the soil of Dilmun, where eight plants grow.

Enki visits the location of the plants with his companion Isimud, who names and cuts pieces from each of the eight plants for Enki to eat. Ninhursaĝa, once again enraged, curses Enki and departs Dilmun. Shortly after, Enki falls gravely ill.

Enki's suffering greatly saddens the Anunnaki, the great gods. Enlil, the lord of the air and Enki's brother, along with all the healing deities, tries to help his brother, to no avail. A fox promises Enlil that she will seek out Ninhursaĝa. At the fox's instigation, the birth goddess begrudgingly returns and brings Enki back to health by putting his head into her lap and birthing eight new gods from each of Enki's eight ailing body parts.

SIGNIFICANCE

The myth of Enki and Ninhursaĝa is well known among mythological scholars due to its many similarities to the biblical story of Adam and Eve. The most obvious correlation is Enki's devouring of forbidden fruit—namely, the eight plants that grow because of his affair with Uttu. Much as Adam and Eve's devouring of the forbidden fruit in the Garden of Eden casts them into an eternity of fallibility and suffering, Enki too is met with considerable suffering after repeatedly being unable to rein in his desires.

In interesting contrast to the biblical story, it is the goddess Ninhursaĝa who extracts a rib from the god Enki in order to spawn life. Scholars have never been able to pinpoint the influence of the myth of Enki and Ninhursaĝa on the biblical story of creation with accuracy, although the ancient Sumerian culture has been seen as a major influence on the Canaanites, an early Middle Eastern people who preceded the Jewish people in the southern Levant.

Many of the details of the myth of Enki and Ninhursaĝa remain open to speculation, both because of varying scholarly interpretation and because of physical damage to the stone that bears the text (see Kramer). For instance, some scholars speculate that there may be a connection between the biblical narrative surrounding the biblical creation of Eve from Adam's rib and the use of the word *ti* ("rib") for Ninti, the goddess of the rib, in the Sumerian myth. The existing fragments from the original text give little information regarding the whereabouts of Ninhursaĝa during Enki's incestuous exploits, the emotions and motives of the major characters, and the exact reasons for Ninhursaĝa's curse and return. Modern renditions, such as that given on the Gateways to Babylon website, often attempt to fill in these gaps. Such accounts sometimes also condense the number of incestuous encounters, omitting the goddess Ninimma, the daughter of Ninkura and mother of Uttu.

Despite such speculation, the myth of Enki and Ninhursaĝa bears resemblance to creation myths that have been discovered from former civilizations all over the world. Throughout world mythology, human life is derived after a continual and developing merger between the forces of the natural world, each of which are subject to the desires and betrayals with which humankind continually struggles.

John Pritchard

BIBLIOGRAPHY

Black, Jeremy A., et al., eds. "Enki and Ninhursaĝa." *Electronic Text Corpus of Sumerian Literature*. Faculty of Oriental Studies, U of Oxford, 2006. Web. 21 June 2013.

Elwell, Walter A., and Philip Wesley Comfort, eds. "Sumerian Creation Myths." *Tyndale Bible Dictionary*. Wheaton: Tyndale, 2001. 330–31. Print.

"Enki and Ninhursag: How Enki Surrendered to the Earth Mother and Queen." *Gateways to Babylon*. N.p., n.d. Web. 21 June 2013.

Kramer, Samuel Noah. "Enki and Ninhursag: The Affairs of the Watergod." *Sumerian Mythology: A Study of Spiritual and Literary Achievement in the Third Millenium B.C.* Rev. ed. Philadelphia: U of Pennsylvania P, 1972. 54–58. Print.

Leick, Gwendolyn. "Enki and Ninhursaga: A Myth of Male Lust?" *Sex and Eroticism in Mesopotamian Literature*. London: Routledge, 1994. 30–41. Print.

Monaghan, Patricia. "Ninhursag." *Encyclopedia of Goddesses and Heroines*. Santa Barbara: ABC-CLIO, 2009. 72–73. Print.

Enuma elish, the Babylonian Creation Myth

Author: Traditional Babylonian
Time Period: 2499 BCE–1000 BCE
Country or Culture: Mesopotamia
Genre: Myth

SUMMARY

In the age when the sky and the earth are still nameless, the gods Apsû and Tiāmat live together as one mass of swirling water. Apsû is the god of fresh water and male fertility, and Tiāmat is the goddess of the sea and of chaos. Other gods, such as the gods of the earth and the sky, begin to form in this body of water.

The young gods inside the water are disorderly, and the commotion they make begins to upset Apsû and Tiāmat. Because of this, Apsû decides to destroy them. Ea, a god of wisdom and magic who is stronger than any of the other young gods, learns of Apsû's plan. Ea uses his magic to put Apsû into a dark sleep and then kills him, claiming himself to have become the chief god in this conquest. He lives with his wife, Damkina, above Apsû's corpse. Damkina then gives birth to Marduk, the god of storms and magic and the patron god of Babylon, who is even more powerful than his father.

Furious about her husband's death, Tiāmat gathers an army and summons eleven monsters to help her take revenge on the new gods. She is a deity of great chaos, and as such, the other gods become fearful of her vengeance. Both Ea and Anu, the god of the sky, confront Tiāmat but are unable to stop her path of destruction. Hopeful word eventually comes from Anšar, the son of Tiāmat, who reports that Marduk is willing to confront the goddess himself. The gods at first doubt Marduk's power, but when he makes a piece of clothing disappear and reappear, they agree to make him their ruler for all time if he succeeds in his quest. Marduk gathers the winds about him, charges Tiāmat in a chariot made of clouds, captures her in a net, and slays her by firing an arrow into her heart and smashing her head with a club. Taking her monsters captive, Marduk divides her body into the earth and the sky, imprisoning her chaotic waters and placing guards to ensure they will never escape.

Marduk then creates cities for the gods to dwell in and transforms Tiāmat's saliva into rain to water the earth. Among the cities, he creates Babylon for himself. He and the other gods also take time to establish the seasons and the months of the year. While the gods at first need to serve Marduk, Ea eventually slays Tiāmat's second husband and uses the dead god's blood to make humans, who will serve all the gods. To praise Marduk further, the other gods build him a new home in Babylon, and he in turn throws a feast to thank them. Marduk, then, is the greatest of the gods, a deity known by fifty throne names, and it is the duty of humans to serve him for all time.

SIGNIFICANCE

The *Enuma elish* is a text from ancient Babylon that was read in ceremonies to celebrate the start of the new year. As the Babylonian city-state was one of the first civilizations to develop in the ancient world, the myths included in the text—dating between the twelfth and the eighteenth century BCE—are also some of the oldest myths to survive in written form.

The narrative of the *Enuma elish* served several important functions for Babylonians. It explains the basic nature of the universe and established the cyclical progression of the years and seasons. It was believed that life comes from water, which was once combined in a giant mass but then was split into salt water and fresh water in a cosmic conflict of the gods. Likewise, chaos (represented in Tiāmat and the danger of the open oceans) and order (represented in the life-giving fresh water of Apsû) were once mingled but were then confined apart from one another. The narrative of the feuding gods provides an explanation for how these splits came to be, and indeed it is the existence of fresh water and safety from the seas that allowed civilizations to develop. The myth also explains the cycle of the seasons, which are declared by the triumphant gods after the defeat of Tiāmat. This victorious order also explains why humans exist in obedient tribute to the deities, with their very birth owed to Marduk's strength. In language, also, Marduk represents reason; the time before the gods is one in which even the universe has no name, while after the defeat of Tiāmat and her second husband, Qingu (Kingu), Marduk is known and celebrated by fifty different names. All of this folded together suggests a world that naturally progresses toward peace and order thanks to the might of Marduk, and by extension a world in which the obedience of humans within the religious and social order of Babylon ensures a future of similar security.

More than just a narrative of creation, however, this myth also served an additional political purpose.

Marduk was the chief god of the city of Babylon, and the elevation of his worship above the worship of other deities coincided with the rise of Babylon to a center of regional power. Around the time the *Enuma elish* seems to have become popular, King Hammurabi of Babylonia engaged in a series of wars that won his city control over Mesopotamian agricultural lands and, along with that, military and economic power. Prior to this, the Sumerian god Enlil had been widely worshipped and was commonly considered the most powerful of all the Mesopotamian deities. His seat of power was rooted in the city of Nippur. The *Enuma elish*, then, shows the close interrelationship between political power and religion in the ancient world, the narrative weaving together and making interdependent the exaltation of Marduk, the origins of Babylon, and the natural order of the seasons.

T. Fleischmann, MFA

BIBLIOGRAPHY

Bratcher, Dennis. "*Enuma Elish*: The Mesopotamian/ Babylonian Creation Myth." *The Voice*. CRI/Voice Inst., 25 Mar. 2013. Web. 30 May 2013.

Burkert, Walter. *Babylon, Memphis, Persepolis*: *Eastern Contexts of Greek Culture*. Cambridge: Harvard UP, 2007. Print.

Dalley, Stephanie, trans. *Myths from Mesopotamia: Creation, the Flood, Gilgamesh, and Others*. Oxford: Oxford UP, 1989. Print.

López-Ruiz, Carolina. "How to Start a Cosmogony: On the Poetics of Beginnings in Greece and the Near East." *Journal of Ancient Near Eastern Religions* 12.1 (2012): 30–48. Print.

Oates, Joan. *Babylon*. New York: Thames, 2008. Print.

◆ Etana, King of Kish

Author: Traditional Babylonian
Time Period: 2499 BCE–1000 BCE
Country or Culture: Mesopotamia
Genre: Legend

PLOT SUMMARY

Etana is the legendary king of the southern Mesopotamian city of Kish who assumes power after a great flood. King Etana is, however, childless and in search of an heir to his throne. The implication is that though his wife is pregnant, she does not possess the ability to give birth. As a result, Etana prays to the sun god Šamaš (Shamash) for assistance. Šamaš is simultaneously sought in prayer by two animals, an eagle and a snake.

The snake prays to Šamaš because the eagle has eaten his children. The sun god helps the serpent avenge the death of his children by maiming and imprisoning the eagle in a deep, mountainside pit. In response to Etana's plea, the sun god then instructs that he go to the eagle's aid in the hopes the bird will assist him in finding an heir.

Over a period of seven months, Etana nurses the eagle back to health and helps him learn to fly again. As a reward for his kindness, the eagle promises Etana he will help him find a magical birth plant that will help his wife produce him an heir. However, the eagle is unable to find the plant, and he and Etana fly to heaven to consult Ištar (Ishtar), the goddess of love and fertility.

SIGNIFICANCE

The ancient Mesopotamian tale of Etana illustrates the Sumerian king Etana's struggle to find a successor to his throne. A historical figure named Etana ruled Kish in the first half of the third millennium BCE. References to the legendary Etana have been found on fragmented clay tablets from as far back as the reign of Sargon of Akkad (2334–2279 BCE) as well as in later fragments from the First Dynasty of Babylon, Middle Assyrian period, and Neo-Assyrian period. Though the known fragments contain only an incomplete narrative, enough of it remains intact to make it one of the oldest remaining pieces of literature from ancient Mesopotamia.

One school of interpretation regards the legend of Etana as a kind of royal propaganda. The themes of suffering, punishment, and rebirth are prominent throughout. There is also some scholarly evidence to suggest a connection to an earlier Sumerian myth about the goddess Inana (Ištar's precursor) quarreling with a serpent and eagle for the rights to the supply of wood from which she seeks to build a throne. The connection, if any, could imply that the author or orator was playing on a familiar narrative theme.

Regardless of what cultural or symbolic tactics Etana utilized, the king's capability as a ruler is well established from literature and artifacts related to the period, as is his accomplishment of uniting the Mesopotamian city-states under one rule. The scene in which Etana is flown to heaven on the eagle's back is believed to have a crucial significance to this era in ancient Mesopotamia.

Ancient illustrations depicting the scene have been found on several archeological finds from the period. Historians have also pointed to Etana's successful rehabilitation of the bird as an illustrative indicator of his ability to tackle complex tasks as a leader.

The outcome of the narrative has never been certain, since the fragments depicting the end have not survived. Analysis of myths that followed in the wake of the legend of Etana has led to a scholarly disagreement as to how the tale may have ended. Disjointed fragments indicate that the king never reached heaven and instead crashed to the ground, while others speculate that the king may have utilized his success in the tale to support his claim to the throne.

No matter how the story ended, the surviving narrative implies that the importance of finding Etana's successor is crucial enough to involve collaboration between the human and animal kingdom, as well as divine counsel. Yet despite the story's assertion of the importance of dynastic rule, historians have not unveiled a steady lineage of hereditary rule following Etana's tenure as leader. While according to a manuscript known as the *Sumerian King List*, the historical Etana did have a son, Balih, who succeeded him as the ruler of Kish, their royal line seems to have ended there.

John Pritchard

BIBLIOGRAPHY

Dalley, Stephanie. *Myths from Mesopotamia: Creation, the Flood, Gilgamesh, and Others*. Rev. ed. Oxford; New York: Oxford UP, 2008.

Ehrlich, Carl S. *From an Antique Land: An Introduction to Ancient Near Eastern Literature*. Lanham: Rowman, 2011. Print.

Hallo, William W. *The World's Oldest Literature: Studies in Sumerian Belles-Lettres*. Leiden: Brill, 2010. Print. Culture and History of the Ancient Near East 35.

Horowitz, Wayne. *Mesopotamian Cosmic Geography*. 2nd rev. ed. Winona Lake: Eisenbrauns, 2011. Print.

Jacobsen, Thorkild, trans. *The Sumerian King List*. 1965. Chicago: U of Chicago P, 1973. Print. Assyrological Studies 11.

Kinnier Wilson, J. V., ed. and trans. *The Legend of Etana*. New ed. Warminster: Aris, 1985. Print.

Novotny, Jamie R. *The Standard Babylonian Etana Epic*. Helsinki: Neo-Assyrian Text Corpus Project, 2001. Print. State Archives of Assyria Cuneiform Texts 2.

◆ Inana and Šu-kale-tuda

Author: Traditional Sumerian
Time Period: 2499 BCE–1000 BCE
Country or Culture: Mesopotamia
Genre: Myth

PLOT SUMMARY

The goddess Inana (Inanna) leaves her holy throne one day and travels up into the mountains. The purpose of her journey from the sky and the earth is to distinguish further between right and wrong, so that she may be able to dispense justice more accurately. Climbing up the mountain, Inana is able to survey the land and its inhabitants. By doing this, she can identify the criminal and the just. She climbs farther and farther up the mountain until she grows weary of questioning and searching.

While Inana is finding a place to rest, the god Enki instructs a raven to perform a variety of agricultural chores around his shrine at Eridug (Eridu). The raven's chores include chopping up kohl for the incantation of the priests, watering a field with a shadoof (pole, counterweights, and water), and cultivating date palms. The raven obeys Enki's orders and performs these tasks as a man would.

As Inana travels around the mountain, a young gardener named Šu-kale-tuda (Shukaletuda) arrives to perform his work. He finds that no plants remain, for he had previously pulled them out by their roots and destroyed them. A storm wind blows the dust of the mountain in his eyes, and he is unable to remove it all. Squinting into the sky and the land, Šu-kale-tuda spots Inana, who is just lying down beneath the shade of a poplar tree. At first, he believes her to be a ghost, but judging from her appearance and divine clothing, Šu-kale-tuda realizes that she is a goddess. He approaches her and, as she sleeps, undresses her and has intercourse with her. When he is finished, he returns to his plot. When the sun rises, Inana awakens and inspects herself. Seeing that she has been violated, she becomes furious. In her anger, she turns all of the water in the wells to blood so that the land is irrigated with blood and the inhabitants have nothing else to drink. She searches the land for the man who has violated her but is unable to locate him.

Nervous that he will be found, Šu-kale-tuda goes to his father and explains to him what he has done. His father repeatedly instructs him to hide among the people of the city, where he can blend in with the others and avoid discovery by the goddess, who is searching up on the mountainsides. Still unable to locate the gardener, Inana summons a series of violent storms. This still does not manage to turn up the culprit, so she blocks the highways. No matter what she does, Inana continues to look in the wrong place for Šu-kale-tuda, who successfully remains hidden in the city.

Discouraged by her inability to locate the man who violated her, Inana goes to Eridug and pleads before the powerful water god Enki for guidance and the ability to bring the man to justice. Enki agrees to help her, and Inana then spans across the whole sky like a rainbow. This allows her to locate Šu-kale-tuda, who is attempting to make himself small and unnoticeable in the mountains. Despite his pleas and attempts to explain what happened, she passes judgment upon him. She states that he is to die but that shepherds and bards will sing his name around the land, so that his name will not be forgotten.

SIGNIFICANCE

The myth of Inana and Šu-kale-tuda concerns the goddess Inana, the most prominent female deity in Sumerian mythology and the patron of the city of Uruk (also known as Erech or Unug) in Sumer. As a goddess, she is associated with a wide range of concepts, including war, fertility, love, justice, and fairness. Many evaluations of her myths take a feminist angle, as she was dominant in Sumerian mythology, sometimes more so than patriarchal deities. She has been adapted as the archetype of female transformation and identity.

Contemporary interpretations of Sumerian Inana mythology have noted the astral aspects of the goddess, particularly her relationship with the planet Venus. Research has shown that although the specifics of Venus's movements in the sky may not have been known at the time, prehistoric southern Mesopotamians may have recognized Venus's unique appearances in the east and in the west at different times of the year as being those of the same celestial body long before other civilizations did. The Inana interpretations come from the movements of Inana within her stories, which correspond with the movements of Venus through the sky. Scholars believe that in this particular myth, Inana may be in her astral manifestation, in terms of both her physicality and her specific movements. She is seen in the eastern and western horizons and then miraculously leaves the sky to search for her attacker. Also, many scholars suggest that

when Šu-kale-tuda is looking to the sky after having mountain dust blown in his eyes, he may be looking to Venus, and that is why he is astounded to see her on the land, near the poplar tree.

In another Inana myth, that of her descent to the underworld, her journey in part describes the setting of Venus in the west and its eventual rising in the east, which corresponds with Inana's ascension from the underworld. Scholars have noted that these astral interpretations of Inana's mythology are simply theories, since ancient Sumerian astral mythology was never codified in antiquity.

Enki and Inana interact frequently in Sumerian mythology. In an earlier myth, he attempts to seduce the goddess, but while he gets drunk, she maintains her virtue. In his drunkenness, the god bestows upon Inana the gifts of his *me*, or decrees of civilized life. Enki was known for helping those who asked him for aid, and true to his character, he helps Inana locate her attacker in this myth.

There are several lines missing from the original text surrounding the tale of the raven and Enki. Scholars are unsure how this diversion relates to the narrative arc of Inana and Šu-kale-tuda as a whole. The two stories do share certain features, such as an emphasis on agriculture and the role played by Enki, but the inclusion of the raven's tale is confounding to scholars, since the bird does not interact with Inana or Šu-kale-tuda or appear to affect the story at all. Therefore, the myth of Inana and Šu-kale-tuda is sometimes examined without the inclusion of the raven.

Patrick G. Cooper

BIBLIOGRAPHY

Black, Jeremy A., et al., eds. "Inana and Šu-kale-tuda." *Electronic Text Corpus of Sumerian Literature*. Faculty of Oriental Studies, U of Oxford, 2006. Web. 24 June 2013.

Cochrane, Ev. *The Many Faces of Venus: The Planet Venus in Ancient Myth and Religion*. Ames: Aeon, 1997. Print.

Cooley, Jeff. "Inana and Sukaletuda: A Sumerian Astral Myth." *Kaskal* 5 (2008): 161–72. Print.

Dalley, Stephanie, trans. *Myths from Mesopotamia: Creation, the Flood, Gilgamesh, and Others*. Oxford: UP, 2009. Print.

Kramer, Samuel Noah, and Diane Wolkstein. *Inanna, Queen of Heaven and Earth: Her Stories and Hymns from Sumer*. New York: Harper, 1983. Print.

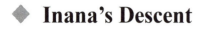

Inana's Descent

Author: Traditional Sumerian
Time Period: 2499 BCE–1000 BCE
Country or Culture: Mesopotamia
Genre: Myth

PLOT SUMMARY

Before she descends to the underworld, the goddess Inana (Inanna) tells her servant Ninšubur (Ninshubur) to lament for her by the ruins and mourn her both in public and in private if she does not return. Ninšubur is also instructed to go and weep first before Enlil (god of air), then Nanna (moon god), and lastly Enki (god of wisdom) in the hope that one of them will bring Inana back from the underworld if she does not return. Inana then journeys to the outer gate of the underworld. At the gate, she sternly calls out for the gatekeeper, Neti, to open the doors.

In all, there are seven gates that Inana must go through. When she goes through the first gate, her *šugurra* (or *shugurra*, "crown of the steppe") is taken from her. At each gate, she must give up another of her powerful possessions: her necklace of lapis beads, the double strand of beads from her breast, her breastplate, her gold bracelet, her lapis measuring tools, and, finally, her royal robe. Each time, she questions the loss of the item and is then rebuked for questioning the ways of the underworld.

Naked, Inana enters the throne room of Ereškigala (Ereshkigal), her older sister and the goddess of the underworld. The judges of the underworld, the Anuna, come up to Inana and pass judgment against her. Their deadly gaze and their shouts of anger and guilt strike her dead, and her body is then hung from a hook like rotting meat.

Three days and three nights go by, and Inana still has not returned from the underworld. Her servant Ninšubur laments at the ruins, beats the drum in the temples, ritually cuts herself, dresses in sackcloth, and visits the gods. Because Inana chose to go to the underworld, from which no one can return, and sought power she should not have, Enlil and Nanna both refuse to help her. However, Enki agrees to release Inana from the underworld. Concerned for the goddess, he creates servants out of dust and commands them to sneak into the underworld. There, they commiserate with the labor-panged Ereškigala and persuade her to release Inana.

As Inana is ascending back to the Great Above, the Anuna seize her and tell her she cannot return without supplying someone to take her place. Then the *galla*, the demons of the underworld, also seize her. These beings know no joy except bringing misery to others. The galla tell Inana they will travel with her to the Great Above and try to take Ninšubur in her place. Inana pleads with them not to take her servant, so the galla state that they will take her sons, Šara (Shara) and Lulal. Inana begs them not to take her sons.

With the galla seizing her, Inana travels to the big apple tree in the city of Uruk (also known as Erech or Unug). There, Inana's husband, Dumuzid, is sitting on his throne, lavishly dressed. Displeased that he is not mourning her, Inana allows the demons to take him. The demons grab him by the thighs and cause a ruckus. Inana freely opens up Dumuzid to the galla. She gives him "the eye of death" and speaks "the word of death" and "the cry of guilt" (Wolkstein and Kramer 71). The galla begin beating Dumuzid and cutting him with axes. Although he tries to escape the galla, the tale ultimately ends with Dumuzid residing in the underworld for six months out of the year and his sister, Ĝeštinana (Geshtinanna), taking his place the other six months.

SIGNIFICANCE

Inana, known as Ištar (Ishtar) in Babylonian mythology, is the most prominent female deity in Sumerian mythology and, as a goddess, represents a range of concepts, from war to love and fertility to healing. Called the Queen of Heaven, she was considered the patron of Uruk, where her most important temple was built.

The story of Inana's descent into the underworld has been interpreted in many different ways. Popular contemporary interpretations have frequently used a feminist lens. These interpretations read the story as empowering for women, particularly in Inana's willful decision to descend to the underworld, knowing that she might not be able to return. In this way, she has become an archetype of feminine transformation and experience. While the text hints at but does not specifically state a reason or purpose for her descent, the feminist interpretation typically views it as a personal journey that she knows she must endure in order to acquire further strength and wisdom. Enlil and Nanna's disapproval of her descent supports this idea and implies that they consider desire for this knowledge hubristic. Some have read the removal of her expensive clothes and jewelry at the gates as Inana stripping away the symbols of who she is.

When Inana does return, feminist interpretations have said that she chooses her husband, Dumuzid, to descend with the galla in order to prove perhaps that he possesses the same feminine strength and wisdom that she has. The annual death and rebirth of Dumuzid has been taken as a representation of the growth and harvest cycle of crops. Along the same lines, Inana's descent and return can be read as a metaphor for the revival of life in the spring. In later, Babylonian versions, Ištar descends to the underworld in order to retrieve Tammuz (the Babylonian Dumuzid), who has already died, and thereby initiates this annual cycle.

The descent to the underworld is a recurring element found in mythologies throughout the world and specifically in the traditional hero's journey. The reasons mythological characters travel to the underworld vary, but some common motifs include searching for one's destiny or retrieving a lost loved one. Metaphorically, the descent usually represents a transformation for the character. When the character returns, he or she is fundamentally changed by the travel and is thereafter a different person, typically with more wisdom and strength. In these cases, the underworld itself is a place of revelation rather than a place of eternal fire and suffering, a concept revisited in many modernist depictions.

Patrick G. Cooper

BIBLIOGRAPHY

Black, Jeremy A., et al. "Inana's Descent to the Underworld." *The Literature of Ancient Sumer*. Oxford: Oxford UP, 2004. 65–76. Print.

Deagon, Andrea. "Inanna's Descent: An Archetype of Feminine Self-Discovery and Transformation." *University of North Carolina Wilmington*. UNC Wilmington, n.d. Web. 30 May 2013.

Murdock, Maureen. *The Heroine's Journey*. Boston: Shambhala, 1990. Print.

Perera, Sylvia Brinton. *Descent to the Goddess: A Way of Initiation for Women*. Toronto: Inner City, 1981. Print.

Smith, Evans Lansing. "Modernism." *The Hero Journey in Literature: Parables of Poesis*. Lanham: UP of America, 1997. 341–452. Print.

Wolkstein, Diane, and Samuel Noah Kramer. "The Descent of Inanna." *Inanna, Queen of Heaven and Earth: Her Stories and Hymns from Sumer*. New York: Harper, 1983. 51–90. Print.

◆ The Journey of Nanna to Nippur

Author: Traditional Sumerian
Time Period: 2499 BCE–1000 BCE
Country or Culture: Mesopotamia
Genre: Myth

PLOT SUMMARY

One day Nanna, the god of the moon, decides to travel to Nippur (Nibru) to visit his parents, Enlil and Ninlil. His father, Enlil, is the patron god of Nippur and the head of the Sumerian pantheon.

Nanna, who is alternatively known as Suen or Acimbabbar depending on the phase of the moon, is the guardian god of the southern Sumerian city of Ur. It is from there that Nanna will begin his journey north along the Euphrates River. Nanna calls on his people to bring reeds, pitch, and rushes to construct his river barge. When it is finished, Nanna's son Utu, the god of the sun, rejoices with his father. Nanna loads his barge with a great quantity and variety of animals. He takes bulls, sheep, goats, and different species of bird and fish on board. Nanna also gathers eggs, lumber, precious metals, and reeds to take to his father.

When his barge is loaded, Nanna sets off for Nippur. He stops at five cities along the Euphrates and its tributaries. At each city, a noblewoman greets the boat and the townspeople attempt to sidetrack the barge from its ultimate destination, but Nanna continues on to Nippur.

Finally, Nanna docks his barge at the quay of Nippur. He calls out to the doorman of his father's house to open the city's gates. Nanna announces all the gifts he has brought to honor his father. With joy, the doorman opens the gates. Enlil gladly welcomes Nanna. He gives his son the sweet cakes Nanna loves, top-quality bread, and beer. Nanna presents the many gifts he has brought from the south. Father and son rejoice in their reunion.

Nanna thanks Enlil for his generous hospitality. He asks his father for divine gifts to bring home with him. Nanna asks Enlil to send a river flood for carp to breed in, barley to grow in his fields, carp to thrive in his ponds, old and new reeds, syrup and wine for his orchards, and the game animals of ibex and wild ram. With great paternal generosity, Enlil agrees to fulfill all of his son's wishes. Wishing each other a long life, Nanna takes his leave from Enlil to depart south for Ur.

SIGNIFICANCE

The myth of Nanna's journey to Nippur is referenced in several surviving texts from ancient Sumer. Sumer was an association of prosperous city-states located in modern-day Iraq. With origins in the fifth millennium BCE, Sumer flourished throughout the third millennium BCE. Nippur is located near the modern-day Iraqi city of Afak, and Nanna's hometown of Ur lies near the modern-day Iraqi town of Nasiriya. In the 1930s, a ziggurat temple dedicated to Nanna was unearthed near Nasiriya.

Around 2500 BCE, Sumerians began to record their myths in the cuneiform writing they had invented by 3000 BCE. Most surviving cuneiform tablets relating the journey of Nanna to Nippur date from the seventeenth century BCE, but scholars agree that the myth was recorded long before, most likely at the end of the third millennium BCE.

The prime significance of the journey of Nanna to Nippur is the mythological elevation and celebration of the river trade to ancient Sumer. Sumerian cities flourished in part because of this trade. A primary route was between southern Sumerian cities such as Ur and northern counterparts such as Nippur. The gifts that Nanna, the guardian deity of Ur, gathers to bring north ceremonially reflect the goods of the marshlands of southern Sumer. Along the banks of the Euphrates, Sumerians raised a variety of domesticated animals. Nanna gathers an impressive flock of them to transport north. The goods Nanna receives as gifts from his father—cakes, fine bread, and beer—reflect the agricultural products grown in the north of Sumer. There, wheat and barley provided the basis for bread and beer.

In the myth, Nanna refuses to trade with the river cities where his barge stops. Scholars have established that trade did historically occur at all of these way stations, but the myth reinforces Nippur's ascendency and Ur's strong allegiance to Nippur and Enlil. The ancient cities of Nippur and Ur were located approximately 125 miles (200 kilometers) apart from each other. Both cities were centers of Sumerian culture, and they competed with each other for cultural and political supremacy. The myth establishes Ur's prominence and wealth in the great variety of goods that Nanna loads onto his barge. But Nanna's pilgrimage to Nippur demonstrates that the prosperity of Ur depends on the continued benediction of Enlil.

R. C. Lutz, PhD

BIBLIOGRAPHY

Bottéro, Jean. *Religion in Ancient Mesopotamia*. Trans. Teresa Lavender Fagan. Chicago: U of Chicago P, 2001. Print.

Ferrara, A. J. *Nanna-Suen's Journey to Nippur*. Rome: Biblical Institute, 1973. Print.

Jacobsen, Thorkild. *The Treasures of Darkness: A History of Mesopotamian Religion*. New Haven: Yale UP, 1976. Print.

Kramer, Samuel Noah. "The Journey of Nanna to Nippur." *Sumerian Mythology*. Rev. ed. Philadelphia: U of Pennsylvania P, 1976. 47–48. Print.

◆ Marduk the Dragon Slayer

Author: Traditional Babylonian
Time Period: 2499 BCE–1000 BCE
Country or Culture: Mesopotamia
Genre: Myth

PLOT SUMMARY

In the beginning, there is only a vast sea. Apsû is in charge of this sea, while the spirit of chaos is embodied in the goddess Tiāmat. Then, the gods, beginning with the god Lahmu and the goddess Lahamu, start to emerge from Apsû's domain. After a long period, more gods come forth, such as Anšar (Anshar) and Kišar (Kishar). Later, the great sky god, An (Anu), and the wise Ea, or Enki—who will become the lord of the earth—emerge from the sea as well. Many more gods come forth, each of whom is powerful and glorious. The gods set out to bring order and control to the forming universe.

Apsû and Tiāmat do not wish to see an end to the chaos. Apsû consults with his son and counsel, Mammu, to determine what can be done about the high gods' activities. Tiāmat sends powerful storms, but the gods are undeterred, and Apsû's projections of power are also ineffective in defeating the high gods. Mammu tells Apsû that defeating the gods is possible, and the two go about plotting how to fight the gods. Ea, who has grown more powerful than his father, overhears Apsû and Mammu and utters an incantation. Apsû falls asleep, while Mammu falls into a daze. Ea kills Apsû by holding him down and captures Mammu, binding him with a rope. Ea then takes his father's crown and other signs of power and claims them for himself. Ea and his wife Damkina then have a son, Marduk (also known as Merodach).

Tiāmat, vengeful at the defeat of Apsû and Mammu, consults with the god Qingu. The two agree to wage full war against Ea and the high gods. They raise an army of fearsome creatures, including serpents, dragons, scorpion men and other monstrosities. In the face of this danger, Ea consults with his father, Anšar, who in turn appeals to An to calm Tiāmat. An, however, senses her wrath and does not approach Tiāmat. Anšar therefore turns to Marduk to stand against the fearful power of Tiāmat and her army. Anšar relieves Marduk of the latter's fear and promises him that he will indeed wound Tiāmat. Anšar also appeals to the other gods and his own counsel to make Marduk their king so that he will have the power to smite Tiāmat.

Marduk takes up a bow and quiver of arrows, a club, and a spear and moves to engage Tiāmat. He creates a number of powerful natural forces—the seven winds—and the powerful thunderstone before climbing into his storm chariot, which is pulled by poisonous horses. The high gods stand by his side as he rides to Tiāmat's lair. He reveals his newfound power to her, using his thunderstone to terrify her supporters. Using a net and the winds at his disposal, Marduk slays Tiāmat the dragon. The rebellious gods, having lost Tiāmat, attempt to retreat but are caught in Marduk's net and stripped of their weapons.

Marduk then divides the dragon's body and uses it to create realms for the gods as well as the earth. He also creates the stars and celestial bodies, including the moon and the constellations. Later, at the behest of Ea, who wants the gods to be revered, Marduk creates humans. Thereafter, he creates the other creatures of the earth as well as the Tigris and Euphrates Rivers and the plants and trees that surround the area.

Meanwhile, all of the gods become linked to Marduk, including the gods that had previously been aligned with Tiāmat. Such actions help bring order to the universe.

SIGNIFICANCE

The story of Marduk is derived from two separate Babylonian sets of tablets—the *Enuma elish* and the *Atrahasis*—both of which were likely written between 1800 and 1500 BCE. The *Enuma elish* (When on high) comprises seven tablets, known as the seven tablets of creation, which were unearthed during the nineteenth century CE. The tablets were incomplete and were pieced together thereafter. It is believed that the story on these tablets dates back to ancient Sumer (ca. 3500–2000 BCE). The elements of the myth focusing on humans,

found on the *Atrahasis* (Extra-wise), are believed to have been written around 1700 BCE, though the story itself likely dates back to Sumerian times. These inconsistencies are evident in the myriad names for such figures as Ea, Tiāmat, and other gods. Even Marduk, although depicted as the most powerful of the gods in every story, has fifty names and aspects in this story, including the name Bel (lord).

The Babylonian tale of the creation of the universe and the gods who oversee it begins in a similar fashion to other ancient civilizations' accounts of creation, with everything in a state of chaos and with no discernible ground or heavens. From this sea of confusion arise the gods, who bring order to the chaos preferred by Tiāmat and Apsû. The elder gods, in the process, combat the evil that would destroy the universe.

Marduk is a complex figure in Mesopotamian mythology. For millennia, he was little more than a minor deity. However, this story elevates him significantly, first as a hero and then as the creator of the universe. At about the same time this story was written, in the eighteenth century BCE, Marduk also became the patron god of the city of Babylon, which was growing in terms of political and cultural power in the region. Meanwhile, the story reduces the role of Enki/Ea—who in ancient Sumerian tradition, predating Babylonia by millennia, was the creator of the universe and at the apex of the gods—to that of a secondary figure while empowering Marduk with Ea's heroism and destiny.

Michael P. Auerbach, MA

BIBLIOGRAPHY

Falk, Daniel K. "Creation Myths in the Ancient Near East: Enuma Elish." *University of Oregon*. U of Oregon, n.d. Web. 3 June 2013.

MacKenzie, Donald A. *Myths of Babylonia and Assyria*. 1915. *Sacred Texts*. Evinity, 2011. Web. 3 June 2013.

"Marduk (God)." *Ancient Mesopotamian Gods and Goddesses*. U of Pennsylvania, n.d. Web. 3 June 2013.

Massey, Gerald. *The Natural Genesis; or, Second Part of* A Book of the Beginnings. London: Williams, 1883. Print.

Railsback, Bruce. "Marduk Creates the World from the Spoils of Battle." *Creation Stories from around the World*. U of Georgia, n.d. Web. 3 June 2013.

Webster, Michael. "The Babylonian Creation Story (*Enuma Elish*)." *World Mythology*. Grand Valley State U, n.d. Web. 3 June 2013.

Nanna and Ningal

Author: Traditional Sumerian
Time Period: 2499 BCE–1000 BCE
Country or Culture: Mesopotamia
Genre: Myth

PLOT SUMMARY

Nanna (Nanna-Suen), the Sumerian god of the moon, travels across the sky each night. This gives order to the natural environment, bringing the spring floods that irrigate and fertilize the fields. Down in the marshlands near the city of Eridu in southern Mesopotamia, a young woman named Ningal falls in love with Nanna. Ningal's mother, Ningikuga, goddess of reeds, carefully watches over her daughter.

One night, Ningal sings a poetic love song to Nanna in the night sky. She tells Nanna how she longs to be in his arms. When Nanna hears Ningal's love song, he falls in love with her. Nanna descends to earth to meet Ningal. As night is fading, Nanna implores Ningal not to wait until the completion of the proper wedding rituals, which will take too long. Instead, he asks her to meet her the next night in the marshes to consummate their love. When Ningal demurs, Nanna promises to bring milk and cheese to her mother's house, but he expresses his desire to visit her without her mother present. Ningal responds that that is also her desire, saying, "O my Nanna, your plaint is sweet, it is the plaint of my heart" (Jacobsen 125), but she continues to insist they wait.

Ningal returns home, and Nanna later sends a traveler to carry a message to Ningal, in which he entices her with the abundance of dairy products and crops in his possession and urges her to join him without delay. Ningal sends the traveler back to Nanna, repeating her insistence that they wait. Only after "he has filled the rivers with the early flood" will she join him as his wife in Ur (126). Nanna sees the wisdom in her words and agrees to wait.

At the end of spring, when the first fruits of the new season are ripening following the floods brought by the moon's cycle, Nanna and Ningal are married at Ur. Afterward, they proceed north up the Euphrates river to the town of Nippur, where Nanna's parents, father Enlil and mother Ninlil, live. Ningal promises Nanna that she will bear two children. Their firstborn, Inana (Ištar or Ishtar), will become the goddess of love and war. Their son, Utu, will become the god of the sun.

SIGNIFICANCE

The story of Nanna and Ningal is a myth from ancient Sumer. Sumerian cities were located in modern-day southern Iraq. Sumerians developed one of the oldest known writing systems, the cuneiform script, by 3000 BCE. This invention allowed Sumerians to transcribe their myths. Sumerian texts were rediscovered and transcribed into English after the middle of the nineteenth century CE, although many of these texts were extremely fragmentary, including the myth of Nanna and Ningal.

As god of the moon, Nanna was one of the principal Sumerian deities. He was also the city god of Ur. Astronomical knowledge of the moon, its phases, and its course across the sky was well understood by the Sumerians. The moon was seen as regulating the cycles of the seasons, particularly the forces of the rain and the two rivers of Mesopotamia, the Euphrates and the Tigris, which were vital to the region's agricultural prosperity. Both rivers run into the Persian Gulf at the southern coast of what was ancient Sumer. The myth opens with an invocation of the significant power and extent of Nanna's rule over natural matters important to the agrarian, river-based Sumerian culture.

Another key significance of the marriage of Nanna and Ningal is its double emphasis on the power of love and its necessary submission under human rule and ritual. Nanna and Ningal love each other with a passion that brooks no delay. They are willing to transgress the marriage rules and rituals of Sumerian society. These rules are shown to apply even to a god and his consort. It is Ningal who comes to insist on following societal rules for the benefit of all involved. She successfully persuades Nanna to agree to wait until the appropriate preparations have been made for their marriage. As social order is restored, both the lovers and the land prosper.

Of special importance in Sumerian mythology are the two children of Nanna and Ningal. Their daughter, Inana, is better known by her Akkadian name, Ištar (Ishtar). Nanna and Ningal's procession upriver to Nanna's parents echoes the subject of another Sumerian myth, the story of Nanna's journey to Nippur. Travel and trade between southern and northern cities such as Ur and Nippur was vitally important in shaping Sumerian society and culture.

R. C. Lutz, PhD

BIBLIOGRAPHY

Black, Jeremey, et al. "A *Balbale* to Nanna (Nanna B)." *Electronic Text Corpus of Sumerian Literature.* Faculty of Oriental Studies, U of Oxford, 19 Dec. 2006. Web. 20 Sept. 2013.

Bottéro, Jean. *Religion in Ancient Mesopotamia*. Trans. Teresa Lavender Fagan. Chicago: U of Chicago P, 2001. Print.

Jacobsen, Thorkild. *The Treasures of Darkness: A History of Mesopotamian Religion*. New Haven: Yale UP, 1976. Print.

Leick, Gwendolyn. *Sex and Eroticism in Mesopotamian Literature*. London: Routledge, 1994. Print.

Stone, Adam. "Nanna/Suen/Sin (god)." *Ancient Mesopotamian Gods and Goddesses*. Oracc and the UK Higher Education Academy, 2013. Web. 20 Sept. 2013.

◆ Ninurta and the Turtle

Author: Traditional Sumerian
Time Period: 2499 BCE–1000 BCE
Country or Culture: Mesopotamia
Genre: Myth

PLOT SUMMARY

Imdugud (or Anzû), the great lion-headed bird, has stolen the powerful Tablet of Destinies from the water god, Enki, and carried it off to the mountains. The tablet can enable the person possessing it to control the *abzu* (*apsû*), the sweet waters that exist beneath the earth's surface. Enki enlists the help of his brother Enlil's son Ninurta, the god of war. Ninurta follows the bird on a great journey into the mountains. He attacks the bird, who after a great battle drops the tablet into the abzu, where it is returned to Enki. Imdugud is defeated and taken captive by Ninurta. Enki praises Ninurta's bravery in defeating Imdugud.

However, brooding at his post near the abzu, Ninurta wishes for more than praise for his victory. Ninurta decides to pursue the Tablet of Destinies and Enki's *me* (divine power) for himself and plots to retrieve it from the abzu. If he succeeds, Ninurta will gain power over the world. He then creates a dark flood wave. Enki is very clever, however. He intuits that Ninurta will attempt to take the tablet and stirs the waters of the abzu, creating his own flood and thereby issuing a warning to Ninurta that he is aware of the war god's intentions. Enki next sends his emissary, Isimud, to confront Ninurta and convince him to rethink his quest for power. Ninurta rebuffs Isimud, striking Enki's minister during their meeting. Obsessed with obtaining the power of Enki through the Tablet of Destinies, Ninurta continues his plans.

Enki decides to punish Ninurta for his arrogance. He creates a turtle out of clay and gives it life. The turtle digs a deep hole in the earth. Enki lures Ninurta into conversation near the trap, and the turtle, still in the hole, reaches out and grabs Ninurta, pulling him inside. Ninurta tries to escape, but the turtle continues to claw at his legs. Enki stands over the hole, mocking his strength and heroic qualities.

Meanwhile, Ninurta's mother, Ninhursaĝa (or Ninhursag; sometimes referred to as Ninmena) sees Enki tormenting and ridiculing Ninurta. She intervenes, rending her garments and reprimanding Enki for his cruel behavior. She reminds him of a past incident in which he, out of greed, decided to eat plants that were forbidden by the gods and, were it not for Ninhursaĝa, would have certainly died. The extant fragments of the myth conclude there, but it is believed that Ninurta is then allowed to reemerge from the hole and goes on to receive glory for his past deeds.

SIGNIFICANCE

The story of Ninurta and the turtle has been compiled from two literary poetic compositions dating back to the second millennium BCE. Only the middle part of the story has been found, leading scholars to attempt to piece together the missing two ends using other stories. For example, how Enki came into possession of the Tablet of Destinies is explained by the belief that Enki wished to exercise his divine right as one of the primary gods; later Babylonian tales establish that Marduk, the offspring of the god Ea (who corresponds to the Sumerian Enki), kills the owner of the tablet, Qingu, and takes possession of it. As there are no other references to Ninurta's pursuit of the tablet, scholars believe that the story concludes with Ninurta learning his lesson from the heroic Enki.

The story of Ninurta, Enki, and the turtle offers a lesson on humility. Ninurta, the god of war, is called upon by his uncle Enki, the great god of the waters, to retrieve the source of Enki's power, the Tablet of Destinies. To his credit, Ninurta goes on a great journey in pursuit of the bird Imdugud and defeats the bird in a heroic fashion. Ninurta rightly receives praise from Enki for this accomplishment but then becomes arrogant, dismissing his uncle's accolades and instead deciding that the *me* generated by the tablet should be his and not Enki's. Ninurta is disrespectful of Enki's emissary, who attempts to convince Ninurta to reconsider his pursuit of the tablet. After much posturing, Ninurta confronts Enki, who simply pushes his nephew into the hole dug by the turtle. This humiliating defeat is only exacerbated by the fact that Enki mocks the "hero's" inability to escape from the pit.

This story, however, is not just about the humbling of Ninurta. Enki, the powerful and clever god, determines that Ninurta wishes to attack him. At first, he shows restraint, offering Isimud as a vehicle by which a confrontation may be avoided. When Ninurta assaults Isimud, Enki devises a clever plot to teach his nephew a lesson. When Ninurta falls into the turtle's pit, however, Enki's own arrogance comes to light as he openly mocks Ninurta's bravery and heroism. Enki is reminded by Ninhursaĝa that the water god himself has in the past made poor decisions that were based on pride and arrogance. When those choices nearly killed Enki, Ninhursaĝa saved him. This aspect of the story characterizes Enki, one of the three most revered gods in Sumerian mythology, as a figure who must demonstrate humility as well.

Michael P. Auerbach, MA

BIBLIOGRAPHY

Black, Jeremy Allen, et al., eds. "Ninurta and the Turtle." *Electronic Text Corpus of Sumerian Literature*. Faculty of Oriental Studies, U of Oxford, 2006. Web. 20 June 2013.

Black, Jeremy Allen, and Anthony Green. *Gods, Demons, and Symbols of Ancient Mesopotamia: An Illustrated Dictionary*. Austin: U of Texas P, 1992. Print.

Jacobsen, Thorkild. *The Treasures of Darkness: A History of Mesopotamian Religion*. New Haven: Yale UP, 1976. Print.

Penglase, Charles. "Ninurta." *Greek Myths and Mesopotamia: Parallels and Influence in the Homeric Hymns and Hesiod*. London: Routledge, 2003. 42–61. Print.

Walton, John H., and Eugene E. Carpenter. "The Tablet of Destinies." *Genesis, Exodus, Leviticus, Numbers, Deuteronomy*. Grand Rapids: Zondervan, 2009. 517. Print.

◆ The Sin of the God Zu

Author: Traditional Assyrian
Time Period: 2499 BCE–1000 BCE
Country or Culture: Mesopotamia
Genre: Myth

PLOT SUMMARY

As the Assyrian myth of the sin of the god Zu exists only in fragmentary form, with key portions of the myth missing or undeciphered, the narrative is cryptic and leaves much to the imagination. Desiring a grander life as a powerful ruler, the aging deity Zu, who is possibly a bird god, decides that he will seize power. Zu attempts to steal the crown, clothing, and *unsimi*—which nineteenth-century translator George Smith identifies as "possibly some talisman or oracle" (114)—belonging to the father of the gods, known by the title of Bel ("lord"). He then prepares to declare war on his fellow deities, hiding himself in his realm and spreading darkness.

The god Anu tells his sons that he who kills Zu will become renowned throughout the world. He encourages his son Vul to pursue Zu, describing the praise Vul will receive for doing so. However, Vul objects to this and tells his father that he will not go. Next, Anu makes a similar speech to the god Nabû (Nebo), son of the goddess Ištar (Ishtar). This god also objects and refuses to go after Zu, repeating Vul's words. The existing transcription of the myth ends there, and it remains unclear whether Zu is killed or whether Vul, Nabû, or another deity rescues the *unsimi*.

SIGNIFICANCE

The myth of the sin of the god Zu was originally written in the Assyrian cuneiform script on a four-column clay tablet. This language evolved from the Sumerian script, the earliest writing system in the world. To create such tablets, a stylus was used to form wedge-shaped inscriptions in a plate of soft clay; the tablets were then baked to harden the text. This method of writing allowed texts to be preserved for thousands of years, albeit often in fragmentary form, as in the case of the tablet recording the myth of Zu. While this narrative remains incomplete, it is nonetheless remarkable in that it sheds some light on the Assyrian pantheon while demonstrating early literary techniques such as the use of repetition.

The myth was first translated into English by George Smith, a British scholar best known for his translation of fragments of the *Epic of Gilgameš*. Smith was a self-taught assistant in the British Museum's Assyriology Department, where he worked under the direction of Sir Henry Rawlinson, cataloging clay tablets discovered at various Mesopotamian sites. The translation of the myth of Zu was one of Smith's last achievements, as he died soon after while on a research trip to Syria.

Smith published his translation of the fragmentary myth of Zu in *The Chaldean Account of Genesis* (1876), a collection of myths that Smith identified as similar to biblical narratives, specifically those about the creation and the great flood. The story of Zu in particular reminded him of the biblical story of Ham and Noah, in which Ham commits an offense against his father while the patriarch is drunk. He also notes that the myth bears some similarities to the Greek myth of the castration of Uranus by his son Cronus.

Although Smith was unable to translate some terms, such as *unsimi*, which prohibited full comprehension of the text, his translations laid the foundation for future research regarding ancient Mesopotamian literature, culture, and mythology. Later scholars identified Zu with the god Anzû, who features prominently in the Sumerian and Akkadian myth about the theft of the Tablet of Destinies.

Sally Driscoll, MLS

BIBLIOGRAPHY

Black, Jeremy, and Anthony Green. *Gods, Demons and Symbols of Ancient Mesopotamia.* Austin: U of Texas P, 1992. Print.

Dalley, Stephanie. *Myths from Mesopotamia: Creation, the Flood, Gilgamesh, and Others.* Rev. ed. Oxford: Oxford UP, 2000. Print.

McCall, Henrietta. *Mesopotamian Myths.* Austin: U of Texas P, 1990. Print.

Penglase, Charles. *Greek Myths and Mesopotamia: Parallels and Influence in the Homeric Hymns and Hesiod.* London: Routledge, 1994. Print.

Smith, George. *The Chaldean Account of Genesis.* London: Scott, 1876. Print.

◆ The Sumerian Creation of Humankind

Author: Traditional Sumerian
Time Period: 2499 BCE–1000 BCE
Country or Culture: Mesopotamia
Genre: Myth

PLOT SUMMARY

The Sumerian gods experience difficulty in procuring their own sustenance, particularly bread, in the wake of the creation of several female deities. They appeal to Enki, the god of water and wisdom. Their complaints initially go unheard, as Enki is asleep when they voice their displeasure. Enki's mother eventually brings the gods' dissatisfaction to her son's attention.

To solve this problem, Enki summons assistants and tasks them with molding new beings from primordial clay. The clay is first thickened under the watchful eye of the earth goddess Ninmah and then fashioned by Enki's assistants into limbs. Ninmah binds the fate of the new creature to the gods, and humankind is born.

Enki arranges a feast for the gods to celebrate the creation of humankind. At the feast, Enki and Ninmah indulge in copious amounts of wine. In her exuberance, Ninmah decides to fashion six individuals from the primordial clay. Among these individuals are a woman who cannot bear children and a sexless person.

Enki too opts to create beings from the clay but is less successful. The clay human forged by Enki is weak in both body and mind, and Enki asks Ninmah's assistance in helping the pathetic creature. Ninmah attempts to talk to Enki's creation and offers it bread to eat. However, the goddess's efforts are in vain. The creature does not answer her, nor does it eat the bread. It is also unable to sit, stand, or walk. After a long debate with Enki, Ninmah curses him for creating such a feeble creature, a fate that Enki accepts.

SIGNIFICANCE

This Sumerian myth illustrates the ancient Sumerian interpretation of the genesis of and place of humankind on earth. The ancient clay tablets on which the myth was transcribed have suffered the deteriorating effects of time, long-distance travel across centuries, and poor preservation. As a result, the narrative of the myth is incomplete; for example, only two of Ninmah's six creations are described, as the tablet itself exists only in fragmentary form. Some scholars have speculated that the goddess's other four creations were as maladjusted as the two known beings, while others have suggested that perhaps they were bestowed with gifts as opposed to flaws. Regardless, the two known creations of Ninmah do not seem to have been cursed with a fate as severe as Enki's mute, functionless man. Despite the scholarly disputes arising from such missing or unclear sections of the narrative, there is widespread scholarly agreement regarding the myth's basic framework.

Scholars frequently compare and contrast the Sumerian myth of the creation of humanity with the creation myths of other cultures that developed in Mesopotamia and the Levant. The myth significantly predates these creation narratives yet shares a number of similarities with them; for instance, in the Sumerian, Babylonian, and Jewish myths, humanity is formed out of preexisting material. The differences between the Sumerian myth and these later narratives likewise shed light on the ways in which these cultures perceived the gods and the place of humans in the world. While the Sumerian myth states that humanity was created to free the gods from their laborious duties, the account found in the Hebrew Bible (corresponding to the Christian Old Testament) explains that one of humankind's responsibilities was to look after the animal kingdom. The Babylonian version describes the birth of humanity as resulting from the spilled blood of a mischievous god after a war among the deities.

The Sumerian myth illustrating the creation of humanity follows a succession of elaborate myths that describe the creation of the natural world, elements, and surrounding universe from the sea. That the creation of humanity follows such an elaborate formation of the natural world—and that it results in flawed and imperfect individuals—may shed some light on not only the ancient Sumerians' extreme reverence for the natural world but also their perception of humanity as flawed in both body and spirit and as eternally charged with doing the bidding of their deities.

John Pritchard

BIBLIOGRAPHY

Black, Jeremy, and Anthony Green. *Gods, Demons, and Symbols of Ancient Mesopotamia: An Illustrated Dictionary*. Austin: U of Texas P, 1992. Print.

Elwell, Walter A., and Philip Wesley Comfort, eds. *Tyndale Bible Dictionary*. Carol Stream: Tyndale, 2001. Print.

Kramer, Samuel Noah. *Sumerian Mythology: A Study of Spiritual and Literary Achievement in the Third Millennium BC*. Rev. ed. Philadelphia: U of Pennsylvania P, 1961. Print.

Leeming, David. *Jealous Gods and Chosen People: The Mythology of the Middle East*. New York: Oxford UP, 2004. Print.

Penglase, Charles. *Greek Myths and Mesopotamia: Parallels and Influence in the Homeric Hymns*. New York: Routledge, 2005. Print.

◆ The Theft of Destiny

Author: Traditional Sumerian
Time Period: 2499 BCE–1000 BCE
Country or Culture: Mesopotamia
Genre: Myth

PLOT SUMMARY

Enlil, the chief god of the Sumerians, is enjoying a few moments of peace and splendor while guarding the Tablet of Destinies. Soon his solitude is interrupted by his children, who come bounding up the hillside carrying an unusual creature, part lion and part eagle with a sharp beak and pointed talons fit to kill. Enlil nervously asks the creature to identify itself, and the creature replies that he is Anzû. The strange creature bows his head and states that he is there to do the god's bidding, which comforts the god. To ease his suspicions further, Enlil retreats to the chamber that holds the Tablet of Destinies and searches the text for any mention of this creature. Finding nothing, he concludes that Anzû must be some novel creation, not a monster from the underworld or elsewhere, and decides that it is safe to employ him as guardian of the Tablet of Destinies.

For a while, Anzû proves to be an obedient and docile guard, but one day he questions with envy why only Enlil may touch the tablet. Enlil replies that he alone may hold it because it is very powerful and would destroy Anzû. The god also fears that should the tablet fall into the wrong hands, it could destroy the world. Anzû feigns complicity, but when Enlil goes to bathe, he steals the tablet and flies away.

Unable to retrieve the tablet himself, Enlil calls a council of other deities, including the gods Enki and Ninurta, and puts them to the challenge. Ninurta is quick to respond, as he desires to prove his worth among the other gods. He travels to the mountains where Anzû is hiding and finds the raging monster clinging powerfully to the tablet, his eyes ablaze and his feathers as sharp as knives. Ninurta aims his bow and releases an arrow. Anzû, however, uses the power granted by the tablet to make the mountains shake and a storm darken the sky. He simply laughs at the arrow before commanding it to turn back toward Ninurta.

Ninurta ducks and aims again. This time the returned arrow strikes him in the arm. He retreats to behind a rock while Anzû shouts out threats and commands him to leave. Finally, Ninurta summons the courage to attack again. He releases one arrow after another until Anzû grows tired and can no longer defend himself. With his last arrow, Ninurta pierces the monster's heart, killing him. The god uses the power of the tablet to call for rain, and as the rain falls, Ninurta recovers the stolen tablet.

SIGNIFICANCE

This retelling of the theft of the Tablet of Destinies is based on one of two Sumerian versions that date as far back as the third millennium BCE. In the other version of the myth, the warrior king Lugalbanda, father of the hero Gilgameš (Gilgamesh), slays Zu (Anzû, also known in some myths as Imdugud) and rescues the Tablet of Destinies. A later Babylonian version begins with the birth of Anzû rather than his delivery to Ellil (Enlil) by his children. The Babylonian version also highlights the danger of battling Anzû, as the gods Girra, Šara (Shara), and Adad are unable to defeat the monstrous bird god, despite being equipped with powerful weapons. Finally, after a plea from his mother, Ninurta rises to the challenge, retrieves the tablet, and thus comes to reign over civilization.

The myth of Anzû's theft of the tablet is valued individually and for its connection to other myths. As one of the earliest texts from Mesopotamia, the myth sheds much insight into the spiritual beliefs and culture of the ancient Sumerians, particularly through its depiction of Enlil and his royal family as divine beings with a wide range of human emotions and characteristics. The many variations on the myth demonstrate the practice of adapting deities and narrative elements to fit a particular empire, region, or period. The Tablet of Destinies remains a spiritual source of supreme power in mythology from one empire to the next, demonstrating the strong influence wielded by the Sumerians. In addition, the themes of the battle between good and evil and of a god's rise to power after slaying a monster seem to have been popularized in Sumerian mythology before spreading to the Babylonians, the ancient Greeks, and other cultures.

The myth is also significant because of its connection to the *Enuma elish*, a foundational Babylonian myth that some scholars identify as the source for key elements of the Hebrew Bible (Christian Old Testament). The *Enuma elish* chronicles the rise to power of Marduk, the chief Babylonian god, and his battle with the gods Tiāmat and Qingu (Kingu) over the Tablet of Destinies.

Sally Driscoll, MLS

BIBLIOGRAPHY

Black, Jeremy, and Anthony Green. *Gods, Demons, and Symbols of Ancient Mesopotamia: An Illustrated Dictionary*. Austin: U of Texas P, 1992. Print.

Dalley, Stephanie, trans. and ed. *Myths from Mesopotamia: Creation, the Flood, Gilgamesh, and Others*. Rev. ed. Oxford: Oxford UP, 2000. Print.

Leick, Gwendolyn. *A Dictionary of Ancient Near Eastern Mythology*. New York: Routledge, 1998. Print.

McCall, Henrietta. *Mesopotamian Myths*. Austin: U of Texas P, 1990. Print.

Pritchard, James B., ed. *Ancient Near Eastern Texts*. Princeton: Princeton UP, 1969. Print.

Weis, Margaret, ed. *Legends: Tales from the Eternal Archives*. Vol. 1. New York: DAW, 1999. Print.

◆ Uta-Napishtim and the Deluge

Author: Traditional Babylonian
Time Period: 2499 BCE–1000 BCE
Country or Culture: Mesopotamia
Genre: Myth

PLOT SUMMARY

The story begins with Gilgameš (Gilgamesh), the great king, uncovering a tablet on which is inscribed the words of a man named Uta-Napishtim (Pir-Napishtim). He recalls how, while living in the city of the sun, he overheard the gods who also lived there discussing completely destroying humanity using wind and water, because humanity had become too wicked and violent. Even Anu, the father of all the gods, advocates this course of action. However, after some reconsideration, some of the gods agree that they will allow one man and his family to survive the flood. The god of the ocean, Ea, approaches Uta-Napishtim, a man known for his goodness and piety, and begs him to give up his possessions and build a great ship that would save his and his family's lives.

Ea also advises Uta-Napishtim to go before the city's elders to warn them that the gods are preparing to destroy humanity. He does so, but is openly mocked by these leaders. Uta-Napishtim returns to his home and builds the ship according to Ea's specifications, drawn as a blueprint in the sand. Once the flat-bottomed ship is complete, it measures 120 cubits (about 180 feet) in length. Uta-Napishtim stocks the ship with the amount of grain Ea recommends and makes room for his family and pairs of every living animal. Ea tells Uta-Napishtim not to fear and to trust that the gods will keep him and the ship's passengers safe.

With the next evening tide, Uta-Napishtim watches as a great dark cloud and flood approach. From the cloud emerge the gods, who attack humanity through the waters. The fury of the flood puts the world into chaos and even gives the gods pause—the speed at which it rises forces them to retreat to higher ground. Ištar (Ishtar), the "Lady of the Gods," laments the gods' action after seeing the devastation it has caused.

After six days and six nights, the flood finally stops rising. On the seventh day, Uta-Napishtim comes out of his shelter and sees nothing but water. He cries at the notion of all other humans being wiped from the earth. The ship comes to rest on top of a mountain. Uta-Napishtim lets fly a dove and then a swallow, but the two birds return, unable to find a perch. Later, he releases a raven, which does not return. Knowing that the waters are receding, Uta-Napishtim lets his passengers disembark. Meanwhile, Bel, the god of sages, is angry to learn that a human was allowed to survive. Ea confronts Bel, telling him that it is proper to punish the sinner but not the entire human race; never again should there be a flood. Bel's anger cools and he boards the ship. Taking Uta-Napishtim and his wife by the hand, Bel decides that the two mortals should become immortal like the gods.

When he finishes reading the tablet, Gilgameš wishes to find Uta-Napishtim and discover the secrets of his immortality. He sets out for Mount Mashu, where he is told he may find his ancestor. Gilgameš is set upon by many challenges and dangers. However, as he is part god and part man, he has great strength and wisdom, protecting him from death. Gilgameš eventually finds Uta-Napishtim and his wife and, after spending some time with them, is told of the secret of immortality. It is contained in a plant, found at the bottom of the sea. If he consumes it for nine days, he will live forever.

Gilgameš finds the plant and departs for home. However, before he can consume it, a serpent steals it. The spirit of his deceased friend Endiku visits Gilgameš to tell him about the Land of the Dead, which all men must enter when they die.

SIGNIFICANCE

The Babylonian version of the great flood is likely a reproduction of a similar story, about Ziusudra and the great flood, offered by the ancient Sumerians, who preceded the Babylonians in the region known as Mesopotamia (between the Tigris and Euphrates Rivers in Asia). This tale is written in poetic form on twelve tablets that date back to around 650 BCE, although the original story of the flood is believed to have originated in the third millennium BCE. Gilgameš was likely an actual historical figure, as he is identified in Sumerian texts as a king of the Uruk era (the early third millennium BCE).

In a variation of the Babylonian myth, Uta-Napishtim tells the story of the deluge directly to Gilgameš. The complete story of Gilgameš tells of how he travels a great distance to learn about Uta-Napishtim's immortality so that he might become immortal himself; however, in this version, he is simply the audience. Also different in this version is Ea's advice to Uta-Napishtim: he instructs the man not to tell anyone in the city of Šuruppak (Shuruppak) about the flood, but instead to say that he has fallen out of Bel's favor and needs to leave. Meanwhile, according to Ea, the rains will produce a great harvest and large quantities of fowl and fish, which will distract the people of the city into believing that they have received a blessing from the gods.

Although the biblical book of Genesis and the *Epic of Gilgameš* are the products of two very different cultures, there are a number of similarities in the retelling of the great flood. Uta-Napishtim and Noah, for example, share a number of characteristics and experiences. Both are righteous and therefore are spared by the god or gods who unleash the flood. Both are told of the flood's coming and are asked to prepare for it by building a ship that will house all of the earth's animals in pairs. Also, both are blessed with long life after the flood—although Noah eventually dies, while Uta-Napishtim becomes immortal.

The stories themselves bear some similarities as well. For example, in both Genesis and the *Epic of Gilgameš*, the god or gods grow weary of the sins and wickedness of humanity. However, both stories say that the gods reconsider and allow for the seed of humanity to survive. Furthermore, both Uta-Napishtim and Noah are chosen to represent humanity not only because of their unwavering piety and faith, but also because they possess the ability to construct such a massive and complex ship.

Uta-Napishtim proves to the gods that he is worthy of their blessing by demonstrating his dedication to their will.

Michael P. Auerbach, MA

BIBLIOGRAPHY

Arnold, Emma Josephine. "How Gilgamesh Learned about the Flood." *Stories of Ancient Peoples*. New York: American Book, 1901. 110–16. Print.

Dalley, Stephanie. *Myths from Mesopotamia: Creation, the Flood, Gilgamesh, and Others*. Rev. ed. New York: Oxford UP. 2008. Print.

George, A. R. *The Epic of Gilgamesh: The Babylonian Epic Poem and Other Texts in Akkadian and Sumerian*. New York: Penguin, 2003. Print.

Jacobs, Thornwell. *The New Science and the Old Religion*. Atlanta: Oglethorpe UP, 1927. Print.

Kramer, Samuel Noah. "Miscellaneous Myths—The Deluge." *Sumerian Mythology*. Philadelphia: American Philos. Soc., 1944. Print.

MacKenzie, Donald A. "Chapter IX: Deluge Legend, the Island of the Blessed, and Hades." *Myths of Babylonia and Assyria*. London: Gresham, 1915. 190–216. Print.

Pliens, J. David. *When the Great Abyss Opened: Classic and Contemporary Readings of Noah's Flood*. New York: Oxford UP, 2003. Print.

Pritchard, James B., and Daniel Edward Fleming. *The Ancient Near East: An Anthology of Texts and Pictures*. Princeton: Princeton UP, 2010. Print.

Spence, Lewis. *Myths and Legends of Babylonia and Assyria*. 1916. New York: Cosimo, 2010. Print.

EAST ASIA

◆ The Adventures of Kintarō, the Golden Boy

Author: Yei Theodora Ozaki
Time Period: 1901 CE–1950 CE
Country or Culture: Japan
Genre: Folktale

PLOT SUMMARY

In ancient Kyoto, the soldier Kintoki falls in love with a beautiful woman, and they marry. Kintoki's enemies at the imperial court cause his downfall, and he dies in despair. His widow flees into the wilderness of the Ashigara Mountains. There, she gives birth to a boy. She names him Kintarō, or "golden boy."

Kintarō is amazingly strong. At age eight, he cuts down trees as efficiently as the woodcutters, who are the only other human inhabitants of the area. His mother gives him a big ax. Kintarō joins the woodcutters for fun, smashing rocks and stones for play as well. The woodcutters call him Wonder-Child and his mother Yama-uba, or "Old Nurse of the Mountains."

Lacking any other children for playmates, Kintarō learns the language of the animals of the mountains. He befriends many of them, and four of them become his followers. They are a bear, a deer, a monkey, and a hare.

Kintarō's games include holding sumo-wrestling matches for his favorite four animals. One day, at one of these matches, the hare wrestles with the monkey, and the deer wrestles with the hare. There are different winners of each match.

Returning from the day's matches, Kintarō and the four animals reach a swollen stream. Wondering how to cross the raging waters, Kintarō proposes to make a bridge for them. Approaching a tall tree on the riverbank, Kintarō grasps its trunk. Pulling hard, he yanks the tree from the ground and casts it across the stream as bridge.

This feat is observed by an old man, dressed as woodcutter, who follows Kintarō home. There, Kintarō parts from the animals and joins his mother. During their conversation about his day, Kintarō tells his mother that he is the strongest of all five companions. The old woodcutter approaches and asks Kintarō for a wrestling bout with him. Their match is a draw.

The old man praises Kintarō's strength. He asks his mother why she has not sent him to the capital of Kyōto to train to become a samurai. Yama-uba replies that this may be her dream, but as Kintarō is a wild boy without formal education, it seems impossible. Now, the man reveals his true identity. He is General Sadamitsu, serving Lord Minamoto no Raikō. He is roaming the countryside in disguise, scouting for strong boys to be trained for his lord's army. He proposes to Kintarō's mother to take the boy and present him to his master.

Yama-uba agrees to this plan, and Kintarō is full of joy at the prospect of becoming a samurai. While his mother is sad at their separation, she is happy for her son's good fortune. Kintarō promises to return and take care of her once he has become a samurai. His four animal friends appear and wish him good luck.

In Kyōto, Minamoto no Raikō agrees to take on Kintarō. Once Kintarō is a young man and a samurai, he becomes the leader of his lord's elite fighter group, the Four Braves. Kintarō's first feat as their leader is to cut off the head of a cannibal monster that has come to terrorize the people near the capital.

Considered a national hero and enjoying power, honor, prestige, and wealth, Kintarō remembers his promise. He builds a house for his mother in Kyōto. She lives there with Kintarō until her death.

SIGNIFICANCE

The Japanese folk hero Kintarō has been extremely popular in his native Japan since at least the seventeenth century CE. In contemporary Japan, dolls of Kintarō, often riding a red carp, are a key part of a family's decorations for the national Children's Day on May 5, if a young boy is part of the family. Most Japanese children can sing the traditional Kintarō song.

Traditionally in Japan, the boy hero has been related to the historic figure of the samurai Sakata no Kintoki (956–1012 CE). He was a retainer of the real Fujiwara-era nobleman Minamoto no Yorimitsu, also called Minamoto no Raikō, who lived from 948 to 1021 CE. Sakata has been identified as one of Minamoto's four key retainers, the Shiten-nō or Four Guardian Kings. Folktales of Kintarō growing into Sakata no Kintoki flourished after the death of the historical samurai.

Many Japanese versions of the origin and birth of Kintarō contain a strong sense of the supernatural. His mother is either a princess, the fairy Yama-uba (Yama-uba is a *yōkai*, or supernatural monster, who appears in Japanese folklore as a crone), or a noblewoman in exile who is called Yama-uba by the woodcutters among whom she comes to live. Kintarō gets his name from the red bib with the yellow character for gold that he wears, according to Japanese folk tradition. These illustrations of Kintarō have existed since the seventeenth century. Tales of Kintarō's exploits focus on his strength, courage, loyalty, and later his filial duty to his mother.

As a beloved folk icon in Japan, Kintarō has become a ubiquitous character in many manga stories, anime movies, and video games. There, the development and treatment of his character vary widely. His strength and good nature are a common element of the many creative versions of Kintarō across contemporary Japanese media versions of this folk hero.

The folktale was first rendered in English by A. B. Mitford in his *Tales of Old Japan*, published in 1871. There, Kintarō's personal name is translated as "Little Wonder," and the focus is on his growing up to become the samurai Sakata Kintoki. In 1908, Yei Theodora Ozaki rendered in English "The Adventures of Kintarō, the Golden Boy," the version followed here. Ozaki's text is one of the most authoritative translations, capturing well the spirit of the Japanese folktale. Numerous other children's books in English tell versions of Kintarō's story. These often focus on his play with his animal friends and their bouts of sumo wrestling.

R. C. Lutz, PhD

BIBLIOGRAPHY

Hearn, Lafcadio. *Glimpses of Unfamiliar Japan*. 1894. North Clarendon: Tuttle, 2009. Print.

McCarthy, Ralph F., and Suhoi Yonai. *Kintaro, the Nature Boy*. Small format ed. New York: Kodansha USA, 2000. Print.

Mitford, A. B. "The History of Sakata Kintoki." *Tales of Old Japan*. 1871. Mineola: Dover, 2005. 189–93. Print.

Ozaki, Yei Theodora. "The Adventures of Kintaro, the Golden Boy." *Japanese Fairy Tales*. 1908. Rutland: Tuttle, 2007. 65–75. Print.

Sakade, Florence, and Yoshio Hayashi. "Kintaro's Adventures." *Kintarō's Adventures and Other Japanese Children's Favorite Stories*. North Clarendon: Tuttle, 2008. 26–42. Print.

The Casting of the Great Bell

Author: Traditional
Time Period: 1001 CE–1500 CE
Country or Culture: China
Genre: Legend

PLOT SUMMARY

Whenthe Ming dynasty emperor Yongle (Yung Lo) moves the Chinese imperial capital from Nanjing (Nanking) to Beijing (Peking), he orders the construction of many new buildings. When the city's bell tower is finished, the emperor orders Guan Yu (Kuan Yü) to cast a suitable bell, "the sound of which should be heard . . . in every part of the city" (Werner 394). Guan Yu, a nobleman, is chosen because of his prior experience in casting guns.

Guan Yu sets to his task with zeal and devotion. Emperor Yongle witnesses the moment when the hot liquid metal rushes into the waiting mold. The emperor withdraws as the metal cools off inside the mold. When the mold is removed, the bell is flawed and unusable.

Even though he is displeased, Yongle orders Guan Yu to conduct a second attempt at creating a bell. Very worried and very carefully, trying to avoid any past mistakes, Guan Yu prepares another casting, but the result is another failure. Enraged, Yongle gives Guan Yu one last chance. Should he fail again, the emperor will have Guan Yu beheaded.

At his home, Guan Yu's only child, his beautiful sixteen-year-old daughter Ge-ai (Ko-ai), learns about this. Deeply devoted to her father, Ge-ai tries to cheer him up and prays for his success. She also consults an astrologer to learn the reasons for the previous failures and the way to avoid them next time. The astrologer tells Ge-ai that the casting will fail again if "the blood of a maiden were not mixed with the ingredients" of the metal for the mold (Werner 397).

On the day of the third attempt, Ge-ai asks and is given permission to witness the process. At the moment that the molten metal rushes into the mold, Ge-ai jumps into the liquid, yelling, "For my father!" (Werner 398). One of her servants tries to catch her but only manages to save one of her shoes. Her father is forcibly restrained from following his daughter into the mold and is "taken home a raving maniac" (398). When the mold is taken off, a perfect bell is revealed. There is no trace of Ge-ai's body.

The bell is suspended for its first ringing in the presence of Emperor Yongle. Its deep boom signals the triumph of the casting. Everybody is shocked when this boom is followed by a low wail, like the sound of a woman crying the word *xié* (*hsieh*), the Chinese word for shoe. To this day, the legend concludes, *xié* is heard after every boom made by the great bell, which is interpreted as Ge-ai asking for her shoe, left behind after her sacrifice for her father.

SIGNIFICANCE

The Chinese legend "The Casting of the Great Bell" developed around the historical casting of a great bell in 1405 CE during the reign of China's Emperor Yongle. In the nineteenth and twentieth century, the legend reached the West from China via three Western authors, but it was first published in Chinese in 1871 in the book *Bai Xiao tu Shuo* (One hundred examples of filial piety) by Yu Baozhen. Excerpts of this book, including "The Casting of the Great Bell," were then translated and published by French Sinologist Claude Philibert Dabry de Thiersant in 1877. From Dabry's book, international writer Lafcadio Hearn translated the legend into English and published it as "The Soul of the Great Bell" in his 1887 anthology *Some Chinese Ghosts*. In 1922, British Sinologist and sociologist Edward Werner rendered a condensed version of Hearn's text as "The Casting of the Great Bell" in his *Myths and Legends of China*.

In China, the legend of the casting of the great bell is popular and significant for three key reasons. First is its illustration of extreme filial piety. Filial piety—the love, devotion, and loyalty of children toward their parents, called *xiào*—is a key Confucian concept and a prime element of Chinese culture. Ge-ai's sacrifice for her father's sake is esteemed as the ultimate extent that love for one's parents can reach.

Second, through the human sacrifice of Ge-ai, the legend expresses criticism of the historic emperor Yongle. Popular in ancient China, human sacrifices to river deities were abolished through the efforts of the fifth-century BCE hydraulic engineer Ximen Bao. Human sacrifices of the servants of a lord after his death were outlawed in 384 BCE. However, facing death, Emperor Yongle continued the tradition of human sacrifices revived by his father after centuries of disuse. Yongle ordered that thirty of his concubines be hanged and then buried with him in 1424. Human sacrifice was outlawed again for members of the royal family in 1464.

Sympathy for Ge-ai in the face of Yongle's threatened punishment of her father subtly critiques the emperor's cruelty.

Third, the motif of Ge-ai's shoe points to her nascent sexual maturity that is thwarted by her self-sacrifice. Among the Han Chinese, foot-binding became popular after the tenth century CE. The tiny shoes holding a woman's bound feet became a sign of a woman's sexual appeal. Ge-ai is sixteen years old and is on the cusp of being married. However, she sacrifices herself for her father, which, in a sense, ritually marries her to the bell. This significance is heightened by the fact that Guan Yu treasures Ge-ai as his only hope "of perpetuating his name and fame" through her eventual offspring (Werner 396). As the bell rings out *xié*, or shoe, in Ge-ai's voice for generations to come, she and her father's lineage have accomplished a version of immortality.

R. C. Lutz, PhD

BIBLIOGRAPHY

Bush, Laurence C. "Some Chinese Ghosts." *Asian Horror Encyclopedia: Asian Horror Culture in Literature, Manga, and Folklore.* Lincoln: Writers Club, 2001. 170–71. Print.

"The Goddess Who Cast the Bell." *Activity Village.* Lindsay Small, 2012. Web. 18 June 2013.

Hearn, Lafcadio. "The Soul of the Great Bell." *Some Chinese Ghosts.* 1887. Mineola: Dover, 2008. Print.

Mooney, Paul. "Big Bell Temple." *National Geographic Traveler: Beijing.* Washington: National Geographic, 2008. 180. Print.

Werner, Edward T. C. "The Casting of the Great Bell." *Myths and Legends of China.* 1922. New York: Dover, 1994. 392–98. Print.

◆ Ch'ŏnjiwangbonp'uri

Author: Traditional
Time Period: 5000 BCE–2500 BCE
Country or Culture: Korea
Genre: Myth

PLOT SUMMARY

Ch'ŏnjiwangbonp'uri (Cheonjiwang Bonpuli), the myth of the king of heaven and earth, is an ancient creation myth from the South Korean island of Jeju (Cheju). As a story based in Jeju's shamanic oral tradition, the myth exists in numerous versions with varying details. However, most versions of the myth share a series of core plot elements.

At the beginning of time, heaven and earth exist together as a uniform void. Suddenly, a gap appears in this void. Light material rises to form the sky, and heavy material sinks down to form the earth. From the sky, a dewdrop falls and mixes with a dewdrop from the earth. Out of this mixture everything in the world is formed, including humanity and the gods. Ch'ŏnji, the king of heaven and earth, awakes to the cry of three roosters. To appease them, Ch'ŏnji creates two suns and two moons.

Ch'ŏnji is drawn into a conflict with the arrogant and exploitative human leader of the mortal world, Sumyŏng Changja. Sumyŏng's power comes from his being the first to tame animals to serve him. In one version of the myth, he is a wicked landowner. Ch'ŏnji defeats Sumyŏng, who must prostrate himself before the king of heaven. The god puts an iron ring on Sumyŏng's head to subdue him, causing the evil man intense pain. After Sumyŏng asks to be decapitated rather than endure the punishment any longer, Ch'ŏnji removes the iron ring and leaves him alone. In another version of the myth, Ch'ŏnji arranges for Sumyŏng's house to be burned, along with those inside.

Ch'ŏnji marries the young human woman Ch'ongmaeng, remaining with her for several days before returning to his home. He tells Ch'ongmaeng to name the two sons she will bear Taebyŏlwang and Sobyŏlwang. He gives her two gourd seeds and a part of his dragon-shaped comb, which will help his sons visit him when they are older.

When Taebyŏlwang and Sobyŏlwang are teenagers, they ask about their father, and their mother reveals his true identity. Hoping to meet their father, the brothers plant the two gourd seeds and climb the vines that soon sprout. They eventually reach heaven, where they play with their father's throne and accidentally break off a piece, thus establishing a tradition in Korea that the ruler's throne be missing that piece. Ch'ŏnji appears and acknowledges his sons.

The king of heaven and earth proposes that Taebyŏlwang and Sobyŏlwang rule over the human world and the underworld. The two brothers settle on a contest to decide who will rule humanity. Sobyŏlwang loses at a riddling game but cheats at the contest to grow a flower from seed, switching his withering plant for Taebyŏlwang's flourishing one. By this trickery, he wins the right to rule humanity.

In one version of the myth, Sobyŏlwang's first act on earth is to kill Sumyŏng and exterminate his family. He is troubled by the chaos created by every plant, animal, human, and ghost having the power of speech, and he is concerned about the low state of morality among humans. The two suns plague humanity with too much heat, and the two moons create too much cold.

Sobyŏlwang asks his brother for help, and Taebyŏlwang readies his bow and two heavy iron arrows. With one arrow, Taebyŏlwang shoots down one sun, and with the other, one of the moons. The stars form from their debris. In another version, both brothers shoot down the extra sun and moon. Next, Taebyŏlwang uses pine dust to silence the speech of all but humans and ghosts.

Before returning to the underworld, Taebyŏlwang classifies light beings as ghosts and heavy ones as humans. Sobyŏlwang neglects to tell Taebyŏlwang about humanity's loose morals. Therefore, Taebyŏlwang does not correct them. While humans are wicked on the earth, good and evil are sorted out in the underworld.

SIGNIFICANCE

As a key part of the oral tradition of Jeju, Ch'ŏnjiwangbonp'uri has continued to be recited by shamans into the twenty-first century. Some of the oldest material of the myth may date back to Neolithic times, when Jeju was first settled. In its existing form, Ch'ŏnjiwangbonp'uri also contains story elements and motifs that indicate Chinese and mainland Korean influence, which suggests that the myth continued to develop over centuries of trade and cultural exchange.

The existing version of Ch'ŏnjiwangbonp'uri was greatly shaped by these cultural influences. As king of heaven and earth, Ch'ŏnji reflects the Chinese Daoist (Taoist) philosophy that proposes such a ruler. Iron, the material from which Ch'ŏnji's ring and Taebyŏlwang's arrows are made, was introduced in the Korean mainland via China and was brought to Jeju from the mainland. Some scholars have further suggested that the myth itself originated in mainland Korea and traveled to Jeju, noting that some mainland creation myths, including the Ch'angsega myth, share elements with Ch'ŏnjiwangbonp'uri.

On Jeju, myths such as the story of the king of heaven and earth are recited by shamans as part of a *kut*, a shamanistic ritual designed to win favors from particular gods. Shamans, who are typically female, perform these rituals by offering food to the deities in question and reciting their myths. Rituals may be designed to ensure prosperity, health, general well-being, or other positive outcomes. After a period of government repression of shamanism on Jeju and in South Korea as a whole in the 1960s and 1970s, there has been a strong revival of shamanism in both places, and traditional rituals and myths such as Ch'ŏnjiwangbonp'uri have been preserved.

R. C. Lutz, PhD

BIBLIOGRAPHY

Choi, Won-Oh. "Shoot for a Sun, Shoot for a Moon." *An Illustrated Guide to Korean Mythology*. Kent: Global Oriental, 2008. 28–37. Print.

"Folk Tales." *Jeju Special Self-Governing Province*. Jeju Special Self-Governing Province, 2007. Web. 4 June 2013.

Hong, Sunyoung, and Anne Hilty. "Ipchun-gut, the Coming of Spring." *Jeju Weekly*. Jeju Weekly, 14 Feb. 2013. Web. 4 June 2013.

Park, Changborn. *Astronomy: Traditional Korean Science*. Seoul: Ewha Womans UP, 2008. Print.

Kim, Soonie, and Anne Hilty. "Rites, Tools, and Offerings—Jeju Shamanist Mythology." *Jeju Weekly*. Jeju Weekly, 14 Mar. 2013. Web. 4 June 2013.

◆ The Dragons

Author: Traditional
Time Period: 999 BCE–1 BCE
Country or Culture: China
Genre: Myth

PLOT SUMMARY

Dragons have been part of Chinese myths for millennia. In "The Dragons," British Sinologist Edward Werner has summarized Chinese dragon myths, and this overview follows Werner's survey. Werner based part of "The Dragons" on the 1913 work *The Dragon in China and Japan* by Dutch scholar Marinus Willem de Visser.

In China, dragons are strongly associated with water. They represent the beneficial effect of rain in supporting human agriculture. They stand for the male principle of the yang in Daoist (Taoist) philosophy. They are strong and good and have great powers. Because they control the rain, they are a key to the prosperity of the community.

Buddhism introduced evil dragons to Chinese mythology. These evil dragons are inspired by the *nāga*, or mythical Buddhist snake. In China, these evil dragons inhabit the mountains only. Their counterparts, the good Chinese dragons, generally live in bodies of water such as rivers and lakes.

The Chinese dragon is considered the king of the scaly reptiles. Typically, a dragon has a horse's head, a snake's tail, wings on its side, and clawed legs. The imperial dragon sports five claws on each leg, the common dragon only three or four.

The features of the dragons resemble parts of other animals in nine specific ways. For example, their horns resemble deer antlers, and their eyes look like those of devils or demons. Their claws are like those of a hawk, and the legs like a tiger's.

Chinese dragons come in all sizes. The smallest are as tiny as silk worms, and the largest "fills the Heaven and the earth" (Werner 209). Dragons have a pearl with them, sometimes carried on a string around their necks. This pearl represents the sun. Dragons undergo many changes in their long lifetime; for example, "a horned dragon" becomes a "flying dragon" in one thousand years (Werner 209).

Dragons are associated with Chinese emperors, including the mythical ancient emperors. Dragon "bones, teeth, and saliva" are beneficial ingredients of traditional Chinese medicine (Werner 209). Dragons can change their form at will and become invisible. In spring, many rise to the sky. They return to their waters in fall. Some ascend into the sky without wings through their mental powers alone.

There are different dragons classified by their function. Celestial dragons support the gods in the heavens, while divine dragons are responsible for wind and rain. Earth dragons carve out the beds of rivers and streams, and some dragons guard treasures hidden from human discovery. There are as many different Buddhist dragons as there are different ocean fish.

Dragons rule the hills, influence feng shui, linger around graves, and are part of Confucian worship rituals. They live in different places, ranging from the deep sea to the dry land.

SIGNIFICANCE

In China, dragon myths have a long tradition. Dragons have played a key part in traditional Chinese culture, folk beliefs, and customs since Neolithic times. The oldest archaeological evidence for Chinese mythological belief in dragons comes from the 1987 discovery of a dragon statue of the Yangshao culture that flourished from around 5000 to 3000 BCE in China's contemporary Henan province. Coiled dragon jade ornaments called *zhulong*, or pig dragons, are typical of the Hongshan culture that existed from 4700 BCE to 2900 BCE in an area that includes modern Inner Mongolia. Inside cairns, or piled up stone artifacts of the Hongshan culture, twentieth-century Japanese excavators found dragon sculptures as well.

In Chinese writing, dragons are first mentioned in the book *Yih king*, first mentioned in 1122 BCE. From this text on, Chinese dragons have been associated with the masculine yang principle. Many Chinese and international scholars believe that dragon myths were based on the discovery of dinosaur bones by ancient Chinese people.

Evil dragons, called *nāga*, became part of Chinese mythology when Buddhism entered China. Traditionally, the first Indian Buddhist missionaries came to China by 265 BCE. Historically, it can be proven that Buddhism has existed in China since the first century CE. Since that time, evil *nāgas* are believed to plague mountains, while benevolent, older Chinese dragons rule water.

Politically, from the Zhou dynasty, lasting from 1046 BCE to 256 BCE, to the end of the last Qing dynasty overthrown in 1912 CE, Chinese emperors embraced the dragon as their imperial emblem. By the Yuan dynasty of the thirteenth and fourteenth century and enforced again in the subsequent Ming dynasty, the five-clawed dragon was exclusively reserved for the emperor. Members of the imperial family and high-ranking nobles could wear emblems with four-clawed dragons, and some other aristocrats and some privileged commoners could wear a dragon emblem with three claws.

In traditional Chinese medicine, dragon parts, primarily derived from dinosaur bones if genuine, have many beneficial applications. The dragon is one of the twelve animals of the Chinese zodiac. People, especially men, born in the year of the dragon are considered especially powerful and lucky. As a result, the years of the dragon are favorites for childbearing among many Chinese.

In modern times, Chinese dragon myths inform two significant folk customs. The first are the dragon boat races. These are performed both at the Duanwu spring festival and at the Lunar, or Chinese, New Year. In dragon boat races, crews of up to twenty members, including paddlers and one striking a drum and another steering the boat, compete in customized watercraft. These boats have dragons' heads at the bow and dragons' tail at the stern.

Dragon dances have traditionally been performed in China on lucky days and on occasions when luck is desired. After a widespread hiatus under communism from 1966 to 1976, dragon dances have since been performed in mainland China. Typically, dragon dances feature dragon puppets of big, supposedly original scale. These big puppets are operated by teams handling its support poles.

R. C. Lutz, PhD

BIBLIOGRAPHY

Christie, Anthony. *Chinese Mythology*. London: Hamlyn, 1968. Print.

"Dragon Articles." *Crystal Dragon of Taiwan*. Crystal Dragon of Taiwan, 2010. Web. 17 May 2013.

Visser, Marinus Willem de. *The Dragon in China and Japan*. Amsterdam: Müller, 1913. Print.

Werner, Edward T. C. "The Dragons." *Myths and Legends of China*. London: Harrap, 1922. 208–10. Print.

Yang, Lihui, et al., eds. *Handbook of Chinese Mythology*. New York: Oxford UP, 2005. Print.

◆ The Fairy Princess of Mount Ophir

Author: Traditional
Time Period: 1001 CE–1500 CE
Country or Culture: Malaysia
Genre: Folktale

PLOT SUMMARY

The wife of Sultan Mahmud Shah, who ruled Malacca in contemporary Malaysia from 1488 to 1511, died, and his courtiers, noblemen, and officers implore him to marry again. They propose he choose a new wife from the daughters of local rulers, but Sultan Mahmud exclaims that he will not marry any ordinary princess: "I want to marry one to whom no other Prince can aspire. . . . I want to ask the Princess Gunung Ledang" (Leyden 276).

Sultan Mahmud prepares to send messengers to carry his marriage proposal to the fairy princess. Among the messengers are Admiral Sang Satia and Tun Mamed (Mamat). In some versions, the messengers include the legendary Malay warrior Hang Tuah.

The messengers climb the mountain Gunung Ledang, called Mount Ophir by Westerners. The ascent is difficult, and at "about the middle of the mountain," Tun Mamed decides to proceed alone with the help of some local men (277). They reach a forest of singing bamboos located so high up in the clouds "that one may touch them" (277). Enchanted, Tun Mamed stops for a while to enjoy his surroundings. Next, he comes upon a magical garden of singing birds and plants. At the center, in a hall made of bones, he encounters an elegant old woman attended by four young women.

Tun Mamed states his mission. The old woman replies that she is Dang Raya Rani, the head attendant of Princess Gunung Ledang. She promises to relay the sultan's marriage request to the princess. Dang Raya Rani and the four younger women then suddenly vanish.

Next, a very old, bent-down woman appears to state the demands of Princess Gunung Ledang, which are that the sultan has to build two bridges, one of gold and one of silver, from Malacca to Gunung Ledang. He must also provide enough gnat and moth hearts to fill seven platters, "a vat of human tears," and a vat of betel juice (280). In addition, the sultan must provide one flask of his own blood (this demand is omitted in some versions) and a vial of his son's blood.

The folktale states that the old woman disappears after stating the demands, and many versions of the tale suggest that the old woman was the princess in disguise.

When Tun Mamed returns and relates the demands to the sultan, the ruler gives up on his marriage quest. He states, "All these requests may be complied with, but the taking of blood is an unpleasant business, and I have no inclination for it at all" (281).

Some versions of the tale continue to tell a background story of the princess. She once married the heroic Malay seafarer Nakhoda Ragam. One day, Ragam tickles his wife, and she stabs him—either accidentally or in anger, depending on the version—with her sewing needle. Ragam dies. His empty boat crashes and its parts form the six islands of Malacca. The princess retires to Mount Ophir, vowing never to marry again, and it is in this state that she receives the sultan's messengers.

SIGNIFICANCE

Many different versions of the tale of the fairy princess of Mount Ophir (Gunung Ledang in Malay) exist in Malaysia, where it is still very popular and is known "Puteri Gunung Ledang." The tale ties a legendary princess from a local creation myth to the unfortunate marriage quest of the historical sultan of Malacca, Mahmud Shah, and is believed to have been originally commissioned as part of a work titled *Sejarah Melayu* (*The Malay Annals*), which was edited and compiled by the Malaysian grand vizier Tun Sri Lanang in 1612 CE. In 2001, the *Sejarah Melayu* was accepted in the United Nations Educational, Scientific and Cultural Organization (UNESCO) Memory of the World Program International Register.

The story of the fairy princess of Mount Ophir, as part of the *Malay Annals*, was published first in English in 1821. In 2013, Malay scholar Sabri Zain compiled a survey of the different traditions and elements of the folktale. Unfortunately, Zain ascribes the wooing of Princess Gunung Ledang to Mahmud Shah's grandfather, Sultan Mansur Shah, which contradicts the original account.

Historically, it is interesting that the folktale credits Mahmud Shah with such great love for his son, Prince Raja Ahmed, that he will not draw his son's blood. In reality, Sultan Mahmud Shah lost Malacca to the Portuguese in 1511 CE and killed his son Ahmed in 1513 for failing to recapture Malacca. The folktale seeks to exonerate Mahmud Shah, who would not harm his son for personal reasons, only to kill him for military failure.

In Malaysia, "Puteri Gunung Ledang" has enjoyed enduring popularity and been adapted for film and stage. The 1961 box-office hit *Puteri Gunong Ledang* stars Elaine Edley as the fairy princess, and Director S. Roomai Noor follows the folktale with some telling differences. The princess appears as her young and beautiful self, and the sultan fulfills the first six conditions; there is no demand for his own blood. He is ready to kill his son in order to obtain his blood, but the sultan gives up on his third attempt. The princess appears to him and scolds him for his cruelty. In the end, the sultan repents and is welcomed by his people.

Malaysian director Saw Teong Hin's 2004 movie *Puteri Gunung Ledang* takes further creative liberties. In this film, Tiara Jacquelina as the princess is in love with heroic warrior Hang Tuah. She puts her conditions to the sultan to convince him to leave her alone, but he refuses to give in until the princess appears to him as he is about to kill his son. The sultan curses the princess and Hang Tuah, and the film leaves open the ending of their love affair.

The film served as the basis of Zahim Albakri's 2006 musical *Puteri Gunung Ledang*, which starred Tiara Jacquelina in three productions from 2006 to 2009. In the musical, the sultan condemns the princess to live alone on Gunung Ledang forever.

R. C. Lutz, PhD

BIBLIOGRAPHY

Brown, C. C. *Sejarah Melayu; or, Malay Annals*. Oxford: Oxford UP, 1970. Print.

Hooker, Virginia Matheson. *A Short History of Malaysia*. Crow's Nest, Australia: Allen, 2003. Print.

Leyden, John, trans. *Malay Annals*. Introd. Thomas S. Raffles. London, 1821. 276–81. Print.

"Puteri Gunung Ledang: The Fairy Princess of Mount Ophir." *Sabrizain.org*. Sabri Zain, n.d. Web. 18 June 2013.

Winstedt, Richard. *The Malay Magician*. London: Routledge, 1951. Print.

◆ The First People

Author: Traditional
Time Period: 501 CE–1000 CE
Country or Culture: Japan
Genre: Myth

PLOT SUMMARY

Out of the "clouds and mists" at the beginning of the universe, the man Izanagi (Izana-gi) and the woman Izanami (Izana-mi) are created (Colum 249). They are the last beings in a succession of deities. In the primeval landscape, they walk onto a rainbow bridge. There, Izanagi casts his spear downward and waterdrops run down the spear's shaft to its tip, where they freeze, forming a place for the couple to stay.

In this place, they have many different children who become "the ancestors of men and women" (250). Yet after Izanami gives birth to the fire children, she falls fatally ill and disappears from the surface of the earth.

Through a cave, Izanagi enters the underworld, called "Meido, Place of Gloom," in search of his wife (250). Underground, in a loud voice, Izanami tells him to stop and not to look at her. Yet Izanami lights a torch and approaches her. He is horrified by her appearance. Her eyes are hollow in her bare skull, and her mouth has no lips.

Angry at her husband's defiance, Izanami vows not to let him return to their children above. Izanagi runs away. He is pursued by Izanami and her fellow "dread dwellers of the Place of Gloom" (250). Izanagi facilitates his escape by throwing bamboo shoots and grapes from his comb to the ground. There, his pursuers stop to eat them. He finally exits the cave and blocks its entrance with a big rock.

Izanami curses him. She announces that as his punishment, she will draw one thousand people down to Meido each day. Undeterred, Izanagi promises he will bring about the birth of fifteen hundred persons each day.

Beyond the cave, Izanagi bathes in a stream to wash off the pollution of the underworld. From the dirt he washes off, people are born. From them, one thousand have to die each day. This necessitates Izanagi to have his followers give birth to fifteen hundred people each day.

Because Izanagi defied Izanami's orders not to look at her in the underworld, and because of her ensuing vengeance, the first couple becomes separated. As consequence, there are "death and separation in the world" ever since their hateful last encounter (251).

SIGNIFICANCE

In *Orpheus: Myths of the World* (1930), Irish author Pádraic Colum published his rendition of the Japanese myth of Izanami and Izanagi as "The First People." In his retelling, Colum takes great creative liberties with the original Japanese creation myth of Izanami and Izanagi, which was first transcribed in Japan by Ō no Yasumaro in the *Kojiki* (Record of ancient matters) in 712 CE. The myth was later made part of the *Nihongi* (Chronicle of Japan), which was compiled and edited by Prince Toneri in 720 CE. Until the early twentieth century, this myth was taught to Japanese children as a historical chronicle of the creation of the Japanese islands and its earliest inhabitants.

Colum's "The First People" condenses and alters the story of Izanami and Izanagi in some significant ways. Omitted is their creation, on the rainbow bridge, of the islands of Japan. Also, in the original, Izanami and Izanagi do not create human children, as in Colum's rendition, but *kami* (spirits or deities).

The death of Izanami from giving birth to fire children, or the fire kami in the Japanese original, is central to the story. It alludes to the historical danger of death from childbirth. Even a deity such as Izanami was not immune to this tragic death.

Izanagi's encounter with Izanami in the underworld is true to the Japanese original. The Japanese people of the Kofun period (ca. 250–535 CE), when the story most

likely originated, did not cremate their dead. Instead, they buried them in impressive tombs, called "tumuli." Some of these tombs have survived to the present day, such as the Daisen Kofun in Osaka. The Kofun people were familiar with the decay of the body after death. They envisioned the underworld as a horrific, dreadful place. Even a deity like Izanami faces bodily decay and disfigurement after death. She so resents her husband seeing her in this awful state that she forever severs ties with him.

Colum's "The First People" omits the creation of the sun goddess Amaterasu, the divine ancestress of the Japanese emperors. In the original, Amaterasu is given birth either by Izanagi and Izanami together or by Izanagi alone after Izanami's death. Both accounts are given in the Japanese chronicles.

Instead, Colum uses elements from the Chinese creation myth of Pangu when he states that people are created from the polluted dirt off Izanagi's body. In the Chinese myth, common people are created from vermin in Pangu's clothes. This presents a similarly discomfiting image totally absent in the Japanese original, in which Izanagi creates only three more kami after his return from the underworld.

In Japan, the story of Izanami and Izanagi is still popular and widely known. The two characters can be found in manga, anime, films, and computer games, for example. In the field of literature, prominent Japanese crime author Natsuo Kirino (pen name of Mariko Hashioka) retold the story from Izanami's female point of view in *Joshinki* (2008; *The Goddess Chronicle*, 2012).

Colum's "The First People" represents an interesting Western rendition of the Japanese myth of Izanami and Izanagi. Colum downplays the divine elements of the story. He focuses instead on the effects of the conflict of the first couple on humanity's ensuing fate.

Colum was drawn to the Japanese story's coincidental similarity to the Greek myth of Orpheus and Eurydice. Both tales feature a lover's travel to the netherworld. In the Greek myth, however, Eurydice retains her beauty, and the two lovers do not fight each other, even after their separation in the underworld. For Izanagi and Izanami, their love ends. This is because Izanagi defies Izanami's plea not to look at her figure, which has become a decomposing corpse. Their divorce definitively separates the world of the living from the world of the dead and introduces the cycle of life and death to the world.

R. C. Lutz, PhD

BIBLIOGRAPHY

Aston, William George, trans. *Nihongi*. London: Routledge, 2011. Print.

Burkert, Walter. *Greek Religion*. Cambridge: Harvard UP, 1985. Print.

Chamberlain, Basil Hall, trans. *The Kojiki*. Kobe: Thompson, 1919: 19–51. Print.

Colum, Pádraic. "The First People." *Orpheus: Myths of the World*. New York: Macmillan, 1930. 249–51. Print.

Kirino, Natsuo. *The Goddess Chronicle*. Trans. Rebecca Copeland. Edinburgh: Canongate, 2012. Print.

Philippi, Donald, trans. *The Kojiki*. Tokyo: U of Tokyo P, 1977: 48–73. Print.

 # Garuda

Author: Traditional
Time Period: 1001 CE–1500 CE
Country or Culture: Indonesia
Genre: Myth

PLOT SUMMARY

Hatched from an egg over a tumultuous period spanning five hundred years, the human-headed eagle Garuda is the son of Kasiapa, one of just a half-dozen divinely enlightened Buddhas, and Winata, the first of Kasiapa's twenty-nine wives. The myth begins in a time prior to Garuda's hatching, with a quarrel between Garuda's mother and Kadru, Kasiapa's second wife. Kadru is a Nagini, one of the cosmic, snakelike gods that appear throughout Hindu and Buddhist mythology with varying motivations and allegiances.

Winata and Kadru quarrel over the color of the tail of the divine horse Ucaistrawa, who was born into the world at the same time as *amrita*, the sacred substance of the gods regarded by ancient Buddhists as the water of life. Kadru believes that the horse has a black tail, while Winata argues that it is completely white. After the two goddesses grow tired of constant quarrelling, they make a pact to inspect the horse to end the debate once and for all. The goddesses also decide that whoever is wrong will become the victor's slave for all eternity.

Kadru deceives Winata by having her snake children spray poison on Ucaistrawa's tail, which turns it from white to black. As a result, Winata loses the pact and is enslaved by Kadru just as her son Garuda is hatching.

In response to his mother's enslavement, Garuda comes of age as a sworn enemy of the Naginis, even devouring many of his Nagini half siblings for sustenance.

Garuda approaches the snakes to inquire what they will accept in exchange for his mother's freedom. The Naginis insist that they will free Winata if Garuda gives them amrita in return, which they implore him to steal from the gods. He complies, and an intricate battle between Garuda and the mythical protectors of the amrita unfolds. In the end, Garuda is victorious and retrieves the amrita.

Garuda's bravery and strength in the clash compels the powerful god Wisnu (Visnu) to ask the bird to become his vehicle. Garuda accepts the gracious offer and, in doing so, takes an illustrious place in the divine hierarchy as the transport of one of the most powerful figures in Hinduism and Buddhism, while simultaneously establishing an inseparable association with the water of life, the elixir of immortality.

SIGNIFICANCE

The intricate myth of Garuda encompasses numerous characters and plot lines that remain intertwined throughout the entire canon of Buddhist mythology. The major narrative throughout illustrates the efforts of the eponymous mythical bird to free his mother from slavery. Garuda, also referred to throughout Indonesian myth as the "Garuda Bird," remains a crucial figure throughout the Buddhist cultures of East Asia in modern times. Although Garuda is depicted in Buddhist mythology as having a human face with the body of an eagle, the bird's appearance varies throughout epochs and particular cultures. Although Garuda appears on state and royal emblems throughout the region, no East Asian nation has embraced the Garuda bird with more exuberance than Indonesia, where he maintains a visible presence in both national and corporate iconography—most notably, as the symbol for the flag carrier for Indonesian air transport, Garuda Indonesia.

Scholars attribute Garuda's longevity to several significant causes. While the amrita he triumphantly recovers to free his mother from captivity has several religious connotations with regard to immortality after death, it was also adopted by the secular founders of Indonesia as an important cultural symbol representing longevity and political stability with regard to the state, its institutions, and its people.

Also, Garuda's divine role as the sole means of transportation for the powerful god Wisnu connotes unity. As an aid to the powerful god, he acts a symbol of unification for all who believe in Wisnu, becoming, in a sense, a divine mascot.

John Pritchard

BIBLIOGRAPHY

Beer, Robert. "The Garuda." *The Handbook of Tibetan Buddhist Symbols*. Chicago: Serindia, 2003. 73–77. Print.

Dowman, Keith. *The Flight of the Garuda: The Dzogchen Tradition of Tibetan Buddhism*. Boston: Wisdom, 2003. Print.

Leeming, David Adams. *A Dictionary of Asian Mythology*. New York: Oxford UP, 2001. Print.

Mishra, P. K., ed. *Studies in Hindu and Buddhist Art*. New Delhi: Abhinav, 1999. Print.

Rose, Carol. *Giants, Monsters, and Dragons: An Encyclopedia of Folklore, Legend, and Myth*. Santa Barbara: ABC-CLIO, 2000. Print.

◆ How a Man Got the Better of Two Foxes

Author: Traditional
Time Period: 501 CE–1000 CE
Country or Culture: Japan
Genre: Folktale

PLOT SUMMARY

One day, a man collecting bark in the mountains comes upon a foxhole. Hiding behind a tree, he observes a fox approaching the foxhole and speaking to another fox in human language. The outside fox makes a promising proposition. The next day, around lunchtime, he will return to the foxhole in the shape of a man. The other fox should change into a horse, and together they will ride into a human settlement on the shoreline. There, the outside fox will sell his companion as a horse and buy valuables and food with the proceeds. When the new owner puts the horse outside to feed on grass, the first fox will return, free the horse, and help it escape. The foxes will then share the spoils equally.

With this knowledge, the man returns to the foxhole the next day and imitates the voice of the first fox. The second fox appears from the foxhole, and as agreed, he transforms himself into a magnificent, reddish-colored horse. In a prosperous village nearby, the man sells this fine horse for a good deal of food and precious things. Afterward, he leaves.

The new owner likes his splendid horse so much that he keeps him inside his house and cuts grass himself to feed his horse rather than allow the horse to graze outside. Because the fox cannot eat grass, he faces starvation. After four days, he manages to escape through the window and run home. Believing the other fox has tricked him, he intends to kill him. However, upon meeting, the two foxes realize they have been cheated by the man and vow to kill him instead.

The man approaches the two foxes and apologizes for his trick. He tells them they would gain nothing from killing him. However, if the foxes let him live, he will brew rice beer for them and worship them for all time. In addition, the man promises that whenever he lands a good catch, he will make the foxes an offer of fish. Finally, he explains that all humans will worship foxes from now on. The foxes believe this offer is a good one, and they accept it. This is the reason, the folktale concludes, why the Ainu and the remainder of the Japanese population revere foxes.

SIGNIFICANCE

The story of the man and the two foxes is a folktale of the Ainu, the indigenous people of northern Japan. Contemporary anthropological and genetic research strongly suggests that the Ainu people were formed by the thirteenth century CE from members of the Satsumon culture of northern Japan and the Okhotsk culture flourishing on the island of Hokkaido and around the Sea of Okhotsk. Because individuals of Ainu descent differ physically from ethnic Japanese, typically having more facial and body hair, round eyes, and lighter skin, they often faced discrimination in Japan.

The best-known version of this tale was told by Ainu storyteller Ishanashte to British Japanologist Basil Hall Chamberlain on July 15, 1887. Hall, who spoke Ainu, recorded the tale in Ainu, translated it into English, and published it in his anthology *Aino Folktales* (1888).

For the Ainu, the significance of the folktale lies in its explanation of the cultural practice of fox worship. This was still practiced at the end of the nineteenth century on Hokkaido. English missionary John Batchelor, an early friend of the Ainu and speaker of their language, reported as late as 1901 that Ainu homes featured fox skulls decorated with wood shavings at the sacred eastern end of the dwellings. Ainu also took fox skulls on journeys as amulets.

Japanese and Western studies of Ainu folklore have confirmed that Ainu folklore distinguished between two kinds of foxes. The rare dark or black fox, called *shitunpe* in the Ainu language, represents a good divine spirit, or *kamui*, even though he is believed to be mischievous or cruel at times. The red fox, called *chironnup*, is more common. However, in Ainu mythology, this fox has the power to change shape and is generally of a negative character. It is interesting that the fox in the folktale changes into a reddish-colored horse. This indicates that he belongs to the shape-shifting, chironnup variety. Even though he has less spiritual power than his benevolent counterpart, he and his companion accept human worship.

In its transcribed form, the folktale is a combination of Ainu material and material adapted from Japanese folklore. Foxes figure prominently in Japanese folktales, in which they can shift shapes and are distinguished by color. Yet use of fox skulls for worship is a unique Ainu feature. The story elements pointing most significantly at Japanese influence are the horse and the rice beer. There is no archaeological evidence for horses among the Ainu of Hokkaido before contact and trading began with the Japanese after the thirteenth century CE. Horses disappeared from Satsumon culture in northern Japan by the tenth century and thus never traveled to Hokkaido. The horse into which the fox changes in the folktale might be inspired by a remote Satsumon collective memory. More likely, it is the result of trade with the Japanese.

Japanese rice beer, often known as sake, was not brewed on Hokkaido before 1868. Some sake may have been brought to the island by Japanese traders prior to that date. However, this story element appears to be a more recent addition. By the time Ishanashte told the folktale to Chamberlain, sake was brewed widely on Hokkaido. It seems reasonable to suggest that the two foxes of the tale were given a fondness for rice beer to ease their acceptance of the man's apology for tricking these two tricksters.

R. C. Lutz, PhD

BIBLIOGRAPHY

Batchelor, John. *The Ainu and Their Folk-lore*. London: Religious Tract Soc., 1901. Print.

Casal, U. A. "The Goblin, Fox and Badger and Other Witch Animals of Japan." *Asian Folklore Studies* 18 (1959): 1–94. Print.

Chamberlain, Basil Hall. "How a Man Got the Better of Two Foxes." *Aino Folk-tales*. 1888. London: Folk-Lore Soc., 2006. 10–12. Print.

Ota, Yuzo. *Basil Hall Chamberlain: Portrait of a Japanologist*. New York: Routledge, 2011. Print.

Siddle, Richard. "From Assimilation to Indigenous Rights: Ainu Resistance since 1869." *Ainu: Spirit of a Northern People*. Ed. William Fitzhugh and Chisato O. Dubreuil. Washington: Natl. Museum of Natural History, 1999. 108–15. Print.

Strong, Sarah. "The Most Revered of Foxes: Knowledge of Animals and Animal Power in an Ainu *Kamui Yukar*." *Asian Ethnology* 68.1 (2009): 27–54. Print.

◆ In the Palace of the Sea God

Author: Traditional
Time Period: 501 CE–1000 CE
Country or Culture: Japan
Genre: Folktale

PLOT SUMMARY

Hoderi and his younger brother, Hoori, are great-grandsons of the Japanese sun goddess, Amaterasu. They excel in two different activities: Hoderi is an excellent fisherman, while Hoori an outstanding hunter. One day, the two brothers decide to switch their occupations. Hoderi fails at hunting and returns his brother's bow and arrow. Hoori cannot catch any fish, but he loses his brother's magic fishhook before he can return it. Hoderi refuses to accept any replacement or the offer of multiple new fishhooks, which grieves Hoori.

Hoori goes to the seashore and tells a friendly old man, Shiko-tsutsu no Oji, about his estrangement from his brother. The old man reassures Hoori with a promise to help repair the situation. Shiko-tsutsu makes a basket for Hoori and lowers him into the sea. Hoori climbs out once he has reached an underwater beach adorned with seaweed. From there, Hoori reaches the palace of the Sea God. He rests outside the palace at a well in the shade of a cassia tree. A young woman, Toyo-tama, spots him there and tells her parents about him. Her father, the Sea God, invites Hoori into the palace and listens to his story. The Sea God summons all the fishes, and Hoderi's fishhook is found in the mouth of a tai fish.

Hoori marries Toyo-tama, but after three years of living under the sea, he becomes homesick. The Sea God gives Hoori the fishhook and advises him on how to return it to Hoderi, also giving him two jewels—one to raise and one to lower the tide—with which to fight his brother should he have to.

As Hoori prepares to leave, his wife reveals that she is about to give birth to their child. She tells Hoori that she will come to the seashore on a stormy day and asks him to build her a hut to give birth in.

Hoori returns home and finds Hoderi, who apologizes for his hostile behavior. Hoori forgives him.

On a stormy day, Toyo-tama comes ashore together with her younger sister. Toyo-tama gives birth to a boy in the hut Hoori has built before taking the form of a dragon and returning to the ocean. When their son reaches adulthood, he marries his aunt, Toyo-tama's younger sister, and they have four sons. One of the four is Kamu-Yamato-Iwate-Biko, who becomes Jimmu Tennō, the first emperor of Japan.

SIGNIFICANCE

This folktale is based on traditional material collected in two Japanese classics. The oldest collection is the *Kojiki*, composed in 712 CE. Commissioned by Japanese empress Gemmei, court writer Ō no Yasumaro recorded the stories told to him by mythology expert Hieda no Are. Sections 28 to 44 of the *Kojiki* contain the oldest written material about the brothers Hoderi and Hoori. The *Nihon Shoki* (or *Nihongi*)—composed under the general editorship of Japanese prince Toneri in 720 CE—includes more variants of the story.

In 1912, F. Hadland Davis published his English text of the folktale in his anthology *Myths and Legends of Japan*. Davis based his rendition mainly on William George Aston's translation of the *Nihongi*, which Davis acknowledges as source. In Davis's hand, the multiple Japanese stories are formed into one streamlined version that contains most events from the original versions. One key omission is Toyo-tama's warning to her husband not to watch her as she gives birth. She does so knowing that while giving birth, she will return to her true dragon, serpent, or crocodile form (depending on the version of the tale). When Hoori disobeys her and sees her thus, Toyo-tama feels forced to leave out of shame. In one version, she and Hoori exchange several love poems thereafter while separated forever.

Historically in Japan, a primary significance of the material rendered in this folktale was to establish an unbroken genealogy confirming the divine origins of Japan's first emperor. By presenting the story of Jimmu's grandfather (Hoori) and father (Hoori's son), descendents of the goddess Amaterasu, both the *Kojiki* and the *Nihon Shoki* confirm the divine origins of Japan's imperial line. This was taught as straight history in Japan until 1945.

In Japanese folklore, the two brothers are widely popular and the subject of many special folk customs. In folktales, Hoori is known primarily by his nickname of Yamasachihiko, or Luck of the Mountain. His nickname comes from his mountain hunting grounds. His travels to meet the sea god Ryūjin and his marriage to the god's daughter Princess Otohime are the subject of a cycle of popular tales still told in Japan. His brother, Hoderi, known in folk tales as Umisachihiko, or Luck of the Sea, is less prominent in the popular Japanese imagination. However, his dance of submission to Hoori, which is part of the folktale material not incorporated in Davis's rendition, is still performed at Japanese folk festivals. In this dance, Hoderi/Umisachihiko performs some acts related to an archetypal jester figure.

In Japan's Shintō religion, there is a cult dedicated to Hoori, who is worshipped as the god of rice and other cereals under his alternate name of Hohodemi, which means "many harvests." This name is derived from the Japanese character that is used to write the first syllable of his name, *ho*, indicating rice or another field crop. It is interesting that the hunter Hoori has become a guardian of farmers. This new occupation may reflect the influence of Buddhism in Japan after the sixth century. Then, society turned away from killing land animals for food and established a traditional diet of rice and fish.

R. C. Lutz, PhD

BIBLIOGRAPHY

Aston, William George, trans. *Nihongi*. 1896. London: Routledge, 2011. Print.

Chamberlain, Basil Hall, trans. *The Kojiki*. Kobe: Thompson, 1919. Print.

Davis, F. Hadland. "In the Palace of the Sea God." *Myths and Legends of Japan*. New York: Crowell, 1912. 34–37. Print.

Kitagawa, Joseph. *Understanding Japanese Religion*. Princeton: Princeton UP, 1987. Print.

Philippi, Donald. *The Kojiki*. Tokyo: U of Tokyo P, 1977. Print.

The Island of Women

Author: Traditional
Time Period: 1501 CE–1700 CE
Country or Culture: Japan
Genre: Folktale

PLOT SUMMARY

The chieftain of the town of Iwanai sets sail with his two sons one day, hoping to hunt down enough sea lions to provide a feast for their people. Though they manage to spear a sea lion, a violent storm then descends upon them, forcing the chieftain to cut the rope attached to the thrashing animal and ride out the waves.

In a short while, the man and his sons come to a gorgeous island. As they approach the shore, a parade of beautiful women comes to meet them. They all carry another, even more beautiful woman, hoisting her above their heads in an ornate chair. This woman is left at the shore to greet the men as her companions return up the hillside. She explains that this island is a land of women, and as such, there are no men there. There is also, she says, something else unusual about the island, which she will not explain. Because of this additional peculiarity, she will allow the men to stay in her house for the remainder of the spring and the summer. When the autumn passes, the men will be made husbands to the women, and when the next spring arrives, they will be sent back home.

The men carry the female chieftain to her home, where she puts them in a fine room surrounded by golden netting. While the men reside in the female chieftain's home, women from all over the hills come to look upon them. Months pass in this manner, until the leaves of the trees begin to change for autumn. When this occurs, the female chieftain comes to take the male chieftain as her husband, explaining that his sons will go to two other women. The men spend the winter as husbands, lying with the women and living among them.

When the spring at last comes, the female chieftain takes her husband aside. She explains to him that the women of this island, unlike the women of his home, grow teeth in their vaginas every year. These teeth appear with the first growth of spring and fall out in the autumn as the leaves change. Because this prevents them from marrying, the women take the wind as their husband, turning their backs to it when it blows and thus becoming pregnant. The girls are raised among them and the boys are killed when they reach the age of men.

Because of all of this, she says, she will send the chieftain and his sons home.

On the last night, however, the female chieftain is overcome with emotion. Knowing she will miss her husband, she asks that he lie with her one last time. The male chieftain, fearing for his safety, crawls into bed with her. Instead of using his body, however, he takes the sheath of his sword and inserts it into the female chieftain to make love with her. The next day, he and his sons sail back to their home, where their wives have been mourning as widows. When they tell the story of the island of women, the male chieftain shows the people his scabbard, the markings of the teeth still upon it.

SIGNIFICANCE

Although the story of an island of women who possess teeth-filled vaginas might seem strange to some modern readers, it is in fact a common motif across world mythology, appearing in a large number of traditions across diverse regions. This particular version comes from the Ainu people, an ethnic group that is indigenous to Japan and Russia, and was allegedly adapted from an earlier Japanese tale. The culture of the Ainu seems to have emerged in the late twelfth century CE as an outgrowth of the earlier Satsumon culture. The story of the island of women was recorded in the late nineteenth century by a British academic named Basil Hall Chamberlain. Unsurprisingly, very similar versions of the myth exist in Japanese culture as well.

Across cultures, the stories of women with teeth in their vaginas are referred to as *vagina dentata* (Latin for "toothed vagina") stories. As with most vagina dentata myths, the Ainu tale is in many ways a reflection of male anxieties and desires. The island of women, a land in which the chieftain and his sons are the only men, is described as a sort of paradise. The women are all gorgeous and all desire the company of the men, having been loved only by the wind for generations, and the land itself is fertile and pleasing. As the only male figures in this land, the men are living a sort of prolonged sexual fantasy, the women gathering to gaze on them while they remain the companions of the most powerful figures in the society. This fantasy, however, is revealed to have a nightmarish component when the female chieftain tells the men of the women's biological peculiarity. Instead of a sexual paradise, the island becomes a land of physical violence. Realizing the fantasy of union with the women will result in a gruesome dismemberment in which the primary sign of their masculinity will be literally ripped away from them. For a man who lives in a position of power within his own society—the main hunter and political leader of his people—the power held by the female chieftain on her island of women is both eroticized and terrifying, the physical threat of her female body representing a metaphorical threat to his role of masculine power. This is further heightened by the fact that he uses his scabbard to lie with the female chieftain, the scabbard being a symbol of masculinity, violence, and leadership that the woman is quickly and easily able to damage.

In the end, the man and his sons return to their island. There, their wives wait in pious respect, cloaked in mourning clothes that signal their devotion to and respect for their male partners. The threat of the island of women is avoided, and the men are still able to function physically and as political leaders. It is unsurprising that the men escape the island both unharmed and having experienced the sexual pleasures the women offer, especially as the tale is told from the perspective of a male-dominated society. The tale of the island of women, like vagina dentata stories in many societies, is primarily an expression of anxiety. As in so many patriarchal cultures, the men's fear is ultimately not a fear of castration or displacement but rather a fear of powerful women, figures who lead their own societies and control their own bodies, upsetting the dominance of men in the process.

T. Fleischmann

BIBLIOGRAPHY

Chamberlain, Basil Hall. *Aino Folk-Tales*. London: Folk-Lore Soc., 1888. Print.

Ishida Eiichirō. "The Island of Women." *Japan Quarterly* 4.4 (1957): 454–60. Print.

Macé, François. "Human Rhythm and Divine Rhythm in Ainu Epics." *Diogenes* 46.1 (1998): 31–42. Print.

Moerman, D. Max. "Demonology and Eroticism: Islands of Women in the Japanese Buddhist Imagination." *Japanese Journal of Religious Studies* 36.2 (2009): 351–80. Print.

Refsing, Kirsten, ed. *Early European Writing on Ainu Culture: Religion and Folklore*. 5 vols. London: Routledge, 2002. Print.

◆ The Korean Cinderella

Author: Shirley Climo
Time Period: 1951 CE–2000 CE
Country or Culture: Korea
Genre: Fairy Tale

PLOT SUMMARY

In feudal Korea, a childless old husband and wife long to have a child. One day, a daughter is born to the old couple, and the father plants a pear tree in front of their home to celebrate her birth. The mother names the child Pear Blossom. As Pear Blossom grows up into a beautiful girl, her mother lovingly raises her. Sadly, one day, Pear Blossom's mother dies.

Following his wife's death, Pear Blossom's father approaches the village matchmaker and remarries. His new wife, Omoni, brings along her daughter, Peony. Peony is the same age as Pear Blossom.

Omoni and Peony mistreat and abuse Pear Blossom. Her old father prefers to look the other way. Omoni makes Pear Blossom perform long, arduous household chores. She gives Pear Blossom only used, worn clothes to wear. Peony, who is less beautiful than Pear Blossom, maliciously teases her stepsister. She calls her Little Pig or Pigling.

To humiliate Pear Blossom, Omoni sets a series of seemingly impossible tasks for her to complete. First, she gives Pear Blossom a jar with a large hole in it and tells her to fetch water with it. Pear Blossom worries about how she will accomplish this until a big frog appears. The frog helps Pear Blossom by serving as plug for the hole. Enraged at Pear Blossom's success when she returns with the water, Omoni abuses her and looks for a new task.

One day, Omoni orders Pear Blossom to polish every grain in a huge sack of rice by the time she and Peony return later that afternoon. Pear Blossom weeps and embraces the pear tree, asking for help. A flock of sparrows flies down from the pear tree and polishes the grains in due time. When Pear Blossom tells Omoni what happened, she sends Peony under the pear tree to catch some of its magic. However, the sparrows fly down and attack Peony. Angry, Omoni starves Pear Blossom for two days.

Pear Blossom is then ordered to weed a huge field before she can join her stepmother and stepsister at a festival. A black ox appears. He quickly eats all the weeds and gives Pear Blossom delicious fruits and candies.

Pear Blossom hastens to the festival. On the way, she moves behind a willow tree to let pass the procession of a feudal magistrate. One of her straw sandals slips off her foot and falls into a creek. The magistrate notices this and sees beautiful Pear Blossom shyly running away from his entourage. He orders his men to retrieve the sandal and falls in love with its unknown bearer.

In the village, the magistrate orders his subordinates to find the sandal's owner. Thinking that Pear Blossom has stolen the sandal, Omoni turns her in. To her great surprise, the magistrate asks Pear Blossom to marry him. He resolutely refuses Omoni's demand that he marry Peony instead.

In the spring, the magistrate asks Pear Blossom's old father for permission to marry her. After the wedding, Pear Blossom is surrounded by sparrows and frogs in her new home. They all call out her name, sounding like *E-wah* in Korean.

SIGNIFICANCE

In *The Korean Cinderella* (1993), American author Shirley Climo combines several Korean variants of the Cinderella fairy tale, which, along with the European versions, share their roots with the classic Greek story of the slave girl Rhodopis in Egypt, transcribed by Strabo in the first century CE. In Korea, the fairy tale retold by Shirley Climo in *The Korean Cinderella* has been popular for centuries. The Korean tale is known by the names of its two principal characters. Depending on how the Korean Hangul script is romanized, Pear Blossom in *The Korean Cinderella* is called Kong-jwi or Kongji. The evil stepsister, Peony, is called Pat-jwi or Patji.

Climo's *The Korean Cinderella* captures the first part of the Korean fairy tale, which exists in many different versions. The inability of Pear Blossom's old father to stand up for his daughter and her subsequent mistreatment at the hands of her stepmother and stepsister are central elements of the story. They subtly critique what happens in a feudal society built on the Confucian ethos of filial loyalty when the person supposedly at the top of the family hierarchy, the father, becomes too weak to fulfill his duties toward his own daughter. This problem is resolved only when the magistrate becomes Pear Blossom's husband and restores social and familial order.

However, in Climo's *The Korean Cinderella*, the author cuts out the horrific second part of the original Korean fairy tale. Traditionally, the story of Kong-jwi and Pat-jwi continues with Pat-jwi's murder of Kong-jwi

after her marriage. After this, Pat-jwi usurps her sister's role as the magistrate's wife, fooling him. Only after several reincarnations does Kong-jwi come back to life as herself. Only then does her husband realize his mistake. In punishment, Pat-jwi is hacked to death. Her pickled meat is consumed by her mother, who dies of shock.

It is obvious why *The Korean Cinderella*, a book intended for children, omits the traditional ending. Interestingly, the full story of Kong-jwi and Pat-jwi corresponds closely to the Vietnamese version of the Cinderella tale, known as the story of Tam and Cam. Similar to *The Korean Cinderella*, contemporary versions of the story of Tam and Cam often abridge the story to cut out the ultimate punishment of the evil stepsister and stepmother. The full extent of the vengeance of the original Korean and Vietnamese fairy tales, which deliver a stark moral message, has been deemed too horrible for young readers and listeners in contemporary times.

In Korea, the material rendered in *The Korean Cinderella* has been adapted into many media. There is the 1951 opera *Kongji Patji* by composer Kim Dai-Hyun. The fairy tale was turned into Korean movies both in 1958 and in 1967. As of 2013, two television series have adapted the story. *My Love Patji* (2006–2007), produced by Lee Jin-Suk, irreverently turns the villain into a spunky contemporary heroine. The situation comedy *All My Love* (2010–11), produced by Kwong Ik Joon, features pop singer Son Ga-in as the Kongji character, called Geumjiin a contemporary setting.

There are other renditions of this Korean fairy tale in English. A reader may look at them to compare their individual focus, but Climo's text still stands out.

R. C. Lutz, PhD

BIBLIOGRAPHY

Adams, Edward. *Korean Cinderella*. Seoul: Seoul International, 1985. Print.

Climo, Shirley. *The Korean Cinderella*. New York: HarperCollins, 1996. Print.

Jolley, Dan. *Pigling: A Cinderella Story*. Minneapolis: Lerner, 2009. Print.

Jones, Horace Leonard, trans. *Strabo: Geography*. 8 vols. Cambridge: Loeb Classical Lib., 1917–30. Print.

Korean Classical Literature Society. *The Story of Kong-jwi & Pat-jwi*. Seoul: Baek Am, 2000. Print.

Roberson, Dongwol Kim. *Congjui & Potjui: Korean Cinderella*. Houston: Good Life, 2009. Print.

Sierra, Judy. "The Story of Tam and Cam." *Cinderella*. Westport: Oryx, 1992. 141–44. Print.

The Magic White Swan

Author: Traditional
Time Period: 1001 CE–1500 CE
Country or Culture: Laos
Genre: Folktale

PLOT SUMMARY

In an indeterminate time, a farmer in Laos goes fishing. He casts his fishing net into the water. Over and over again, the net comes up empty. On his final try, he feels that his net is very heavy. When the farmer looks at his catch, it is a beautiful white pebble. Impressed by its perfection, he takes the pebble home. There, he places it on an altar situated above his head. He eats dinner and goes to bed.

The next morning, the pebble has changed into a white swan. The swan talks to the farmer and tells him that it will transport him to a gorgeous setting filled with flowers, of which he can take as many home as he pleases.

Thus, the farmer gets on the swan's back. The swan flies to the garden with the farmer. There, the farmer enjoys all the beautiful flowers. He picks one and is surprised by its heavy weight. The next flower he picks feels even heavier, and so does the third.

Out of concern for the swan that will have to carry him and his flowers home, the farmer stops picking flowers. He does not want to overburden the swan. The swan flies the farmer to his home and then vanishes. To his surprise, the farmer finds the flowers have turned to gold, making him a rich man.

A friend of the farmer hears of his sudden wealth. He asks how he acquired such riches, and the farmer tells him the true story. On the next day, the farmer's friend goes to the river to fish. He casts out his net three times, pulling it up empty each time. On his last attempt, he finds a white pebble in the net. He takes this pebble along and puts it into his room.

The next morning, the white pebble has transformed into a beautiful white swan. The swan tells the man that he will take him to a flower garden. The man gets on the swan's back and is flown to the flower garden. There, the man picks three heavy flowers. He has no concern for how this weight will burden the swan and proceeds to pick two full armloads of flowers.

He tells the swan to fly home so he can deposit the flowers he has picked and then return for another run. The swan has difficulties rising into the air with his load

but just about makes it to the man's home in a wobbly flight. There, the man tells the swan to wait for him while he drops off his load at home. When he comes out again, the tired swan has flown off. Still, the man rejoices at all the golden flowers he has picked. However, when he looks at them inside his home, he finds not gold but a bunch of ordinary flowers.

SIGNIFICANCE

"The Magic White Swan" is a folktale from Laos, a country in Southeast Asia. Traditionally, the story has been told by the lowland Lao people as a moral tale to educate children and other members of the community. By 2002, Laotian-Thai folklore scholar Wajuppa Tossa had transcribed and translated the folktale as told by Laotian storyteller Sivilay Sopha in Laos. In 2008, the Magic White Swan was included in the print anthology *Lao Folktales*.

"The Magic White Swan" is designed to teach a rich variety of moral lessons. First, there is emphasis on determination. Even though the farmer's net comes up empty many times, he does not give up. Among the lowland Lao farmers, fishing the lakes and rivers of the country, including the Mekong, has been an important source of food. For his determination, the farmer is rewarded at his last attempt.

"The Magic White Swan" also teaches appreciation and reverence for natural beauty. When the farmer finds the heavy white pebble in his net, he does not toss it aside for its apparent lack of utilitarian use. Instead, he is awed by its beauty and reverently puts it on his altar at home. This altar is characteristically placed high on the wall above his head. Among Southeast Asian Buddhist people, the head is strongly revered as being closest to the spirit of the Buddha. Here, the farmer shows proper reverence. In contrast, his friend merely puts his pebble at an unspecified and insignificant area of his home, indicating he does not give its position much consideration.

The folktale further teaches the core Buddhist value of compassion for all other living things. The farmer stops picking the heavy flowers out of his concern for the swan. He limits his pursuit to a reasonable scale. On the other hand, his friend treats the magic swan as a mere pack animal.

"The Magic Swan" also encourages openness and honesty among friends. When asked about the source of his new wealth, the farmer tells his friend the true story.

The folktale teaches a lesson about the second man that the storyteller's audience can all understand: he does meet the magic white swan despite his obviously greedy intentions, but he fails the tests of compassion, humility, and reverence and is punished appropriately.

"The Magic White Swan" was possibly influenced by Hinduism. The Hindu goddess of wisdom, Sarasvatī, travels on a white swan. In Buddhism, which came to Laos by the seventh century CE, Sarasvatī is a guardian of Buddhist teachings. Laos is home to the swan goose that migrates from northern Asia in fall. The presence of this swan, which is not white, may have helped Sarasvatī's mythical white swan enter Lao folklore.

R. C. Lutz, PhD

BIBLIOGRAPHY

Koret, Peter. "Books in Search: Convention and Creativity in Traditional Lao Literature." *The Canon in Southeast Asian Literature*. Ed. David Smyth. Richmond, UK: Curzon, 2000. 210–33. Print.

---. "Laos." *South-East Asia*. Ed. Alastair Dingwall. Lincolnwood: Passport, 1995. 120–53. Print.

Ong, Walter S. *Orality and Literacy: The Technologizing of the Word*. Rpt. London: Routledge, 1991. Print.

Sopha, Sivilay. "The Magic White Swan." Trans. Wajuppa Tossa. *Lao Folktales*. Ed. Margaret Read MacDonald. Westport: Libraries Unlimited, 2008. 18–19. Print.

Zipes, Jack. *The Great Fairy Tale Tradition*. New York: Norton, 2001. Print.

◆ The Magnanimous Girl

Author: Songling Pu
Time Period: 1701 CE–1850 CE
Country or Culture: China
Genre: Folktale

PLOT SUMMARY

In the village of Jinling (Chin-ling) lives a gifted but poor scholar named Gu (Ku). Because he does not want to leave his aging mother alone, he works as writer and painter from home. At twenty-five, he is still single. One day, an old woman and her beautiful young daughter move into the house opposite Gu's home.

A little later, Gu meets the young woman in his home. She does not speak to him but silently stands her ground. His mother informs Gu that the young woman has borrowed her scissors and tape measure. Gu's mother is confident that her neighbor's family has a good background despite their poverty. The young woman told Gu's mother that she does not want to marry because she will not leave her old mother. Gu's mother believes she would be a good wife for Gu.

When visiting them, Gu's mother learns that they live off the income generated from the daughter's "ten fingers" (Giles 161), meaning her tailoring and needlework. When Gu's mother broaches the subject of a match with Gu, the young woman repeats her refusal. Gu and his mother let the matter drop.

Soon after, a young man appears and asks Gu for a picture. The young man becomes Gu's best friend. He finds the young woman next door beautiful but stern.

Gu's mother tells Gu that the young woman has come to beg for rice and asks Gu to bring them some. When Gu does so, the young woman does not thank him. However, she comes to help Gu's mother with her chores. One day, Gu's mother falls sick with a leg abscess. The young woman tenderly cares for her. Gu's mother wishes for a daughter-in-law as devoted as she is. The young woman rejects this praise and states, "Your son is a hundred times more filial than I, a poor widow's only daughter" (Giles 162). When Gu thanks her profusely, she rebukes him. She tells him that she did not thank him for their rice, so he should not thank her now.

Gu falls in love with the young woman, but she does not reciprocate. One day, she enters Gu's home as Gu sits with his friend, whom she dislikes intensely. Suddenly, getting angry at Gu's friend's words, she draws knife from her robe. Gu's friend jumps up and runs away. The young woman follows him outside and throws her dagger into the air. There is a streak of light resembling a rainbow, and something falls to the ground. When Gu looks at it, he sees the severed head and the body of a white fox. "There is your friend," the young woman tells Gu, and she insists this man caused her to destroy him (Giles 163).

The young woman leaves and refuses to discuss her magic skills with Gu. When Gu asks her to marry him, she refuses. The next day, Gu goes to her house to ask her again. He finds the house empty, and the young woman and her mother have disappeared forever.

SIGNIFICANCE

The story of the magnanimous girl is based on a Chinese folktale written by Songling Pu (P'u Sung-ling) and collected in Pu's 1740 collection, *Liaozhai Zhiyi* (*Strange Stories from a Chinese Studio*, 1880). Pu states self-depreciatingly that he mostly collected the tales from storytellers or ancient sources; however, contemporary scholars have established that Pu was most likely the principal author of his *Strange Stories*, just drawing on traditional sources for inspiration.

In 1880, British diplomat Herbert Giles published an English translation of Pu's work. In his rendition, "The Magnanimous Girl," Giles removed the strong sexual content of Pu's original story. In 2008, Sidney L. Sondergard published *Strange Tales from Liaozhai*, for which he faithfully translated Pu's full original. Sondergard titled his rendition of the story of the magnanimous girl "The Swordswoman."

The story of the magnanimous girl is a moving tale of filial piety and devotion, the supernatural, and unrequited love. Giles's rendition captures the original message that reciprocal actions of good will are more important than profuse declarations of gratitude. As Giles renders the folktale, there is a strong feeling of romantic despair. Giles's version of the tale fits well with the Victorian moral attitudes common to Britain and the United States at the time of its publication.

"The Swordswoman," Sondergard's full translation, reveals sexual content that must have shocked the nineteenth-century British translator. "The Swordswoman" makes clear that the white fox, disguised as young man, inflames homosexual desire in Gu. After becoming friends, the young men start teasing each other. This goes on until "Gu lasciviously embraced the young man, who put up no resistance, and they indulged in sexual pleasures" (Sondergard 292). This turn of events makes perfect sense according to traditional Chinese fox lore, in which foxes are depicted as very crafty in their desire to achieve immortality. As a short cut, the foxes change into human form to "seduce men in order to drain them of their *jing*, or sexual essence" (Sondergard xxiv). Traditionally, foxes change into beautiful women. In Pu's tale, the white fox changes into a young man to seduce Gu.

This plot detail makes clear why the young woman hates the young man hanging around Gu to the point that she decides to kill him. It is not only because fox-human relations are usually harmful for the human man in Chinese folklore and mythology that the young woman saves Gu. It is also out of romantic jealousy on the young woman's part.

Sondergard's "The Swordswoman" also reveals that the young woman agrees to have intercourse with Gu after she kills the white fox. She is even willing to bear him a child. Her limitation is that she cannot nurse the baby. For this reason, she counsels Gu not to marry her but to hire a wet nurse for the child and say it is adopted. Gu does as told, and a baby boy is born to them. Then, the young woman disappears after foretelling the truth that Gu will die young but his son will carry on his family line. The full version of the Chinese folktale strongly ties Pu's tale to traditional Chinese lore about shape-shifting foxes.

R. C. Lutz, PhD

BIBLIOGRAPHY

Chang, Chun-shu, and Shelley Hsueh-lun Chang. *Redefining History: Ghosts, Spirits, and Human Society in P'u Sung-ling's World, 1640–1715*. Ann Arbor: U of Michigan P, 1998. Print.

Giles, Herbert A., trans. "The Magnanimous Girl." *Strange Stories from a Chinese Studio*. London: De La Rue, 1880. 160–64. Print.

Sondergard, Sidney L. "The Swordswoman." *Strange Tales from Liaozhai*. Vol. 1. Fremont: Jain, 2008. 290–99. Print.

Werner, Edward T. C. "The Magnanimous Girl." *Myths and Legends of China*. London: Harrap, 1922. 376–79. Print.

Zeitlin, Judith. *Historian of the Strange: Pu Songling and the Chinese Classical Tale*. Stanford: Stanford UP, 1993. Print.

◆ Origin of the Tiger

Author: Traditional
Time Period: 1001 CE–1500 CE
Country or Culture: Cambodia
Genre: Folktale

PLOT SUMMARY

A great king rules an unnamed, wealthy kingdom in an indeterminate time. He has a wise and beautiful queen and is supported by four chief ministers and the royal astrologer, as well as other court officials. Over time, the king becomes worried that he, like everyone else in his court, knows nothing about magic. The king believes that magic is essential to defend his kingdom from any potential invaders.

One day, holding court in the morning, the king decides to learn magic from the wise man Tisabamokkha.

Tisabamokkha lives in the distant northwestern Indian kingdom of Takkasila. Accordingly, the king and his closest retinue depart for Takkasila. There, Tisabamokkha instructs them in magic, particularly the changing of oneself into different animals or celestial beings.

When they complete their education from Tisabamokkha, the king decides that he and his companions should leave for home. Three days into their return journey, they get lost in a great forest. There they begin to run out of food, having exhausted their supplies, and rely on only the roots and berries they can find. Worried that they all may die of starvation, the king calls his companions together to ask for their advice. The royal astrologer suggests that all of them should turn into a single tiger. This tiger could eat forest animals for nourishment. Once they return to their kingdom, they would change back into humans.

The king and his companions agree to this idea. The king questions each member of his entourage, asking which part of the tiger they want to be. The four chief ministers want to become the four legs of the tiger. The astrologer wishes to become the tiger's tail. The queen wants to be his body. The king is left to become the head of the tiger.

Each member of the king's party recites the magic spells necessary for the transformation, and a royal tiger is formed. The hungry royal tiger catches deer and antelope to feed on. He leads such a happy and fulfilled life that he never returns to the king's native land.

This transformation into the royal tiger is the origin of tigers, the strongest of all animals. On the hunt, the tiger is guided by his tail, representing the royal astrologer. His agile body is provided by the queen. His four strong, clawed legs are provided by the four chief ministers. The king gives the tiger his majestic and powerful head, making the tiger the greatest of all kings.

SIGNIFICANCE

The origin of the tiger is a Cambodian folktale. It was told orally for centuries in this Southeast Asian country before being transcribed and translated into French in the 1920s. The Buddhist journal *Soleil du Cambodge* (sun of Cambodia) published the French translation of this and other Cambodian folktales in one of its editions, which can still be found in France. In 1956, a German translation of the tiger folktale was published in East Germany. In the twenty-first century, the American anthropologist and ethnomusicologist Toni Shapiro-Phim

has provided an English rendition of the tale on a website hosted by Cornell University, where Shapiro-Phim earned her degree in 1994.

According to Shapiro-Phim, the great significance of this popular Cambodian folktale lies in its message that people need to cooperate for the benefit of the common good. The king cannot use magic alone to defend his country from potential invaders, nor can he become a tiger alone. Instead, he needs the cooperation of his queen, his chief ministers, and his royal astrologer.

At the same time, Shapiro-Phim asserts, the Cambodian folktale expresses a warning to its audience: people should not forget their origins and their original motivation to band together to aid their community. The story of the tiger is a cautionary tale of what happens when people forget their responsibilities. People should not turn their backs on society once they achieve remarkable success. This success is metaphorically expressed by the king's group turning into a tiger.

Shapiro-Phim points out that the name of the Indian teacher, Tisabamokkha, means "great teacher" in Pali, an ancient language associated with Buddhist teachings. She identifies Takkasila as a northwestern Indian location. This underlines the fact that Buddhism reached Cambodia from India, which in turn greatly influenced Cambodian, or Khmer, society and culture.

The historic Cambodian association of India as a center of great learning is stressed in the tiger folktale by the fact that the king himself embarks upon a journey to be taught in that foreign land. Learning magic is symbolic of obtaining wisdom, both spiritual and practical, to defend his own country.

Upon their return voyage, the king's group is still relatively far from their own kingdom when faced with starvation. Their tiger's diet of antelope signifies this. While some antelope species are native to India, they do not live farther east in the deep jungles of Southeast Asia. Thus, the king and his retinue are far from home when they transform into a magic royal tiger and forget their return. This signifies how far estranged from their country their success has made them, and how forgetful of their initial mission and overall duty they have become.

The Cambodian origin of the tiger represents an origin myth, an educational story, and a cautionary tale all in one. Shapiro-Phim's English rendition has made this folktale accessible to Cambodians in the diaspora. Her work attests to the tale's survival despite the horrors of the Killing Fields, when the Khmer Rouge sought to exterminate all of Cambodia's traditional culture, among many other crimes, during their murderous reign of terror from 1975 to 1979.

R. C. Lutz, PhD

BIBLIOGRAPHY

Baker, Demaz Tep. *Khmer Legends*. Parker: Outskirts, 2009. Print.

Ong, Walter J. *Orality and Literacy: The Technologizing of the Word*. 1982. New York: Routledge, 1991. Print.

Roveda, Vittorio. *Images of the Gods: Khmer Mythology in Cambodia, Thailand, and Laos*. Warren: Floating World Editions, 2005. Print.

Shapiro, Toni. "Cambodian Folktales: Origin of the Tiger." *Southeast Asia Program*. Cornell U: Mario Einaudi Center for Intl. Studies, n.d. Web. 20 May 2013.

Shapiro-Phim, Toni. "Mediating Cambodian History, the Sacred and the Earth." *Dance, Human Rights, and Social Justice: Dignity in Motion*. Ed. Naomi Jackson and Toni Shapiro-Phim. Lanham: Scarecrow, 2008. 304–323. Print.

◆ Pangu Creates the World

Author: Xu Zheng
Time Period: 1 CE–500 CE
Country or Culture: China
Genre: Myth

PLOT SUMMARY

The Chinese Daoist (Taoist) world creation myth about Pangu (Panku) exists in many different versions, with newer ones adding details to the oldest two transcribed in the third century CE. In the beginning, the world resembles an opaque swirling mass inside an egg. Inside this egg, Pangu is born. After eighteen thousand years, the egg breaks open. This happens either by itself or by Pangu wielding an ax from the inside, causing the shell to break.

As the egg splits, the primordial mass of the universe separates, either by itself or through Pangu's ax. The result of this separation is shown to correspond to the Daoist principle of yin and yang. The clear part of the primordial mass of the world becomes the sky, or the heavens, expressing the male yang force. The murky part of the universe coalesces into the earth, resembling the female yin force.

Pangu stands in the middle of the emerged world. In the oldest version, he transforms himself by growing taller and bigger nine times every day, and acts like a god in heaven and as a wise man on earth. The universe expands. Every day for eighteen thousand years, the sky moves away from the earth by one *zhang* (3.2 meters or 10.5 feet), the earth grows one zhang wider, and Pangu grows taller by one zhang. He is often depicted as a hairy giant with horns on his head, wearing fur clothing. Later versions of the myth give Pangu four magical companions during this time: the turtle, the *qilin* or Chinese fire-unicorn, the dragon, and the phoenix.

After eighteen thousand years of growing, Pangu dies. In death, his body transforms itself to create the features of the world. Every intangible and tangible part of his body contributes to the creation of the known universe.

Pangu's breath becomes the wind and the clouds, and his voice becomes the thunder. His left eye changes into the sun, and his right eye into the moon. His four extremities become the four directions of the compass. His main body transforms into five mountains. His blood turns into rivers and his sinews bestow features to the surface of the land. Pangu's muscles become the fertile soil of fields. The hair and beard of Pangu turn into stars and planets. His skin and the hair on it become grasses and trees.

Pangu's teeth and bones become bronze and jade rocks. His semen and his bone marrow turn into pearls and precious gemstones. From his sweat, rain and lakes are created. Finally, either the worms in his body or the insects dwelling in his fur clothes become the common people of the world.

SIGNIFICANCE

The two oldest versions of the Chinese myth about Pangu creating the world were written down by the Chinese Daoist author Xu Zheng (220–265 CE). The first part of the myth, with the cosmic egg breaking apart, is found in Xu's chronicle *Sanwu liji* (record of the three and five). The second part, Pangu's postmortem transformation into the features of the world, is told in Xu's fragment *Wu yun li nianji* (annals of the five-phase cycles). Later classical writers added to the myth in their own works.

The oral origins and traditions of Pangu are subject to great contemporary scholarly debate. Some scholars believe that the myth's core tale of the division of heaven and earth can be traced back to the Paleolithic, or Stone

Age, in China. Evidence for this may be provided by the layout of the burial site of a fifth-millennium BCE shaman of China's Yangshao culture found in Henan Province, China. This grave features a cosmogram with a separate round heaven and a square earth.

The transformation of Pangu's body to make up the parts of the universe is likely to have been influenced by a similar myth, the Purusha sukta. This hymn is found in the tenth book, or mandala, of the Indian epic the *Rig Veda*. Here, the cosmic being Purusha creates the world from the tangible and intangible parts of his body. This act is strikingly similar to Pangu's second act of creation. Though there are many variants in the details, there are stunning similarities. Both Purusha and Pangu, for example, create the sun from their eyes. After the *Rig Veda* was composed in the period from 1700 to 1100 BCE, it was passed down by an exact oral tradition for over two millennia. Many scholars believe knowledge of its myths not only travelled west to the Middle East and Europe, but to China as well. This view is supported by the evidence of a Pangu myth among the Miao and Yao people of southern China. From them, the myth may have travelled further north in China.

In the Pangu creation myth, the separation of the universe follows the core Daoist doctrine of the two complementary forces of yin and yang that order all life and existence. For this reason, many scholars believe that the Chinese Daoists, who began to flourish as an organized philosophical movement by the late second century CE, used some older myth material to give their myth of Pangu its distinct Daoist shape. In the form written down first by Xu Zheng, the Pangu myth describes how the Daoist order of the world came into existence.

Even though Daoism became very influential in China by the first half of the first millennium CE, Pangu's myth never became a universally recognized or literally believed creation story in China. However, in the wake of Japan's contact with China, especially during the Tang dynasty beginning in the seventh century CE, the myth of Pangu arrived in Japan. There, it strongly influenced Japanese creation mythology. Many scholars see significant Chinese influence on authentic Japanese myths transcribed in the opening of Japan's Kojiki (711–712 CE), which tells of the beginning of the world. For example, when Izanagi-no-Mikoto washes his left eye, he gives birth to the sun goddess Amaterasu, the divine ancestress of Japan's imperial line. As Izanagi washes his right eye, Tsukuyomi, the moon god, is born. The parallel to the transformation of Pangu's

eyes is obvious. Yet Izanagi gives birth to a third deity, Susanoo the storm god, through his nose, indicating the persistence of original Japanese myth material in the Kojiki as well.

R. C. Lutz, PhD

BIBLIOGRAPHY

Chang, Kwang-chih. *Art, Myth, and Ritual: The Path to Political Authority in China*. Cambridge: Harvard UP, 1983. Print.

---. "Mythology, China's Origins, and the Xia Dynasty." *The Cambridge History of Ancient China*. Ed. Michael Loewe and Edward L. Shaughnessy. New York: Cambridge UP, 1999. 65–70. Print.

"Chinese Creation Myths." *Crystalinks*. Ellie Crystal, n.d. Web. 20 May 2013.

"Creation of Heaven and Earth by Pangu." *China Daily*. China Daily, 7 Mar. 2011. Web. 20 May 2013.

Yang, Lihui, and Deming An. *Handbook of Chinese Mythology*. New York: Oxford UP, 2008. 63–66. Print.

◆ Prince Mountain and Princess Mountain

Author: Traditional
Time Period: 1001 CE–1500 CE
Country or Culture: Laos
Genre: Legend

PLOT SUMMARY

In ancient times, a poor woodcutter and his wife abandon their twelve daughters in the forest because they cannot provide for them. An ogress finds the twelve girls and takes them home. There, she raises them together with her own daughter, Kang Hi.

When grown up, the young women escape from the ogress and reach a city. There, the king falls in love with them. He marries all twelve of them. When the ogress hears this, she becomes furious. She changes herself into a beautiful woman and approaches the king. He makes her his queen.

The ogress starves herself, and the king worries for her life. She changes herself into an astrologer and tells the king that the twelve sisters are the source of the queen's illness. To save her, she tells the king that he must take out the eyes of the twelve sisters as a sacrifice and send them away. The king complies with this advice. The ogress sends the eyes to her daughter, and the sisters are locked up in a cave.

The twelve sisters are all pregnant. One by one, they each give birth to a child. Out of starvation, eleven of them eat each baby as it is born. Only the twelfth sister, who has retained one eye, refuses to eat this meat. Her son is the only child who survives. Eventually, they all are fed grains of rice by a wild rooster.

When the boy grows up, he visits the city. There, the king recognizes him as his son. He names him Prince Phutthasen and keeps him in his palace. In secret, Phutthasen brings food to his mother and aunts in the cave every day.

The ogress discovers Prince Phutthasen's identity and decides to kill him. She tells the king that the only cure for her new illness is at her home with her daughter and that Phutthasen should fetch it. The king agrees, and Phutthasen is given a flying horse for the journey. The ogress also gives him a letter to her daughter. In this letter, she asks her daughter to kill Phutthasen.

While Phutthasen rests on his journey, a hermit discovers the letter, reads it, and changes its wording. It now announces the prince as husband for Kang Hi. When Kang Hi reads the letter from Phutthasen, she is happy. She shows him her palace, the eyes of his mother and aunts, and the heart of the ogress, among other magic things. Phutthasen organizes a banquet, makes everybody else fall into a drunken sleep, and escapes with the eyes, the ogress's heart, and the magic things. Kang Hi awakes and pursues him. He stops her first with a bamboo forest, then an impassable magic river. Giving up, Kang Hi curses the prince: "May you die for love, just as I have done" (Nattavong 127). Returning home, she dies of a broken heart.

Phutthasen returns the eyes to the twelve sisters and restores their sight with a drop of magic lemon juice. When the ogress sees Phutthasen return to the palace, she changes into her true form and tries to kill him. Phutthasen pierces her heart with his sword, killing her instantly. He takes his leave from his elders and returns to his wife.

Finding Kang Hi dead, he falls face down and dies with his head at her feet. Seeing this, the deities feel this offends the cosmic order: if women heard this story, they would never trust men again. So, they rearrange the prince's body so that he lies on his back, implicitly putting his feet at Kang Hi's head. In this position, the legend concludes, the prince and the princess have become Phu Phra, Prince Mountain, and Phu Nang, Princess Mountain.

SIGNIFICANCE

"Prince Mountain and Princess Mountain" is a legend from the former royal city of Luang Prabang in Laos, a country in Southeast Asia. It explains the legendary origin of two mountains facing Luang Prabang across the Mekong River. These are called indeed Prince Mountain and Princess Mountain (Phu Phra and Phu Nang).

The original composers of the legend used material from the *Jataka* tales to tell this story. The *Jataka* are moral tales that relate episodes from Buddha's previous incarnations. When Buddhism reached Southeast Asia, local people added their own apocryphal stories to the canonical, originally Indian *Jataka* tales. Buddhism entered Laos around the seventh and eighth centuries CE, and it flourished as the state religion of the first Lao kingdom, founded in 1353 CE. From that time until 1560, Luang Prabang was the capital. The legend of Prince Mountain and Princess Mountain is likely to have originated during the cultural heyday of the city. The tale has been recorded, transcribed, and translated into English by Lao scholar Samrit Buasisavath. It was published as "Phu Phra and Phu Nang" in 1992. A second, more widely available English text of the tale can be found in the 2008 anthology *Lao Folktales*. However, this version cuts out the most horrific detail of the legend, the filicidal cannibalism of eleven of the sisters. Apart from this expurgation, the tale follows the traditional version.

As Buddhist moral tale, "Prince Mountain and Princess Mountain" strongly emphasizes filial duty. Prince Phutthasen devotedly cares for his elders, his mother and his aunts, bringing them food at the risk of being punished. It is interesting that in doing so, he must defy his father. Yet he obeys the father in traveling to Kang Hi's place. There, the prince places filial duty to his mother above his marital happiness. Only when he has avenged his mother and his aunts does he return to his wife. The deities reward him for this. Rather than being left dead prostrating himself at the feet of his wife, the prince regally lies on his back.

R. C. Lutz, PhD

BIBLIOGRAPHY

Buasisavath, Samrit. "Phu Phra and Phu Nang." *The Great Gourd of Heaven: A Selection of the Folk-Tales and Stories of Laos*. Ed. Roisin O. Boyle and Thavisack Phanmatanh. Vientiane: Vannasin Magazine, 1992. 9–17. Print.

Heywood, Denise. *Ancient Luang Prabang*. Bangkok: River, 2006. Print.

Koret, Peter. "Books in Search: Convention and Creativity in Traditional Lao Literature." *The Canon in Southeast Asian Literature*. Ed. David Smyth. Richmond: Curzon, 2000. 210–33. Print.

Nattavong, Kongdeuane. "Phu Pha Phu Nang: Prince Mountain and Princess Mountain." Trans. Wajuppa Tossa. *Lao Folktales*. Ed. Margaret Read MacDonald. Westport: Libraries Unlimited, 2008. 125–27. Print.

Tossa, Wajuppa, comp. "Phu Phra Phu Nang (Prince Mountain and Princess Mountain)." *Lao Folk Literature Course*. Center for Southeast Asian Studies, Northern Illinois U, 2002. Web. 26 June 2013.

◆ The Spirit of the Lotus Lily

Author: Traditional
Time Period: 1701 CE–1850 CE
Country or Culture: Japan
Genre: Folktale

PLOT SUMMARY

One day in feudal Japan, a deadly disease breaks out in Kyoto. It quickly spreads east into Idzumi (Izumo) Province. There, it strikes the lord of Koriyama. His wife and son fall critically ill as well. Because the lord of Koriyama is very popular, common people come to his castle to learn of his fate. They camp in the castle moats, which are left dry in this period of peace.

Soon, the lord's highest official, Tada Samon, receives a mountain recluse, called a *yamabushi*. He tells Samon that the lord's illness is caused by an evil spirit. The spirit could only enter the castle because its moats are dry and no lotus flowers grow in the water that should fill them up. The yamabushi offers to help: "I shall enter the castle to-day and pray that the evil spirit of sickness leave; and I ask that I may be allowed to plant lotuses in the northern moats" (Smith 269).

Samon agrees. The people help clean and fix the northern moats. After his ablutions and prayers, the yamabushi supervises their filling with water and planting of lotuses. The task done, he vanishes. The lord of Koriyama and his family soon recover. The people rejoice and name the place the Lotus Castle.

When the lord dies eventually, his son succeeds him but neglects the lotus flowers. One day in August, when the lotus flowers are in full bloom, a young samurai passes by. He sees two beautiful young boys playing on the bank of the moat. When he warns them that this is dangerous, they jump into the water and disappear. The samurai is sure he has seen two *kappa*, or water imps. He informs the castle. Yet when the moats are cleaned and dragged, no kappa are found, and people ridicule the samurai.

One evening a few weeks later, another samurai, Murata Ippai, admires the lotus flowers. Suddenly, he sees a group of about a dozen naked boys playing around the edge of the moat, splashing each other with water. Ippai is convinced these are kappa and determines to kill them all.

When Ippai approaches the boys with his sword drawn, the boys look almost natural. They are beautiful, and a scent of lotus lilies wafts from their bodies. Steeling his resolve, Ippai falls upon the boys. He "slash[es] right and left among the supposed kappas" and is sure he hit many bodies (272). When he looks around, a colorful mist arises, almost blinding him.

Ippai resolves to wait there until morning. At dawn, he sees nothing but lotus stalks rising from the water, their flowers cut off. Ippai realizes that he has killed not kappa but the spirits of the lotus. As the lotus saved the lord of Koriyama and his son, Ippai's master, the samurai has committed a heinous crime. He realizes that he "must appease the spirits by disembowelling [him]self" (273). Ippai says a prayer and commits ritual suicide. However, from this day on, "no more lotus spirits [are] seen" (273).

SIGNIFICANCE

"The Spirit of the Lotus Lily" is a Japanese folktale collected by English amateur naturalist Richard Gordon Smith, who published it in his 1908 anthology *Ancient Tales and Folk-Lore of Japan*. Smith states that this tale was told to him by the Japanese storyteller Fukuga and that it was about two hundred years old. It is a local folktale from Izumo Province (mistranscribed "Idzumi" by Smith), part of contemporary Shimane Prefecture in Japan.

"The Spirit of the Lotus Lily" illustrates archaic and traditional Japanese attitudes toward diseases, their causes, and their spread. It adds a variant to the lore of the kappa. With its climactic scene, "The Spirit of the Lotus Lily" offers some rare, subtle popular criticism of the samurai class.

The conviction that physical illnesses are caused and spread by spiritual pollution has very deep, ancient roots in Japanese culture. An important part of traditional treatment of serious illnesses has been the chanting of prayers. Just as the yamabushi performs a powerful exorcism for the lord of Koriyama and his family in "The Spirit of the Lotus Lily," Japanese families would seek spiritual help for ill members. In "Curable Cancers and Fatal Ulcers: Attitudes toward Cancer in Japan," Susan and Bruce Long show that even contemporary Japanese people may perceive physical illness as a polluting force.

The lotus lilies of the folktale represent a powerful defense from spiritual pollution and thus illness. In Asia, reverence for the lotus flower is particularly strong in the Indian-originated religions of Hinduism and Buddhism. There, the lotus flower is seen as symbol of purity. The introduction of Buddhism in Japan spurred the cultivation of lotus flowers there.

"The Spirit of the Lotus Lily" adds a significant local variant to the folklore of the popular Japanese kappa, or water imps. The spirits of the lotus flower are mistaken for kappa that appear to have transformed into humans. Kappa are mythological child-sized water goblins with both humanlike and reptilian features. Traditionally, kappa are said to draw people and livestock under water to eat their livers and souls, but they have also mischievous and popular characteristics. As folklorist Michael Foster shows, by the late twentieth century, kappa had become a cute informal symbol of Japan and were used to promote a clean natural environment.

In "The Spirit of the Lotus Lily," kappa are viewed with suspicion. However, the sheer brutality with which samurai Murata Ippai cuts down those naked boys he considers kappa hints at criticism of the samurai class by the common people. With stern self-discipline bordering on the psychopathological, Ippai convinces himself that it is his duty to kill the supposed kappa. "Seeing how innocent and unsuspecting the children looked," Ippai is not moved to pity (Smith 272). Instead, he thinks that "he would not be acting up to the determination of a samurai if he changed his mind"—that is, spared the boys (272). For his mistake in killing the loyal, lifesaving lotus spirits, he has to die. In feudal Japan, samurai

wielded great powers over commoners and cultivated a haughty attitude toward them. It is not surprising that a folktale, popular among commoners over two centuries, might include such veiled criticism.

R. C. Lutz, PhD

BIBLIOGRAPHY

Foster, Michael Dylan. "The Metamorphosis of the Kappa: Transformation of Folklore to Folklorism in Japan." *Asian Folklore Studies* 57.1 (1998): 1–24. Print.

---. *Pandemonium and Parade: Japanese Monsters and the Culture of Yokai*. Berkeley: U of California P, 2008. Print.

Long, Susan, and Bruce Long. „Curable Cancers and Fatal Ulcers: Japanese Attitudes toward Cancer." *Social Science and Medicine* 16.24 (1982): 2101–8. Print.

Manthorpe, Victoria, ed. *Travels in the Land of the Gods (1898–1907): The Japanese Diaries of Richard Gordon Smith*. Upper Saddle River: Prentice, 1986. Print.

Smith, Richard Gordon. "The Spirit of the Lotus Lily." *Ancient Tales and Folk-Lore of Japan*. London: Black, 1908. 267–73. Print.

 Urashima Tarō

Author: Traditional
Time Period: 501 CE–1000 CE
Country or Culture: Japan
Genre: Folktale

PLOT SUMMARY

One day in spring, the young fisherman Urashima Tarō (sometimes referred to as Urashimako) sets out to fish in the sea from his small boat. He waits all day but does not catch any fish. Suddenly, he catches a turtle. Knowing that turtles are considered sacred creatures, he releases it back into the water.

After failing to catch any fish, Urashima falls asleep in his boat. He is awakened by the daughter of the dragon god, who has the body of a beautiful young woman. She reveals that she had been the turtle that Urashima released. Out of gratitude, the daughter of the dragon invites Urashima to come live with her in her father's underwater castle, where she will become his wife.

Overjoyed and enticed by her great beauty, Urashima agrees. The dragon god's daughter summons a huge turtle. On its back, they ride to the dragon god's palace, where they live happily together for some time.

Eventually, however, Urashima becomes homesick. He asks the dragon god's daughter to let him return to his village, look at his parents, and return right away to her. Though she is saddened by Urashima's request, she agrees to it, giving him a casket that will protect him but that he must never open.

Urashima and the dragon god's daughter part, and Urashima is transported to his village. There, he feels very alienated. The villagers have strange features and dress strangely. His father's dwelling no longer exists, and even the fields of his childhood have gone. Believing he had been away for only three years, Urashima is puzzled by the many ways in which the village changed during his absence.

Finally, Urashima encounters an old man. The old man states that when he was a boy, his father told him that Urashima's parents died of grief over the death of their son, who was deemed lost at sea. Since that time, four hundred years have passed. Urashima realizes he has lived for centuries in a fairyland. He longs to return to his wife, but not knowing how to return to the dragon god's palace, he sits on the shore despondently and waits for the arrival of the turtle. The turtle never comes.

In agony, Urashima remembers the casket the dragon god's daughter gave him. Ignoring her warning not to open it, he begins to unravel the string of silk that binds it shut. Suddenly, a white cloud emerges from the box. As it rises into the sky, four hundred years catch up with Urashima in a moment, and the fisherman rapidly ages and dies.

SIGNIFICANCE

The core of the narrative of Urashima Tarō was first transcribed in about 713 CE in Tango Province, part of contemporary Japan's Kyoto Prefecture. This text survives in a fragment from *Tango fudoki itsubun* (Local records of Tango Province), which refers to Urashima by the name Shima no Ko. The story of Urashima was later included in Japan's early chronicle *Nihon shoki* (720; *Nihongi*, 1896), edited by Prince Toneri. *Nihon shoki* identifies Urashima's marriage to the dragon god's daughter as a historical event that took place in the autumn of 478 CE. In this version, Urashima goes down into the sea to live with his wife and never returns

Another eighth-century version of the story of Urashima is found in the poem "Urashima of Mizunoé," written by Japanese poet Takahashi no Mushimaro and collected in the anthology *Manyōshū* (ca. 759 CE; *The Manyōshū*, 1965). The poet was particularly interested in collecting local folktales and myths and rendering them in poetic form. This version also includes Urashima's return to his village and his death from sudden old age after he foolishly opens the magic box.

The folktale was later translated into English and published in various collections of Japanese folklore, including Alexander Otto and Theodore S. Holbrooke's *Mythological Japan* (1902), F. Hadland Davis's *Myths and Legends of Japan* (1900), and Donna Rosenberg's *Folklore, Myths, and Legends* (1996). American folklorists often compare the tale of Urashima to American writer Washington Irving's 1819 story "Rip Van Winkle," in which the titular character falls asleep in the forest and wakes twenty years later.

In Japan, the tale of Urashima has enjoyed enduring popularity. Statues of Urashima riding the turtle, sometimes as old man, are found in many coastal Japanese cities, and a shrine dedicated to the fisherman is a popular tourist destination in Kyoto Prefecture. Part of the tale's attraction comes from traditional Japanese reverence of the sea turtle, considered a symbol of longevity and good luck. Drifting algae on the shells of old sea turtles are seen as resembling the long beard of an old man. Occasionally, sea turtles that come on land are offered gifts of sake in appreciation for the good fortune they bring.

R. C. Lutz, PhD

BIBLIOGRAPHY

Aston, William George. *Nihongi*. London, 1896. Print.

Davis, F. Hadland. "Urashima." *Myths and Legends of Japan*. New York: Crowell, 1912. 323–28. Print.

Keene, Donald, trans. "Urashima of Mizunoé." *The Manyōshū*. New York: Columbia UP, 1965. 216–18. Print.

Otto, Alexander F., and Theodore S. Holbrooke. "Urashima (The Japanese Rip Van Winkle)." *Mythological Japan*. Philadelphia: Drexel Biddle, 1902. 28–29. Print.

Rosenberg, Donna. "Taro Urashima, the Young Fisherman." *Folklore, Myths, and Legends: A World Perspective*. Chicago: NTC, 1997. 421–31. Print.

Water War

Author: Traditional
Time Period: 999 BCE–1 BCE
Country or Culture: China
Genre: Myth

PLOT SUMMARY

The water god Gong Gong (Kung Kung) unleashes torrential rains and floods that devastate the earth and cause great loss of human and animal life. The other gods are afraid of Gong Gong. The exception is Zhu Rong (Zurong or Chu Jung), the fire god.

Zhu Rong opposes Gong Gong's plan to make the earth a water-dominated world and challenges Gong Gong to a celestial battle. The two gods rise into the sky to wrestle with each other for days. The sky shakes with thunder; lightning flickers across it. Finally, the two combatants end up "crack[ing] the dome of heaven" itself (Collier 44).

With the battle a draw, Gong Gong challenges Zhu Rong to resume their fight on earth. Gong Gong places his best soldiers on a huge raft constructed from bamboo stalks. Zhu Rong attacks with a pillar of fire. The fire surges inside the hollow bamboo reeds, burning the raft and thus drowning Gong Gong's soldiers.

Gong Gong summons his sea monsters. These include turtles, crabs, and lobsters that have "huge horns and wings like bats" (45). They are protected by armor and raise a wall of water to drown the fire god. In retaliation, Zhu Rong exhales a fierce blast of fire, burning Gong Gong's sea monsters to death inside their armor.

Gong Gong flees west amid the rejoicing of all other gods. Enraged, Gong Gong rams his head into the top of Mount Buzhou (Buzhow or Puchou). This splinters off the mountain peak, which flies upward and tears a big hole in the sky.

This rends open the dome of heaven. Through the fissures and the hole, "deadly creatures from beyond the heavens" sweep down upon the earth (47), where Gong Gong's impact has also torn open the earth's crust. Mountains explode, and fire and smoke emerge from the earth. The land is hit by earthquakes, forest fires, and breaking dams. The gods, including Zhu Rong, look helplessly at this great destruction.

The goddess Nüwa angrily intervenes. She gathers rocks of the "five sacred colors" (47) and melts them down together. With this mixture, Nüwa patches up the sky. Next, Nüwa gathers river rushes to put into the fiery cracks on the earth. Their ashes plug up the cracks, and the earth settles down. With more rushes Nüwa dams the raging rivers. Finally, Nüwa cuts off the legs of a deceased giant turtle of Gong Gong's defeated army. She uses the legs as pillars to hold up the sky. As she puts up the northwestern pillar, the earth tilts from west to east.

To calm humanity, Nüwa creates a flute. It has twelve bamboo reeds tied together to look like the tail of a phoenix. Nüwa teaches humanity to play this instrument, which brings forth "clear, soothing notes" (47).

It is because of the war that the earth is still unstable. Its new tilt causes the moon and the stars to move across the sky in a northwesterly direction, and Chinese rivers to flow from the west down to the east.

SIGNIFICANCE

"Water War," by Irene Dea Collier, is an English rendition of a Chinese myth. The story draws on classic Chinese sources to present the myth of the earth's near-destruction by a divine war and its rescue by the goddess Nüwa. The oldest surviving written reference to this myth is found in the section "Tianwen" ("Heavenly Questions") of the classic Chinese anthology *Chu Ci* (*Ch'u Tz'u*), written in the third century BCE by Qu Yuan (Ch'ü Yüan).

The second Chinese classic reference to the myth is found in the sixth chapter of the book *Huainanzi* (*Huainan Tzu*), by Prince Liu An of the second century BCE. The two versions by Qu Yuan and Liu An differ in detail. Collier has formed a successful synthesis of the myth into English.

The key themes of "Water War" are the near-fatal consequences for all life on earth that result from an epic battle between two gods and the world's rescue by Nüwa. Here, the personification of strong natural forces—water and fire—into deities is a classic global mythological element. The capricious quest for dominance by Gong Gong, the water god, threatens the world. Its only counterpart is provided by Zhu Rong, the god of fire. This represents the Chinese Daoist (Taoist) philosophical emphasis on balance in life, here between water and fire. This theme of balance is especially prominent in Liu An's story.

"Water War" expresses the classic theme in Chinese mythology that humanity is endangered by the capriciousness and excesses of the various deities. Storms and floods threatened traditional Chinese life. In Chinese mythology, these phenomena were attributed to violent deities.

The idea that the sky itself gets damaged in the myth points at an apocalyptic cataclysm threatening all of humanity and the natural environment. Large natural disasters, including earthquakes and huge floods, have been common in the areas populated by Chinese people since ancient times. The starkly envisioned consequences of the gods' careless struggle, and Gong Gong's willful ramming of Mount Buzhou, represent a powerful image of natural disaster dwarfing even the might of most gods.

Collier's text stresses the idea of a gender struggle. While male gods are violent, unrestrained, and careless, and damage the very fabric of the universe, the goddess Nüwa is the only one able to restore order. Nüwa uses traditional Daoist magic—five sacred colors of rocks—to plug the hole in the heavens. She employs techniques in quenching fires and restoring dams that relate both to real ancient methods to deal with these calamities and to Daoism. As Sinologist Anthony Christie points out, the reeds represent the element of water and the ashes that quench the fires relate to the element of earth. The balance of water and earth is restored by Nüwa.

"Water War" contains elements of an origin myth to explain the course of the stars and the shape of the earth. As indeed two of China's largest rivers, the Yangzi (Yangtze) and the Yellow River (Huang He), flow west to east, the myth provides a supernatural rationale for geographic reality. Finally, Nüwa's flute, the sheng, is a real traditional Chinese musical instrument.

R. C. Lutz, PhD

BIBLIOGRAPHY

Birrell, Anne. *Chinese Mythology: An Introduction.* Baltimore: Johns Hopkins UP, 1993. 97–98. Print.

Christie, Anthony. *Chinese Mythology.* 1968. Rev. ed. New York: Bedrick, 1987. 86–87. Print.

Collier, Irene Dea. "Water War." *Chinese Mythology Rocks!* Berkeley Heights: Enslow, 2012. 42–51. Print.

Hawkes, David, trans. and ed. *The Songs of the South: An Anthology of Ancient Chinese Poems by Qu Yuan and Other Poets.* 1959. New York: Penguin Classics, 2012. Print.

Le Blanc, Charles. *Huai-nan Tzu.* Hong Kong: Hong Kong UP, 1985. Print.

Lianshan, Chen. "War between Zhuanxu and Gonggong." *Chinese Myths and Legends.* Trans. Zhang Fengru and Chen Shanshan. New York: Cambridge UP, 2011. 79–81. Print.

---. "Nüwa Mending the Heaven." *Chinese Myths and Legends.* Trans. Zhang Fengru and Chen Shanshan. New York: Cambridge UP, 2011. 11–16. Print.

Yang, Lihui, Deming An, and Jessica Anderson Turner. *Handbook of Chinese Mythology.* New York: Oxford UP, 2005. Print.

◆ The Weaver Maiden and the Herdsman

Author: Traditional
Time Period: 999 BCE–1 BCE
Country or Culture: Korea
Genre: Myth

PLOT SUMMARY

A beautiful princess named Chih Nü, known as the weaver maiden, lives in the heavens and weaves diligently on her loom every day, producing fabrics that are both beautiful and strong. Her father, the Sun, is pleased with her attention to her work, but he is also worried that she spends too much time toiling at her loom.

One day he realizes that she has grown into a woman of marriageable age. The Sun is pleased and is certain that marriage will help his daughter regulate her time at the loom. Together with his advisers, he arranges a marriage for Chih Nü with a young man known as Niu Lang, the herdsman. Niu Lang spends every day herding cows as diligently as Chih Nü weaves cloth, and Niu Lang's father is delighted to find a woman whose hard work is equal to his son's.

The two are married, and they are so happy together that they begin to neglect their duties. Chih Nü stops weaving, and Niu Lang's cows wander loose into the palace gardens. They spend every day with each other rather than doing their work.

The Sun becomes very upset, and he scolds Chih Nü and Niu Lang and forbids them to see each other. He forces Chih Nü to live in the west and Niu Lang to live in the east, with the River of Heaven separating them. The husband and wife are so upset that they beg the Sun to change his mind, and each promises to attend faithfully to his or her duties. Finally the Sun relents and tells them that as long as they never neglect their duties again, they can meet each other once each year, on the seventh day of the seventh month.

When a year has passed and the time comes for the couple to meet, they stand on opposite banks of the River of Heaven, but the river is so wide that they cannot cross to see each other. No bridges span the river, and there are no boats, so the two begin to weep at their misfortune. Because they live in the heavens, their tears become rain that waters the earth below. Their ceaseless weeping causes floods, and the animals become worried. After much discussion, the crows and magpies decide to fly to the heavens and form a bridge that Chih Nü and Niu Lang can cross to see each other. The birds spread their wings, and the two lovers are able to step across from bird to bird. They rejoice in seeing each other, and when the dawn of the next day breaks, they part, promising to meet again on the same day every year.

SIGNIFICANCE

The myth of the weaver maiden and the herdsman helped early Koreans explain a natural phenomenon. The River of Heaven in this myth is the Milky Way, and the weaver maiden and the herdsman represent the stars Vega and Altair respectively. Once each year, these two stars are especially visible on each side of the Milky Way, and on the seventh day of the seventh month of the lunisolar calendar, Koreans celebrate this event during the Chilseok festival. This festival occurs at the start of the monsoon season, and the impending rain is considered to be the tears of the lovers: either tears of joy upon meeting on the day before Chilseok or tears of parting the day after Chilseok. Festivities include dancing and singing, and traditionally women pray to the weaver maiden for help with needlework. Men consider it a time when the god of agriculture comes to check on the harvest and decide his share. Koreans traditionally eat wheat-based foods such as noodles and wheat cake during Chilseok, since it is perceived to be one of the last chances to enjoy such foods before the cold winds of the season arrive.

The prevalence of Confucian thought in Korea is also evident in this myth, indicating that the myth evolved as Chinese influence spread throughout the region. Under Confucianism, the family consisted of a cohesive unit with a central male authority. The family as a group was considered more important than any one individual, and the family's most important job was to preserve the household according to the traditional Confucian system. Within this system, the most important relationship was the relationship between parent and child. Children were expected to obey their parents even over their spouses; this was one of the central Confucian

tenets, known as filial piety. In the myth, Chih Nü disobeys her father by abandoning her work for her new husband, thereby neglecting her filial duty. In doing so, she disrupts the order of the Confucian family, and so her father must separate the couple and reestablish the family order.

In modern times, traditional mythology and folklore have been used as a way for Koreans living outside of Korea to reconnect with their heritage. In addition, the myth of the weaver maiden and the herdsman has been used to represent the divide between North Korea and South Korea. South Koreans who believe in reunification have equated the two countries with the two lovers who have been forced apart. In this metaphor, the reunification of the two nations would represent the reunification of the family.

This myth also calls attention to the shared cultural heritage of China, Korea, and Japan. A remarkably similar story can be found in Chinese mythology, and this myth inspired a Japanese version and a related festival. The Japanese Tanabata festival celebrates the reunion of the lovers Orihime, the weaver maiden, and Hikoboshi, the herdsman. These similarities are evidence of the exchange of ideas and culture between the three countries.

Haley Blum, MA

BIBLIOGRAPHY

"Chilseok." *Encyclopedia of Korean Folklore and Traditional Culture*. National Folk Museum of Korea, n.d. Web. 14 May 2013.

Colum, Pádraic. "Weaver Maiden and the Herdsman." *Orpheus: Myths of the World*. New York: Macmillan, 1930. 239–41. Print.

Han, Suzanne Crowder. *Korean Folk and Fairy Tales*. Elizabeth: Hollym, 1991. Print.

Jager, Sheila Miyoshi. "Women, Resistance and the Divided Nation: The Romantic Rhetoric of Korean Reunification." *Journal of Asian Studies* 55.1 (1996): 3–21. Print.

Sakata, Shane. "Tanabata—Festival of Star Crossed Lovers." *Nihon Sun*. Nihon Sun, n.d. Web. 15 May 2013.

Stephens, John. "Korean Tales." *The Greenwood Encyclopedia of Folktales and Fairy Tales*. Ed. Donald Haase. Vol. 2. Westport: Greenwood, 2008. 546–48. Print.

Williams, C. A. S. *Encyclopedia of Chinese Symbolism and Art Motives*. New York: Julian, 1960. Print.

Yinglong, the Winged Dragon

Author: Traditional
Time Period: 5000 BCE–2500 BCE
Country or Culture: China
Genre: Myth

PLOT SUMMARY

China's legendary ancient emperor Huangdi, called the Yellow Emperor, is devoted to making life better for his fellow humans and subjects. However, he has to fight many enemies, including gods and demons. In his battles, Huangdi is supported by the winged dragon Yinglong (or Ying-lung, meaning "responding dragon"). Yinglong is one of the oldest existing dragons, as indicated by the immensity of his wings. Dragons take three thousand years to mature. During that time, they transform from small water snakes and develop wings.

Huangdi and Yinglong are opposed by a band of demon brothers. Their leader is the evil rebel Chiyou, the inventor of weapons, who has a human body and a bull's head. His eighty-one brothers are half human, half beast. Chiyou provides his brothers with strong weapons, including near-invincible lances.

Chiyou, ungrateful after Huangdi makes him god of war, rebels against the Yellow Emperor. In one account, Yinglong is responsible for Huangdi's first victory. Yinglong attacks Chiyou's army from above, sending a deluge of flood rains to destroy everything below. Yet Chiyou rises again in alliance with Fengbo, god of wind, and Yushi, god of rain.

There are different versions of the outcome of the myth. According to one account, despite Yinglong's ability to control rain, he is useless against Fengbo and Yushi. The battle is won by the intervention of Huangdi's daughter Ba. Her lightning strikes dry up the storms that were raised by Fengbo and Yushi. She defeats the enemies, allowing Huangdi to kill Chiyou.

In another version, the victory belongs to Yinglong. The winged dragon dominates the battlefield from above. He flaps his giant wings and causes fierce rains to drench the opposing army. He launches numerous airborne attacks, using his fangs, tail, and the storm to destroy Chiyou's host.

After Huangdi triumphs over Chiyou, Yinglong helps restore the land by drawing drainage tunnels in the earth with his tail. Once Huangdi dies, however, Yinglong no longer serves humanity. People have to cope with floods and droughts on their own. Unable to go back to heaven, Yinglong stays in southern China, where it rains a lot because of his presence.

SIGNIFICANCE

Yinglong, the winged dragon is a popular Chinese mythological creature with roots in the Neolithic age. In written form, myths involving Yinglong can be found in classic Chinese texts dating back to the fourth century BCE. In one of its oldest written forms, the myth of Yinglong's support for Huangdi has survived in *Shan hai jing* (*The Classic of Mountains and Seas*). Contemporary scholars believe that this compilation was written down first in the fourth century BCE.

The earliest surviving written reference to *The Classic of Mountains and Seas* is by China's great historian Sima Qian (145 BCE–86 BCE) in the first century BCE. He sought to separate historical information from its primarily mythical accounts. For Sima Qian, Huangdi is the first Chinese emperor who may have been a historical person. By tradition, he lived around the twenty-seventh century BCE. According to most contemporary scholars, Liu Xiang was the first editor of the *Classic*. Xiang was an imperial court bibliographer of the Western Han dynasty who lived from around 77 BCE to 6 BCE. His son, Liu Xin (53 BCE– 23 CE), wrote the earliest preface to the classic. More than three centuries later, between 310 and 324 CE, Guo Pu published his annotated version of the classic.

In imperial China, Yinglong was believed to have a very powerful effect on rain and able to cause both flooding and drought. Guo Pu notices that the myth of Yinglong's support for Huangdi in battle inspired people to make clay figures of Yinglong to implore the dragon for rain, a tradition that continued into the early twentieth century.

This Chinese folk belief is echoed by *The Classic of Mountains and Seas* itself. The text states that after people appeal to Yinglong for rain, he defeats Chiyou: "When there is a drought, people make an image of Responding Dragon, and they receive a heavy rainfall" (Birrell 162).

Indeed, the interplay of rain, storm, and drought are core to the myth of Yinglong. These were natural effects that essentially influenced life and welfare of traditional Chinese agrarian society. While normal amounts of rain sustained life, its abundance in floods or its absence in droughts threatened human survival.

R. C. Lutz, PhD

BIBLIOGRAPHY

Birrel, Anne, trans. *The Classic of Mountains and Seas.* New York: Penguin, 1999. Print.

Chen, Lianshan. "War between Emperor Huangdi and Chiyou." *Myths and Legends of China.* New York: Cambridge UP, 2011. 53–60. Print.

Strassberg, Richard E. *A Chinese Bestiary: Strange Creatures from the Guideways through Mountains and Seas.* Berkeley: U of California P, 2002. Print.

Visser, Marinus Willem de. *The Dragon in China and Japan.* Amsterdam: Müller, 1913. Print.

Yang, Lihui, et al., eds. *Handbook of Chinese Mythology.* New York: Oxford UP, 2005. Print.

Yu Rebuilds the Earth

Author: Traditional
Time Period: 999 BCE–1 BCE
Country or Culture: China
Genre: Myth

PLOT SUMMARY

The Yellow Emperor rules over China, and while he does his best to support his people and bring them happiness, he is unable to prevent the terrible flooding that unleashes itself again and again onto the land. The only trick he has is to gather magic dirt, which he drops into the floodwaters to absorb them, but this dirt is never enough to keep the destruction back.

One day, his son Kun steals the magic dirt, thinking he will be able to help the people better than his father can. Kun travels all over China, dropping the dirt and building dams. The mounds of magic dirt swell as they absorb water, and the farmers gather these mounds and spread them across their fields. Unfortunately, Kun's dams regularly burst open and flood the fields once again. When the Yellow Emperor learns that his son has stolen the magic dirt, he sends the fire god, Zhu Rong, to kill him. Zhu Rong chases Kun all the way to the glaciers at the end of the world, slices him with his sword, and leaves his body to freeze. After several years, the Yellow Emperor sends Zhu Rong back to check on the body. When the fire god cuts open the ice to expose Kun,

however, he accidentally slices the body again, releasing a gigantic dragon that had been inside. This dragon is Yu the Great, the son of Kun, and he magically knows all the things that Kun knew in life.

Yu has the same desires as his father, but he knows that the Yellow Emperor will not tolerate any betrayal or lies. Thus, Yu goes to the emperor and asks his permission to fight the floods. The Yellow Emperor eventually agrees, giving Yu a large dragon and a magic turtle to accompany him on his quest. Yu then carefully measures the earth and divides it into nine regions. With the turtle carrying the magic dirt and the dragon helping him carve canals into the landscape, he travels through all of China, gradually redirecting the rivers to the sea. This work is long and arduous and takes a severe toll on Yu's body. He appears as a human while laboring so as not to frighten the farmers, and as he continues to rebuild the earth, his body shrivels and becomes malformed. He also loses his wife and son, who abandon him because of his obsession with fighting the floods.

In the end, Yu manages to build up the farms and repair the land from the horrendous floods. From then on, the people are safe from the floods and able to grow vast amounts of food. The people are so thankful that the Yellow Emperor decides to name Yu his successor. As the new emperor, Yu ushers in the Xia dynasty, and his subjects never forget to thank Yu for the great sacrifices he has made for them.

SIGNIFICANCE

The myth of Yu as a legendary leader, traversing the expanses of China and carving the landscape apart with a dragon and a giant turtle, is based on the historical leader Yu, who reigned around 2000 BCE. A great deal of time separates modern audiences from the story of Yu, so historical details are somewhat difficult to separate from the legendary figure who appears in the myth. It is generally accepted that Yu lived during a period of intense flooding in central China, especially in his home along the Yellow River. His father battled the floods by building dams but was not able to prevent the destruction before his death. Yu, however, came up with a plan to build irrigation canals that both worked with the natural flow of the water and supported local agriculture. By directing the floods in this manner, he helped to usher in a period of prosperity in his homeland. These accomplishments made Yu so popular that the emperor, Shun, made Yu his successor instead of his own son. Yu would go on to initiate a patrilineal tradition, establishing the first dynasty in Chinese history, the Xia dynasty, by naming his firstborn son emperor.

The shift from historical reality to mythological tale indicates a great deal about the impact Yu had on Chinese culture and politics. In the fictional narrative, Yu does not simply create a system of irrigation in his own land but rather radically restructures the entirety of the Chinese landscape and geography. In addition to this, he is the first figure to map all of China and the first leader to divide the land into the nine provinces. This is an intense and systematic level of ordering that contrasts with the disorder and chaos brought about by the floods. Tied in with the development of the first dynasty and the establishment of a political system that would endure for thousands of years, Yu came to represent the righteousness and prosperity made possible through an organized, structured civilization. This is further stressed by linking Yu to the Yellow Emperor; while the legendary ruler seems to have actually been many generations behind Yu, the close linking of the two famed leaders further emphasizes the importance of the dynasty system and the value of the emperors' accomplishments.

Throughout China, local myths praising Yu and linking regional leadership to the legendary emperor became increasingly popular in the centuries following his death. As his mythology expanded and the divide between the historical reality and the fantastical narratives grew wider, the diverse stories of Yu continued to influence the development of Chinese politics and culture. A figure of great sacrifice and pure morals, Yu would be praised throughout Chinese history by many thinkers, including the philosopher Confucius, as an ideal leader and citizen.

T. Fleischmann, MFA

BIBLIOGRAPHY

Birrell, Anne. *Chinese Mythology: An Introduction.* Baltimore: Johns Hopkins UP, 1993. Print.

Collier, Irene Dea. *Chinese Mythology.* Berkeley Heights: Enslow, 2001. Print.

Lee, Jacob. "Xia Dynasty." *History Reference Center.* EBSCOhost, 2007. Web. 2 July 2013.

Lewis, Mark Edward. *The Flood Myths of Early China.* Albany: State U of New York P, 2006. Print.

Suh, Kyung-Ho. Rev. of *The Flood Myths of Early China*, by Mark Edward Lewis. *China Review International* 15.1 (2008): 125–31. Print.

INDIA

Brahmā the Creator

Author: Traditional
Time Period: 1 CE–500 CE
Country or Culture: India
Genre: Myth

PLOT SUMMARY

Brahmā is an important god of creation in the Hindu pantheon. His name comes from the root word *brahman*, referring to abstract sacred power, which in turn comes from the root word *brh*, signifying growth and development. Traditionally, Brahmā is revered both as an abstract underlying power and as a concrete deity capable of acting in the mundane world.

Brahmā is the protagonist of several of the best-known creation stories in the wide and varied Hindu mythological canon. In one, Brahmā as an abstract force creates a universe consisting of primal waters. He plants a small golden seed into this watery existence, and it grows into a golden egg known as Hiranyagarbha. In some texts, the egg is said to rest on a lotus growing out of the navel of the god Visnu (Vishnu). When this egg breaks open, its top forms the heavens;

its bottom, the earth; and the portion between the two pieces, the sky.

Brahmā as a concrete manifestation emerges from this egg and continues the work of forming the universe. According to some sources, he brings some beings into existence on his own, without the aid of a mother counterpart. These include a number of sages who are said to have been born from his mind and deified representations of emotions that come from parts of his body.

Most of the universe, however, is populated with help from a mother figure. In one popular tale, Brahmā creates Sarasvatī, a goddess representing wisdom and the fecund powers of the earth. As soon as she emerges, he finds her very attractive and wants to have sex with her. She coyly demurs and becomes a cow to hide from him. He then assumes the form of a bull, and their union generates all cattle. They next transform into a mare and a stallion, and horses come into being. This playful game of hide and seek continues until the earth is populated by all existing forms of life.

Brahmā in his concrete manifestation is represented as a red or pink male figure, often depicted riding on a sacred goose. According to some myths, Brahmā grows a new head for each direction Sarasvatī teasingly flees

186

from him. By the time the world is populated, he has heads looking north, south, east, west, and above. However, he loses the fifth head, the one looking up. In some myths, this head is too radiant or radiates beams of light that are so bright that they offend the other gods. In others, he becomes involved in a dispute with Visnu and Śiva (Shiva) as to who is the most powerful being, and Śiva takes on an aggressive manifestation that chops off Brahmā's fifth head.

Although the gods themselves come to dispute his ultimate authority, Brahmā has been believed to be the progenitor of all beings throughout much of Indian history. Since he is their ultimate cause, all Hindu gods are sometimes considered manifestations of Brahmā. Therefore, he is sometimes known by the reverent title Pitāmaha, meaning "grandfather."

SIGNIFICANCE

Brahmā is one of the main deities of traditional Hinduism. In his role as the world creator, he forms the Trimūrti, or triumvirate, along with Visnu, the world sustainer, and Śiva, the world destroyer. Information about Brahmā can be found in a number of sacred Sanskrit texts. Chief among these is the *Brahmā Sūtra*, also known as the *Vedānta Sūtra*. Consisting of 555 verses, it is an examination of the nature of Brahmā and a summary of several popular Upanishads, including the *Chāndogya Upanishad*. The *Brahmā Sūtra* is credited to the scholar Bādarāyana, who is sometimes identified with the saint Vyāsa, the traditional author of the Mahābhārata. The age of the text is a subject of much debate, with some scholars claiming that the *Brahmā Sūtra* was written as late as 400 CE and others placing its date of composition as early as 500 BCE.

Bronze and stone statues of Brahmā were created in India and the Indianized states of Southeast Asia during the early medieval period (ca. 500 CE–1200 CE). They generally depict him with four heads and four arms. The repetition of the number four is sometimes interpreted as symbolizing the four main Vedic texts. Brahmā is often shown holding stylized objects such as a scepter, a lotus, a book of the Vedas, and a necklace of beads used to count time. Art from this early medieval period often features the entire Trimūrti. Such pieces sometimes depict the three gods on their mounts, with Brahmā riding a goose, Visnu upon the mythical bird Garuda, and Śiva atop a bull.

Brahmā worship decreased after the early medieval period. Some scholars have suggested that Brahmā's association with the concrete, created world caused this decline, as worshippers had become more interested in ascetic spiritual pursuits focused on Visnu and Śiva. According to some Hindu beliefs, Brahmā has the ability to grant immortality but is not able to give the gift of spiritual release, as are Visnu and Śiva. Hindus began to seek liberation from samsāra, the cycle of death and rebirth, so worshippers became more focused on the other two gods of the Trimūrti. Today, only a few temples are dedicated to Brahmā, whereas Visnu and Śiva remain popular subjects of veneration.

Adam Berger, PhD

BIBLIOGRAPHY

Dimmit, Cornelia, and J. A. B. Van Buitenen. *Classical Hindu Mythology*. Philadelphia: Temple UP, 1978. Print.
Hemenway, Priya. *Hindu Gods*. San Francisco: Chronicle, 2003. Print.
Johnson, W. J. *A Dictionary of Hinduism*. Oxford: Oxford UP, 2009. Print.
Jones, Constance A., and James D. Ryan. *Encyclopedia of Hinduism*. New York: Infobase, 2007. Print.
Māni, Vettam. *Purānic Encyclopaedia*. New Delhi: Motilal Banarsidass, 1975. Print.
Shattuck, Cybelle. *Hinduism*. New York: Routledge, 1999. Print.
Sullivan, Bruce. *Historical Dictionary of Hinduism*. London: Scarecrow, 1997. Print.
Wilkins, W. J. *Hindu Mythology*. London: Curzon, 1973. Print.

◆ The Creation of the Ganges

Author: Traditional
Time Period: 1 CE–500 CE
Country or Culture: India
Genre: Myth

PLOT SUMMARY

King Sagara seeks to declare himself ruler of the world by performing a ceremony involving the sacrifice of a horse. Indra, the supreme ruler of the gods and the god of rain, thwarts Sagara's plan by stealing his horse and making it seem as if the horse was stolen by a powerful sage named Kapila. Sagara's sixty thousand sons go to Kapila's home and attack the sage with boulders and arrows. When Kapila awakens from meditation, he becomes angry and uses mystical fire to reduce Sagara's sons to ashes. Saddened by the loss of his sons, Sagara learns that the only way his sons can journey to heaven is if Gaṅgā, the river goddess, descends to earth and purifies their ashes with her waters.

The sage Bhagīratha, the great-great-great-grandson of Sagara, travels to the region of the Himalayas now known as Gangotri and remains in the forest for more than one thousand years, practicing austerities to honor the gods. Eventually, Brahmā visits Bhagīratha and tells him that he will grant him any wish in return for his devotion and austerity. Bhagīratha asks for the goddess Gaṅgā to descend to earth to purify the ashes of his ancestors, and Brahmā agrees to order Gaṅgā to do so.

Gaṅgā is the daughter of Himalaya, the lord of snow, and has never descended to earth because she knows that her rushing waters would destroy the land. She tells Bhagīratha that she can safely come to earth only if the god Śiva (Shiva) uses his head to break her fall from heaven. Bhagīratha spends a year worshipping Śiva until the god brings him up to his heavenly realm and speaks to him. Moved by his plight, Śiva agrees to help Bhagīratha, and he travels to the peak of the Himalayas and orders Gaṅgā to descend.

Angered by Śiva's orders, Gaṅgā determines that she will allow her full force to fall upon him and sweep him away. As Gaṅgā's waters fall from heaven, Śiva allows the waters to fall into the locks of his hair, thus deflecting the force of the water and causing Gaṅgā to break into streams, reducing her power. Each of the streams has mystical properties and can purify even the most malevolent impurity. Gaṅgā breaks into seven streams, four of which are named the Gladdener, the Purifier, the Lotus-Clad, and the Fair. Three of the streams flow to the east, three flow to the west, and the purest and strongest stream follows Bhagīratha, who rides ahead of the flowing water in his chariot and leads it to the spot where Kapila destroyed Sagara's sons. When the water reaches this location, the ashes of the fallen sons are purified, and the sixty thousand rise into heaven.

SIGNIFICANCE

The myth of the creation of the Ganges River is an example of an important type of mythology found around the world: mythology concerning the essential natural resources of a particular culture. Myths of this type are common in agricultural societies that are tied by necessity to prominent features of the environment. The

evolution of Indian culture followed the Ganges from the Himalayas through the continent; important towns and cities emerged on the banks of the river, and people used it for food and water as well as trade and travel. Given the cultural, economic, political, and social importance of the Ganges, as well as other rivers in India, it is not surprising that Hindu mythology reflects this historical relationship and has imbued these phenomena with spiritual and mythological significance.

The heavenly origins of the Ganges establish the river as a bridge between the physical world of the earth and the world of the gods; therefore, the river became an important symbolic location for individuals to honor the gods. The association of the river with the goddess Gaṅgā also provided a focus for the prayers and hopes of those who made their lives on the river. Fishers hoping for a bountiful harvest or travelers hoping that their boats would reach their destinations without incident could therefore direct their prayers toward the patron gods and goddesses seen as responsible for providing the river's bounty and controlling the dangerous waters.

Associations between the Ganges and the process of cleansing or purifying might have derived simply from the use of the river's water to cleanse the bodies and food of the ancient people in riparian communities. Bacteriological studies of the Ganges have shown that the dissolved minerals within the river have antiseptic properties. These minerals aid in killing harmful bacteria and enhance the cleansing of bodies and clothing. Ganges water has been shown to kill the germs that cause the disease cholera, for instance, and likely has similar effects on other pathogens. The antiseptic qualities of the river's waters must have been more potent in the preindustrial age, before pollution of the river was widespread. In any case, the legend of the Ganges purifying the ashes of Sagara's sixty thousand sons has been integrated into the death rituals of the Indian people, and the ashes of the dead are still submerged in the Ganges by families hoping that the waters will purify the bodies of their departed loved ones.

Hindu mythology surrounding the Ganges not only honors the importance of the river but also explains, in mythological terms, features of the landscape that must have mystified those who first came to live along the banks of the river. Before modern science could explain the path of the river through studies of the density of substrate materials and other features of the environment, the ancient Hindus postulated that the river's shape and qualities reflected the nature of their gods, which was akin to the notion that the very existence of the river had seemingly mystical effects on their lives.

Micah Issitt

BIBLIOGRAPHY

Darian, Steven G. *The Ganges in Myth and History*. Honolulu: UP of Hawaii, 1978. Print.

Lewin, Ted. *Sacred River: The Ganges of India*. New York: Houghton, 1995. Print.

Narayan, Madukkarai K. V. *Exploring the Hindu Mind: Cultural Reflection and Symbolism*. New Dehli: Readworthy, 2009. Print.

Nelson, Lance E. ed. *Purifying the Earthly Body of God: Religion and Ecology in Hindu India*. Albany: State U of New York P, 1998. Print.

Shiva, Vadana. *Water Wars: Privatization, Pollution, and Profit*. Cambridge: Southend, 2002. Print.

◆ Damayantī's Choice

Author: Traditional
Time Period: 1 CE–500 CE
Country or Culture: India
Genre: Myth

PLOT SUMMARY

The Mahābhārata is a lengthy and complicated set of interwoven tales. The main plot is driven by the struggle between two factions to gain control of a northern Indian kingdom. These two groups, the Kauravas and Pāndavas, use diplomacy, trickery, and violence to defeat one another and gain political superiority.

In one episode, the two factions gamble with magical dice. The dice belong to a dishonest ally of the Kauravas named Shakuni, who uses them to cause the Pāndavas to lose everything, including their own freedom and that of their collective wife, Draupadī. After the Kaurava brothers mistreat Draupadī, she appeals to the god Krishna, who intervenes on her behalf. This moves the leader of the Kaurava family to free the Pāndavas, but they are sent into exile in the forest for twelve years.

The Pāndava brothers are deeply ashamed of having been lured into the Kaurava trap through their desire to gamble. While they are in the forest, the Pāndavas are visited by a number of wise men, who tell them stories of others' sufferings. One of the men, the venerated

sage Brihadaswa, tells the Pāndavas the story of Nala and Damayantī. The first part of the story is often called "Damayantī's Choice."

The sage describes how once upon a time a king of Vidarbha had a daughter named Damayantī. She was considered the most beautiful woman in the world, and people everywhere spoke of her grace and virtue. Meanwhile, there was a king of the Nishādha tribe who had a son named Nala. Nala was also said to have excellent personal qualities. Hearing wonderful tales of the princess Damayantī, he fell in love with her.

One day, the prince catches a golden goose (or swan) with magical powers. It agrees to go to Damayantī and tell her of Nala's passion for her. Once it finds Damayantī, the goose tells her of a handsome prince who wishes to marry her. Damayantī replies that she is not interested if the man is not Nala, as she secretly loves him. When the bird says it is Nala, Damayantī is overjoyed.

In time, Damayantī's father, the king of Vidarbha, announces that there will be a tournament of suitors so that the princess can choose a husband. Hundreds of princes from all over India come to try to win Damayantī's hand in marriage. She is so beautiful that even several of the gods want her for a wife, including Agni, the god of fire; Indra, the sky god; Varuna, the lord of the celestial ocean and the underworld; and Yama, the god of death.

On his way to the tournament, Nala comes across four glorious chariots. He knows that no mortals can ride in such splendid vehicles, so he bows down in worship. The gods in the chariots charge him with delivering Damayantī the message that they are coming to win her hand as a bride. When Nala mysteriously finds himself in Damayantī's room at the palace, he delivers the news of the immortal suitors. She responds by telling Nala to be at the tournament, as she wants him, and the choice is hers to make.

Knowing that Damayantī favors Nala, the four gods take on his appearance to trick her, so that there are five suitors at the tournament who look like Nala. Damayantī responds by appealing to all the gods to give her the power to tell her true love from the imposters. She then notices that only one has a shadow and sweat on his forehead and that the flower garland he wears is slightly faded. Damayantī realizes that this man is the real Nala, as his minor imperfections mark him as truly human, allowing her to distinguish him from the four gods who seek to mislead her.

SIGNIFICANCE

Along with the Rāmāyana, the Mahābhārata is one of the two great classical Indian epics. According to traditional belief, the writing of Mahābhārata is attributed to the renowned sage Vyasa, as are other Hindu holy books, including the Vedas and Puranas. Modern scholarship has determined that the Mahābhārata was, in fact, composed over many centuries, combining a number of stories that were passed along orally through generations, and that it has been written and rewritten numerous times. The version of the Mahābhārata as it is known today probably took shape around the fourth century CE, and its earliest forms probably date back to before 500 BCE.

The Mahābhārata is acknowledged as one of the most popular compilations of tales of all time, and it remains a favorite story cycle in much of Asia. In India's medieval period, lasting from approximately the eight century to the eighteenth century CE, it was translated into many languages throughout the Indian subcontinent and Southeast Asia, strongly influencing the literary traditions of many cultures in the region. In some places, including the state of Tamil Nadu in southern India, episodes of the Mahābhārata form the basis for still-active temple cults.

Although it is peripheral to the main narrative of the struggle between the Kauravas and Pāndavas, the story of Damayantī and Nala has always been considered one of the most enjoyable parts of the overall epic. The first part, often known as "Damayantī's Choice," is a romantic story, a tribute to the power of love. Moreover, it is a testament to what it means to be human and to have imperfections, and to the fact that these imperfections are lovable.

"Damayantī's Choice" is just the beginning of the account of Damayantī and Nala. The rest of the story recounts how the goddess Kālī, jealous of the couple's love, infects Nala with a destructive desire to gamble. Despite Nala's ill luck, Damayantī's love remains true. Overall, the story of Damayantī and Nala is a tale of the ups and downs of human fortunes, fittingly told to the Pāndavas as they are living in exile in the forest.

As a result of her commitment to her husband in bad times as well as good, Damayantī is regarded as a model of fidelity. This makes her an important symbol of the feminine ideal, as medieval Indian culture believed that a wife should be selflessly devoted to her husband no matter what his fate. The appeal of the story of Damayantī and Nala, then, lies not only in its romantic beginning but also in its depiction of the enduring and patient nature of true love.

Adam Berger, PhD

BIBLIOGRAPHY

Dimmitt, Cornelia, and J. A. B. Van Buitenen. *Classical Hindu Mythology*. Philadelphia: Temple UP, 1978. Print.

Flood, Gavin. *The Blackwell Companion to Hinduism*. Malden: Blackwell, 2003. Print.

Guerber, H. A. *The Book of the Epic: The World's Great Epics Told in Story*. Philadelphia: Lippincott, 1913. Print.

Johnson, Robert. *Femininity Lost and Regained*. New York: Harper, 1990. Print.

Jones, Constance, and James Ryan. *Encyclopedia of Hinduism*. New York: Facts On File, 2007. Print.

Shattuck, Cybelle. *Hinduism*. New York: Routledge, 1999. Print.

Sullivan, Bruce. *Historical Dictionary of Hinduism*. London: Scarecrow, 1997. Print.

Van Buitenen, J. A. B., trans. and ed. *The Mahābhārata*. Vol. 2. Chicago: U of Chicago P, 1975. Print.

Van Nooten, Barend. *The Mahābhārata: Attributed to Krishna Dvaipāyana Vyāsa*. New York: Twayne, 1971. Print.

Wilkins, W. J. *Hindu Mythology*. London: Curzon, 1973. Print.

◆ Draupadī

Author: Traditional
Time Period: 1 CE–500 CE
Country or Culture: India
Genre: Myth

PLOT SUMMARY

Draupadī is an important female character in the classic Indian story the Mahābhārata. The Mahābhārata is a complex tale of the struggle of different factions competing for succession to the throne of a northern Indian kingdom called Kuruksetra. The two principal opposing sets are rival cousins, the Pāndavas and the Kauravas. The two main sides draw other families into their struggle in a dynamic and baroque series of alliances.

In this complicated tale, Draupadī is the beautiful and intelligent daughter of Drupada, king of a region along the Ganges River called Pāñcāla. Born from the fire of a sacred ritual sacrifice and associated with mystical powers, Draupadī is also said to be an incarnation of the goddess Sri (sometimes associated with Laksmī, or Lakshmi), who represents kingly power and the right to continued succession.

Eager to forge an alliance with a militarily powerful family, King Drupada holds a tournament so that suitors can show off their skills to his daughter. She will then choose as her husband the champion who most impresses her; the man of her choice will therefore become a protector of the kingdom. After one of the five Pāndava brothers, Arjuna, wins an archery contest, Draupadī chooses him to be her groom. When Arjuna explains to his mother that he has won a contest, she misunderstands him; thinking he has won treasure, she admonishes him to share equally with his brothers. Arjuna follows his mother's instructions, and all five brothers marry the princess Draupadī. Eventually she gives birth to five sons, one sired by each husband.

In a major turning point in the Mahābhārata, the villain Śakuni entices the Pāndava brothers to play a game of dice against the Kauravas. Unbeknownst to the players, the dice used have been carved from the leg bone of Śakuni's father, and he can magically control the outcome of their rolls. Yudhisthira, the eldest of the Pāndava brothers, gradually loses all of his property and then his freedom and that of his brothers. In the end, he loses Draupadī as well. As the Kauravas seek to strip her of her clothes to shame her, the god Krsna (Krishna) intervenes and gives her an endless number of garments. In his shame, the patriarch of the Kauravas frees the Pāndava brothers. Draupadī is so insulted by the crude actions of the Kauravas, however, that she vows revenge.

The members of the Pāndava clan, including Draupadī, are exiled to the forest for twelve years. When the thirteenth year comes, however, Draupadī encourages the men in her family to go to war against the Kauravas. When Krsna comes to try to make peace, she argues against him, saying that the Pāndavas must fight to uphold her honor.

The Pāndavas are victorious in the ensuing campaign, known as the Kuruksetra War. However, Draupadī's five sons are killed in combat by the great warrior Aśvatthāmā. She vows to fast until Aśvatthāmā is caught and killed. Eventually, he is caught, but Draupadī shows him mercy, taking a jewel he wears on his head instead of his life.

In the end, Draupadī follows her five husbands in their quest for world renunciation. They try to climb the sacred Mount Meru, but this feat is physically too much for Draupadī, and she dies in the attempt. In death, she is reunited with her family in the heavenly realm.

SIGNIFICANCE

The Mahābhārata is one of the most enduring works of art from the Indian subcontinent. Along with the roughly contemporaneous Rāmāyana, the Mahābhārata is definitive of classical Sanskrit literature, offering a fascinating window into what life was like in early medieval India. Dating it, however, can be problematic. The epic is traditionally credited to the great scholar Vyāsa, who is said to have been an incarnation of the god Visnu (Vishnu) as well as the scribe who first wrote down the holy Hindu texts, the Vedas and Puranas. However, modern scholars have concluded that the Mahābhārata was composed in pieces that were repeatedly redacted and mainly passed down through the generations in a tradition of oral storytelling. The existing version of the Mahābhārata probably took shape around the fourth century CE, and its earliest forms probably date back to before 500 BCE

The events of Draupadī's life set into motion some of the central plots of the Mahābhārata. Foremost, it is her humiliation by the Kauravas and her desire for revenge that drive the Pāndavas to fight the Kauravas. This culminates in the great Kuruksetra War, the definitive conflict in the epic. Therefore, Draupadī is known to many as the chief instigator of the Kuruksetra War and one of its main victims, since her five sons are killed in its battles. As many scholars have noted, this is a typical pattern in Sanskrit literature, wherein the fates of women often cause reactions among the main protagonists and antagonists that drive the overall plotlines of the tales.

Draupadī has been one of India's favorite literary heroines since the early medieval period. She represents a woman who both endures great trials and gains divine intervention to help her overcome injustice. However, she has also been a somewhat controversial figure. Her marriage to all five Pāndava brothers is an exceedingly rare act of polyandry within the Sanskrit tradition, and it is an act that some conservative Hindus have considered blasphemous. Nonetheless, the popular appeal of the Draupadī character endures.

In some places, Draupadī's admirers have elevated her to a divine role. For instance, she is worshipped as a goddess in some parts of the southern Indian state of Tamil Nadu, where elements of the Mahābhārata story that pertain to Draupadī's life are acted out ritually in temple plays. Such rituals also include feats of extreme endurance, such as fire walking. Expressions of religious fervor such as possession by spirits also take place during these rituals, with the afflicted individuals talking in the voices of characters from the Mahābhārata.

Adam Berger, PhD

BIBLIOGRAPHY

Dimmitt, Cornelia, and J. A. B. Van Buitenen. *Classical Hindu Mythology*. Philadelphia: Temple UP, 1978. Print.

Leemings, David Adam. *Mythology: The Voyage of the Hero*. New York: Oxford UP, 1998. Print.

Shattuck, Cybelle. *Hinduism*. New York: Routledge, 1999. Print.

Van Buitenen, J. A. B. *The Mahābhārata*. Chicago: U of Chicago P, 1973. Print.

Wilkins, W. J. *Hindu Mythology*. London: Curzon, 1973. Print.

◆ Durgā

Author: Traditional
Time Period: 1 CE–500 CE
Country or Culture: India
Genre: Myth

PLOT SUMMARY

Stories of the goddess Durgā are found in a number of Hindu sacred scriptures. They all follow a similar pattern. First, a demonic being gains magical powers through ascetic feats. Second, the demon uses these powers to defeat the gods. Third, the gods combine their strengths to create a many-armed female defender, Durgā, and each god gives her his magical weapon to fight the demon. In the end, Durgā defeats massive evil armies and then the ruling demon himself.

The best known of the Durgā stories comes from the Devī Māhātmya purānic text. It recounts how a demon named Mahisāsura (also known as Mahisā and Durgāma), who often appears in the form of a giant buffalo but can change his shape at will, attains great powers through meditation and ascetic endurance. Because of his spiritual achievements, he is given the opportunity to ask for a magical boon from Brahmā, the creator. He asks for immortality, and Brahmā decrees that he can never be killed by god or man.

Mahisāsura wages war on the gods for hundreds of years and eventually defeats them, throwing them out of heaven and forcing them to live in exile in the forests. In a final act of desperation, the gods appeal to the three most powerful gods, Brahmā, Śiva (Shiva), and Visnu (Vishnu), to help them overthrow the usurping demon. These three gods know that they cannot beat Mahisāsura because of his magical boon. Cunningly, they create a female warrior to avenge them, for, as a female, she is neither god nor man and therefore unaffected by Mahisāsura's magical protection.

Durgā is a beautiful, multi-armed woman, who rides a fierce lion (sometimes translated as tiger). The gods arm her with their characteristic weapons. Śiva gives her his trident, Agni his fire dart, Indra his thunderbolt, and so forth, so that she wields the most powerful armaments in the cosmos. Durgā drinks copious quantities of wine, making her eyes red, and she is intoxicated as she enters into battle.

With her arms constantly moving but her face still and serene, Durgā calmly laughs as she destroys Mahisāsura's millions of troops. Eventually, Durgā and Mahisāsura face each other on the field of battle. After a fierce struggle, Durgā knocks down the demon king, chops his head off, and kills the spirit escaping from his decapitated body. Thus, she ends Mahisāsura's reign of terror, restores the gods to their proper places, and renews the cosmic order.

SIGNIFICANCE

Durgā is discussed in a number of Sanskrit Hindu scriptural sources, or Purānas. One of the first accounts of Durgā comes from the *Mārkandeya Purāna*, which may date back to as early as the fourth century CE. Stories about this warrior-goddess are prominent in the Devī Māhātmya section of the *Mārkandeya Purāna*, which was written down by the sage Mārkandeya in the fifth century CE. Her deeds also form an important part of the *Devī Bhāgavata Purāna*, which is traditionally attributed to Vyāsa, the nominal author of the Mahābhārata. While the *Devī Bhāgavata Purāna*'s actual origins are not fully understood, it was likely compiled sometime between the sixth and fourteenth centuries CE. The *Skanda Purāna*, which is mainly about the exploits of the god Śiva and his kin, also contains details about Durgā. This text is thought to date back to the eleventh or twelfth century CE.

Although she is a lesser divinity compared to the primary gods Brahmā, Śiva, and Visnu, the goddess Durgā has been a popularly important figure in the vast and diverse Hindu pantheon for the past two millennia. In some regions of the Indian subcontinent, particularly the northeast, she is highly revered. Like Pārvatī, the goddess in her manifestation as the wife of the god Śiva, Durgā is associated with human, plant, and animal fertility. Durgā is also considered a divine protector, able to calmly fight off dangerous forces to protect those unable to protect themselves.

Durgā Pūjā, the autumnal festival in her honor, is one of the most important religious holidays in the Indian states of Assam and West Bengal. Images of Durgā, made of clay from ritually sacred rivers, are venerated in households during Durgā Pūjā. At the end of the holiday, these idols are paraded to the rivers and thrown in, signifying the cycle of death and rebirth. Durgā Pūjā is very important socially because married daughters, who traditionally move to live in their husbands' households, return to their childhood homes and enjoy the seasonal festivities with their own families.

Although Durgā is an extremely popular divinity in parts of India, she also contradicts typical Hindu sensibilities. This is particularly true regarding traditional gender roles. In most parts of the Indian subcontinent, it is considered appropriate for women to be protected by men. In the case of Durgā, this norm is reversed, as she has to fight to avenge the honor of the vanquished male gods. Not only does she engage in warfare, which is highly unusual for females in India, but she does so while intoxicated on wine—and heavy drinking is considered scandalous for high-caste Hindu women. Furthermore, the way she is worshipped reflects her marginality. It is traditional for Durgā's worshippers to give her offerings of meat and blood, which are otherwise believed to be polluting to high-caste Hindus.

Adam Berger, PhD

BIBLIOGRAPHY

Coburn, Thomas B. *Encountering the Goddess: A Translation of the Māhātmya and a Study of Its Interpretation*. Albany: State U of New York P, 1991. Print.

Hemenway, Priya. *Hindu Gods: The Spirit of the Divine*. San Francisco: Chronicle, 2003. Print.

Jones, Constance, and James D. Ryan. *Encyclopedia of Hinduism*. New York: Infobase, 2007. Print.

Kinsley, David. *Hindu Goddesses: Visions of the Divine Feminine*. Berkeley: U of California P, 1986. Print.

Māni, Vettam. *Purānic Encyclopaedia*. New Delhi: Motilal Banarsidass, 1975. Print.

McDaniel, June. *Offering Flowers, Feeding Skulls: Popular Goddess Worship in West Bengal*. Oxford: Oxford UP, 2004. Print.

Shattuck, Cybelle. *Hinduism*. London: Routledge, 1999. Print.

Wilkins, W. J. *Hindu Mythology: Vedic and Purānic*. London: Curzon, 1973. Print.

◆ Gotama's Attainment

Author: Traditional
Time Period: 1 CE–500 CE
Country or Culture: India
Genre: Myth

PLOT SUMMARY

In the fifth or sixth century BCE, a child is born in the village of Lumbinī, in present-day southern Nepal, to a local leader named Śuddhodana Gotama (sometimes spelled Gautama) and a noblewoman named Māyādevī, who dies shortly after the boy was born. A sage named Asita notices marks on the baby that indicate he is destined for greatness: he will become a great political leader or religious man. The boy is named Siddhārtha, meaning "one who has accomplished every goal."

Śuddhodana prefers that Siddhārtha become a great leader instead of a religious thinker and shelters him from any misery that might inspire him to seek spiritual answers. On trips from the palace, however, Siddhārtha witnesses scenes that inspire spiritual curiosity, and when he sees a holy man meditating, he decides to become a spiritual seeker.

At sixteen, Siddhārtha marries a lovely young woman named Yasodharā. Although he deeply cares for her, he cannot forget his dream of becoming a holy man. When Yasodharā bears his first son, Siddhārtha has a vision that the baby is a fetter holding him back, and he determines to leave the palace and seek spiritual answers.

Siddhārtha sets out and finds a teacher named Ālāra Kālāma, who teaches him to meditate on nothingness. Siddhārtha soon surpasses his teacher, but he also finds the practice unsatisfying. He then meets a guru named Udraka Rāmaputra, who teaches him to live in a state that is neither perception nor nonperception. Again, Siddhārtha becomes adept at this but finds it unfulfilling. He then lives a deeply ascetic lifestyle for six years, starving himself nearly to death in the process.

One day he notices how emaciated he is and realizes that starving himself is not teaching him anything. He comes upon a village woman named Sujātā, who gives him food in a golden bowl. Afterward, he goes to bathe in the river, and when he places the golden bowl into the river, it floats away. Siddhārtha takes this as a sign that he is close to a spiritual awakening.

He sets out for a deer park to meditate. As he approaches the site, animals follow him to bear witness to the miracle about to happen. He sits down under a fig tree to contemplate a middle way between asceticism and worldly life. As he does so, the evil spirit Mārā, king of illusions, attempts to distract him.

Mārā first causes the ground to shake, which scares off the animals, but Siddhārtha ignores the threat. Mārā then tells Siddhārtha that his father's kingdom has been taken by his cruel cousin and that he must save it, but Siddhārtha again ignores him. Enraged, Mārā commands his army of evil spirits to attack Siddhārtha with weapons, but they are unable to strike him.

Mārā grows exasperated and yells that this is his own place and that Siddhārtha must leave. In response, Siddhārtha touches the ground, and the earth bears witness to the fact that he has gained sufficient spiritual merit to remain in meditation. Mārā then tries to tempt Siddhārtha by commanding his beautiful daughters to dance and flirt around him. Siddhārtha simply sits and meditates on the middle path. At the twentieth hour of mediation, he comes to enlightenment. Rays of brilliant light emanate from his head. Thereafter Siddhārtha is known as the Buddha, "the awakened one."

SIGNIFICANCE

The foundation myth of the Buddhist religion, this story describes the moment that Siddhārtha transcended ordinary human perception to attain spiritual enlightenment. In order to appreciate the significance of the myth, it is necessary to understand the socioreligious environment into which Siddhārtha was born. In the sixth century BCE, religious change was taking place throughout India, and perhaps prompted by a wave of urbanization and concurrent political upheaval, many thinkers began to question the supremacy of the established religion. Spiritual seekers explored a variety of philosophical and meditative techniques to uncover deeper truths about the nature of the universe. This new wave of spiritual exploration became known as the Upanishadic era, reflecting that teachings were passed orally from teacher to

student. (*Upanishads* derives from the prefix *upa*, meaning "approach"; the word *ni*, meaning "near"; and the root verb *shad*, meaning "to sit.") Around the time that the Buddha was born, some of these Upanishads were beginning to be written down. Siddhārtha Gotama's quest for spiritual fulfillment outside the normal social order, then, was very much in keeping with his time.

According to the myth, the Buddha remained seated for seven days after his enlightenment, with the snakelike being Mucalinda providing him shelter from the elements. The Buddha's first thought was that the knowledge of the essential truth of the universe could not be taught. At that point, the gods intervened and begged him to go forth and teach what he had learned for the betterment of all beings in the universe.

For the rest of his life, forty-five years according to some sources, the Buddha did just that. He wandered around northern India, preaching the insights he had gained through meditation and converting many men and women to his new sect. In the centuries after his death, the Buddha's religion grew exponentially, even gaining the patronage of powerful emperors.

Adam Berger, PhD

BIBLIOGRAPHY

Bercholz, Samuel, and Sherab Chödzin Kohn, eds. *The Buddha and His Teachings*. Boston: Shambhala, 2003. Print.

Carrithers, Michael. *The Buddha: A Very Short Introduction*. Oxford: Oxford UP, 2001. Print.

Flood, Gavin D. *The Blackwell Companion to Hinduism*. Malden: Blackwell, 2003. Print.

Gowans, Christopher W. *Philosophy of the Buddha*. New York: Routledge, 2007. Print.

Sullivan, Bruce. *Historical Dictionary of Hinduism*. London: Scarecrow, 1997. Print.

◆ The Heavenly Nymph and Her Mortal Husband

Author: Traditional
Time Period: 2499 BCE–1000 BCE; 999 BCE–1 BCE; 1 CE–500 CE
Country or Culture: India
Genre: Myth

PLOT SUMMARY

For more than twenty-five hundred years, the love story of Urvaśī (Urvashi) and Purūravas informed South Asian literature, and there have been slight plot variations in the different renditions. Most versions begin by explaining that Urvaśī, the most beautiful of the *apsaras* (heavenly nymphs), has grown bored of living in heaven. According to Hindu mythology, their role is to dance to the music played by their male counterparts, the *gandharvas* (celestial musicians), and thereby give dramatic flourish to the gods' divine activities.

Urvaśī's ambition to experience life among mortals is unusual for a denizen of the heavenly realm. In some versions of the tale, Urvaśī first comes to earth because she is cursed by the Vedic gods Mitra, deity of alliance and friendship, and Varuna, lord of justice and the underworld. According to this plotline, Urvaśī is expelled from heaven because she sexually inflames both of the gods and makes them jealous of one another.

Whether her trip to earth is voluntary or forced, Urvaśī comes to enjoy it and travels with her two beloved pet lambs (or goats in some accounts). One day, she happens to meet a king named Purūravas. He is handsome, honest, and noble. The celestial nymph and the mortal king fall deeply in love as soon as they lay eyes on one another.

Purūravas asks Urvaśī to marry him, and she agrees on three conditions. First, he must allow her to keep her pets, because she cherishes them as if they were her own children. Second, she must never see him naked. Third, she must eat only ghee (clarified butter), because she is a creature of heaven, not a mortal.

In her absence, the denizens of the heavenly realm begin to complain that their lives are not the same without Urvaśī among them. The apsaras and gandharvas grow discontent and decide to win her back to their heavenly home. Viśvāvasu (Vishvavasu), head of the gandharvas, knows of the contract between Urvaśī and Purūravas and hatches a plan to exploit it.

Viśvāvasu goes to earth and steals one of Urvaśī's pets in the middle of the night. When she hears it crying out, Urvaśī wails and complains that she is living in a world without noble protectors. Seeking to please his beloved wife, Purūravas leaps up from his bed without dressing to get the animal back. Just as he does so, the gandharvas cause a bolt of lightning to illuminate the bedchamber, and Urvaśī sees her husband naked and disappears to heaven.

When Purūravas triumphantly returns to show his wife that both animals are safe, he cannot find her anywhere. He wanders around crazed, looking for her. Eventually Urvaśī takes pity on him and tells him to go to the spot where they first met at the end of the year. When he does, Purūravas finds his wife there, and they make love for the night. A son is born of this union. This pattern continues a total of five times, with the pair meeting once a year and a son being born from each tryst.

After many years, the celestial beings grow sympathetic to the couple's desire to live together. They present Purūravas with a pan of fire. Following their instructions, he eventually makes the appropriate fire sacrifices and receives his boon. When the gods are pleased with his offerings, Purūravas is allowed to go to heaven and unite with his beloved Urvaśī.

SIGNIFICANCE

The story of the apsara Urvaśī and her mortal husband, the legendary King Purūravas, is one of the oldest tales in Hindu mythology. It makes its first appearance in the *Rig Veda*, composed around 1500 BCE, which is considered the most venerable text in the Hindu canon. The *Rig Veda* contains over a thousand hymns to various gods, meant to be recited in precisely prescribed manners to maintain the well-being of the universe. Although the story of these two lovers is a minor part of the great Vedic tome, it endured through the centuries as a perennial favorite while other aspects of Vedic mythology faded from memory.

The story makes another appearance in the late Vedic compendium *Śatapatha Brāhmana* (*Shatapatha Brahmana*). As was often the case with the early Hindu works, the *Śatapatha Brāhmana* was communicated orally for centuries prior to being written down, probably beginning to circulate around the eighth century BCE and recorded around the sixth century BCE. The *Śatapatha Brāhmana* marks the transition of Hinduism from the Vedic to the Upanishadic period. Its inclusion of the love story of Urvaśī and Purūravas is evidence that the appeal of the tale transcended that of the Vedic form of worship, which was beginning to fade away at the time the *Śatapatha Brāhmana* was committed to writing.

The story gained renewed popularity during the reign of the Gupta dynasty, which controlled much of the subcontinent during the fourth through sixth centuries CE and is often considered the high point of Indian civilization. The tale of Urvaśī and Purūravas is recounted in the classic Sanskrit epic the Mahābhārata. Traditionally ascribed to the legendary sage Vyāsa, the Mahābhārata is generally considered a synthesis of several stories passed along orally from as early as the eighth century BCE until its recording sometime around the fourth century CE. The inclusion of the myth of Urvaśī and Purūravas in this Gupta-era literary gem ensured its preservation for future generations.

The Mahābhārata is considered one of the greatest works of literature India ever produced. However, many scholars hold another piece, written around the same time as the Mahābhārata, to be the fullest expression of the myth. The prolific Gupta-era writer Kālidāsa is widely regarded as the master of the Sanskrit language. Although little is known about his life, it is assumed he lived sometime in the fourth century CE, as he is strongly associated with Gupta emperor Chandra Gupta II, who came to power around 375 CE. One of his most celebrated dramatic pieces, the *Vikramōrvaśīyam* (*Vikramōrvashīyam*) is a play about Urvaśī and Purūravas. A far longer and clearly creative rendition, it is nonetheless certainly based on the traditional myth.

The myth found its way into some of the holiest texts of the early medieval period as well. The Purānas, which evidence a return among Hindus to a more theistic or deity-centered form of worship than was current during the earlier Upanishadic period, were likely written sometime during the first five centuries of the Common Era. The Urvaśī and Purūravas story is included in the religiously significant *Bhāghavata Purāna*, the *Matsya Purāna*, and the *Visnu Purāna* (*Vishnu Purāna*).

The importance of the myth to later medieval Hindus is clear from its inclusion in the *Kathāsaritsāgara* (ca. 1063 BCE–81 CE). This tome is a compendium of the most popular stories from ancient India compiled by the sage Somadeva for Queen Sūryavatī of Kashmir. The Urvaśī and Purūravas myth's appearance in this early medieval survey of South Asian literature shows that it retained its popular appeal for more than twenty-five hundred years after it first appeared in the *Rig Veda*.

Adam Berger, PhD

BIBLIOGRAPHY

Dimmit, Cornelia, and J. A. B. van Buitenen, eds. and trans. "Purūravas and Urvaśī." *Classical Hindu Mythology: A Reader in the Sanskrit Purānas*. Philadelphia: Temple UP, 1978. 271–73. Print.

Johnson, W. J. *Dictionary of Hinduism*. Oxford: Oxford UP, 2009. Print.

Klostermaier, Klaus. *A Survey of Hinduism*. Albany: State U of New York P, 2007. Print.

Miller, Barbara. *Theater of Memory: The Plays of Kalidasa*. New York: Colombia UP, 1984. Print.

Mills, Margaret, Peter Claus, and Sarah Diamond. *South Asian Folklore*. New York: Routledge, 2003. Print.

Saletore, R. N. *Encyclopedia of Indian Culture*. New Delhi: Sterling, 1983. Print.

Sullivan, Bruce. *Historical Dictionary of Hinduism*. London: Scarecrow, 1997. Print.

◆ The Incarnations of Visnu

Author: Traditional
Time Period: 1 CE–500 CE
Country or Culture: India
Genre: Myth

PLOT SUMMARY

The blue-skinned god Visnu (Vishnu) is the supreme being, residing in Vaikuntha, the eternal home of enlightened souls. Alongside the great gods Brahmā, the creator of all things, and Śiva (Shiva), the destroyer, Visnu is the preserver, and as such, he is intimately tied to all aspects of the cosmos.

On occasion, the forces of evil become more prominent. When this happens, it is necessary for Visnu to take another form, or incarnation, so that he might make things right again. The first time this occurs is when a horrendous flood overtakes the earth. Before the rains begin, Visnu takes the form of a fish called Matsya and informs the first man, Manu, of the coming disaster, advising him to take shelter on a large boat. When the rains fall, Matsya pulls the boat to safety. Soon after this, a sage curses the gods so that they lose their powers and immortality. Visnu tells them that the way to regain their power is to churn the enormous ocean of milk, using a mountain to stir the waters. When the mountain proves too large to move, Visnu takes the form of Kurma, a giant turtle, and carries the cliffs on his back.

After restoring the powers of the gods, Visnu faces an even greater challenge. A horrible demon steals the entire earth, hiding it in swirling, dark waters. In order to retrieve it, Visnu takes the form of Varāha, a ferocious boar, and slaughters the demon; he then carries the earth between his tusks in order to return it. However, the brother of the demon is furious about the slaughter, and he causes volcanoes to erupt and rivers to run violently. He even tortures his own son, who is a follower of Visnu. Unwilling to accept this, Visnu takes the form of Narasimha, a powerful creature that is half man and half lion, and kills that demon as well.

The deaths of these demons mark the end of the first age, but the second age is no more peaceful, as the tyrannical king Bali, one of the Asuras (counterparts of the gods who are in constant conflict with them), reigns on earth. Visnu cleverly takes the form of Vāmana, a dwarf, and asks the king to give him as much land as he can cover in three steps. When the king agrees, Vāmana transforms into a giant and takes three enormous steps that cover all of the land and the sky. After winning the world back from Bali, he appears as Paraśurāma (Parashurama), a sage armed with a gigantic ax, and uses his power to overcome wicked armies, even holding back the advancing seas in order to keep them from flooding the lands. After this, Visnu takes the form of Rāma, an ideal human who is able to triumph over any temptation that might bring him to evil and who is strong enough to defeat the powerful demon Rāvana in battle, ending the second age. For his next two avatars, Visnu likewise takes forms that resemble humans. First, he appears as Krsna (Krishna), a divine prince and warrior with many wives, whose life initiates the third age. After that, he appears as Buddha, the enlightened spiritual leader who founds the transcendental practice that is today called Buddhism.

These nine incarnations of Visnu vary wildly from one another, yet they are not all the forms that he will take. Someday, the end of the current era will come. At that time, Visnu will take the form of his tenth incarnation, Kalki, a powerful being riding a white horse. With his flaming sword raised high above his head, Kalki will defeat evil and usher in the end of our time.

SIGNIFICANCE

The Hindu god Visnu is one of the most widely worshipped deities in world history, and over thousands of years, the sacred Hindu texts that describe him have had a significant impact on international culture, particularly in the Indian subcontinent. In part because his mythology has spread so far in both space and time, the stories of the incarnations of Visnu are varied, with some sources listing many more forms of the god or including different incarnations within this set of ten, called the *daśāvatāra* (*dashavatara*). The particular version of the daśāvatāra listed above is perhaps more widely worshipped and accepted than any other form, and the oldest incarnations come from the authoritative Purānas, ancient Hindu texts that describe the creation of the universe and the origins of the gods.

Even within this daśāvatāra, there is incredible diversity among the incarnations. Some reference fanciful and entertaining stories, such as his incarnations as Varāha and Kurma, and seem to speak primarily to the might and power of Visnu and, by extension, the strength of the religion built around him. These earlier incarnations help establish the nature of the universe, with Visnu promising salvation and spiritual enlightenment and overcoming the wickedness of the demons. Within the Purānas, they also weave together Hindu cosmology with historical information, philosophy, and politics. Later incarnations steer away from mythological beasts and instead take their inspiration from adjacent religious traditions and actual leaders. This is perhaps most evident with the eighth and ninth incarnations. It appears likely that Krsna was a living person, a political leader who, after death, slowly grew in influence until he was absorbed into the daśāvatāra. This absorption allowed Hindu political and spiritual leaders to consolidate power while maintaining religious cohesion. Today, Krsna remains the most widely worshipped Hindu deity, and because many traditions consider him to be a part of the daśāvatāra, that worship is also directed toward Visnu. Buddha seems to have entered the daśāvatāra through a similar path. As the influence of the historical spiritual leader and his teachings spread, different Hindu practices accepted him as an incarnation of their supreme being rather than as a competing and incongruent force, allowing both spiritual traditions to coexist and preserving the power of Hinduism.

At one point slaying world-ending demons and at another teaching compassion, the forms that Visnu assumes can differ radically from one another. Within the complex Hindu mythology, however, the preserver god remains a consistent force of righteousness, and the variety of his incarnations is a reminder that the universe itself is a place as much of contradiction and violence as of redemption.

T. Fleischmann, MFA

BIBLIOGRAPHY

Bansal, Sunita Pant. *Hindu Gods and Goddesses*. New Delhi: Smriti, 2005. Print.

Basu, Anustup. "The 'Indian' Monotheism." *Boundary 2* 39.2 (2012): 111–41. Print.

Germer, Lucie. "Vishnu: God of Power." *Vanished Civilizations*. Spec. issue of *Calliope* 2.5 (1992): 33–35. Print.

Lal, Vinay. "Avatars (Incarnations or Descents) of Vishnu." *Manas: India and Its Neighbors*. UCLA, n.d. Web. 1 July 2013.

Zaehner, R. C. *Hinduism*. 2nd ed. New York: Oxford UP, 1966. Print.

◆ Matsya and the Great Flood

Author: Traditional
Time Period: 1 CE–500 CE
Country or Culture: India
Genre: Myth

PLOT SUMMARY

Matsya and the Great Flood is an important story in Hindu mythology. It describes the end of the world in a cataclysmic deluge and the salvation of life by the efforts of an honest man acting on the instructions of a deity manifested in the form of a giant fish.

Manu, depicted either as a great king or the only honest man, is bathing in a river when he accidentally catches a very small fish with a single horn growing from its head. The unusual fish, named Matsya, has the magical ability to speak. He asks Manu to protect him from the bigger fish in the river. In exchange, Matsya promises to save Manu from an impending flood.

Manu takes the small horned fish home and puts him in a bowl of water. The fish is happy there, but he soon outgrows it. Manu then puts him in a pitcher of water; this works fine for a time, until it becomes too small. Next, Manu puts the fish in a well, but Matsya soon grows too big for it. He then releases the fish into a pond, where Matsya continues to expand in size. Matsya is freed into the Ganges River, but he outgrows even that. Finally, Manu helps Matsya into the ocean, and the fish grows to be very huge indeed.

Manu regularly visits Matsya in the ocean. One day when Manu is meeting with him, Matsya says that the end of the world is near. He instructs Manu to build a great ship with a strong rope attached to the bow and to gather all the species of the world. Manu has a moment of doubt, wondering if the giant horned fish might be a demon trying to trick him. Matsya then reveals himself to be a deity, either Visnu (Vishnu) or Brahmā, depending on the version of the tale.

Heeding Matsya's advice, Manu is ready with a huge ship stocked with all the species of the world by the time the deluge begins. As the waters rise and flood the earth, Manu's ship floats safely on the waves. Matsya tells Manu to fasten the rope to his horn, and the gigantic fish pulls the ship to safety. Eventually, the mighty fish drags the boat to the highest mountain in the world, and Manu ties the rope to a tree on its peak, securely anchoring the ship until the storm ends.

When the waters recede, the species on Manu's boat repopulate the earth with their various kinds. Manu thanks Matsya for saving the world, but he says that he wishes there were a way to continue the survival of humanity. Matsya miraculously provides Manu with a wife, and they have children from whom all the people of the new world are descended.

SIGNIFICANCE

Apocalyptic flood myths are found throughout the world. The best known of these to a Western audience is the Jewish story of Noah's Ark; the South Asian tale of Matsya and the Great Flood is its Hindu equivalent. In all myths of this kind, a righteous man is chosen by a benevolent deity to build a boat capable of sheltering the animals of the world from the storm's destructive powers. By following the god's orders, the chosen man is able to save the species of the world and allow them to regenerate when the flood waters recede.

The tale appears in various Hindu religious texts. These include the late Vedic *Śatapatha Brāhmana*, written in its final form in the fourth century BCE; the Mahābhārata epic, which was finalized in the Gupta period around 300 CE; and the *Bhāgavata Purāna* and *Matsya Purāna* from around 500 CE. Some scholars speculate that the myth actually came into popular circulation much earlier, since its principal human protagonist, Manu, is mentioned in the *Rig Veda*. The *Rig Veda* was compiled around 1500 BCE and reflects materials that date back still further into Indian prehistory.

There are variations in all of these retellings of the story. One key difference between versions of the myth has bolstered the argument that it is in fact a very ancient tale. In some variants of the story, the giant fish Matsya is revealed to be Visnu, the world preserver. In others, he is identified with Brahmā, the world creator. This may indicate that there was an older version of the myth in which the supernatural fish was not identified with a god, and that the detail that Matsya is a manifestation of either Brahmā or Visnu—specifically the first avatar of Visnu—was added much later.

Though the story's history is not fully understood, it is clearly very important to the overall body of Hindu mythology. In Hindu cosmology, time is circular rather than linear. Worlds are created and destroyed, then created again, in an endless pattern. One common measurement of mythological time according to the Mahābhārata and later texts is an eon, called a *kalpa*. This is stated to be a day in the life of Brahmā, or equivalent to 4.32 billion years.

One kalpa is divided into fourteen *manvantaras*, or ages of Manu. In each manvantara, the world is repopulated through the heroic efforts of Manu, acting with the assistance of the benevolent giant fish Matsya. Each world eventually becomes corrupt and is destroyed by the great flood, and the manvantara cycle starts over again. The myth of Matsya and the Great Flood is therefore instrumental in shaping the Hindu perception of cosmological time.

The myth's human protagonist, Manu, is considered to be the ancestor of all living people. He is also credited with authoring the *Mānava Dharma Śāstra*, the most important Hindu text outlining laws and duties. As such, Manu is held to be not only the progenitor of humanity, but also of legal order. In each age, and on the advice of Matsya, Manu saves life on earth, regenerates humankind, and gives his descendents the gift of civilization.

Adam Berger, PhD

BIBLIOGRAPHY

Dimmit, Cornelia, and J. A. B. Van Buitenen. *Classical Hindu Mythology*. Philadelphia: Temple UP, 1978. Print.

Johnson, W. J. *Dictionary of Hinduism*. Oxford: Oxford UP, 2009. Print.

Jones, Constance, and James D. Ryan. *Encyclopedia of Hinduism*. New York: Infobase, 2007. Print.

Klostermaier, Klaus K. *A Survey of Hinduism*. Albany: State U of New York P, 2007. Print.

Leeming, David A. *The World of Myth*. New York: Oxford UP, 1992. Print.

Saletore, Rajaram Narayan. *Encyclopaedia of Indian Culture*. New Delhi: Sterling, 1983. Print.

Sullivan, Bruce M. *Historical Dictionary of Hinduism*. London: Scarecrow, 1997. Print.

EUROPE

BRITISH ISLES

Beowulf and the Battle with Grendel

Author: Traditional
Time Period: 501 CE–1000 CE
Country or Culture: England
Genre: Legend

PLOT SUMMARY

In the anonymous Anglo-Saxon epic that bears his name, the Geat warrior Beowulf (who hails from a Scandinavian land) faces and vanquishes three monsters: Grendel, Grendel's mother, and a dragon. The most famous and influential of these battles is the first, during which Beowulf mortally wounds the murderous creature known as Grendel in Heorot (Herot), the hall of the Danish king Hroðgar (Hrothgar). Until the arrival of Beowulf and his companions, Heorot has lain empty because of Grendel's predations on the Danes. Beowulf, a famed monster-slayer, crosses the sea with the Geats in order to rid Hroðgar's realm of the demonic creature.

The episode opens with Grendel journeying from his home in the swamps far from Heorot. The monster has

traveled this route many times in the past and always with the same result of brutally murdering Hroðgar's men and terrorizing the Danes. This night will end differently, however, for the men asleep in Heorot are not Danes, but Geats accompanied by the watchful Beowulf.

Grendel silently and swiftly sneaks across the empty moors to Heorot only to rip the doors of the great hall from their hinges. When he assails his first victim, the monster rips the man apart, chews him up, drinks his blood, and gobbles his remains. Eerily, Grendel's destructive entrance and violent attack do not seem to disturb the men sleeping in Heorot. The only one aware of his presence is Beowulf, who witnesses the murder of his companion but does not intervene. Only when the monster reaches for the great warrior lying on the floor does Beowulf respond.

Earlier in the epic, Beowulf vows to Hroðgar and the Danes that he will fight the monster unarmed. He reasons that Grendel fears no man and bears no weapon, and so must be dealt with in kind. True to his word, Beowulf seizes the monster's grasping claw in his bare hands. Shocked and suddenly filled with fear because he has "met a man whose hands were harder" (line 753),

Grendel attempts to flee the warrior's grip. Beowulf stands up in order to get a surer grasp on the monster, break his claws, and kill him. The intensity of their struggle and the monster's frantic shrieks shake Heorot to its shingles, terrifying the Danes.

As Grendel's moaning becomes louder and his attempts to escape become more desperate, Beowulf's companions wake and try to join the fray. Strapping on shields and drawing blades, they discover their weapons have been enchanted by the monster: "that sin-stained demon / Had bewitched all men's weapons, laid spells / That blunted every mortal man's blade" (lines 803–5). Despite his sorcery, Grendel is no match for Beowulf's power. For the first and last time, the monster realizes that his mortal foe is filled with divine strength and that he is being punished by God through Beowulf's deeds. Even so, the creature manages to pull himself from the warrior's clasp, tearing his arm from his body. He escapes back to his swamp and dies of his wounds.

Beowulf hangs the dismembered limb from Heorot's rafters. On the morning after the battle, warriors from many lands converge on Hroðgar's hall to see the monstrous claw and to track Grendel's bloody footprints to the edges of his swamp. They marvel at the gore he leaves behind and rejoice at his doom.

SIGNIFICANCE

Beowulf is an epic poem written in England sometime between the eighth and eleventh centuries CE. It was composed in the Old English language commonly referred to as Anglo-Saxon, a Germanic predecessor to the modern English language. Its author remains unknown. Though English in origin, the work describes events occurring in Scandinavia and conveys values characteristic of the Scandinavian groups that invaded the British Isles in the early years of the Common Era.

One of the decidedly Anglo-Saxon themes running throughout *Beowulf* is individuality as an indication of one's superiority or wretchedness. In the battle between the warrior and Grendel, both characters are described as singular examples of mortal beings. The distinction between them is that Beowulf is a civilized man who lives and acts to preserve the common good of others who share a commitment to social order. Grendel, on the other hand, is profoundly isolated both by his gruesome deeds and by his lineage as a descendent of Cain, the first murderer in human history according to the Judeo-Christian Bible.

Grendel is one of the most compelling characters in comparative literature. The monster is described throughout *Beowulf* in language that conveys violence and cruelty. Grendel's bloodthirsty nature results from his status as creature that even God hates. In this passage, for example, Grendel is "snarling and fierce" (line 725). He is "forever joyless" and moves "angrily" (720, 723) while "hoping to kill (712)." The sight of warriors vulnerable and helpless as they sleep in Hroðgar's hall makes him "hot / With the thought of food and the feasting his belly / Would soon know" (733–35). In addition to the merciless and animalistic language used to describe the monster, the poem further emphasizes his separateness from humans by identifying his lair as a place far from Heorot, a "miserable hole at the bottom of the marsh" isolated even from the air breathed by men and other earthly creatures.

In contrast, Beowulf possesses social and political status among other men. Though a great warrior, he does not lead his people. Rather, he remains "Higlac's brave follower" (line 813). Even so, Beowulf is a "mighty protector of men" (790) whose defeat of Grendel grants him "new glory" (819) precisely because he fulfills his promise to another tribe: "the Danes / Had been served as he'd boasted he'd serve them" (828–29). The language of hierarchy and service underscores the idea that Beowulf, though an exemplary fighter, still belongs to a larger community bound by oaths and other shared expectations that recognizes the preserving power of sacrifice.

Beowulf's deference to these ideas is so complete that he fights Grendel without weapons, relying instead on the righteousness of his cause to lead him to victory. Some scholars claim that the overtly Christian allusions and ideas evident in *Beowulf*, such as the references to hell and an almighty being watching over human affairs, are later additions to the original poem. Readers must decide for themselves whether these additions reinforce or undermine the depiction of Beowulf's excellences.

G. Matthews, MA

BIBLIOGRAPHY

Benson, Larry. "The Originality of *Beowulf*." *The Interpretation of Narrative*. Cambridge: Harvard UP, 1970. 1–44. Print.

Irving, Edward B., Jr. "Christian and Pagan Elements." *A Beowulf Handbook*. Ed. Robert E. Bjork and John D. Niles. Lincoln: U of Nebraska P, 1998. 175–92. Print.

Niles, John D. "Beowulf's Great Hall." *History Today* 56.10 (2006): 40–44. Print.

Raffel, Burton, trans. *Beowulf.* New York: New Amer. Lib., 1963. Print.

Tolkien, J. R. R. "Beowulf: The Monsters and the Critics." *Proceedings of the British Academy* 22 (1936): 245–95. Print.

The Birth of Bran

Author: James Stephens
Time Period: 999 BCE–1 BCE; 1 CE–500 CE
Country or Culture: Ireland
Genre: Folktale

PLOT SUMMARY

This tale from the vast and ancient Fenian cycle describes the birth of Fionn mac Cumhaill's beloved hounds. Fionn is a powerful chieftain who rules over the Fianna, a federation of Celtic clans.

Fionn's mother and aunt, Muirne and Tuiren (Uirne), pay him a visit. Tuiren's beauty inspires such admiration in the men of the Fianna that they long only to gaze upon her. Despite their adoration, Fionn's aunt agrees to marry Iollan Eachtach, a man from neighboring Ulster. Before Fionn will consent to this match, though, he makes the Ulsterman agree to a single condition: if ever Tuiren is unhappy, then Iollan must send her back to the Fianna or lose his life. Tuiren is given away by one of Fionn's clansmen, Lugaidh, who is also in love with her.

Iollan takes Tuiren to live among his people in Ulster. Iollan's former lover, Uct Dealv, learns of his marriage. Uct Dealv is one of the Shí, or fairy people. Enraged by Iollan's betrayal, she magically transforms herself to look like one of Fionn's messengers. Thus disguised, the Shí woman approaches Iollan claiming to bear a message for Tuiren.

Leading Tuiren away from Ulster, Uct Dealv strikes her with a magic hazel stick. Tuiren assumes the form of a terrified, quivering hound. The Shí woman fastens a chain around the dog's neck and drags her westward. As they travel, Uct Dealv chastises Tuiren for being a usurper and sweetheart thief, and promises to make miserable her remaining days by taking her to Fergus Fionnliath, a man notorious for his hatred of all dogs.

Once at his doorstep, Uct Dealv declares that the pathetic hound belongs to Fionn, who demands that Fergus take care of the dog until the Fianna chief arrives to reclaim her. Fergus orders his servant to comfort the shivering hound. The servant fails, and Fergus, who fears Fionn's wrath should he discover his dog unhappy and ill, himself takes charge of the poor beast. Fergus hugs and kisses the hound to stop her shivering, and man and dog grow to love one another.

Eventually, Fionn learns that his aunt no longer resides in Ulster. He demands her return or Iollan's head. The Ulsterman, suspecting that his former lover had a hand in his bride's disappearance, confronts Uct Dealv. She admits to abducting Tuiren and agrees to return her to Fionn only if Iollan consents to be her lover. He accepts and Tuiren is transformed back into her womanly form. She returns to the Fianna with the pups born to her when she was a hound, Bran and Sceólan, and marries Lugaidh, her true love.

Fergus Fionnliath, heartsick at the loss of his beloved canine companion, spends the next year in bed. Fionn's gift of a new puppy restores him.

SIGNIFICANCE

James Stephens was an Irish writer from Dublin whose major published work appeared in the first half of the twentieth century. His books were notable for their deep immersion in Irish folklore and mythology. Some, such as *The Crock of Gold* (1912), synthesized Irish themes and lore with contemporary life. Others, such as *Irish Fairy Tales* (1923), which includes "The Birth of Bran," were retellings of well-known Irish stories, specifically the first half of the Fenian cycle of tales. Scottish and Manx versions of these stories also exist.

Stephens wrote during an era of intensified European and American interest in Irish culture, especially Irish language, music, literature, and drama. This renewed attention to native Irish arts grew out of wider exposure to the cause for Irish independence and people's identification with Irish heritage. Many Irish writers, like Stephens, explored the relevance of Irish and, more broadly, Celtic interests to contemporary life.

"The Birth of Bran" exhibits the hallmarks of Stephens's elliptical narrative style. He was renowned for writing stories that seemed to meander and stray from an expected plot, and this tale demonstrates this quality. For example, though the title refers to the birth of the legendary hound Bran, the heart of the story is the idea of transformation, both physical and emotional; Bran and Sceólan's birth is only mentioned in passing.

Transformation is a persistent theme in Celtic lore and often serves as a punishment for mortals who offend the magical fairy people. Stephens evokes this tradition and elaborates on it in "The Birth of Bran." While the Shí Uct Dealv magically transforms Fionn's aunt Tuiren into a hound, Fergus Fionnliath's hatred of dogs is transformed into love by the affection that develops between him and the queenly dog. In Stephens's version of this myth, transformation results in both debasement as well as personal growth.

Stephens also uses this story to show that animals and people are bound by more than utility or codependence. Rather, as the relationship between Fionn, Bran, and Sceólan suggests, the affinity between them is familial and essential. Fergus Fionnliath's change of heart toward the hound Tuiren dramatically emphasizes this point because the former dog-hater becomes ill when the queen changes back into a woman and leaves him.

Ultimately, Stephens uses the relationship between dogs and men to make a point about loyalty. The Ulsterman Iollan exhibits the changeable nature of the human heart when he turns his back on Uct Dealv to marry the beautiful Tuiren. Ironically, it is the mercurial and temperamental Shí who teaches the mortal about romantic constancy. In addition, it is out of loyalty to Fionn that Fergus comforts the quivering dog, and in so doing, he undergoes a profound change of heart.

The introduction of Bran and Sceólan to the larger narrative of Stephens's *Irish Fairy Tales* marks a turning point in the plot. As indicated in "The Birth of Bran," these hounds are loyal as dogs but are also as intelligent as human beings, and they play crucial roles in Fionn's courtship of his bride Saeve and in the upbringing of their son, the poet Oisín.

G. Matthews, MA

BIBLIOGRAPHY

Bramsbäck, Birgit. *James Stephens: A Literary and Bibliographical Study*. 1959. Cambridge: Harvard UP, 1977. Print.

Carrassi, Vito. *The Irish Fairy Tale: A Narrative Tradition from the Middle Ages to Yeats and Stephens*. Lanham: John Cabot UP, 2012. Print.

Martin, Augustine. *James Stephens: A Critical Study*. Totowa: Rowman, 1977. Print.

Reinhard, John R., and Vernam E. Hull. "Bran and Sceolang." *Speculum* 11.1 (1936): 42–58. Print.

Richardson, H. D. "The Irish Wolf-Dog." *Irish Penny Journal* 1.45 (1841): 353–55. Print.

Stephens, James. "The Birth of Bran." *Irish Fairy Tales*. New York: Macmillan, 1923. 102–21. Print.

---. Introduction. *The Return of the Hero*. By Darrell Figgis. New York: Boni, 1930. ix–xv. Print.

◆ Childe Rowland

Author: Joseph Jacobs
Time Period: 1851 CE–1900 CE
Country or Culture: England
Genre: Folktale

PLOT SUMMARY

Childe Rowland, Burd Ellen, and their two brothers play ball outside of a church. As they run back and forth, Childe Rowland kicks the ball so hard that it flies over the building and Burd Ellen goes racing off to fetch it. When their sister fails to return, the brothers go searching for her, but Burd Ellen is nowhere to be found.

Not knowing what to do, the eldest brother seeks advice from the warlock Merlin. The old man tells him that the sister must have run around the church "widdershins"—that is, in the opposite direction of the sun. If she did this, he explains, the king of Elfland would have been able to abduct her and hold her captive in the Dark Tower. Merlin then tells the eldest brother that it is possible to save Ellen, but only if the brother is able to follow very specific rules while in Elfland. The brother understands that he is risking his life but agrees to learn the rules and takes off in search of his sister.

Days pass, and when the eldest brother does not return, the middle brother likewise seeks the advice of Merlin. He is given the same instructions and disappears in search of his siblings, also failing to return.

When Childe Rowland decides that it is up to him to save all three siblings, his mother, the queen, at first refuses, scared of having no children left. Eventually, however, Childe Rowland convinces her and seeks out the advice of the warlock Merlin, who tells him that he must obey two very simple rules. First, he must chop off the head of anyone he meets on the way to save Burd Ellen; second, he must abstain from eating any food or drinking liquid while in Elfland. To help him with this, the queen gives Childe Rowland his father's sword, giving it her blessing to ensure it will always strike true.

Childe Rowland then marches into the land of the fairies. There, he encounters three people—a horse-herd, a cowherd, and a hen-wife— chopping the heads off of all three after asking them for further directions. The hen-wife teaches him the spell to enter the Dark Tower, which he performs successfully.

In the twilight of the Dark Tower, Childe Rowland sees precious stones and ornate decorations hanging from the ceiling as his sister, Burd Ellen, combs her hair among the jewels. She tells him that the eldest and middle brothers had made it to the Dark Tower, but the king of Elfland cast a spell on them and they now lie in a deathlike sleep. Childe Rowland tells Burd Ellen that he is hungry from his journey, and while she wants to warn him not to eat, a spell makes her fetch him rich bread and milk without saying a word. Just as he is about to feast, however, he remembers Merlin's advice and throws the food to the ground.

At that moment, the king of Elfland enters and threatens to kill Childe Rowland. The boy draws the sword that is enchanted with his mother's blessing and battles the king, bringing him to his knees. Childe Rowland then demands that the king release him and his siblings, and after a few incantations are spoken, the four children are able to leave the Dark Tower, returning safely home once again.

SIGNIFICANCE

The version of "Childe Rowland" that remains the most popular today is as Joseph Jacobs told it in 1892. Earlier versions had been popular for centuries, with Scottish ballads of the fairy tale existing in oral histories and elements of the narrative inspiring playwright William Shakespeare. It was Jacobs, however, who compiled these variations together, providing a somewhat definitive narrative.

Jacobs also provided some commentary on the fairy tale. In his understanding, the roots of "Childe Rowland" reflect wars in prehistoric England. From the perspective of the queen's children, the king of Elfland represented a foreign army who raided their land and stole a young woman to become a bride (in essence, a slave) in the Dark Tower. Jacobs further suggests that the fairy tale is rooted at the historical moment when popular paganism fell under the rising influence of

Christianity, so that the fairies of Elfland represent the "threat" of paganism in the face of the new monotheistic religion.

Viewed through this lens, "Childe Rowland" is as much about the enduring power of the family as it is about the danger of foreign influences. The darkest elements of the narrative—the intention to make the young Burd Ellen a slave wife, for instance—are obscured by the inclusion of the mystical details, such as the magical nature of the Dark Tower and the superstitious disappearance that results from walking around a church "widdershins." These supernatural elements both reference the pagan religions that Jacobs sources into the fairy tale while also making the story friendlier to children (even if the grotesque violence of beheadings remains). The elements also highlight the power of the family, masculinity, and Christianity; it is the mother's blessing on the father's sword that allows Childe Rowland to defeat the king of Elfland, for instance, and an improper engagement with a religious building (the widdershins walk) that initiates all the problems. When considered in historical context, these themes are reflected on an even more basic level, with the political violence and tribal warfare of prehistoric England making tight family bonds and a firm sense of local community necessary for small groups of people to survive.

In this sense, the character of Childe Rowland is ultimately one of great hope. The youngest child—the weakest and least experienced in the world—is able to defeat the powerful magic of the king of Elfland and save the future of his family. While the xenophobic fear of outsiders and different spiritual beliefs is rooted in the past, the hope that our loved ones will protect us remains today, and it is in that hope that "Childe Rowland" has continued to earn its audience.

T. Fleischmann, MFA

BIBLIOGRAPHY

Bily, Cynthia A. "Joseph Jacobs." *Guide to Literary Masters & Their Works* (2007): 1. *Literary Reference Center.* Web. 10 May 2013.

"English Fairy Tales." *Literary World* 21 (1890): 439. Print.

Jacobs, Joseph. "Childe Rowland." *English Fairy Tales.* London: Nutt, 1890. 117–24. Print.

Shah, Idries. *World Tales.* London: Octagon, 1991. Print.

Tatar, Maria. Introduction. *The Classic Fairy Tales.* New York: Norton, 1999. ix–xviii. Print.

◆ The Combat of Fer Díad and Cúchulainn

Author: Traditional Celtic
Time Period: 999 BCE–1 BCE; 1 CE–500 CE
Country or Culture: Ireland
Genre: Legend

PLOT SUMMARY

The queen of Connacht, Medb, wants to steal the famed brown bull of Cúailnge (Cooley), which is being guarded by the warrior Cúchulainn (also spelled Cuchulain) of Ulster. She decides to send Cúchulainn's friend and foster brother, Fer Díad (Ferdiad), to do battle with him. Cúchulainn has thus far slain every warrior sent to battle him in defense of the bull, but Fer Díad and Cúchulainn trained together and are seen as an equal match in combat. When Fer Díad refuses to fight Cúchulainn, Medb sends men to taunt Fer Díad and shame him into going into battle.

In order to defend his honor, Fer Díad goes to Medb's camp, where he is given strong liquor until he is drunk. Medb promises him great rewards, including her own daughter to wed, if he defeats Cúchulainn. She lies to him and says that Cúchulainn has heard of Fer Díad's challenge and welcomes the opportunity to slay him. Although he does not believe her, Fer Díad finally agrees to fight Cúchulainn. Fergus, the former king of Ulster, overhears and goes to warn Cúchulainn that Fer Díad will be coming the next day to offer battle. Cúchulainn is disheartened to hear that his comrade wishes to fight him, but he knows he has to continue defending the brown bull of Cúailnge, even if it means killing his dear friend.

That night, Fer Díad has a fitful sleep and awakes early to prepare for his travel to the ford where he will battle Cúchulainn. His charioteer, Id, readies the horses and weapons, and Cúchulainn's charioteer, Láeg, does the same. When the men meet for battle at the ford, Fer Díad calls out to Cúchulainn, asking him what brought him out to fight. He reminds Cúchulainn that during their training, he was always the inferior warrior. Cúchulainn tries to talk Fer Díad out of the fight, saying that they were once brothers and Medb is only using him as a pawn. Still, Fer Díad insists that they fight.

The men fight for three days, taking breaks at night to rest and heal their wounds. On the first two nights, they share a fire and display much camaraderie. After the third day of fighting, in which they fight with heavy shields and swords, the men sleep in separate camps.

Fer Díad awakes the fourth day knowing it will be the decisive day of combat. He dresses himself in his heaviest armor, including an iron kilt with heavy shielding around the midsection. Fer Díad fears that today Cúchulainn will use the dreaded *gáe bulga*, a spear that is thrown using the foot and ejects numerous barbs after piercing a person's body. This weapon was used by Cúchulainn to kill many of his enemies. Cúchulainn sees Fer Díad practicing for battle and tells Láeg to ready the *gáe bulga*.

During the battle, Fer Díad gains the upper hand several times. After he seriously wounds Cúchulainn, two invisible spirits named Indolb and Dolb come to Cúchulainn's aid. Once Fer Díad realizes the spirits are there, he becomes furious and kills them both. Cúchulainn calls for Láeg to prepare the *gáe bulga*, which he sends downstream to him. Fer Díad tries to shield himself from the deadly spear, but Cúchulainn sends it with all of his might. The *gáe bulga* pierces the iron kilt, shatters Fer Díad's shield, and enters his stomach, spreading the barbs throughout his body.

As he lies dying, Fer Díad accuses Cúchulainn of an unfair battle. Cúchulainn carries Fer Díad to the north side of the ford so that he will die advancing in combat, not retreating. There, Cúchulainn sings laments to his comrade and foster brother.

SIGNIFICANCE

It is important to examine the legend of the combat of Fer Díad and Cúchulainn in the context of the Ulster cycle of Irish mythology. The Ulster cycle is an epic series of legends, traditionally set in Northern Ireland around the time of Jesus Christ, that focus on the Ulaid tribe, headed by King Conchobar, and its conflict with the rival Connachta tribe, led by Queen Medb. One of the central stories of the Ulster cycle is the *Táin Bó Cúailnge*, widely known as *The Cattle Raid of Cooley*. Cattle were a main source of currency during this time, and in this story, Queen Medb is determined to steal Conchobar's treasured bull. Cattle and bulls are also symbols of fertility in Celtic mythology, so by stealing Conchobar's bull, Medb would also be taking away from his tribe's vigor.

Much of the Ulster cycle was compiled during the time when pagan Ireland was transitioning to its Christian period, and the legends contain a considerable amount of mythological content, such as the invisible spirits that aid Cúchulainn and the great bull of Ulster. Because of a curse put upon the men of Ulster, where the Ulaid reside, the seventeen-year-old Cúchulainn is the only warrior able to resist the armies sent by Medb.

The story of the combat of Fer Díad and Cúchulainn marks the climax of *The Cattle Raid of Cooley*.

Cúchulainn is one of the most important figures in Irish mythology and the central character of the Ulster cycle. He is the son of the god Lugh and possesses superhuman strength. In most legends, Cúchulainn is born with seven fingers on each hand, seven toes on each foot, and seven pupils in each eye. He is celebrated for his extraordinary deeds and battle prowess at a young age. One of the most well-known aspects of his legend is his berserker rage, during which his body takes on a monstrous appearance and his violent anger becomes uncontrollable. In *The Cattle Raid of Cooley*, the exiled former king Fergus recounts to Medb many of Cúchulainn's heroic exploits.

In Irish culture, Cúchulainn is used as an archetype of good character and honorable traits. He appears frequently in works of art, music, and literature. During the height of the troubles in Ireland, both the Irish nationalists and Ulster unionists used him as a symbol of their movements. He was used frequently as a character by Irish author and poet William Butler Yeats. Critics believe that Yeats used the legends of Cúchulainn as a theme to reflect the plight of Irish people at the time and to inspire hope in them.

Patrick G. Cooper

BIBLIOGRAPHY

Gantz, Jeffrey. *Early Irish Myths and Sagas*. New York: Penguin, 1982. Print.

Joe, Jimmy. "Ulaid Cycle." *Timeless Myths*. Timeless Myths, 24 June 2006. Web. 7 May 2013.

Kinsella, Thomas, trans. *The Táin: Translated from the Irish Epic Táin Bó Cuailnge*. Oxford: Oxford UP, 2002. Print.

Mountain, Harry. *The Celtic Encyclopedia*. Vol. 3. Boca Raton: Universal, 1998. Print.

◆ Culhwch and Olwen: Hunting the Twrch Trwyth

Author: Traditional
Time Period: 1001 CE–1500 CE
Country or Culture: Wales
Genre: Legend

PLOT SUMMARY

When Culhwch declines to marry his stepsister, his stepmother curses him so that the only woman he can marry is Olwen, the daughter of Ysbaddaden, king of the giants. Ysbaddaden is fated to die when his daughter marries, so to prevent this, he declares that Culhwch must first complete forty tasks. The greatest and potentially most dangerous of these tasks is acquiring the razor, comb, and shears that the Twrch Trwyth, a former king who has been transformed into a boar, keeps between his ears. Only with these legendary implements can Ysbaddaden's hair and beard be groomed.

Half of Ysbaddaden's forty challenges to Culhwch relate in some way to the hunt for the Twrch Trwyth, and many of these mention the monstrous boar by name. Most of the tasks associated with the boar hunt address the people, animals, and equipment the hopeful groom will require to undertake the hunt in the first place, and the most significant among them is procuring the assistance of King Arthur and his huntsmen. As Arthur is Culhwch's cousin, Culhwch is easily able to enlist his aid. Once allied with Culhwch, Arthur and his men take over the hunt for the Twrch Trwyth and all the challenges related to it.

Arthur and his knights criss-cross kingdoms in Ireland, Wales, England, France, and Brittany to secure the aid of several heroes Ysbaddaden has identified as necessary partners in the boar hunt. Some of these men have access to mysterious objects needed for the hunt; for instance, the Irish king Odgar appeals to his steward Diwrnach to give up a magical cauldron. Others possess magical abilities, such as the shape-shifter and interpreter Gwrhyr, who can assume the shape of a bird and speak the boar language of the Twrch Trwyth's brood. With Arthur's retinue assembled, the hunt begins in Ireland, where the Twrch Trwyth and his seven children live.

Arthur's men pursue the Twrch Trwyth and his brood for two days. They are unsuccessful, and the boar devastates the Irish countryside. Arthur himself pursues the Twrch Trwyth for nine days and nights but kills only one piglet. The king sends Gwrhyr to parley with the boars. The Twrch Trwyth's son Grugyn Silver-Bristle refuses their terms and declares that his father will only part with the razor, comb, and scissors between his ears upon his death. The boars then swim across the sea to lay waste to Arthur's own lands in Wales.

Once in Wales, the boars and Arthur's men wage war across the landscape. After both sides suffer devastating losses, the huntsmen overtake the Twrch Trwyth in Wales at the mouth of the Severn River. Driving the boar into the river, Arthur's men retrieve the razors and scissors from between his ears, but the Twrch Trwyth escapes before they can get the comb. Arthur finally corners the beast in Cornwall and takes the comb. Driven into the sea by two monstrous hounds, the Twrch Trwyth disappears. His whereabouts remain unknown.

SIGNIFICANCE

The legend of Culhwch and Olwen is one of eleven stories included in a collection of Welsh myths and folktales commonly referred to as the *Mabinogion*. While scholars agree that this collection was gathered during the fourteenth and fifteenth centuries, the legend of Culhwch and Olwen was probably composed around the eleventh century, as references to some of the events and characters described in it appear in other Welsh works predating the arrangement of the *Mabinogion*.

The Culhwch and Olwen tale is a unique contribution to Arthurian literature for several reasons. First, it is of Welsh origin and so locates Arthur's life and exploits in specifically Welsh contexts, especially in terms of landscapes and medieval tribal customs. Along these lines, it is also an extraordinary example of an onomastic tale, in which names of people and places are cited in order to imbue with a special significance the real locations in which these epic events are said to have occurred. For example, in the episode described here, in which Arthur and his men hunt for the Twrch Trwyth, the names of Arthur's companions, the boar's children, the lands they traverse, and the places where they wage war are recorded in detail. As a result, real places in Ireland and Wales assume mythical importance and lend historical credibility to the astonishing events set in these locales.

The story of the hunting of the Twrch Trwyth contains very old mythical themes that resonate in multiple folklore traditions and that can be traced in subsequent literary works, such as *Sir Gawain and the Green Knight* (late fourteenth century) and *Moby-Dick* (1851). The idea that the chief giant Ysbaddaden must die before Olwen and Culhwch can marry calls to mind the mechanism of divine succession in Greek mythology, wherein the Olympian deities overthrow the Titans and so establish a new order. Ysbaddaden does not willingly embrace death; he refuses to accept that Culhwch's marriage to Olwen is preordained. The apparent impossibility of the deeds demanded of the hero by the giant

underscore Ysbaddaden's refusal to accept fate, Culhwch and Olwen's as well as his own.

The hunt for the Twrch Trwyth corresponds to Ysbaddaden's refusal of Culhwch in the sense that the boar and the giant king both possess something necessary to initiate great change in the world. Ysbaddaden has his daughter Olwen, while the Twrch Trwyth possesses the implements that Arthur's men will use to vanquish the giant. Likewise, as his son Grugyn Silver-Bristle makes clear, the great boar will only give up the razor, scissors, and comb upon his death. It is unclear why these monstrous beings must die in order for change to occur, though readers may speculate that their deaths prepare the way for a new kind of power structure based on civilized kinship rather than brutality. After all, earlier in the tale, Ysbaddaden greets Arthur's men by throwing spears at them, and the Twrch Trwyth was a human king before God transformed him into a boar on account of his sins.

G. Matthews, MA

BIBLIOGRAPHY

Bromwich, Rachel, and D. Simon Evans, eds. *Culhwch and Olwen: An Edition and Study of the Oldest Arthurian Tale*. Cardiff: U of Wales P, 1992. Print.

Jones, Gwyn. *Kings, Beasts and Heroes*. London: Oxford UP, 1972. Print.

Jones, Gwyn, and Thomas Jones, trans. *The Mabinogion*. Rev. ed. London: Dent, 1974. Print.

Sheehan, Sarah. "Giants, Boar-Hunts, and Barbering: Masculinity in *Culhwch ac Olwen*." *Arthuriana* 15.3 (2005): 3–25. Print.

Wilson, Anne. *The Magical Quest: The Use of Magic in Arthurian Romance*. Manchester: Manchester UP, 1988. Print.

◆ The Death of King Arthur

Author: Sir Thomas Malory
Time Period: 1001 CE–1500 CE
Country or Culture: England
Genre: Legend

PLOT SUMMARY

Written between 1469 and 1470, Sir Thomas Malory's *Le Morte D'Arthur* is the best-known and most influential version of the Arthurian legend. The entirety of the work traces the legend from before Arthur's birth through the downfall of the once-famous king and his Knights of the Round Table.

The story of the death of Arthur begins with Sir Mordred and Sir Agravain stirring up dissonance between King Arthur and Sir Lancelot (sometimes spelled Launcelot). The two knights attempt to sway Sir Gaheris, Sir Gareth, and Sir Gawain (Gawaine), three of Arthur and Lancelot's most honorable followers, to reveal an inappropriate relationship between Lancelot and Queen Guinevere (Guenever or Guenevere). Gaheris and Gareth refuse to interfere, citing loyalty to both the king and his strongest knight, while Gawain's attempts to dissuade them fail. Mordred and Agravain convince Arthur to test Lancelot's and his wife's fidelity. Lancelot is warned, but believing in his own innocence, he meets Guinevere alone. When Arthur's enemies break in on Lancelot and Guinevere, Lancelot trounces them and kills all except Mordred. This attack splits the Knights of the Round Table into two warring groups: those who support Arthur and Mordred and those who support Lancelot.

Arthur feels that he must burn the queen at the stake for treason, as her presumed adultery might produce an heir to the throne who is not the king's progeny. While Gawain refuses to be a part of the execution, Lancelot sweeps in and rescues Guinevere, taking her to a safe hiding place. Lancelot's rescue mission leads to the deaths of many more of Arthur's knights. Gaheris and Gareth, unarmed and hidden in the crowd, are among the casualties. Though Guinevere is saved, the kingdom is torn apart.

Arthur's grief at the deaths of his knights is devastating. He cries, "And much more am I sorrier for my good knights' loss than for the loss of my fair queen" (481). Gawain's woe is even stronger, and he vows to revenge the deaths of his brothers. Lancelot and Arthur begin to recruit armies to fight against each other, and shortly after, war commences. Eventually, Lancelot goes to Arthur and swears that he has never betrayed the king with a physical relationship with Guinevere. The war becomes one that seeks to defend Lancelot's honor more than Guinevere's, with Gawain fighting more staunchly than Arthur, who has lost his heart for the battle.

The war continues until the pope orders Arthur to take Guinevere back into his good graces. He does this, but Lancelot is exiled from the kingdom. Lancelot leaves for France, taking one hundred knights with

him. The banishment does not cure Gawain's desire for vengeance, however, and Lancelot is attacked in France. The battles continue back and forth until Gawain and Lancelot meet on the field, and Gawain is sorely injured.

While Arthur is occupied fighting with Lancelot, Mordred has taken over Arthur's kingdom, spread rumors of his death, and attempted to force Guinevere to marry him. Arthur and Gawain return home to overcome Mordred, but Gawain, who has not fully recovered from the injuries Lancelot gave him, succumbs to further physical distress. On his deathbed, he writes Lancelot, asking the noble knight to seek out his tomb and requesting his assistance in Arthur's conflict with Mordred.

Mordred and Arthur almost reach a truce, but a last battle ensues. King Arthur overcomes Mordred, but he is mortally injured as well. Knowing he is near the end, Arthur asks to be placed on a barge that will sail to Avalon (Avilion). Malory concludes his story with the likelihood that the female mourners on the barge bury Arthur's body at a hermitage chapel; other versions of the legend leave open the possibility of Arthur's return to glory.

SIGNIFICANCE

Malory's Arthurian tale is one of the first recorded British versions, and it is based on earlier French and English poetic and prose sources. The depressing tone of the story may be the main reason Malory chose this format, since early tragic pieces tended to be prose. The numerous reprintings of Malory's novel in the two centuries following its initial publication kept more attention on this work than on the many earlier versions. In part because of this, Malory's work became the main influence on later versions of the tale after receiving renewed attention in the nineteenth century.

The final chapter of Malory's work tells the story of Arthur's death, which is the culmination of the broken fellowship between Arthur's knights. The internal struggles are evidenced at the beginning of the chapter as Agravain and Mordred try to stir trouble between Arthur and Lancelot, effectively causing problems between Gawain and his brothers as well. The dissenting groups go their own ways, and Mordred and Agravain seek out the king to plant the seeds of distrust.

Cracks continue to fissure the Round Table when Lancelot kills thirteen knights, including Agravain, in his escape from Guinevere's chambers. Arthur commands

Gawain, Gaheris, and Gareth to aid him in the execution of his queen, but all three, torn in loyalty between their king and his most honorable knight, ask to be excused. Lancelot's rescue of the queen, which includes the brief fight that leaves Gareth and Gaheris dead, leads to Arthur's grief-stricken plea: "For now have I lost the fairest fellowship of noble knights that ever Christian king held together. Alas, my good knights be slain and gone away from me, that now within these two days I have lost nigh forty knights, and also the noble fellowship of Sir Lancelot and his blood; for now may I never more hold them together" (481).

The deaths of Gawain's brothers result in the most devastating break in the fellowship. Gawain swears revenge on Lancelot. The ensuing wars between Arthur and Lancelot, in fact, become as much about Gawain's anger as Arthur's need to reestablish his honor. The Round Table is finally truly broken when Gawain and Lancelot battle, leaving Gawain with the wound that will eventually lead to his death.

King Arthur's own gullibility in leaving Mordred as "ruler of all England" (505) is the last fracture in his rule. While Arthur fights Lancelot in a distant land, Mordred has taken over his kingdom, spread rumors of his death, and attempted to marry his wife. The knight who started the discord is the cause of its end, as well as the ends of Gawain and Arthur. Gawain dies after being wounded in battle, but a bright note appears as he writes Lancelot asking for reconciliation. The deaths of Arthur and Mordred at each other's hands complete the rift in the kingdom that Mordred began.

Theresa L. Stowell, PhD

BIBLIOGRAPHY

Johnson, David, and Elaine Treharne. *Readings in Medieval Texts: Interpreting Old and Middle English Literature*. Oxford: Oxford UP, 2005. Print.

Lupack, Alan. *The Oxford Guide to Arthurian Literature and Legend*. Oxford: Oxford UP, 2005. Print.

Malory, Sir Thomas. *Le Morte Darthur*. Ed. Stephen H. A. Shepherd. New York: Norton, 2004. Print.

---. "The Death of Arthur." *Le Morte Darthur: The Winchester Manuscript*. Ed. Helen Cooper. Oxford: Oxford UP, 1998. 468–527. Print.

Philip, Neil. *Myths and Legends Explained*. London: DK, 2007. Print.

◆ The Fisher King

Author: Traditional
Time Period: 1001 CE–1500 CE
Country or Culture: England
Genre: Legend

PLOT SUMMARY

Many versions of the legend of the Holy Grail describe the Grail, or Sangreal, as the cup used by Jesus Christ at the Last Supper. Jesus gives the cup to Joseph of Arimathea, a holy man said to have donated his tomb to Jesus, and Joseph takes the cup to Europe, where it is passed down through the generations and guarded by holy men. For many years, pilgrims are able to observe the Grail, until one of the guardians falters by looking sinfully upon a young woman. He is immediately wounded by the sacred lance of Christ, a wound that cannot be healed. The guardian of the Grail becomes known as Le Roi Pecheur, or the Fisher King (a corruption of Le Roi Pécheur, "the Sinner King"), and both the Fisher King and the Grail vanish from public view.

Later, in the days of King Arthur, the magician Merlin sends the king a message telling him to seek the Grail, as the knight capable of achieving the deed is alive and of the right age. When the Knights of the Round Table gather at the vigil of Pentecost, they suddenly hear "a clap of thunder" and witness "a bright light burst[ing] forth," and "the Holy Gra[il], covered with white samite" (Leeming 119), floats through the hall and then vanishes. Sir Gawain promises to seek the Grail for a year and a day, returning only after he has seen it, and most of the other knights follow suit. Arthur laments the lost fellowship of the hall.

Sir Percival (Perceval), another of Arthur's knights, happens upon a lake where he finds a fisherman who is "richly dressed, but pale and sad" (119). The fisherman directs Percival to an opulent castle, where he is graciously received. In the hall, he finds four hundred "grave and silent" knights, who all rise and bow at his arrival. The master of the castle, who greatly resembles the fisherman, sits by the fire and appears to be ill with "some wasting disease" (120). Percival next witnesses a mysterious procession, as a servant carrying a blood-stained lance; beautiful maidens carrying velvet cushions, a stand, and other items; and Queen Repance, carrying a precious vessel, enter the room. The onlookers whisper that the vessel is the Holy Grail, and Percival stares in astonishment. The procession ends, and a bounty of food and drink is produced from the vessel, but the master eats very little. Though the castle's master and servants both seem to expect something from Percival, they say nothing, and he asks no questions about anything he sees. Percival spends the night at the castle; as he departs the next morning, a voice calls out to curse his failure to perform the good work set before him.

Next, Sir Gawain visits the same castle, and he too witnesses the marvelous procession. However, he recognizes one of the maidens, who once spoke to him about the Grail and requested that if he should ever see her with five other women, he should "fail not to ask what they did there" (121). Gawain watches as three drops of blood fall from the spear into a tray the youths have placed on a table. Unable to contain his wonder, he entreats his host to explain the meaning of "this great company, and these marvels" (122). At this, everyone in the hall immediately jumps up to rejoice. The Fisher King congratulates Gawain; by asking the meaning of what he saw, he has achieved what Percival did not and delivered the people from God's punishment.

SIGNIFICANCE

This version of the story, as retold by David Adams Leeming, is a composite of several other stories, a fact that nicely reflects the Grail story's evolution since it first appeared in northern Europe in the late twelfth century. The story is one of many tales associated with the large body of literature known as Arthurian legend. One early version is *Perceval, the Story of the Grail* by the poet Chrétien de Troyes, but this is not considered the authoritative text because the tale is unfinished and likely existed in prior oral and Celtic sources. Moreover, within fifty years of its emergence in literary form, the story gave rise to numerous and conflicting variants (Bryant 2). Consequently, there is little consensus on what the Grail actually was—it is variously represented as a platter, a cauldron, and a chalice—and which knight achieves the quest. In most versions, either Sir Percival or Sir Galahad is successful; Leeming's version is unusual in casting Gawain as the hero.

There has also been much debate regarding the significance of the Fisher King, and because the Grail story is believed to have both pagan and Christian roots, interpretations of the Fisher King center on the relative influence of those two traditions. In Leeming's composite, the Fisher King is implied to be the Christian heir of the fallen guardian originally wounded by the sacred lance.

This medieval king is thus understood to inherit the wound and must wait for an upstanding knight to heal it. The king also says at the end of Leeming's excerpt that the people of his land have suffered from the fact that they "live, and yet are dead," because God punished them after "one brother smote the other for his land" (122). According to scholar Jessie Weston in her 1920 study *From Ritual to Romance*, the convention of a hero needing to ask the right question to restore an afflicted king and his people derives from pagan fertility rituals. The cup or similar object in these rituals symbolizes the abundance and nourishment that both land and people require to flourish, and the Fisher King is an enchanted leader in need of restoration by a hero. Weston argues that the procession in the story was originally part of a pagan ritual that was eventually incorporated into Christian practice, which then suppressed the original pagan symbols to overlay the story with a new meaning. Many scholars have since followed and built upon Weston's seminal thesis.

Ashleigh Imus, PhD

BIBLIOGRAPHY

Bryant, Nigel. *The Legend of the Grail*. Cambridge: Brewer, 2004. Print.

Leeming, David Adams. *Mythology: The Voyage of the Hero*. 3rd ed. New York: Oxford UP, 1998. Print.

Loomis, Roger Sherman. *The Grail: From Celtic Myth to Christian Symbol*. New York: Columbia UP, 1963. Print.

Umland, Rebecca A., and Samuel J. Umland. *The Use of Arthurian Legend in Hollywood Film: From Connecticut Yankees to Fisher Kings*. Westport: Greenwood, 1996. Print.

Weston, Jessie L. *From Ritual to Romance*. Cambridge: Cambridge UP, 1920. Print.

◆ # Havelok and Godard

Author: Traditional
Time Period: 1001 CE–1500 CE
Country or Culture: England
Genre: Legend

PLOT SUMMARY

A powerful and respected king named Birkabeyn (or Birkabein) rules Denmark. Birkabeyn loves his three children, Swanborow, Elfleda the Fair, and Havelok, his young son and heir to the realm. When death comes for the king, he is terribly upset at the prospect of leaving his three children unprotected and fatherless. Birkabeyn prays to God for wisdom and guidance on how to ensure the children's safety. He decides to entrust the children to a faithful advisor and friend, Jarl Godard.

Birkabeyn instructs Godard to keep his three royal children safe until Havelok is old enough to be knighted and crowned king. Godard takes an oath that he will rule over Denmark and keep the land safe until Havelok comes of age. Shortly after, King Birkabeyn dies, comforted by the belief that Godard will keep his beloved children and country safe. After the king's funeral, Godard assumes rule over Denmark and hides the children away in a castle where they can be kept in secret. But Godard betrays his oath, and the castle becomes a prison for the children.

Godard quickly begins taking action to strip the royal rights of Swanborow, Elfleda, and Havelok. He orders that only a minimum amount of food and clothes be supplied to the imprisoned children, so they will die of starvation and cold. Finding this slow method of death to be taking too long, Godard decides to kill them himself. When he enters the children's room, Havelok throws himself down before Godard and begs for food and clothes. Havelok's pleas have no effect on Godard, who coldly seizes the two girls and cuts their throats.

Havelok is terrified and begs Godard for mercy. He cries that if Godard will let him live, he will flee the kingdom and leave Denmark forever. This sparks some compassion in Godard, but the ruthless man knows he will never be safe as long as Havelok lives. Godard promises riches and freedom to a naïve fisherman named Grim in exchange for secretly taking the boy and throwing him into the sea with an anchor tied around his neck. Grim agrees and binds Havelok with cords, sticks a rag in his mouth, and throws him into a sack. He carries the boy to his cottage, where he tells his wife, Dame Leve, about the agreement he has made with Godard. The promise of riches excites her, and she throws Havelok into a corner, nearly breaking his head.

At midnight, Grim and Dame Leve awake to complete the task. When they enter the room where they had thrown Havelok, they are terrified to see a bright gleam shining around the boy and coming from his mouth. On his right shoulder is a cross of red gold, a symbol of true royalty. They untie Havelok and begin weeping in front of the boy. They plead with Havelok, stating that they will hide him from Godard in return for their lives. Havelok demands food and rest, which the couple provide.

The next morning, Grim steals away to Godard to tell him that the task is complete and that Havelok is dead. When he asks for his reward, Godard laughs in his face and tells him to flee before he has him hanged for the murder of Havelok. Grim returns home and tells his wife about Godard's betrayal. Worried for their safety, they decide to flee Denmark with Havelok and their five children. After selling all of their possessions, they sail for England, where they all arrive safely.

SIGNIFICANCE

The story of Havelok and Godard comes from a larger poetic work commonly titled *Havelok the Dane*, an early Middle English romance. It is considered by many scholars to be part of the Matter of England, the collection of localized English romances in medieval literature. *Havelok the Dane* dates back to between 1280 and 1310 CE and is believed to be a compilation or composite of various Anglo-Norman sources, the earliest of them being Geoffrey Gaimar's *L'estoire des Engleis*, written around 1140 CE.

Havelock the Dane concerns the merging of two kingdoms, Denmark and England. It contains similar dual plots involving kings being betrayed after death and the rightful heir to the throne being dispossessed. In England, the traitor Godrich takes the throne away from Princess Goldeboru (Goldborough or Goldeburgh). This parallels what occurs in the story of Havelok and Godard. Later in the story, Havelok marries Goldeboru and defeats both usurpers, claiming his kingship in Denmark and England. They go on to have over a dozen children, all of whom become kings and queens.

Scholars have noted the ideological way in which the story creates an integrated Anglo-Danish kingdom in the period following the Viking raids. While in reality the Vikings invaded and pillaged England, *Havelok the Dane* provides a revisionist history wherein the union of Havelok and Goldeboru consolidates the two kingdoms. Some argue that this story was meant to reflect the validity of Danish rule over England in the eleventh century. This makes the story relevant to studies of Englishness and a unified English identity.

Some examinations of *Havelok the Dane* have given much attention to his physical body and its role in the narrative. Havelok's body is literally a sign of power and kingship. Light streams from his mouth, and a *kynmerk*, the red, cross-shaped birthmark on his shoulder, display his divinely appointed status. In later parts of the story, Havelok's body, strength, and appetite are described as being much greater than those of ordinary men.

Scholar Donna Crawford goes further, stating that Havelok's body is meant to represent England itself and its vulnerability. This is an example of body politic, a metaphor for hierarchical social entities with the corporate head at the top, or, in this particular case, the king. Throughout the story, connections are made between the perils facing Havelok and their social context. At the end, Havelok is safe, and the lands he comes to rule over are thoroughly incorporated.

Patrick G. Cooper

BIBLIOGRAPHY

Barron, W. R. J. *English Medieval Romance*. London: Longman, 1987. Print.

Crawford, Donna. "The Vulnerable Body of *Havelok the Dane*." *Medieval Forum*. English Dept., San Francisco State U, 2009. Print.

Drake, Graham, Ronald B. Herzman, and Eve Salisbury, eds. *Four Romances of England*. Kalamazoo: Medieval Inst., 1999. Print.

Ebbutt, Maud Isabel. "Havelok the Dane." *Hero-Myths and Legends of the British Race*. London: Harrap, 1910. 73–94. Print.

Kleinman, Scott. "The Legend of Havelok the Dane and the Historiography of East Anglia." *Studies in Philology* 100.3 (2003): 245–77. Print.

Shepherd, Stephen H. A., ed. *Middle English Romances*. New York: Norton, 1994. Print.

◆ King Arthur and Guinevere

Author: Sir Thomas Malory
Time Period: 1001 CE–1500 CE
Country or Culture: England
Genre: Legend

PLOT SUMMARY

Although he is revealed to be Britain's true king through a supernatural test, Arthur is not accepted as sovereign by the barons who served the former ruler, Uther Pendragon. Because Arthur's royal lineage is not yet common knowledge, the lords question his right to the kingship.

Merlin—renowned seer, enchanter, and former adviser to Uther—gains the loyalty of some of the barons by openly affirming Arthur to be Uther's son and rightful heir. Others, however, challenge Arthur's claim to the throne and declare war. Arthur proves himself in battle and gains victory over the rebels, thereby establishing his regal authority and military supremacy. During the early days of his reign—and for most of his life—Arthur depends on Merlin's counsel. Yet in one fatal instance, he goes against the advice of his mentor, which eventually leads to the downfall of his kingdom.

The young king complains to Merlin that the lords and knights under his command are pestering him to marry. Merlin agrees with Arthur's vassals. Now that Arthur is a man of power and property, a wife is necessary for producing an undisputed successor to the throne. When Merlin asks Arthur if he has a woman in mind, the king replies that he has fallen in love with Guinevere (Guenever or Guenevere), the daughter of King Leodegrance of Cameliard (sometimes spelled Lodegreance of Camelard). He also notes that Leodegrance possesses the Round Table that once belonged to Uther. Merlin is dismayed at Arthur's choice of bride. He warns the king that Guinevere is "not wholesome" (50) and prophesies that she will become entangled in a love affair with Lancelot, a chivalric hero who will play a key role in the quest for the Holy Grail. The king, however, has his heart set on Guinevere.

Merlin recognizes the futility of trying to convince Arthur that wedding Guinevere is a mistake. Accepting the inevitable, the seer agrees to act as a matchmaker and sets out to Cameliard with a band of knights to negotiate the marriage agreement with King Leodegrance. Leodegrance is overjoyed at the prospect of his daughter being joined to so powerful a ruler as Arthur and does not hesitate to accept Merlin's proposal of a match. To seal the bargain, he offers a hundred of his knights and the "Table Round" as Guinevere's dowry. Their mission accomplished, Merlin and the king's men ride back to London with Guinevere, the Round Table, and a contingent of Leodegrance's knights.

SIGNIFICANCE

A pivotal event in Arthurian legend, the story of Arthur's marriage to Guinevere was written by Sir Thomas Malory while he was imprisoned in Newgate Prison from 1468 to 1471. A nobleman, courtier, soldier, and adventurer, he was familiar with the three cultural constructs of medieval society that underpin the tale of Arthur and his queen—feudalism, chivalry, and courtly love. Existing from the ninth to fifteenth centuries, feudalism arose from the lack of a centralized government and was characterized by a reciprocal relationship between a lord and his vassal that included military and economic advantages. This relationship was necessary because vulnerable landowners frequently needed the military might overlords could provide to throw off invaders. In return for protection, the vassals would swear an oath of loyalty to the overlord.

The association between Arthur and Leodegrance is an example of a feudalistic relationship, one that dates back to Uther's reign. After Uther's death, Leodegrance remains faithful to Arthur. In return for the loyalty of his father's old friend, Arthur comes to Leodegrance's aid when King Royns of West Britain invades his lands. The past and the present unite as the two warriors rout Ryons's invading force. Arthur's subsequent proposal of marriage to Guinevere further solidifies the alliance between Arthur and the king of Cameliard. In becoming the overlord's father-in-law, Leodegrance ensures that he will hold an influential place in Arthur's court.

Leodegrance's fealty and Guinevere's hand are not the only prizes Arthur attains through his arranged marriage. The fabled Round Table—which had once belonged to Arthur's father and was given to Leodegrance for safekeeping upon Uther's death—is not only a valuable asset in Guinevere's dowry but also destined to become the focal point of Arthur's court. The shape of the table highlights the equality of the members of the prestigious fellowship. All the knights who are privileged to sit at the table take the same chivalric pledge—to protect the weak, honor their fellow knights, serve their lord faithfully, and fear God. The table also serves as a launching point for the men as they leave the court in search of adventure and renown.

The social convention of courtly love is tied to the concept of chivalry. It is defined as a form of idealized love between men and women of the medieval nobility. A knight was expected to perform feats of valor in order to be worthy of the favor of his lady, whom he idealized, elevating her supposed virtues. This attitude is exemplified when Arthur characterizes Guinevere as "the most valiant and fairest" among women, even though he does not know her well (50). Indeed, Arthur's profession of love seems to be based more on necessity (his barons are insisting that he marry) than on a real desire to wed Guinevere. Love, however, is not necessarily the primary reason for the union between Arthur and Guinevere.

Instead, their marriage, agreed upon by Merlin and Leodegrance, amounts to a beneficial political arrangement for both Leodegrance and Arthur. Guinevere has no say in the situation. She is a pawn in a system that is controlled by powerful men. Consequently, she is required to marry a man she respects but does not love. This arrangement has grave consequences when, several years later, Guinevere and Lancelot's relationship, originally built on the ideal of courtly love, seems to cross the line into adultery. Their betrayal of Arthur contributes both to the destruction of his kingdom and to his death.

Pegge Bochynski, MA

BIBLIOGRAPHY

Baines, Keith. *Malory's Le Morte D'Arthur.* New York: New American Lib., 1962. Print.

Davies, Rees. *Lords and Lordships in the British Isles in the Late Middle Ages.* New York: Oxford UP, 2009. Print.

Malory, Sir Thomas. "The Wedding of King Arthur." *Le Morte Darthur: The Winchester Manuscript.* Ed. Helen Cooper. Oxford: Oxford UP, 1998. 50–57. Print.

Norris, J. Lacy, ed. *The Arthurian Encyclopedia.* New York: Bedrick, 1986. Print.

Wollock, Jennifer G. *Rethinking Chivalry and Courtly Love.* Santa Barbara: Praeger, 2011. Print.

◆ King Arthur's Round Table

Author: Traditional
Time Period: 1001 CE–1500 CE
Country or Culture: England
Genre: Legend

PLOT SUMMARY

Folklorist Andrew Lang's "How the Round Table Began" provides a brief history of King Arthur's center of political and military power. This portion of Arthur's legend begins with his marriage to Guinevere (Guenevere or Guenever), a princess of Cameliard, where her father, Leodegrance, is king. Arthur's advisers have been urging him to marry, but he wants the magician Merlin's input. When Merlin asks Arthur whether he has a favorite, Arthur claims Guinevere owns his heart. The magician cautions him about the "goodness" of the princess but acknowledges that the heart cannot be changed (25). Despite his poor opinion of the girl, Merlin goes to

Guinevere's father for consent. Her father is so pleased with the offer that he gives Arthur "the Round Table which Uther Pendragon gave me, where a hundred and fifty Knights can sit at one time" as a dowry. He also notes that he does not have enough knights to fill the table anyway.

King Arthur is thrilled with the combination of his queen and the Round Table, so he sends his trusted knight Lancelot to greet and retrieve his bride. It quickly becomes apparent that the Round Table holds 150 knights and that Arthur needs bodies to fill the spots, so he sends Merlin out to find "fifty of the bravest and most famous Knights that can be found throughout the land" (26). Fulfilling this quest is harder than expected, and Merlin returns with only twenty-eight. After being blessed by the bishop of Canterbury, the knights pledge Arthur their loyalty, and their names are carved into their chairs in gold to mark their places at the table.

The table begins to fill as additional men come to Arthur asking to become part of his entourage. His nephew Gawain (Gawaine) is the first, asking to be made a knight on Arthur's wedding day. After Gawain, a poor cowherd asks a boon of Arthur. His son, Tor, wants to become a knight, and the poor man reminds the king that he has made a promise "that at the time of your marriage you would give any man the gift he should ask for" (27). Arthur immediately knights the boy, so with the addition of Gawain the day after, he has thirty knights. The founding of the Round Table ends with this addition to Arthur's followers.

SIGNIFICANCE

The legend of King Arthur's Round Table changes in minor ways depending on the version of the story; however, its symbolism remains consistent throughout the literature, and this version includes important irony and foreshadowing for the rest of the king's story.

The Round Table is mentioned first in the version of Arthur's story relayed by the Norman poet Wace in the early to middle part of the twelfth century. In Wace's tale, Arthur's warrior skills and his chivalrous qualities are clearly established before the creation of the Round Table, drawing knights. As scholar Alan Lupack contends, Wace brings the Round Table in to illustrate Arthur's desire to provide his companions with a sense of equality. Wace's version of the table's origin, which claims that Arthur had the table made, contradicts the origin presented in many other forms of the tale, in which Merlin originally creates the table for Arthur's

father, Uther Pendragon, who then passes the table to Guinevere's father, and Leodegrance gives it to Arthur as Guinevere's dowry.

There is also some discrepancy regarding how many knights the table holds. One idea is that the Round Table reflects Joseph of Arimathea's Grail table and the one used for the Last Supper, which creates a direct tie to the quest for the Holy Grail. In the variants based on this concept, the table holds fifty or fifty-two, including a spare seat either for the Grail winner or to represent the one occupied by the traitorous disciple Judas. Later tales increase the number of knights at the table, ranging from 140 knights up to 250. Regardless, the larger the number, the more difficult the table is to fill. Merlin's ability to find only twenty-eight worthy men in this account is a clear illustration of the problem.

Regardless of its origins or how many knights it holds, the Round Table is particularly important in Arthurian legend for the wide range of symbolic meanings that it represents. The chivalry of the knights is the most obvious ideal symbolized by the Round Table. The group of men associated with Arthur as seen as "uncorrupted and incorruptible" (Finke and Shichtman 179). A second meaning assigned to the Round Table is the political symbol of a developing kingdom with a reach to the world, as seen in the circular shape being representative of the earth. A more specific connection is imputed to Galahad in John Hardyng's version. In the book *King Arthur and the Myth of History*, Laurie Finke and Martin Shichtman suggest that the Round Table is "the material embodiment of the principles of genealogy" that then sets up Galahad's worth as a knight (155).

The story of the Round Table told in this version also provides irony and foreshadowing. First, there is the question of the table's connection to Guinevere. When Arthur tells Merlin whom he wants to marry, Merlin indicates that he would prefer to find a better woman. Her own father even comments that he is surprised that a man of such lofty position would be interested in his daughter. These foreshadowing clues provide a hint about Guinevere's later indiscretions. In addition, Leodegrance's comment in this story that he does not have enough knights to fill the table anyway is further evidence of irony, suggesting that the table, a bride gift, is another undesirable burden that he will gladly unload on his unsuspecting son-in-law. Next, Arthur's early trust in Lancelot is also ironic, considering he sends the knight who will eventually betray him to escort his future wife.

Finally, Arthur sends Merlin out to find fifty knights, but the magician is only able to find twenty-eight. Despite Arthur's request for "the bravest and most famous Knights," he ends up initiating Tor, the unknown son of a "poor man."

The story of King Arthur's Round Table is just one small piece of the whole legend, but it is important in the way it establishes the reputation of Arthur's knights, in its introduction to Arthur's queen, and in its ironic foreshadowing of events that occur later in the literature.

Theresa L. Stowell, PhD

BIBLIOGRAPHY

Finke, Laurie A., and Martin B. Shichtman. *King Arthur and the Myth of History*. Gainesville: UP of Florida, 2004. Print.

Kennedy, Edward Donald, ed. *King Arthur: A Casebook*. New York: Garland, 1996. Print.

Lacy, Norris J., Geoffrey Ashe, and Debra N. Mancoff. *The Arthurian Handbook*. 2nd ed. New York: Garland, 1997. Print.

Lang, Andrew, ed. "How the Round Table Began." *King Arthur: Tales of the Round Table*. London: Longmans, 1902. 25–28. Print.

Lupack, Alan. *The Oxford Guide to Arthurian Literature and Legend*. Oxford: Oxford UP, 2005. Print.

White, Richard, ed. *King Arthur in Legend and History*. New York: Routledge, 1998. Print.

◆ The Legend of Tuan mac Carell

Author: Traditional Celtic
Time Period: 501 CE–1000 CE; 1001 CE–1500 CE
Country or Culture: Ireland
Genre: Myth

PLOT SUMMARY

Tuan mac Carell (Cairill), an old pagan warrior, is one day visited by Saint Finnen, an Irish abbot. Tuan lives close to Finnen's monastery in County Donegal, and the abbot decides to stop by and become acquainted with the old warrior. At first, Tuan refuses to let Finnen inside his home, so the abbot waits and fasts on Tuan's doorstep for an entire Sunday. Finally, Tuan welcomes him in, and the two become friends.

Finnen returns to his monastery and tells his monks about Tuan and the stories of old Ireland the warrior has shared with them. Shortly after, Tuan visits the monastery, and the monks encourage him to tell them the history of Ireland. He begins by telling them about his lineage. He explains that he is Tuan, son of Carell, but that he was once son of Starn, the brother of an early settler of Ireland. This settler was named Partholan, and he and his people were wiped out by a horrible plague. Tuan was the only one to survive the pestilence. Alone, Tuan wandered through barren towns and sheltered in empty fortresses, constantly avoiding wolves. He states that he lived like this for twenty-two years until old age settled in.

New settlers known as Nemedians arrived in Ireland, led by Nemed, another brother of Starn. Tuan, now "decrepit" and "miserable" (Rolleston 99), avoided these new people. Then, one day, he awoke and found himself transformed into a young stag. This filled Tuan's heart with joy, and he became the king of all the deer in Ireland. He then explains that during his time as a deer, he saw Nemed and all of his people inexplicably die. On his own once more, he grew old and became weak once again. Then one day, while standing at the mouth of the cave where he dwelled, Tuan found himself transformed into a young wild boar.

Tuan went on to become king of all of the boar herds of Ireland. He lived an active and plentiful life, roaming Ireland with other boars. One day, he sensed another transformation coming on. He returned to Ulster, where all of his other transformations had taken place. There, he waited until his body would be renewed once again. Old age settled in as it had before, and when Tuan transformed, he became "a great eagle of the sea" (Rolleston 100). Again, he had been rejuvenated with youthful vigor.

During this time, Tuan explains, Semion, son of Stariat, came to inhabit Ireland and gave rise to three tribes who thrived for many years. The Tuatha Dé Danann (race of the goddess Dana) also arrived around this time but were later conquered by the Milesians. Throughout these waves of settlers and conquerors, Tuan kept his eagle shape. When he finally felt another transformation coming on, he fasted for nine days. When he awoke on the tenth day, he had been changed into a salmon. Eventually, a fisherman caught him and gave him to the wife of Carell. She then ate Tuan, who passed through her womb and was born again as Tuan, son of Carell.

SIGNIFICANCE

The legend of Tuan mac Carell comes from *Lebor na h-Uidre* (*Book of the Dun Cow*), one of the oldest surviving manuscripts in Irish literature. The manuscript supposedly derives its unique name from the original vellum, made of the hide of a treasured cow at the monastery of Clonmacnoise, County Offaly. Scholars believe Irish monks at the monastery assembled the manuscript around 1100, compiling older manuscripts and oral lore, both factual and legendary. Its contents mainly date back to between the seventh and ninth centuries, although this particular legend takes place during the sixth.

The legend is used to communicate the waves of settlers and invaders that came to Ireland, dating back to pre-Christian times. Tuan's recounting of these settlers begins with the people of Partholan, who were supposedly the first to arrive in Ireland following the biblical flood described in the book of Genesis. Earlier Irish texts state that the Partholanians, as well as the subsequent Nemedians, came from the cryptic realm of the dead. In later texts created following the Christianization of Ireland, these early peoples are said to be descendants of biblical figures from Spain or Scythia.

The legend contains the theme of the transmigration of the soul through different bodies (also known as metempsychosis), a frequent occurrence in Celtic mythology. Throughout the legend, Tuan transforms from human to animal and back again. Through each transformation, he maintains the intelligence, experiences, and memories from his past lives. The Welsh story of Taliesin is very similar to Tuan's. He too transforms into different animals to survive, and during his last embodiment as a grain, he is eaten by a hen, who later gives birth to him in human form. Both of these stories reflect the Celtic belief that everyone and everything possesses a spirit, plants and animals included, and that mortals can undergo transformation.

The Celtic belief in the transmigration of the soul differs from other, more traditional concepts of reincarnation. Hindus, for example, believe that how a person lived life dictates the type of being of his or her next reincarnation, but all memory and experience is lost in the person's new form. According to some classical authors, the druids of Gaul believed that the soul lives on after death and is sent into another being, although that being is not necessarily of this world. Just as in Tuan's repeated transmigrations, all memory, experience, and intelligence would be maintained in the new being.

Patrick G. Cooper

BIBLIOGRAPHY

Dooley, Ann, and Harry Roe, trans. *Tales of the Elders of Ireland*. Oxford: Oxford UP, 2008. Print.

Ellis, Peter Berresford. *Celtic Myths and Legends*. Philadelphia: Running, 2002. Print.

MacCulloch, John Arnott. *The Religion of the Ancient Celts*. Mineola: Dover, 2012. Print.

Rolleston, Thomas William. "The Legend of Tuan mac Carell." *Myths and Legends of the Celtic Race*. London: Constable, 1911. 96–100. Print.

"The Story of Tuan mac Carell." *Eleusinianm*. Richard Alan Scott-Robinson, 2011. Web. 28 May 2013.

◆ The Marriage of Sir Gawain

Author: Traditional
Time Period: 1001 CE–1500 CE
Country or Culture: England
Genre: Legend

PLOT SUMMARY

Maud Isabel Ebbutt's "The Marriage of Sir Gawayne" begins at King Arthur's court during the Christmas season. A bored Arthur upbraids his knights for their sloth, threatening to stay at the table "till some adventure be undertaken" (267). As the knights defend themselves against this charge, a sobbing maiden appears before them and begs for vengeance on a giant who drove away her lover and mistreated her in his castle. When the giant released her, he mocked her threat of justice at the hands of King Arthur.

Provoked by the report of the giant's scorn, King Arthur sets forth the next day to challenge him, but the giant's magic powers disable the king. The giant then offers to release the king on the condition that he returns on New Year's Day with the correct answer to the question, "What thing is it that all women most desire?" (270). The humiliated king has no choice but to accept the terms, and he travels around the land, receiving all manner of responses as women relate to him their desire for wealth, beautiful clothing, handsome lovers, and so forth. Sensing that he has not yet received the right answer, the king sadly returns at the appointed time. On the way, he meets a hideously ugly old woman. After he apologizes for ignoring her, she promises to reveal the true answer if he agrees to give her whatever she requests. King Arthur accepts her offer, is told the correct reply, and returns to the giant, who is enraged to realize that his own sister has betrayed him by revealing the answer. The king departs and returns to the loathly lady who requests that Arthur find a young, brave, handsome, and courteous knight to marry her. Utterly dejected, Arthur returns to his castle at Carlisle, where his nephew Sir Gawain (here spelled "Gawayne") gallantly offers to marry the hag.

The next day, Arthur arranges a hunting party to keep his knights from noticing their journey to transport the loathly lady to the castle. Unfortunately, Sir Kay notices the lady's scarlet dress and proceeds to mock and deride her, but Sir Gawain interrupts to defend the lady's dignity. Arthur is forced to reveal his promise to provide a handsome and courteous knight as the husband for the lady, and Gawain again nobly steps forward as Kay persists with his bad manners. The knights bring the lady back to Carlisle, where a somber wedding ensues, but Gawain's courtesy ensures that no one dares to be disrespectful of his new wife.

Later that evening in the bedroom, Gawain's sadness prompts the lady to question his silence. Turning toward her, Gawain is amazed to find a beautiful young maiden with black eyes and long curly hair. She explains that a witch has cast a spell on her that transforms her into a hideous old woman for half of each day, and Gawain must choose whether to have her "fair by day and ugly by night, or hideous by day and beauteous by night" (282). Gawayne first chooses to have her true form at night, but when the lady explains the disadvantages of this choice, he quickly changes his mind. She again points out the problems with his second choice, at which point he offers to allow her to decide. She immediately rejoices and informs him that with this answer, he has completely broken the spell and restored her true form. She then explains that her father had married a witch, who cast a spell on her and her brother. Both are now free thanks to Gawain's courtesy and wisdom. The next morning, the happy couple present themselves to the court, and all rejoice at the blissful news.

SIGNIFICANCE

Ebbutt's early twentieth-century version heightens the moral tone of this medieval English story, which was originally a parody of romance tales and ideology. In some medieval versions, often called simply "The Loathly Lady," the element of parody is evident in details such as the hag's bad manners at her own wedding, which offend everyone. Furthermore, the idea of actual female sovereignty was likely considered a joke in the Middle Ages, a humorous commentary on the tension between the sexes in an era in which male dominance was assumed as part of the proper order of society. For a medieval audience, the fantasy of female sovereignty came from tales of romance and courtly love, or more accurately, *fin amor* (pure love), according to which brave knights swore to serve their ladies, analogous to how such knights took oaths to serve their lords in war. The idea of serving one's lady, however, was more of a narrative ideology than a reality: a knight served his lady to prove his courtliness, but men did not grant sovereignty to women in the way that Gawain does for the hag, whose appearance was likely a source of humor as well. One famous version of the story appears in Geoffrey Chaucer's *Canterbury Tales*, where the incontrovertible Wife of Bath tells the story as a way of displaying her desire for both power and traditional romance.

Ebbutt wrote in a period in which many anthologists greatly desired to recast legends and fairy tales in didactic terms as part of a movement to create national cultural identities, a movement that evolved in part through the revival of traditional popular stories. With this goal, Ebbutt discards the humorous details and heightens the moral tone by, for example, beginning the story with a preface emphasizing the rare value of not just courtesy but "gentle courtesy" (265)—that is, the respectful treatment of maidens and others of lower status. Gone is the loathly lady's uncouth behavior, which Ebbutt replaces with details like Kay's ungracious mockery that Arthur must finally interrupt by threatening him with banishment. With these details, Ebbutt transforms Gawain into a true hero and exalts with a new seriousness the virtues of courtesy and loyalty to all who merit such respect.

Ashleigh Imus, PhD

BIBLIOGRAPHY

Chaucer, Geoffrey. *The Selected Canterbury Tales: A New Verse Translation.* Trans. Sheila Fisher. New York: Norton, 2011. Print.

Ebbutt, M. I. "The Marriage of Sir Gawayne." *Hero-Myths & Legends of the British Race.* London: Harrap, 1920. 265–85. Print.

Hahn, Thomas. *Sir Gawain: Eleven Romances and Tales.* Kalamazoo: Medieval Institute Pub., 1995. Print.

Matthews, John. *Sir Gawain: Knight of the Goddess.* Rochester: Inner Traditions, 2003. Print.

Passmore, Elizabeth S., and Susan Carter. *The English "Loathly Lady" Tales: Boundaries, Traditions, Motifs.* Kalamazoo: Medieval Institute Pub., 2007. Print.

The Mermaid

Author: J. F. Campbell
Time Period: 1901 CE–1950 CE
Country or Culture: Scotland; Ireland
Genre: Folktale

PLOT SUMMARY

A childless blacksmith meets and makes a deal with a mermaid: in exchange for fish, he will give her his firstborn son on the child's third birthday. After several days, the smith catches a magical fish, who instructs the smith to bury three bones found in its head. If he does so, the fish explains, his wife, mare, and dog will each give birth to three offspring.

The man's wife gives birth to triplet sons, but when the children turn three, he goes back on his deal with the mermaid. Twice he pretends to have forgotten to bring the child to her, and twice he is forgiven. When the time comes for the boy to be turned over to the mermaid, his father tells of his commitment, and though the boy is willing, his father will not let him go. Instead, the boy and his brothers leave home to make their own way in the world. Their father gives each boy a magical horse, a hound, a club, and a sword to help him on his way.

After traveling for some time, the brothers part ways. The oldest brother's adventures begin when he encounters a wolf, a hawk, and a fox. He gains blessings from them that will help him in a time of need. Shortly afterward, the boy comes to a herder's hut and takes on a job tending cattle. The youth is warned to stay away from a certain fenced area, but he ignores the advice and learns the reason for the counsel when he sees a fearsome giant. The giant steals three cows, but the boy overpowers him through trickery and is rewarded with the giant's wealth. The boy next faces the giant's two brothers and their mother, emerging victorious each time.

The day after the giants' mother dies, the herder shares the news that the king's daughter has been threatened by a great, three-headed sea dragon. The young man pretends not to care but rides in to protect the girl, since out of all the men in the kingdom, only the king's cook has volunteered to protect her. The king sends his daughter, the cook, and fourteen warriors to the seashore, but the guards flee when the smith's son rides out of the sky wearing glittering armor. For three days, the hero repeats a pattern of frightening the guards, napping with his head in the princess's lap, waking when she cuts off a piece of his flesh (the tip of an ear, the tip of a finger, and a piece of scalp), cutting off one of the dragon's heads, and then riding off into the horizon. Each time, the cook takes credit for the monster's defeat. After finally slaying the sea dragon, the hero learns that the princess and the cook will be wed, but he travels home confidently, undaunted by this setback.

The young man soon proves that he is the true hero and marries the princess. They live happily together for some time, until one day when they decide to travel to the seashore. The mermaid appears and swallows the hero, claiming the child the blacksmith promised her years before. However, his wife tricks the mermaid into revealing him three times, and on the third occasion, he escapes. The mermaid responds by swallowing the wife and fleeing, but after a long journey, the man is able to reclaim his wife and kill the mermaid once and for all.

SIGNIFICANCE

The story of the mermaid and the blacksmith's son was told by Scottish scholar John Francis Campbell in his posthumously published volume *The Celtic Dragon Myth* (1911), which collects mythology and folklore from Celtic and other sources and assembles them into a cohesive narrative. The number three plays a significant role in this narrative. The old blacksmith lives with three companions: his wife, a mare, and a dog. When he meets the mermaid while fishing, she asks him to give her his eldest son when the boy reaches the age of three. For three days in a row, the smith goes fishing and catches a fish who pleads for release. After eating a portion of the fish, the smith buries three of its bones. Three trees then grow in the places where the bones were buried, and nine (three times three) months later the smith becomes the father of triplet sons.

The number three continues to be central as the oldest boy leaves home with his brothers. They come across a road that branches in three directions, and each takes a different path. The oldest son's story continues to focus on threes as he gains three powers, conquers three giants, and gains three fortunes. Then, the hero defeats the three-headed dragon who threatens the princess over the course of three days.

The number three is a common motif in many forms of folklore. Some scholars interpret the number as representing the beginning, middle, and end, and it likewise suggests the Holy Trinity of the Father, the Son, and the Holy Spirit in Christianity and the trio of the sun, earth, and moon. The number is also found in various myths, proverbs, and other narratives across the globe. This story is significant partially because of its use of the number three as a unifying motif.

Theresa L. Stowell, PhD

BIBLIOGRAPHY

Campbell, J. F. *The Celtic Dragon Myth*. Edinburgh: Grant, 1911. Print.

Haase, Donald. *The Greenwood Encyclopedia of Folktales and Fairy Tales*. Westport: Greenwood, 2008. Print.

Leeming, David Adams, and Marion Sader. *Storytelling Encyclopedia*. Phoenix: Oryx, 1997. Print.

Matthews, John. *Classic Celtic Fairy Tales*. London: Blandford, 1997. Print.

Zipes, Jack. *The Oxford Companion to Fairy Tales*. New York: Oxford UP, 2003. Print.

The Morrígu

Author: Traditional Celtic
Time Period: 999 BCE–1 BCE; 1 CE–500 CE
Country or Culture: Ireland
Genre: Myth

PLOT SUMMARY

Before the coming of the Gaels to Ireland, the Morrígu, also known as the Great Queen and the Crow of Battle, lives in the hill of Tara, or Teamhair. She is able to appear in many forms, including those of a large black crow and of three sisters. She has a great cooking spit that holds three types of food: a chunk of raw meat, a chunk of cooked meat, and a slab of butter. The food on this spit never diminishes. One day, nine outlaws go to the Morrígu and ask her to make them a spit of their own. She creates for them a spit that holds nine ribs, from which the outlaws eat every night.

The Morrígu has a son, Mechi, who is killed by Mac Cécht on Magh Fertaige. It is said that Mechi had three hearts, each with a serpent running through it, and that if Mac Cécht did not kill Mechi, the serpents in his hearts would have grown out of his body and devastated Ireland. Thus, after slaying him, Mac Cécht takes Mechi's three hearts and burns them on Magh Luathad, the Plain of Ashes. He throws the ashes of the three hearts into a stream, which begins boiling and kills every living creature within it.

The Morrígu is often seen aiding in or instigating battles around Ireland. She frequently intervenes in the life of the great warrior Cúchulainn (Cuchulain), defender of Ulster. When he is only a child, the Morrígu appears to him after he has fallen under the spell of a shadow enchantment. She taunts him until he is angry enough to get to his feet and cut off the head of the shadow that is suppressing him. When the king Conchobar mac Nessa of Ulster is rousing his men during the war for the bull of Cúailgne, he orders that the Morrígu be sent to aid Cúchulainn.

During the Battle of Moira (or Magh Rath), as the king of Ireland does battle against the king of Ulster, the Morrígu transforms into her crow form and flies around the king of Ulster until he becomes confused and attacks his own warriors. In a later battle, she performs a similar trick on the king of Leinster.

She often meddles in cattle disputes and thievery as well. One time, Cúchulainn spots her stealing a cow from the hill of Cruachan, and the two begin to quarrel over the beast. On another occasion, she aids a druid named Talchinem in the acquisition of a bull that his wife wishes to have. The Morrígu also steals a cow from a woman named Odras and takes it to the cave of Cruachan. Odras pursues the Morrígu but eventually grows tired and falls asleep in a forest. The Morrígu casts a spell over the sleeping Odras and transforms her into a pool of water that flows into a river.

SIGNIFICANCE

The figure called the Morrígu, also known as Morrígan, appears frequently in Irish mythology, particularly in the Ulster cycle of legends. She is one of the Tuatha Dé Danann (people of the goddess Dana) and is often interpreted as a goddess of battle, strife, and fertility, making her a goddess of both life and death. She can appear in different forms, including the form of a trio of goddesses: the Morrígu herself, Badb (crow), and either Macha (crow) or Nemain (frenzy).

As a goddess of battle, the Morrígu's role is often as a premonition of death and an influence on the outcome of battles. During battles, she often appears in the form of a crow, which is a symbol of death in Celtic mythology. Some accounts even have her feeding on the bodies of the dead after battles. In this way, she was seen as a harbinger of death, much like the Valkyries of Norse mythology, who would select the soldiers who were to die in battle. One way she serves as an omen of death is by appearing as the washer at the ford, who can be seen washing the bloody clothes or armor of men who will later die in battle. There are many stories of her washing the bloodied armor of Cúchulainn before his death. Once he recognizes that it is his armor being washed, he knows that he is doomed.

The Morrígu has an interesting relationship with the warrior Cúchulainn. She appears to him often, and in many of those instances, he fails to recognize her. Some accounts state that she becomes so enraged when Cúchulainn fails to identify her that she brings about his death by interfering during a battle. After he dies, she appears on his corpse in the form of a crow. Many interpretations blame Cúchulainn's demise on his inability to recognize the Morrígu's feminine power.

Other interpretations of the Morrígu depict her as less of a war goddess and more of a protector and guardian of soldiers during a battle. She uses her magic to influence the outcome of battles, thus providing kings with military aid. Helping certain rulers defeat their enemies makes her a goddess of sovereignty. The Morrígu's association with cattle helps identify her as a fertility and sovereignty goddess. In Celtic mythology, cattle are symbols of fertility, and the prosperity of a tribe was directly reflected in its thriving herd of cattle.

Many myths associate the Morrígu with bands of Irish warrior-hunters who engaged in a lawless lifestyle and may have worshipped her. She provides food for them, and the symbol of her cooking spit further associates her with fertility. Other interpretations present a more metaphorical reading of the Morrígu's food and spit, depicting them as symbols of her wisdom.

Patrick G. Cooper

BIBLIOGRAPHY

Billington, Sandra, and Miranda Green, eds. *The Concept of the Goddess*. New York: Routledge, 1996. Print.

Clark, Rosalind. *The Great Queens: Irish Goddesses from the Morrígan to Cathleen ní Houlihan*. Lanham: Rowman, 1992. Print.

Gregory, Augusta. "The Morrigu." *Gods and Fighting Men*. London: Murray, 1905. 84–85. Print.

Hennessey, W. M. "The Ancient Irish Goddess of War." *Revue Celtique* 1 (1870): 32+. *Internet Sacred Text Archive*. Web. 10 May 2013.

Jones, Mary. "Morrigan." *Jones' Celtic Encyclopedia*. Jones, 2003. Web. 10 May 2013.

◆ Oisín's Mother

Author: James Stephens
Time Period: 999 BCE–1 BCE; 1 CE–500 CE
Country or Culture: Ireland
Genre: Folktale

PLOT SUMMARY

Fionn mac Cumhaill, chief of the Fianna-Finn band of warriors, calls an end to a hunt when a fawn leaps out nearby. Fionn and his two dogs, Bran and Sceolan, pursue the fawn, leaving behind the rest of the warriors. The chase is long, and Fionn has never seen his dogs absorbed in such a state of pursuit. When they reach a valley, the fawn suddenly stops running and rests peacefully on the grass as if it were unafraid of Fionn and the two dogs.

Fionn prepares to strike, but then the dogs start licking the fawn's face and rubbing their snouts against its neck. Fionn lowers his spear and watches in astonishment as the fawn lovingly plays with the dogs. The three animals frolic around Fionn, and then the fawn approaches him and affectionately places its muzzle in his palm. Fionn returns to his home at Allen of Leinster, where people are surprised to see their chief with a fawn in tow. The rest of the Fianna agree that the fawn should be treated as the pet of their band. Some believe that the fawn came from the Shí, the Celtic otherworld.

As Fionn prepares for sleep that night, a girl enters his room. Fionn has never seen a girl so beautiful in all his life, and he immediately knows that he will never leave her side. The girl says that her name is Saeve (Sadb) and that she is a woman of Faery. She explains how the Black Magician of the Men of God put his eye on her, so that wherever she looks, the magician is there. She confesses her love for Fionn and asks for his protection, which he grants with a fierce devotion.

Fionn becomes fully dedicated to Saeve. He ceases to hunt and looks over the Fianna no more. His entire world becomes Saeve. He continues on like this until the Norse Lochlannachs attempt an invasion of Ireland. Fionn marches against them with the Fianna-Finn and drives them back to their ships. He returns to his home victorious, eager to see Saeve.

When he arrives at Allen, he finds his keep in disarray and Saeve nowhere to be seen. Fionn's butler, Gariv Crona'n, confesses that Saeve has disappeared. He explains that a man resembling Fionn had arrived with two dogs similar in look to Bran and Sceo'lan. Against the wishes of the guards, Saeve ran to the man. When she reached him, he touched her with a hazel rod, turning her into a fawn. When the guards and servants of the keep ran to save her, she, the man, and the dogs all disappeared.

Many years pass, and Fionn continues to search for the fawn. One day, Fionn's dogs discover a young boy. They protect the boy from the other dogs, an act that tells Fionn that the boy is special. The boy does not speak the Irish language, but in his eyes Fionn recognizes the same look Saeve gave him years before. Knowing the boy to be his son, Fionn takes him in and protects him.

Once the boy learns the language, he explains that he came from the Shí, where he lived with a fawn. He states that one day the Black Magician took the fawn away, and as hard as he tried, he was not able to follow. He collapsed on the ground, and when he awoke, Fionn's dogs had found him. The boy is given the name Oisín, meaning "Little Fawn," and he grows up to become a great warrior and the chief poet of the Irish people.

SIGNIFICANCE

This Irish folk tale is part of the Fenian cycle of Celtic mythology. The stories of the Fenian cycle are primarily concerned with the heroic exploits of some of the most beloved and essential characters of Irish folklore, particularly Fionn and his son Oisín, who narrates much of the cycle. Experts believe that the stories of the Fenian cycle take place around the third century in the south and east of Ireland and that the recording of this lore began in the twelfth century, when Christian monks began documenting Irish history.

Many of the Fenian cycle stories involve warriors hunting, battling enemies of Ireland, and encountering the spirit world. Some stories take place in the Celtic otherworld, which is similar to the realm of spirits and deities in other mythologies, although it holds no religious connotations. In the story of Oisín's mother, the world is referred to as the Shí, which is another name for the land of the fairies (or faeries). While modern depictions of fairies present them as small, winged creatures

often out to cause mischief, the ancient Irish saw them as spirits who possessed magical powers and lived in hills and mounds or on an island far off to the west.

Oisín was one of the few mortals who lived in the land of the fairies. There he had children with a fairy queen named Niamh. One of the most famous accounts of Oisín is the narrative poem *The Wanderings of Oisin*, by Irish poet William Butler Yeats. This piece, first published in 1889, is in the form of a dialogue between Oisín and Saint Patrick, who is credited with converting pagan Ireland to Christianity.

One particularly well-known version of the tale of Oisín and his mother was recorded by James Stephens, a renowned Irish novelist and poet. Much of his work was devoted to the retelling of classic Irish myths and fairy tales, which Stephens infused with his own style and humor. In 1937, Stephens reached a new audience through a series of broadcasts on the British Broadcasting Corporation. He continued these broadcasts until his death in 1950.

Patrick G. Cooper

BIBLIOGRAPHY

Heaney, Marie. *Nine Waves: A Book of Irish Legends*. London: Faber, 1995. Print.

"Irish Legend: Oisin's Mother and the Dark Druid." *The Epoch Times*. Epoch Times International, 6 June 2006. Web. 5 May 2013.

Joe, Jimmy. "Fenian Cycle." *Timeless Myths*. Timeless Myths, 6 Jan. 2009. Web. 4 May 2013.

Kennedy, Patrick. *Legendary Fictions of the Irish Celts*. 1866. New York: Blom, 1969. Print.

Stephens, James. *Irish Fairy Tales*. New York: Macmillan, 1920. Print.

Yeats, William Butler. *Collected Poems*. London: Collector's Lib., 2010. Print.

◆ The Order of Scáthach

Author: Traditional Celtic
Time Period: 999 BCE–1 BCE; 1 CE–500 CE
Country or Culture: Ireland
Genre: Myth

PLOT SUMMARY

The greatest of the men under King Conchobar in Ulster is his nephew Cúchulainn. Although he is younger than many of the other men, he defeats any challengers who test his force, wisdom, and quickness. The men of Ulster become worried that Cúchulainn will steal their wives and sleep with their daughters, so they decide to find him a woman to marry.

Conchobar sends out nine men to each province of Erinn (Ireland) to find Cúchulainn a bride. These men search for a year but cannot find a woman suitable for him. The warrior does have a particular woman on his mind though: Emer, the daughter of chieftain Forgall the Wily. He goes to address Emer and to prove to her his worthiness. When Forgall is told that Cúchulainn had been speaking with his daughter, he knows that she is in love with him. He disguises himself as a foreigner and seeks counsel with Conchobar. The men of Ulster, including Cúchulainn, welcome him. Forgall states to Conchobar that Cúchulainn could become one of the greatest warriors of Europe if he receives training in Scotland from King Domnall the Soldierly and the revered warrior woman Scáthach. Forgall thinks this ordeal will be too much for the young warrior, and hopes he will not come back alive. Cúchulainn consents to the training and bids farewell to Emer.

After completing his training in spear-fighting techniques with Domnall, Cúchulainn travels west to the home of Scáthach. Cúchulainn endures several hardships on his way to her, including travels through the Plain of Ill-Luck and the Perilous Glen. At the house, Scáthach's daughter Uathach pretends to be a servant and brings him food and drink. He is aroused by her, and takes hold of her, accidentally breaking one her fingers. One of Scáthach's champions, Cochar, comes to defend Uathach, but he is no match for Cúchulainn, who cuts off his head. Sorry for killing one of her best men, Cúchulainn pledges allegiance to Scáthach and promises to defend her army.

During the training of Cúchulainn, Scáthach is at war with a female warrior chieftain named Aífe. Cúchulainn joins a battle and, after defeating many of her men, he takes Aífe hostage and makes her grant him three wishes: never to attack Scáthach again, to sleep with him, and to bear him a son. Aífe complies, and Cúchulainn gives her a gold ring to give to his son, with instructions that he come find Cúchulainn in Ireland when the ring fits his finger.

Cúchulainn returns to Scáthach and there revives himself and completes his training. She teaches him many fighting feats using chariots, spears, ropes, and more. Eventually Cúchulainn is called to return to his own land, but before he leaves, Scáthach tells him his future and sings to him.

In Ulster, Cúchulainn finds an army of men set against him by Forgall, who still will not let Cúchulainn marry his daughter. Cúchulainn defeats Forgall's forces and Forgall himself falls from a wall and dies. Cúchulainn takes Emer away with him, and they are wed and never parted again.

SIGNIFICANCE

This tale is part of "The Wooing of Emer" of the Ulster cycle of Irish mythology. The legends of this cycle are usually set in the provinces of Ulster and Connacht around the time of Christ. They tend to deal with the heroic exploits of King Conchobar and Cúchulainn. There is a short and long revision of this legend, with the long one being one of the lengthiest stories in the Ulster cycle. It is considered an introductory story to the legend of Táin Bó Cúailnge, also known as "The Cattle Raid of Cooley," which is one of the central tales of the Ulster cycle.

A total of eight manuscripts of "The Wooing of Emer" exist, which has led scholars to believe it was a favorite legend of the Irish. Wooing or courtship stories appear frequently in the Ulster cycle, alongside tales of feasts, births, and battles. The longest version appears in the Book of Leinster, a text that dates to the tenth or eleventh century.

Cúchulainn was the most prominent hero of the cycle. Much of the cycle's legends are concerned with his life, and many contemporary examinations see him as an archetypal Irish hero. Following his training as outlined in this legend, Cúchulainn goes on to defeat his foster brother Fer Díad (Ferdiad), who also trained under Scáthach, who was one of the great warrior women of Irish legend.

Scáthach was said to have lived on an island off of Scotland, where she trained warriors in the fighting skills they needed to become great heroes. She alone could teach a variety of martial arts, including chariot-feat, salmon-feat, and thunder-feat. Cúchulainn's feared spear, the Gae Bulga, was given to him by Scáthach. This mythical weapon has been compared to King Arthur's sword Excalibur, which he also received from a woman. With the Gae Bulga, Cúchulainn slew many men in single combat, including his foster brother Ferdiad.

In some tales, Scáthach was also able to tell warriors what would befall them in the future, like she does in the story above. In some accounts of this story, however, she refuses to tell Cúchulainn his future, because she knows he will murder his son, Connal. Different versions also have Scáthach as Connal's mother, rather than Aife.

Researchers have used the Irish legends of women warriors such as Scáthach to argue that women participated in battles alongside men, while others contest these claims due to laws of the time that limited women's activities. Either way, Scáthach was a powerful female warrior and essential character of the Ulster cycle.

Patrick G. Cooper

BIBLIOGRAPHY

Caldecott, Moyra. *Women in Celtic Myth: Tales of Extraordinary Women from the Ancient Celtic Tradition.* Rochester: Destiny, 1992. Print.

Gantz, Jeffrey. *Early Irish Myths and Sagas.* New York: Penguin, 1982. Print.

Gregory, Augusta. *Cuchulain of Muirthemne.* 1902. Whitefish: Kessinger, 2010. Print.

Kinsella, Thomas, trans. *The Táin: Translated From the Irish Epic Táin Bó Cúailnge.* Oxford: Oxford UP, 2002. Print.

"The Wooing of Emer by Cú Chulainn." Trans. Kuno Meyer. *CELT: Corpus of Electronic Texts.* University College, Cork, 2011. Web. 13 June 2013.

◆ Sir Galahad and the Holy Grail

Author: Traditional
Time Period: 1001 CE–1500 CE
Country or Culture: England
Genre: Legend

PLOT SUMMARY

With roots in Celtic legend, the Holy Grail has been variously represented as a stone, dish, cup, caldron, and platter. During the Middle Ages, however, the vessel was understood to be the chalice associated with the Last Supper, brought to Britain by Joseph of Arimathea. In the Vulgate cycle of Arthurian romances, the Holy Grail is the object of a sacred quest undertaken by Arthur's knights, the foremost of whom is Lancelot's illegitimate son, Galahad.

During the dangerous journey, Galahad and his fellow knights Perceval (Percival) and Bors encounter a ship waiting by the shore. When they board the boat, they discover the Holy Grail, covered in red samite and sitting on a silver table. Galahad is so overcome by the sacred object's presence that he prays that God will take him to heaven at that moment. A voice promises to honor the young knight's request in due time.

The ship transports the seekers to the island of Sarras. As they attempt to remove the silver table from the ship, Galahad calls on a lame man to help them. The crippled man protests that he has been using crutches for ten years. Nevertheless, Galahad bids him rise, and the man discovers that he can walk unaided. The old man's recovery causes a stir in the city, which displeases the king. Instead of honoring Galahad and his fellow knights, he imprisons them. After a year elapses, the king, near death, frees the three knights and asks for their forgiveness.

Galahad replaces the dead ruler as king and orders that a shrine be created for the Grail. A year after his coronation, Galahad enters the room where the Grail is displayed and has a vision of a bishop, surrounded by angels, kneeling before the silver table. The bishop tells Galahad that his request to see the unveiled Grail is about to be granted and that he will be taken to heaven soon afterward. Rejoicing, Galahad bids farewell to Perceval and Bors and asks Bors to remind Lancelot of his vow to live a virtuous life. As Galahad kneels before the Grail, he dies, and the sacred vessel, gripped by a disembodied hand, vanishes.

Mourning Galahad, Perceval adopts the habit of a hermit, while Bors continues to a secular life. After Perceval's death, Bors returns to Camelot. He tells the story of the Holy Grail to Arthur and his court, and also gives Galahad's message to Lancelot. Grief stricken, Lancelot agrees to keep his promise to his son but continues to live a sinful life. Galahad's adventure brings the search for the Holy Grail to a close, and the decline of Arthur's kingdom begins.

SIGNIFICANCE

While the quest for the Holy Grail is one of the most enduring legacies of medieval Arthurian literature, the story's origin is found in Celtic myth. One example is the Welsh tale of Bran the Blessed's horn of plenty, a magic receptacle that provides physical and spiritual nourishment to those deemed worthy. By the late twelfth century, Christianity's influence became evident in French poet Chrétien de Troyes's version of the Grail adventure, which focuses on Perceval. The Prose Lancelot, or Vulgate cycle, a collection of early thirteenth-century stories penned by unknown authors, portrays Galahad as the only knight to achieve the Grail quest.

Galahad's prominence in the Vulgate cycle's Grail narrative is connected to the rise of the Knights Templar, highly skilled warrior monks who fought during the thirteenth-century Crusades. Bernard of Clairvaux, reformer of the Cistercian monastic order, outlined the Rule of the Knights Templar in 1129. The rule defined the ideal Christian knight as a man who was brave, wise, virtuous, and committed to God. The Vulgate cycle's portrayal of Galahad as a man of strength, courage, and purity embodies traits prized by the Templars. In addition, Galahad is sometimes seen in art carrying a white shield painted with a red cross, which is the traditional symbol of the Templars. Galahad exhibits messianic qualities as well. The tale of his healing of the elderly man echoes Jesus's healing of the paralytic in John 5:1–15. Within this context, the figure of Galahad is analogous to the son of God.

The Christianization of the Grail legend not only elevates Galahad as the most Christlike of Arthur's knights but also highlights the Grail's association with the Eucharist (or Holy Communion). During the mass celebrated by the mysterious bishop, Galahad is granted his request to view what the Grail holds. Instead of the host (bread or wafer) commonly used during Eucharist, the contents of the vessel are indescribable. Galahad reacts with uncontrolled trembling as he beholds the vision. His behavior is similar to that of a mystic who is so engulfed by the transcendent that he can no longer live on earth.

Over the centuries, Galahad's search for the Holy Grail has continued to capture the public imagination. Sir Thomas Malory's *Le Morte D'Arthur* (1485), Alfred, Lord Tennyson's *Idylls of the King* (1859–85), T. H. White's *The Once and Future King* (1958), and the film *Monty Python and the Holy Grail* (1975) all reference the Vulgate cycle version of the Galahad narrative, but each reinterprets the story to reflect the times in which they were written or produced.

Pegge Bochynski

BIBLIOGRAPHY

Barber, Richard. *The Holy Grail: Imagination and Belief.* Cambridge: Harvard UP, 2004. Print.

Day, David. *The Search for King Arthur.* New York: Facts On File, 1998. Print.

Jung, Emma, and Marie-Louise von Franz. *The Grail Legend.* Princeton: Princeton UP, 2005. Print.

Loomis, Roger Sherman. *The Grail: From Celtic Myth to Christian Symbol.* Princeton: Princeton UP, 1991. Print.

White, Richard, ed. *King Arthur in Legend and History.* New York: Routledge, 1997. Print.

◆ Sir Gammer Vans

Author: Joseph Jacobs
Time Period: 1851 CE–1900 CE
Country or Culture: England
Genre: Fairy Tale

PLOT SUMMARY

While sailing over mountaintops, an anonymous narrator meets two men riding on one horse. He asks them if they know whether a woman who had been hanged for drowning herself in feathers is dead. The two men plead ignorance on this matter and refer the speaker to Sir Gammer Vans, a more reliable source for information on the subject. Asking for directions, the narrator learns that the man he seeks is easy to find because he lives in a solitary brick house made of flints in the middle of several buildings just like it.

When the narrator finally meets Sir Gammer Vans, he discovers that the man is a giant and a bottle-maker. As such, Sir Gammer Vans makes his appearance as all giant bottle-makers do—by jumping out of a tiny bottle situated behind the door of his home. Sir Gammer Vans invites the narrator to join him for a breakfast of sliced beer and cold veal in a cup. A small dog eats the crumbs that fall from the table.

The narrator demands that Sir Gammer Vans hang the dog under the table. The giant declines because the dog had killed a hare the day before. He offers to prove it to the narrator by showing him the hare, alive, in a basket that he keeps out in his yard. They commence to walk through Sir Gammer Vans's garden, a place teeming with wonders including a fox hatching eagle's eggs, an iron apple tree bearing pears and lead, and wooden switches threshing tobacco.

The threshing switches become so agitated at the approach of the narrator and Sir Gammer Vans that a plug of tobacco hurls through the garden wall and blasts a hole through a dog. The narrator jumps the gate, turns the dog inside out, and proceeds to follow Sir Gammer Vans to a deer park. The narrator produces a royal warrant permitting him to shoot venison for the crown's table and commences to shoot at a herd of deer.

The narrator breaks several ribs by shooting his arrow, but whether they are his own or his target's remains unclear. Regardless, the speaker loses his arrow only to recover it in the hollow of a tree where he disturbs a covey of partridges living in a beehive. The narrator fires at the birds and kills several of them as well as a flying salmon from which he makes an apple pie.

SIGNIFICANCE

The American folklorist Joseph Jacobs included "Sir Gammer Vans" in his 1894 publication *More English Fairy Tales*. He cites a book compiled by English scholar Joseph Halliwell-Phillipps, *Popular Rhymes and Nursery Tales* (published in the mid-1840s), as his source for this strange tale. But the roots of this unique, nonsensical account likely extend back to an anonymous seventeenth-century English tract titled "A Strange and Wonderful Relation of the Old Woman Who Was Drowned at Ratcliff-Highway a Fortnight Ago."

This earlier iteration of "Sir Gammer Vans" was known to the Anglo-Irish authors Jonathan Swift and Oliver Goldsmith, and it contains many details present in Jacobs's tale. For example, like "Sir Gammer Vans," the older tale features an anonymous narrator and opens with contradictions that prepare readers for the nonsense that characterizes the story. Various absurdities ensue: a dead horse runs, apples fill an empty cart, and a party of sleeping people playing nine-pins eats a freezing hot roasted pudding. Sir Gammer Vans does not appear in this version of the story, however. Instead, readers encounter the bottle-making giant Sir John Vangs, his wife Gammer Vangs, and their son, who is an old woman.

"Sir Gammer Vans" clearly uses storytelling techniques evident in the earlier version of the account. By consistently presenting nonsensical observations, events, and exchanges, the narrator conveys a curious sense of order throughout the piece. The very title of the tale suggests this notion, as it conflates Sir John and Gammer Vangs from the earlier story into one character,

a man with a knightly title whose first name is an antiquated English term for *grandmother*.

Unlike its source, however, "Sir Gammer Vans" abandons any conventional plot trajectory and instead crowds the tale with non sequiturs. While "A Strange and Wonderful Relation of the Old Woman Who Was Drowned" describes a series of nonsensical contradictions, its narrator returns to his original question about the drowned woman. This repetition grounds the plot in the speaker's quest for an answer to his query. In "Sir Gammer Vans," on the other hand, the question that opens the tale never recurs, and each turn of events spontaneously leads to other unexpected events. The plot even leaves behind the title character by its conclusion.

Readers may be baffled by "Sir Gammer Vans" and question the meaning of the story and whether it was simply an exercise in nonsense composition. There are many possible critical approaches to this curious work. One such approach is to recognize that nineteenth-century scholars likely discovered and transmitted the story during an era when nonsense literature in English—especially by authors such as Edward Lear and Lewis Carroll—enjoyed tremendous popularity. The nineteenth century also marked a period when readers were interested in folklore and mythology. Another reading might consider conventions of courtly literature evident in the tale, as suggested by the giant's knightly title and the deer hunt, while yet another might explore the violence that runs throughout the tale.

G. Matthews, MA

BIBLIOGRAPHY

Briggs, Katharine. *British Folk Tales and Legends: A Sampler*. London: Routledge, 2002. Print.

Halliwell, J. O., ed. "Notices of Fugitive Tracts and Chap-Books." *Early English Poetry, Ballads, and Popular Literature of the Middle Ages, Edited from the Original Manuscripts and Scarce Publications*. Vol. 29. London: Percy Soc., 1851. 1–96. Print.

Jacobs, Joseph, ed. "Sir Gammer Vans." *More English Fairy Tales*. New York: Putnam's, 1922. 43–45. Print.

Malcolm, Noel. *The Origins of English Nonsense*. London: Harper, 1997. Print.

Nash, Walter. *The Language of Humour: Style and Technique in Comic Discourse*. London: Longman, 1985. Print.

Sewell, Elizabeth. *The Field of Nonsense*. London: Chatto, 1952. Print.

The Story of Saint Kenelm

Author: Traditional
Time Period: 1001 CE–1500 CE
Country or Culture: England
Genre: Legend

PLOT SUMMARY

"The Story of Saint Kenelm" tells of the boy-king St. Kenelm (or Cynhelm), the son of King Coenwulf (Kenulf) and rightful ruler of the Anglo-Saxon kingdom of Mercia in what is now the West Midlands of England. According to the legend, the lover of St. Kenelm's ambitious sister Quendreda (Quendryth or Kendrida) murders Kenelm at her request when the boy is only nine years old. In the woods near the Clent Hills, the lover cuts off the boy's head with a long knife and then buries the head along with the body and knife under a bush in the forest. St. Kenelm has hardly been buried when, a thousand miles away, a white dove flies into St. Peter's Basilica in Rome. The dove carries a scroll in its bill and presents it on the high altar. The scroll tells of St. Kenelm's murder and the body's location.

The pontiff tells the churchmen of Mercia about the message and instructs them to make a thorough search for the prince's body. Everyone from priests to the bishop of Mercia look diligently around the forest for the slain boy. Eventually, the search party comes across a cow mournfully standing near a patch of freshly turned sod. There, they dig and find the body of the murdered prince. When they lift the body, the bells of the neighboring churches begin ringing and a spring of water flows out from the excavated ground. Shortly after, the Chapel of St. Kenelm at Romsley is built beside the spring. On the doors of the chapel are carvings of a childlike figure wearing a crown and holding a book.

SIGNIFICANCE

"The Story of Saint Kenelm" concerns the legend of the murdered boy-king and the land where his body was allegedly found. The account of St. Kenelm come primarily from a twelfth-century manuscript found at Winchcombe Abbey, claiming to be based on the accounts of a Worcester monk. According to that manuscript, King Coenwulf of Mercia died in 819 CE and was survived by two daughters and a seven-year-old son named Kenelm. The boy was chosen to succeed his father, which made the daughter Quendreda envious. She plotted with her lover, Askeberd (Askobert), who was also Kenelm's tutor and guardian, to kill her brother so she could become queen. While on a hunting trip in the forests of Worcestershire, Quendreda and Askeberd saw their opportunity when Kenelm rested beneath a tree. Askeberd dug a grave in preparation before assassinating the young boy.

Several fantastical elements surround the hagiography of St. Kenelm. The manuscript states that the night before the ill-fated hunting expedition, Kenelm has an ominous dream in which he climbs and sits atop a large tree from which he can see his whole realm. Three corners of the kingdom bow to him, but the fourth chops the tree down. Kenelm turns into a white bird and flies away. Before Askeberd can kill the sleeping prince, the legend states that Kenelm awakes and thrusts a stick into the ground, which later flowers and grows into a large ash tree, known as St. Kenelm's Ash. Another part of the legend states that when Askeberd cuts Kenelm's head off, Kenelm's soul transforms into the white dove that carries the scroll to St. Peter's Basilica. In some accounts, the boy martyr dies singing the hymn "Te Deum." Later versions of the legend also relate that the cow that found Kenelm's body produces double the usual milk, and the grass she eats replenishes itself nightly. Others recount that Quendreda's eyes fall out as the bells ring for her brother's passing, and she dies a terrible death.

This legend seems to bear little resemblance to the facts known about the real Kenelm. Kenelm in fact signed several of his father's charters between 798 and 811 CE and owned land in Glastonbury, and some scholars believe that he died fighting the Welsh in 812. All of this would indicate that Kenelm would not have been a child at the time of his death. Local historians even argue that there were two Kenelms: the older may have been the one who died in battle, and the younger is believed to have been the son of his distant cousin and successor, Coenwulf of Mercia. Many believe that the younger was in fact the Kenelm who was canonized. Historical records also show that at the time of the king's death, Kenelm's sister Quendreda had already become an abbess.

The site of St. Kenelm's supposed murder became the location of the annual St. Kenelm's feast, held on July 17, and over time a hamlet grew around it, populated mainly with pilgrims. During the reign of King Edward I, folklorist Hugh Miller recounts, the hamlet's population grew numerous and the chapel received many gifts of silver and gold. Pilgrimages to the location were frequent, and many travelers drank from the spring's sacred water to cure their ills.

In holy art, St. Kenelm is sometimes depicted as a boy in royal robes holding a lily or as a young boy with a crown and a holy book. During the Middle Ages, he was a highly venerated saint throughout England, but in contemporary times, his following is essentially found in Worcestershire. When King Henry VIII initiated the age of Reformation, he seized Winchcombe Abbey, and gradually the hamlet dissolved. According to Miller's account, Bishop Latimer broke down the well and pilgrimages to the location ceased, but the annual feast ran until 1784. In 1815, the foundations of an ancient monastery in Winchcombe were excavated. It was there that the body of St. Kenelm was said to be interred near his father. They found a small stone coffin beside a larger one, and inside were bone fragments, a half-grown human skull, and a long-bladed knife.

In literature, the prophetic dream and death of St. Kenelm are referenced in Geoffrey Chaucer's *Canterbury Tales* in "The Nun's Priest's Tale." English poet Francis Brett Young penned the long-form poem "The Ballad of St. Kenelm, AD 821," published in his 1944 collection *The Island*.

Patrick G. Cooper

BIBLIOGRAPHY

Chambers, Roger. *The Story of St. Kenelm: Prince, King, and Martyr*. Cornwall: Exposure, 2007. Print.

De Voragine, Jacobus. "The Life of S. Kenelm." *The Golden Legend*. Vol. 4. Trans. William Caxton. Ed. F. S. Ellis. London: Dent, 1900. 60–66. Print.

Hartland, Edwin Sidney. "The Legend of St. Kenelm." *Transactions of the Bristol and Gloucestershire Archaeological Society*. U of California, Berkeley, 18 Mar. 2010. Web. 17 June 2013.

Love, Rosalind C., trans. *Three Eleventh-Century Anglo-Latin Saints' Lives: Vita S. Birini, Vite et Miracula S. Kenelmi, Vita S. Rumwoldi*. Oxford: Oxford UP, 1996. Print.

Miller, Hugh. "The Story of Saint Kenelm." *English Fairy and Other Folk Tales*. Ed. Edwin Sidney Hartland. London: Scott, 1890. Print.

Price, John. *St. Kenelm's Trail*. Waltham Cross: John Merrill Foundation, 2008. Print.

Smith, Mike, and David Taylor. "The Crown and the Well: The Divine King and the Re-Discovery of a 'Lost' Well." *At the Edge*. IndigoGroup.co.uk, 2001. Web. 16 July 2013.

◆ The Story of the Young Cuckoo

Author: Padriac Colum
Time Period: 999 BCE–1 BCE; 1 CE–500 CE
Country or Culture: Ireland
Genre: Folktale

PLOT SUMMARY

A young cuckoo screams in frustration while he frantically tries to squeeze through the narrow opening of a hollow tree in order to free himself. While other birds whose children have already left the nest live joyful lives, the young cuckoo's foster-parents have taken care of him for too long and are now old and tired. When they hear his screams of frustration, they are reminded of the sound a hawk. Frightened, they fly away although they express regret for abandoning their foster-child.

The foster-parents built their nest inside a hollow tree that contained a small opening. The young cuckoo grew up there because his birth-mother had laid egg on the ground and carried it up the hollow tree in her beak and placed it in the nest. Although this strange egg pushed out their own young birds, the foster-parents treated the bizarre-looking bird as their own child, but they were tired after collecting food for him.

The cuckoo thrived in the hollow tree, but when it came time for him to leave the nest, he could not fit through the small opening. Before fleeing, the foster-parents had brought him food until he had grown so big there was no longer any room for them inside the hollow. With their home overtaken by the peculiar bird and startled by the scream, the foster-parents vow to never return to the hollow tree.

While the young cuckoo attempts to make his way out, a curious woodpecker stops by and asks how the bird got in there. The cuckoo explains that he had been born there, and then he opened his mouth wide and asks the woodpecker to give him some food. The woodpecker denies the request and explains that he has trouble enough finding food for himself. The young cuckoo continues to struggle at the opening in the tree and lets out another scream. Then the woodpecker advises the cuckoo not to draw too much attention to himself with all of the screaming because other creatures might mistake him for a young hawk and rip him apart.

Desperate to get out of the tree, the cuckoo asks the woodpecker what he is supposed to do. The woodpecker replies that the cuckoo has to do what is in his nature. The cuckoo replies that it is his nature to swing on high branches, spread his wings and soar over the land, and be alone with the sound of his own voice. After this declaration, the cuckoo cries "Cuckoo, cuckoo, cuckoo!"

The woodpecker leaves the cuckoo with a warning that a storm is approaching. With renewed energy, the cuckoo struggles against the tree's opening but more forcefully than before. Just then, a bolt of lightning strikes the hollow tree and tears away the opening. The young cuckoo falls from the tree and lands on the wet grass. He walks clumsily among the blue bellflowers and comments on the amount of fire and noise that it took to free him: "What a world!"

SIGNIFICANCE

Padriac Colum's "The Story of Young Cuckoo" is featured in the children's novel *The King of Ireland's Son* (1916). Colum was a poet, playwright, and novelist who wrote many of his own interpretations of classic Irish legends and folktales. He was a leading figure in the Irish Literary Revival, which was a literary movement in the late nineteenth and early twentieth centuries when interest was renewed in Ireland's Gaelic heritage. In *The King of Ireland's Son*, Colum writes about the eldest of the king's sons and his endeavors to win the hand of Fedelma, the Enchanter's Daughter. The book features several Irish folktales, including "The Story of the Young Cuckoo."

Celtic mythology contains several beliefs concerning cuckoo birds, also known as "gowks." Cuckoos are common migrating birds around Europe and they typically appear in early April and coincide with the arrival of spring, so their call is often synonymous with violent storms, much like the one that frees the young cuckoo in the folktale. Young boys often imitate the cuckoo's call (an early April Fools' Day joke) to trick others into thinking a storm is coming.

The birds are often depicted with supernatural powers. Many believe that their call can summon the souls of the dead and that the birds are able to move between the worlds of the living and the dead. Other legends portray the cuckoo as being able to foretell when a person will marry and how many children he or she will have. It is considered a bad omen if a cuckoo's call is heard while fasting or hungry, but it is a good sign if the call is heard after a feast.

The cuckoo appears in other tales as a sign of spring, warm weather, and harvest. Swiss legend says that a cuckoo cannot sing until April 3 and never after midsummer. In Great Britain, legends tell of cuckoos transforming into hawks at the end of spring and reverting back to their original form every April. This legend was a likely influence on Colum and can be seen in the young cuckoo's hawk-like scream in the story.

A real-life attribute of the cuckoo bird that is used in the story is its brood parasitic nature. Brood parasites manipulate members of the same or different species to raise their young, and cuckoos lay their eggs in the nests of other birds for that purpose. The cuckoo's brood parasitic behavior was first observed by Aristotle in the fourth century BCE. He believed that this trait made the cuckoo resourceful by nature. The young cuckoo in Colum's story, however, needs advice from the woodpecker in order to be truly free.

Patrick G. Cooper

BIBLIOGRAPHY

Anderson, Glynn. *Birds of Ireland: Facts, Folklore & History*. Cork: Collins, 2009. Print.

Armstrong, Richard. "Cuckoos and Cuckoldry." *Engines of Our Ingenuity.* John Lienhard, n.d. Web. 30 May 2013.

Collins, Richard. "The Cuckoo: Ireland's Most Scandalous Bird!" *RTÉ Radio*. RTÉ Commercial Enterprises, n.d. Web 30 May 2013.

Colum, Pádraic. *The King of Ireland's Son.* Mineola: Dover, 1997. Print.

Glassie, Henry, ed. *Irish Folktales*. New York: Pantheon, 1997. Print.

GRECO-ROMAN WORLD

◆ Achilles and the Stern Waters of Styx

Author: Statius
Time Period: 1 CE–500 CE
Country or Culture: Rome
Genre: Myth

PLOT SUMMARY

In Statius's *Achilleid*, an unfinished Roman poem of the first century CE, the link between the Greek hero Achilles (Akhilleus)and the River Styx is not elaborated as an explicit event but is alluded to as part of the larger myth of Achilles's life and death. Statius intended to represent the life of Achilles until his death in the Trojan War at the hands of his enemy Paris, who stole Helen, the wife of Menelaus, and thus precipitated the conflict between the Greeks and the Trojans. The completed portions of Statius's poem recount the failed attempts of Thetis, mother of Achilles, to protect her son from joining the Greek forces and meeting his death.

The poem begins with Thetis, a sea nymph, who laments the presence of the war ships traveling to Troy.

Thetis has learned from a prophecy that her son Achilles will be called to fight and that if he goes to war, he will meet certain death. To prevent this, she first appeals unsuccessfully to Neptune, god of the sea, to destroy the ship carrying Paris and Helen. She then goes to retrieve Achilles from his guardian, the centaur Chiron (Kheiron). She hides him on the island of Scyros (Skyros) and urges him to disguise himself by dressing as a girl. Achilles refuses until he encounters the beautiful Deidamia, daughter of King Lycomedes, at which point he agrees to cross-dress so that he may become closer to the object of his love.

Disguised as a girl, Achilles is entrusted to the care of King Lycomedes, and Thetis departs. Eventually, Achilles and Deidamia develop a love relationship. She conspires to maintain his disguise, becomes pregnant, and bears a child. During this time, the Greek warriors travel to gather forces and become aware of Achilles's absence. When a prophet reveals the young man's presence on Scyros, the Greek heroes Ulysses and Diomede expose Achilles's true identity by offering him weapons as gifts, which he readily accepts. Achilles and Deidamia are then married, after which Achilles departs for war. The story breaks off in book 2 after Achilles recounts his youthful years and his rearing by Chiron.

In the narrative, Statius alludes to the River Styx in relation to Achilles several times. The first appears in book 1 when Thetis entreats Chiron, begging him to reveal the whereabouts of her son Achilles. In this scene, Thetis laments that her sleep has been troubled, and she has had "terrible portents from the gods and fearful panics" (519) because she senses the doom to come. She states, "I seem to take my son down to the void of Tartarus, and dip him a second time in the springs of Styx" (519). She refers to the magical river later in book 1 when she attempts to convince Achilles to disguise himself as a girl. She urges him to acquiesce and accept the disguise "if at thy birth I fortified thee with the stern waters of the Styx" (529). The final reference appears as the Greek warriors wonder at the absence of the great Achilles, describing him as follows: "Whom else did a Nereid take by stealth through the Stygian waters and make his fair limbs impenetrable to steel?" (545). In these passages, Statius refers to a long-established Greek myth according to which Thetis, learning the prophecy of Achilles's early death, attempts to protect her infant son by immersing his body in the Styx, a supernatural river bordering the earth and the underworld. The waters make Achilles invulnerable to mortal wounds, but he remains vulnerable on his left heel, where his mother held him as she dipped the rest of his body in the enchanted water.

SIGNIFICANCE

One of the most important mythological heroes in Western civilization, Achilles appears most prominently in Homer's *Iliad*, an eighth-century BCE Greek epic poem that highlights the conflicts of Achilles with his Greek comrades and with the enemy Trojans. A Roman poet writing centuries after Homer in the first century CE, Statius (like many Roman poets) adapted Greek mythological material partly in an attempt to create a Latin literary tradition worthy of the Greek epic models. Thus, the myths surrounding Achilles, who was already a major hero by the time Statius wrote, offered appropriate subject matter, and the *Achilleid* aims to develop the hero's life by recounting his youth with his mother prior to the war.

The story of Achilles's vulnerability clearly became a central part of the Greco-Roman mythological tradition. Interestingly, however, neither Homer nor Statius recount the death of Achilles, which, according to myth, occurs at the hands of Paris, who shoots a poisoned arrow into Achilles's unprotected left heel, causing him to die. Other prominent writers do offer this part of the story, including the Roman poet Ovid, who recounts the hero's death in book 12 of the *Metamorphoses.*

Whereas the ancient story of Achilles's heel emphasizes the literal sense of the hero's weak mortal spot, the legacy of this myth has proved most enduring for its medical and metaphorical significance. As the myth survived into the modern age, his heel was applied to anatomy: the calcaneal tendon of the lower leg, which extends and attaches the gastrocnemius and soleus muscles to the bone, is commonly referred to as the Achilles tendon. Perhaps most powerful, however, is the metaphorical significance of "Achilles' heel," which has come to signify any flaw or weakness that in the context of great strength can lead to failure or ruin. Just as the great Greek hero died because of a small yet fatal flaw, people and even societies are sometimes described as possessing an Achilles' heel—a single, powerful weakness that can precipitate downfall or disaster.

Ashleigh Imus, PhD

BIBLIOGRAPHY

Cook, Elizabeth. *Achilles.* New York: Picador, 2002. Print.

Corey, Dale. *From Achilles' Heel to Zeus' Shield.* New York: Fawcett Columbine, 1993. Print.

Fantuzzi, Marco. *Achilles in Love: Intertextual Studies.* Oxford: Oxford UP, 2012. Print.

Heslin, P. J. *The Transvestite Achilles: Gender and Genre in Statius'* Achilleid. Cambridge: Cambridge UP, 2005. Print.

Homer. *The Iliad.* Trans. Edward McCrorie. Baltimore: Johns Hopkins UP, 2012. Print.

Ovid. *Metamorphoses.* Trans. A. D. Melville. Oxford: Oxford UP, 1986. Print.

Statius. *Statius.* Vol 2. Trans. J. H. Mozley. Cambridge: Harvard UP, 1989. Print.

◆ Apollo Establishes His Temple at Delphi

Author: Ovid
Time Period: 1 CE–500 CE
Country or Culture: Rome
Genre: Myth

PLOT SUMMARY

After the creation of the earth, sky, waters, and other elements come the ages of humanity, beginning with the golden age and continuing through the silver, bronze, and iron ages. As the world degenerates into sin and vice in the iron age, Jupiter sends a flood to wipe out humanity and to begin life on earth again.

However, the chief god allows a virtuous couple, Deucalion and Pyrrha, to survive the flood. When the waters recede, the couple realizes that they are the sole surviving humans on Earth, so they pray to the goddess Themis for counsel on how to propagate the human race once again. The goddess instructs them to cast their mothers' bones behind them. Puzzled, Pyrrha fears that she is being asked to offend her mother's spirit by disrespecting her bones, but Deucalion soon realizes that the goddess is referring to the stones of the earth. The couple immediately throws stones behind them; as the rocks land, they slowly begin to take the shape of humans, with Deucalion's stones becoming men and Pyrrha's stones transforming into women. In this way, humans are restored.

Other species emerge from the warmth and heat of the earth following the flood, some of which replicate creatures in existence prior to the flood and others of which are new and strange. One of these new species is a giant snake (sometimes referred to as a dragon) known as Python. This beast terrorizes the humans until the god Apollo, a deity linked to the sun and prophecy and representing the medicinal, poetic, and musical arts, kills the snake with his arrows. To preserve the memory of this great victory, Apollo then establishes the Pythian athletic games.

In some retellings of the deeds of Apollo, the god kills Python because the serpent is preventing him from reaching Delphi, where an oracle of Themis resides. After killing the snake, Apollo claims the oracle as his own, establishing his temple at Delphi. Over time, many humans visit the oracle, seeking knowledge of future events, and her prophecies come to shape the lives of many legendary rulers and heroes.

SIGNIFICANCE

The myth of Apollo's defeat of Python and establishment of his temple at Delphi is found in numerous classical Greek and Roman sources, though the details of the myth vary considerably. One particularly memorable account of the origin of Python derives from the *Metamorphoses*, a compilation of myths composed by the Roman poet Ovid early in the first century CE. Although Ovid mentions Apollo as a central figure in the

re-creation of the world after Jupiter's flood and discusses the slaying of Python, he does not mention the founding of the temple at Delphi. There are at least two possible reasons for this. First, Ovid was likely aware that his readers were already well familiar with the story of Apollo's temple at Delphi. Many accounts of Apollo's defeat of Python and subsequent founding of the temple precede Ovid's version, including a hymn to Apollo frequently attributed to the eighth-century BCE Greek poet Homer, which explains that Apollo is sometimes called Pythian Apollo because of his victory. The Greek writer Pseudo-Apollodorus, in his *Bibliotheca* (*The Library*), chronicles Apollo's journey to Delphi and defeat of the snake. Given Apollo's well-established identity, Ovid did not need to repeat in detail the story of the temple's founding at Delphi.

Second, Ovid may have left out the founding of the temple in keeping with his pattern of representing the gods in nontraditional terms. The Roman poet concludes his account of Apollo's slaying of Python by referencing the oak or other leaves the god uses to adorn his hair and that of victorious athletes; the poet notes that the god has yet to begin using laurels for that purpose. With this conclusion, Ovid segues into the story of Apollo and the nymph Daphne, to which he dedicates significant attention. The most obvious purpose of this story is to explain the origin of the laurel tree and Apollo's use of its leaves: Apollo falls in love with Daphne after Cupid strikes him with an arrow. The god chases her through the woods, begging her to acknowledge and accept his love. Just as he is about to overcome her, Daphne prays to her father, Peneus, to save her, which he does by transforming her into a laurel tree. Apollo then embraces the tree and makes its leaves the sign of his honor.

In this story, Ovid does much to undercut the traditional image of Apollo as a serious, manly guardian of oracular truth, health, and high culture, an image that the myth of Apollo's defeat of the serpent and establishment of the temple presents in a more straightforward manner. Apollo falls in love with Daphne only because of his quarrel with Cupid, whom Apollo scorns based on his own prowess in archery, and when chasing the nymph, the god boasts of his power and claims to love Daphne but then laments that he, the god of healing, cannot cure himself of love. The effect of this story, which immediately follows the account of Apollo's victory over Python in the *Metamorphoses*, is to undercut the seriousness and authority traditionally associated with Apollo. This undermining is typical of Ovid's treatment of the gods in the *Metamorphoses* and indicates not only his urbane style but also the shifting cultural attitudes of his Roman audience in the Augustan age.

Ashleigh Imus, PhD

BIBLIOGRAPHY

Apollodorus. *The Library of Greek Mythology.* Trans. Robin Hard. Oxford: Oxford UP, 1997. Print.

Broad, William J. *The Oracle: The Lost Secrets and Hidden Message of Ancient Delphi.* New York: Penguin, 2006. Print.

Homer. *The Homeric Hymns.* Trans. Jules Cashford. London: Penguin, 2003. Print.

Ovid. *Metamorphoses.* Trans. A. D. Melville. Oxford: Oxford UP, 1986. Print.

Solomon, Jon, ed. *Apollo: Origins and Influences.* Tucson: U of Arizona P, 1994. Print.

◆ Athena and the Birth of Erichthonius

Author: Pseudo-Apollodorus
Time Period: 1 CE–500 CE
Country or Culture: Greece
Genre: Myth

PLOT SUMMARY

The patron deity of the city of Athens, Athena is a powerful goddess of wisdom and warfare and an ally to just heroes and soldiers. She is also a virgin goddess, and her virginity is considered a mark of her virtue and strength. One day, Athena seeks out Hephaestus, the god of smiths, in order to obtain new weapons from him. Though Hephaestus has made many weapons for fellow gods before, when he sees Athena, he is so overcome by love and lust for the goddess that he begins to chase her. When he finally throws himself upon her, Athena manages to defend herself and fight off the sexual assault, although Hephaestus does ejaculate onto her leg in the process. Disgusted by this, Athena uses a piece of wool to wipe his semen onto the ground. The earth welcomes it, and from this union Erichthonius is born.

Erichthonius has the upper body of a human and the lower body of a snake. When Athena sees him, she decides to raise him in secret, hoping to make him an immortal like herself despite the fact that he is not her true son. She places the baby in a wicker basket in order to hide him from the other gods and gives him to Pandrosus (Pandrosos,) the daughter of the Athenian king, Cecrops (Kekrôps). Athena orders Pandrosus never to open the basket, trusting that the young woman, a faithful follower of the goddess, will obey her.

However, Cecrops's other daughters, Herse and Aglaurus (Aglauros), are not as obedient as their sister is. They are overcome by curiosity about what might be in the basket and eventually convince Pandrosus to let them open it. The sisters are driven mad by the sight of the serpent child and the holy wrath of Athena, and they throw themselves off the side of the Acropolis of Athens, perishing on the city streets. Athena then raises Erichthonius herself, training the young man in politics and military strategy. When he comes of age, he overthrows Amphictyon, who had usurped the throne of Athens, and becomes ruler of the city, establishing festivals and temples that will praise Athena for all time.

SIGNIFICANCE

The myth of the birth of Erichthonius is one of the most dominant myths concerning the history of Athens, and the establishment of the mythic king as the city's ruler was an important moment in the legend of the metropolis. It is notable, then, that the myth is only superficially concerned with Erichthonius and masculine rulers and instead focuses on the virgin goddess and her priestesses.

Athena occupies a complicated and uniquely gendered role within the Greek pantheon. She is a goddess of warfare and heroism, qualities typically associated with masculinity by the ancient Greeks. While Athena is famously beautiful, she does not engage in the affairs, marriages, and scandalous romances that occupy the other gods and goddesses. These tensions between traditional ideas of gender and gendered behavior are likely rooted far back in the history of Greek mythology. Some scholars believe that the goddess originated in ancient, largely lost matriarchal religions and was subsumed into the patriarchal Greek pantheon centuries later. Discrete ideas regarding gender and sexuality, then, remained unresolved in the mythology of Athena.

In the myth of the birth of Erichthonius, an elaborate moral of chastity and deference is woven into the baby's origin. Athena uses her strength and military knowledge to fend off the attack by Hephaestus, and it is the earth rather than the body of the goddess that carries the child. In this way, her supposedly masculine qualities of strength and fortitude are seen as being in the service of her divine and untouched femininity, while the magical birth of Erichthonius allows her to raise a child without sacrificing her virginity. Likewise, Pandrosus and her sisters are not only royal citizens of Athens but also priestesses of Athena, ostensibly devoted to her worship above all else. In being given the wicker basket and the command to remain ignorant of its contents, the girls are expected to exhibit both strength of will and ultimate subservience, qualities that would make them ideal women in the ethics of the Athenian cult.

Ultimately, only Pandrosus exhibits these qualities, and her sisters are driven to madness and death by their sins. Pandrosus, however, was celebrated in Athenian cults for centuries; a temple dedicated to her existed alongside one of Athena's own temples, and a yearly ritual in the city involved young women carrying baskets through the temple without opening them to view the contents. While it is often relatively easy to apply stereotypical ideas regarding gender to the gods and goddesses of Greek mythology, in the myth of the birth of Erichthonius, the complex character of Athena precludes any such simplifications. Instead, the myth presents a tale of power woven into subservience and of masculinity bolstering femininity, the priestesses and the goddess abstaining from sexuality and physical pleasure in order to bring about the divine birth of the legendary king.

T. Fleischmann, MFA

BIBLIOGRAPHY

"Athena and the Birth of Erichthonius." *Theoi Greek Mythology*. Aaron J. Atsma, 2011. Web. 28 May 2013.

Deacy, Susan. *Athena*. New York: Routledge, 2008. Print.

Georgievska-Shine, Aneta. "From Ovid's Cecrops to Rubens's City of God in *The Finding of Erichthonius*." *Art Bulletin* 86.1 (2004): 58–74. Print.

Neils, Jennifer, ed. *Worshipping Athena: Panathenaia and Parthenon*. Madison: U of Wisconsin P, 1996. Print.

Rigoglioso, Marguerite. *The Cult of Divine Birth in Ancient Greece*. New York: Palgrave, 2009. Print.

◆ Bellerophon and the Battle with Chimera

Author: Homer; Pindar; Hesiod
Time Period: 1 CE–500 CE
Country or Culture: Greece
Genre: Myth

PLOT SUMMARY

Born of Eurynomê, queen of Corinth, and the god Poseidon, Bellerophon is raised as the son of King Glaucus (Glaukos) and trained to become an expert horseman. As a young man, he learns of the existence of the great winged horse Pegasus (Pêgasos) and becomes determined to capture the animal. He spends a night on an altar dedicated to the goddess Athena, during which he dreams of a golden bridle capable of subduing Pegasus. Upon awakening, Bellerophon discovers the bridle in his hands. Pegasus eventually comes into the city of Corinth to drink from the fountain of Pirene (Peirênê), and the young man uses the bridle to capture and ride the horse.

In light of his success, Bellerophon approaches Pittheus, king of Troezen, to ask for his daughter's hand in marriage. The king agrees to the match, but Bellerophon accidentally kills a man prior to the wedding. In accordance with custom, Bellerophon is banished. He next travels to Argos and asks that city's king, Proteus, to purify him of the crime he has committed. Proteus agrees, but after Bellerophon spurns the unwanted advances of the queen, Stheneboea, she tells her husband that their guest attempted to seduce her. This angers the king, who devises a plan to dispose of Bellerophon.

As breaking the laws of hospitality was considered an affront to the gods, Proteus pretends to remain a friend of Bellerophon, asking the young man to deliver a letter on his behalf to King Iobates of Lycia, the queen's father. The letter describes Bellerophon's alleged actions against Iobates's daughter. Bellerophon flies atop Pegasus to Iobates's kingdom and is well received by the king. However, when Iobates reads the letter, he turns against his guest just as Proteus intended. Still bound by the belief that one should not harm a guest, Iobates instead asks Bellerophon to undertake a seemingly impossible challenge. The king charges the hero with killing the Chimera (Khimaira), a vicious, fire-breathing monster with the heads of a lion, a goat, and a snake, which has killed many in the kingdom.

Out of pity for the people of Lycia, Bellerophon accepts the challenge. Flying on Pegasus and using his considerable archery skills, he succeeds in slaying the monster. Iobates next asks Bellerophon to engage Lycia's enemy, the neighboring Solymi people. When Bellerophon easily defeats the Solymi, Iobates asks him to fight the Amazons. Bellerophon again emerges victorious, this time thanks to a flood sent by Poseidon. Having failed to kill Bellerophon indirectly, Iobates next sends his own army to defeat the young hero. When Bellerophon returns to Lycia unharmed, Iobates realizes that the young man clearly has the favor of the gods and gives Bellerophon half of his kingdom as well as the hand of his daughter, Philonoe.

Although Bellerophon becomes known as an honorable man and a beloved ruler, his success against the Chimera and his other foes makes him arrogant. Wanting to meet the gods, Bellerophon attempts to fly Pegasus to the top of Mount Olympus, where they reside. The king of all the gods, Zeus, punishes Bellerophon for this action by knocking the hero from Pegasus. Severely injured from the fall, Bellerophon is left to walk the earth alone for the rest of his life, shunned by humans and gods alike.

SIGNIFICANCE

The tale of Bellerophon illustrates the relationship between mortals and the gods in Greek mythology. Like many heroes known for performing seemingly impossible tasks, including Heracles and Perseus, Bellerophon is the son of a god and a mortal woman. This semidivine heritage gives the young hero great strength, agility, and intelligence, and it also provides him with a degree of divine support and protection. At first, he uses these attributes for adventure, relying on both his skills and divine assistance to capture Pegasus. He later uses his great strength and skill to defeat the deadly Chimera and save the people of Lycia.

As befits one who has received aid from Athena, the goddess of wisdom and honorable warfare, Bellerophon remains honorable throughout his adventures. When Stheneboea attempts to seduce him, Bellerophon refuses, obeying the customs governing the conduct of guests and keeping true to his heritage. Though he encounters deceit and wickedness, the son of Poseidon cannot be defeated so easily; the scores of men sent to kill him meet the same fate as the Chimera.

Although a respectful and honorable hero in his early years, Bellerophon eventually grows arrogant and presumptuous as a result of his success. Inspired by the blessings he has received, Bellerophon believes himself to be worthy of visiting and living among the gods. His semidivine nature does grant him the gods' favor, but as a mortal, he is still unworthy of approaching Mount Olympus. His punishment for his presumption is harsh: he is sent back to earth to live out his days as an outcast, while the purer Pegasus, also a son of Poseidon, is granted entrance to Olympus.

Bellerophon's fate reflects the ancient Greek concern with hubris, excessive arrogance or pride, which proves to be the downfall of humans and demigods in many myths. In particular, the theme of a mortal attempting to reach a realm belonging only to the divine recurs throughout Greek mythology, as in the myth of Icarus, who falls to his death after flying too close to the sun. In attempting to approach Mount Olympus, Bellerophon oversteps the bounds of his semidivine existence and faces the appropriate consequences. Despite being the child of a god and a hero among humans, he loses the favor of both the gods and humanity. Bellerophon spends the rest of his life walking the earth in solitude, enjoying the company of neither mortals nor immortals.

Michael P. Auerbach, MA

BIBLIOGRAPHY

"Bellerophontes." *Theoi Greek Mythology*. Aaron J. Atsma, 2011. Web. 24 May 2013.

Hunt, J. M. "Bellerophon." *Greek Mythology*. San Diego State U, 1 Jan. 1996. Web. 24 May 2013.

Lieberman, Erez. "Bellerophon." *Encyclopedia Mythica*. Encyclopedia Mythica, 2 Jan. 2004. Web. 24 May 2013.

Parker, Janet, and Julie Stanton, eds. *Mythology: Myths, Legends, and Fantasies*. Cape Town: Struik, 2007. Print.

Peterson, Amy T., and David J. Dunworth. *Mythology in Our Midst: A Guide to Cultural References*. Westport: Greenwood, 2004. Print.

◆ The Birth of Zeus

Author: Hesiod
Time Period: 999 BCE–1 BCE
Country or Culture: Greece
Genre: Myth

PLOT SUMMARY

Before the age of the Olympian gods, the universe is ruled by Gaia and Uranus, the earth goddess and sky god, and their children, the Titans. One of the Titans, Cronus, overthrows Uranus, and he and his sister Rhea become the king and queen of the gods, initiating a long period of peace and celebration in their realm.

While it is the duty of the Titans to give birth to more gods and goddesses, Cronus learns that just as he overthrew his own father, one of his children would someday come to overthrow him. Unwilling to give up his power or his physical relations with his wife, he insists on swallowing up their children the moment they are born. One after the other, Cronus swallows Hestia, Hades, Demeter, Poseidon, and finally Hera, imprisoning some of the most powerful deities inside of his stomach before they even have the chance to see a full day. While the gods and goddesses do not die, they remain weak and unable to usurp their father.

Rhea is distressed by her husband's violent actions and seeks the advice of her parents, Gaia and Uranus. These gods agree to help Rhea not only for her benefit and for the benefit of their grandchildren but also because Cronus had overthrown and castrated Uranus years before. They know that if they can save only one infant from Cronus, that child will grow to overthrow him, securing their revenge.

On the advice of her parents, Rhea travels to the island of Crete as soon as she is ready to give birth. There, Gaia herself receives the child Zeus from Rhea, covering him with her protective arms and hurrying him to a sacred, hidden cave in the heavy forests of Mount Aigion. There, Gaia promises to use her powers and the strength of the earth to raise the child into the mighty god he is destined to become. Just as quickly, Rhea wraps a large stone in a swaddling cloth, holding it as though it were a living child, and returns to her home. She gives this stone to Cronus, who swallows it whole without another thought. With Cronus tricked, the infant Zeus is finally safe, able to grow and gain strength until he will one day overthrow his father and become king of the gods himself.

SIGNIFICANCE

The myth of the birth of Zeus comes to the modern day through the ancient Greek poet Hesiod's *Theogony*, a work composed in the seventh or eighth century BCE that charts the rise of the Olympian gods to dominance and their overthrow of the more ancient Titans. The *Theogony* is a foundational text in understanding power within Greek mythology. Through its narrative, Hesiod combines divergent myths into one cohesive text,

demonstrating how and why the Greek pantheon came to be.

The narrative of the birth of Zeus is a key moment in the transfer of power from the Titans to the Olympians, set in a long tradition of deceit, betrayal, and violence. While Zeus would eventually need to form an army and overthrow his father by brute force, the subtle tricks of his mother and grandmother are equally significant in establishing his dominance. Like that of many leaders in ancient Greek mythology, the power of Zeus comes from several sources. He has a divine right to the throne of Olympus, his leadership having been prophesied well before his birth, and he eventually claims that right through military might. However, his birth also shows a blessing by divine women and the earth. Rhea and Gaia are two of the most ancient and powerful female forces in Greek mythology, with Gaia representing the essential power of the earth itself. Neither goddess rules with the same force as her husband, but both represent the necessity of the female counterpart in establishing political and mythological power. This is particularly significant as they are both the consorts of former rulers and queens of the gods, yet they choose to use their powers to usher in the age of Zeus rather than preserve the reign of their male counterparts.

The role of Gaia and Rhea in this myth of power ultimately points to the patriarchal nature of Greek society and mythology. Only a single male will rule in the Greek pantheon at any moment, and Zeus himself will eventually be called the father of all gods (a symbolic fatherhood for the most part, although he does father many deities). Yet in the story of his birth, it is the female deities who truly influence the course of mythology, holding all the power by tricking Cronus and relying on the protection of the earth to safeguard the infant god. However, the strength of the goddesses is subverted into the rule of gods (and men), and despite all their wit, Rhea and Gaia will find themselves eventually displaced from power once more, Zeus banishing the Titans as soon as his reign is established. Within the context of the *Theogony*, the story of the birth of Zeus is a justification of these inevitabilities. The mythological Greek world, much like the Greek political world, will become a place of male supremacy and power. By describing the most ancient and powerful feminine forces as supporting this eventual patriarchy, Hesiod both recognizes and subverts the value of the goddesses.

T. Fleischmann, MFA

BIBLIOGRAPHY

Garrison, Daniel H. "Hesiod." *Critical Survey of Poetry: European Poets*. Ed. Rosemary M. Canfield Reisman. 4th ed. Vol. 2. Pasadena: Salem, 2011. 465–71. Print.

López-Ruiz, Carolina. "How to Start a Cosmogony: On the Poetics of Beginnings in Greece and the Near East." *Journal of Ancient Near Eastern Religions* 12.1 (2012): 30–48. Print.

Munn, Mark H. *The Mother of the Gods, Athens, and the Tyranny of Asia: A Study of Sovereignty in Ancient Religion*. Berkeley: U of California P, 2006. Print.

"Rhea and the Birth of Her Children." *Theoi Greek Mythology*. Aaron J. Atsma, 2011. Web. 20 June 2013.

Shapiro, H. A. *The Cambridge Companion to Archaic Greece*. Cambridge: Cambridge UP, 2007. Print.

◆ Cadmus Sowing the Dragon's Teeth

Author: Ovid
Time Period: 999 BCE–1 BCE; 1 CE–500 CE
Country or Culture: Rome
Genre: Myth

PLOT SUMMARY

The story of Cadmus begins in book 3 of Ovid's *Metamorphosis*, where it develops from the tale of Jupiter's seduction of the Tyrian maiden Europa at the end of book 2. The god Jupiter, known for seducing human women, desires Europa, daughter of King Agenor. To conceal his infidelity, Jupiter disguises himself as a gentle white bull and joins a herd of other animals, prompting Europa to admire the bull's beauty and calm nature. Europa eventually climbs onto the animal's back and is promptly whisked away to Crete. At the opening of book 3, Jupiter reveals himself to Europa, while her father, King Agenor, sends her brother Cadmus to find the lost girl. When Cadmus fails to find her, he avoids the king's presumed anger and consults Apollo's oracle to discover where he should establish his new home. The oracle tells Cadmus that when he finds an unyoked cow, he should follow her and found his city in the place where she rests in the grass. Obeying these instructions, Cadmus locates the spot and sends his men to find water to perform a sacrifice to Jupiter.

The men set forth and discover a cave with plentiful water gushing from its rocks. Within the cave lies "a snake of Mars" with flashing eyes, a gold crest, and "triple rows of teeth" (53). As the Tyrian men dip their pails into the water, a giant snake emerges from the cave and slaughters all of the men with its fierce venom and crushing coils. When his men fail to return, Cadmus follows their tracks and discovers their slain bodies and the menacing serpent. He first hurls a rock, which misses the snake, but his javelin pierces the animal's body. Not yet dead, the enraged serpent attacks Cadmus, who finally defeats it by lancing it against a tree.

No sooner than the serpent is slain, however, a mysterious voice declares, "Why, Cadmus, why / stare at the snake you've slain? You too shall be / a snake and stared at" (53–54). Wondering at the meaning of this pronouncement, Cadmus stands terrified until the goddess Minerva appears and instructs him to plant the serpent's teeth, "from which a future people should arise" (54). Cadmus follows this command and soon witnesses some spearheads emerging from the soil, followed by plumed helmets and a "growing crop of men in mail" (54). Cadmus takes up arms to defend himself against the fearful warriors. One of the soldiers then cries out, "Lay down your arms," telling them "Take no part / In civil strife" (54), but the others ignore this warning and proceed to slaughter one another. Only five men survive, including Echion, who follows Minerva's command to lay down his arms. These men become Cadmus's partners in founding the new city of Thebes.

SIGNIFICANCE

The story of Cadmus did not originate with the Roman poet Ovid, but rather was widely known to earlier Greek sources. The Greek writer Pseudo-Apollodorus tells the story in his second-century BCE *Bibliotheca* (*Library*). His account largely matches that of Ovid, except that he reports that Cadmus throws stones at the warriors that spring from the earth. The soldiers believe the stones originate among themselves, which motivates them to destroy one another. As punishment, Cadmus must serve Ares, the god of war. Numerous other Greek and Roman writers, including the second-century CE Roman mythographer Pseudo-Hyginus, also tell versions of the story.

Ovid was a major Roman poet during the reign of Augustus (27 BCE–14 CE), and his *Metamorphoses* is one of the most important works of Latin poetry. His inclusion of the Cadmus story attests to the importance of the myth in the ancient Greco-Roman tradition. Thebes was indeed a crucial city in Greek mythology as it was the seat of many famous characters and events, including the myths of Oedipus, the adventures of Heracles, and the rise of Dionysus (the god of wine), among others. Ovid weaves many such notable characters into Cadmus's story to develop the significance of his victory over the serpent. After founding the city of Thebes with the help of the few surviving soldiers, Cadmus marries Harmonia, and all seems to go well until the tragedies begin: first, Ovid presents the story of Cadmus's grandson Actaeon, who is transformed into a stag by the goddess Diana as punishment for spying on her while bathing. Next, Cadmus's daughter Semele is impregnated by the philandering Jupiter and punished cruelly by his wife, Juno, who causes Semele to ask Jupiter, who has promised to grant her any wish, to reveal his full power to her. Unable to break his promise, Jupiter's revelation causes Semele to perish, but he saves her unborn child by implanting it into his thigh. Semele's sister Ino raises the boy child upon his birth.

This son turns out to be Bacchus, the Roman god of wine corresponding to the Greek Dionysus. Ovid next tells a series of stories in which various characters deny the divine origin and power of this new god and pay dearly for the impiety. First, Pentheus, son of Echion, scorns Bacchus and is torn apart by Theban worshippers of the god. Next, the daughters of Minyas refuse to participate in the Bacchic rites, instead remaining indoors to tell stories, for which Bacchus transforms them into bats. Cadmus's daughter Ino is then punished by Juno for her faithfulness to Bacchus, whose power has been legitimated. Juno orders the Furies to drive Ino and her husband, Athamas, mad. Crazed, Athamas murders his own son, which then causes Ino to hurl herself and her other child off a cliff into the ocean. Venus convinces Neptune, god of the sea, to make both the boy and his mother immortal.

Grieving these misfortunes, Cadmus and his wife depart from Thebes to become pilgrims. One day, Cadmus wonders if the great snake he had once slain was sacred, and he wishes to become a snake if his misfortunes have resulted from the gods' vengeance. With this wish, both Cadmus and his wife immediately metamorphose into peaceful, harmless snakes, thus fulfilling the prophecy Cadmus had heard upon slaying the serpent.

Ashleigh Imus, PhD

BIBLIOGRAPHY

Baldwin, James. "Cadmus and Europa." *Old Greek Stories*. New York: American Book Co., 1895. 75–87. Print.

Calasso, Roberto. *The Marriage of Cadmus and Harmony*. London: Vintage, 1994. Print.

Hofmann, Michael, and James Lasdun, eds. *After Ovid: New Metamorphoses*. New York: Farrar, 1995. Print.

Ovid. *Metamorphoses*. Trans. A. D. Melville. Oxford: Oxford UP, 1986. Print.

Pseudo-Apollodorus. *Library of Greek Mythology*. Trans. Robin Hard. Oxford: Oxford UP, 1997. Print.

◆ Cronus and the Birth of the Cosmos

Author: Orphica
Time Period: 999 BCE–1 BCE; 1 CE–500 CE
Country or Culture: Greece
Genre: Myth

PLOT SUMMARY

At the very beginning, there is simply creation, the divine matter of the universe brought into existence. Once this divine matter exists, it is necessary to sort it out and order it into different components. Because of this, at the same moment creation begins, Cronus and Ananke are brought into being. Cronus is time, a winged creature with the body of a serpent and the heads of a human, a lion, and a bull. He begins the process of organizing the universe, clarifying that this is the beginning of all things. Ananke is inevitability and fate, and her presence shows that all things will progress forward and an end will one day come.

To organize the universe further, Cronus creates a giant egg out of the divine matter. He and Ananke begin to circle the giant egg, squeezing it tightly with their bodies. Eventually, the force of their motion begins to separate the egg, and so also the universe, into its disparate atoms. When this force is great enough, the atoms become three elements. The lightest of the atoms become the bright light of the heavens, the heaviest float down to become the earth and the waters, and the remainder float between as the wind of chaos. Because all of these elements are set spinning by Cronus and Ananke, they still spin today, the stars and the universe in constant motion.

As the matter of the universe is split in this way, from the great egg also emerges Phanes, the deity of procreation and birth. Phanes has golden wings and a body entwined with a snake's, and with his birth, day is created. Phanes gives further order and logic to the universe, for with his daughter Nyx (the deity of night), he sets in place the cycle of birth and death, of sunrise and nightfall, that comes to define existence.

At the moment of its creation, the universe is both confused and disordered, a mass of undifferentiated divine matter. It is Cronus and Ananke's ordering of the universe that initiates the development of the organized cosmos of Greek myth, with Phanes giving power to all the deities to come and passing his scepter on to Zeus, the eventual king of the Olympian gods.

SIGNIFICANCE

The story of Cronus and the cosmic egg belongs to a theological tradition that is today called the Orphic cosmogony. Orphism seems to have first thrived in ancient Greece during the sixth century BCE, although most records of this practice come from secondhand sources composed as late as the second or third century CE. Unlike many other religions and cults in ancient Greece, Orphism focused on the individual soul, reincarnation, and the path to salvation. Orphic cults were dedicated to the mythological poet Orpheus, who in legend traveled to the underworld but later returned to the land of the living. The core of the religion was based on writings referred to by modern scholars as Orphica, poems supposedly written by Orpheus that tell of the gods and their origins.

Because most Orphic texts have been largely lost to time, the exact nature of the narrative of Cronus is somewhat unclear. Some retellings, for instance, describe the formation of water and earth as preceding the birth of Cronus. A number of renditions make it clear that Cronus directly created Aether, the personification of the divine air that the gods breathe, while others suggest that Aether emerged from the splitting of the cosmic egg. Within these narrative variations, however, the philosophy associated with Cronus and the cosmic egg remains relatively consistent.

For the Orphics, the cosmic egg was an important indicator that the physical universe reflected spirituality. Rather than being purely abstract ideas, the religious beliefs of the Orphics were rooted in the material reality of life itself. The cosmic egg, for instance, is a primordial substance that contains all the matter of existence, expressed in the physical nature of the earth. Cronus as time divides this matter into discrete components, but that does not mean the substances are no longer related. Instead, light comes along with darkness and life with death. This duality was an important philosophical concept within Orphism, and adherents believed that by following this philosophy and participating in the associated rites, they might eventually transcend such splits and come to understand the duality of their own natures. The Orphic emphasis on duality is further reflected in Phanes, who is often described as an androgynous being containing both male and female elements. So clearly rooted in the primordial substance of the cosmic egg and transcending divisions of gender, Phanes escapes the dualities inherent in the world even as he exists in it.

As was true of many ancient Greek theologies, Orphism seems to have shifted and evolved over time, as the Orphic philosophers and writers wrestled with the complicated philosophy and metaphors of the origin myths. Almost always, however, the different interpretations point directly back to Cronus and his cosmic egg. The mythological union of all matter and its inevitable split supply the foundational metaphor for a worldview as interested in life and reunification as it was in death and destined transformation.

T. Fleischmann, MFA

BIBLIOGRAPHY

"Chronus and Aeon." *Theoi Greek Mythology*. Aaron J. Atsma, 2011. Web. 29 May 2013.

James, E. O. *Creation and Cosmology: A Historical and Comparative Inquiry*. Boston: Brill, 1997. Print.

Leeming, David Adams. *Creation Myths of the World: An Encyclopedia*. Santa Barbara: ABC-CLIO, 2010. Print.

"Orpheus and Eurydice." *Masterplots*. Ed. Laurence W. Mazzeno. 4th ed. Vol. 8. Pasadena: Salem, 2010. 4229–31. Print.

Rice, David G., and John E. Stambaugh. *Sources for the Study of Greek Religion*. Atlanta: Soc. of Bib. Lit., 2009. Print.

◆ The Death of Ajax

Author: Sophocles
Time Period: 999 BCE–1 BCE
Country or Culture: Greece
Genre: Myth

PLOT SUMMARY

As documented in Homer's *Iliad* and in subsequent dramatic interpretations attributed to Sophocles, the Greek soldier Ajax is an important figure of the Trojan War. The son of Telamon, the king of Salamis, Ajax is also known as Ajax the Greater, and he can trace his lineage directly to Zeus. Ajax is a hulking figure, reticent in speech and aggressive in battle. Among his most significant accomplishments, Ajax is credited with defeating Hector, a powerful prince of Troy.

Achilles, the most powerful warrior of the Greek armies, is killed by the Trojan prince Paris, whom Apollo aids in finding Achilles's weakness, his heel. Ajax and Odysseus lead an assault against the Trojans to reclaim Achilles's body for burial. Following their successful return with Achilles's body, Ajax and Odysseus have a dispute over who will take possession of Achilles's armor, which had been manufactured by Hephaestus and imbued with magical powers. In order to prevent bloodshed, Ajax and Odysseus agree to plead their case before the kings of Greece and to allow impartial judges to decide which warrior will receive the armor. Though Ajax was a close friend to Achilles and is in some respects a more successful warrior than Odysseus, Odysseus is more intelligent and a better orator; he is therefore successful in convincing the judges that he is deserving of the armor.

Ajax, outraged by the decision of the judges and believing the results of the vote have been fixed, is determined to kill the leaders of the Greek army and Odysseus, now his sworn enemy. However, Athena intervenes and places Ajax under a spell. Led astray by Athena's illusion, Ajax goes mad, slaughtering a herd of sheep he believes to be the Greek kings Agamemnon and Menelaus. He captures another sheep, which he believes to be Odysseus, and plans to torture his captive before executing him.

When Athena removes the illusion, Ajax is gripped by intense grief and suffering at his dishonor. After some discussion with his wife, Tecmessa, and a group of warriors from Salamis, Ajax travels alone to a shaded grove where he kills himself, using the sword he had won from his duel with Hector. After his death, Menelaus and Agamemnon refuse to allow Ajax's body to be buried, calling him a traitor, but Ajax's half brother, Teucer, argues for the right to bury his dead brother. The conflict ends with the intervention of Odysseus, who convinces Agamemnon and Menelaus to allow the burial.

SIGNIFICANCE

Sophocles's play *Ajax* was most likely written in the mid-fifth century BCE (ca. 440 BCE) at a time when Greek culture was in a state of political and social flux. The philosophical movement of the sophists introduced a variety of new artistic, cultural, and social ideas while the political situation was unstable as Greece prepared for the Peloponnesian War (431–404 BCE). Sophocles does not show the audience the contest between Ajax and Odysseus to determine who will win the divine armor of Achilles, but the difference between the two warriors is a mirror of changing values in Greece at the time the play was written. Odysseus represents the ascension of a new age, in which rhetoric, guile, cunning, and intelligence have eclipsed the traditional values of honor, courage, bravery, and duty. Ajax is a member of the old guard, and his downfall represents both the failings of traditional values and the sense of loss and tragedy as the new age begins to wipe away the virtues of the past.

The first half of Sophocles's play focuses on Ajax's dramatic suicide, beginning with his realization that he has brought dishonor upon himself in his hatred of his enemies. In Ajax's speech to Tecmessa and the Salaminian warriors, he displays for the audience the tragedy inherent in the fall of the noble values he embodies:

> What pleasure is there in living day after day,
> Edging slowly back and forth toward death?
> Anyone who warms their heart with the glow
> Of flickering hope is worth nothing at all.
> The noble man should either live with honor
> Or die with honor. That is all there is to be said.
> (Meineck and Woodruff 1.475–80)

Ajax's suicide comes at the midpoint of the play, and the remaining half is dedicated largely to the lengthy argument between Agamemnon and Ajax's half brother regarding the right to bury Ajax as a hero despite the severity of his attempted crimes. Literary critics have noted that the dialogue of the play, concerning the argument over the dispensation of Ajax's body, seems petty and dull in comparison to the drama of the hero's death. As the dramatic, poetic language of the first half blends into the more banal and measured discussion of the second half, the audience is presented with an example of a world in flux, where the heroism embodied by men like Ajax must be considered a feature of the past. Odysseus eventually intervenes on Ajax's behalf, thus representing the blend of the traditional and modern models of the hero. In Odysseus, we see that the heroic qualities embodied in the literal, physical heroism of Ajax can exist also as mental qualities, embodied in the eloquent rhetoric of Odysseus.

Also embedded within Sophocles's *Ajax* is a cautionary message about the nature of war and violence. In his efforts to defeat his enemies, Ajax unwittingly murders helpless and innocent victims embodied by a herd of sheep, a species often used to invoke the ideals of purity and innocence in Western philosophy. The intervention of the goddess Athena may also represent the unforeseeable twists of fate that can and often do bring about unexpected results to one's actions. The lesson that can be derived from this tragedy is that once engaged in a cycle of violence, unforeseen events will occur, resulting in unintended tragedies that are beyond one's control. The traditional counter to evil, embodied by Ajax, is to answer the evil actions of others with evil actions of the same measure. The intervention of fate twists Ajax's actions and turns his retribution back upon himself.

Micah Issitt

BIBLIOGRAPHY

Beer, Josh. *Sophocles and the Tragedy of Athenian Democracy*. Westport: Greenwood, 2004. Print.

Jebb, Richard C., ed. *The Ajax*. Vol. 7 of *Sophocles: The Plays and Fragments*. 1896. New York: Cambridge UP, 2010. Print.

---, trans. *Sophocles: Plays – Ajax*. Ed. Patricia E. Easterling. London: Bristol Classical, 2004. Print.

Meineck, Peter, and Paul Woodruff, trans. *Four Tragedies*. By Sophocles. Indianapolis: Hackett, 2007. Print.

Mills, S. P. "The Death of Ajax." *Classical Journal* 76.2 (1980–81): 129–35. Print.

Raphael, Frederic, and Kenneth McLeish, trans. "Ajax." *Sophocles, 1*. Ed. David R. Slavitt and Palmer Bovie. Philadelphia: U of Pennsylvania P, 1998. Print.

Winnington-Ingram, R. P. *Sophocles: An Interpretation*. New York: Cambridge UP, 1998. Print.

◆ The Divine Loves of Zeus

Author: Hesiod
Time Period: 999 BCE–1 BCE
Country or Culture: Greece
Genre: Myth

PLOT SUMMARY

Zeus is the king of the gods, a deity of thunder and lightning who resides on Mount Olympus and looks down on all creation. Many humans praise Zeus for his might in battle and his brave leadership, but he is equally well known for his insatiable desires and his many, many affairs with mortals and gods alike.

The first goddess Zeus takes as a wife is the Titan Metis. It has been prophesied that Metis will bear a son with even greater power than Zeus's. When she becomes pregnant, Zeus fears that her child will overthrow him just as he had overthrown his own father, and he decides to eat Metis. She does give birth to a child, although it is the goddess Athena rather than a warrior boy, and Zeus releases Athena from his body while keeping Metis imprisoned. Satisfied that he has made the right choice, he then turns his attention to the Titan Themis. With this goddess, he fathers the gods of the seasons, fate, justice, and order, filling the magical realm with beautiful, young creatures. He soon seduces Eurynome, who gives birth to the Graces, and Demeter, who gives birth to gorgeous Persephone. From there, still lustful in heart, he comes to the sacred bed of Mnemosyne, who lives in a secluded home away from the other gods. For nine nights, Zeus and Mnemosyne embrace, and from this union come the nine muses. He then fathers Apollo and Artemis with Leto and chases down Asteria, another Titan goddess.

Perhaps the greatest romance of Zeus's life, and certainly the one that lasts the longest, is his marriage to Hera, his sister and eternal consort. During the long war in which Zeus and the Olympian gods overthrow the rule of the Titans, Hera and Zeus run away to wed one another in secret. Joined together, Hera is the queen of the gods and Zeus their king. However, the rare beauty and power Hera possesses are not enough to satisfy the notoriously lustful Zeus, and he immediately returns to his old ways, causing his wife great stress and his conquests much torment at the hands of the jealous goddess. When Zeus seduces the goddess Aphrodite, for instance, Hera discovers the affair and places her hands on Aphrodite's swollen abdomen, cursing their child with ugliness. However, this does little to deter Zeus from further affairs. When he meets the goddess Persephone, he even scorns the advances of Hera and many of the beautiful Titans, ignoring their seductions in order to transform himself into a large serpent and lie with the virginal Persephone.

Some of Zeus's many divine loves willingly approach the powerful king of the gods, some are slowly seduced by his might and persistence, and still others are violently overpowered. The one thing that remains consistent, however, is that Zeus no sooner seduces a new beauty than he loses interest, a new consort on his mind and a new target vulnerable to Hera's jealous rages.

SIGNIFICANCE

The countless romances and affairs of Zeus form the core of many Greek myths, with the lustful whims of Zeus and the jealousy of Hera initiating a significant portion of the ancient Greek narratives. While these myths are often presented with a humorous edge to them, when viewed in succession, the violent misogyny and patriarchy of the stories becomes painfully clear.

The ancient Greek myths, including the canonical versions compiled by the poet Hesiod in the seventh or eighth century BCE, often present the seductions and affairs of Zeus in neutral tones, the god simply getting up to his old tricks once again. In reality, however, Zeus is performing a long string of sexual assaults, overpowering women who do not wish to sleep with him and going to great lengths in order to trick young virgins into becoming his consorts. The Titan Metis, for instance, is rewarded with violence and eternal imprisonment after her encounter with Zeus, while Asteria turns into a bird in a desperate attempt to flee him. Even his wife and sister, Hera, resists his advances for years before Zeus finally turns himself into a bird in order to get close enough to the goddess that he can overpower and rape her. A great number of the goddesses (not to mention a majority of the mortals and nymphs) with whom Zeus shares a romance, then, are actually unwilling women who, within the patriarchal world of Greek mythology and culture, have no choice but to become the temporary playthings of the father god.

This deeply problematic portrayal of romance does not end with Zeus, however. Despite having faced the brunt of Zeus's attentions in the past, Hera has no sympathy for the women he takes as lovers and typically goes to incredible lengths to punish them for bringing shame onto her. Hera is a goddess who champions and protects wives, and one might assume that she would turn her anger toward Zeus while defending these wronged women. Instead, however, Zeus regularly faces few repercussions while Hera, a goddess who never betrays her husband despite his infidelities, focuses some of the most powerful rage in the mythological realm onto the hapless and abandoned consorts.

The affairs of Zeus are so numerous that a large number of deities in the Greek pantheon owe their lineage to him. Furthermore, the gods and goddesses who do not come directly from the bloodline of Zeus still regularly refer to him as the father of all gods, suggesting that his symbolic role as patriarch is more significant than the actual lineage of many deities. Sitting atop Mount Olympus and looking down on a world filled with women he might abuse and objectify, Zeus is a prime example of a dangerous patriarch, whose position of cultural, political, and familial privilege serves only to satisfy his own indulgent fancies at great cost to the women he supposedly loves.

T. Fleischmann, MFA

BIBLIOGRAPHY

Caviness, Alys. "Hera." *Gods, Goddesses, and Mythology*. Ed. C. Scott Littleton. Vol. 5. New York: Marshall, 2005. Print.

Evelyn-White, Hugh, trans. *Hesiod, the Homeric Hymns, and Homerica*. Cambridge: Harvard UP, 1943. Print.

"Hera Wrath." *Theoi Greek Mythology*. Aaron J. Atsma, 2011. Web. 20 June 2013.

Lies, Betty Bonham. *Earth's Daughters: Stories of Women in Classical Mythology*. Golden: Fulcrum, 1999. Print.

"Loves of Zeus." *Theoi Greek Mythology*. Aaron J. Atsma, 2011. Web. 20 June 2013.

◆ Gaia and the Castration of Uranus

Author: Hesiod
Time Period: 1 CE–500 CE
Country or Culture: Greece
Genre: Myth

PLOT SUMMARY

Gaia (Gaea) is the goddess of the earth, a massive and powerful deity who predates almost all the other gods.

As the earth, she creates Uranus (Ouranos), the god of the sky, to cover her and to provide a home for the deities yet to come. After she forms Uranus, she also joins with him in order to give birth to more gods and goddesses. These gods are the twelve Titans, and while they are all mighty, the most terrible and cunning of them is Cronus (Kronos), who immediately comes to hate his father for his lecherous and forceful nature.

Once the Titans are born, Gaia continues to couple with Uranus. She gives birth to the Cyclopes (Kyklopes), which are gigantic monsters with only one eye, and the Hecatoncheires (Hekatonkheires), three horrible gods with fifty heads and one hundred arms each. The Hecatoncheires are the most terrible creation to come from the union of Gaia and Uranus, and because of their horrific strength, Uranus begins to hate them the moment they are born. Rather than facing the monstrosities he has created, he hides them deep inside Gaia's body, refusing to let them crawl into the light for even a moment and openly boasting about his clever trick.

Living beneath the ground and at the ends of the earth takes a terrible toll on these gods, who should, by right, be able to see the sky that is their father. Likewise, the strain of holding her sons inside of her causes Gaia incredible pain. To solve this, she creates a giant sickle out of flint and speaks to all of her children, telling them that their father is wicked and that together they should punish him. It was Uranus who first did evil things, she urges them, and so it is only fair that they retaliate. Most of the children are terrified of Uranus and remain silent, but headstrong Cronus rises and agrees to assist her.

When Uranus next comes to lie with Gaia, Cronus is waiting with the sickle in hand. Uranus brings the night with him, and as he approaches Gaia, he exposes his entire body to the darkness. At the last minute, Cronus reaches out, grabbing his father's genitals with one hand and using the jagged sickle to cut them off. He then tosses the severed genitals behind him. As the blood sputters out of Uranus, it falls on Gaia, and once more, children are born of their union, including the giants and the nymphs of the ash trees.

SIGNIFICANCE

Among the varying narratives of the gods in Greek mythology, Hesiod's *Theogony* stands as one of the most lasting and influential origin stories. Likely written around the seventh or eighth century BCE, the *Theogony* synthesizes a number of oral literary traditions and mythologies, both Greek and Eastern, bringing the divergent stories together into one cohesive narrative. It is in this work that the poet Hesiod relates the story of Gaia and the castration of Uranus.

On a grander scale, Hesiod's *Theogony* is the story of order arising from chaos, with the universe slowly forming out of a primordial disorder and the reign of Zeus, the king of the gods, eventually being established. At the moment when Gaia conspires to castrate Uranus, the mythological and physical universes have barely emerged from the disorder of creation. Because of this, the distinctions between physicality and abstraction, as well as between the bodies of the gods and the bodies of the earth, remain hazy. Gaia is the first deity to emerge from the chaos, and in this myth, she can be understood both as a powerful spiritual entity and as the object of the earth itself. Similarly, her husband, Uranus, is both a god and the actual sky, and when Gaia creates him, one imagines him both a husband lying in a bed with his wife and the sky lying as a blanket above the earth. The birth and imprisonment of the monstrous children follows a similar logic, with Uranus hiding them within Gaia, suggesting both their burial under the earth and their return to her womb.

This confusion of ideas and objects, of bodies and natural elements, is much more pronounced at the beginning of the myth than it is by the time Zeus claims power. Likewise, the seemingly natural order of families and devotion that will cement itself in Greek society is confused here: by necessity of Gaia and Uranus being the first gods, she is both his mother and his wife, and their children will come to mate with their siblings and parents alike. The original gods are an extended family that chaotically turns in on itself, copulating with and maiming one another, returning to wombs and birthing new children out of blood. The very act of Uranus coming to mate with Gaia drives her to destroy him. This confusion and mayhem makes it so that the natural world and the social world are both places of danger in the pre-Olympian chaos, with earth, wife, and mother rising up to castrate sky, husband, and son.

Ultimately, Uranus does lose his power, castrated by the son who would come to overthrow him (Cronus) and who in turn would come to be overthrown by his son Zeus. In narratives to follow, Uranus will even cease to maintain his godlike persona, his name for centuries operating primarily as a placeholder for the physical sky rather than its humanlike incarnation. Greek mythology remains a world driven by violence and natural metaphors, just as Greek society remained a place of war and slavery. Hesiod, however, draws freely from those myths to suggest that a logic was emerging, even if it was a logic rooted in the almost unimaginable chaos that birthed Gaia and Uranus.

T. Fleischmann, MFA

BIBLIOGRAPHY

Cottrell, Alan. "Hesiod." *Cyclopedia of World Authors*. Ed. Frank N. Magill and Tracy Irons-Georges. 4th rev. ed. Vol. 3. Pasadena: Salem, 2003. 1481. Print.

"Gaea: Greek Goddess of Earth." *Theoi Greek Mythology*. Aaron J. Atsma, 2011. Web. 24 May 2013.

Garrison, Daniel H. "Hesiod." *Critical Survey of Poetry: European Poets*. Ed. Rosemary M. Canfield Reisman. 4th ed. Vol. 2. Pasadena: Salem, 2011. 465-71. Print.

Graf, Fritz. *Greek Mythology: An Introduction*. Baltimore: Johns Hopkins UP, 1993. Print.

Koning, Hugo H. "The Other Poet: The Ancient Reception of Hesiod." *Mnemosyne* 64.3 (2011): 527–28. Print.

Vernant, Jean-Pierre. "One . . . Two . . . Three: *Erōs*." *Before Sexuality: The Construction of Erotic Experience in the Ancient Greek World*. Ed. David M. Halperin, John J. Winkler, and Froma I. Zeitlin. Princeton: Princeton UP, 1990. 465-78. Print.

Wender, Dorothea. Introduction. *Hesiod and Theognis*. Trans. Wender. New York: Penguin, 1976. 11–22. Print.

◆ Helen of Troy

Author: Homer
Time Period: 999 BCE–1 BCE
Country or Culture: Greece
Genre: Myth

PLOT SUMMARY

In the midst of the Trojan War, the army of Greece has gathered to lay siege to the famed city of Troy. The army has been there nearly a decade, and their aim is to reclaim Helen, the most beautiful woman in the world and a daughter of the god Zeus. Helen's beauty has earned her countless suitors, of whom the king of Sparta chose Menelaus to be her husband. However, the Trojan prince Paris came to the city of Sparta years after the marriage, supposedly on a friendly mission between the two cities but with the secret goal of seducing Helen. With the help of the goddess of love, Aphrodite, he won Helen's heart and returned with her to Troy. Enraged, Menelaus gathered his massive armies and began the assault that now takes place.

The Trojan army advances from the gates of the city to meet the rallied Greek forces. Paris offers himself in one-on-one combat against any Greek warrior. Menelaus then steps forward from the Greek army and volunteers himself as Paris's opponent. At first, Paris fears the famous warrior and tries to retreat from the battle, but his brother Hector chastises him for his lack of bravery, and he acquiesces. Paris and Menelaus agree that their duel will decide for good the outcome of the war, with the winner receiving Helen as a wife.

In the palace tower, the messenger goddess Iris visits Helen. Disguised as Paris's sister, Iris inspires in Helen longing for her husband and her old Greek home and convinces Helen that she should watch the battle. Although Helen willfully ran away with Paris, she regrets the harm and misfortune that her romance has brought upon the Greeks, feeling great shame for her actions. She joins Priam, Paris's father, alongside other lords of the city at the gates of Troy. There, she points out the famed warriors of Greece to them. Moments before the battle begins, Priam is overcome with worry and has to leave, fearful of seeing his own son's death.

Menelaus and Paris begin their vicious battle. They first attack each other with spears, and then Menelaus breaks his sword over Paris's helmet. It seems as though Menelaus will win back his wife when he manages to grab hold of the stunned Paris's helmet. However, Aphrodite intervenes and breaks the helmet's straps, setting Paris free again. Menelaus is about to stab Paris with his spear when Aphrodite uses her magic to spirit Paris away, placing him safely in his bed, where she also summons Helen. Although Helen is ashamed that Paris has abandoned the battle in this way, she lies with him while the soldiers of both armies search for the missing warrior. Unable to find him, the Greeks insist that they have won and demand that Helen be returned to them.

SIGNIFICANCE

As the most beautiful woman in the ancient Greek world, Helen has a long and varied history, with poets telling and retelling her story throughout the ages and Greek cults worshipping her as a goddess. This particular episode in Helen's life comes from the epic poem the *Iliad*, attributed to the poet Homer and believed to have been composed in the eighth century BCE, one of the most influential narratives in world literature.

The *Iliad* is a story of heroes and of fate, with warriors and generals willing to wage decade-long battles in order to earn their glory and protect their pride. Helen, as the daughter of Zeus and the most beautiful woman in the world, would certainly have been a valued queen and wife in Greek society. However, the extremes of the battle fought over her companionship have much more to do with prideful vengeance than with her actual companionship, and even the gods themselves influence the war in pursuit of the fame and honor that comes with their side winning. As Menelaus and Paris finally agree to a duel to settle their grievance, the lesser soldiers collapse in relief, finally believing they might go home rather than continue to battle for someone else's dignity.

In addition to narrating the war itself, this particular section reveals quite a bit about the characters of Paris and Helen, two lovers whose hasty decisions have resulted in the long siege. For her part, Helen is remorseful, and she realizes that her selfish behavior brings her shame rather than glory. When she looks upon the battlefield, the absence of her brothers inspires fear, not that they have died but rather that they did not come to defend her honor in the first place. While Helen worries, however, Paris comes across in a much worse light. He is initially unwilling to face Menelaus directly in battle, despite having affronted the man's pride by seducing his wife, and only agrees to do so when his brother calls him a coward. When he finally does engage in the battle, he quickly begins to lose and needs to be rescued by Aphrodite. The involvement of gods in the wars of ancient Greece often led to glorious moments in which the might of the deities would bless the human warriors. Paris, however, is shamed by his rescue, as Aphrodite—a goddess of love, not battle—carries him away like a weakling rather than bolstering his strength.

In the epic of valor and dignity that is the *Iliad*, Helen and Paris are hardly inspirational figures. Instead, this moment serves as a counterpoint to the bravery of the other warriors. Love and beauty play important roles, and Aphrodite does heavily influence the outcome of the war. However, the real heroes of Homer's epic are those who stake their claims broadly and fight for their own honor, not those who hide in bed with their beautiful wives at the day's end.

T. Fleischmann, MFA

BIBLIOGRAPHY

Doyle, A. "'Unhappily Ever After?': The Problem of Helen in Odyssey 4." *Akroterion* 55 (2010): 1–18. Print.

Forman, Robert J. "Homer." *Magill's Survey of World Literature*. Ed. Steven G. Kellman. Rev. ed. Vol. 3. Pasadena: Salem, 2009. 1205–13. Print.

Homer. *The Iliad*. Trans. A. T. Murray. Cambridge: Harvard UP, 1924. Print.

Roisman, Joseph. "Greek Perspectives on the Justness and Merits of the Trojan War." *College Literature* 35.4 (2008): 97–109. Print.

Talbot, John. "Speaking for Homer." *New Criterion* 31.1 (2012): 24–30. Print.

Weigel, James, Jr. "Iliad." *Masterplots*. Ed. Laurence W. Mazzeno. 4th ed. Vol. 5. Pasadena: Salem, 2011. 2808–12. Print.

Hera and the Seduction of Zeus

Author: Homer
Time Period: 999 BCE–1 BCE
Country or Culture: Greece
Genre: Myth

PLOT SUMMARY

In the tenth year of the Trojan War, the Greek army lays siege to the city of Troy. While the gods have been heavily involved in the battle up to this point, the king of all gods, Zeus, has declared that they are no longer allowed to visit the battlefield. The goddess Hera, however, is a passionate supporter of the Greeks. Years before, the Trojan prince Paris had judged a beauty contest between Hera and two other goddesses and ultimately selected Aphrodite as the most beautiful of all the deities. To bribe him, Aphrodite had offered the most beautiful woman in the world as his bride. Paris seduces the woman, the Greek queen Helen, and takes her to Troy, beginning the decade-long war. Years later, Hera's pride is still injured by this contest, and so she does everything she can to take vengeance on Paris and his city.

After Zeus forbids the gods from interfering in the battle, Hera quickly devises a plan. She looks out across the land and sees Zeus, her husband and brother, relaxing on Mount Ida, a mountain near the city of Troy. She realizes that if she makes herself beautiful enough, she might seduce him and thereby exhaust him and lure him into sleep.

Hera dresses in her fanciest clothing but decides she needs something extra to ensure that the seduction will work. She then visits Aphrodite, the goddess of love and beauty and a supporter of Troy, and asks for some of the unparalleled beauty and charm that the goddess possesses. Speaking sweetly to Aphrodite and behaving as if they are allies, Hera explains that she is headed to visit the Titans, gods who had warred with the Olympians in the distant past, and seeks to mend the rift that had developed between them. Aphrodite agrees that this a wonderful plan and quickly gives Hera a breastband that radiates with longing and lust.

Hera puts on the enchanted breastband and speeds across the earth, making sure to cross Mount Ida. Zeus sees her and is overcome with longing for his wife. He asks Hera to stay with him, but Hera tells him she is going to visit the Titan Okeanos, feigning indifference to her husband. Zeus, however, continues to urge her, and after only a moment Hera agrees to lie down with him. When Zeus soon falls asleep, Hera's plan is proven a success, and she is able to direct her attention back to the Trojan War.

SIGNIFICANCE

Hera's seduction of Zeus takes place in the second half of the epic poem the *Iliad*, believed to have been composed by the Greek poet Homer in the eighth century BCE. Chronicling the final days of the Trojan War, the epic is a narrative of heroes and of gods, of grand victories and tragic defeats, and has remained influential in Western literature through the present day.

Although it takes place during the ongoing war, the story of Hera's seduction of Zeus is fairly far removed from the battle itself. While Hera schemes in order to affect the outcome of the war, her actual plotting and motivations take place in the realm of Olympus, far away from the mortals. Within the *Iliad*, the gods are often portrayed in parallel to the humans, behaving with just as much selfishness and pettiness in their motivations. Hera goes out of her way to influence the war, for instance, but in reality she truly hopes not to defeat the Trojans but to shame Aphrodite, who had bested her in a beauty contest. Likewise, she pretends throughout the myth that she is traveling to the ends of the world in order to heal the rift between the Olympian gods and the

Titans, which formed during the legendary war known as the Titanomachy. This war was one of the most violent and significant events in Greek mythological history, establishing the pantheon and placing Zeus in power. For Hera to mend the division it caused would be a great and noble deed. Her real intention, however, is incredibly shallow; she wants to look pretty in order to seduce her husband and exhaust him so she can secretly aid the Greeks while he is asleep.

Hera is not the only god to come off poorly in this myth. Aphrodite, who knows that Hera despises her after the beauty contest, falls for the goddess's ploy with hardly any convincing, her gullibility becoming her most recognizable trait. Zeus, likewise, is supposedly the king of the gods and the mightiest of all the deities, yet he spends the entirety of the myth relaxing on Mount Ida. A jealous and shallow Hera, a lethargic and wanton Zeus, and a naïve Aphrodite, then, are the main players in this myth. The enormity of the greatest mythological war behind them and the reality of the decade-long bloodshed of the Trojan War beneath them, the deities of ancient Greece can do nothing more than fuss over romance and superficial beauty. Perhaps the most ludicrous aspect of the myth is not their behavior, however, but the fact that their own trifling actions come to define the course of the war and, ultimately, of human history. Homer's narrative is entertaining and engaging, but moments such as Hera's seduction of Zeus add an additional depth to that amusement, suggesting a dark tension between the desperate intentions of humanity and the uncaring whims of the gods.

T. Fleischmann, MFA

BIBLIOGRAPHY

Forman, Robert J. "Iliad." *Magill's Survey of World Literature*. Ed. Steven G. Kellman. Rev. ed. Vol. 3. Pasadena: Salem, 2009. 1207–9. Print.

Knox, Bernard. "Introduction." *The Iliad*. New York: Penguin, 1991. 3–64. Print.

"Stories of Hera." *Theoi Greek Mythology*. Aaron J. Atsma, 2011. Web. 5 June 2013.

Weigel, James, Jr. "Iliad." *Masterplots*. Ed Laurence W. Mazzeno. 4th ed. Vol. 5. Pasadena: Salem, 2010. 2808–12. Print.

Willcock, Malcolm M. *A Companion to the* Iliad. Chicago: U of Chicago P, 1976.

◆ Jove's Great Deluge

Author: Ovid
Time Period: 1 CE–500 CE
Country or Culture: Rome
Genre: Myth

PLOT SUMMARY

The great sky god Jove looks down on the world and is furious, seeing nothing but mortals entangled in their selfish and wicked deeds. Turning to the other gods, he declares that it is not enough to simply slay the most sinful of the humans, but rather that they all must die. Some gods protest, insisting that without humans there will be no one to worship them and tend to their temples. Jove, however, is caught up in his rage, declaring that he will create new mortals who do not behave in such shameful ways.

At once, Jove begins to summon a massive flood. He decides not to use his thunderbolts, knowing that they might engulf the entire universe in flames, bringing even his own existence to an end. Instead, he hides away all winds but the south wind, which gathers up moisture and pours rain down onto the earth, and great streams rush from Jove's scowling face. As storms batter fields and cities, Jove calls on Neptune, the god of the ocean, to join him. Neptune and the gods of the rivers strike the earth with all their force, unleashing their full power so that water rushes over every bit of land; even the greatest mansions and towers are taken by the violent tides. In little time, the earth is a scene of pure chaos, men clinging to the highest branches while lions and tigers wash by and dolphins are battered against the trunks of trees. With nothing but shoreless and violent ocean, nearly all mortals quickly perish.

Amid this chaos, however, the heights of Mount Parnassus on Phocis still rise, and two surviving people, Deucalion and Pyrrha, slowly row their boat up to the standing temple there. There, they immediately begin their worship of the nymphs, the mountain, and the goddess Themis.

When Jove sees these two good and just mortals, he calls off the storms. He forces the clouds and the rivers to retreat, allowing the sun to shine once more and the earth, slowly, to be exposed again. On the drying earth, Deucalion and Pyrrha are overtaken by grief, lamenting their fate to one another and questioning what their role might be as the only survivors of a lost world. Being

pious people, they turn to the oracles, arriving at the nearest temple and asking Themis for guidance, hoping to learn how they might bring about other mortals once more. The oracle tells them that they must depart from the temple, remove their clothes, and toss the bones of their mother behind them. While Pyrrha at first despairs at disrespecting her mother so, Deucalion reminds her that an oracle would never instruct a wicked deed. In little time, they realize that their original mother is the earth and that her bones must be the stones at their feet. Leaving the temple, then, they scatter stones behind them, and as those stones hit the ground, they slowly expand and take on the soft and living form of humans, a trail of men behind Deucalion and women behind Pyrrha.

SIGNIFICANCE

Presented in the first book of Ovid's *Metamorphoses*, the story of the great deluge is one of the first major events in Roman mythology, setting the tone for the violent and irrational world that will emerge from the chaotic seas.

Ovid's long poem is a foundational text in Western literature. Written in Latin, it chronicles Roman mythology from the creation of the universe up through Ovid's present day, the reign of Julius Caesar. Through the text, Ovid brings together hundreds of influential myths from Greek and Roman mythology, offering thematic arcs that bring the disparate narratives together. Several core ideas emerge, including the importance of transformation in Roman culture and a heavy emphasis on love and violence as the animating forces of the world. Set at the core of the myths to follow, the story of the flood makes clear that in this violent and passionate existence, the gods themselves have little more rationality and self-control than humans.

Nothing, perhaps, makes this clearer than the extreme and willful actions of Jove, the king of the gods and supposedly a force of wisdom in the universe. Jove's violent actions that begin this myth are rooted in the foolish mistakes of only a few humans, Jove having been treated with disrespect by a mortal who hosted the god and tried to murder Jove in his sleep. Deciding that this one action damns all of humanity, Jove ignores the advice of the other gods and the pleas of all mortals, destroying the earth and wiping out the beauty of his own creation. The scene of destruction is as violent as it is humorous, with Ovid finding some comic relief in the images of lions floating by stranded Romans and helpless men clinging to ropes. This comedy is not callous, but rather in line with the broader picture Ovid paints. Jove is an irrational god taken by a whim, and his frustration at being treated with disrespect results in a storm of world-ending destruction.

Readers should understand this as being supremely unjust to the mortals, just as a mortal had behaved unjustly to Jove. To make this hypocrisy clear, Ovid includes the pious mortals Deucalion—the son of Prometheus—and his wife, Pyrrha. Ignorant of the indulgent whims of the gods and pure in soul, they float in the great flood, hapless and trusting of a god who would destroy them for the sins of their neighbors. In some versions of the myth, Prometheus—who is credited with having created the first humans from clay—warns his son about the coming flood, giving Deucalion enough time to build a boat that will save him and his wife. Nevertheless, Deucalion and Pyrrha are still left to the whims of the gods.

Far from an instructive text praising the worth of the gods and demanding human devotion, then, Ovid provides us with a myth in which the universe itself is as uncaring and irrational as we could possibly imagine. It is a world, after all, where it seems possible that the gods would arbitrarily demand the desecration of Pyrrha's mother in order to repopulate the earth. With this extreme example of destruction and death at its core, Ovid's *Metamorphoses* is able to go on through the entirety of Roman mythology, showing again and again that the gods and universe they create is as fickle, emotional, and absurd as the mortals that inhabit it.

T. Fleischmann, MFA

BIBLIOGRAPHY

Bate, M. S. "Tempestuous Poetry: Storms in Ovid's *Metamorphoses, Heroides,* and *Tristia*." *Mnemosyne* 57.3 (2004): 295–310. Print.

Fletcher, K. F. B. "Ovidian 'Correction' of the Biblical Flood?" *Classical Philology* 105.2 (2010): 209–13. Print.

Harrison, Stephen. "Bimillenary Ovid: Some Recent Versions of the *Metamorphoses*." *Translation & Literature* 13.2 (2004): 251–67. Print.

Kline, A. S., trans. *Metamorphoses*. By Ovid. *Ovid Collection*. U of Virginia, 2000. Web. 9 Sept. 2013.

Mazzeno, Laurence W., ed. "*Metamorphoses* – Ovid." *Masterplots*. 4th ed. Vol. 7. Pasadena: Salem, 2011. 3651–52. Print.

More, Brookes, trans. *Metamorphoses*. By Ovid. Boston: Cornhill, 1922. Print.

◆ King Oedipus Is Revealed

Author: Sophocles
Time Period: 999 BCE–1 BCE
Country or Culture: Greece
Genre: Myth

PLOT SUMMARY

When Oedipus is born, a prophecy states that he will kill his father, King Laius of Thebes, and marry his mother. In response, Laius abandons Oedipus on the side of a mountain. Through many turns of events, however, the prophecy comes true; Oedipus unknowingly kills Laius and takes his mother as his wife, fathering several children with her. When the truth of his union is revealed, Oedipus stabs out his own eyes and goes into exile, wandering with his daughter Antigone. Eventually, the exiled Oedipus and Antigone arrive at Colonus, a grove of trees outside of the city of Athens.

While Oedipus rests at Colonus, an Athenian man warns him that the grove is a sacred place to the Furies, vengeful and frightening winged deities. When Oedipus insists on staying rather than fleeing the Furies, the Athenian man sends for the king of his city, Theseus. Slowly, other Athenians realize that Oedipus is the cursed king of Thebes, and they urge him to leave their land rather than bring misfortune upon it. Oedipus, however, insists on staying, claiming that he has a message to give to Theseus and reminding everyone of his good intentions and of all the adversity he has suffered.

Oedipus's second daughter, Ismene, arrives with terrible news: the sons of Oedipus have battled over who will become the ruler of Thebes, and the Oracle of Delphi has prophesied horrible tragedies in the city if Oedipus is not buried there. Theseus also arrives, but rather than banish Oedipus from the grove of the Furies, he welcomes him and offers sanctuary. Oedipus says that he will stay there, revealing that the site of his burial will bring great fortune to the city in which he dies and that he has chosen Athens for this honor rather than Thebes, where his sons foolishly war.

When Theseus leaves, several people arrive at Colonus and attempt to convince Oedipus to return to Thebes. First, Oedipus's uncle and brother-in-law, Creon, tries to trick him into returning, but Oedipus knows that Creon seeks only selfish gains and so refuses. Creon then abducts Ismene and Antigone, intending to take them back to Thebes in an attempt to lure Oedipus there. Theseus, however, returns to the grove before Creon can depart and demands to know his intentions. Creon lies, claiming he is trying to save Athens from the curse that follows Oedipus, but Theseus sees through the deceit and rescues the daughters. Oedipus's son Polynices also arrives and begs for his father's blessing, but Oedipus turns him away, cursing his son to a violent death.

The thunder of Zeus sounds across the sky, and Oedipus knows that the time for his death has come. He makes Theseus promise to hide his body and keep its burial a secret so that he might bless Athens. With Theseus alone accompanying him, Oedipus at last dies. Afterward, Theseus urges the mourning daughters to return to Thebes and end the violence that has begun there.

SIGNIFICANCE

This rendition of the myth of the legendary Greek king Oedipus originated in the work of Sophocles, a Greek playwright whose tragedies form some of the foundations of Western literature. Sophocles composed the play *Oedipus at Colonus* (ca. 401 BCE) in the final days of his life, and it completes the story of Oedipus's life as told in Sophocles's famous trilogy of Theban plays, which also includes *Oedipus the King* (ca. 429 BCE) and *Antigone* (ca. 441 BCE).

While the other Theban plays are heavy on action and violence, *Oedipus at Colonus* is a more quiet and contemplative work. It primarily concerns Oedipus as a tragic figure facing a harsh fate. He is already beaten and beleaguered, having experienced the unimaginable trauma of murdering his father and sleeping with his mother, and by his arrival at Colonus he is blind, destitute, and elderly as well. He is also, however, a man of surprising strength and certitude. Throughout the play he continually insists that he is innocent, not of the crimes themselves but of the intent to commit them; Oedipus did not know that the man he killed was his father, nor did he know that the woman he married was his mother. In this way, he makes a careful distinction, taking responsibility for the horrible deeds he unwittingly perpetrated while also emphasizing the importance of intent. Broken in body but not in spirit, he has paid his dues.

Oedipus's role is highlighted by the other characters and the environment in which he spends his final days.

The grove is a home to the Furies, terrifying winged deities that carry out the dark deeds of fate and curse those who break their solemn oaths. Considering the prophecies that have haunted Oedipus throughout his life, the Furies could in theory be his most feared enemies. Instead, however, he finds safety and refuge in their grove, suggesting that he has already faced his fate and has no debt left to pay. Likewise, the Oracle of Delphi—a priestess who speaks prophecies given to her by Apollo—comments on his death, confirming that the city of his burial will receive protection, while those without his interned body will encounter destruction. Oedipus in death, then, is in many ways the inverse of Oedipus in life. His deceased body will function as a holy blessing and a boon to its city, while his living self was a cursed monstrosity, bringing destruction to wherever he lived. This echoes the fact that his sins in life were physical in nature but also somewhat spiritually pure, rendered so by his ignorance.

Oedipus at Colonus is a complicated and nuanced work, its message tailored to the audience of Sophocles, a people entangled in war, the selfish motives of their leaders, and the cruel mechanisms of fate in a violent society. As a figure supremely downtrodden, Oedipus rises out this grand tragedy to promise something like hope, his death a final demonstration that pure intentions and repentance might still hold some promise in an uncaring world.

T. Fleischmann

BIBLIOGRAPHY

Buller, Jeffrey L. "Sophocles." *Magill's Survey of World Literature*. Ed. Steven G. Kellman. Rev. ed. Vol 6. Pasadena: Salem, 2009. 2440–46. Print.

Holtze, Elizabeth A. "Sophocles." *Research Guide to Biography and Criticism*. Ed. Walton Beacham. Vol. 3. Washington: Research, 1986. 589–93. Print.

Sophocles. *Oedipus at Colonus*. Trans. F. Storr. *Internet Classics Archive*. Massachusetts Inst. of Technology, n.d. Web. 29 May 2013.

Stone, Laura M. "Classical Greek and Roman Drama." *Critical Survey of Drama*. Ed. Carl Rollyson. 2nd rev. ed. Vol. 8. Pasadena: Salem, 2003. 3949–87. Print.

Weigel, James, Jr. "Oedipus at Colonus." *Masterplots*. Ed. Laurence W. Mazzeno. 4th ed. Vol. 8. Pasadena: Salem, 2010. 4083–86.

The Line and the Cave

Author: Plato
Time Period: 999 BCE–1 BCE
Country or Culture: Greece
Genre: Myth

PLOT SUMMARY

The line and the cave are separate but related allegories in Plato's *Republic*. During the discussion between Socrates and Glaucon on the "Form of the Good," knowledge, truth, and other related subjects, Socrates introduces a theoretical line. He divides it into two unequal sections to represent the visible world and the larger intelligible world. He then divides each section again in similar proportions. The first visible section represents likenesses or images, such as shadows, reflections of people, animals, objects, and so forth. The second section represents the concrete objects whose likenesses form the first section. The men then agree that these two sections represent different degrees of truth and that they can be viewed as an analogy for the relationship between opinions and knowledge. The third section represents mathematical and scientific thinking, which uses ideas in the form of models and hypotheses to uncover principles. The larger fourth section represents the dialectic (philosophy), which relies on ideas to reach other ideas, rather than models, images, or concrete objects. In this way, Plato argues that philosophy is a higher level of thinking.

The allegory of the cave begins with Socrates describing a cave where humans are imprisoned with chains in such a way that they cannot move and can only view what is in front of them. Behind them is a fire and nearby is a road and wall that serves as a stage. Behind the wall, men pass by carrying various types of vessels, statues of animals, and other objects. The chained prisoners see only the shadows of these figures. To the prisoners, the shadows are reality and thus represent truth. According to Socrates, when the prisoners are released and see the actual people and objects, they will be confused about what is real. Outside of the cave, in the sunlight, they will be blinded by the truth. Only when their eyes adjust will they be able to begin to contemplate reality and the power of the truth.

Socrates explains to Glaucon that this allegory represents the journey of the soul into the intellectual world. He states that in the intellectual spectrum, virtue represents beauty, reason, and truth, and only a person who puts forth the needed effort by thinking and acting rationally will be able to see the light. He then presents two types of blindness—that which occurs while moving from the bright sunlight into darkness and that which occurs when moving from darkness into bright sunlight—and equates the time needed to adjust to each allegorical circumstance with varying degrees of learning.

SIGNIFICANCE

Although Plato's cave and line narratives are sometimes referred to as myths, they are better described as allegories or parables that he injected into the greater dialogue carried out between Socrates and Glaucon in his philosophical masterpiece the *Republic*. The line allegory can be found in chapter 6 and the cave allegory in chapter 7. Plato did not write the *Republic* in chapters, however, and so these divisions represent a much later organization.

Plato used these allegories to elevate the role of dialectic (philosophy) in Greek society and education, where the emphasis during Plato's lifetime was, instead, on gymnastics and the glorification of physical beauty. While he believed the study of philosophy would benefit all, he felt it was uniquely beneficial to politicians. Plato maintained that leaders trained in dialectic and rationality could rule the state with "virtue and wisdom . . . the true blessings of life" rather than being distracted by the temptations of "silver and gold" (183). For Plato, the ideal education combines music and gymnastics and progresses through all of the major sciences—arithmetic, astronomy, geometry, and harmonics, or music theory. He believed that education should culminate in five years of philosophy after an individual fulfilled the expected fifteen years of military or political service. Notably, Plato believed that women should also be encouraged to study philosophy. Only when a person understood the difference between the four stages of knowledge as indicated by the line analogy—two levels of visible or sensual objects and two levels of the intelligible world—will he or she be able to grasp the "Form of the Good," or justice and truth. In particular, Plato argued for his fellow Greeks to learn how to differentiate between opinions and facts, symbolized in the cave analogy by images and concrete objects. This distinction remains a major component of critical thinking skills today.

The line and cave allegories serve as foundational narratives in education, phenomenology, metaphysics, epistemology, and other branches of philosophy; they have also influenced religion and politics. The cave allegory in particular has served as a common motif in the arts, sciences, and literature for two millennia—used either metaphorically or overtly to call attention to the problem of ignorance or immoral behavior in humankind.

Sally Driscoll, MLS

BIBLIOGRAPHY

Audi, Robert, ed. "Divided Line." *The Cambridge Dictionary of Philosophy*. 2nd ed. Cambridge: Cambridge UP, 1999. Print.

Lampert, Laurence. "Images of the Greatest Study: Sun, Line, Cave." *How Philosophy Became Socratic: A Study of Plato's* Protagoras, Charmides, *and* Republic. Chicago: U of Chicago P, 2010. 348–74. Print.

Plato. *The Republic*. Trans. Benjamin Jowett. Ed. Joslyn T. Pine. Mineola: Dover, 2000. Print.

Williams, Leaun. "Plato and Education." *The SAGE Handbook of Philosophy of Education*. Ed. Richard Bailey, et. al. London: Sage, 2010. Print.

◆ The Love of Aphrodite and Anchises

Author: Anonymous
Time Period: 999 BCE–1 BCE
Country or Culture: Greece
Genre: Myth

PLOT SUMMARY

"The Homeric Hymn to Aphrodite" begins by describing the limits of the goddess's powers, which do not affect her fellow goddesses Athena, Artemis, and Hestia because they are utterly unconcerned with matters of love. Aphrodite's power affects all others, and she is particularly known for causing the gods to fall in love with mortals. These unions produce children who are mortal and thus subject to death, which causes the gods great sorrow. To give Aphrodite a taste of her own medicine, Zeus, the king of the gods, decides to make her fall in love with the mortal Anchises, a Trojan hero and shepherd.

Struck with desire, Aphrodite prepares herself with divine oils, rich clothing, and jewelry and flies through the clouds to Mount Ida, where she appears before Anchises as a noble, mortal maiden. Suspecting she is a goddess, Anchises addresses her as such, asking for her favor and promising to sacrifice to her. Aphrodite denies her divine nature, claiming instead to be the daughter of the Phrygian king Otreus and a devotee of Artemis. She tells Anchises that she was taken away from her band of nymphs and maidens by the god Hermes, who delivered her to Anchises because she is destined to be his bride. She requests that he present her to his family and send a messenger to her people, the Phrygians, to announce their marriage. She claims that her family will send gifts and gold as a dowry.

Still believing that Aphrodite is mortal, Anchises agrees to the marriage, and the two copulate. After their encounter, Aphrodite causes her lover to fall asleep while she restores her appearance to her full divine splendor. She awakens Anchises and commands him to look upon her. Recognizing the goddess, Anchises is astonished and hides his face with his cloak. He says that he had suspected that she was a goddess and begs for her pity, acknowledging that mortal men who consort with goddesses often face unpleasant consequences.

Aphrodite reassures him that he need not fear the gods and declares that a glorious son will result from their union. This son will be named Aeneas and will be as beautiful as the gods. Aphrodite then gives examples of gods who have granted immortality to mortals, sometimes with unfavorable results. She tells Anchises that she will not make him immortal because he will soon be old and she would not want such a husband. Moreover, she blames him for the shame she will feel when her divine peers mock her for enduring the same abasement that she so frequently inflicted on them and for her resulting pregnancy. Aphrodite tells Anchises that as soon as the child is born, he will be handed over to mountain nymphs, who will raise him for the first years of his life, and that she will present the child to Anchises when he is five years old. At the conclusion of the hymn, Aphrodite commands Anchises to tell everyone that the child's mother is one of the wood nymphs, and she warns him that if he foolishly identifies her as the boy's true mother, he will face the wrath of Zeus.

SIGNIFICANCE

An essential part of the Greek mythological corpus, the Homeric hymns are generally dated between the seventh and sixth centuries BCE. The hymns are of unknown authorship but are described as "Homeric" because they share characteristics of meter and dialect with the eighth-century BCE Greek epics the *Iliad* and the *Odyssey*, which are commonly attributed to the poet Homer. The major significance of the hymn to Aphrodite is twofold. First, the hymn describes the origin of the hero Aeneas, who, although not central in Greek mythology, became one of the most important heroes in Roman culture. In the *Iliad*, Aeneas is a member of the force fighting against the Greeks in the Trojan War, and although not a major character, he is repeatedly saved from death through the interventions of Aphrodite and other gods. Aeneas is most notable in his role as protagonist of the *Aeneid*, an epic composed by the Roman poet Virgil between 29 and 19 BCE. This poem narrates the Trojan War from the perspective not of the Greeks, as in the Homeric epics, but of the Trojans, a natural choice given that the Romans credited Aeneas with settling the region that would become Rome following his escape from Troy.

The second and most significant feature of the hymn is what it reveals about the mythological relationships among the gods and between gods and mortals. Aphrodite's love affair with Anchises occurs because of an act of retaliation by Zeus, who himself, along with many other gods, has been the victim of Aphrodite's power. These power games indicate that the gods are not omniscient and are subject to all-too-human emotions such as lust and anger. Furthermore, the revelation of Aphrodite's true identity after her encounter with Anchises constitutes an epiphany scene, a common element of ancient Greek literature. The goddess's deceit, interaction with Anchises, and revelation in which she blames the human man for her humiliation and warns him not to speak of the encounter reveal a formulaic pattern found in many other epiphany scenes. The purpose of these scenes is certainly to entertain but also to affirm the gods' unequivocal and often unjust power over mortals, even if the deities are also partially driven by forces beyond their control.

Ashleigh Imus, PhD

BIBLIOGRAPHY

Bergren, Ann L. "The Homeric Hymn to Aphrodite: Tradition and Rhetoric, Praise and Blame." *Classical Antiquity* 8.1 (1989): 1–41. Print.

Evelyn-White, Hugh G., trans. *Hesiod, the Homeric Hymns, and Homerica*. Cambridge: Harvard UP, 1954. Print.

Faulkner, Andrew. *The Homeric Hymn to Aphrodite: Introduction, Text, and Commentary*. Oxford: Oxford UP, 2008. Print.

---. *The Homeric Hymns: Interpretive Essays*. Oxford: Oxford UP, 2011. Print.

Richardson, N. J. *Three Homeric Hymns: To Apollo, Hermes, and Aphrodite; Hymns 3, 4, and 5*. Cambridge: Cambridge UP, 2010. Print.

◆ The Myth of Atlantis

Author: Plato
Time Period: 999 BCE–1 BCE
Country or Culture: Greece
Genre: Myth

PLOT SUMMARY

At the beginning of time, when the gods are first forming the earth, the island city of Atlantis is given to the sea god Poseidon. Atlantis is a massive and fertile island, larger than many kingdoms. To rule this land, Poseidon takes a mortal wife, Cleito, and builds her a gorgeous home at its center. He also carves the island into rings of water and land, each one circling Cleito's palace, so that she will be protected and so the people of Atlantis will have hot and cold springs for bathing and drinking.

From its earliest days, Atlantis is a prosperous and peaceful nation. Cleito bears ten sons, five pairs of twins; the oldest, named Atlas, is made the king of the island, and his brothers all rule as princes over different regions. Atlas inherits Cleito's home at the center of Atlantis and, from it, is able to look down on the rich mines and fruitful fields of his kingdom. He is also able to establish lucrative trade routes that spread from his island all over the world, the gains of which benefit all of his people. When Atlas dies, his first son takes over the throne, starting a long succession of peaceful rulers, every one of whom adds to the riches of the kingdom. Soon, Atlantis is one of the wealthiest lands on earth, guarded by massive walls and protected by Poseidon.

Under the guidance of the sea god, the rulers of Atlantis follow a strict set of rules, which are carved into the walls of Poseidon's greatest temple. In this temple, the ten rulers of Atlantis, representing the original ten sons of Cleito, regularly meet. They begin every council by committing themselves once again to Poseidon's laws, burning a sacrificial bull to the god and pouring wine over a sacred fire as they pledge their obedience. With these oaths confirmed, the people of Atlantis then bring them their quarrels, and the ten rulers bring down judgment based on the codes set forth by Poseidon.

For many years, the leaders follow these rules and honor Poseidon, and their kingdom prospers. Over time, however, the rulers begin to abandon the god's guidance, and the strength of the kingdom falters. Desiring more power, the rulers gather their armies and send them out to Asia and Europe to seize land. As other rival rulers begin to fall, the Athenians bravely fight back, eventually driving the armies of Atlantis back to their island and freeing the lands they have overtaken, including the mighty kingdom of Egypt. As soon as the armies of Atlantis return home, defeated and weary, the island itself is plagued by earthquakes and massive storms. Within only a day's time, the island cracks and sinks into the sea, and the people of Atlantis are never heard from again.

SIGNIFICANCE

The myth of Atlantis continues to captivate audiences thousands of years after it was first recorded, with people in the modern day still debating the island's theoretical historical origin and location. These debates have given rise to a large number of conjectures, including a popular nineteenth-century European belief that the Maya and Aztec people were somehow linked to the mythological island and more recent pseudoscientific arguments that Antarctica is the site of sunken kingdom. The original version of the myth is equally ambiguous, and ancient people were as skeptical of the existence of Atlantis as most audiences are today.

The story of Atlantis as told above comes from the Greek philosopher Plato's texts *Timaeus* and *Critias*. In these philosophical works, Plato describes a Greek man named Solon visiting Egypt and uncovering the myth of the island, which has been lost to Greek culture. The descriptions of the city's origin, its ancient history, and the eventual clash between Atlantis and the civilized society of Athens are all folded into a longer philosophical text exploring the nature of existence and, in particular, the physical components that make up the cosmos (such as air, water, fire, and earth). Plato writes this text as a dialogue, an imagined conversation between several different philosophers, and is therefore able to present a variety of hypothetical ideas with which he does not necessarily agree. Thus, while it is entirely possible that he believed in the existence of Atlantis and championed its history as truth, it is also possible that he saw the story as a convenient fiction, a captivating myth with a strong moral that could be used to explore his broader ideas. In this sense, the story of the people of Atlantis abandoning their god and attacking Athens is a story of a kingdom that loses sight of the fundamental laws of the universe and, as a result, crumbles into the sea, its physical nature literally destroyed by its spiritual failings. Athens, by contrast, is presented as an ordered and pious society, a people who worship their gods and uphold the ancient laws they have inherited. In the reality of Plato's time, Athens was becoming increasingly violent and warlike, resembling the Atlantis of the myth more than the just nation of its own history. By telling the history of the fall of Atlantis, Plato seems to be offering a warning, suggesting that the leaders of Athens must take heed if they do not want their city to meet a similar fate.

The tension between a historical Atlantis and an Atlantis that exists as a philosophical metaphor has allowed the ancient city to remain a source of fascination for thousands of years. Just as engrossing as the story of a lost civilization are the ideas we attach to that myth. With only a few scant details describing the island, people from Plato onward have spoken of the lost land in order to defend their gods and impart their politics. Regardless whether Plato himself believed the war between Atlantis and Athens to have occurred, his recounting of that battle has forever lodged in the Western imagination the question of what Atlantis might have been and what it means for such a land to have been lost.

T. Fleischmann, MFA

BIBLIOGRAPHY

"Atlantis . . . Did Plato Know the Truth?" *Monkeyshines on Mysteries in History*. Ed. Phyllis Barkas Goldman. Greensboro: Monkeyshines, 2003. 40–41. Print.

Hefner, Alan G. "Atlantis: The Myth." *Encyclopedia Mythica*. Encyclopedia Mythica, 31 Jan. 2004. Web. 24 June 2013.

McInerny, Dennis Q. "Plato." *Magill's Survey of World Literature*. Ed. Steven G. Kellman. Rev. ed. Vol. 5. Pasadena: Salem, 2009. 2042–49. Print.

Plato. *The Dialogues of Plato:* The Republic, Timaeus, Critias. Trans. Benjamin Jowett. 3rd ed. Vol. 3. Oxford: Clarendon, 1892. Print.

Vidal-Naquet, Pierre. "Atlantis and the Nations." Trans. Janet Lloyd. *Critical Inquiry* 18.2 (1992): 300–326. Print.

◈ The Myth of Er

Author: Plato
Time Period: 999 BCE–1 BCE
Country or Culture: Greece
Genre: Myth

PLOT SUMMARY

Er, a Pamphylian soldier, is killed in battle. After he is buried, his soul leaves his body and journeys to the afterworld in the company of other souls. The afterworld has two openings in the ground and two openings in the heavens. In between the two sets of openings are judges who sentence souls to heaven or hell based on the good or bad deeds they have committed on earth. The judges tell Er that he is to observe all he can of the afterworld and tell people on earth what it is like. Er sees that the souls rising out of the ground are crying, dusty, and travelworn, whereas the souls departing from the heavens are clean, bright, and full of praise regarding heaven's delights and beauty.

Er then learns about the judgments made in the afterlife. For every wrong committed, a wrongdoer is made to suffer the same act ten times over, while a good deed yields a tenfold payment in kind; the punishment or reward is meted out over a thousand-year period, which represents ten human lifespans of one hundred years each. A member of Er's company asks another soul if he knows about the punishment received by Ardiaeus the Great, who had murdered his elderly father and older brother and committed other horrendous crimes one thousand years earlier. The spirit replies that he saw Ardiaeus and other tyrants attempt to leave to leave the underworld before their punishment was completed. Instead of being admitted to the opening leading to heaven, Ardiaeus and the others were bound, whipped, dragged along the road, carded like wool, and cast back into hell.

Er then journeys with the party of souls to the heavens, where they reach a bright light purer than a rainbow. He describes the light as a heavenly belt that holds the universe together. Extending from its ends is the steel spindle of Necessity. The whorl to which the spindle is attached is composed of seven others all fitted together inside one another, representing the stars, moon, Saturn, Mercury, Venus, Mars, and Jupiter. On top of the spindles are the Sirens, who are singing or humming. They are accompanied by Lachesis, Clotho, and Atropos, the three Fates.

Er and his companions are then greeted by an Interpreter, or prophet. The Interpreter takes a handful of numbered lots from Lachesis and tosses them at the souls. They each pick up the closest one and thus receive a number—except for Er, who is not allowed to choose a lot. The Interpreter then spreads out a selection of animal and human lives representing a wide spectrum of nature and gives instructions to the group about choosing a new life based on the order of their numbers. Those souls who have descended from heaven, and thus have not witnessed suffering on earth or in hell, choose lives based on greed, lust, or another evil, while those who do not want to duplicate their earthly suffering choose lives they think will allow them to avoid the hardships they have already experienced. Er witnesses the reincarnation of several souls, including Orpheus, who chooses to become a swan rather than undergo birth to a woman, as women had been his murderers, and Odysseus, who draws the last lot and chooses the life of an ordinary man in contrast to his rather ambitious life full of strife. Er then returns to his own body on earth while the others continue on their journeys to other worlds.

SIGNIFICANCE

The myth of Er represents the imagination of the ancient Greek philosopher Plato (ca. 428–347 BCE) and forms the end of the final chapter (chapter 10) in his profound classic the *Republic*. As with the rest of the book, the narrative is written in the form of a Socratic dialogue, narrated by Socrates to Glaucon, Plato's brother.

While the primary emphasis of the *Republic* is the exploration of the meaning and nature of justice, the myth of Er deals mostly with the consequences of living a just or unjust life. It is one of the first narratives that argues for the immortality of the soul and describes a day of judgment, when rewards or punishments are meted out in the afterlife for choices made on earth. For these reasons, the narrative is considered to have exerted much influence on early Christianity and its leading proponents, such as Saint Augustine and Clement of Alexandria; however, all but a few Gnostic Christian sects rejected the notion of reincarnation portrayed in the myth.

As part of a foundational work in philosophy, the myth of Er has been highly influential in the development and study of ethics, metaphysics, and other philosophical disciplines. Of its many themes and arguments, free will and the related issue of nature versus nurture continue to be debated as they were during Plato's time. In the narrative, Plato stresses the need for philosophical reasoning in making sound moral choices. He also suggests that humans are free to make their own choices in life, although he puts forth the idea that society and experience shape those decisions. For example, Er tells about witnessing the souls of Greeks who have chosen to be reincarnated as greedy criminals because they had not been exposed to those evils while in the heavenly afterlife. Er also mentions the decision made by the Trojan war hero Ajax to be reincarnated as a lion because of his experience with human injustice. Apparently, Plato envisioned Ajax as still feeling bitter about Odysseus being awarded Achilles's armor instead of himself, one of several references to Homer's *Iliad* or *Odyssey*. Scholars have historically debated Plato's reasons for including the myth of Er in the *Republic*, as it seems to contradict the work's main proposition that a moral life is worth living without any overt or ulterior punishments or rewards.

Sally Driscoll, MLS

BIBLIOGRAPHY

Annas, Julia. "Book Ten." *An Introduction to Plato's* Republic. Oxford: Oxford UP, 1981. 335–54. Print.

Blackburn, Simon. "The Farewell Myth." *Plato's* Republic*: A Biography*. New York: Atlantic, 2006. 158–62. Print.

Halliwell, Francis Stephen. "The Life-and-Death Journey of the Soul: Interpreting the Myth of Er." *The Cambridge Companion to Plato's* Republic. Ed. G. R. F. Ferrari. Cambridge: Cambridge UP, 2007. 445–73. Print.

Partenie, Catalin, "Plato's Myths." *Stanford Encyclopedia of Philosophy*. Stanford U, 20 Sept. 2011. Web. 29 May 2013.

Plato. *Plato's* Republic. Trans. Benjamin Jowett. 1873. Mills: Agora, 1997. Print.

---. *The Republic*. Trans. Reginald E. Allen. New Haven: Yale UP, 2006. Print.

◆ Pandora and the Great Jar

Author: Hesiod
Time Period: 999 BCE–1 BCE
Country or Culture: Greece
Genre: Myth

PLOT SUMMARY

The Greek poet Hesiod tells the story of Pandora in two texts written circa 700 BCE: the *Theogony*, a poem about the origins of the gods, and *Works and Days*, a poem that addresses agricultural practice. In the *Theogony*, the titan Prometheus angers Zeus by stealing fire from the gods and giving it to humans. In retaliation, Zeus orders Hephaestus, blacksmith of the gods, to fashion a shy maiden out of earth. The goddess Athena clothes her with silver garments and a beautiful veil and adorns her hair with garlands. Athena also places on her head a golden crown wrought with fine detail by Hephaestus himself. When Zeus presents the woman to the other gods and men, they are astonished at the sight. Hesiod elaborates by describing the maiden as the origin of "the deadly race and tribe of women who live amongst mortal men to their great trouble, no helpmeets in hateful poverty, but only in wealth" (123). The poet likens this female scourge to mischievous drones who enjoy the fruit of the other bees' labor, and he describes the misfortune of men whether they marry or not: those who do not marry have no one to help them in old age, while those who do marry risk the misfortune of difficult children who cause unceasing worry. Hesiod concludes this brief story by affirming that through this punishment, not even Prometheus could overcome the power of Zeus.

In *Works and Days*, Hesiod also begins the story with Prometheus's theft of fire, but he elaborates on the tale by adding several plot details and embellished rhetoric. After Zeus discovers Prometheus's crime, he proclaims that he will give to men "an evil thing in which they may all be glad of heart while they embrace their own destruction" (7). Zeus orders Hephaestus to create a maiden out of earth and commands that the maiden resemble the goddesses in appearance. Athena instructs the maiden in needlework and weaving, Aphrodite endows her with beauty and a sense of longing, and Hermes is instructed "to put in her a shameless mind and a deceitful nature" (7). The gods follow the commands of Zeus, who names the maiden Pandora (meaning "all-endowed") because she was given gifts from the gods of Olympus. Zeus then sends Pandora to Epimetheus, Prometheus's brother, who forgets Prometheus's previous warning never to accept a gift from the gods. She brings with her a jar full of the gods' gifts, which are in fact nothing but evil and suffering. When she removes the lid from the jar, she releases "ills and hard toil and heavy sicknesses" (9), which had previously been unknown to humans. Only hope remains behind in the jar; otherwise, the earth is plagued by evils of every sort. Hesiod concludes this version by affirming that Zeus's will cannot be escaped.

SIGNIFICANCE

Both versions of this ancient Greek myth function as etiologies of evil and suffering in the world. Yet although each version places the blame squarely on women, as represented by Pandora, the stories emphasize different elements. In the *Theogony*, Hesiod does not mention Pandora by name but emphasizes that the woman created by Hephaestus is a punishment; by her very nature, she causes inevitable evil to men whether they marry or not. In this story, all women bring suffering to men, and Hesiod thus implies that women are the source of all suffering in the world. The better-known version of the myth, recounted in *Works and Days*, also describes the maiden as evil, but this story includes the important new detail of the jar containing the sufferings that Pandora releases when she removes the lid. In this version, Pandora is evil and her actions bring about suffering, but she is not exactly the embodiment of all evils.

Notwithstanding these differences, the image of woman suffers greatly in both versions, which portray her as unequivocally bad. In this sense, the story is analogous to other etiological myths, most notably the story of Adam and Eve in the Hebrew Bible (Christian Old Testament). In this story, Adam and Eve are the first humans created by God, and they live in perfect innocence and harmony in the Garden of Eden until Eve violates God's commandment not to eat the fruit of the tree of knowledge. Deceived by a serpent, Eve eats the fruit and persuades Adam to do the same. God punishes the couple by banishing them from the garden and forcing them to live on earth, where they must suffer pain and hardship as a consequence of Eve's sin. Here too, woman is portrayed as the cause of the world's suffering.

Interestingly, however, Hesiod's myth includes an important difference, which is that Zeus engineers the creation of Pandora as a punishment for Prometheus's theft. This act implies that Zeus himself is responsible for the etiology of evil and suffering, given that he deliberately commands Hephaestus to create such a maiden. Moreover, the theft of fire indicates that some type of evil, or at least wrongdoing, existed prior to the advent of Pandora. As readers and scholars have noted, these and other ambiguous details pose intriguing interpretive puzzles regarding this myth.

Ashleigh Imus, PhD

BIBLIOGRAPHY

Hesiod, et al. *Hesiod, the Homeric Hymns, and Homerica*. Trans. Hugh G. Evelyn-White. Cambridge: Harvard UP, 1954. Print.

Lev Kenaan, Vered. *Pandora's Senses: The Feminine Character of the Ancient Text*. Madison: U of Wisconsin P, 2008. Print.

Panofsky, Dora. *Pandora's Box: The Changing Aspects of a Mythical Symbol*. Princeton: Princeton UP, 1978. Print.

Phipps, W. E. "Eve and Pandora Contrasted." *Theology Today* 45.1 (1988): 34–48. Print.

Zeitlin, Froma. *Playing the Other: Gender and Society in Classical Greek Literature*. Chicago: U of Chicago P, 1996. Print.

◆ Prometheus and the Theft of Fire

Author: Hesiod
Time Period: 999 BCE–1 BCE
Country or Culture: Greece
Genre: Myth

PLOT SUMMARY

As the gods of ancient Greece gather to eat, the Titan Prometheus decides to play a trick on Zeus, the god of thunder and the leader of the Olympian pantheon. Prometheus places two food offerings before Zeus, the first a delicious piece of beef hidden inside of a revolting ox's stomach and the second the hard bone of a bull wrapped in delectable fat. Zeus selects the second piece of food, and because of this humans begin to sacrifice bones wrapped in fat to him while keeping the tastiest and most nourishing food for themselves.

Zeus is furious at this deception and decides to punish the humans, even though it was truly Prometheus who wronged him. First, he takes away the secret of the crops. Were humans to know this secret, they could work only a single day and create enough food to feed themselves for the entire year, freeing large spans of time for relaxation and celebration. He also takes away fire, which the humans need to cook their food. Prometheus sees the harsh punishments Zeus is inflicting on the humans and decides to come to their aid, using a giant rod from a fennel plant to steal fire from Zeus and return it to the mortals.

When Zeus sees that Prometheus has again made a fool of him in order to benefit the humans, he decides further punishments are needed. He then summons the god Hephaistos and tells him to gather mud and water and mold them into a form much like that of a human man. Zeus then has Hephaistos place human strength and a pretty voice inside of the form, modeling it after the goddesses. This creature of mud becomes a creature of flesh, whom Zeus names Pandora. Zeus is pleased that he has created something that will cause the human men great pain.

Zeus then instructs the messenger of the gods, Hermes, to deliver Pandora to Epimetheus, the brother of Prometheus and a Titan who also often aids the mortals. Prometheus, expecting such a trick, had already visited Epimetheus and warned him never to accept a gift from Zeus, for such a gift would likely be a trap rather than an actual boon. Epimetheus, however, is so pleased by the sight of Pandora and the seeming generosity of Zeus that he accepts the gift. It is only later, after Pandora reveals her true nature, that Epimetheus understands the mistake he has made and the humans are punished once more for the meddling of the gods. Prometheus himself is chained to a mountain and forced to endure the daily torture of an eagle eating his liver. As he is immortal, his liver grows back each night, providing a new meal for the eagle and fresh punishment for the Titan who dared to disobey the ruler of the gods.

SIGNIFICANCE

Before the birth of the Olympian gods who dominate Greek mythology, another pantheon of gods called the Titans ruled the universe. While most of the Titans were essentially banished from Greek mythology after Zeus led his rebellion against them, Prometheus lingered, playing a significant role in clarifying the relationship between the gods and humans.

Arguably more than any other Greek deity, Prometheus is defined by his strong alliance with mortals. He continually risks his own safety and power in order to support humans and, in some accounts, is even responsible for their creation. The myth of Prometheus's theft of fire is no exception; even though Zeus clearly holds greater power than Prometheus, the Titan still dares to trick the Olympian, secreting away the vital resource so that humans will be able to continue developing their civilization. While this is in character for Prometheus, the cruelty with which Zeus casts his punishment on the humans seems to contradict some later depictions of the thunder god. This particular myth, however, takes place in the early days of Olympian rule, and the tension between Zeus and Prometheus is meant not to define Zeus for all time but rather to define the unclear relationship between humanity and the deities. As foils, neither Zeus nor Prometheus entirely trumps the other; instead, fire is taken away and given back, the secrets of agriculture are both partially hidden and partially revealed, and the punishment of Pandora is as much a gift as it is a curse. The myth, then, highlights the ambiguity of the relationship between humans and a pantheon of gods who are at once both loving and spiteful.

The idea of a god such as Prometheus rallying for humans despite the uncaring attitude of more powerful deities resonated with writers and artists for centuries, and he eventually became a symbol of the human pursuit of scientific knowledge. On a basic level, the control of fire is one of the first technologies that humans developed, and the ability to stay warm and cook food allowed for the early development of civilization. The myth of Prometheus asserts the necessity of such pursuits while suggesting that they are not so easily earned and often come with their own unique consequences, just as the acquisition of fire results in the creation of Pandora. A range of more modern works continue with this idea, among them Mary Shelley's nineteenth-century novel *Frankenstein; or, The Modern Prometheus*, in which a scientist pushes the limits of knowledge in order to create life out of death, only to achieve disastrous and disturbing results.

T. Fleischmann, MFA

BIBLIOGRAPHY

"Pandora, in Greek Mythology." *Columbia Electronic Encyclopedia*. 6th ed. *Literary Reference Center*. Web. 6 June 2013.

Power, Carl, and John E. J. Rasko. "Whither Prometheus' Liver? Greek Myth and the Science of Regeneration." *Annals of Internal Medicine* 149.6 (2008): 421–26. Print.

"Prometheus: The Theft of Fire and Instruction of Men in the Arts." *Theoi Greek Mythology*. Aaron J. Atsma, 2011. Web. 6 June 2013.

"Prometheus Unbound." *Benet's Reader's Encyclopedia*. New York: Harper, 1996. 833. Print.

Weigel, James, Jr. "Prometheus Bound." *Masterplots*. Ed. Laurence W. Mazzeno. 4th ed. Vol. 9. Pasadena: Salem, 2010. 4731–33. Print.

The Prophecy of Paris

Author: Pseudo-Apollodorus
Time Period: 1 CE–500 CE
Country or Culture: Greece
Genre: Myth

PLOT SUMMARY

King Priam and Queen Hecuba are rulers of the great city of Troy, a powerful military and cultural center. Priam fathers many children, both with Hecuba and with other wives and mistresses, most of whom go on to live happy and prosperous lives. When his wife is pregnant with a new child, however, she experiences a horrible dream in which she goes into labor and a flaming torch emerges from her body. Not knowing what the dream might portend, Priam and Hecuba summon the seer Aesacus, a son from Priam's first marriage. Having learned the secrets of dreams from a young age, Aesacus tells them that the flaming torch signals the eventual destruction of Troy, which the baby will bring about.

On the day the baby is born, Aesacus is struck by a further prophecy, declaring that a child born to the royal family on that day must be killed in order to keep the city safe. Priam and Hecuba, however, cannot bring themselves to harm such a defenseless child themselves. Instead, they summon their chief shepherd, Agelaus, and ask him to take the baby away and to leave him exposed to the elements. The shepherd takes the baby to Mount Ida and abandons him there, hoping that nature will do the deed for him. Shortly after Agelaus walks away, however, a powerful female bear approaches the baby, suckling him and providing him with warmth for many days. When Agelaus returns to determine the fate of the child, he is amazed to find him still alive. The shepherd is so moved by the baby's survival that he places him in his backpack and returns home, naming the child Paris and deciding to raise him as his own son.

Unaware of his royal lineage, Paris is able to grow up in Agelaus's household, unharmed by the prophets that warned of the damage he would cause. He is a strikingly beautiful and strong child who impresses everyone he meets. He even gains the nickname Alexander (meaning "the one who protects men") after encountering a group of livestock thieves and defeating them singlehandedly. Enjoying his life among the animals and even marrying a nymph, the headstrong young Paris blissfully pursues his own desires, entirely unaware that his actions will one day lead to the destruction of one of the greatest cities on earth.

SIGNIFICANCE

This story of the birth and prophecy of Paris comes to the modern day primarily through an account in book 3 of the *Bibliotheca* (*The Library*). A multivolume text chronicling the expanse of Greek mythology and legends, the *Bibliotheca* is written in brief and straightforward prose, eschewing the overwrought drama and language of some other Greek mythological histories in order to create a version of the history that appears more "factual."

Many other classical writers took up the story of Paris, and indeed, his narrative and the downfall of Troy are central to the Greek poet Homer's classic *Iliad*. Paris himself encounters almost all of the major figures of Greek mythology, angering as many gods and goddesses as he pleases and crossing paths with the greatest kings and warriors of his time. Here, however, the writer of the *Bibliotheca*—traditionally believed to be Apollodorus, though this is now considered incorrect—focuses entirely on the prophecy surrounding the birth of Paris and, in doing so, concentrates on the tension between the desires of the mortals and the decrees of the gods.

Before Paris is even brought into the world, the gods communicate the clear, unambiguous message that he will bring about the downfall of Troy. Aesacus, a member of Priam's family, first makes this declaration, while in other versions of the myth, a sibyl of the god Apollo or Paris's sister Cassandra gives the omen. It is evident then, through both the word of the god and the prophecy of the family, that Paris will bring doom to the kingdom; however, Priam and Hecuba are unable to follow the advice they are given. What begins instead is a series of events in which the mortals fail to heed the warnings of the gods and, as a result, ensure their own deaths. This narrative is interesting because even as the gods warn that Paris should be killed, they also seem to conspire to keep him alive. For instance, the young prince is left on Mount Ida, a location sacred to the gods and goddesses, and is mystically protected by a gigantic bear. When he somehow survives exposure to the elements, the shepherd takes pity on the baby and decides to raise him. These events call attention to the core lesson of the myth: although Hecuba and Priam believe they might outwit the god's omen, in reality it is not a warning but the announcement of a divine plan. The outcome is already written, even as the parents do their best to avoid it.

While the actual logic and schemes of the gods remain unspoken in this brief narrative from the *Bibliotheca*, ancient readers familiar with the long dramas between Paris and various deities would have known the dominant themes of his life. In Greek mythology, the gods themselves are often as fickle as the humans, their whims and fancies likely to result in massive destruction and widespread war. As the story of the prophecy of Paris shows, however, even when the actions of the gods seem impulsive or arbitrary, the mortals are still doomed to follow the prophesied path and meet whatever violent ending awaits them.

T. Fleischmann, MFA

BIBLIOGRAPHY

Anderson, Michael John. *The Fall of Troy in Early Greek Poetry and Art*. Oxford: Oxford UP, 1997. Print.

Bryce, Trevor R. "The Trojan War: Is There Truth behind the Legend?" *Near Eastern Archaeology* 65.3 (2002): 182–95. Print.

Hard, Robin. "The Birth and Early Life of Paris, and His Judgement of the Three Goddesses." *The Routledge Handbook of Greek Mythology*. London: Routledge, 2004. 441–44. Print.

"Paris, in Greek Mythology." *Columbia Electronic Encyclopedia*. 6th ed. (2013): 1. *Literary Reference Center*. Web. 26 June 2013.

Pseudo-Apollodorus. *The Library*. Vol. 2. Trans. James George Frazer. Ed. G. P. Goold. 1922. Cambridge: Loeb Classical Lib., 1996. Print.

◆ The Sack of Troy

Author: Virgil
Time Period: 1 CE–500 CE
Country or Culture: Rome
Genre: Myth

PLOT SUMMARY

During the Trojan War, Greek military forces lay siege to the city of Troy for ten fruitless years. Finally, the Greek leaders develop a plan to defeat their enemy once and for all. They construct a giant wooden horse, and the best warriors hide inside its hollow body. After presenting the horse as a peace offering, the remaining Greeks depart to lie in wait on the island of Tenedos. The Trojans debate whether to accept the horse, and the priest Laocoön runs down from the citadel to urge the Trojans not to trust the gift, which will surely lead to their downfall. He declares, "Men of Troy, trust not the horse. Whatever it be, I fear the Greeks, even when bringing gifts" (Virgil 319; bk. 2). With these words, he hurls his spear into the horse's wooden flank.

Next, a band of young Trojan men appears with a Greek stranger they have captured. The stranger, Sinon, spins a long tale of mistreatment at the hands of his fellow Greeks: his kinsman Palamedes was killed, and Sinon himself was harassed by the Greek hero Ulysses and chosen to be sacrificed to the gods. He claims to have fled his impending death and begs the Trojans for mercy. Priam, king of the Trojans, treats Sinon kindly and asks him to explain the massive gift. Sinon declares that the Greeks built the horse in atonement to the goddess Minerva because their warriors Diomedes and Ulysses had defiled her temple. Sinon claims that the Trojans' acceptance of the gift will make them victorious in war.

Nearly persuaded, the Trojans are fully convinced after they witness a final, terrible portent: from the ocean, two deadly serpents approach the beach, "licking with quivering tongues their hissing mouths" (331). Once ashore, they immediately attack Laocoön and his two young sons, killing them. The Trojans interpret this as divine punishment for Laocoön's disrespect of the horse, so they haul the structure into the city and begin to celebrate their victory.

That night as the Trojans sleep, the departed Greeks return and unite with the warriors whom Sinon has freed from within the horse. Just as the Greeks begin to storm the city, the Trojan Aeneas, a son of the goddess Venus, has a dream in which the slain Trojan hero Hector announces that their city is falling. He commands Aeneas to take his household gods and flee, and he prophesies that Aeneas will wander the seas but eventually establish a "mighty city" (337). Aeneas wakes and attempts to fight the Greeks as the city burns. He and a few companions slay enemies and steal their armor to disguise themselves. This ruse works temporarily, but they are soon attacked by Trojans who mistake them for Greeks.

Greek forces destroy Priam's castle, breaking through the doors and murdering Priam's son Polites and then Priam himself. Aeneas nearly kills Helen, the Greek beauty whose seduction by the Trojan prince Paris began the hostilities, but Venus prevents him and urges him to flee the city. Aeneas's father, Anchises, at first refuses to leave but is quickly persuaded by an omen. When the family has nearly reached the gates, Aeneas discovers that his wife, Creusa, is missing. He rushes back to search the city, and her ghost suddenly appears. In a moving farewell, she describes her fate and prophesies his happy future of kingship and a royal wife by "the Lydian Tiber" (369). After trying and failing to embrace the ghost of Creusa three times, Aeneas escapes the city with his father, his son, and many other Trojan companions.

SIGNIFICANCE

The Roman poet Virgil's account of the fall of Troy appears in book 2 of the *Aeneid*, when Aeneas recounts the story to the Carthaginian queen Dido and her court. As a mythological event, the sack of Troy had been long established in Greek culture prior to Virgil's retelling in the *Aeneid*, which was written between 29 and 19 BCE. The most notable account appears in Homer's eighth-century BCE epic poem the *Iliad*, which tells the story of the Trojan War from the point of view of the Greek heroes, with emphasis on the warrior Achilles and his struggles with his Greek comrades. As a Roman poet writing approximately seven centuries after Homer, Virgil had very different objectives in representing the sack of Troy. Because ancient Roman culture drew so heavily on Greek antecedents, Roman writers frequently used Greek source material and strove to distinguish their achievements from those of their Greek predecessors while matching the greatness of Greek culture. Writing at the dawn of the Roman Empire, Virgil was commissioned by the emperor Augustus to write the *Aeneid* as an epic representing the empire's origins and greatness—an epic that would rival the Greek classics.

Through his devotion to duty and his successful founding of Rome, Aeneas is meant to embody the greatness of the empire. Thus, the hero renders the perspective of the Trojans—the mythological ancestors of the Romans—in the ancient war, which Virgil portrays with dramatic brilliance in book 2 as he describes the horrors of Laocoön's death, the burning city, the deaths of Priam and his son, and the apparitions of Hector and Creusa. Through these details, Virgil not only creates a Roman version of an old myth but also renders the psychological inner life of his heroes. Aeneas is not simply a one-dimensional warrior driven by duty. He often experiences doubts and apprehension, which make his character and Virgil's portrayal of the making of empire both fascinating and more complex than the characterization in the Greek epics.

Ashleigh Imus, PhD

BIBLIOGRAPHY

Haynes, French Leo. "Shakespeare and the Troy Story." *Howard College Bulletin* 80.3 (1922): 67–131. Print.

Knight, W. F. Jackson. *Vergil, Epic, and Anthropology: Comprising Vergil's Troy, Cumaean Gates, and the Holy City of the East*. New York: Barnes, 1967. Print.

Lapham, Lewis H., and Peter T. Struck, eds. *The End of the World*. New York: St. Martin's, 1998. Print.

Miller, Frank Justus, trans. *Two Dramatizations from Vergil*. Chicago: U of Chicago P, 1908. Print.

Virgil. *Virgil:* Eclogues, Georgics, Aeneid *I–VI*. Trans. H. Rushton Fairclough. Cambridge: Harvard UP, 1999. Print.

 # The Statue of Pygmalion

Author: Ovid
Time Period: 1 CE–500 CE
Country or Culture: Rome
Genre: Myth

PLOT SUMMARY

Ovid's story of the artist Pygmalion appears in book 10 of the *Metamorphoses* in the context of Venus's punishment of the Propoetides, the daughters of Propoetus who deny Venus's power and are thus forced to become prostitutes. Disgusted by the women's immorality, Pygmalion rejects all women and decides to live a celibate life. Instead, rather than seek a truly virtuous woman, he uses his art to carve the snow-white likeness of a perfect woman. The result is so stunningly beautiful that passion inflames him, and he touches the stone as if it were a real woman: "caresses it, believes / The firm new flesh beneath his fingers yields, / And fears the limbs may darken with a bruise" (233). He speaks lovingly to the statue and brings it gifts of shells and stones, birds and flowers. He dresses the figure in lovely clothes and jewels and lays her "on a couch of purple silk, / Called her his darling, cushioning her head, / As if she relished it, on softest down" (233).

Soon after, the island of Cyprus, where Pygmalion lives, celebrates the festival of Venus. Worshippers burn incense and sacrifice animals. After making his offering, Pygmalion prays to the goddess, but he is not bold enough to ask that his statue come to life, so he humbly entreats Venus to make the stone "the living likeness of my ivory girl" (233). But Venus understands his true wish and sends forth a good omen: the flame at her altar burns brightly and leaps up three times. Encouraged, Pygmalion returns home to kiss the statue that lies on his couch. Miraculously, her form beneath his touch begins to soften, like wax melting in the sun. As the statue increasingly resembles a living being, Pygmalion is "torn with wonder and misgiving, / Delight and terror that it was not true!" (234), until he finally realizes that the statue is indeed a living woman. Overjoyed, he expresses deep gratitude to Venus as he observes his shy maiden blush modestly in response to his kisses. Venus blesses the union she has made, and nine months later, the couple produce a daughter named Paphos, which eventually becomes the name of an island as well.

SIGNIFICANCE

The original myth of Pygmalion is Greek, but the Roman poet Ovid offers his unique and compelling treatment in the *Metamorphoses*, his first-century collection of ancient Greek and Roman myths, considered his finest achievement and one of the most important literary texts of Western civilization. The idea of bringing to life one's artistic creation evidently fascinated ancient Greek audiences, as the theme recurs in several other ancient myths as well, including the story of Daedalus and the creation of Pandora, among others. Moreover, this intriguing theme has informed subsequent Western literary classics from Carlo Collodi's *The Adventures of Pinocchio* to Mary Shelley's *Frankenstein*. Part of the allure lies in the notions of ambition, ideal beauty, and the divine potential of humans to create a living being from inanimate material. Implicit in this ambition and power is the understanding that art can seduce an artist in delightful but dangerous ways.

With remarkable depth, Ovid's treatment explores this seduction by framing the story of Pygmalion within a larger narrative structure that implies the story as a commentary on its teller. The myth of Pygmalion is told by Orpheus, a famed musician who narrates most of the stories of book 10. After his wife, Eurydice, dies from a snakebite wound shortly after their marriage,

Orpheus is inconsolable and resolves to visit Pluto and Persephone, king and queen of the underworld Hades, to persuade them to return his wife to the land of the living. In Hades, Orpheus performs a song so moving that it amazes the bodiless shades, who cease all activity and weep. Unable to refuse Orpheus's request, Pluto and Persephone agree to return Eurydice to the world on the condition that Orpheus not look back at his wife as they travel out of the underworld. If he does, she must return to Hades forever. They begin the arduous journey, and at the last moment, Orpheus cannot help himself as he glances back at Eurydice.

The rest of book 10 can be understood as Orpheus's response to his loss. He is so devastated that he rejects all women and decides to love young men instead. His first two stories are about homosexual love; he introduces the theme of illicit desire in the brief anecdote about the Propoetides. Pygmalion's reaction to these women is strikingly similar to Orpheus's response to the loss of Eurydice: both men reject all women. The link is made even more significant by the fact that both are artists who use their talent to defy the laws of nature: Orpheus seduces the powers of death to bring Eurydice back to life, whereas Pygmalion creates the perfect sculpture and brings it to life through his devotion to Venus. The difference, of course, is that Orpheus fails, whereas Pygmalion succeeds. Unable to control his world and his emotions through his art, Orpheus fails to truly understand the limits of artistic genius, and his story of Pygmalion shows that he does not learn from this fatal mistake (Heath 369). Instead, he holds on to his fantasy of artistic talent as all-powerful by exalting Pygmalion, a man who hypocritically claims concern for morality but is attracted to his statue based on its physical beauty alone (Anderson 269). Moreover, in some versions of this story, the statue-woman is named Galatea, but she remains nameless in Ovid's version, which underscores her objectification. These details demonstrate why Ovid's version of the myth remains unmatched in sophistication and psychological depth.

Ashleigh Imus, PhD

BIBLIOGRAPHY

Anderson, William S. "Aspects of Love in Ovid's 'Metamorphoses.'" *Classical Journal* 90.3 (1995): 265–69. Print.

Heath, John. "The Stupor of Orpheus: Ovid's *Metamorphoses* 10.64–71." *Classical Journal* 91.4 (1996): 353–70. Print.

Miller, J. Hillis. *Versions of Pygmalion.* Cambridge: Harvard UP, 1990. Print.

Ovid. *Metamorphoses.* Trans. A. D. Melville. New York: Oxford UP, 1986. Print.

Stoichita, Victor I. *The Pygmalion Effect: From Ovid to Hitchcock.* Chicago: U of Chicago P, 2008. Print.

◆ The Twelfth Labor: Hercules and Cerberus

Author: Seneca
Time Period: 1 CE–500 CE
Country or Culture: Rome
Genre: Myth

PLOT SUMMARY

Hercules is a warrior of legendary might, the son of the great god Jupiter and a mortal woman. At the bidding of Jupiter's jealous wife, the goddess Juno, Hercules is ordered by Eurystheus, king of Argos, to perform twelve daunting tasks.

Having completed eleven labors, each one seemingly impossible, Hercules now faces his final task. This labor is perhaps the most frightening of all: Hercules is ordered to enter the underworld, defeat the fearsome demon dog Cerberus, and bring the creature back to Eurystheus in submission. This three-headed beast waits inside the land of the dead, guarding the only exit so that the souls of the deceased cannot escape back into the world of the living and wandering mortals are likewise kept at bay.

Hercules descends into the underworld via a chasm located where Sparta meets the sea. He reaches Tartarus, the home of Pluto, god of the underworld, and approaches the river Styx, where Charon, the ferryman, is carrying shades across the water. Hercules pushes through the crowd of waiting shades and demands that Charon carry him across. When Charon objects, Hercules subdues him and steals his boat.

On the other side of the river is the home of Pluto, where Cerberus stands guard. Upon seeing Hercules, Cerberus bays so loudly that even the ghosts are frightened by him, and as he growls, Hercules sees the snakes and vipers that twirl around the dog's shaggy head and entwine themselves within its tail. As Hercules lunges toward the beast, however, even Cerberus experiences a moment of fear, realizing the mortal's strength. Wearing the head and hide of the Nemean lion, which he slew in his first labor, Hercules begins to pound Cerberus viciously with his club, sparing none of his great strength in the onslaught. After a long while, Cerberus is eventually so exhausted that he yields, lowering all three of his menacing heads onto the ground in surrender.

As Pluto and his wife, Proserpine, look on and shiver, Hercules demands a gift, and they give him the hero Theseus, whom they previously trapped in the underworld. Hercules then binds Cerberus in chains and, accompanied by Theseus, leads the shamed beast away from the underworld. While at first Cerberus is calm, exhausted and beaten from the long battle, as soon as Hercules crosses into the light of the sun, the beast is roused again, having never seen such intense light. The dog kicks up his legs and struggles to drag Hercules back to Pluto with him, but Hercules summons the last of his strength and, with Theseus's help, overcomes the beast yet again. Hercules leads the defeated animal to Eurystheus, completing his twelfth labor.

SIGNIFICANCE

Hercules is perhaps the most famous hero of Greek and Roman mythology, and the tales of his labors continue to inspire literature and theater in the modern day. As the final labor in his long quest, his battle with Cerberus intensifies the struggle between mortality and godliness that so often defines the hero. The first-century CE Roman playwright Seneca tells this story in his play *Hercules Furens.* Unlike earlier versions of the story, in which Hercules (known in Greek as Heracles) kills his family in a fit of madness and is sentenced to perform his twelve labors as penance, Seneca's retelling has Hercules succumb to insanity and commit his murders immediately after completing his last labor. In Seneca's version, both the labors and Hercules's ensuing madness are orchestrated by Juno as a result of her hatred for her husband's son.

Although his father is Jupiter, the most powerful god in the Roman pantheon, Hercules also has a mortal mother, which makes him a mortal rather than an undying deity. He is, however, an incredibly powerful and gifted warrior, which puts him in a somewhat unusual liminal space between immortality and humanity. Because of his hybrid nature, Hercules manages to represent the highest aspirations of humanity as well as its limitations, both of which are brought into extreme tension when he battles Cerberus. While Hercules fights an incredible number of fierce and deadly beasts during his labors, gods among them, the battle with Cerberus is significant because of the dog's role in mythology. Guarding the border between the underworld and the land of the living, Cerberus literally protects the line between life and death. He is also a creature that only desires living meat, a feature that emphasizes his role as an enemy of mortals and a friend to the dead. For Hercules to overcome the beast is for him to overpower the force that would keep him dead were his physical life to end.

Even though Hercules does manage to defeat the beast, he does not change the order of the Roman universe as a whole. Cerberus is terrified and upset by his voyage into the living world, and the very sight of sunlight seems to be even more upsetting to him than his defeat by the hero. However, in most versions of the story (though not Seneca's), as soon as Hercules shows the defeated animal to Eurystheus, he returns Cerberus to the underworld, allowing him once again to protect the barrier between life and death. These concessions speak both to the strength of Hercules and to the importance of the order of the world. Hercules is a legendary hero, the greatest in all mythology, and as such, he reluctantly wins the respect of the gods and an immortal position among them; in later antiquity, cults worshipping Hercules as a god became somewhat popular. However, the forces he overcomes rise again to power, with Cerberus continuing to stand guard beside the god Pluto for all time. Hercules is a folk hero, a mortal man who rises to greatness, and his myth stands as testament to the possibility of godliness in all mortals as well as to the incredible losses and suffering that await on the path to deification.

T. Fleischmann, MFA

BIBLIOGRAPHY

Genovese, E. N. "Hercules and His Twelve Labors." *Masterplots*. Ed. Laurence W. Mazzeno. 4th ed. Vol. 5. Pasadena: Salem, 2010. 2554–56. Print.

Henry, Elisabeth. *Orpheus with His Lute: Poetry and the Renewal of Life*. Carbondale: Southern Illinois UP, 1992. Print.

Lutz, R. C. "Seneca the Younger." *Magill's Survey of World Literature*. Ed. Steven G. Kellman. Rev. ed. Vol. 5. Pasadena: Salem, 2009. 2325–30. Print.

Morgan, Pauline. "Hercules and His Twelve Labors." *Cyclopedia of Literary Places*. Ed. R. Baird Shuman and R. Kent Rasmussen. Vol. 2. Pasadena: Salem, 2003. 517–18. Print.

Seneca. *Hercules Furens. Seneca's Tragedies*. Trans. Frank Justus Miller. Vol. 1. London: Heinemann, 1917. 1–119. Print.

◆ The Vengeance of Medea

Author: Euripides
Time Period: 999 BCE–1 BCE
Country or Culture: Greece
Genre: Myth

PLOT SUMMARY

In the Greek city of Corinth, the Colchian princess Medea is mourning her abandonment by Jason, the former leader of the Argonauts, and his subsequent marriage to King Creon's daughter, Glauce. While full of self-pity over the rejection, Medea is also actively plotting her revenge. Having previously killed her brother, she has a taste for more bloodshed.

Believing Medea to be an emotionally unstable sorceress, Creon announces that he is banishing her and her two sons from Corinth to protect himself and the newlywed couple from her wrath. A life in exile means that she and her children will face either homelessness or slavery, as she cannot return home to the father and homeland she spurned to marry Jason. She pleads with the king to let her stay just one more day, and he reluctantly complies, although when he is out of sight she announces her plans for murderous revenge.

Jason offers Medea money so that she will not be penniless; he otherwise remains heartless toward her plight. Medea lashes out at him for his repulsive behavior, reminding him of the deeds she committed on his behalf: she slew the dragon that protected the Golden Fleece and thus saved his life, allowing him to fulfill his mission, return to Iolcus, and claim his inheritance to the throne of his uncle Pelias. She was also responsible for encouraging the daughters of Pelias to kill their father so that Jason could take power. She also reminds him that she fulfilled their marriage contract by bearing two sons and that he is breaking sacred oaths by leaving her. Jason counters that all of these deeds were not the work of her hands but the work of the gods and further claims that her love for him was also dictated by the gods.

As Medea's anger continues to fester, she is visited by Aegeus, the king of Athens. He tells her about his unhappy, childless marriage, and Medea promises to help him bring children into the world with her magic potions. In exchange, he must promise to provide her with a safe home in Athens and to neither turn her over to her enemies nor cast her out no matter what she does.

Medea then carries through with her plan to kill Glauce, giving the princess a poisonous robe and gold headdress. After the young bride dons the items, the crown lights her hair and scalp on fire while the robe begins to eat through her skin, and neither can be removed. When King Creon attempts to remove the garments, he too succumbs to their poison.

Finally, Medea kills her two children with a sword, claiming that she must do so because they have no father, home, or future. As Jason discovers the gruesome act, Medea escapes with the bodies of her children in a chariot, headed safely toward Athens.

SIGNIFICANCE

The myth about the vengeance of Medea is the subject of the Greek playwright Euripides's play *Medea*, first performed in 431 BCE. Euripides and his fellow Greeks were well aware of the details of the myth, as it formed part of the well-known mythological history of Jason and the Argonauts. Prior to the writing of *Medea*, however, the betrayed princess was typically viewed as a wicked sorceress and a weak, irrational, and selfish mother. Euripides, however, portrays her as a more sympathetic victim in his play, which debuted at the annual Dionysia festival in Athens.

The motives for Euripides's sensitive treatment are clearly stated by Medea, who was once a princess and sacrificed everything for Jason. She protests the patriarchal society that allows husbands to divorce their wives at whim but prohibits women from doing the same. She complains about how women must give up their bodies and their lives, only to be abandoned when their husbands decide to remarry for more power or wealth. Medea states that by killing her children, she is not only preventing them from enduring decades of suffering and pain but also committing the horrendous deed herself out of love before someone else can kill them out of hatred. In presenting the injustice of the fate of Medea in particular, Euripides calls attention to the unjust nature of a society that would doom a woman and her children to lives of slavery or homelessness.

As a female character living in a patriarchal society who plays an active role in determining her own fate, Medea has often been viewed through a feminist lens. Other interpreters read her as a wicked witch whose

revenge against her husband represents an almost unimaginable and unspeakable side of human nature. Today, the term "Medea syndrome" is sometimes used to describe instances in which a woman responds to betrayal or conflict by using her children to take revenge against her partner.

Sally Driscoll, MLS

BIBLIOGRAPHY

Bates, Alfred, ed. *Greek Drama*. Vol. 1. London: Athenian Soc., 1903. Print.

Euripides. *Euripides'* Medea*: A New Translation*. Trans. Diane J. Rayor. Cambridge: Cambridge UP, 2013. Print.

---. *Medea*. Trans. E. P. Coleridge. *Internet Classics Archive*. Massachusetts Institute of Technology, n.d. Web. 27 June 2013.

"Medea." *The Oxford Classical Dictionary*. Ed. Simon Hornblower and Antony Spawforth. 3rd ed. Oxford: Oxford UP, 1996. 944–45. Print.

Schwab, Gustav. "The Story of the Argonauts." *Gods and Heroes of Ancient Greece*. New York: Random, 2011. 86–142. Print.

◆ Zeus and the Titan War

Author: Hesiod
Time Period: 999 BCE–1 BCE
Country or Culture: Greece
Genre: Myth

PLOT SUMMARY.

The powerful god Zeus wages war against the Titans. Among them is his father, the deity Cronus. Cronus is the ruler of all things and the bearer of tremendous power. However, he fears that one of his children might overthrow his leadership. Because of this, he devoured all of his offspring up until Zeus, who was secretly saved by his mother, Rhea. When Zeus grew and became powerful, he rescued his siblings from the stomach of Cronus and began the war that rages, gathering the other gods of Mount Olympus to be his allies.

The war is fiercely fought and violent, and although it rages for ten years, neither side begins to conquer the other. Seeing the intensity of the battle, Gaia suggests that Zeus rescue the Hecatoncheires from their prison within the earth. These mighty creatures are the children of Gaia and Uranus, each having one hundred arms and unmatchable strength. Zeus revives them from the deep caves of Tartarus and treats them to delicious food and drink. Zeus makes his plea when the creatures are strong again, explaining that the other children of Cronus have fought alongside him for a decade, but that without the assistance of the Hecatoncheires, the Titans will remain in power. The Hecatoncheires agree, noting that it was not until Zeus attempted to claim power that they were rescued from the abyss, and the terrifying creatures quickly join the battle. They raise gigantic boulders above their fifty heads as the Olympians charge forth with renewed energy, the very sky and the seas shaking from their ferocity and the blows they lay upon the Titans.

In this new onslaught, Zeus hurls his lightning against the Titans, and the powers of the various gods make the elements turn against themselves. The upper airs of the sky burn with intense flames and the oceans boil over with frenzied heat. Among the tornados and earthquakes that rock the land, the sounds of crashing are so intense that it seems as though the earth itself must be colliding with the sky above. The most powerful creatures in the battle, however, are not the Titans or the Olympians, but the Hecatoncheires, who hurl hundreds of rocks at the Titans, burying the gods in the earth and binding them with chains. With the Titans subdued, the Hecatoncheires are able to drag them so far underground that they reach Tartarus again. His father vanquished, Zeus is then able to claim power for himself, declaring that the sea god Poseidon should build a gate around the Titans and that the Hecatoncheires should stand watch over the ancient gods, ensuring that they will never attempt to reclaim power from the god of thunder.

SIGNIFICANCE

Told in the *Theogony* of the Greek poet Hesiod, the story of Zeus's rise to power and the overthrow of the Titan leaders is a foundational story in Greek mythology. The *Theogony* (ca. 700 BCE) is a long narrative poem that brings together diverse oral histories. Arguably one of the first attempts to do so in written language, the text details the creation of the cosmos and of the gods, setting in place the groundwork on which all future Greek mythological narratives would rely.

Because of the foundational nature of the text, examining the specifics of Zeus's rebellion also reveals a great deal about the ethics that drive Greek mythology. In the Olympian world (the world that Zeus establishes

and in which most Greek myths are set), Zeus is the ultimate father of both the gods and the humans, the authority figure to which all other deities and mortals must defer. A patriarch in the truest sense, he reflects the power structures of Greek families and politics, with men holding almost all of the agency and political strength and women relegated to minor roles. This rule, while understood as being unquestionable in most mythology, needs to have a firm foundation to explain it. Zeus does not exactly have a pure moral case to make in the *Theogony*: Cronus acts like a tyrant in many regards (the behavior that theoretically justifies the war), but so too will Zeus at times, and the violence Cronus brings on the cosmos as its ultimate ruler is no greater than the bloodshed Zeus will unleash from Mount Olympus. The justification for the patriarchy is not so much a justification of morality, then, but rather one of might.

Zeus, as Cronus did before him, manages to become the ruler simply because he is the strongest figure, and the myth of his war with the Titans is a long proof of that strength. In terms of his conflict with other masculine figures, he manages both to unleash extreme violence on the Titans and to function as a savior of the fearsome Hecatoncheires. These hundred-armed creatures turn the tides of the battle with their legendary strength, but it is Zeus who unleashes them and, importantly, Zeus who commands them to stand guard over the Titans in the end. In this way, the god of thunder manages to demonstrate both physical might and political leadership over the strongest male figures in the pantheon. Likewise, the deference of the female figures remains central to his triumph. Rhea and Gaia, his mother and grandmother, are the most powerful goddesses in Greek mythology, and both offer their loyal assistance to Zeus rather than to his father. The significance of the women in the transfer of power cannot be underestimated: without Rhea, Zeus would have been swallowed up with his siblings, and without Gaia, the Hecatoncheires would never have been released. The goddesses never scheme to gain their own power, however, but rather only to secure the power of the thunder god.

This decade-long battle of earth-shaking violence both concludes the most ancient portion of Greek mythology and establishes the power dynamics that remain through the end of the ancient Greek empire. Zeus is the father of all gods and the final power in Greek mythology, ruling from Mount Olympus in nearly unquestioned power. The narrative of Hesiod is a reminder that, even as the Greeks developed democracy and built their legendary culture, extreme violence and oppressive patriarchy remained at its core.

T. Fleischmann, MFA

BIBLIOGRAPHY

Atsma, Aaron J. "Titanes." *Theoi Greek Mythology.* Theoi Project, 2011. Web. 27 June 2013.

Boys-Stones, G. R., and J. H. Haubold, eds. *Plato and Hesiod.* Oxford: Oxford UP, 2010. Print.

Garrison, Daniel H. "Hesiod." *Critical Survey of Poetry.* 2nd rev. ed. Pasadena: Salem, 2002. 1–6. Print.

Koning, Hugo H. "The Other Poet: The Ancient Reception of Hesiod." *Mnemosyne* 64.3 (2011): 527–28. Print.

Shapiro, H. A. *The Cambridge Companion to Archaic Greece.* Cambridge: Cambridge UP, 2007. Print.

NORSE WORLD

◆ The Aesir-Vanir War

Author: Traditional Norse
Time Period: 1001 CE–1500 CE
Country or Culture: Scandinavia
Genre: Myth

PLOT SUMMARY

Two of the nine worlds within the universe, Asgard and Vanaheim, are occupied by two races of the gods (the Aesir and the Vanir, respectively). The Aesir and the Vanir coexist in relative harmony, but long ago, such was not the case. The two races entered into a brutal war, a conflict started over the Vanir goddess Freya (Freyja).

One day, Odin, the highest god, was monitoring the nine worlds for evil when his son Heimdall came to him to share his discovery of Vanaheim. The Vanir, he divulged, are peaceable gods who use magic and witchcraft to defeat their enemies rather than the strength of arms and muscle. Heimdall was concerned that the magic the Vanir practice, *seidr* (which could alter the destiny of those against whom it was used), could be a threat to Asgard. Heimdall suggested that he go to meet Freya, the daughter of Njord, the ruler of the Vanir, as

Odin's emissary in the hope that the two races of gods could coexist peacefully.

Seidr is a dark and unsavory form of magic only practiced by women. In fact (unbeknownst to Heimdall), Odin had met Freya while Heimdall was traveling and, disguised as a woman, had received training in *seidr*. Despite its disreputable connotation, *seidr* captured the attention of many in Asgard. The Aesir were drawn to Freya's powers, putting aside their own virtues and honor to be with Freya and to learn her craft. Fearing that Freya and *seidr* would destroy Asgard, Odin dubbed her Gullveig (meaning "gold greed") and decided to put Freya to death. The Aesir attempted to execute her three times, but like Odin, Freya has the power of resurrection: she rose repeatedly from the ashes of the fire into which she was thrown.

Meanwhile, the Vanir, seeing the brutal fashion in which the Aesir attempted to kill Freya, grew angry with the Aesir. The two races of gods entered into a brutal war that lasted many years. The Aesir used their physical skills and weaponry against the Vanir, while Freya's people utilized dark magic. Neither side gained a major advantage, however. Eventually, the two war-weary parties agreed to a truce. The Aesir and Vanir exchanged "hostages": Freya, her brother Freyr, and the great Njord were sent to Asgard, while Odin sent the timid Hoenir and the very wise Mimir to Vanaheim. Additionally, as a sign of their accord, the Aesir and Vanir agreed to meet and spit into a cauldron. The saliva was used to create a new god, Kvasir, who represents long-standing harmony between the Aesir and Vanir.

While Njord, Freya, and Freyr are seen as valuable contributors to Asgard (although Freya has romantic relationships with many of the Aesir, including Odin), Hoenir and Mimir did not fare as well in Vanaheim. Hoenir rarely spoke up when consulted by the Vanir leaders and, even when he did, offered little. The Vanir decided that their end of the arrangement was unfair and beheaded Mimir. They sent the head back to Asgard. Odin preserved it, however, and Mimir's head continued to counsel Odin thereafter. Eventually, Hoenir became a great leader among the Vanir.

SIGNIFICANCE

The Norse myth about the war between Asgard and Vanaheim is one of greed, paranoia, and brutality. These characteristics are common among humans, but what is significant is that the gods of Asgard demonstrate them. The Aesir are expected to demonstrate nobility and honorable behavior, but their discovery of the Vanir (who, according to the story, are peaceful) inspires them to abandon their traditions and to seek knowledge about *seidr*, a form of witchcraft that they knew to be dark and disreputable. Even Odin, the greatest of the Aesir, allowed himself to be bewitched by Freya's magic.

The story also shows the degree to which the Aesir fear losing their high status among the known worlds in the Norse universe. The Aesir constantly monitor the other worlds to ensure that they pose no threat to Asgard before they find Vanaheim. Despite the fact that the Vanir are perfectly content to coexist with Asgard in peace, Odin and the Aesir see a potential threat from the Vanir and therefore seek access to *seidr* to counter this perceived threat.

At the center of the war is Freya. Throughout Norse mythology, she is seen as a figure who is both attractive and disruptive. For example, when Heimdall reports on the Vanir to Odin, he includes an alleged romantic link between Freya and her brother, Freyr. After she joins the Aesir following the war, she is romantically connected to several Aesir, including Odin. Furthermore, although the Vanir women are all seemingly capable of practicing

seidr, the Aesir are particularly interested in Freya's abilities.

The war that erupts between the two races of gods begins when the Aesir brutally torture and kill Freya, whom Odin accuses of attempting to take the precious belongings of the Aesir. The war is drawn out and exhausting for both the Aesir and the Vanir. Neither race can claim an advantage, a fact indicative of the relative parity between the two. After the war's conclusion, the Aesir and Vanir exchange hostages, a tradition in the Norse world, and create Kvasir. Other tales of the Aesir and Vanir that take place after this war indicate that the two races remain in relative harmony with one another thereafter.

Michael P. Auerbach, MA

BIBLIOGRAPHY

Davidson, H. R. Ellis. *Gods and Myths of Northern Europe*. New York: Penguin, 1964. Print.

Grimes, Heilan Yvette. *The Norse Myths.* Boston: Hollow Earth, 2010. Print.

Lindow, John. *Norse Mythology: A Guide to Gods, Heroes, Rituals, and Beliefs*. New York: Oxford UP, 2002. Print.

Littleton, C. Scott. "Vanir." *Gods, Goddesses and Mythology*. Tarrytown: Cavendish, 2005. 1404–7. Print.

McCoy, Dan. "The Aesir-Vanir War." *Norse Mythology*. Norse Mythology, 2013. Web. 9 Jun 2013.

◆ Brynhildr, the Norse Valkyrie

Author: Traditional Norse
Time Period: 1001 CE–1500 CE
Country or Culture: Scandinavia
Genre: Myth

PLOT SUMMARY

Brynhildr (also known as Brynhild or Brunhilde) is one of the Valkyries, mighty warrior goddesses whose responsibility it is to decide who will live or die in battle and to deliver casualties to the majestic hall known as Valhalla, in the world of Asgard. Brynhildr is following a great battle among mortals and chooses Hjálmgunnarr to die. Hjálmgunnarr, however, has the favor of the great god Odin, who promises that he will win the battle. Brynhildr's defiance enrages Odin.

To punish her, Odin sentences her to sleep forever in a mountaintop castle, Hindafjall (Hindarfell), where she is surrounded by a wall of fire and protected by a dragon named Fáfnir. The only way for her to escape this fate is for her to marry a mortal, whom Brynhildr vows must be a man who lives without fear. While she sleeps, a brave hero named Sigurðr (Sigurd) is sent on a mission to kill Fáfnir. He then learns of Hindafjall's prisoner and rides to the castle out of curiosity. Walking through the wall of fire, Sigurðr comes across the sleeping Brynhildr and is captivated by her beauty.

Cutting through her armor, Sigurðr awakens Brynhildr. They agree to become engaged, but he does not free her from captivity. However, he vows to do so once he returns from delivering the treasure that was guarded by Fáfnir to his ally, King Gjúki. Before he leaves, he gives her a symbol of his promise to her, the magic ring Andvaranautr, from among the treasures that Fáfnir safeguarded. The ring is cursed, however, and because of that curse, Sigurðr becomes fated to forget his love. Gjúki's daughter Guðrún (Gudrun) falls in love with Sigurðr. Sigurðr still remembers his love for Brynhildr and spurns Guðrún. With the help of her mother, the witch Grimhíldr, Guðrún gives a magic potion to Sigurðr, making him forget his true love and instead fall in love with Guðrún.

Guðrún's brother Gunnarr wants to marry Brynhildr himself but is afraid to travel through the flames that surround her dwelling. Grimhíldr again intervenes, changing Sigurðr's appearance to that of Gunnarr. Under the spell, Sigurðr (as Gunnarr) rides through the flames and convinces Brynhildr that she should instead marry Gunnarr. She gives the impostor Andvaranautr. Over time, the effects of Grimhíldr's magic dissipate, and Sigurðr returns to his normal self, remembering his love for Brynhildr, but by this time she is married to Guðrún.

Years later, Guðrún reveals to Brynhildr Sigurðr's deception. Blinded by her rage, Brynhildr urges Gunnarr to kill Sigurðr. Bound by an oath, Gunnarr instead convinces his younger brother to commit the crime. (In one version, Sigurðr slays this brother just as he is being cut down.) As Sigurðr's body is laid to rest, Brynhildr, consumed by grief, throws herself upon Sigurðr's funeral pyre so that she can be with Sigurðr forever in the afterlife.

SIGNIFICANCE

Brynhildr's story is one of love, beauty, bravery, strength, and deception. The two main characters, Brynhildr and Sigurðr, demonstrate each of these characteristics. Brynhildr, for example, is described as a woman of incredible beauty (evidenced by her status as one of Odin's few handmaidens) and power. When Sigurðr finds her, he is first drawn to her golden hair, which is falling out of her helmet. When he removes the helmet, and her locks fall free, he is even more attracted. She is also clad in armor, which demonstrates her great physical strength; when he cuts away her chain mail clothing, he reveals her physical beauty. At the sight of this beautiful and strong woman, Sigurðr falls in love. When she awakes, Brynhildr quickly shares that love at the sight of the man who has freed her.

Bravery is also a trait demonstrated by both of the main characters. Unfortunately, Brynhildr's bravery and defiance are to blame for her imprisonment. As a Valkyrie, she is responsible for choosing who would die in battle. However, she defiantly chooses a combatant who has Odin's favor, and she is punished for her decision. Meanwhile, Sigurðr is so fearless that he rides his horse through the wall of flame that keeps Brynhildr hidden from the world. He also confronts and kills the terrible dragon that guards the castle in which the sleeping Brynhildr is imprisoned. In fact, when the fearful Gunnar wants to marry Brynhildr, he needs Sigurðr's innate bravery to return to Hindafjall for his would-be wife.

Both Sigurðr and Brynhildr, cursed because of the ring the former gave the latter, fall victim to the deception and betrayal of the other characters in the story. Sigurðr unwittingly succumbs to two magic spells that make him both spurn his true love and force her into the arms of another. Brynhildr, unaware that her betrothed is under the influence of magic, becomes enraged at his actions and brings about his death. She still loves him, however, and upon his death takes her own life as well so that they can be together forever.

In light of these themes, the story of Brynhildr has survived the ages, appearing in various incarnations in art, literature, music, and even popular culture. The themes of this story found their way into a number of Scandinavian poems during the twelfth and thirteenth centuries. In the eighteenth century, composer Richard Wagner used the Brynhildr epic in *Der Ring des Nibelungen*, a four-opera cycle including what is considered his most well-known piece, *Die Walküre* (The Valkyrie). The themes of the Brynhildr story (as well as characters resembling her) have appeared in modern comic books and television shows, and Wagner's iconic piece composed in her honor has been featured in a wide range of films and productions.

Michael P. Auerbach, MA

BIBLIOGRAPHY

"Brynhild." *Elizabeth A. Sackler Center for Feminist Art.* Brooklyn Museum, 13 Apr. 2007. Web. 24 May 2013.

Byock, Jesse L., trans. and ed. *The Saga of the Volsungs: The Norse Epic of Sigurd the Dragon Slayer.* Berkeley: U of California P, 2012. Print.

Littleton, C. Scott, ed. *Gods, Goddesses, and Mythology.* Vol. 10. Tarrytown: Cavendish, 2005. Print.

Mackenzie, Donald A. *Teutonic Myth and Legend.* London: Gresham, 1912. Print.

"The Ring Cycle by Wagner." *Metropolitan Opera.* Metropolitan Opera, 2013. Web. 24 May 2013.

Smart, Anthony E. "Brunhilde." *Encyclopedia Mythica.* Encyclopedia Mythica, 30 Mar. 2001. Web. 24 May 2013.

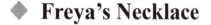

Freya's Necklace

Author: Traditional Norse
Time Period: 1001 CE–1500 CE
Country or Culture: Scandinavia
Genre: Myth

PLOT SUMMARY

While out for a walk on the borders of her palace grounds in Asgard Freya (Freyja)—the Norse goddess of love, beauty, and fertility—encounters dwarfs creating a beautiful golden necklace. Her weakness for beautiful objects, jewelry in particular, compels her to offer the dwarfs whatever sum of silver they desire in exchange for the necklace, which was known as Brisingamen (Brísingamen or Brísing amen), or the Brising necklace, an object of tremendous pride and value within the dwarf kingdom.

The dwarfs refuse the goddess's offer, insisting that no amount of silver is of equal value to the golden necklace. Freya, ultimately driven to madness by her desire for the necklace, offers to reward the dwarfs with any treasure in the world they would accept in exchange for it.

The dwarfs say that only the love of Freya herself is worthy of the beautiful necklace, and they insist she wed four of them for one day and one night each in exchange for it. Though she is married to Óðr (Ód or Odur), Freya

accepts. None of the other gods are aware of the goddess's illicit pact, particularly as she hides the necklace in shame upon return to her palace.

It is revealed, however, that Loki, the Norse god of mischief, secretly witnessed the pact between Freya and the dwarfs. He promptly informs Óðr of his wife's misdeeds. Enraged, Óðr demands the necklace be brought to him as proof of Freya's infidelity.

Loki procures the necklace from Freya as she sleeps and reveals it to Óðr, who, distraught, abandons Aesir for distant lands, leaving the necklace behind. Freya awakes to find both her necklace and husband gone, and tearfully asks Odin, king of the Norse gods, for forgiveness. Odin grants Freya forgiveness and demands a penance, commanding Freya to wear the necklace for eternity while searching for her lost love Óðr. Freya's eternal tears of sorrow, according to the myth, turn into gold when they land on the earth and amber when they reach the sea.

SIGNIFICANCE

The tale of Freya's necklace illustrates the importance placed on fidelity and loyalty in Scandinavian culture. The goddess's callous abandonment of her family and kingdom in the face of tangible beauty and eventual eternal punishment is a stark portrayal of the potential dangers inherent in infidelity.

The story takes on some complexity because in Norse mythology, Freya's husband Óðr is considered a human personification of Odin, the king of the Aesir (Æsir) gods and ruler of the mythical kingdom of Asgard. As a result, Freya is unfaithful to not only her husband, but to Odin, and it is from him she must seek forgiveness and ultimately penance. This fact offers some important insight into the perception of marriage in Norse mythology, illustrating that it is both a personal and divine commitment.

Some scholars contend that Óðr is the personification of Odin's lust for Freya, whereas Odin himself is rarely if ever viewed in a carnal context in Norse mythology. The conflation of one god with another is not uncommon in Norse mythology, however, and Freya herself assumes other roles in later myths in German and Scandinavian mythology.

There is archaeological evidence that points to the significance of the Brisingamen as a symbol of maternity (Littleton 533). Necklaces similar in appearance to its description in the myth appear on fertility statues dating back to 3000 BCE. Some scholars have theorized that the Brisingamen may have represented an infant's passage through the birth canal.

While the god Loki has a complex role throughout Norse mythology, his role in the myth of Freya's necklace can be interpreted a variety of ways. Loki is present in several myths either directly causing or witnessing the gods' more calamitous episodes. In the myth of Freya's necklace, however, Loki is not only a divine spectator but a defender of righteousness. While Loki's penchant for mischief appears in other Norse myths, in the myth of Freya's necklace he does not appear to have any selfish aims. Loki's talents as a shape-shifter also play a prominent role in this myth when he transforms himself into a flea in order to recover the Brisingamen from Freya's neck as she sleeps.

John Pritchard

BIBLIOGRAPHY

Blumetti, Robert. *The Book of Balder Rising: A Modern Perspective on the Norse Religion.* New York: iUniverse, 2006. Print.

Grundy, Stephan. "Freyja and Frigg." *The Concept of the Goddess.* Ed. Sandra Billington and Miranda Green. New York: Routledge, 1999. Print.

Keary, Annie, and Eliza Keary. *The Heroes of Asgard: Tales from Scandinavian Mythology.* New York: Macmillan, 1893. Print.

Lindow, John. *Norse Mythology: A Guide to Gods, Heroes, Rituals, and Beliefs.* Oxford: Oxford UP, 2001. Print.

Littleton, C. Scott. *Gods, Goddesses, and Mythology.* Vol. 4. New York: Cavendish, 2005. Print.

Näsström, Britt-Mari. "Freyja—A Goddess with Many Names." *The Concept of the Goddess.* Ed. Sandra Billington and Miranda Green. New York: Routledge, 1999. Print.

◆ How Thor Fought the Giant Hrungnir

Author: Traditional Norse
Time Period: 1001 CE–1500 CE
Country or Culture: Scandinavia
Genre: Myth

PLOT SUMMARY

The famous Norse tale of the god Thor's battle with the giant Hrungnir opens with a horse race. Hrungnir challenges Odin, the most powerful of all Norse gods, to a race in response to Odin's boast about the prowess of his horse. The spectacular race eventually leads the two men inside the gates of Asgard, the walled fortress that is home to many of the gods.

At race's end, the two convene in a great hall and proceed to drink large amounts of wine. In short time, Hrungnir becomes inebriated and begins to insult the gods of Asgard. The giant's insults anger Odin, who is already perturbed by Hrungnir's mockery of his horse. Yet with Asgard's sacred rites of hospitality in place, the gods have no choice but to tolerate Hrungnir's insults and boasts for many more servings of wine. However, their indignation at their drunken guest's behavior eventually gives way, and mighty Thor, son of Odin, is summoned to rid Asgard's great hall of the giant.

Hrungnir scoffs at Thor's requests that he depart, knowing that because he himself is unarmed, any attack on him by Thor would be deemed cowardly by the gods of Asgard. He nonetheless challenges Thor to a duel at a later date, which Thor enthusiastically accepts.

Hrungnir's fellow giants are frightened at the thought of the duel, or holmgang. They understand that if Thor is victorious, he will be able to make war on them for all time, as Hrungnir, the biggest and most intimidating among them, would no longer be alive to protect them. To inspire Hrungnir, his fellow giants fashion him another giant out of clay to fight alongside him. Thor also enlists an ally, his associate Thjálfi, and sends him ahead to survey the battle scene before his arrival. Thjálfi instructs Hrungnir to stand on his shield in case Thor opts to attack him from underground. The advice is a trick that renders Hrungnir vulnerable, and Thor instead attacks from the sky, while Thjálfi dispatches the clay giant with ease.

While Thor defeats Hrungnir without contest, his victory is not without casualty. Hrungnir's weapon is shattered in the attack, and a piece becomes lodged in Thor's head. Also, Thor's neck becomes trapped under the dead Hrungnir's giant foot, which eventually is lifted off by Thor's son, Magni. Thor rewards the boy by giving him Hrungnir's horse, an act that earns Thor the scorn of Odin, who feels entitled to the horse himself.

SIGNIFICANCE

Some scholars believe that much of the mythology surrounding Thor contains messages that were aimed at instructing young warriors about the customs surrounding warfare. This is evidenced by both the formal nature with which both combatants schedule their duel and the careful preparation each opposing party takes leading up to the battle.

The construction of Hrungnir's clay giant illustrates the notion that enemies in war are capable of going to great lengths to thwart their opponents. Even the ostensible heroes of the myth, Thor and the gods of Asgard, are not above what could potentially be viewed as stretching the rules of combat, as illustrated by the ruse employed by Thjálfi, which is the main reason for Thor's victory.

The narrative's numerous illustrations of natural phenomena, particularly during the fantastic introductory steeplechase and the travels of Thor, the god of thunder, which quake the skies and lash the land, are common in nearly all Norse myths pertaining to incidences of combat and violent aggression from the gods. As noted by Kevin Crossley-Holland in *The Norse Myths*, there is even etymological evidence for this connection, as the Old Norse word for thunder was used interchangeably for the word for cart, or chariot. There is also a cultural significance to the remnants of Hrungnir's stone weapon remaining lodged in Thor's head at the end of the battle. The clash of stone and metal creates fire, which many cultures closely associated with lighting, a meteorological event for which they had scant explanation.

There are many Norse scholars who point to Thor's fight with Hrungnir as a possible initiation for the god himself, suggesting that the myth is a tale of a younger Thor that establishes his prowess and the esteem in which he is held in later myths. This may be additionally illustrated by the fact that Thor's son, Magni, who at the myth's end saves his father's life by freeing him from under Hrungnir's giant foot, is described as merely three days old. Additional appearances by Magni in Norse mythology outside of this particular tale are few and far between.

John Pritchard

BIBLIOGRAPHY

Anderson, Rasmus Björn. *Norse Mythology; or, The Religion of Our Forefathers, Containing All the Myths of the Eddas, Systematized and Interpreted*. Chicago: Griggs, 1875. Print.

Crossley-Holland, Kevin. *The Norse Myths*. New York: Pantheon, 1980. Print.

Dumézil, Georges. *Gods of the Ancient Northmen*. Ed. and trans. Einar Haugen. Berkeley: U of California P, 1973. Print.

Mabie, Hamilton Wright. *Norse Stories Retold from the Eddas*. Boston: Roberts, 1882. Print.

◆ Loki and the Dwarfs

Author: Traditional
Time Period: 1001 CE–1500 CE
Country or Culture: Scandinavia
Genre: Myth

PLOT SUMMARY

Loki is a troublesome and impish god, always trying to be a nuisance. One day, he finds himself bored and, in order to amuse himself, cuts off the beautiful golden hair of the goddess Sif. When her husband, the thunder god Thor, finds out what Loki has done, he is enraged. Thor grabs Loki and threatens to beat him, but Loki quickly develops a plan, offering to descend into the caves of the dwarfs to see if they can fashion new golden hair for the goddess. Thor agrees and sends Loki off.

Once Loki enters the underground land of the dwarfs, he tracks down the sons of the dwarf Ivaldi. These dwarfs are so skilled that they quickly create not only stunning golden hair for Sif but also an incredibly fast ship (Skídbladnir) that always catches the wind and can be folded up so tightly that it can fit inside a pocket. After finishing the ship, Ivaldi's sons go a step further, creating the deadliest and most dangerous spear (Gungnir) that has ever existed. When Loki sees these marvelous creations, he realizes that there is great potential for mischief in the caves and decides to stay in the land of the dwarfs a moment longer.

Loki then tracks down two more dwarfs, Brokkr and Sindri (or Eitri), who are brothers. He immediately begins to tease them, bragging about the wondrous creations he has just acquired and insisting that the brothers could never create anything on par with what the sons of Ivaldi could create. When the brothers protest, Loki bets his own head against them. They set to work, hammering away beside the hot fires, and Loki departs only to take the form of a fly and return to their shop. As Sindri hammers, Loki stings him on the hand. However, the brothers are still able to create a golden boar (Gullinbursti) that can speed through land, water, and air, his coat always shining with a bright light. As Brokkr continues working and throws gold onto the fire, Loki bites him on the neck. Undistracted, Brokkr forms a golden ring (Draupnir) that magically creates eight more golden rings every ninth night.

Sindri and Brokkr then begin their final project, a creation even more magnificent than the others. When they are about to begin, Loki stings Brokkr on the eye. Sindri, however, is still able to work, creating a wondrous hammer (Mjölnir) that always hits true and even returns to its owner when thrown. However, as Brokkr had been distracted, the handle of the hammer comes out slightly shorter than it should be. Even with this flaw, however, the brothers are confident in their creations, and they head to the hall of the gods to collect their debt.

Before the dwarfs arrive, Loki approaches the gathered gods and offers them the treasures, dividing the hammer, the ship, and the other rare creations among the gods Thor, Frey, and Odin. Despite this bit of bribery, the gods still decide that Loki has lost his bet, and the dwarfs pull out their knives with the intention of cutting off his head. Loki, however, makes one last plea, pointing out that he had not wagered his neck, and so instead the dwarfs amuse themselves with sewing his mouth shut before returning home.

SIGNIFICANCE

The god Loki holds a complex role within Norse mythology. While a deity and a regular figure in Asgard, the realm of the gods, he is also a foil to the leaders of the Norse pantheon. In contrast to Thor, the god of thunder and Loki's most recurrent nemesis, Loki is the god of lightning, standing for chaos and frivolity in the seriously ordered mythology of Asgard. In many early myths, this mischievousness remains playful and often actually benefits the gods. By the foretold end of Asgard, however, Loki will rise in power and lead an army of ice giants against those gods, destroying them once and for all.

The story of Loki cutting the hair of Sif reflects the complicated role of the lightning god. This tale is told in the *Prose Edda*, a compilation of Norse stories from the thirteenth century CE that provides many of the definitive versions of the myths. As with many of Loki's myths, its primary function is that of entertainment. The act of cutting off Sif's hair, for instance, would strike audiences as particularly devious, not only because the goddess's hair was of legendary beauty but also because having a shorn head was a punishment in Norse society, meant to shame women. Those familiar with Loki's other stories would enjoy the familiar pattern set into place, with the god first breaking a social code in something

like a prank, then relying too heavily on his wits in a dangerous situation, and finally facing the punishment he thought he would avoid all along. The humor and the light sense of danger—even if Loki's head is cut off, the myth's audience knows he will certainly find a way to come back—drive the plot forward. At the same time, however, a greater theme is subtly reinforced.

Loki actively brings unpleasantness upon the other gods, but his schemes also regularly benefit them. When he finishes with the dwarfs, for instance, he does not keep their magnificent gifts for himself; rather, he offers them to Thor and the other gods who regularly punish him. This is particularly significant because the hammer that the dwarfs create, Mjölnir, becomes Thor's legendary weapon, capable of destroying entire mountains and acting as a first line of defense between the gods of Asgard and the frost giants.

While it seems somewhat odd that Loki would not abscond with such treasures for himself, it is also in line with the general themes of Norse mythology. The disorder and playfulness that Loki represents are not simple distractions but instead important counterpoints to the rigid world order of Thor. Just as Loki's eventual role in the destruction of Asgard is inevitable, a necessary tragedy in the cycle of the world, so too do his small acts of destruction in their own way move the world forward. Loki tricks the dwarfs into creating the hammer he gives Thor, only to battle that fearsome weapon himself at the end of the world. Neither contradiction nor inconsistency, these small details speak to the reality of living in a world in which destruction is understood to be as significant as creation and chaos as necessary as order.

T. Fleischmann, MFA

BIBLIOGRAPHY

Janik, Vicki K. *Fools and Jesters in Literature, Art, and History: A Bio-Bibliographical Sourcebook.* Westport: Greenwood, 1998. Print.

Kowalski, Kathiann M. "Sealed Lips." *Dig* 8.9 (2006): 33. Print.

Krasskova, Galina. *Exploring the Northern Tradition: A Guide to the Gods, Lore, Rites, and Celebrations from the Norse, German, and Anglo-Saxon Traditions.* Franklin Lakes: New Page, 2005. Print.

"Loki and the Dwarves." *Norse-Mythology.org.* Dan McCoy, n.d. Web. 3 June 2013.

Mackin, Jeanne. "The Comedy Divine." *American Letters and Commentary* 15 (2003): 57–61. Print.

Loki Bound

Author: Traditional Norse
Time Period: 1001 CE–1500 CE
Country or Culture: Scandinavia
Genre: Myth

PLOT SUMMARY

In Norse mythology, Loki's relationship with the gods is somewhat unclear: he is a shape-shifter and the son of the giant Farbauti but is also considered a member of the Aesir, the tribe of the gods. Loki's trickery and deception are sometimes beneficial to the gods, but he tends to undermine them more often than help them. What is clear, however, is that Loki frequently uses his various disguises and his cunning to make the gods turn on one another. The gods, taking a degree of enjoyment from their harsh punishment of Loki, inadvertently make him bitter and resentful toward them, ultimately driving him to seek their destruction.

One of Loki's most infamous actions in this regard is the murder of the god Balder, one of the wisest and most revered gods. The son of Odin, he is known for his courage, generosity, and good will. Balder dreams that he will be killed, however, and Odin goes to the underworld, Helheim, where he speaks to a dead prophet and learns of a prophecy that Balder will indeed fall to misfortune. Balder's mother, Frigg, attempts to protect her son by soliciting a promise from every living thing not to kill him. She does not, however, approach mistletoe, thinking it too small to be considered a threat. Loki becomes aware of this oversight and fashions a spear with a mistletoe tip. He gives the poisoned spear to the blind god Hod, who, unaware that he is being deceived, is convinced to throw the spear at Balder and kills him.

The god Hermod rides to Helheim to convince the keeper of the dead, Hel, to release Balder. Hel tells Hermod that if every living being weeps for Balder, she will release him. Loki prevents this condition from being fulfilled by disguising himself as a giantess named Tokk and refusing to mourn Balder's death; Balder therefore remains in Helheim until Ragnarok, the time when the gods will fight the giants for control of the universe.

When the gods are made aware of Loki's role in Balder's death, they bring him to a cave, along with two of his sons. They transform one of Loki's sons into a wolf, who then proceeds to slaughter his brother. The gods use the slain sons' entrails to forge a chain that is used to tie Loki to three rocks positioned under a poisonous snake, which drips deadly venom on Loki in the hope that he will ingest it and die. Loki's wife, Sigyn, catches the venom in a bowl to prevent his death; but whenever she moves away to dump the bowl's contents, the snake's venom splashes on his face, causing him to writhe and struggle and resulting in earthquakes. Loki is bound to this fate until Ragnarok, when he will be freed from the chain to fight alongside the giants against the gods who have punished him.

SIGNIFICANCE

The story of Loki's punishment by the gods is one of the more prominent tales in which the character is presented in a negative, if not evil, light. In fact, Loki's binding to the three rocks demonstrates the gods' ultimate anger for Loki's many acts of deception. At times, Loki's lies and tricks are nefarious but sometimes beneficial to the gods; for example, in one story, he uses his cunning to rebuild the world of the gods, Asgard. In this light, Loki is initially seen as a companion to the great gods, even though he occasionally embarrasses them through his trickery. The foster brother of Odin himself, Loki is allowed to live among the gods even though he is not a god himself.

However, Loki's tricks gradually become more malicious in nature, however, and the gods' apparent pleasure at his torture and punishment serve to harden Loki against them. His fall from grace is made complete when he plots to kill one of Asgard's most popular gods, Balder, and then, after facilitating Balder's death, disguises himself and asks Hel to keep Balder in the underworld. Based on these actions, Loki becomes a powerful enemy of the gods.

Loki's punishment for his role in Balder's death—and his deception to keep Balder from returning from the underworld—is severe. Odin and his fellow deities brutally kill two of Loki's sons and confine him to a torturous situation from which he would not be freed for millennia. Although the two sons are depicted in other stories as evil, the use of their entrails in Loki's punishment is nonetheless cruel. At this point of the story, Loki, despite his wicked actions, becomes a victim of the gods' mercilessness. In fact, Loki even seems redeemable, given his wife's unquestioned loyalty to him; she remains at Loki's side throughout his imprisonment to prevent him from being killed by the snake that sits above him.

Loki's release from his punishment will only be for the purpose of Ragnarok. At this epic battle between the gods and the giants, the cosmos will be destroyed and rebuilt by the victor. Although Loki is a member of the community of the gods, he is a giant by birth. When Ragnarok arrives and the universe is at an end, Loki vows to fight alongside the giants, not just because he himself is a giant but also because he has become empowered by his rage to fight against those who imprisoned him.

Michael P. Auerbach, MA

BIBLIOGRAPHY

Bradish, Sarah Powers. "Fenris Wolf: Loki's Children." *Old Norse Stories*. New York: American Book Co., 1900. 43–44. Print.

"The Death of Baldur." *Norse Mythology*. Dan McCoy, 2013. Web. 22 Apr. 2013.

"Loki." *Encyclopedia Britannica*. Encyclopedia Britannica, 2013. Web. 22 Apr. 2013.

"Loki Bound." *Norse Mythology*. Dan McCoy, 2013. Web. 22 Apr. 2013.

"Ragnarok: The End of the World." *Norse Mythology*. Dan McCoy, 2013. Web. 24 Apr. 2013.

Short, William R. "Loki." *Hurstwic Norse Mythology*. Hurstwic, 2013. Web. 22 Apr. 2013.

◆ The Nine Worlds of the Norse

Author: Traditional Norse
Time Period: 1001 CE–1500 CE
Country or Culture: Scandinavia
Genre: Myth

PLOT SUMMARY

The Norse universe is separated into three vertical levels that contain nine distinct worlds. All of these worlds are intertwined in the roots and branches of the great world-tree, Yggdrasil. The worlds are not side by side but rather separated by great distances, mountains, valleys, and other obstacles that exist within Yggdrasil's roots and branches.

The first level contains the highest beings. At the very top of this level is the world of Asgard, occupied by the gods, known as the Aesir. This world is commanded by the father of all gods, Odin. Among the other Aesir are Thor (the god of thunder) and Balder (the god of beauty). Also occupying this first level is Vanaheim, the world of the Vanir. Long ago, the gods of the Vanir and Aesir tribes engaged in a brutal war, but they have since agreed to coexist peacefully. The third world within the first level, Alfheim, is occupied by the god Frey and the light elves.

The second level includes the world in which humans live. This world, Midgard ("middle earth"), is connected to Asgard by way of a great rainbow bridge, Bifröst. Also present in this second level is the world of the giants, Jotunheim. The Jotuns have been frequent enemies of Asgard; Midgard itself was forged from the corpse of the first Jotun, Ymir, who was killed by Odin and his brothers. There are exceptions to this rivalry, however: Loki was born a Jotun but is allowed to live in Asgard. In addition to Midgard and Jotunheim, there is Svartalfheim, the home of the dark elves. Finally, there is the world of Nidavellir, where the dwarves live. The dwarves constructed some of the Aesir's most powerful possessions, including Thor's hammer and Odin's spear.

Beneath the second level are the worlds of fire and frost: Muspelheim and Niflheim, respectively. Muspelheim, which lies at the southernmost position of Yggdrasil, is ruled by the giant Surt. At Ragnarok, the battle at the end of the world, Surt will rise up to fight his sworn enemy, Asgard. On Muspelheim's northern border, separated by a gulf called Ginnunga Gap, lies Niflheim, the world of primordial ice. Niflheim contains the spring Hvergelmir, from which all rivers come. In fact, even the tree of Yggdrasil has a root that draws from it. It is also said that the realm of the dead, Helheim (ruled by the female monster Hel), exists within Niflheim. In some interpretations of the nine worlds, Helheim is itself a distinct world, while Svartalheim is not referenced.

SIGNIFICANCE

The nine worlds of the Norse universe were first collectively identified in early medieval poems known as the Eddas. With the exception of Midgard, these worlds are invisible to humans. However, the influences of the other eight worlds on Midgard help give them definition for humans. For example, many scenes of nature, such as thick forests, are seen as part of Jotunheim. Also, Asgard is seen in the sky, while Helheim, the underworld, is associated with the grave (hence its placement underground).

Although all of the worlds within Yggdrasil are ruled by Odin and the gods of Asgard, the nine Norse worlds comprise a network of distinct regions, each of which interacts in some way with other worlds. At times, these interactions are negative. For example, the worlds of the giants (Jotunheim) and the highest gods (Asgard) are most often in conflict. When Ragnarok takes place, the two realms will continue their war and, in the process, destroy the universe. Similarly, the fire giants of Muspelheim will also take up arms against Asgard when Ragnarok takes place. At other times, the worlds come into contact with another, with localized, minor effects. For example, the dwarves of Nidavellir are said to have made great crafts for occupants of the other worlds, especially Asgard.

The nine worlds' interactions also explain the cycle of life, both for mortals and immortals. Ymir, the great giant from which Midgard was created, is himself created by the convergence of fire and ice at Ginnunga gap. Odin is also a product of the collective power of Niflheim and Muspelheim: he is a descendent of a primordial cow that formed at the meeting point between Muspelheim and Niflheim.

Humans are the creatures most influenced by the interaction between the nine worlds. Humans have a direct link to Asgard via the rainbow bridge of Bifröst. Furthermore, when the bravest human warriors die, they are carried from Midgard to either Odin's great hall, Valhalla, or Freya's hall, Sessrumnir, both located in Asgard, where they are honored for their feats. If the souls of the dead are not brought to these places of honor in Asgard, however, they are brought to Helheim.

Michael P. Auerbach, MA

BIBLIOGRAPHY

"The Aesir-Vanir War." *Norse-Mythology.org*. Dan Mc-Coy, 2013. Web. 29 May 2013.

Daly, Kathleen N. "Nine Worlds." *Norse Mythology A to Z*. 3rd ed. New York: Chelsea, 2010. 73. Print.

Hollander, Lee Milton, trans. *The Poetic Edda*. Vol. 1. 1962. Austin: U of Texas P, 2004. Print.

Lindemans, Micha F. "Nine Worlds." *Encyclopedia Mythica*. Encyclopedia Mythica, 27 Dec. 1998. Web. 29 May 2013.

Lindow, John. *Handbook of Norse Mythology*. Santa Barbara: ABC-CLIO, 2001. Print.

"The Nine Worlds." *Norse-Mythology.org*. Dan McCoy, 2013. Web. 29 May 2013.

The Norse Creation of the Cosmos

Author: Traditional Norse
Time Period: 1001 CE–1500 CE
Country or Culture: Scandinavia
Genre: Myth

PLOT SUMMARY

Between Muspelheim, the land of fire, and Niflheim, the land of ice, there is a vast nothingness. Empty, dark, and soundless, this abyss is called Ginnungagap, and the void there is filled only with chaos.

Over time, the licking flames of Muspelheim and the icy tendrils of Niflheim begin to move toward each other, reaching across Ginnungagap. As the heat touches the ice for the very first time, a single droplet of water melts off of a glacier, landing in the chaos. As more droplets of water fall, they slowly form into Ymir, a terrible and powerful giant who is both man and woman. When the creature sweats, the perspiration falls to the ground and makes even more giants, who begin to populate the void of Ginnungagap.

Still the great masses of ice and burning flames continue to move closer to one another. As more of the ice melts, a gigantic cow named Audhumla is formed. She lumbers over to Ymir and provides the giant with milk, sustaining the godlike being's strength. To keep herself alive, she licks the salty ice around Ginnungagap. As her tongue wears away the ice over time, the first god, Buri, is exposed within it. Buri's son, Bor, marries the daughter of one of the great giants. Their children are both gods and giants at once, and they are named Odin, Vili, and Ve. Odin is a powerful god of war, victory, wisdom, and magic. Vili and Ve, as Odin's siblings, are also expressions of the great god himself, Vili being a force of strong will and Ve a force of sanctity.

Knowing that the giants are a threat, Odin, Vili, and Ve slaughter Ymir. When he is dead, they create the world out of his corpse. His flesh becomes the dirt, his hair the plants, his blood the oceans and rivers, and his brain the clouds that float above. The sky itself they make out of his empty skull, which four dwarves hold above their heads so that it can stretch over all creation, one dwarf at each of the cardinal directions. In this new world, the gods then create two humans, Ask and Embla, from the trunks of trees. Pleased with what they have done, the gods build a fence around their home, which they call Asgard, hoping that it will protect them from the giants who still roam throughout the cosmos.

SIGNIFICANCE

As is the case in many world mythologies, the story of the creation of the cosmos indicates a great deal about the underlying philosophy that guided Norse culture. This particular narrative of creation and destruction was first recorded in a text called the *Prose Edda*, an Icelandic transcription of oral myths written in the thirteenth century.

Perhaps the tale's greatest theme is the recurrent lesson that creation can only come from destruction and consequently that all destruction can lead to further creation. As in many spiritual and mythological traditions, there is a void at the onset of Norse mythology. Rather than existence rising spontaneously out of the void, however, the origins of the world are based in the slow destruction of two neighboring realities, Niflheim and Muspelheim. In these two worlds, the opposing primal forces of ice and fire, both themselves destructive energies, come together within the emptiness that is existence. The substance they create in their meeting is the same substance from which the first life is formed.

The intimate linking of creation and destruction does not end on this elemental level but rather continues into the origins of the earth itself. The first gods slaughter the first giant and then use the creature's corporeal form to craft the world, while the offspring of this giant will one day return to destroy the earth again. Even before the creation of humans, the forces of Norse mythology are turning in on themselves, destroying one another in order to create new life. The giants and the gods have no clear reason to be instant enemies, but they must naturally turn against one another so that further creation and life can occur. The fact that the sky, the land, and the sea are all built out of the giant's body further emphasizes this fact, making the elements of the earth once again metaphors for the duality of life and death that rests at the center of Norse mythology.

On the whole, the world created through the destructive meeting of Niflheim and Muspelheim is a world that is in constant motion. The very substances of life are all built out of the dead bodies of the past. Likewise, humans too shall one day die so that new life will come from their forms, just as Norse mythology itself moves toward Ragnarok, a prophesized world-ending destruction that will give way to another creation, another meeting of fire and ice within the void. Cyclical rather than linear, the cosmos of Norse mythology is a complicated place in which death is no more than an expression of life and creation is simply another aspect of the ongoing destruction of the world.

T. Fleischmann, MFA

BIBLIOGRAPHY

Acker, Paul, and Carolyne Larrington, eds. *The Poetic Edda: Essays on Old Norse Mythology*. New York: Routledge, 2002. Print.

McCoy, Dan. "The Creation of the Cosmos." *NorseMythology.org*. McCoy, n.d. Web. 1 July 2013.

"Scandinavian Mythology." *Funk & Wagnalls New World Encyclopedia*. World Almanac Educ. Group, 2009. Web. 1 July 2013.

Zorins, Kimberly. "The Eddas: Iceland's Books of Lore." *The Norse Gods*. Spec. issue of *Calliope* 13.5 (2003): 11–16. Print.

◆ Odin's Discovery of the Runes

Author: Traditional Norse
Time Period: 1001 CE–1500 CE
Country or Culture: Scandinavia
Genre: Myth

PLOT SUMMARY

Odin is one of the most powerful Norse gods, drawing his might from wisdom, poetry, and magic. Along with many of the gods, he lives in Asgard, one of nine realms held in the sprawling branches of Yggdrasil, a magnificent and holy ash tree. The roots of Yggdrasil curl into the earth and the Well of Urd, a bottomless well filled with enchanted water that swirls with the magic of the universe.

The Well of Urd is also home to the Norns, powerful maidens who can control the destiny of gods and humans alike. They have many magical abilities and duties, including tending to the health of Yggdrasil itself, but one of their most significant acts involves carving runes into the trunk of the mighty tree. These runes are ancient symbols that allow one to interact directly with the cosmic forces of existence. When the Norns add a new rune to the bark of the tree, the entire course of history is altered. Time and time again, Odin watches this ritual, and he slowly becomes obsessed with gaining such powerful knowledge for himself.

Odin knows that wisdom as great at that held in the runes cannot be easily gained. Because of this, he goes to great lengths in order to prove himself worthy of this new magic. First, he hangs himself upside down from one of Yggdrasil's branches and stares directly into the murky waters of the Well of Urd. Then, he takes his spear and pierces it into his side. Finally, he instructs the other gods to leave him there unbothered regardless of how much he seems to be suffering, insisting that they do not even bring him a sip of water. As nine days pass, Odin continually calls out to the runes, his voice growing raspier and raspier as he approaches death.

At long last, the waters begin to swirl, and the runes reveal themselves to Odin. He at once memorizes not only the shapes of the runes but also the ancient and mystical meanings attached to them. The revelation of the knowledge surpasses the pain of his body. Although he is already a formidable god, this new wisdom expands Odin's power beyond the limits of his own imagination, and with only an incantation, he is now able to raise the dead, heal injured bodies, bind his enemies in battle, and summon love in one he desires.

SIGNIFICANCE

Odin is a recurrent god in the Norse pantheon, present from the creation of the earth and humans onward. Though he is a deity of war and destruction, much of his power comes not from violent battle but from his rich sources of wisdom and magical knowledge. His status as an early deity provides him with some innate mystical abilities, but Norse mythology makes clear that most of his powerful wisdom is attained through self-sacrifice (he even trades an eye for knowledge at one point), situating the acquisition of sacred learning as a holy pursuit.

In the myth of Odin's discovery of the runes, the god not only sacrifices his body but also goes through a form of death and rebirth. The sacrifice required to obtain the knowledge of the runes is both expected and accepted; Odin does not attempt to learn the runes through any other method, and he clearly tells the other gods that he will appear to be in extreme pain while going through his ritual. Similarly, the myth makes clear that Odin approaches death by the ninth day of his hanging (nine being a holy number in Norse mythology), thus linking the acquisition of the runic knowledge with a symbolic

rebirth. Odin craves the information that the runes provide, knowledge that includes the ability to bring people back from death; it is evident to the god, then, that he must put himself through a similar process in order to understand such ancient wisdom.

The history of runes in the Norse world is also significant in understanding this myth. Runic inscriptions were used by people in the region from around the first century CE, although they were replaced by the Latin alphabet with the introduction of Christianity around a millennium later. The myth of Odin's discovery of the runes is one of many included in the *Poetic Edda*, a compilation of Norse mythology written after Christianity came to dominate the Norse world. When Odin accesses the secret knowledge of the runes, then, he is also in a way accessing the secret knowledge of the people and spiritual beliefs that existed prior to Christianity. These belief systems, displaced by time, have become in legend even more powerful and mystical, much like the Norns, who are hidden from the universe but still influence the course of history. Odin, then, goes through ancient rites of self-sacrifice and bodily harm in order to gain equally ancient knowledge, thus reviving it into his world.

While Christianity was widespread by the recording of the *Poetic Edda* in the thirteenth century CE, the worship of Odin and other ancient gods remained common for several centuries, especially in rural areas. The myth of his discovery of the runes manages ultimately to encapsulate this tension; described in the Latin alphabet, Odin hangs from a mystical ash tree, peering into a murky past for a wisdom he trusts is not quite lost yet.

T. Fleischmann, MFA

BIBLIOGRAPHY

Gard, Carolyn J. "Runes." *Calliope* 13.5 (2003): 17. Print.

Krasskova, Galina. *Exploring the Northern Tradition: A Guide to the Gods, Lords, Rites, and Celebrations from the Norse, German, and Anglo-Saxon Traditions.* Franklin Lakes: Career, 2005. Print.

"Odin's Discovery of the Runes." *Norse-Mythology.org.* Dan McCoy, 2013. Web. 4 June 2013.

Ross, Margaret Clunies. *A History of Old Norse Poetry and Poetics.* Suffolk: Brewer, 2005. Print.

Starkey, Kathryn. "Imagining an Early Odin." *Scandinavian Studies* 71.4 (1999): 373–93. Print.

The Otter's Ransom

Author: Traditional Norse
Time Period: 1001 CE–1500 CE
Country or Culture: Scandinavia
Genre: Myth

PLOT SUMMARY

Three Asas (residents of Asgard)—the gods Odin, Hoenir (or Vili), and Loki—decide to explore the rest of the world. During their trip, they visit Midgard, where humans live. They walk along a river and come across an otter that has killed and has begun to eat a salmon. Loki throws a stone and kills the otter. The gods skin the otter, and Loki wears the pelt on his shoulder.

The three later come across an estate. They ask the owner, Hreidmar, if they may rest there, offering the salmon they found as compensation. Hreidmar, however, sees the pelt on Loki's shoulder and recognizes it as that of his son, Otr (Otter), who can transform into the animal. Hreidmar, unaware that these men are gods, calls for his other sons, Fáfnir and Regin, and the three take the Asas into custody for murdering Otter. The Asas offer to pay a ransom in exchange for their lives—as much money as Hreidmar demands. Hreidmar agrees, telling the Asas that they must fill Otr's pelt with gold, covering the skin with gold as well. Loki leaves to find the ransom while Odin and Hoenir remain in captivity.

Loki goes to the land of the dark elves in pursuit of a treasure kept by the dwarf Andvari. Andvari disguises himself as a fish, but Loki captures him and demands the treasure. Andvari gives him the gold but attempts to retain a ring, which Loki demands as well. Andvari tells Loki that the ring is cursed and it will bring great misfortune to anyone who would possess it. Loki fills the pelt with the treasure and covers the skin with more gold. He returns to Hreidmar, who notices that a single hair of his son's pelt is not covered. The ring is placed on the hair, and the father accepts the ransom. The Asas are then freed.

When the Asas depart, Hreidmar refuses to share the gold with his sons, and they then plot to kill their father. Afterward, Fáfnir and Regin fight with one another for the treasure. Regin is driven out while Fafnir keeps the gold. Regin plots to retake the treasure but needs the help of the great king Sigurðr (Sigurd) to kill Fáfnir, who has become a great dragon or serpent. Fáfnir takes up residence at a castle, where he defends the treasure of Andvari and keeps watch over a sleeping Brynhildr (who, in another tale, betrays Odin and is put into a deep sleep as punishment). Sigurðr agrees to help Regin and, after a great battle with the dragon, kills Fáfnir and takes the gold. Regin has Sigurðr cut out and roast his brother's heart. After Regin drinks the blood that comes from the heart, he is given the ability to understand the language of birds. The birds sing about his deceptiveness and acts of betrayal. Over time, the curse is fulfilled repeatedly, as great tragedy befalls those who take possession of the ring.

SIGNIFICANCE

The story of the otter's ransom and the treasure of Andvari is the point of origin for many tales in Norse mythology. This story is taken from "Skáldskaparmál," the second book in the collection of poems titled the *Prose Edda*. The *Prose Edda*, which is attributed to Icelandic poet and politician Snorri Sturluson, is believed to be one of the most integral texts in Norse mythology and dates from about 1200 CE.

"The Otter's Ransom" is one of the few stories in Norse mythology in which humans who are imbued with special gifts interact with and influence gods. In this case, the gods make the mistake of killing a human (albeit one disguised as an otter), and the human's father is then able to capture and make demands of the gods. In Norse mythology, humans must endure death and hardship at the will of the gods, but in this tale, the roles are reversed when Hreidmar is able to inflict hardship upon the gods.

The story is also significant as the foundation of many other major tales in Norse mythology. For example, Sigurðr's role in the tale overlaps another major story: the tale of Brynhildr the Valkyrie. One of the most noble of Norse figures, Sigurðr in the tale of Brynhildr rescues a beautiful woman when he discovers the treasure of Andvari. He bravely smites the dragon that imprisons her and that guards the treasure. The dragon is in fact Fáfnir, the son of Hreidmar, who helped kill his father in order to steal the treasure that he later took from his brother.

The curse of Andvari's treasure also plays a role in other stories in Norse mythology. Some literary analysts have concluded that J. R. R Tolkien, author of the classic *Lord of the Rings* trilogy, may have been influenced by "The Otter's Ransom." His use of the One Ring, which is the cause of great suffering, may have been modeled after Andvari's ring. Andvari, after all, initially tried to keep it from Loki, and any person who possessed it as part of the treasure would have suffered greatly. Although Tolkien never confirmed this theory, these similarities, as well as the presence of many other parallels between Norse mythology Tolkien's works, are significant.

Michael P. Auerbach, MA

BIBLIOGRAPHY

Anderson, Rasmus Björn. *Norse Mythology*. Princeton: Princeton UP, 2008. Print.

Byock, Jesse L., trans. *The Prose Edda*. By Snorri Sturluson. New York: Penguin, 2005. Print.

---, trans. and ed. *The Saga of the Volsungs: The Norse Epic of Sigurd the Dragon Slayer*. Berkeley: U of California P, 2012. Print.

Davidson, H. R. Ellis. *Scandinavian Mythology*. London: Hamlyn, 1994. Print.

Fee, Christopher R. "The Norse Dragon-Slayer Hero." *Mythology in the Middle Ages: Heroic Tales of Monsters, Magic, and Might*. Santa Barbara: Praeger, 2011. 3–26. Print.

Lindow, John. *Norse Mythology: A Guide to the Gods, Heroes, Rituals, and Beliefs*. New York: Oxford UP, 2001. Print.

Wettstein, Martin. "Norse Elements in the Work of J. R. R. Tolkien." *Academia*. Academia.edu, Oct. 2002. Web. 4 June 2013.

◆ Ragnarok

Author: Traditional Norse
Time Period: 1001 CE–1500 CE
Country or Culture: Scandinavia
Genre: Myth

PLOT SUMMARY

Throughout time, dark dreams and prophecies have foretold the eventual end of the gods and the universe. For many years, the gods are able to ignore these prophecies, none of the promised omens having yet occurred. This all changes when the trickster god Loki maliciously slaughters the god Balder, a tragic murder that was prophesied as the start of Ragnarok, the battle that will end the gods. Loki is chained to a massive rock as punishment, and the gods have no choice but to wait for their coming destruction.

The great god Odin, wise in his ways, does his best to prepare for the end, even though he knows that the Norse deities will surely lose their lives. As he waits for the arrival of Loki and his army of giants, he gathers the most famed human warriors to assist him. Those humans who do not join Odin learn of their coming fate and abandon hope, leaving their labor unfinished and turning against their own families. Gods and humans alike are caught in a dark despair, the prophesied long winter comes, and for three successive seasons the snow falls in darkness without the relief of summer. Finally, when it seems the depression can run no deeper, Loki and his wolf son, Fenrir, break free of their chains and lead the attack on the gods.

The god Heimdall is the guard of Asgard, the realm of the deities, and he is the first to see Loki and Fenrir arriving on a ship of the dead, with countless giants behind them. As the gods and humans ready themselves at Heimdall's warning, the giants set to tearing apart the very cosmos itself. Fenrir opens his mouth so wide that he gobbles up the sun, tearing through the landscape and eating sky and earth alike. One giant with a flaming sword swings it so broadly that he scorches all the landscapes of the earth. The gods fight back, but they quickly fall, and even the great thunder god Thor is defeated by a sea serpent. Eventually, the land sinks back into the sea, and the void that preceded creation, called Ginnungagap, is all that remains once more.

The destruction of Ragnarok is total, but it is not lasting. After some time, the land again rises out of the sea, Balder returns from death, and the earth becomes more fertile than it has ever been. In this new, pristine creation, two new humans are created, and the cycle of the cosmos continues onward as it always has.

SIGNIFICANCE

The story of Ragnarok presents all the gods and forces of Norse mythology at their furthest extremes. The wise Odin, known for his knowledge and sagacious learning, is left helpless and despondent in the face of prophesied destruction. Thor, the mightiest warrior, takes hold of his legendary hammer to lead the defense but quickly meets his death. The brave and holy Balder, a figure often described as emanating a white light, is both widely loved and the first to die. Loki, a deity who often only causes mischief and even assists the gods at opportune moments, is transformed into a monster of destruction, leading the forces of chaos against the holy realm of Asgard. Even the landscape itself is pushed to its limits, the primordial nothingness of Ginnungagap overtaking existence and the sea immersing the land in a reversal of the Norse creation myth, which depicts the earth rising out of water.

All of these dramatic events and reversals upend what is commonly presented in Norse mythology. Notably, however, these violent changes are not a surprise but rather the outcome of a prophecy that has always been with the gods, suggesting that all of the deities and cosmic forces had the potential for such upheavals from the start. Ragnarok is a story of creation reaching its natural extremes, the sin of Loki and the heroism of Thor both magnified to their breaking points. Rather than allowing audiences to understand these extremes as signaling a conclusion, however, the myth heavily emphasizes a cyclical view of the world. No sooner has Ragnarok ended and the universe itself ceased to exist than it is born again, Ginnungagap fading into life and Balder, the first to die, becoming the first also to return. Even the name Ragnarok suggests this, being sometimes written as *Ragnarøkkr*, "twilight of the gods," rather than the more common *Ragnarök*, "fate of the gods" or "doom of the gods."

As striking as the massive destruction of Ragnarok is, the eventual rebirth of humanity and gods alike is equally important to this myth of the Norse doomsday. Upheaval and violent change are devastating forces throughout Norse mythology, but they are also necessary agents of renewal. With the world wiped clean, it can be born again, even more fertile and giving than it was in the past. In turn, this new existence can fade once more, meeting a destructive but essential end in a new Ragnarok that will likewise begin another cycle. While many Western traditions emphasize a linear narrative, Norse mythology eschews this tendency, instead suggesting that no matter how devastating the chaos of Loki and the failure of the heroes may be, the same point at which one thing ends is often the moment at which something better is allowed to begin.

T. Fleischmann, MFA

BIBLIOGRAPHY

De Rose, Peter L., and Jane Garry. "Death or Departure of the Gods, Motif A192, and Return, Motif A193." *Archetypes and Motifs in Folklore and Literature: A Handbook*. Ed. Garry and Hasan El-Shamy. Armonk: Sharpe, 2005. 17–23. Print.

Pálsson, Hermann. Rev. of *Ragnarok: An Investigation into Old Norse Concepts of the Fate of the Gods*, by John Stanley Martin. *Modern Language Review* 71.4 (1976): 975–76. Print.

Price, Neil. "Passing into Poetry: Viking-Age Mortuary Drama and the Origins of Norse Mythology." *Medieval Archaeology* 54.1 (2010): 123–56. Print.

"Ragnarok." *Norse-Mythology.org*. Dan McCoy, n.d. Web. 3 June 2013.

Stookey, Lorena. *Thematic Guide to World Mythology*. Westport: Greenwood, 2004. Print.

◆ The Theft of Mjölnir

Author: Traditional Norse
Time Period: 1001 CE–1500 CE
Country or Culture: Scandinavia
Genre: Myth

PLOT SUMMARY

One day, the thunder god Thor falls asleep under a tree. When he awakes, he instinctively reaches for his magic hammer, Mjölnir, which is usually attached to his belt. It is not there. He looks all over his estate, asking for help from his fellow gods, but no one can locate the hammer, which is used to defend all of Asgard, the realm of the gods. More and more gods join the search, to no avail.

Thor, becoming angrier and more frustrated, begins to believe that Mjölnir has been stolen from him. He initially accuses the trickster Loki, whom Thor believes is the only person in Asgard who could profit from Mjölnir's disappearance. Loki, however, is innocent of the theft, and he suggests that the two consult with the fertility goddess Freya. She does not know the whereabouts of Mjölnir but lends them her falcon dress so that they may conduct a search from above. Loki takes the falcon dress and flies toward Jotunheim, the world of the giants. He spies on the giant world, believing that Thrym and the other giants, who are enemies of Asgard, have stolen Mjölnir.

Loki confronts the giant Thrym, who admits to stealing the hammer but says it is hidden so deep in the mountains of Jotunheim that no one, save Thrym, may find it. The cunning trickster asks Thrym what he would like in exchange for Mjolnir. Thrym replies that there is nothing in Asgard he would want in exchange for this great weapon. However, Loki is very persuasive, and Thrym finally tells him that if the gods will give him the beautiful Freya's hand in marriage, he will return Mjölnir. Loki knows that he cannot convince the gods to approve of such an arrangement but agrees nonetheless. He returns to Thor, who tells Loki that he may be able to convince Freya to agree if doing so would safeguard Asgard with the return of the hammer.

When Freya and her father vehemently reject Thor's proposal, Thor and Loki must find another course of action. Loki devises a plan whereby they would deliver an impostor to Thrym to trick the giant into returning Mjölnir. The gods agree that the one who lost the hammer, Thor himself, must don Freya's wedding dress. He reluctantly agrees, and Loki takes the disguised god to Jotunheim and presents him to Thrym. A great celebration is planned among the Jotun, but Loki tells Thrym to tell his fellow giants not to raise "Freya's" veil or otherwise touch her. The unsuspecting Jotun begin the feast, and Thrym, true to his part of the bargain, digs up and carries forth Mjölnir. He gives it to his supposed bride. With Mjölnir back in his hands, Thor removes his disguise, kills Thrym, and destroys the banquet hall. Thor and Loki return to Asgard with the hammer safely in tow.

SIGNIFICANCE

Loki is one of the most enigmatic figures in Norse mythology. He is not a god—his father, in fact, is a Jotun, which explains why, in Heilan Yvette Grimes's account, Thrym attempts to convince Loki to let him retain the hammer. In other accounts, Thrym merely uses the hammer to blackmail the gods into sending Freya to him. Loki is famous for his trickery, which is frequently used to turn the gods against one another. In fact, in one story, Loki facilitates the murder of the beloved god Balder, which results in his torture and imprisonment at the hands of the greatest of gods, Odin.

This story, however, demonstrates how Loki's cunning and trickery is sometimes used for the benefit of Asgard. Indeed, Loki is innocent of the theft. In fact, he shows great loyalty to Thor and the rest of the gods, playing an active and willing role in locating the lost hammer. Moreover, in older accounts, only Loki and Freya are entrusted with the knowledge of Mjölnir's

disappearance until after Loki tries to retrieve it from Thrym. Despite Thrym's attempt to convince Loki to look away and allow the Jotun to retain Mjölnir, which is so powerful that it can be used by the Jotun to destroy their mortal enemies in Asgard, Loki becomes defiant and angry with Thrym for making such an attempt. Furthermore, Loki even goes before Odin and the other highest gods in Asgard to gain support for his plan to regain Mjölnir. In this story, such acts are characteristic of a loyal subject of Asgard, willing to help the gods protect themselves from the Jotun.

The story of the theft of Mjölnir also shows the great power of the gods. In particular, the power of Thor is demonstrated. Thor is the defender of both Asgard and Midgard, the world in which humans live. He is known as a rugged and very strong god, capable of lifting great weights. Additionally empowered by Mjölnir, he is an extremely powerful god; in some Norse tribal traditions, he supplants Odin as the greatest of the gods.

In this tale, Thor, Odin, and other gods work in concert to address a major threat. Mjölnir is said to level mountains, create lightning, and cause great storms. The Jotun, longtime enemies of the gods, would have Asgard's greatest weapon to use against them. Were it not for Loki's trickery, and the gullibility of Thrym, the collective dominance of the gods would be challenged.

Michael P. Auerbach, MA

BIBLIOGRAPHY

Ashliman, D. L. "The Lay of Thrym from the Poetic Edda." *Folklore and Mythology Electronic Texts*. U. of Pittsburgh, 20 Nov. 2009. Web. 13 May 2013.

Bray, Olive, ed. and trans. "The Lay of Thrym." *The Elder or Poetic Edda*. London: King's Weighthouse Rooms, 1908. 127–37. Print. Viking Club Translation ser. 2.

Colum, Pádraic. "How Thor and Loki Befooled Thrym the Giant." *The Children of Odin*. New York: Macmillan, 1920. 116–23. Print.

Grimes, Heilan Yvette. "The Stealing of Thor's Hammer." *The Norse Myths*. Boston: Hollow Earth, 2010. 176–84. Print.

Littleton, C. Scott, ed. *Gods, Goddesses, and Mythology*. Vol. 10. Tarrytown: Cavendish, 2005. Print.

WESTERN EUROPE

◆ The Death of Roland

Author: Traditional
Time Period: 1001 CE–1500 CE
Country or Culture: France
Genre: Legend

PLOT SUMMARY

Emperor Charlemagne of France and his army of Christians have conquered all of the Muslims in Spain except for those in the city of Saragossa. The Muslim king of that city, Marsile, sends ambassadors to the emperor with offerings of peace. The men tell Charlemagne that Marsile is willing to convert to Christianity if the emperor leaves Spain. Charlemagne consults his council, chief of them the great military leader Roland. Although he advises his emperor not to trust Marsile, Charlemagne believes the Muslim king is asking for mercy.

Roland's stepfather Ganelon is nominated against his will to be the messenger to Marsile. Roland volunteers to lead the rear guard back to France through the mountain passes. With him is the knight Oliver and the archbishop Turpin. Angered that Roland selected him as

messenger, Ganelon rides toward Saragossa and overtakes Marsile's ambassadors. He plots with the Muslims to get revenge on his stepson. They make a plan to ambush Roland and the rear guard as they pass through the Pyrenees Mountains. Ganelon lies to Marsile, telling him that Charlemagne intends to conquer Saragossa and split Spain between Roland and the Muslim king.

Roland leads the rear guard, which is made up of twenty thousand Franks. He rides his horse Veillantif and take his sword Durendala and his magic Olifant horn, which he can blow to summon reinforcements. When the troops reach Roncevaux Pass in the mountains, the Muslims ambush them. Despite pleading from Oliver, Roland refuses to blow his horn because he sees it as a dishonor to France if they cannot defeat the Muslim army themselves. Roland rallies his troops and rouses them with the war cry of their emperor.

The battle is fierce, and both sides fight viciously. Roland kills the nephew of King Marsile, who had boasted that he would behead Roland. Wherever the fighting is fiercest, Roland swings Durendala and turns the tide of the battle. Thousands of men on both sides lie dead, and the victorious Franks mourn their fallen comrades. This is when King Marsile rides in with his main army and the battle begins anew. As this second battle rages, the weather in France turns violent; the citizens know that the death of Roland is near. The Franks fight hard, however, and the second army of Muslims is defeated. After the second battle, only sixty Franks remained.

The third Muslim army then appears, and Roland knows he must blow the horn. He knows that the emperor will not get there in time to save them, but at least their deaths can be avenged. Roland blows the horn three times. The second time he blows so hard the veins in his temple burst. The third blow is so faint that Charlemagne knows that Roland is in real peril.

Accepting that he and his troops will not survive the day, Roland rushes into battle and slays the only son of King Marsile. When the king counterattacks, Roland cuts off his right hand. Roland feels death drawing near and begins praying to his guardian angel Gabriel. He climbs a small hill and falls under two pine trees. A Muslim soldier creeps up and tries to steal Durendala. This rouses Roland, and he smashes Olifant over the soldier's head, killing him. He then makes his confession and prays to heaven for mercy. He dies with his head bowed and hands clasped, awaiting deliverance to paradise. Charlemagne later finds Roland's body, which is brought to a great cathedral in France for burial.

SIGNIFICANCE

"The Death of Roland" is taken from *Chanson de Roland* (*The Song of Roland*), the oldest surviving major work of French literature, and the Matter of France, which is a body of stories concerned with the history of the country. It is also considered the greatest medieval poem written in French. Although no exact composition date is known, scholars estimate that the poem was written sometime between the late eleventh century and the middle of the twelfth century; the first English translation was published in 1880. The poem describes historical events that occurred in 778 during the reign of the French emperor Charlemagne, who was one of the first Christian kings. The summary above specifically details the Battle of Roncevaux, when Spaniards defeated Charlemagne's rear guard in the Pyrenees Mountains on the border of France and Spain.

The Battle of Roncevaux did actually occur, although *The Song of Roland* presents a romanticized view of Charlemagne's reign. Also embellished is the historical

figure of Roland. In real life, Roland did serve under Charlemagne as the military governor in charge of defending the border frontiers between France and Britain at the time. The only historical account of Roland is in the ninth-century work *Vita Karoli Magni* (*Life of Charlemagne*), a biography of Charlemagne written by his courtier Einhard. According to the book, Roland did die during the ambush in the Pyrenees. Besides his appointment and the date of his death, few details about the real Roland exist.

In *The Song of Roland*, his character represents the embodiment of the noble Christian warrior who is conscious of his responsibilities to both God and his king. When he knows he is going to die, Roland courageously defends his men and then leaves the gruesome battlefield to give his confession to Christ. He admits being too proud to blow the horn for reinforcements, but he does not see his sacrifice as being in vain, for he was fighting for Christianity and died a martyr. Pride and impetuousness were his only flaws.

The themes present in *The Song of Roland* focus on duty and the conquering of good in the face of evil. Read as a precursor to the Crusades, the Franks are good because they are fighting for the spread of Christianity, while the Spanish Muslims represent evil. The sense of loyalty and duty Roland possesses for both Charlemagne and God is powerful and drives the character through battle and prayer. Roland was Charlemagne's vassal, meaning he would be completely loyal to him in exchange for protection and vengeance should he be killed in battle. For his devotion and service, angels carry Roland to heaven at the end of the story.

Patrick G. Cooper

BIBLIOGRAPHY

Brault, Gerard J. *Song of Roland: An Analytical Edition.* Vol. 1. University Park: Penn State UP, 2003.

Einhard. *The Life of Charlemagne.* Whitefish: Kessinger, 2010. Print.

Heer, Friedrich. *Medieval World: Europe 1100–1350.* New York: Welcome Rain, 1998. Print.

Smith, Nicole. "The Song of Roland: An Analysis of Medieval Lord and Vassal Relationships." *Article Myriad.* Article Myriad, 6 Dec. 2011. Web. 22 May 2013.

"The Song of Roland." Trans. John O'Hagan. *Internet History Sourcebooks.* Fordham U, Aug. 1998. Web. 22 May 2013.

Diamonds and Toads

Author: Charles Perrault
Time Period: 1501 CE–1700 CE
Country or Culture: France
Genre: Fairy Tale

PLOT SUMMARY

A widow has two daughters. The elder daughter, named Fanny, is a mirror image of her mother, and people often mistake the two. They are also similar in their mean-spirited dispositions. The younger daughter resembles her father. She is beautiful and always kindhearted, unlike her older sister. The widow adores her elder daughter, but she dislikes the younger daughter, gives her many chores to do, and forces her to eat in the kitchen, away from herself and Fanny.

One of the younger daughter's most difficult chore is to draw water from a fountain a great distance from the house, which she has to do twice a day. One day, a poor old woman walks up to the fountain and begs the younger daughter for a drink of water. She is glad to show the old woman some kindness and happily holds the pitcher up to the woman's mouth. After having quenched her thirst, the old woman praises the girl for her good manners and kindness. This old woman turns out to be a fairy, and she gives the girl a gift, stating that every time that the girl speaks, either a flower or a jewel will come out of her mouth.

The girl returns home and is scolded by her mother for being away at the fountain for so long. The girl apologizes for her delay, and when she speaks, two roses, two pearls, and two diamonds come from her mouth. The mother is shocked and demands the girl tell her how this has come to be. As more flowers and jewels fall from her mouth, the girl tells her mother about the old woman at the fountain.

The mother calls for Fanny to witness the miraculous flowers and jewels as they come from her sister's mouth. Then she instructs Fanny to go to the fountain and generously give the old woman some water so that she too can summon riches. At first, Fanny refuses to perform such a menial chore as fetching water, but then the mother berates her into going.

Shortly after Fanny arrives, an attractively dressed woman walks out of the woods. She comes up to Fanny and asks her for a drink of water. This is the same fairy that rewarded the younger daughter for her kindness, but she is now disguised with the air and attire of a princess. In a sassy, proud tone, Fanny mocks the woman but states she can drink some water if she truly wishes. Because of Fanny's rude behavior, the fairy gives her a gift similar to that of the younger daughter, but when Fanny opens her mouth, a snake or a toad will come from it.

Fanny returns to her mother, and when Fanny greets her, two vipers and two frogs spring from Fanny's mouth. Blaming the younger daughter for this trickery, the mother runs to beat her. The younger daughter runs into the woods and hides. There, the king's son, returning from a hunting trip, finds her and is immediately taken with her beauty. She tells him of her plight and of how the fairy has gifted her with jewels and flowers. While she tells the prince this story, he falls in love with her and takes her back to his father's palace, where they are wed.

As for Fanny, she is disowned by her mother and dies alone in a corner of the woods.

SIGNIFICANCE

"Diamonds and Toads" was written in 1697 by French author Charles Perrault. Perrault is considered the founding father of the modern fairy-tale genre. His works were derived from preexisting folk and fairy tales that he imbued with his own subtexts and subject matter. Some of his most influential fairy tales have become timeless classics, including "Little Red Riding Hood," "Cinderella," and "Puss in Boots."

His story "Diamonds and Toads" contains common folkloric and fairy-tale motifs, such as that of the kind and unkind girls, which can be found in tales from Russia and Scandinavia and throughout western Europe. It is a simple moral theme in which one girl, usually a daughter, is rewarded for her kindness and generosity, while another, usually her sister or stepsister, is punished in some way for her insolence or cruelty. The story varies depending on the culture in which it is told.

Another common motif found in "Diamonds and Toads" and throughout world folklore is the magical benefactor who provides an unlucky girl with a means of escaping her harsh reality. In this case, the magical being is the fairy, but in other stories, these benefactors appear as elves, ogres, and other fantasy beings. By providing the younger sister with the gift of creating flowers and jewels, the fairy helps her out of her unhappy life with her mother and older sister. Moreover, the girl goes on to become a princess, while the unkind Fanny dies alone in the woods. The appearance of magical beings like the fairy also helps infuse such tales with an appealing sense of enchantment.

The moral of the blessing and the curse bestowed by the fairy in the story has been interpreted as having the same meaning as the familiar maxim "If you don't have anything nice to say, don't say it at all." The younger sister speaks kindly to the disguised fairy, so she is rewarded. Fanny, on the other hand, is rude and she mocks the fairy. She is then cursed to have snakes and toads come out of her mouth whenever she speaks.

Patrick G. Cooper

BIBLIOGRAPHY

Bettelheim, Bruno. *The Uses of Enchantment: The Meaning and Importance of Fairy Tales*. New York: Vintage, 2010. Print.

Birkhäuser-Oeri, Sibylle. *The Mother: Archetypal Image in Fairy Tales*. Toronto: Inner City, 1988. Print.

Lang, Andrew, ed. "Toads and Diamonds." *The Blue Fairy Book*. New York: Dover, 1965. Print.

Perrault, Charles. *The Complete Fairy Tales of Charles Perrault*. Trans. Neil Philip and Nicoletta Simborowski. New York: Clarion, 1993. Print.

Roberts, Warren Everett. *The Tale of the Kind and the Unkind Girls: AA-TH 480 and Related Titles*. Detroit: Wayne State UP, 1994. Print.

◆ El Cid

Author: Traditional
Time Period: 1851 CE–1900 CE
Country or Culture: Spain
Genre: Legend

PLOT SUMMARY

After his banishment by King Alfonso, El Cid ("the Lord") wins several victories over the Moors. Following one such victory, Cid sends a messenger to the king with a gift of thirty horses. While waiting for the messenger to return, Cid and his band of warriors encamp in the forest of Tebar. The count of Barcelona, Raymond Berenger (also known as Ramón Berenguer), hears of Cid's location and readies to take arms against the intruder. When Cid hears of Raymond's intentions, he sends the count a message of peace, stating that he means no harm and

wishes to pass through the woods of Tebar without any trouble.

Despite this, Raymond still sees Cid's intrusion on his land as an insult to his honor, so Cid rallies his soldiers and instructs them to collect whatever booty they can. He delivers a rousing speech to his men, telling them how much more skilled they are than Raymond's troops. When Raymond's troops start to descend upon them, Cid gives the order to charge. Within an hour, Cid and his men are victorious. Their spoils include one thousand marks of silver and the legendary sword Colada.

Count Raymond is put under guard, but Cid offers him the opportunity to leave a free man. Raymond refuses and fasts for three days. He says he would rather die than eat Cid's food. It is only after Cid offers him two knights with which to travel that Raymond agrees to leave. After feasting, the count and his two knights ride away in peace.

Later in Cid's life, he is brought before a court of King Alfonso to plead his case against his sons-in-law, Ferrando and Diego Gonzalez. These brothers beat Cid's daughters, Elvira and Sol, and abandoned them, so he demands they return to him his swords and three thousand marks of gold and silver. The court grants Cid his wishes, but Cid demands the brothers be further punished. The Count Garcia is present in the court and states that because of Cid's long beard, the brothers Gonzalez did not believe the daughters were of nobility. Cid retorts that his beard is a gift from God and no enemy has ever plucked a hair from it.

Ferrando Gonzalez explains that he and his brother were justified in the beating of Cid's daughters, for they believed them to be of low estate, not the daughters of emperors or kings. Then Pero Bermuez, one of Cid's knights, testifies against Ferrando, stating that the man is a coward and a traitor who fled in battle against the Moors. Bermuez recounts another tale in which Ferrando hid from an unchained lion that threatened Cid as he slept. Ferrando could only hide in fear from the beast while Bermuez and the other knights protected their lord.

Diego stands and reaffirms his and his brother's noble birth and explains that there was nothing wrong with how they treated Cid's daughters. After much back and forth, the king declares that the Gonzalez brothers must fight their challengers. Bermuez fights Ferrando using his lance. The knight bests him, and Ferrando calls for mercy, which is given. Martin Antolinez, another of

Cid's knights, takes on Diego. The knight easily bests Diego, who sees no chance for survival but to flee on his horse. Cid and his men are victorious.

El Cid returns with his knights to Valencia, where the citizens rejoice to see their champion. After his daughters are avenged, Cid marries them to the noblemen Navarre and Aragon.

SIGNIFICANCE

These stories are part of *El cantar de mío Cid*, which translates to *The Song of My Cid*. Commonly referred to in English as *The Poem of the Cid*, this work is the oldest preserved Castilian Spanish epic poem. Written between 1195 and 1207, the epic tells the story of the national hero of Spain, Rodrigo Díaz de Vivar, commonly referred to as El Cid. It is set during the reconquest of Spain from the Moors, in an Islamo-Judeo-Christian multicultural landscape.

In the beginning of the poem, Cid is accused of stealing, and King Alfonso takes away his titles and land. He is given a royal pardon after the conquest of Valencia (a city in eastern Spain that was Islamic at the time), and he is named the lord of the city. To help solidify his new lordship, he marries his daughters to the noble Gonzalez brothers, who beat them and leave them for dead. Throughout *The Poem of Cid*, the pattern of loss and restoration recurs.

The poem is unique for its time for several reasons. For one, there are no supernatural elements. While other legendary heroes have the support of magical benefactors, such as fairies or gods, Cid survives on his own strength, wisdom, and strategy. He is injured and even makes a few mistakes, which makes him a hero who is much more human and relatable than other heroes of medieval literature. Also, the fictionalized adventures in the work are historically accurate, even if the original author took certain liberties.

Although the exploits may be dramatized, Cid was a real Castilian nobleman and military leader. Some scholars believe that the historical Cid was a mercenary who cared less about honor and more about his own land and riches. The Cid in the poem, however, functions as an exemplary hero. He embodies all of the heroic virtues that the poet perhaps saw lacking in contemporary medieval Spanish society. Despite being banished, Cid is loyal to his king and always fights on the Christian side. He is an ideal lord and vassal within the historical context of feudal Spain. The historical Cid died in 1099, when the Almoravids invaded Valencia. His body lies in the Burgos Cathedral in Burgos, Spain.

Patrick G. Cooper

BIBLIOGRAPHY

Barton, Simon, and Richard Fletcher. *The World of El Cid: Chronicles of the Spanish Reconquest*. New York: Manchester UP, 2000. Print.

Chasca, Edmund de. *The Poem of the Cid*. Boston: Twayne, 1976. Print.

Hamilton, Rita, Janet Perry, and Ian Michael. *The Poem of the Cid*. New York: Penguin, 1975. Print.

Nelson, Lynn Harry. "Rodrigo Diaz de Bivar, El Cid." *Medieval History Lecture Index*. Virtual Library, 2001. Web. 19 May 2013.

---. "Thoughts on Reading *El Cid*." *Medieval History Lecture Index*. Virtual Library, 2001. Web. 19 May 2013.

Rabb, Kate Milner. "Selections from the Poem of the Cid." *National Epics*. Authorama, n.d. Web. 19 May 2013.

◆ The Emperor's New Clothes

Author: Hans Christian Andersen
Time Period: 1851 CE–1900 CE
Country or Culture: Denmark
Genre: Fairy Tale

PLOT SUMMARY

The story begins by introducing an emperor who loves clothes so much that he devotes all his attention and his money to what he wears. His obsession is such that he is said to have a different ensemble for each hour of the day and is often found in his dressing room. Visitors commonly come to the emperor's town, so it is not unusual when two strangers arrive claiming to be master weavers, capable of producing the finest fabrics and patterns. Moreover, the weavers claim to have a special power: their cloth is "invisible to every person who [is] not fit for the office he held, or who [is] impossibly dull" (263). The emperor immediately orders the weavers, who are in fact swindlers, to produce such clothes for him so that he can discover who in his kingdom is incompetent or foolish. He pays the swindlers a large advance and provides them with costly silk and gold thread. They immediately set up their equipment and begin to weave, but there does not appear to be anything on their looms.

The emperor soon wishes to check on the weavers' progress but decides to send someone else first, choosing a faithful minister for the task. When the swindlers point to the loom, commenting on the splendid colors and design, the minister fails to see anything and wonders to himself, "Is it possible that I am a fool? I have never thought so, and nobody must know it. Am I not fit for my post? It will never do to say that I cannot see the stuff" (264–65). So the minster praises the work and listens intently as the swindlers describe the pattern so that he can report back to the emperor.

The swindlers soon demand more money for their work, which the emperor grants. When the emperor sends another minister to check on the weavers' progress, this man also wonders at his inability to see anything and concludes that he must be incompetent since he is not a fool. Like the first minister, he praises the swindlers' nonexistent work. Finally, the emperor himself, accompanied by his ministers, visits the swindlers and is shocked to find that he can see nothing, worrying that he is not fit to be the emperor. Regardless, he and his ministers make a good show of praising the beautiful cloth, and the emperor is advised to wear the clothes for an upcoming important procession.

The night before the procession, the swindlers make a grand show of working with great urgency to complete the emperor's clothes in time, staying up all night and burning sixteen candles. In the morning, they pretend to hold the clothes in the air and to dress the emperor, who goes along with the pretense. Everyone in attendance praises the emperor's fine appearance, and as the procession begins, the chamberlains pretend to hold the emperor's train. The spectators in the streets all marvel aloud at the emperor's new clothes. The only exception is a little child who loudly exclaims that the emperor is not wearing any clothes. In response, the child's father says, "Oh, listen to the innocent," but people begin to repeat the child's words, murmuring, "A child says he has nothing on!" (268). Finally, the crowd begins to repeat the child's pronouncement. The emperor realizes that the child has spoken the truth, but instead of acknowledging it, he insists to himself that the procession must continue, "so he [holds] himself stiffer than ever, and the chamberlains [hold] up the invisible train" (268).

SIGNIFICANCE

Since its publication in Copenhagen, Denmark, in the first half of the nineteenth century, "The Emperor's New Clothes" has remained a popular fairy tale throughout the world, with numerous translations in many countries. This popularity derives from the story's enduring messages about the folly of social pretense and the power of honest vision. People are subject to rules that govern social behavior; these rules sometimes dictate the acceptance of social situations that people do not truly support or believe but still support for the sake of relationships, credibility, or social status. "The Emperor's New Clothes" satirizes this phenomenon to show what can happen when social pretense goes too far. The emperor and virtually all of his subjects are drawn into the swindlers' scheme, not just because they care too much about what others think of them. The point is that the scheme itself dramatizes and plays on the fear of social failure because the swindlers claim that seeing the cloth depends on two crucial elements of social acceptance: competence and intelligence. The child's act of seeing and voicing the truth occurs in part because children are less subject to the social pressures manipulated by the swindlers. The child is therefore more honest and emerges as a model of courage and conviction surrounded by cowardly adults, not least the emperor whose vanity initiated the fiasco in the first place.

This vanity is also part of the story's implicit political satire. The emperor's obsession with his appearance and implicit distrust of his own judgment of his servants make him vulnerable to the swindlers. These are serious flaws in a ruler and imply that he is concerned primarily with himself rather than with the protection of his subjects, a dangerous condition for any society. The story acknowledges these flaws in the first paragraph by mentioning that the emperor "care[s] nothing about his soldiers, nor for the theater," and unlike other emperors, he dwells in his dressing room rather than in government offices (263). Thus, the story satirizes not merely the foolishness of social pretense, but also the danger and hypocrisy of such pretense in political contexts.

Ashleigh Imus, PhD

BIBLIOGRAPHY

Andersen, Hans Christian. *Andersen's Fairy Tales.* Trans. E. V. Lucas and H. B. Pauli. New York: Grosset, 1945. Print.

Prince, Alison. *Hans Christian Andersen: The Fan Dancer.* London: Allison, 1998. Print.

Robbins, Hollis. "The Emperor's New Critique." *New Literary History* 34.4 (2003): 659–75. Print.

Tatar, Maria. *The Annotated Hans Christian Andersen.* New York: Norton, 2008. Print.

Zipes, Jack. *Hans Christian Anderson: The Misunderstood Storyteller.* New York: Routledge, 2005. Print.

The Enchanted Maiden

Author: Consiglieri Pedroso
Time Period: 1851 CE–1900 CE
Country or Culture: Portugal
Genre: Fairy Tale

PLOT SUMMARY

In Europe, there lives a man with three daughters. As is local custom, when the man's oldest daughter wishes to get married, the father hangs a gold ball at his door. This gold ball is meant to deter any potential suitor who believes the daughter is too rich for him. One day, a prince passes by and sees the gold ball. He asks the father for his daughter's hand in marriage and the father joyfully agrees.

This custom is repeated to marry the second daughter to a prince as well. When the youngest daughter later asks to get married, however, the father cannot afford another gold ball so they agree on a silver ball. A passing prince rejects the young woman, seeing the silver ball as beneath his station. One suitor, though, believes that the third daughter is just right for him and marries her. As a result, the older two sisters break off communications with the youngest.

The third daughter eventually has a baby girl. She becomes ill, and her husband leaves their home to get her medicine. While he is out, three fairies ask for shelter in their home, and the young mother permits them to stay. Before they take their leave, the fairies approach the baby. The first fairy touches the girl with her divining rod and promises she will become the most beautiful woman in the world. The second fairy promises that she will become the richest. The third fairy gives her the ability to create flowers from her lips. As their final gift, the fairies turn the modest home into a richly furnished palace. When the older two sisters learn of this, they become friends with the third one once again. Her daughter, the enchanted maiden, becomes more beautiful every day.

Years pass, and one of the older sisters has a daughter—the enchanted maiden's cousin—who is betrothed to a prince. When this prince meets the enchanted maiden, however, he falls in love with her and rejects his fiancée. When the prince falls sick and his physicians send him abroad, the enchanted maiden climbs a high tower to see him for as long as possible. The rejected fiancée attacks the enchanted maiden and plucks out the eyes of her adversary with a pointed rod.

Blinded, the enchanted maiden finds shelter with a kindly man. The prince returns, and the former fiancée says that she is the enchanted maiden. He does not believe her, but she repeats her claim. Being blind, the enchanted maiden does not dare to approach the prince. When the prince is ready to marry his former fiancée, the enchanted maiden sends her cousin a proposal. For her wedding, she will furnish the bride with a nosegay—a flower bouquet—in exchange for her eyes. The other woman agrees.

The enchanted maiden dresses in black and veils her face. She approaches the palace and meets the prince, beseeching him not to get married. The prince replies that he must go through with the wedding because the guests have been invited. The enchanted maiden then shows the prince her hand with the ring he gave her, and the prince lifts her veil and recognizes his true fiancée. The enchanted maiden uses the fairies' divining rod, still in her possession, to change into rich clothes.

The prince tells his wedding guests: "I lost something, and instead I bought another. I have now recovered that which I lost. Which ought I to make use of—that which I lost, or what I bought?" (Pedroso 40). The guests agree the prince should use what he recovered. The prince goes back to the enchanted maiden. She explains to the guests all that happened to her, and the two are married.

SIGNIFICANCE

The Portuguese fairy tale "The Enchanted Maiden" is part of the anthology *Portuguese Folk-Tales* published by Portuguese academic Consiglieri Pedroso in 1882. Centuries old, many of these folktales and fairy tales were told to Pedroso by storytellers, mostly older women, so he could transcribe them. By 1882, Pedroso was persuaded to select thirty of his collected tales, including "The Enchanted Maiden." These were translated into English by Henrietta Monteiro and published by the American Folk Lore Society.

In his introduction to *Portuguese Folk-Tales*, the editor W. R. S. Ralston praised Pedroso's tales for their authenticity. For Ralston, one significant indication of this was that like "The Enchanted Maiden," these tales lacked literary finesse and finish. Instead, their "occasional clumsiness and obscurity, their frequent forgetfulness of their original meaning" attested to their original, unadulterated form (Pedroso i). Significantly, "The Enchanted Maiden" illustrates strong adherence to social order and subtly criticizes class snobbery. Through the actions of the prince of the second generation of lovers, the fairy tale implicitly critiques male romantic behavior.

First in "The Enchanted Maiden" is the story of the third daughter who finds marital happiness by adjusting her desires to the material means of her family. The fairy tale conveys a strong, significant obedience to social status and order among its characters. The plot ultimately rewards the third daughter for her modesty. From here, the fairy tale moves on to serve as a criticism of the two sisters married to princes. First, they reject their younger sister because she has married a man below the status of their own husbands. Once the fortunes of the third sister change, however, her sisters reestablish contact. This both satirizes and critiques social behavior.

With the next generation of characters, the original three sisters disappear from the plot and are replaced by their children. For Ralston, this points at the authenticity of the tale. An orally transmitted story does not polish its narrative as fully as would be expected from a published, edited tale.

From a feminist perspective, it is interesting that the prince appears of a rather fickle and indecisive character. Enamored of the beauty of the enchanted maiden, he abandons his previous engagement to her cousin. Even though he does not believe the cousin later on, he eventually agrees to marry her. When recognizing his true love, the enchanted maiden, he leaves the decision whom to marry to his wedding guests! This certainly connotes a significant critique of male behavior in this Portuguese fairy tale.

R. C. Lutz, PhD

BIBLIOGRAPHY

Cardigos, Isabel. *Catalogue of Portuguese Folktales.* Helsinki: Suomalainen Tiedeakatemia, 2006. Print.

---. *In and Out of Enchantment: Blood Symbolism and Gender in Portuguese Fairytales.* Helsinki: Suomalainen Tiedeakatemia, 1996. Print.

Ong, Walter S. *Orality and Literacy: The Technologizing of the Word.* New York: Routledge, 1991. Print.

Pedroso, Consiglieri, comp. *Portuguese Folk-Tales.* Trans. Henrietta Monteiro. Introd. W. R. S. Ralston. New York: Folk Lore Soc., 1882. 37–40. Print.

Sellers, Charles. *Tales from the Lands of Nuts and Grapes (Spanish and Portuguese Folklore).* Charleston: BiblioLife, 2011. Print.

◆ The Gingerbread Man

Author: Peter Christen Asbjørnsen
Time Period: 1851 CE–1900 CE
Country or Culture: Norway
Genre: Fairy Tale

PLOT SUMMARY

The tale begins with a mother who is making pancakes to feed her brood of seven children. As she prepares the meal, she uses "new milk," which presumably leads not only to a pleasing-looking cake, but one that can think and act independently. As this best-looking pancake lies sizzling in the pan, all seven of the children beg for a taste, with each child asking more convincingly than the one before: from the first child's request of "Oh, give me a bit of pancake, mother, I am so hungry!" to the last child's "Ah, do! dear, good, kind, nice, sweet, darling mother" (Asbjørnsen 62), there is a lesson not only in counting but in flattery. Listening to the mother and her children, the cake becomes afraid and «turn[s] itself» to cook both sides before jumping out of the frying pan and rolling out the door and away from the house.

The family pursues the tasty morsel, but the pancake escapes, only to meet a variety of additional characters who want to devour it. These characters include a man, a hen, a cock, a duck, a goose, a gander, and a pig. As the pancake interacts with each new character, the character expresses the desire to eat the tempting morsel, but the pancake is smarter. By the time the pancake meets the gander, it has mocked each character with a taunt similar to the one it delivers the gander: "When I have run away from Goody Poody and the goodman and seven squalling children, and from Manny Panny, and Henny Penny, and Cocky Locky, and Ducky Lucky, and Goosey Poosey, I must run away from you too, Gander Pander" (66). The pancake is finally outwitted when the pig, who is smart enough to avoid asking if he can eat it, offers protective services. The story ends when the pig carries the pancake across a stream and "swallow[s] the pancake in one gulp" (67).

SIGNIFICANCE

Peter Christen Asbjørnsen's version of the Gingerbread Man fairy tale is a Norwegian story originally titled *Pannekaken*, or "The Pancake." Though an earlier version of the tale had been published in the American children's periodical *St. Nicholas Magazine* in 1875, the story was translated into English by H. L. Brækstad in the 1881 book *Round the Yule Log: Norwegian Folk and Fairy Tales*.

One of the main reasons for this story's continuing significance is its popularity across cultures. Versions of this Norwegian tale have been retold in Germany, England, Ireland, Scotland, Russia, and the United States. Slight changes are made from translation to translation, but all variations are cumulative (or chain) tales and are combined with the talking beast (or animal) tale. The dual form makes "The Pancake" ideal for children for several reasons.

Repetition of ideas is the key ingredient in a cumulative tale. In Asbjørnsen's version of the story, the repetition begins with the seven children requesting a taste of the treat. The first child begins the litany with a simple appeal, «Oh, give me a bit of pancake, mother, I am so hungry!» (62). The second child adds a bit of flattery, «Ah, do! dear, mother,» and by the time the seventh child calls for a sample, the request has burgeoned into «Ah, do! dear, good, kind, nice, sweet, darling mother» (62). This set of cumulative queries opens readers to expect more snowballing repetition as the story progresses, and the pancake provides just that as it interacts with a human and various animals it encounters in its bid for freedom.

The pancake first meets a man who greets the pancake and asks it to slow down so that he can eat it. The pancake taunts the man, saying, «When I have run away from Goody Poody and the goodman and seven squalling children, I must run away from you too, Manny Panny» (65). The pancake's road is populated by several animals, however, so he will not escape so easily. After running from the man, the pancake meets a hen, a cock, a duck, a goose, a gander, and a pig. The seven children are the preview for the pancake's seven later pursuers and his rhyming names for them. Similarly, the pancake's taunts to the man are the preview for the cumulative jeers the pancake says to each of the animals it meets. By the time the pancake comes upon the pig, however, it has met its match. The pig convinces the

pancake that traveling together through the woods is safer, and when they come upon a body of water, the pig persuades the pancake to ride across the stream on his snout, which results in the pig gobbling the pancake up and ultimately ending the story.

A second element is the crossover of tale types apparent in the talking animal tale type. The talking beast tale provides a mixture of popular elements that are also found in stories such as Mother Goose rhymes, fairy tales, and noodlehead tales. The rhyming elements echo the poetry found in Mother Goose tales; the pancake (or cookie) that grows legs or turns itself to cook and then flees from those who want to eat it reflects the magical aspect of the fairy tale; and characters who are easily outsmarted by a pancake is reminiscent of the noodlehead tale. Furthermore, «The Pancake» contains easily recognizable animals from other folktales. Asbjørnsen's Norwegian and several oral German variations of the tale have a pig outwitting the pancake; however, at least one Scottish version has a wee bannock (which is a small loaf of flat bread) being eaten by a toad while another has the cake devoured by a fox who is then shot by a hunter. The fox is a common adversary and is found not only in the Scottish tale, but it also appears in Irish, English, and American adaptations.

No matter what ultimately consumes the pancake, the story's simple format, talking animals, and humorous rhymes maintain its popularity throughout the Western world.

Theresa L. Stowell, PhD

BIBLIOGRAPHY

Asbjørnsen, Peter Christen. «Pannekaken.» *Round the Yule Log: Norwegian Folk and Fairy Tales*. Trans. H. L. Brækstad. London, 1881. 62–67. Print.

Ashliman, D. L., trans. and ed. «The Runaway Pancake: Folktales of Aarne-Thompson-Uther Type 2025.» *Folklore and Mythology Electronic Texts*. U of Pittsburgh, 13 Aug. 2010. Web. 28 June 2013.

Davidson, Hilda Ellis, and Anna Chaudhri, eds. *A Companion to the Fairy Tale*. Cambridge: Brewer, 2006. Print.

Heiner, Heidi Anne. "The Annotated Gingerbread Man." *SurLaLune fairytales.com*. SurLaLune Fairy Tales, 9 July 2007. Web. 12 July 2013.

Thomas, Joyce. "'Catch if you can': The Cumulative Tale." *A Companion to the Fairy Tale*. Ed. Hilda Ellis Davidson and Anna Chaudhri. Cambridge: Brewer, 2006. 123–36. Print.

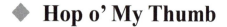

Hop o' My Thumb

Author: Charles Perrault
Time Period: 1501 CE–1700 CE
Country or Culture: France
Genre: Fairy Tale

PLOT SUMMARY

A husband and wife who work as woodcutters have seven sons, and this number of children burdens them greatly. What worries them the most is that their youngest son is abnormally small, no larger than a thumb, and barely ever speaks. Because of his stature, his parents call him Little Thumb. Although he is always blamed for everything wrong in the house, Little Thumb is secretly far more intelligent than all of his brothers combined.

The parents cannot provide for their children, so the father suggests that they leave them in the woods. Unbeknownst to them, Little Thumb is hiding in the room, listening to them devise the plan. He gets up early and sneaks away to the riverside, where he collects several white pebbles. Shortly after he returns home, the whole family goes into the woods as planned.

When the children are not looking, the parents disappear into the winding bushes, leaving the children alone and lost. The other children begin to cry, but Little Thumb does not. He tells his brothers not to be afraid, for he will lead them home: as the family walked through the woods, he dropped the white pebbles along the way, leaving a trail. The mother and father arrive home to find that the lord of the manor has sent them ten crowns. The mother prepares a feast, and as they eat, the parents lament the fact that they left their children in the woods. The children are outside listening to their mother's regrets, and after a while, they cry out to her. The mother is relieved they are alive.

Eventually the family spends the ten crowns. Again, the parents decide that the only way to survive is to leave their children in the woods. Little Thumb overhears their scheme again and steals a piece of bread with which to leave a trail of crumbs. The parents bring them into the thickest part of the woods and leave them. When Little Thumb tries to locate the trail of crumbs, he finds that birds have eaten them.

Night comes, and the children walk until they reach a house. A woman answers the door, and Little Thumb tells her about their dilemma. She warns them that her husband is an ogre who eats children, but she agrees to hide them for a while. When the ogre comes home, the children hide under the bed. The ogre, however, smells the children and snatches them up. He decides he will eat them the following day and orders his wife to put them to bed.

The ogre has seven daughters, who sleep with golden crowns on their heads. After the ogre has fallen asleep, Little Thumb takes the seven bonnets worn by his brothers and switches them with the gold crowns worn by the daughters. The ogre wakes around midnight and groggily gropes around in the dark until he feels the bonnets. He then cuts the throats of each of his daughters. He does not discover his mistake until the morning, by which time Little Thumb and his brothers have escaped. The ogre quickly puts on his magical boots that allow him to travel at great speed and pursues the boys.

He eventually becomes exhausted and falls asleep on top of a rock under which the boys happen to be hiding. Little Thumb quietly steals the ogre's boots, which magically shrink to his size; he quickly returns to the ogre's house, explaining to the ogre's wife that a gang of thieves overpowered the ogre and will kill him if they are not given riches. The frightened woman gives Little Thumb all of their riches, and he returns to his parents' house, where he is received with great joy.

In other versions of the fairy tale, Little Thumb uses the magical boots to become a messenger for the king. He is paid a great sum of money to carry orders to the king's army. After saving up his wealth, Little Thumb returns home.

SIGNIFICANCE

"Hop o' My Thumb" first appeared in French author Charles Perrault's 1697 collection of fairy tales, *Histoires ou contes du temps passé* (Stories or fairy tales from past times). At the time, fairy tales were popular with those who frequented Parisian salons. Perrault is considered to be the originator of the modern fairy-tale genre, and many of his stories remain popular.

The theme of a small boy defeating an ogre can be found frequently in fairy tales, and it has its own indexing number, 327B, in the Aarne-Thompson classification system, which is used by folklorists to index recurring themes and narrative structures in folklore and fairy tales. Other stories of this type include the French story "The Bee and the Orange Tree" (written by Madame Marie-Catherine d'Aulnoy) and the Norwegian story "Boots and the Troll." The tale of Hansel and Gretel is often placed in this type, since, much like an ogre, the witch in that story intends to eat the children. Child abandonment is also a recurring theme found in 327B stories.

Perrault helped bring the word *ogre* into wide use. The word is French in origin, and although there are many different theories, scholars believe it may be derived from the name of the Greek river god Oiagros (or Oeagrus). Perrault uses ogres in several of his stories and even introduces an ogress, or female ogre, in his version of the story of Sleeping Beauty.

As the main character, Little Thumb is smarter than his brothers and the ogre, and as the story progresses, he grows even wiser. In the beginning, it takes him all night to think of the plan to make a trail with pebbles, but near the end, he is quickly able to think of how to save himself and his brothers while also acquiring all of the ogre's riches. He saves his family from poverty and death through his wits. Through the story he transforms from the scolded, disliked youngest son into the hero.

The number seven appears frequently in fairy tales, perhaps most notably in the fairy tale of Snow White and the seven dwarfs. In "Hop o' My Thumb," the woodcutters and the ogre each have seven children, and the ogre's magic boots are known as the "boots of seven leagues." Scholars believe the number symbolizes completeness, being derived from the seven days of Judeo-Christian creation as well as the seven planets of Greek antiquity.

Patrick G. Cooper

BIBLIOGRAPHY

Bettelheim, Bruno. *The Uses of Enchantment: The Meaning and Importance of Fairy Tales*. New York: Vintage, 2010. Print.

Crossen, Kendra, and Marie-Louise von Franz. *The Interpretation of Fairy Tales*. Boston: Shambhala, 1996. Print.

Perrault, Charles. *The Complete Fairy Tales of Charles Perrault*. Trans. Neil Philip and Nicoletta Simborowski. New York: Clarion, 1993. Print.

Roberts, Anna. "In the Dark Wood: Abuse Themes in Common Fairy Tales." *Northern Lights*. Northern State U, 2003. Web. 31 July 2012.

Tatar, Maria M. *Off with Their Heads! Fairy Tales and the Culture of Childhood*. Princeton: Princeton UP, 1992. Print.

◆ Little Red Cap

Author: Jacob and Wilhelm Grimm
Time Period: 1701 CE–1850 CE
Country or Culture: Germany
Genre: Fairy Tale

PLOT SUMMARY

"Rotkäppchen" or "Little Red Cap," better known as "Little Red Riding Hood," is the version of the story recorded by Jacob and Wilhelm Grimm in their 1812 volume of German folktales. The tale starts by introducing a well-loved maiden who has a special connection with her grandmother. The grandmother often bestows presents on the girl, including "a little cap of red velvet" (13) that the girl wears at all times, leading to the nickname Little Red Cap. The girl's adventure begins when her mother sends her on a mission to take food to her sick grandmother. As she leaves, she is cautioned by her mother to follow the direct path to her grandmother's cottage and to pay attention to social niceties.

As soon as Little Red Cap enters the woods outside of her village, she encounters a charming wolf who inquires about her mission. Naively, the girl reveals her destination and the purpose of her trip. The wolf shrewdly recognizes the potential of two victims and distracts Red with the enticements of the forest. Disregarding her mother's earlier admonitions, the girl leaves the trodden path to pick flowers for her ailing relative. The wolf, in the meantime, hurries to the grandmother's cottage, consumes his first meal, and disguises himself in the old woman's clothes and bed.

Little Red Cap eventually comes back to the purpose of her trip and reaches her grandmother's home. Upon entering, she senses that all is not well and begins to question the wolf: "Oh, Grandmother, what big ears you have! . . . Oh, Grandmother, what big hands you have! . . . Oh, Grandmother, what a big, scary mouth you have!" (Grimm 15). Unfortunately for Little Red Cap, the wolf is so fast that she is eaten before she can react further.

The ending of the story varies from version to version from this point. Some stories conclude with the deaths of Little Red Cap and her grandmother. Some introduce a huntsman who saves them. The Grimm brothers' version continues with the huntsman, who cuts the wolf's belly open, freeing both the girl and her grandmother. The three then weigh the wolf down by loading his stomach with rocks, which eventually kill him when he awakens and attempts escape. Each human character receives a boon: the huntsman skins the beast for its pelt, the grandmother enjoys the contents of the basket brought by her grandchild, and the girl acknowledges a lesson learned and vows to heed her mother's guidance in the future. The Grimm version adds one last note to the story, however. In this extra piece, Little Red Cap has returned to her grandmother's cottage with another basket of goodies. Once more, she meets a wolf, but this time she flees. Upon reaching her grandmother's house, she shares her predicament, and together the two women outsmart and kill the wolf.

SIGNIFICANCE

"Little Red Cap" is often interpreted as the story of a young woman who moves from the innocence of childhood to the recognition of sexual maturity. Though the tale originates in oral tradition, there are numerous literary versions from across the world, with the German version by the Grimm brothers being one of the most commonly recognized.

One of the most notable fairy-tale motifs relevant to this story is the repetition of the number three. This starts with the characters. The story begins with a child, her mother, and her grandmother, representing women from all stages of life. There are also three male stereotypes: the charming wolf who entices the girl to stray from her moral upbringing; the heroic huntsman, often viewed as a father figure, who frees the girl and her grandmother; and the second, more obviously villainous wolf, who is outsmarted by the women. The characters also reflect the three sets of rules given to Little Red Cap by her mother: set off early (practical), "don't stray from the path" (moral; Grimm 14), and be polite upon entering the grandmother's home (social). Finally, there are three clearly symbolic locales in the story: the town where Little Red Cap lives (civilization), the woods that separate the village from her grandmother's cottage (the uncivilized wasteland), and the cottage itself (home/safety).

The motif of three, combined with possible broader symbolic meanings, also connects to three possible purposes for the story, based on the point when the story was collected. Zohar Shavit argues that Charles Perrault's 1697 version was written for adult entertainment purposes, the Grimm brothers' story is more pedagogical, and later variations told as children's amusement are more "protective" in nature (322), softening the narrative for an audience of children that is more sheltered.

One of the most common interpretations of the story focuses on a sexual interaction between the characters. In this vein of criticism, the red cap represents the child's movement into sexual maturity. Catherine Orenstein argues that the tale can be twisted "to portray a seduction by a temptress, the rape of a virgin or the passage of a young girl into womanhood" (4). Perrault's version ends with a moral that warns women about the dangers inherent in being involved with men, while the Grimm brothers shine a more positive light on men, as the huntsman enters the story to rescue Little Red Cap and her grandmother. However, their story becomes ambiguous regarding women's need for male protection when the women overcome the second wolf on their own. The suggestion may be that a dose of charm—as utilized by the first wolf, who does devour the women—may mislead, but aggression, as demonstrated by the second wolf's approach, will ultimately lead to the demise of the wolf's lecherous plans, along with the wolf himself.

Theresa L. Stowell, PhD

BIBLIOGRAPHY

Dundes, Alan, ed. *Little Red Riding Hood: A Casebook*. Madison: U of Wisconsin P, 1989. Print.

Grimm, Jacob, and Wilhelm Grimm. "Little Red Cap." Tatar, *Classic* 13–16.

Orenstein, Catherine. *Little Red Riding Hood Uncloaked: Sex, Morality, and the Evolution of a Fairy Tale*. New York: Basic, 2002. Print.

Shavit, Zohar. "The Concept of Childhood and Children's Folk Tales: Test Case—'Little Red Riding Hood.'" Tatar, *Classic* 317–32.

Tatar, Maria, ed. *The Classic Fairy Tales*. New York: Norton, 1999. Print.

---. *The Hard Facts of the Grimms' Fairy Tales*. Exp. 2nd ed. Princeton: Princeton UP, 2003. Print.

Zipes, Jack. *The Trials and Tribulations of Little Red Riding Hood: Versions of the Tale in Sociocultural Context*. South Hadley: Bergin, 1983. Print.

◆ Petrosinella

Author: Giambattista Basile
Time Period: 1501 CE–1700 CE
Country or Culture: Italy
Genre: Fairy Tale

PLOT SUMMARY

"Petrosinella" begins with a pregnant woman, Pascadozia, who has a craving for a "beautiful bed of parsley" (475) in the vegetable patch of the ogress who lives next door. When she cannot resist the craving any longer, she sneaks into the garden and steals the delicacy. Pascadozia does this several times before the ogress catches her and threatens that she will only let her go if Pascadozia gives up the child she is carrying. Fearful for her life, the mother-to-be quickly agrees. Soon after, Pascadozia has a daughter whom she names Petrosinella, because of "a pretty birthmark on her breast the shape of a tuft of parsley" (475).

When the girl's seventh birthday comes, the ogress seizes the opportunity to claim the child by telling the girl to remind her mother of the promise. Pascadozia attempts to refuse only once and then sends her child to the ogress. Petrosinella is imprisoned in a tower that has only one access point, a small window at its peak, which can only be reached when the ogress climbs the girl's rope of hair.

One day, a prince comes upon the tower and falls in love with its prisoner. After several days of innocent interaction, the two begin to meet on a regular basis, pursuing amorous activities during their trysts. As their nightly encounters escalate, they plan an escape. Meanwhile, the ogress is given the news that her ward is conducting an affair. In her anger, the ogress becomes indiscreet in a discussion with the hag who had shared the news, and she reveals information about an enchantment she has cast on three acorns that are hidden in the tower. The spell blocks any attempts at escape. Fortunately for the young lovers, Petrosinella overhears and finds the magical objects.

When the couple escapes, the neighbor alerts the ogress to their departure. Petrosinella is not without ability though, and she uses the enchanted acorns, one at a time, to stall the ogress's path as she and her lover flee. The first acorn turns into a Corsican hound that attacks the ogress, but the ogress easily outmaneuvers it. The second acorn becomes a ferocious lion that turns cowardly when the ogress possesses a donkey and runs

toward it. Her disguise becomes her downfall when the third acorn turns into a wolf that gobbles her up, mistaking her for a donkey, as she has not had time to change back into her original form.

The young couple's travels culminate in an arrival at the prince's home kingdom, where they marry and cherish the lesson that "one hour in a safe harbor can make you forget one hundred years of storms" (479).

SIGNIFICANCE

A young girl kidnapped and trapped in a tower, a pregnant woman whose cravings endanger those closest to her, and a set of three enchanted objects are not uncommon motifs in both oral and recorded folktales from across Europe, Asia, and Africa. Italian folklorist Giambattista Basile's story "Petrosinella" (ca. 1634–36), which captures all three motifs, is one of the best-known and earliest recorded variations of the maiden-in-the-tower tale, and later versions often copied the basic aspects of the tale while adding to or modifying the plot and characters to fit the new story.

The motif of locking a girl in a tower to protect her from puberty and sexual activities is not surprising considering Basile's story or later tales that warn against the dangers of sexual interaction. Basile's Petrosinella is only seven years old when she is taken from her mother, but other versions have the girl closer to adolescence when she is imprisoned. For example, in the 1698 tale by Charlotte-Rose de la Force, Persinette is taken from her parents shortly after her birth, but when she reaches twelve years old, the fairy decides "to shield [Persinette] from her destiny" (480). Friedrich Schultz's 1790 "Rapunzel" is almost identical to de la Force's tale. The Grimm brothers' sorceress also raises the girl Rapunzel from infancy but interns her in a tower when she reaches the age of twelve. Obviously, incarcerating the child does not protect her, as in all variations the prince finds her, falls in love with her, and gains access not only to the tower but also to the girl herself. If one considers an adult audience, all of the authors are clear in the revelation of sexual activity, which results in either escape, as in Basile's story, or in pregnancy and exile, as in German variants by Schultz and the Grimms.

The idea that the pregnant woman's cravings must be satisfied was also familiar in folklore and superstition. Strong appetites for exotic or unusual fare would have told the audience that the woman at the beginning of the story is pregnant, and many cultures held superstitious beliefs that a pregnant woman whose cravings were not met would be touched by evil in some way. One possibility would be through miscarriage. One could interpret the theft of the newborn daughter by fairy, sorceress, or ogress as a version of miscarriage, since the woman who bore the child was not allowed to raise her. The later claiming of the daughter, as in Basile's story, would have been just as devastating for her mother, who had raised the child for seven years only to lose her because of those early cravings.

The three enchanted acorns are another recognizable motif based partially on the common use of the triad and its importance in spiritual symbolism. The ogress enchants the acorns to strengthen the girl's imprisonment; however, when the girl and her lover co-opt the magical objects, they are used as a means both of escape and of destroying the ogress. In this story, the acorns turn into three animals that frighten and ultimately devour the monstrous mother figure. In Thomas Crane's "The Fair Angiola," a late nineteenth-century Italian retelling, the witch is outwitted through the use of three magical objects stolen by the Rapunzel figure and her prince. In Crane's tale, the witch's three balls of yarn transform into a mountain of soap, a mountain of nails, and a wild flood.

Whether the version of the tale is Italian, French, German, or from another culture outside of Europe, the story of a girl hidden in a tower by a primarily evil substitute mother figure remains universally appealing, partially because readers can find recognizable motifs, characters, and conventions in each retelling.

Theresa L. Stowell, PhD

BIBLIOGRAPHY

Ashliman, D. L. *Folk and Fairy Tales: A Handbook.* Westport: Greenwood, 2004. Print.

Basile, Giambattista. "Petrosinella." Zipes 475–79.

Bettelheim, Bruno. *The Uses of Enchantment: The Meaning and Importance of Fairy Tales.* New York: Vintage, 1976. Print.

Brown, Mary Ellen, and Bruce A. Rosenberg. *Encyclopedia of Folklore and Literature.* Santa Barbara: ABC-CLIO, 1998. Print.

Crane, Thomas Frederick. "Fair Angiola." *Italian Popular Tales.* London: Macmillan, 1885. 26–29. Print.

De la Force, Charlotte. "Persinette." Zipes 479–84.

Schultz, Friedrich. "Rapunzel." Zipes 484–89.

Zipes, Jack, ed. *The Great Fairy Tale Tradition: From Straparola and Basile to the Brothers Grimm.* New York: Norton, 2001. Print.

◆ Princess Belle-Étoile

Author: Marie-Catherine d'Aulnoy
Time Period: 1501 CE–1700 CE
Country or Culture: France
Genre: Fairy Tale

PLOT SUMMARY

In Europe, in an indeterminate time, a princess falls on hard times. Widowed with three young daughters, she decides to raise her children humbly, opening an inn to earn an income. One day, a poor old woman arrives at the inn and requests a big meal. The princess and her daughters, Roussette, Brunette, and Blondine, serve the woman. After having eaten, the penniless old woman reveals that she is a fairy and promises to grant the first wishes that the daughters make without thinking of her.

When a king and his entourage come to the inn several months later, the three daughters each make impulsive wishes. Roussette wishes to marry the royal admiral, Brunette wishes to marry the king's brother, and Blondine wishes to marry the king. Blondine also wishes to bear her new husband three children who will have stars on their foreheads and whose hair will fall in golden curls and drop precious stones. Their first wishes come true with a triple marriage at the inn that night.

At the king's palace, the king's mother, while outwardly calm, is furious at her son's apparently poor choice of a wife. She allies with Roussette, who is bitterly jealous at the lower status of her admiral husband. Before Blondine and Brunette give birth, the king and his brother head to war. Brunette dies giving birth to her son. Blondine has triplets, two boys and a girl, just as she had wished. Roussette approaches the king's mother and proposes that they exchange Blondine's children for three puppies and kill all four children. The king's mother agrees and charges her servant Feintise to carry out the plot. Feintise does not kill the four babies but puts them out to sea in a small boat during a major storm. Believing she gave birth to dogs, Blondine moves back to her mother.

At sea, a pirate picks up the babies. He and his wife, Corsine, raise them as their own. The precious stones gained from combing the hair of Blondine's children allow them to live well. Blondine's daughter is named Belle-Étoile (Beautiful Star), and her brothers are named Petit-Soleil (Little Sun) and Heureux (Cheerful); Brunette's son is called Chéri (Beloved).

As teenagers, the four children learn they are adopted. They sail off to find their parents. Belle-Étoile and Chéri deny their mutual love, still believing they are siblings. The fairy guides their boat to their father's city. He welcomes and houses them without recognizing them. However, the king's mother suspects the truth. Feintise confesses her failure to kill the children fifteen years earlier and promises to destroy the four young people.

Feintise places three subsequent wishes in Princess Belle-Étoile's heart. First, she makes Belle-Étoile desire dancing water, which gives its drinker long-lasting beauty but is extremely dangerous to obtain. Chéri, wanting to impress Belle-Étoile, fetches the water. He nearly dies in the attempt but succeeds after the fairy, disguised as a dove, summons forest animals to dig a tunnel for him to the source of the dancing water. Next, Feintise induces Belle-Étoile to want a singing apple capable of bestowing special powers on its owner. Chéri succeeds in finding the singing apple, as the fairy, again as dove, advises him to don a suit of mirrors to chase away the dragon that guards this treasure. Finally, Cheri tries to bring Belle-Étoile a little green bird that can answer all questions, but he fails in this quest after he is immobilized inside the bird's perching rock, as are his cousins Heureux and Petit-Soleil. Belle-Étoile, aided by the dove-fairy and disguised as a man, captures the green bird and frees the others.

They return to the palace just as the king is preparing to remarry. Roussette sends someone to fetch Blondine and her three dogs, all four on leashes. The little green bird reveals the truth about the four youngsters and Feintise's treachery. The king reconciles with Blondine, gently dismissing his intended new bride. His mother is locked up in a tower. Roussette, Feintise, and the dogs are thrown into a dungeon, where they die. Princess Belle-Étoile and Prince Chéri marry. Blondine's mother reveals her royal status, pleasing the king.

SIGNIFICANCE

In 1698, French noblewoman Marie-Catherine d'Aulnoy published the tale of Princess Belle-Étoile in her anthology *Contes nouveaux ou les fées à la mode* (New tales or fashionable fairies). D'Aulnoy based her fairy tale upon an older Italian source, "Ancilotto, King of Provino," which was published by Italian fairy-tale collector Giovanni Francesco Straparola in his 1550 anthology *Le piacevoli notti* (*The Facetious Nights by Straparola*, 1901). From this Italian source, different versions spread to many European countries. "Princess Belle-Étoile" has significant additions by d'Aulnoy. The most accessible, full translation of d'Aulnoy's version of "Princess Belle-Étoile" was written by Anne Macdonell and Elizabeth Lee for their 1892 anthology *The Fairy Tales of Madame D'Aulnoy*, which is the source for this synopsis.

"Princess Belle-Étoile" is significant for two key reasons. First, it presents greatly empowered women for its time. Second, it critiques absolutist feudal monarchy. Princess Belle-Étoile and her royal grandmother show remarkable resilience and autonomy. When her grandmother loses her position as princess for unknown reasons, she rescues herself and her three daughters by leveraging her talent as a cook and opening up an inn. This represents a remarkable choice for a female character in a seventeenth-century French fairy tale. It may have been influenced by Marie-Catherine d'Aulnoy's own fall from grace. Of noble birth, d'Aulnoy removed herself for some time from aristocratic French society after her husband, Baron d'Aulnoy, was falsely accused of treason in 1669. When her husband was acquitted, the couple separated. After returning to Paris, Marie-Catherine d'Aulnoy supported herself by writing.

The unfortunate princess is d'Aulnoy's own addition to her Italian source material. Princess Belle-Étoile herself, disguised as a man, is the heroine who saves her brothers and cousin from the trap of the little bird. She is more thoughtful than her counterpart in the Italian source. Her romance with Prince Chéri is also d'Aulnoy's creation. In all their endeavors, the good characters are aided by the fairy. She is welcomed as an old woman at the inn and is the second powerful female character d'Aulnoy creatively incorporates into the tale.

As d'Aulnoy witnessed the intrigues at the court of French king Louis XIV firsthand, her social criticism of absolutist monarchy is well grounded. When Roussette, Brunette, and Blondine marry, their mother, a former princess, refuses to go to the palace with them. She tells the king that, as she already knows of the turmoil of court life, she prefers to continue to live simply at the inn. Even the pirate who adopts the four children is shown to be a kind and generous father figure, especially in contrast to the wicked and scheming queen mother, who is motivated only by her impression that Blondine is of low rank.

R. C. Lutz, PhD

BIBLIOGRAPHY

D'Aulnoy, Marie Catherine. "Princess Belle-Etoile." *The Fairy Tales of Madame D'Aulnoy*. Trans. Anne Macdonell and Elizabeth Lee. London: Lawrence, 1892. Print.

DeGraff, Amy Vanderlyn. *The Tower and the Well: A Psychological Interpretation of the Fairy Tales of Madame D'Aulnoy*. Birmingham: Summa, 1984. Print.

Hannon, Patricia. "A Politics of Disguise: Marie-Catherine d'Aulnoy's 'Belle-Etoile' and the Narrative Structure of Ambivalence." *Anxious Power*. Ed. Carol Singley and Susan Sweeney. Albany: State U of New York P, 1993. 73–90. Print.

Seifert, Lewis. *Fairy Tales, Sexuality and Gender in France, 1690–1715: Nostalgic Utopias*. Cambridge: Cambridge UP, 1996. Print.

Straparola, Giovanni Francesco. "Ancilotto, King of Provino." *The Facetious Nights by Straparola*. Trans. W. G. Waters. London: Society of Bibliophiles, 1901. Print.

Princess Rosette

Author: Marie-Catherine d'Aulnoy
Time Period: 1501 CE–1700 CE
Country or Culture: France
Genre: Fairy Tale

PLOT SUMMARY

Once upon a time, there live a king and queen who are friends with the fairies. Their first two children are boys, and the two young men live in good health, just as the fairies predicted. Later, they have another child, a daughter named Rosette. Princess Rosette is a beautiful little girl whose beauty endears her to anyone she encounters. The queen consults with the fairies as to the future of her daughter, but the fairies are unusually reluctant to give an answer. The queen presses for a response, and the chief fairy finally tells her that they believe that Rosette may one day be responsible for the deaths of both of the princes.

The queen eventually tells the king of the fairies' unsettling report. Upon the advice of an old hermit, they lock Rosette in a tower and vow never to release her. Still, the king, queen, and princes visit their dear Rosette every day. The boys do not know why she is locked in the tower but remain loyal to their parents' wishes.

Eventually, the king and queen die, leaving the elder prince to assume the throne. He decides to free his sister and allow her to marry.

The princess loves life outside of the tower. One day, while enjoying the outdoors with her green dog, Fretillon, she comes across a peacock. Drawn to the bird's beautiful colors, she decides that she will marry the king of the peacocks one day. Rosette has many suitors, and she treats each one with respect and kindness but remains dedicated to the idea that she will one day marry the king of the peacocks. Eventually, her brothers set out to find the Peacock King, leaving her in charge of the kingdom.

After a long journey, the king and the prince arrive at the realm of the Peacock King, whom they learn is not a bird but a handsome man clad in peacock feathers. The Peacock King meets with the two men, who show him a picture of their sister and offer her in marriage. The Peacock King agrees to the match but says that if she is not as beautiful as her portrait, the two men will be killed. Agreeing to his terms, the brothers allow themselves to be imprisoned while the Peacock King meets the princess. They send word to Princess Rosette, who boards a ship to her betrothed's kingdom. Along the way, however, Rosette's nurse offers the ship's captain a great sum of money to throw Rosette overboard so that the nurse's daughter, disguised as Rosette, can be presented to the Peacock King. The boatman agrees and throws the princess and her dog overboard. However, the princess and her pet survive, floating on her bed on the ocean.

Meanwhile, the nurse's ugly and rude daughter is met by the Peacock King's entourage. The Peacock King is excited to meet her, but when he sees that she is nothing like the picture he was shown, he sentences Rosette's brothers to death. As this verdict is issued, Rosette is rescued from the sea by a kind, poor old man. She tells him her story and that she believes the Peacock King to be responsible for having her thrown into the sea. Rosette takes a basket and ties it around her dog's neck, commanding her pet to fetch a great deal of food from the Peacock King's pantry. The dog goes back and forth between the king's kitchen and the man's house, bringing more and more food to the man and Rosette while the Peacock King goes without. One day, one of the king's advisers witnesses the dog's theft and follows it back to the man's hut. The adviser reports his findings to the king, who sends his guards to capture the strangers who have stolen his food and bring them back to the palace. Upon seeing Rosette and learning her name, the king realizes that she is the true princess, and he immediately frees her brothers from captivity. The scheming nurse and her accomplices are forgiven, the good man is allowed to live in the palace for the rest of his life, and the Peacock King and Princess Rosette are married.

SIGNIFICANCE

The fairy tale of Princess Rosette was composed in the late seventeenth century by French writer Marie-Catherine, baroness d'Aulnoy (often known simply as Marie-Catherine d'Aulnoy). At the age of fifteen or sixteen, she was forced to marry a wealthy baron who was more than twice her age. The baron was eventually charged with treason against the king, but the men whose testimony led to his indictment later recanted; historians have since speculated that d'Aulnoy or a member of her family had convinced the men to testify against her husband, with whom she was very unhappy. She lived apart from her husband following his release, becoming a well-known author of travelogues, histories, and fairy tales.

D'Aulnoy wrote two collections of fairy tales, some of the earliest such works published in Europe. Rosette's tale was included in the 1697 collection *Les contes des fées* (Fairy tales). This collection and the subsequent work, *Contes nouveaux ou les fées à la mode* (1698; New tales or fairies in fashion), were later translated into English many times throughout the following centuries.

The story of Princess Rosette is typical of many of d'Aulnoy's works, which are typically fantastical and feature humorous subplots and characters—in this case, for example, a green dog and an entire kingdom of people dressed as peacocks. Such tales contributed to the increasing popularity of fairy tales during the centuries following their publication. Many playwrights and musicians of the nineteenth century in particular were heavily influenced by works such as those of d'Aulnoy and embellished upon her stories in their own productions. Even in the twentieth and twenty-first centuries, fairy tales such as the story of Princess Rosette continue to influence literature, music, stage productions, and films.

Michael P. Auerbach, MA

BIBLIOGRAPHY

Buczkowski, Paul. "The First Precise English Translation of Madame d'Aulnoy's Fairy Tales." *Marvels and Tales* 23.1 (2009): n. pag. Web. 27 June 2013.

D'Aulnoy, Marie-Catherine. *The Fairy Tales of Madame d'Aulnoy, Newly Done into English*. Trans. Annie MacDonell. London: Lawrence, 1892. Print.

DeGraff, Amy Vanderlyn. *The Tower and the Well: A Psychological Interpretation of the Fairy Tales of Madame d'Aulnoy*. Birmingham: Summa, 1984. Print.

Windling, Terri. "Les Contes des Fees: The Literary Fairy Tales of France." *Journal of Mythic Arts*. Endicott Studio, 2000. Web. 27 June 2013.

Zipes, Jack. *Fairy Tale as Myth, Myth as Fairy Tale*. Lexington: U of Kentucky P, 2002. Print.

◆ Snow-White and Rose-Red

Author: Andrew Lang
Time Period: 1701 CE–1850 CE; 1851 CE–1900 CE
Country or Culture: Germany
Genre: Fairy Tale

PLOT SUMMARY

Andrew Lang's "Snow-White and Rose-Red" begins with a poor widow and her two devoted daughters, Snow-white and Rose-red, named for the two rose trees growing in the widow's garden. Snow-white is quiet and enjoys helping her mother at home, whereas Rose-red loves to run and play in the fields. The girls live harmoniously with their mother and with the beasts of the wood and often sleep outside safely. One morning, they wake up outdoors and see a child dressed in white robes near where they had lain. The child soon vanishes, after which the girls realize they had slept close to a precipice and might well have fallen over it the previous night. Their mother tells them that the child in the shining robe was a guardian angel.

One winter evening at home, the family hears a knock at the door. Rose-red opens it to discover a black bear. The girls flee in terror, but the bear assures them that he is safe and that he only wishes to come in from the cold. The mother treats him kindly, inviting him to warm himself by the fire, and she reassures her daughters that the bear is safe. The daughters gradually become comfortable and begin to play with the bear, pulling his fur and rolling about. The beast spends the night on the hearth and departs in the morning. He eventually becomes their regular evening guest.

Spring arrives, and the bear announces that he must leave to protect his treasure from dwarfs that live underground during winter but will soon emerge to steal it. As he departs, he catches a piece of his fur in the door knocker, and Snow-white thinks that she catches a glimpse gold underneath it.

One day, the girls happen upon a dwarf jumping up and down trying to free his beard, which has become stuck in a cleft of wood under a fallen tree. When the girls accost the creature, he verbally abuses them, but they help him anyway, eventually cutting off his beard to release him. The dwarf upbraids the girls for cutting his beard and scurries off with a bag of gold. The daughters encounter the dwarf twice more: the first time, his beard is stuck once again, this time in a fishing line. The girls help him by again cutting the beard, and again the dwarf insults them as he runs off with a bag of pearls. The second time, the dwarf is nearly carried off by an eagle, but the girls hold onto him so that the bird simply flies away. This time, dwarf reacts by screaming at the girls for tearing his coat. Snow-white and Rose-red go on their way, but as they return from their errands in town, they see the dwarf emptying his bag of pearls. As usual, the dwarf screams at the girls until the black bear suddenly appears and kills him. The bear then catches up with the girls, who had fled in fear, and he suddenly changes into a prince dressed all in gold. He reveals that he is a king's son who had been enchanted to live as a bear as long as the dwarf was alive. Snow-white then marries the prince, and Rose-red marries his brother. The brides divide the dwarf's treasure, and their mother lives happily with them and preserves her two beloved rose trees.

SIGNIFICANCE

This version of the tale comes from the *Blue Fairy Book*, published in 1889 by the Scottish writer Andrew Lang. Lang worked in numerous genres but became best known for his series of twelve "fairy books," whose titles each include the name of a different color. The first in the series, the *Blue Fairy Book* was quite successful and enabled Lang to produce the subsequent volumes. The books include tales from different cultures and time periods. Overall, the series was produced by and represents the Western European cultural fascination with folklore and traditional tales during the eighteenth and nineteenth centuries.

The story of Snow-white and Rose-red falls into a familiar category of fairy tales: the coming-of-age tale involving a test by an enchanted prince who initially appears as a bear or some other beast. The most famous story of this tale type is "Beauty and the Beast," but

there are many other versions, such as the Norwegian tale "East o' the Sun and West o' the Moon," which is remarkably similar to the story of Snow-white and Rose-red. In both stories, the prince appears as a bear who arrives at the house of the girls to initiate the test. In "Snow-white and Rose-red," the test entails displaying courage and kindness; the girls succeed as they are willing to befriend the bear and to help the dwarf repeatedly despite his ingratitude. The daughters thus embody the perfection symbolized by the rose.

Still, there are other forces at work: the guardian angel figure suggests an element of supernatural protection, and the bear himself finally kills the dwarf and frees himself from the enchantment. These forces raise the question of the meaning of the daughters' kindness to the dwarf given that destroying him signifies the prince's liberation. Notably, in earlier versions of the tale, the girls simply discover the dwarf's treasure and bring it back to their families. The elements of the magical bear and the marriage are later additions that shift the focus of the tale.

Ashleigh Imus, PhD

BIBLIOGRAPHY

Grimm, Jacob, and Wilhelm Grimm. *Household Tales.* Trans. Margaret Hunt. London: Bell, 1884. Print.

Heiner, Heidi Anne. "The Annotated Snow White and Rose Red." *SurLaLuneFairyTales.org.* SurLaLune Fairy Tales, 28 Nov. 2008. Web. 12 July 2013.

Lang, Andrew. *The Blue Fairy Book.* Philadelphia: McKay, 1921. Print.

Rudman, Masha. "Review of Snow-White and Rose-Red and Other Andrew Lang Tales." *Reading Teacher* 27.8 (1974): 849. Print.

Zipes, Jack. *The Great Fairy Tale Tradition: From Straparola and Basile to the Brothers Grimm.* New York: Norton, 2001. Print.

◆ Thumbelina

Author: Hans Christian Andersen
Time Period: 1851 CE–1900 CE
Country or Culture: Denmark
Genre: Fairy Tale

PLOT SUMMARY

"Thumbelina" begins with a woman who wishes to have a child but cannot, so she consults a fairy, who tells her to plant a special grain of barley. The barley produces a flower with red and gold leaves, and as soon as the woman kisses the flower, it opens. Sitting on the stamens is "a very delicate and graceful little maiden" (45). The woman names her Thumbelina for her tiny size and makes her a bed from a walnut shell. One night, an ugly toad mother sneaks into the house and spies Thumbelina. Wanting a wife for her son, the toad takes Thumbelina away in her walnut bed. She places the maiden on a water lily in a stream and then prepares for the wedding. When Thumbelina wakes, the mother comes and announces that the girl will marry her ugly son, prompting Thumbelina to weep bitterly.

When the toads leave, the fish swimming around the lily pad take pity on Thumbelina and decide to help her by nibbling through the stem's leaf. Once free, Thumbelina sails downstream away from the toads. She passes through towns and is admired by birds flying above her. A butterfly joins her on her leaf, and Thumbelina ties it to the leaf with her sash. Suddenly, a cockchafer snatches Thumbelina away to a tree, gives her honey, and praises her beauty. But when the other cockchafers say that Thumbelina is ugly, the first one believes them and leaves Thumbelina on a daisy, where the poor maiden weeps with sorrow.

Thumbelina lives alone in the forest for the summer, eating honey and drinking dew. But when winter comes, she wanders in an empty grain field until she arrives at the house of a friendly mouse, who invites her to stay for the chilly season. Soon, the mouse informs Thumbalina that a wealthy mole who wears a velvet coat and has a large house will come to visit, but he is blind, so Thumbelina must be sure to tell him excellent stories. The mole falls in love with Thumbelina, but she finds him dull. While walking in an underground passage, they find a dead swallow, which moves Thumbelina to great pity because of her fondness for the birds who once sang to her so beautifully. Visiting the bird again on her own, she discovers that it is not dead but merely stunned from the cold.

Thumbelina nurses the swallow back to its full strength, and in the spring, it invites her to fly away with it. Afraid of offending the mouse, she refuses. But soon after, Thumbelina learns that the mouse has arranged her marriage to the mole. As the wedding draws near, Thumbelina bids the sun farewell and again meets the swallow. This time, she agrees to fly south. When they arrive in a warm country near a lake, the swallow places Thumbelina on a lovely white flower. There, she is delighted to find a tiny man very similar to her. He wears a gold crown, and when he sees Thumbelina, he asks her to marry him and become queen of all the flowers.

A large host of tiny flower people attends their wedding. Thumbelina receives wings as a gift, and her new husband renames her Maia. The swallow sings a lovely wedding song but feels sad when he flies back to Denmark. There, his nest is "over the window of a house in which dwelt the writer of fairy tales. The swallow sang, 'Tweet, tweet,' and from his song came the whole story" (56).

SIGNIFICANCE

A nineteenth-century Danish fairy tale, "Thumbelina" was written by Hans Christian Andersen during a cultural period of Western European fascination with collections of fairy tales and folktales. Beginning in the eighteenth century, writers produced anthologies of folk and fairy tales as a way of contributing to the cultural distinctiveness of their nations, and part of this cultural project included presenting the stories as moral exempla. In the famous collections of the Brothers Grimm in Germany, of Andersen in Denmark, and of many other anthologists, stories were offered as lessons and entertainment for young people, but they were also intended to reflect the cultural uniqueness of particular countries.

In this context, "Thumbelina" was not well received by critics in part because it lacks an explicit moral lesson; instead, it emphasizes the maiden's fanciful adventures with various animals and her desire not to marry the toad and the mole. The woman at the story's beginning who desires to have a child evidently fails, and the little man who finally becomes Thumbelina's husband is declared to be "the angel of the flower; for a tiny man and a tiny woman dwell in every flower; and this was the king of them all" (56). This latter detail is emblematic of the story's interest in fantastic details and romance rather than in morality. The story ends happily as Thumbelina finally wins her perfect prince.

This romantic ending, however, implies the values of independence and of finding one's place. Thumbelina repeatedly rejects the marriages arranged for her largely because the animal mates are unsuitable: the toad is ugly, and the tedious mole shuns the sunlight that Thumbelina loves so much. Although she is frequently acted upon rather than taking matters into her own hands, Thumbelina finds ways to escape the undesirable situations she meets, and her acceptance of the flower angel as a husband represents her totally free choice of whom to marry. With this romantic ending, Andersen presents a lesson that was perhaps a bit modern for audiences who desired more traditional tales.

Ashleigh Imus, PhD

BIBLIOGRAPHY

Andersen, Hans Christian. *Fairy Tales.* New York: Orion, 1958. Print.

Churchwell, Sarah. "Justice and Punishment in Fairytales." *Guardian* 14 Oct. 2009, Great Fairytales sec.: 34. Print.

Opie, Iona, and Peter Opie. *The Classic Fairy Tales.* New York: Oxford UP, 1974. Print.

Sale, Roger. *Fairy Tales and After: From Snow White to E. B. White.* Cambridge: Harvard UP, 1978. Print.

Zipes, Jack. *Breaking the Magic Spell: Radical Theories of Folk and Fairy Tales.* Lexington: UP of Kentucky, 2002. Print.

CENTRAL AND EASTERN EUROPE

◆ Baba Yaga

Author: Verra Xenophontovna Kalamatiano de Blumenthal
Time Period: 1851 CE–1900 CE
Country or Culture: Russia
Genre: Folktale

PLOT SUMMARY

Verra Xenophontovna Kalamatiano de Blumenthal's version of "Baba Yaga" begins by introducing a peasant man and his twin children, a boy and a girl. When their mother dies, the husband mourns for more than two years before he remarries and has more children. Jealous of her stepchildren, the new wife orders them to go to her grandmother "who lives in the forest in a hut on hen's feet. You will do everything she wants you to, and she will give you sweet things to eat and you will be happy" (de Blumenthal 119). The twins decide to go to their own grandmother, who tells them that the other grandmother is really a wicked witch. She advises them to be kind, avoid speaking badly of anyone, and "not despise helping the weakest, and always

hope that for you, too, there will be the needed help" (120). With that, she feeds the children and sends them on their way.

In the forest, the children arrive at a hut that "stood on tiny hen's feet, and at the top was a rooster's head" (120). The children command the hut to face them, and inside they observe the witch resting. Despite their fear, the children politely inform the witch of their willingness to serve her. The witch replies that satisfactory service will bring reward, but "if not, I shall eat you up" (121). She orders the girl to spin thread and the boy to fill a tub using a sieve. As the girl weeps, mice appear and offer to help her if she gives them cookies. She does, and they tell her to find a black cat, give it some ham, and it will also help them. The girl then finds her brother distraught as he fails to fill the tub. Birds appear and ask for breadcrumbs. When the children comply, the birds advise them to cover the sieve with clay. The plan works, and they fill the tub.

The children finally meet the cat and feed it some ham. The cat then gives the children a towel and a comb, telling them to run from the witch and throw down the objects behind them when she pursues them. The towel will become a river, and the comb will transform into a dark wood with magic protective powers. Baba Yaga returns and is forced to acknowledge the children's success but says that tomorrow "your work will be more difficult and I hope I shall eat you up" (123).

The next morning, the children are given more tasks but instead take the towel and comb and run off. They overcome every obstacle—pursuing dogs, a closed gate, and treacherous tree branches—with kindness and generosity. When Baba Yaga finds the children gone, she beats the cat and asks it why it let the orphans go. The cat replies that the children fed her "some good ham" (124). Likewise, the dogs, the gate, and the birch tree all praise the children's kindness. Baba Yaga then hurriedly decides to pursue the children on her broomstick. The children throw the towel behind them, and a river blocks Baba Yaga until she finds a shallow crossing. But the comb becomes a dark, impenetrable forest, and the witch is forced to return home without her servants. The children reunite with their father, who sends his evil wife away, and "from that time he watched over their happiness and never neglected them any more" (127).

SIGNIFICANCE

The tale of Baba Yaga was originally collected by Russian folklorist Alexander Afanasyev (1826–71) in the mid-nineteenth century, and stories of Baba Yaga are common throughout central and eastern Europe with the character being portrayed primarily as the malevolent figure found in de Blumenthal's rendering. Baba Yaga is highly ambiguous in the tradition overall, however, and de Blumenthal's notes define the name *Baba Yaga* as meaning "grandmother witch" (151). Baba Yaga represents in Russian folklore a mother goddess figure or a crone who can be wicked or benevolent, and when benevolent, she is often both terrifying and wise. In some retellings, she is a wise hag who offers magical gifts or profound advice.

In the Russian tale of Vasalisa the Wise, Baba Yaga is clearly not a one-dimensional witch but a frightening goddess figure. Poet and psychoanalyst Clarissa Pinkola Estés tells a version of this story, which is in fact an analogue of the Cinderella tale, underscoring Baba Yaga's ambiguous power. In this tale, with a plot similar to de

Blumenthal's story, Vasalisa's mother dies but leaves the girl a doll that she promises will help her in times of trouble. When Vasalisa's father remarries a widow with two daughters, the new women abuse Vasalisa and finally decide to put out the fire so they will have an excuse to send her to Baba Yaga, the keeper of fire. On the way to Baba Yaga's wild hut that stands on chicken legs, Vasalisa encounters three horsemen. The white and red horsemen ride past Vasalisa, but the black one enters the hut and causes night to come. As in de Blumenthal's story, Baba Yaga demands difficult tasks, and Vasalisa performs them with the help of her magic doll so that Baba Yaga finally agrees to hand over the fire. Vasalisa returns home with the fire, which magically burns the evil stepmother and stepsisters to death.

In this story, Baba Yaga as keeper of the fire and as hostess of the three horsemen (who represent day, sunrise, and night) emerges as a fearful yet just earth goddess, an essential figure for Vasalisa's initiation into adulthood and her victory over her oppressors. This version of the story also suggests that the magic powers of the towel and comb in de Blumenthal's tale stem from Baba Yaga herself, even though the children's kindness is also a pivotal force. Both tales thus present Baba Yaga as a supernatural elemental figure whose ferocity and magic provide a crucial test of human survival and who serves as a conduit of growth.

Ashleigh Imus, PhD

BIBLIOGRAPHY

"Baba Yaga." *Old Russia*. Oldrussia.net, n.d. Web. 17 June 2013.

De Blumenthal, Verra Xenophontovna Kalamatiano. "Baba Yaga." *Folk Tales from the Russian*. Chicago: Rand, McNally, 1903. 118–27. Print.

Estés, Clarissa Pinkola. «The Doll in Her Pocket: Vasalisa the Wise.» *Women Who Run with the Wolves: Myths and Stories of the Wild Woman Archetype*. New York: Ballantine, 1995. Print.

Hubbs, Joanna. *Mother Russia: The Feminine Myth in Russian Culture*. Bloomington: Indiana UP, 1993. Print.

Johns, Andreas. *Baba Yaga: The Ambiguous Mother and Witch of the Russian Folktale*. New York: Lang, 2004. Print.

The Boys with the Golden Stars

Author: Andrew Lang
Time Period: 1851 CE–1900 CE
Country or Culture: Romania
Genre: Folktale

PLOT SUMMARY

There is a herdsman who has three daughters, Anna, Stana, and Laptitza. While all three possess great beauty, Laptitza, the youngest, is more stunning than her two sisters combined. The three sisters are picking strawberries one day when the emperor and some of his friends ride by on horses. As the men pass, Anna tells her sisters that if one of those men will make her his wife, she will bake him a loaf of bread that will keep him young and brave forever. Stana says if one chooses her as his wife, she will weave him a shirt that will protect him from any dragon. Laptitza states that she will give her husband twin boys, each with a golden star on his forehead that shines as bright as the sun. The emperor turns to Laptitza and says he will take her as his wife. They ride away and are wed the next morning. For three days and three nights, the kingdom rejoices.

The emperor's stepmother, who has a daughter with her first husband, hates Laptitza, for she had always thought that the emperor would marry her daughter. The stepmother convinces her brother, who is the king of a neighboring country, to declare war against the emperor in order to get him away from his new bride. The emperor assembles his forces, and they swiftly defeat the enemy. While he is away, Laptitza gives birth to twin boys, each with golden hair and a bright star on his forehead. The stepmother quickly steals the babies away and buries them in a hole. When the emperor returns, he sees no baby sons, so he begrudgingly has to punish Laptitza. He orders her to be buried up to her neck so others can see what happens to those who deceive the emperor. Days later, the emperor takes the stepmother's daughter for his bride.

From the spot where the babies are buried grow two aspen trees. The stepmother wishes to remove them, but the emperor insists that they be allowed to grow so he can enjoy their sight from his window. The aspens grow three times quicker than a normal tree, and the emperor delights in them. The empress finally convinces him to cut down the trees, but he insists that their wood be used

to make beds. These beds are made, and the emperor sleeps soundly on his, but the empress is kept awake by the cracking made by the wood. She thinks the beds are mocking her, so the next day the empress has the beds burned.

Two sparks fly up from the flames and fall into a great river. These sparks turn into two little fishes with identical golden scales. One morning, the emperor's fishermen come to the river and cast their nets in; they are stunned at the sight of the two golden fishes. The two fishes plead with the men not to take them to the palace, where they will be eaten. They ask the men to collect dew from the leaves and allow them to swim in it, and then allow them to dry in the sun. The fishermen comply with their wishes and the fish transform into twin boys with golden hair and bright stars on their foreheads.

The boys grow thrice as fast as normal children in age, wisdom, and knowledge until the day they ask to be taken to the emperor. They are led to the palace and force their way into the emperor's hall. The king and queen are at first angered by this insolent duo, but then the twins begin to tell their story. When they reach the end, they remove their caps to reveal the golden hair and bright stars. The emperor knows they are his sons and he takes Laptitza as his wife again.

SIGNIFICANCE

"The Boys with the Golden Stars" is a Romanian fairy tale made popular by Scottish folklorist Andrew Lang in his collection of fairy tales *The Violet Fairy Book*, first published in 1901. Lang contributed greatly to the study of folklore, fairy tales, and anthropology and published over a dozen books on the subject. He was also a poet, historian, and literary critic.

This story contains several motifs and narrative elements that appear in fairy tales throughout the world. The boys' ability to change shape to elude the nefarious stepmother is a fantastical trick that happens commonly in fairy tales—a pattern is usually followed in which the pursued transforms several times in an effort to evade the pursuer. There are variations of this type of chase, such as when a character transforms to avoid a spell or break a curse.

Another prevalent recurring motif in "The Boys with the Golden Stars" is the evil stepmother. In this story, she is the one who has the boys first hidden away from the emperor so that her own daughter can become queen. Stepmothers are often portrayed as evil in fairy tales and modern interpretations of this motif have varied. Some interpret the stepmother as another half of the actual mother that contains all of the attributes the child dislikes. One historical explanation points out that, centuries ago, women often died during childbirth and the father had to remarry to provide for his children. In the case of "The Boys with the Golden Stars," the stepmother performs evil to secure her own daughter with a royal inheritance.

The idea of a woman giving birth to special children with abnormal qualities after she has promised to do so, and then having the children stolen away from her, also appears repeatedly in fairy tales. This story also features the heavy use of the number three, which is a number that commonly appears in fairy tales and folklore. This recurrence is known as the "rule of three." In this story, the herdsman has three daughters, the kingdom rejoices for three days and three nights following the marriage, and the boys grew three times as fast as normal.

Patrick G. Cooper

BIBLIOGRAPHY

Bottigheimer, Ruth B. *Fairy Tales: A New History*. Albany: State U of New York P, 2009. Print.

Lang, Andrew. "The Boys with the Golden Stars." *The Violet Fairy Book*. London: Longmans, 1901. 299–310. Print.

Mawr, E. B. *Romanian Fairy Tales and Legends*. Hong Kong: Forgotten, 2008. Print.

Tatar, Maria. *The Hard Facts of the Grimms' Fairy Tales*. Princeton: Princeton UP, 2003. Print.

---. *The Annotated Classic Fairy Tales*. New York: Norton, 2002. Print.

 Cinderella

Author: Konstantin Pavlov
Time Period: 1851 CE–1900 CE
Country or Culture: Bulgaria
Genre: Fairy Tale

PLOT SUMMARY

The Bulgarian rendition of the fairy tale of Cinderella opens with several young women laughing and talking, seated in a circle making textiles with hand weaving tools around a large hole in the earth. The group is warned by a mysterious old man who approaches them as they work to exercise caution: if the one of the girls drops her spindle and weaving tools inside the hole, her mother will be transformed into a cow. Such is the fate that befalls Cinderella, described as the most beautiful girl of the group, who accidentally drops her spindle into the earth and returns home to find her mother transformed into a cow.

Cinderella's father eventually remarries a widow who has a daughter of her own. The girl's new stepmother is a bitter taskmaster who is also envious of Cinderella's beauty and industry, particularly in comparison to that of her own daughter. Out of spite and jealously, the stepmother refuses to let her new stepdaughter bathe, tame her hair, or change her clothing. The harsh demands of her new chores and inability to clean up eventually rob Cinderella of all her beauty.

The stepmother assigns Cinderella a nearly impossible daily task, demanding that she create a spool of yarn from a bag of raw fiber with nothing but her bare hands. When Cinderella's stepsister covertly discovers Cinderella's mother, as a cow, assisting her with this task by chewing the fiber into fine yarn, the stepmother insists that the cow be slaughtered and eaten.

Before her death, the cow insists that Cinderella preserve her bones and visit her grave if she needs assistance in the future. Cinderella eats none of the meat, but disposes of the bones as instructed. The tale continues with Cinderella's next task, in which she is charged with cleaning her stepmother's entire home before she returns from church, including the kitchen, fireplace, and innumerable small grains of millet that the stepmother purposely scatters throughout the abode to make her chore more difficult. Cinderella rushes to her mother's grave for assistance, whereupon two pigeons adorn her with a beautiful gown made of gold, and urge her to attend church while they tend to her many chores at home.

Magically restored to her original beauty, Cinderella catches the eye of all in attendance, notably the emperor's son, who fails to meet the girl before she rushes home immediately at the service's end to anticipate her stepmother's arrival. The stepmother and stepdaughter are shocked to find the numerous tasks completed.

When the scene repeats itself the following week, Cinderella this time loses a shoe from her magic golden ensemble in her haste to return home before her stepmother and stepsister. The emperor's son retrieves the shoe, and decides to travel throughout the countryside to find the woman to whom it belongs. After the shoe fails to fit the foot of every other girl in the village, the emperor's son discovers Cinderella being held prisoner beneath her stepmother's trough, and slips the shoe on her foot. The two marry, and the stepmother is punished for her harsh treatment of Cinderella.

SIGNIFICANCE

Pavlov's Bulgarian rendition of the classic fairy tale bears several similarities to the lessons and implications outlined in the Grimms' version, despite basic differences in plot.

Where the Brothers Grimm version illustrates Cinderella's divine aid in the form of a fairy godmother, the Bulgarian counterpart is the girl's actual mother transformed into a cow, a standard domestic animal in traditional Western cultures. Household tasks common throughout preindustrial Bulgaria, such as the transformation of flax into yarn, are also included. The story also describes common domestic tasks required of young women and young children of the time period, notably spinning fiber into thread and cleaning and tending to fireplaces. It is in fact from the dirt and grime that cover the young girl from cleaning fireplace cinders that her stepmother nicknames her Cinderella, the Bulgarian translation of which is Pepelezka.

Despite the fairy tale's adaptation to the culture of Southern Europe, the major traditional themes of the Cinderella fairy tale remain in place. The tale cautions respect for one's parents and family in its depiction of a harsh life after Cinderella's mother is transformed and killed.

While Cinderella can be examined in a variety of sociological and cultural ways, the Bulgarian version adheres to the basic plot that has followed nearly all cultural renditions of the Cinderella tale throughout history, notably the providentially or magically supplied escape from the pitfalls of rural life and the ascension over its perceived persecutions to the comforts of the upper or ruling class.

A religious connotation can also be found in the story, indicating that faith in the forces of good can allow believers to eventually ascend to a happier life.

John Pritchard

BIBLIOGRAPHY

Dundes, Alan, ed. *Cinderella: A Casebook*. Madison: U of Wisconsin P, 1988. Print.

Grimm, Jacob, and Wilhelm Grimm. *Cinderella and Other Tales by the Brothers Grimm*. Ed. Julia Simon-Kerr. New York: Harper, 2005. Print.

Lefebvre, Benjamin, ed. *Textual Transformations in Children's Literature: Adaptations, Translations, Reconsiderations*. New York: Routledge, 2013. Print.

Pavlof, Konstantin. "Cinderella (Pepelezhka)." *Sixty Folk-Tales from Exclusively Slavonic Sources*. Trans. A. H. Wratislaw. Boston: Houghton, 1890. 181–86. Print.

◆ The Dragon and the Prince

Author: Traditional
Time Period: 1851 CE–1900 CE
Country or Culture: Serbia
Genre: Folktale

PLOT SUMMARY

The emperor's eldest son goes out hunting one day and encounters a hare. He pursues the animal into a water mill, where it reveals itself to be a dragon and devours him. Then, the middle son goes hunting, and he too sees a hare spring from a bush. He pursues the hare to the same water mill and is also devoured by the dragon inside.

When the third and youngest son goes hunting, he also pursues the hare to the water mill but does not chase it inside. He continues hunting for other game and eventually returns to the water mill, where he finds an old woman. When he asks about the hare, the old woman explains that it is actually a dragon. The prince realizes that the dragon is responsible for the disappearance of his brothers, and he asks the old woman to help him find the source of the dragon's strength so that he can defeat the beast. The old woman agrees, and the prince returns to the palace.

When the dragon returns, the old woman asks him where he gets his strength. After lying twice, he explains that his strength resides in the neighboring empire, inside a dragon that lives in a lake. Inside the dragon is a boar, inside the boar is a pigeon, and inside the pigeon lies his power. The next day, the old woman tells the prince all she has learned, and the prince sets out to find the lake.

After traveling to the neighboring empire, the prince disguises himself as a shepherd and asks the emperor for work. The emperor tasks him with caring for the sheep in the pasture by the edge of the lake but warns him that every shepherd who ventured too close to the lake never returned. The prince gathers the sheep and takes with him two hounds that can catch a boar and a falcon that can catch a pigeon. When the prince arrives at the lake, he calls out a challenge to the dragon. The two battle until late into the day but stop when the dragon becomes too hot. The prince says that he could go on fighting if the emperor's daughter kissed him on the forehead, and the dragon retreats into the lake.

The townspeople are astonished when the prince returns from the lake, for no shepherd has survived the dragon before. The next day, he returns to the lake, and this time, the emperor sends two men to spy on him and report on how he handles the dragon. Again, they battle but stop when the dragon becomes too hot. The prince repeats that he could go on fighting if the emperor's daughter kissed him. The two men tell the emperor what happened, and he instructs his daughter to go with the prince the following day.

The prince again returns to the lake, this time accompanied by the emperor's daughter. The dragon fights the prince again, and when they both become too tired to go on, the emperor's daughter kisses the prince, giving him the strength to smash the dragon into pieces. When he does so, a wild boar runs out. The prince's hounds overtake the boar and tear it apart. A pigeon flies out of the boar's remains, and the prince's falcon overtakes the bird and returns it to the prince. The prince demands to know where his brothers are, and the pigeon tells him that they are locked in a vault inside the water mill.

The prince marries the emperor's daughter and is supplied with a large escort back to his father's empire. The caravan stops at the water mill, and the prince opens the vault. His brothers emerge, along with a multitude of people. Together, they return to their father's palace, where they live happily for many years.

SIGNIFICANCE

The tale of the dragon and the prince originated in Serbia and was introduced to English-speaking audiences by English scholar Albert Henry Wratislaw, who included the story in his 1890 collection *Sixty Folk-Tales from Exclusively Slavonic Sources*. The story includes several classic motifs common to folktales and fairy tales, including a dragon, the repetition of the number three, and a prince who is rewarded with a bride for his good deeds.

Dragons appear frequently in fairy tales and myths throughout the world. In many Asian cultures, dragons are often described as benign creatures. In European folklore, on the other hand, dragons are typically depicted as malevolent creatures that manipulate and feast on humans. In the Serbian tale of the dragon and the prince, the dragon enjoys tricking and imprisoning hunters and lying to the old woman when she asks about the source of his strength.

The number three is used frequently in folktales and fairy tales and is also a sacred number in many religions; for example, Christianity features the Holy Trinity, while Hinduism features a triad known as the Trimūrti. The motif of the recurring use of the number is commonly known as the "rule of three." In this tale, the emperor has three sons, the prince faces the dragon in the lake three times, and the first dragon's power is hidden within three shells: the lake dragon, the boar, and the pigeon.

Often in fairy tales, a prince sets out to rescue a damsel in distress and claim her as his bride. The tale of the dragon and the prince, however, presents a slight deviation on this motif. Rather than seeking to rescue a woman, the prince sets out to rescue his two brothers. He does marry the princess at the end of the story, but she is instead given to him as a reward for slaying the lake dragon. The princess even seems disinterested in the prince at first and only begrudgingly accompanies him to the lake at the will of her father.

The dragon at the water mill is able to transform himself into a hare in order to trick the first two princes into a trap. Transformation, or shape-shifting, occurs frequently in myths and fairy tales throughout the world. Typically this fantastic trick is used to escape harm or to break some kind of curse. One motif within shape-shifting is the transformation chase, in which a person or creature shape-shifts several times while being chased in an attempt to escape. The dragon plays with this motif, transforming himself into a hare specifically so that the princes will chase after him. In this way, the Serbian tale of the dragon and the prince modifies and subverts the traditional fairy-tale narrative.

Patrick G. Cooper

BIBLIOGRAPHY

Bottigheimer, Ruth B. *Fairy Tales: A New History*. New York: State U of New York P, 2009. Print.

Falkayn, David, ed. *Serbian Fairy Tales*. Havertown: Athena, 2004. Print.

Lüthi, Max. *The European Folktale: Form and Nature*. Indiana: Indiana UP, 1986. Print.

Wratislaw, Albert Henry, trans. "The Dragon and the Prince." *Sixty Folk-Tales from Exclusively Slavonic Sources*. London, 1889. 224–30. Print.

◆ Father Frost

Author: Verra Xenophontovna Kalamatiano de Blumenthal
Time Period: 1851 CE–1900 CE
Country or Culture: Russia
Genre: Folktale

PLOT SUMMARY

The Russian tale "Father Frost," recorded for an English-speaking audience by Vera Xenophontovna Kalamatiano de Blumenthal, shares a familiar set of character types in its story of reward and punishment.

The story starts with a family that includes a selfish and thoughtless stepmother and her spoiled daughter, as well as a weak father and his virtuous daughter. Despite doing everything she is told, this daughter, who is "good and kind," receives "no other reward than reproach" (Blumenthal 141). The stepmother is so jealous of the girl that she sends her ineffectual husband on a mission to abandon his daughter in the winter woods, where, she anticipates, the girl will die. The girl's father is so pathetic in his subservience to his wife that though he "wish[es] to cover [the girl] with a sheepskin in order to protect her from the cold," he does not do so, because "he [is] afraid." As he leaves, the narrator attempts to forgive him for his weakness by commenting that the father is "a good man" who does "not care to see his daughter's death" (142).

After being left out in the freezing wild without even a blanket to keep herself warm, the girl is visited by Father Frost. The king of winter approaches her and asks if she can identify him. Because she is upright and well trained, she responds courteously and denies her own discomfort in a desire to honor him, even when he challenges her goodness with an assault of icy temperatures. Father Frost is wise and understands her true state, so, "charmed" (Blumenthal 143) by her attitude, he takes pity on her and rewards her generously with many riches. Upon donning "a blue 'sarafan' ornamented with silver and pearls" (145), the girl's loveliness shines like the sun.

Meanwhile, her stepmother is home preparing the girl's funeral meal. As the stepmother works, a little dog crows, "Bow-Wow! bow-wow! the old man's daughter is on her way home, beautiful and happy as never before, and the old woman's daughter is wicked as ever before" (Blumenthal 145). The woman alternately beats and attempts to bribe the dog with food to tell her that

her daughter will be rewarded while her stepdaughter will be found dead. When her husband comes home with his daughter and her gifts, the woman sees an opportunity to gain riches for her own child and sends him back to the cold wilderness with her own daughter.

The story ends with a predictable twist. The woman's daughter is as rude and shortsighted as her mother, so Father Frost, disgusted by the girl's attitude, freezes her to death. Though crushed by her child's demise, the woman finally accepts her own culpability and learns a lesson about the dangers of evil and jealous attitudes.

SIGNIFICANCE

For centuries after Russia opened to Christianity, Russian folktales were discouraged by the church, the government, and upper levels of society, partially because of their connection to pagan beliefs. In the nineteenth century, however, several literary, art, and music figures, such as Alexander Pushkin, began to acknowledge the power of the oral tales, bringing them to the attention of literary study. True study of Russian folklore began to be regarded as an important contribution to literature with Vladimir Propp's *Morfologija skazki* (1928; *Morphology of the Folktale*, 1958) as well as his later works. Propp makes several points about the "Father Frost" story: first, the tale is part of a cycle focusing on the motif of the victimized child from a previous wife; second, there are several variations of the story, with one version using Father Frost as the magical figure, while other accounts use a bear or a wood goblin; and finally, regardless of the specific character who fulfills the role in the story, the story structure remains the same. Propp's claim coincided with Stith Thompson's first revision of Antti Aarne's categorization of folktales, also in 1928, and connected "Father Frost" to Aarne-Thompson tale type 480, the tale of the kind and unkind girls. Additionally, the tale's universal appeal becomes clear in the ways the characters fulfill several of Thompson's motifs as laid out in his *Motif-Index of Folk-Literature* (1932–36).

A list of thirty-one "functions" of various folktale characters was compiled and defined by Propp in *Morphology*. Among the functions this story contains are function 8, "villany," in which "the villain causes harm or injury to a member of a family"; function 11, "departure," in which "the hero leaves home," either willingly or unwillingly; function 12, the "first function of the donor," in which "the hero is tested, interrogated, attacked, etc., which prepares the way for his receiving either a magical agent or helper"; function 13, the "hero's reaction," in which "the hero reacts to the actions of the future donor"; function 29, "transfiguration," in which "the hero is given a new appearance"; and function 30, "punishment," in which "the villain is punished" (Propp 122–23). The girl's deliverance into the wild by her father fits functions 8 and 11, her interaction with Father Frost mesh with functions 12 and 13, and her reward of riches and transformation when she puts on the gown from Father Frost is function 29. Blumenthal's version of the tale ends with the stepmother's recognition of her own complicity in her daughter's death, thus fulfilling function 30.

Thompson's traditional motifs, which are not usually applied to Russian folklore, are nevertheless also evident in the characters of the story. The cruel stepmother who cares only for her own child to the detriment of her husband's child is probably the most obvious character type. This stepmother not only mocks the virtuous girl but orders her husband to abandon his daughter in the woods with the full knowledge and hope that the girl will freeze to death. Further, her abuse of the dog as it predicts the future demonstrates motif W185, "violence of temper," and her greed and jealousy are evident when she sends her daughter out to gain riches. In contrast to the stepmother, the man's daughter possesses a variety of Thompson's "favorable traits of character," including "kindness" (W10), "patience" (W26), and "obedience" (W31), and she is rewarded for these positive traits. Finally, the talking dog fits Thompson's motifs of "prophetic animals" (B140) and "speaking animals" (B210).

Theresa L. Stowell, PhD

BIBLIOGRAPHY

Blumenthal, Verra Xenophontovna Kalamatiano de. *Folk Tales from the Russian*. Chicago: Rand, 1903. Print.

Marshall, Bonnie C., trans. *The Snow Maiden and Other Russian Tales*. Westport: Libs. Unltd., 2004. Print.

Propp, Vladimir. "The Structure of Russian Fairy Tales." *International Folkloristics: Classic Contributions by the Founders of Folklore*. Ed. Alan Dundes. New York: Rowman, 1999. 119–30. Print.

Riordan, James. "Russian Fairy Tales and Their Collectors." *A Companion to the Fairy Tale*. Ed. Hilda Ellis Davidson and Anna Chaudhri. Rochester: Brewer, 2003. 217–25. Print.

Sherman, Josepha. *World Folklore for Storytellers: Tales of Wonder, Wisdom, Fools, and Heroes*. Armonk: Sharpe, 2009. Print.

Thompson, Stith. *Motif-Index of Folk-Literature: A Classification of Narrative Elements in Folktales, Ballads, Myths, Fables, Medieval Romances, Exempla, Fabliaux, Jest-Books, and Local Legends*. Rev. and enl. ed. 6 vols. Bloomington: Indiana UP, 1955–58. *Ruthenia*. Web. 7 June 2013.

◆ The Feather of Finist the Falcon

Author: Alexander Afanasyev
Time Period: 1851 CE–1900 CE
Country or Culture: Russia
Genre: Folktale

PLOT SUMMARY

A merchant is leaving for the fair one day and asks his three daughters what they wish him to bring back for them. His older two daughters request dresses, but his youngest daughter, Marya, asks for the feather of Finist the Falcon. The merchant goes to the fair twice but is only able to bring back what his older daughters requested. He asks Marya if she wants anything besides the feather of Finist, but she remains steadfast in her desire for it.

During the father's third visit to the fair, he is able to acquire the feather of Finist the Falcon. In exchange for the feather, the father must promise that Marya will marry Finist. Perhaps attracted by his own feather, Finist visits the young girl's bedroom at night and woos her. He explains that his feathers will allow her to disguise herself if she wishes. During the falcon's visit, the other two sisters listen in on their conversation. Finist visits Marya often, and the older sisters become very suspicious. They eventually tell their father that they think Marya has a lover, but he does not believe them.

One day, the older daughters set a trap with knives in the window so that the falcon will be injured when he visits Marya again. Finist arrives and is hurt; before he leaves, however, he tells his love that she must search for him, noting that it will be an arduous journey that will wear out three pairs of iron shoes and three iron staves. The falcon leaves, and when he does not return to her, Marya sets out to find him.

The first place she comes to is the hut of a witch, often known as Baba Yaga. The witch gives the girl expensive gifts, such as a silver spinning wheel and a golden spindle, and then instructs her to visit another witch. This second witch gives the girl a silver dish and a golden egg and then instructs her to go see yet another witch. This witch also gives Marya expensive and magical gifts, such as a golden embroidery frame and a needle that sews itself. This final witch instructs the girl to go to the castle, where Finist the Falcon is planning to marry another girl.

In some versions of the story, Marya trades all of the witches' gifts to Finist's would-be princess in exchange for a night with him. In another variation, the girl sees the princess trying to wash the blood from the injured Finist's shirt and washes it herself in exchange for a night alone with him. In both versions, before allowing Marya to spend the night with Finist, the princess puts a magical pin in his hair to keep him asleep. This way, the two cannot fall in love. On the third night, the pin falls out of Finist's hair, and he awakes and recognizes the young girl. Finist marries Marya, his true love.

In a different version of the tale, Finist asks the nobles which girl he should marry: the one who sold him or the one who bought him. The nobles declare he should marry the one who bought him. In others, Marya returns home to her father and sisters. When the family attends church, Marya goes with Finist, dressed in her fine feather clothes; her sisters do not recognize her, and when they return home, they tell her stories of a prince and princess who were at church. The third time they go to church like this, the father sees Finist's carriage outside the door and realizes that Marya married the falcon.

SIGNIFICANCE

The most popular telling of "The Feather of Finist the Falcon" appears in the highly influential collection *Russian Fairy Tales*, collected by Russian folklorist Alexander Afanasyev and published by him between 1855 and 1863. Throughout his career, Afanasyev recorded and collected over six hundred Russian folktales and fairy tales. He grouped these stories according to their themes, imagery, and style. His work was a major contribution to the distribution and legitimization of Russian peasant culture and folk belief.

In the Aarne-Thompson classification system of recurring plot patterns and narrative structures in folklore, "The Feather of Finist the Falcon" is classified as type 432, in which the prince or lover is a bird. The

stories classified as type 432 typically contain a woman who falls in love with a nobleman in the shape of a bird who is wounded by a trap. The woman then seeks out the wounded bird, cures him, and ultimately marries him.

In Russian folklore, birds are typically interpreted as beings of wisdom and knowledge. Many times these birds transform into humans or share physical traits with humans, such as the prophetic Gamayun bird, who has a human head. Falcons appear throughout world mythology and are typically used as symbols for the gods or messengers. The powerful Egyptian god Horus has the head of a falcon, and in Norse mythology, the goddesses Frigg and Freyja both have cloaks of falcon feathers that allow them to fly.

One of the most famous figures of Russian folklore, the Baba Yaga, appears in this story as well. She appears frequently in various folktales of the Russian and Slavic languages. She is commonly depicted as an old woman who lives in the forest in a house on two chicken legs. She is a rather ambivalent figure who either hinders those who seek her out or provides them aid. In the case of Marya, she provides her with gifts to bribe Finist's princess.

Another common fairy-tale element in this story is the use of the number three, often referred to as the rule of three. Like in "The Feather of Finist the Falcon," other tales frequently have the youngest of three children becoming the hero. Additionally, Marya's father must go to fair three times to get the feather, Marya is given gifts by three witches, and Finist does not awake until the third night.

Patrick G. Cooper

BIBLIOGRAPHY

Afanasyev, Alexander. "The Feather of Finist, the Bright Falcon." *Russian Fairy Tales*. Trans. Norbert Guterman. New York: Pantheon, 1945. 580–87. Print.

Field, Anne. "Russian Folktales." *Book Links* 9.5 (2000): 52–57. Print.

Heiner, Heidi Anne. "The Feather of Finist the Falcon." *Russian Wonder Tales by Post Wheeler*. SurLaLune Fairy Tales, 8 May 2005. Web. 19 May 2013.

Johns, Andreas. *Baba Yaga: The Ambiguous Mother and Witch of the Russian Folktale*. New York: Lang, 2004. Print.

Post, Wheeler. *Russian Fairy Tales*. New York: Senate, 1996. Print.

The Firebird, the Horse of Power, and the Princess Vasilissa

Author: Traditional
Time Period: 1851 CE–1900 CE
Country or Culture: Russia
Genre: Folktale

PLOT SUMMARY

A young archer in the service of the czar is riding through a lush forest when he notices that no birds are singing. As he wonders what has become of the birds, he comes across a large golden feather. The archer realizes that a mighty firebird has flown through the forest and scared away the other birds.

The archer's horse pleads with the archer to leave the feather, for taking it will only lead to trouble. But the archer takes the feather anyway, with the intent of giving it to the czar. The czar is pleased with the feather but tells the archer that he now wishes for his servant to retrieve the firebird itself. He warns that if the archer does not comply, he will cut off the young man's head. Distraught and fearing death, the archer follows the advice of his horse and arranges for one hundred sacks of maize to be scattered over an open field at midnight. This is done, and the archer climbs up an oak tree while the horse waits in the field.

The firebird sweeps in and begins grazing on the maize as the horse creeps closer and closer. When he gets close enough to the bird, the horse steps on one of its wings. The bird struggles, but the archer binds it and takes it to the czar, who is pleased, knowing that no other czar has ever captured a firebird. But the czar is not yet satisfied, and he next orders the archer to travel to the land of Never and bring back Princess Vasilissa, whom the czar wants to marry.

Again, the archer is distraught, but his horse tells him to ask the czar for a silver tent and plenty of rich wine and food. The czar grants the request, and the archer and his horse leave for the land of Never. After several days, they arrive, and the archer sets up the tent on the shore and unpacks the delicious food and wine. The silver tent catches Princess Vasilissa's eye as she is rowing a boat near the shore. When she approaches the tent, the archer invites her in to feast and drink wine. The wine and food are heavy and eventually make the princess fall asleep.

Once she is sleeping, the archer carries her back to the czar.

When she wakes, the princess is upset at the sight of the old czar. She tells him that she will not get married unless she has her wedding dress, which is hidden beneath a rock in the middle of the sea. The archer is sent to retrieve it. He cannot reach the rock, but the horse persuades a large lobster to get the dress for them. The princess next tells the czar that she will not marry until the one who captured her is thrown into boiling water, and he hurries to fulfill this condition, ordering his servants to fill a large cauldron with boiling water. Before the archer can be thrown into the water, Princess Vasilissa waves her hand over it and casts a spell. The czar's servants seize the archer to throw him into the cauldron, but he breaks free of them and, following his horse's advice, jumps into the cauldron of his own free will. The water does not harm him, and the archer comes out of the cauldron more handsome than before.

Believing that the cauldron will make him young again, the czar dives into the water and is boiled to death. The archer becomes the new czar and marries the princess. A golden stable is built for his horse.

SIGNIFICANCE

The story of the archer's encounters with the firebird, the horse of power, and Princess Vasilissa is a folktale rich with adventure and familiar motifs of the hero's journey. A traditional tale originating in Russia, it was included in the influential collection *Russian Fairy Tales*, compiled by folklorist Alexander Afansyev and published between 1855 and 1863. A particularly memorable version of the tale was collected by Arthur Ransome in his 1916 collection *Old Peter's Russian Tales*.

Firebirds, known popularly as "phoenixes," are prominent beings in Russian folklore and fairy tales. These birds are typically described as having plumage that emits a bright red-and-orange glow. At the end of its life cycle, a firebird is said to build a nest in which it burns itself alive. From the ashes, a newborn firebird emerges. Variations on the firebird exist in the folklore of other countries, including France and Ireland. In the Aarne-Thompson classification and indexing system for folk and fairy tales, stories of the firebird fall under type 550, the quest for the golden bird or firebird.

Firebirds symbolize many things in Russian folklore. Sometimes the bird is a symbol of divinity or wealth, while other times it is a harbinger of doom. In some stories, the bird brings hope and charity to those in need. In the tale of the archer, taking the firebird's feather to the czar begins a chain reaction of difficult tasks and threats of beheading. The archer should have listened to his horse, and he avoids his gruesome fate only with the horse's help. The sight of the golden feather inspires greed in the czar, which ultimately leads to his downfall.

Horses likewise appear throughout folklore and fairy tales of various cultures, often serving as the supernatural aids of heroes. From the flying Pegasus of Greek mythology to the eight-legged Sleipnir of Norse mythology, horses often play a significant role. The archer's horse of power continuously devises all of the plans to accomplish the czar's tasks, saving the archer's life multiple times. Despite the archer's initial disregard for the horse's advice, the faithful steed continues to aid him in his transformation into a leader.

Patrick G. Cooper

BIBLIOGRAPHY

Afanasyev, Alexander. "The Firebird and Princess Vasilisa." *Russian Fairy Tales*. Trans. Norbert Guterman. New York: Pantheon, 1976. 494–97. Print.

Gilchrist, Cherry. *Russian Magic: Living Folk Traditions of an Enchanted Landscape*. Wheaton: Quest, 2009. Print.

Ransome, Arthur, ed. "The Fire-Bird, the Horse of Power, and the Princess Vasilissa." *Old Peter's Russian Tales*. 1916. London: Abela, 2010. 227–42. Print.

"Tales Similar to Firebird." *SurLaLune FairyTales*. Heidi Anne Heiner, 10 July 2007. Web. 19 July 2013.

Wheeler, Post. *Russian Fairy Tales*. New York: Senate, 1996. Print.

◆ Ilya Muromets and the Dragon

Author: Alexander Afanasyev
Time Period: 1851 CE–1900 CE
Country or Culture: Russia
Genre: Folktale

PLOT SUMMARY

A peasant couple, who have saved up a considerable amount of money, decide to have a child. After praying to God, the wife becomes pregnant. When the child is born, his legs do not work properly. Years go by, and when the child, Ilya, reaches his eighteenth birthday, his legs still do not function.

One day while the parents are out working, a beggar-pilgrim comes to their house. Ilya is home alone, and when the old man asks for alms, he explains that his legs do not work and that he cannot bring anything. The old man enters the house and demands that the young man rise from his bed and fetch a pitcher. Wondrously, Ilya does just so. The old man then has Ilya fill the pitcher with water and instructs him to drink all of it. Once Ilya finishes drinking, the old man tells him to refill the pitcher. Ilya goes to fetch more water, and each time he grasps a tree for support, he ends up pulling it out of the ground. Ilya can feel a new strength coursing through him. In fear of Ilya becoming uncontrollably strong, the pilgrim drinks half of the second pitcher's water and commands Ilya to drink the remaining half. This lessens Ilya's strength. The beggar praises God and leaves.

Ilya grows bored with lying around and starts digging up the whole forest. When his parents return from work, they are shocked at what their son has done. The czar learns of the boy's feats and summons him to Kiev to display his strength. Ilya sees the czar's beautiful daughter and wants to marry her.

The czar leaves one day to visit another king. This king tells the czar that his daughter is being drained of life by a twelve-headed dragon. The czar knows that Ilya is powerful enough to kill the dragon, so he goes back home and calls Ilya before him. Ilya agrees to the task. From the stables, he selects the only horse that does not stumble when he pats it on the back. He rides for a time until he comes to a very tall and steep mountain made of sand. At the top he finds a sign indicating three roads: one will force him to go hungry, the second will force his horse to go hungry, and the third will lead to death. Having faith in himself, he takes the third road.

The road leads Ilya to a thick forest, where he finds the home of Baba Yaga. The old witch attacks Ilya with a scythe, but he bests her. She eventually invites him in, where she feeds him. He stays the night, and in the morning, Baba Yaga sends him off with a letter to her sister, so that she will not also attack him. This second Baba Yaga warns Ilya about Nightingale the Robber (Solovey-Razboynik), who makes his nest atop seven oak trees and can deafen a person with his whistling. Ilya is not affected by Nightingale's voice, though, and he manages to capture the creature in his satchel.

When he arrives at the palace, Ilya shows the king that he has caught Nightingale. The king then pleads for him to slay the twelve-headed dragon that is sucking the energy from his daughter. Ilya attacks, and with each blow another of the beast's heads falls off until none are left and it is dead. With the task completed, Ilya returns to his kingdom, where he weds the czar's daughter.

SIGNIFICANCE

This story, recorded in the nineteenth century by folklorist Alexander Afanasyev, is one of many medieval tales concerned with the Russian epic hero Ilya Muromets. He is celebrated in numerous Russian epic poems and tales for achieving a number of feats, and he is considered the greatest *bogatyr*, a term applied to the great folk heroes of Kievan Rus, a medieval Slavic state. In other versions of the tale of his origins, Ilya's grandfather puts a curse on him that makes him unable to walk, and this enchantment is not lifted until he is thirty-three years old. Scholars believe that while Ilya's heroic exploits belong to the realm of epic fiction, he may have been based on a twelfth-century warrior known as Chobitko, who earned this name for beating his enemies with a *chobot* (boot). Later in life, Chobitko became a monk in Kiev and was canonized in 1643 as Saint Ilya Muromets.

While little is known of Chobitko's life, records do mention a peasant upbringing and paralysis as a youth. He was a member of the royal bodyguard and fought against the Tatars until he eventually retired and took up a life devoted to religion. When his remains were examined in 1988, scholars found that he was above average height and had an incurable spine defect. Examination of his wounds showed that Chobitko may have been killed when the Mongols besieged Kiev in 1204.

The great amount of evidence of Ilya's existence has helped make him a very popular character. Since being canonized in the seventeenth century, Ilya has remained a very popular saint among Russians. He has been the protagonist of many works of literature, films, works of art, and even cartoons. The residents of the village of Karacharof, believed to be Ilya's birthplace—Ilya Muromets's name comes from the nearest town, Murom—consider themselves direct descendants of the hero.

Several recurring themes and narrative structures appear in the tale of Ilya and the dragon. One prominent example is the rule of three, in which the protagonist is tasked with three challenges or obstacles. This appears frequently in folklore and fairy tales. Ilya must take three trips with the pitchers of water to heal his legs and gain strength, and when he begins his journey, he must select from three paths and overcome three obstacles (two witches and the Nightingale). In other versions of the tale, three pilgrims make thirty-three-year-old Ilya strong.

The Baba Yaga who appears in this story is one of the most famous beings in Russian folklore. Her name is used as a general term for a witch; typically she is depicted as an old woman who lives deep in the forest inside a house with a hidden front door. When visitors reach out to her for help, she either aids them or hinders their journey. Here, both incarnations of Baba Yaga help Ilya achieve his goal to slay the dragon and marry the czar's daughter.

Patrick G. Cooper

BIBLIOGRAPHY

Avanova, Tatyana, and James Bailey, trans. *An Anthology of Russian Folk Epics*. Armonk: Sharpe, 1998. Print.

Balina, Marina, Helena Goscilo, and Mark Lipovetsky, eds. *Politicizing Magic: An Anthology of Russian and Soviet Tales*. Evanston: Northwestern UP, 2005. Print.

Hapgood, Isabel Florence. *The Epic Songs of Russia*. 1916. New York: Scribner, 1969. Print.

Johns, Andreas. *Baba Yaga: The Ambiguous Mother and Witch of the Russian Folktale*. New York: Lang, 2004. Print.

◆ King Kojata

Author: Andrew Lang
Time Period: 1851 CE–1900 CE
Country or Culture: Russia
Genre: Fairy Tale

PLOT SUMMARY

King Kojata lives a happy life with his queen, and the couple's only grievance is that they have been unable to produce an heir. One day, while King Kojata is touring his land, he grows thirsty. He comes to a spring with a jug floating in it, but when he tries to grab the jug, it eludes him. The king decides to drink straight from the spring, but when he lowers his head, a creature grabs his beard and refuses to let go. The creature says he will only release the king if he promises to give the creature something that will be waiting for him when he returns home.

Unable to fathom what the creature could mean, the king agrees to his condition. When he returns home, he is shocked to discover that his queen has given birth to a son, Prince Milan. Realizing that he will have to give away his son, King Kojata keeps his promise a secret. Years go by, and the prince grows into a young man. One day, while he is in the woods, an old man appears before the prince and tells him about the deal his father had made. The prince returns home and tells his father what the old man said. The king finally admits the truth, and determined to make good on the promise, the prince sets out to find the creature.

Eventually, the prince comes to a lake where he finds clothes strewn along the shore and thirty ducks swimming. The prince takes one set of clothes and hides in the bushes. When the ducks come ashore, they change into women and clothe themselves, but the thirtieth duck remains in the water until the prince returns her clothing to her. She explains that she is Hyacinthia, the youngest daughter of the creature, and that she will help the prince in his dealings with her father.

After Prince Milan arrives in the creature's underground realm, the creature assigns him the seemingly impossible task of building a marble palace in one night and warns that the prince will lose his head if he does not comply. The despairing prince goes to his room, and Hyacinthia comes to him in the form of a bee. She promises she will build the palace for him, and miraculously, she does. The creature then demands that the prince pick out his youngest daughter from the rest of his identical brood. Hyacinthia aids the prince by placing a fly on her cheek so that she can be identified. The prince is then ordered to make the creature a pair of boots. The prince and the young woman have no shoemaking skills, so they flee.

The creature's servants chase after them, so Hyacinthia first turns herself into a river and the prince into a bridge and then transforms them into a thick forest with many paths. The servants become lost and turn back. The creature himself then gives chase, so Hyacinthia, knowing her father will not be able to pass a church, turns herself into a church and the prince into a monk. Disguised as the monk, the prince tells the creature that they had passed by, so he turns back.

Prince Milan and Hyacinthia come to a city. The prince insists on visiting the city's king and queen, but the young woman warns him not to kiss their child, for if he does so he will forget her. He kisses the child anyway, and the heartbroken Hyacinthia turns herself into a

flower in the hope of being trampled. An old man picks her, however, and takes her home. Eventually, she turns back into a young woman and tells the old man about her predicament. He explains that the prince is about to marry, so Hyacinthia puts two doves inside the wedding cake. The doves cause the prince to remember everything that had happened, and he runs to meet Hyacinthia. Together, they return to King Kojata's kingdom.

SIGNIFICANCE

"King Kojata" is a Russian fairy tale made popular by Scottish writer and anthropologist Andrew Lang, who published the tale in his 1892 collection *The Green Fairy Book*. Lang later published a shorter variant titled "The Unlooked-For Prince" in his 1900 collection *The Grey Fairy Book*. There is also a Polish variant known by the title "Prince Unexpected," which was collected by scholar Albert Henry Wratislaw in his book *Sixty Folk-Tales from Exclusively Slavonic Sources* (1889).

The fairy tale contains several motifs found throughout world mythology and folklore, including that of a child who is unwittingly promised by one of the parents in exchange for something else. As in the case of King Kojata, the parent is often deceived into promising away his or her child. Another prevalent recurring motif found in this fairy tale is the transformation chase, in which a character shape-shifts in order to evade a pursuer, typically taking on several different forms during a single chase. In this story, it is Hyacinthia who transforms herself and the prince to elude the creature and his servants. Other variations of the transformation chase include shape-shifting in order to lift a curse, dodge a spell, or become powerful enough to defeat a foe. Hyacinthia also shape-shifts so that she can sneak away to the prince's room and aid him in accomplishing his tasks.

Hyacinthia is particularly interesting in that she fills a traditional fairy-tale role yet, unlike female characters in many beloved stories, is not particularly weak or submissive. Traditionally, women in fairy tales were often depicted as fragile damsels in distress or as evil witches. This female character, however, performs more heroics than the prince does. The prince cannot accomplish his impossible tasks without her, and she again saves his life during the transformation chase. Hyacinthia acts as the prince's romantic interest and magical helper, but at the same time, she is also the true hero of the story.

Patrick G. Cooper

BIBLIOGRAPHY

Bettelheim, Bruno. *The Uses of Enchantment: The Meaning and Importance of Fairy Tales*. New York: Vintage, 2010. Print.

Bottigheimer, Ruth B. *Fairy Tales: A New History*. New York: State U of New York P, 2009. Print.

Haase, Donald, ed. *Fairy Tales and Feminism: New Approaches*. Detroit: Wayne State UP, 2004. Print.

Lang, Andrew, ed. "King Kojata." *The Green Fairy Book*. London: Longmans, 1899. 202–15. Print.

---, ed. "The Unlooked-For Prince." *The Grey Fairy Book*. London: Longmans, 1900. 300–308. Print.

The Lime Tree

Author: Traditional
Time Period: 1851 CE–1900 CE
Country or Culture: Russia
Genre: Folktale

PLOT SUMMARY

Vanyusha is sitting with his grandfather one day and asks him why bears' paws are similar to the hands and feet of humans. The grandfather tells him a tale that was passed down from ancient people explaining that bears were once like the Orthodox Christians they are now.

The grandfather recounts that a poor peasant lived in a cottage with no horses or livestock and no wood to warm his house in the winter. When the cold came, the peasant took his ax and went into the woods to cut his own firewood. He came across an enchanted lime tree and prepared to cut it down.

He struck the tree with his ax, and the lime tree spoke in a human voice. The tree stated that he could give the cottager anything he wanted, including riches and a wife. The peasant asked that the lime tree make him wealthier than all of the peasants in his village, and the lime tree told him to go home and find all that he wished for. The peasant returned home and discovered a new house with horses and storerooms full of corn. He was not impressed, however, with the wife the lime tree had provided him. She was not beautiful enough for him, so he decided to ask the lime tree for a better-looking bride.

The lime tree granted his wish, and when the peasant returned home, he found a satisfactory wife. Together, the peasant and his wife lived comfortably, but he soon began to long for authority in addition to wealth.

He returned to the lime tree and asked it to make him the head of his borough; the lime tree complied and the peasant was granted the position. Still unsatisfied, however, the peasant once again returned to the lime tree and asked it to make him a lord. The peasant was content with this for a bit, but while he enjoyed throwing parties for other gentlemen in his position, he soon longed to become an official.

Again, the peasant visited the lime tree, and once again, the tree granted his desire, albeit more impatiently this time. As before, the peasant's new title did not satisfy him for long, and he was soon asking the tree to make him a lord-lieutenant. The lime tree stated that this request was difficult to fulfill, but it begrudgingly elevated the peasant to an even loftier title. He was given a state of inheritance and enjoyed great riches with this position. The peasant quickly became discontent, finally wishing to be made a king. So, once again, he returned to the lime tree to make his request. The lime tree tried to persuade him to recant that wish, explaining that the peasant should reflect on where he started out and be content with how rich and powerful he had become. But even when the lime tree asserted that only God could choose the king, the peasant continued to insist. Frustrated, the lime tree declared that this wish was impossible; it took back everything he had given before angrily turning the peasant and his wife into bears.

The grandfather explains to Vanyusha that the moral of the story is to be content with what you have, because greed and desire will cause you to lose everything.

SIGNIFICANCE

"The Lime Tree" is a Slavonic moral story containing some fantastical elements such as a talking tree and transformations. It was made popular by A. H. Wratislaw in his collection *Sixty Folk-Tales from Exclusively Slavonic Stories*, published in 1890. In his introduction to the story, Wratislaw explains that it is a variation of the Brothers Grimm tale "The Fisherman and His Wife," in which a poor fisherman's wife repeatedly coaxes him into asking a magical flounder to grant them wishes. When the wife asks to become God, the flounder takes everything he has given them away, much like what happens to the peasant in this story.

There are several other variations of this tale of discontent and greed, including one from Japan involving a stonecutter and a spirit and one from Russia involving an old man and a fish. While "The Lime Tree" focuses on one man's greed, other variations involve some amount of marital discord between a husband and his wife, who is typically portrayed as power hungry.

Making and granting wishes is a recurring motif of fairy tales and folklore from all corners of the globe. Mystical creatures such as fairies, demons, and genies typically grant wishes, but sometimes magical items such as rings or, in this case, a lime tree can grant them. Trees have been essential in much of the world's mythologies and religions. They oftentimes were given sacred meanings and depicted as symbols of growth, death, and resurrection. This led to the popular Tree of Life image that is found in several mythologies. Many cultures also have "wish trees," which are individual trees typically designated by locals and presented with offerings for the fulfillment of wishes.

Limes and lime trees also have their significance in mythology, fairy tales, and customs. The heart-shaped lime tree leaf has led the tree to become associated with love and its related symbolism, including fidelity and justice. In Scandinavian mythology, the lime tree is associated with Freya, the goddess of love. The German epic poem "Nibelungenlied" contains a character Sieglinde, which can be translated as "lime tree of victory."

Besides being a morality tale, "The Lime Tree" also acts as a bear creation story, specifically explaining how bears got their humanlike paws. Another famous folktale, "The Bear's Tail," explains why bears do not have tails. Bears appear in a myriad of fairy tales and folktales from around the world, the most famous one being, of course, "Goldilocks and the Three Bears."

Patrick G. Cooper

BIBLIOGRAPHY

Albuisson, Pierre. "The Dance Lime Tree and Its Symbolism." *Tilleuls à Danser*. Trans. Marcia Hadjimarkos. Tilleuls-a-danser.eu, n.d. PDF file.

Ashliman, D. L., trans. "Dissatisfaction and Greed." *Folklore and Mythology Electronic Texts*. U of Pittsburgh, 22 Mar. 2013. Web. 15 June 2013.

Heiner, Heidi Anne. "The Annotated Fisherman and His Wife." *SurLaLune Fairy Tales*. SurLaLune Fairy Tales, 17 Sept. 2007. Web. 15 June 2013.

Luthi, Max. *The European Folktale: Form and Nature.* Bloomington: Indiana UP, 1986. Print.

Wratislaw, A. H., trans. "The Lime Tree." *Sixty Folk-Tales from Exclusively Slavonic Sources*. Boston: Houghton, 1890. 164–67. Print.

◆ Prince Bayaya

Author: Božena Němcová
Time Period: 1701 CE–1850 CE
Country or Culture: Czech Republic
Genre: Fairy Tale

PLOT SUMMARY

In a European kingdom, a queen gives birth to twin boys while her husband is away at war. The older twin loves to ride on his horse, which is as old as he is. The younger twin prefers to play indoors and quickly becomes his mother's favorite. When the twins are seven, their father returns home. The queen lies to her husband, telling him that her favorite son is actually their firstborn child. This makes the younger son heir to the throne. At seventeen, the older twin decides to leave home. To his surprise, his horse speaks to him and encourages him to strike out on his own.

The prince and his horse ride off until they come to a magic rock. The horse strikes the rock three times with its hooves. The rock opens and reveals a stable inside. The horse instructs the prince to disguise himself and enter the service of the king of a nearby city. If the prince needs help, he should approach the rock and hit it three times. The prince puts on an eye patch and pretends to be mute. The local king hires him out of pity. Because he is mute and ugly in his disguise, the widowed king allows Bayaya to entertain his three daughters, Zdobena, Budinka, and Slavena.

One day the king reveals his predicament to Bayaya. Many years prior, three dragons had threatened the kingdom. To ward off their attack, the king promised to give the dragons his three daughters once they reached womanhood. Now the dragons have returned to demand their sacrifice. Bayaya goes to the rock, strikes it three times, and reveals the problem to his horse. His horse tells him that it was because of the dragons that he brought Bayaya to this kingdom. The horse tells Bayaya to come back the next morning. When Bayaya returns, the horse instructs him to unearth a chest, which is filled with three outfits and a shining sword fit for a knight.

When Zdobena arrives at the rock to be sacrificed to the first dragon, Bayaya appears, nicely dressed and riding his horse. He slays the dragon and rides off before anyone can speak to him. Bayaya slays the second dragon on the second day, saving Budinka. On the third day, Bayaya slays the third dragon to save Slavena. Slavena approaches the knight to thank him, but the horse runs off before Bayaya can speak

Soon afterward, a neighboring kingdom declares war. The king summons all his nobles and promises his daughters to those who help him. They all march off to battle. Bayaya goes to the magic rock. His horse tells him to join the battle the next day in a white suit. Bayaya fights valiantly, defeating the enemy and helping to end the war. Bayaya is injured during the fighting, and the king uses a piece of his cape to wrap the wound. Before the king can thank the white knight for his help, Bayaya and his horse ride off.

With the war won, the king decides to select husbands for his daughters from all the nobles who fought for him. From the palace balcony, each princess will throw a golden apple at the noblemen, who are all lined up below. Whoever receives the apple will marry that princess. Bayaya takes his place inconspicuously at the end of the line.

Zdobena and Budinka throw their apples first. They land at Bayaya's feet, but he slyly kicks them toward two other lucky suitors. However, Slavena's apple rolls straight to Bayaya's feet, and he picks it up. Slavena is distraught that she has to marry an ugly mute. On their wedding night, Bayaya's horse bids him farewell. When Bayaya enters Slavena's chambers, the princess recognizes him as the shining knight who rescued her and her sisters and is overjoyed. The newlyweds soon travel to Bayaya's kingdom. There, Bayaya discovers that his brother has died, and Bayaya becomes king.

SIGNIFICANCE

In its original Czech, "Prince Bayaya" was first published in 1848 in the collection of Czech fairy tales *Národní báchorky a powěsti* (National tales and legends) by Božena Němcová. The Austrian Czech author Němcová strongly identified with her mother's Czech heritage and was a key figure in the Czech national revival. During Němcová's lifetime, the region that became the Czech Republic in 1993 was part of the Austrian empire. Němcová began collecting, transcribing, and editing Czech fairy tales such as the story of Prince Bayaya. Many scholars believe Němcová often inserted her own creative ideas into these traditional fairy tales, which in a sense became her own work. Němcová's version of "Prince Bayaya" is thought to be an amalgamation of several shorter tales.

American writer Parker Fillmore included his English translation of the story of Prince Bayaya in the anthology *Czechoslovak Fairy Tales* (1919). Fillmore admits that he altered the stories somewhat to appeal to the tastes of American children. Although not a literal translation, Fillmore's rendition of "Prince Bayaya" remains one of the most accessible versions of this Czech fairy tale in English.

Significantly, "Prince Bayaya" incorporates many popular elements of European fairy tales in its elaborate story of a slighted prince who eventually finds happiness. In so doing, "Prince Bayaya" illustrates well the form and function of traditional fairy tales. For example, "Prince Bayaya" begins with the common European fairy tale motif of a young protagonist who is cheated out of his birthright. He finds the support of a magical, anthropomorphic animal, another common element of traditional European fairy tales.

From an archetypal point of view, Prince Bayaya embarks on a quest leading to his rite of passage. By accepting the demand of his loyal supernatural horse, who insists that that Bayaya humble himself in the service of a foreign king, Bayaya temporarily loses his elevated social status. He is symbolically wounded by his disguise as pale, one-eyed, and mute youth. Through this plot element, the fairy tale expresses the collective hope that any real disadvantaged person may rise up in life.

In his true identity, Prince Bayaya is a shining knight. Slaying dragons, Bayaya rescues the three princesses. From a psychological view, Prince Bayaya's fulfillment of his desires is delayed until he has reached full adulthood. This is illustrated by his horse's condition that he not reveal his true identity until all of his tasks are accomplished. For its happy ending, "Prince Bayaya" relies on the motif of a fortunate marriage and the final assumption of the prince's birthright.

R. C. Lutz, PhD

BIBLIOGRAPHY

Fillmore, Parker. "Prince Bayaya." *Czechoslovak Fairy Tales*. New York: Harcourt, 1919. 77–98. Print.

Francikova, Dasa. „Female Friends in Nineteenth-Century Bohemia: Troubles with Affectionate Writing and 'Patriotic Relationships.'" *Journal of Women's History* 12.3 (2000): 23–28. Print.

Iggers, Wilma Abeles. *Women of Prague*. Providence: Berghahn, 1995. Print.

Němcová, Božena. *The Grandmother*. Trans. Gregor Frances. Prague: Vitalis, 2006. Print.

Součková, Milada. *The Czech Romantics*. The Hague: Mouton, 1958. Print.

Princess Miranda and Prince Hero

Author: Traditional
Time Period: 1851 CE–1900 CE
Country or Culture: Poland
Genre: Fairytale

PLOT SUMMARY

A beautiful princess named Miranda lives on an island with twelve loyal maidens. Visitors to the island speak of Miranda's incredible beauty, and over time she gains a number of subjects as well as a palace of white marble in which to live. Many princes travel to the island to woo her, but she is not interested in any of them. If any of the princes become forceful in their advances, Miranda turns them to ice with her gaze. She dreams of a young, gallant knight who will be her husband.

One day the king of the underground realm, Kosciey, emerges from his kingdom and surveys the upper realms. With a telescope he gazes at Miranda's island, where he sees the marble palace and Miranda, who is sound asleep. Kosciey is struck by her beauty and transports himself to the island. As he advances on Miranda's palace, she calls together her army to fight against him. But Kosciey has poisonous breath and uses it to put Miranda's army to sleep. He closes in on the princess, so she uses her gaze to turn the wicked man to ice and quickly retreats to her palace.

Kosciey escapes from the ice and uses his breath to make all of the inhabitants of the island fall asleep, except Miranda. Afraid to get too close to her because of her icy gaze, Kosciey surrounds her palace with an iron rampart and stations a twelve-headed dragon to guard the gate. Months pass, and Miranda's kingdom becomes a desert. Plants grow around her sleeping army as their armor rusts. The princess takes refuge in a room inside a palace tower and pleads to the stars, moon, and sun for help.

The sun tells her to take comfort, for her savior and lover who appeared in her dreams, Prince Hero, is coming from the bottom of the sea to defeat Kosciey. Then the sun speaks to Hero and explains to him that Kosciey cannot be defeated by normal means. The sun tells Hero where to find a mace and a magical horse that will take him to an old woman named Jandza, who alone can tell him how to defeat Kosciey and save Miranda's kingdom.

Prince Hero finds the mace and magical horse behind iron doors in an eastern field. The horse speaks to Hero and tells him that the magical mace will strike unseen wherever he commands. Hero mounts the steed, and they arrive before sunset at the home of Jandza in an ancient forest. The old woman explains to Hero how he can defeat Kosciey. She tells him that he must go to the island of Everlasting Life, where he will find an oak tree under which is buried a coffer that contains a hare who is sitting atop a gray duck. Inside the duck is an egg, and in that egg is the life of Kosciey. When Hero breaks the egg, Kosciey will die.

The magical horse leads Hero to the island of Everlasting Life, where he finds the coffer, takes out the hare by its ears, and retrieves the egg from the duck. When he travels to Miranda's island, the twelve-headed dragon is still guarding the gate, so Hero commands the mace to kill the beast. It strikes a thousand blows until the dragon finally tears itself apart with its own claws. Once Hero enters the palace, Kosciey attacks and overpowers him. Hero crushes the egg, and Kosciey instantly falls dead.

The enchanter's spell is broken, and the denizens of the island wake up. Prince Hero and Princess Miranda are married, and the whole island feasts, dances, and rejoices.

SIGNIFICANCE

The fairy tale of Princess Miranda and Prince Hero was first collected by author A. J. Gliński in his book *Polish Fairy Tales* (1862). The stories were originally told to Gliński by the peasants of the eastern provinces of Poland, and scholars believe many of the tales date back to primitive times. Many of the stories are remarkably similar to German, Celtic, and Indian folktales.

The fairy tale is a fairly straightforward story of the forces of good conquering the forces of evil, but scholars have interpreted the story as an allegory of Poland, which for years was oppressed by German militarism. The character of Princess Miranda, therefore, symbolizes the spirit of Poland as she surveys all of the despair and devastation around her and waits for a hero. Prince Hero is a typical Prince Charming, a stock character found frequently in fairy tales and folklore. This formulaic hero completes an arduous quest in order to rescue the princess from an evil being.

Polish folklore often contains elements of witchcraft, and Jandza, Prince Hero's magical benefactor, appears frequently in various forms throughout Polish and Russian fairy tales. Her name translates to "fury," but variations of the name appear in different languages and commonly translate into something close to "old witch." She is often depicted as a powerful witch and a goddess of wisdom and death who is mostly benevolent and who helps those who are able to find her. Her house rests atop chicken legs, and the door is always hidden from those who try to come inside.

Dragons are also prominent in Polish folklore and tales from other European cultures. The Wawel dragon that was said to terrorize ancient Kraków is the most famous dragon of Polish legend. Much like the twelve-headed dragon of the fairy tale of Princess Miranda and Prince Hero, dragons in European folklore were generally depicted as evil. This is in sharp contrast to Asian dragons, which were often benign creatures. It was not until modern times that European dragons were depicted in literature and film in a more positive light.

Patrick G. Cooper

BIBLIOGRAPHY

Asala, Joanne. *Polish Folklore and Myth*. Iowa City: Penfield, 2001. Print.

Johns, Andreas. *Baba Yaga: The Ambiguous Mother and Witch of the Russian Folktale*. New York: Lang, 2004. Print.

Knab, Sophie Hodorowicz. *Polish Customs, Traditions, and Folklore*. New York: Hippocrene, 1999. Print.

Lüthi, Max. *The European Folktale: Form and Nature*. Bloomington: Indiana UP, 1986. Print.

Monte, Richard. *The Dragon of Kraków and Other Polish Stories*. London: Lincoln, 2008. Print.

Srna, Jana, et al. "Polish Fairy Tales Translated from A. J. Gliński." *Project Gutenberg*. Project Gutenberg Literary Archive Foundation, 8 July 2011. Web. 4 June 2013.

APPENDIXES

MYTHOLOGY IN THE CLASSROOM

With the great interest in mythology—both classical and comparative—a plethora of books have emerged appealing not only to the general reader but also to teachers and students. The books in this series are part of this profusion. How then are teachers and students to make the best use of the reference works in this series?

In order to evaluate the role that volumes in this series would play in a classroom course, it may be useful to briefly outline the goals and challenges in teaching a mythology course. There are basically two major approaches. At a minimal level students should become competent in recognizing the stories, characteristics, and attributes (many instructors would include visual representations here) of mythological characters. Such competency should also allow students to recognize allusions from later literature and art to contemporary political slogans and commercials. Here, textbooks with summaries of the stories would serve the purpose. Through this basic recognition of the stories and allusions it is argued that students will improve their reading and understanding of texts. The second approach is to read translations of the primary texts of mythology. This approach teaches a different type of reading in which students encounter multiple levels of meaning, nonlinear presentation, archaic thought patterns, and so forth. Such an approach is challenging both for students and teachers.

Other challenges confront instructors of mythology courses. These courses call upon instructors to be knowledgeable in more areas of expertise than any other course that they teach: language and literature, myth theory, archeology and art, history, anthropology, and psychology, to name a few. In comparative or world myth courses, instructors often teach stories that are outside their field of expertise. How then do the volumes of this series address these goals and challenges?

A brief overview of the format of each volume gives a starting point in answering this question. Each volume consists of articles summarizing and analyzing myths, fairy tales, legends, sagas, and folktales on a certain theme (e.g., love, heroes) from various cultures around the world. Each article, where possible, highlights an interpretative or theoretical approach. Part of the article focuses on cross-cultural comparisons and closely analyzes at least one retelling of the tale in art, film, music, and so forth.

COMPARATIVE MYTHOLOGY

Given the diversity of the texts and genres, these volumes would appeal more to a comparative mythology course rather than to a classical mythology class, although instructors in the latter course could still refer their students to relevant articles on Greco-Roman myths. In comparing myths from different cultures, scholars have focused on accounting for the similarities between them. In this respect, many myth courses outline two basic approaches: diffusion and similar thought patterns. The diffusionist approach received its greatest impetus from the discovery of the Indo-European languages in the late 1700s and the subsequent development of I-E linguistics in the following century. Just as linguists could compare words and grammatical and syntactical forms and attempt to reconstruct a protolanguage, those analyzing mythology also hoped to work out relations between mythologies. The method often involves locating common elements that are unique to the two myths being compared. An example would be the birds sent out in the Mesopotamian and biblical flood stories. If enough of these unique common elements can be found, then a genetic relationship can be posited about the two myths. The other approach postulates that the similarities between myths arise from similar thought patterns. Thus Carl Jung posited the universal unconscious and its archetypes, and Joseph Campbell regarded myths as following his monomythic pattern. Yet interpreters of mythology must also take context into account (and the best interpreters of either stripe do). Sources need to be evaluated; learning as much as one can about the dating, storytellers, and audience is a necessity. Differences between the stories should also be explored in detail (discussed below under Interpretative Approaches).

For a comparative mythology course, the articles in these volumes could serve as a basis for the exploration of a theme. Whether the student has been reading primary sources or a summary of the tale, the article furnishes a starting point for obtaining a deeper understanding of the story under consideration. The articles are written by scholars knowledgeable in their respective fields. This aspect of expertise is one of the major challenges in the teaching of comparative mythology, as noted above. Apart from calling in colleagues who are experts in their fields, such articles as are found here fulfill this pressing need. They show how a scholar who studies the culture from which the story arises interprets the tale. Clearly understanding the ways in which the culture understood the story is the first step in any comparison. The articles also give references for further reading so that students can explore the tale from different perspectives.

Once the myth has been explored in detail from the culture's viewpoint, the volumes offer various comparisons. The summary versions allow students to look for other similar stories without having to read the often longer primary sources. The subdivisions of the themes (e.g., lover's quest, tales of transformation, animal lovers) allow the student to focus on a more detailed comparison. From the articles, the students then could go to the primary sources, again gaining from the article a preliminary understanding of how the myths are or were understood within their cultures.

Summary versions of the myth, fairy tale, legend, or folktale also allow the students to encounter the tale in multiple versions. Primary sources often do not present a complete version of the tale but rather focus on a part. Summaries can provide an overall presentation with variations. Students then would be able to choose the most interesting source or version for comparison. As each version may have different emphases, it is crucial for students to understand not only how the story is interpreted within the culture, but also how the culture's understanding of the tale has developed and evolved over time. The later versions of the story also show how later generations have adapted the tale or another culture has assimilated the tale into their culture.

INTERPRETATIVE APPROACHES

As noted earlier, the authors of the articles, where possible, have highlighted their interpretive or theoretical approach. These include the following theories: nature, etiological, ritual, charter, Freudian, Jungian, and structuralist theories. Folktales as well as many myths and other tales are also analyzable in terms of Vladimir Propp's "wonder tale" pattern, and hero stories can be fit into Campbell's or other hero patterns. Folklorists have cataloged the different types of folktales. Feminist analyses also abound. These theories are universalist, i.e., *all* myths are explained by the theory. However, most instructors employ an eclectic approach in which several theories are used in interpreting a myth. Since myths are multivalent, theories are applicable at different levels in the story. Thus, for example, the Demeter-Persephone story can be examined in connection with nature theory (goddess as explanation for the growth of vegetation),

etiological theory (origin of seasons), ritual theory (origin of the Eleusinian Mysteries and in relation to marriage), and psychological theories (e.g., Jung's great mother archetype).

However, many universalist approaches often focus on similarities and force disparate material into a "one-mould-fits-all" pattern. Thus, some recent scholarship has reacted against these universalist theories, arguing that context and culture-specific aspects of a tale are undermined by such approaches. In these reactions, differences play just as important a role as similarities. In fact, differences may be of great interest in revealing aspects of a culture not found in the other culture being compared.[1]

In the end, however, a middle ground between similarities and differences would offer a productive way of comparing myths. After all, there must be some basic similarity to compare. Differences would then provide a more nuanced comparison. The articles deal with both universalist and culture-specific approaches. Students will thus be able to choose the most interesting method to follow in comparing the tales.

FAIRY TALES IN THE COLLEGE CLASSROOM

The inclusion of fairy and other tales, in contrast to myth, will also offer the student interesting comparisons. Much of the study of the fairy tale and folklore has focused on identifying types and motifs within the tales. Developing from the work of Antti Aarne and Stith Thompson, folklorists have been cataloging the stories of the world into type and motif. Unfortunately, this scholarly revolution has for the most part bypassed studies in classical mythology.[2] In this respect, the inclusion of fairy tales in this volume in part provides an opportunity to assimilate the findings of folklorists.

While distinctions between these genres are made, folktale story patterns often appear in other genres. Thus, a definition of a fairy tale or folktale might include that it takes place in the timeless past ("once upon a time"), has protagonists with common names (e.g., Jack), and contains helpers (e.g., fairies, magical objects) and hinderers (e.g., ogres). A myth, however, might be defined as a story about the gods and heroes from a definite locale, and so on. Nevertheless, similar story patterns turn up in both genres. For example, the Oedipus myth is type 931 (hereafter AT 931) in Aarne and Thompson's 1961 publication *The Types of the Folktale*. Although it is often difficult to determine whether there are any tendencies in stories moving from one genre to another, William Hansen in *Ariadne's Thread* (2002) has argued that "genre variance" usually moves from folktales (indefinite place and time) to legend or myth in a definite place (e.g., Oedipus in Thebes).[3] As folklorists have cataloged various traditional genres from around the world, the analysis of stories into types and motifs offers a thorough method to find comparisons.

One example may be given here. The story of Cupid and Psyche in Lucius Apuleius's *Metamorphoses* has often been regarded as "the most fairy tale–like of all ancient stories." Even with its mythological coloring (e.g., the god Cupid as the male protagonist and the goddess Venus filling the role of the witch or evil stepmother), the story can be clearly classified as AT 425B (*The Disenchanted Husband*), a subtype of AT 425 (*The Search for the Lost Husband*). In AT 425B, a marriage is arranged for the heroine to an enchanted husband; a taboo is imposed by the husband, but the bride violates this and thus loses her husband. In her search for her husband, the heroine meets a witch-goddess who imposes seemingly impossible tasks upon her. With the help of her husband or others, she accomplishes these tasks and wins him back. An examination of AT 425B will lead the student to numerous parallels from around the world. Then the student will be able to explore themes found in these parallels, e.g., the theme of anxiety over arranged marriages—it is not surprising that another subtype of AT 425 is AT 425A (*The Monster [Animal] as Bridegroom*), the Beauty and the Beast theme (which has its own subtype, AT 425C). Again, the differences must be explored as well. Another interesting theme to explore is that these stories focus on women and were told by women. An old woman relates the tale of Cupid and Psyche in Apuleius, describing it as one of her "old women's tales," the precursor of "old wives' tales." Much feminist criticism has focused on female storytellers and the themes connected with women (e.g., arranged marriages, incest). While we must be careful not to project more recent ideas into the past, the examination of similar stories in a variety of genres offers students a mutually illuminating way to approach these stories.[4]

These then are some ways in which these volumes may be incorporated into a mythology course.

NOTES

1. See Bruce Lincoln's essay, "Theses on Comparison," in his *Gods and Demons, Priests and Scholars: Critical Explorations in the History of Religions* (2012), pages 121 to 130. See also Daya Krishna's essay, "Comparative Philosophy: What It Is and What It Ought to Be," in *Interpreting across Boundaries: New Essays in Comparative Philosophy*, edited by Gerald J. Larson and Eliot Deutsch (1988), pages seventy-one to eighty-three. While the latter is strictly about philosophy, much of Krishna's arguments are relevant for comparative studies in general.

2. See William F. Hansen's essay, "Mythology and Folktale Typology: Chronicle of a Failed Scholarly Revolution," in the *Journal of Folklore Research*, volume thirty-four (1997), pages 275 to 280.

3. William F. Hansen, *Ariadne's Thread: A Guide to International Tales Found in Classical Literature* (2002). See pages eight to nine on genre variance and pages fifteen to sixteen on the movement of story patterns from folktale to legend or myth.

4. The material in this paragraph is indebted to Hansen's (supra note three) analysis of AT 425 and the Cupid and Psyche story on pages one hundred to 114. He summarizes four parallel stories and cites the literature that will lead students to further sources. Marina Warner's *From the Beast to the Blonde: On Fairy Tales and their Tellers* (1994), among others, explores the Cupid and Psyche story in light of the Beauty and Beast theme, focusing on the role of the heroine as well as female storytellers. See in particular chapters two and seventeen.

LESSON PLAN

CREATION STORIES: A COMPARATIVE ANALYSIS

Students analyze the origin of humans and the natural world in Maya and Egyptian creation myths. In addition, students analyze metaphor and language in the representation of the human and natural world.

Materials: E. A. Wallis Budge's "The Legend of the God Neb-er-tcher, and the History of Creation"; Dennis Tedlock's *Popol Vuh*, Part 4.

Overview Questions

Every culture in the world is rooted in multiple creation myths to explain the beginnings of the human, animal, and natural world. These primordial questions often ground spiritual or religious belief. What is the mythic message these creation stories tell of their cultures?

Discussion Questions

1. How is the form of storytelling different in the selections from "The Legend of the God Neb-er-tcher" and the *Popol Vuh*? Who are the speakers?

2. In creation myths, the use of metaphor often attributes human characteristics to nature or the animal world. What human characteristics are used? What perspectives on creation are depicted in these metaphors?

3. In the two creation myths, what is the relationship between the human and natural worlds? Are they in harmony or disjunction? Which animals are mentioned in the stories? How are they depicted?

4. What is the order of phenomena in the human and nonhuman spheres? What is atop this order? What place does the earth hold in this order?

5. The stories of Neb-er-tcher and of the Maya creator gods depict differing powers of creation and destruction. Is creation a benevolent or violent event in these stories? Why?

6. Creation myths often speak to human truths of love, fear, and power. What is the spiritual (or spirit) dimension described in the stories?

Comparative Study

How do these creation myths compare with stories of creation in your own cultural background? The story of Neb-er-tcher and the *Popol Vuh* are rooted in a divine relation between nature and the human world. What is the significance of the natural word in creation myths in your culture?

Response Paper

Word length and additional requirements set by Instructor. Students answer the research question in the Overview Questions. Students state a thesis and use as evidence passages from the primary source document as well as support from supplemental materials assigned in the lesson.

TIMELINE

BCE	
4000–2270	Sumerian civilization begins
3000–1500	Minoan period in Greece
2649–2181	Old Kingdom in Egypt
2600–2470	Reign of Gilgameš (Gilgamesh), first dynasty of Uruk
2055–1650	Middle Kingdom in Egypt
1792–1750	Hammurabi's reign, height of Babylonian Empire
1600–1100	Bronze Age in Greece
1540–1070	Olmec civilization in Central America
1500	Aryans invade India; Vedic period begins
1360	The Assyrians conquer the lands of Mesopotamia
1250	Moses leads Israelite slaves from Egypt, establishes monotheistic worship at Mt. Sinai (formerly sacred to the Mesopotamian moon god Sîn)
1200–1000	Earliest Hindu literature, the *Rig-Veda*
1200–900	Early Vedic period
1100	Trojan War
900–600	Late Vedic period
800–700	Birth and life of Homer, the Greek epic poet
600–400	Athens is the center of Greece
599–500	Laozi (Lao-Tzu), founder of Daoism (Taoism), active in China
590–527	Birth and life of Mahāvīra, founder of Jainism
563–483	Birth and life of Siddhartha Gautama, the Buddha, founder of Buddhism
551–479	Konguzi (Confucius)
509–31	The Roman Republic
500	Purāṇas, Hindu religious texts, begin to be compiled
356–323	Birth and life of Alexander the Great
31	Roman Empire is established
CE	
30–33	Jesus of Nazareth preaches in Galilee
200–300	Hindu tales of the *Pañcatantra* (*Panchatantra*) composed
250–900	Maya civilization in Central America
400–499	King Arthur, legendary Briton ruler, active in British Isles
476	The Roman Empire falls
500–600	Teotihuacán, Mesoamerican city, grows to 200,000 and influences rest of Mesoamerica

528	Buddhism is officially recognized as the state religion in Silla on the Korean Peninsula
570–682	Birth and life of the prophet Muhammad, founder of Islam
593–622	Prince Shōtoku writes his commentaries on the Buddhist sutras in Japan
629–645	Xuanzang (Hsüan-tsang) travels to India and Southeast Asia, advancing the spread of Buddhism
632–750	Islam spreads to the Near East, North Africa, Spain, and France
700–800	Swahili culture emerges on the East African coast
700–1000	The Viking Age of expansion in Europe, North Atlantic islands, and Asia Minor
762–1055	Founded by the Abbasid caliphate, Baghdad is cultural center of the Islamic world
796–804	Single volumes of the Bible that include the Old and New Testaments begin to be published in France
800	*The Book of Kells* is created in Ireland
850	Ife, in contemporary Nigeria, flourishes as a center of Yoruba culture
850–860	The first version of "Cinderella" composed in China
900–1050	*Beowulf* is recorded by Anglo-Saxon scribes in the British Isles
900-1100	Topiltzin-Quetzalcóatl, legendary Toltec ruler, active in Central America
1000	The Puranic age of Hindu literature ends
1090–1150	The Iroquois Confederacy in North America forges the Great Law of Peace
1325–1521	Aztec empire in Central America
1350–1400	*Sir Gawain and the Green Knight* composed by unknown author in England
1438–1532	Inca Empire in South America
1492	Christopher Columbus explores Hispaniola
1518–1521	Hernán Cortés conquers the Aztec Empire
1623	William Shakespeare's collection of plays are published in the First Folio
1634–1636	Giambattista Basile publishes *Lo cunto de li cunti* (The tale of tales) in Italy
1697	Marie-Catherine d'Aulnoy introduces the term *conte de fées* ("fairy tales") in France
1697	Charles Perrault publishes "Le petit chaperon rouge" ("Little Red Riding Hood") in France
1740	Gabrielle-Suzanne de Villeneuve publishes "La belle et la bête" ("Beauty and the Beast") in France
1812	Jacob and Wilhelm Grimm publish *Kinder- und Hausmärchen* (Children's and household tales) in Germany
1835	Hans Christina Anderson publishes *Eventyr fortalte for børn* (Fairy tales told for children) in Denmark
1889	Andrew Lang publishes *The Blue Fairy Book*, the first of his *Fairy Book* series in England

GUIDE TO ONLINE RESOURCES

Akhet: The Horizon to Ancient Egypt

http://www.akhet.co.uk/mainpage.php

Offers a diverse set of selected texts, including mythology, and photos of masks, sculpture, tombs, and temples. Highly illustrative, the site offers an excellent survey of Egyptian objects.

American Folklore

http://www.americanfolklore.net

Presents a large collection of full-text entries covering all major areas of traditional North American literature. Includes African American, Asian American, and Native American literature, as well as traditional works from Mexico, Latin America, and Canada.

Encyclopedia Mythica

http://www.pantheon.org

Provides A-to-Z reference information on the major mythology and folklore subjects and regions, organized by continent and by major subjects in the literature. The site also offers special sections on bestiary literature, an image gallery, and genealogical tables from various pantheons and prominent houses.

International World History Project

http://history-world.org

Offers introductory articles on all major geographical and cultural areas of interest for background research on ancient civilizations, including Mesopotamia, western and eastern Asia, early Europe, and the Americas.

Internet Sacred Text Archive

http://www.sacred-texts.com

Includes the full text of publications in all major areas of mythology, folklore, and religion, including many esoteric and occult topics across cultures.

Luminarium: Anthology of English Literature

http://www.luminarium.org

Offers full-text selections encompassing the medieval era through the Restoration. Many of the major legends and myths are covered, with an introduction, a list of online texts, and links to study resources.

Perseus Digital Library

http://www.perseus.tufts.edu/hopper/collections

Full-text literature concentrated in the areas of Greek and Roman, German, and Renaissance subjects. Literature varies across the arts, historical periods, and religions.

SurLaLune

http://www.surlalunefairytales.com

An introduction to the major fairy tales and folklore literature. Offering selected full-text entries of many major tales, each title is annotated with its history, a list of similar tales across cultures, and a bibliography. Many articles include a gallery of illustrations and book covers. A forum is available for discussion.

Theoi Greek Mythology

http://www.theoi.com

Contains over 1500 pages on Greek literature, family trees, and illustrations. An excellent resource for primary source literature with introductory material and annotations. The illustration library includes Greek and Roman art from the classical period as well as European paintings and sculpture.

BIBLIOGRAPHY

Aarne, Antti, and Stith Thompson. *The Types of the Folktale: A Classification and Bibliography*. 2nd rev. ed. Helsinki: Academia Scientarum Fennica, 1961. Print.

Abrahams, Roger D. *African Folktales: Traditional Stories of the Black World*. New York: Pantheon, 1983. Print.

Adkins, Arthur. *Merit and Responsibility: A Study in Greek Values*. Oxford: Clarendon, 1960. Print.

Bacchilega, Cristina. "An Introduction to the 'Innocent Persecuted Heroine' Fairy Tale." *Western Folklore* 52.1 (1993): 1–12. Print.

---. *Postmodern Fairy Tales: Gender and Narrative Strategies*. Philadelphia: U of Pennsylvania P, 1997. Print.

Barber, Richard A. *A Companion to World Mythology*. New York: Delacorte, 1979. Print.

Barthes, Roland. "Myth Today." *Mythologies*. Trans. Annette Lavers. New York: Noonday, 1972. 109–59. Print.

Bettelheim, Bruno. *The Uses of Enchantment: The Meaning and Importance of Fairy Tales*. New York: Vintage, 2010. Print.

Bierhorst, John. *The Mythology of Mexico and Central America*. New York: Morrow, 1990. Print.

---. *The Mythology of South America*. New York: Oxford UP, 2002. Print.

Bierlein, John Francis. *Parallel Myths*. New York: Ballantine, 1994. Print.

Black, Jeremy Allen, and Anthony Green. *Gods, Demons, and Symbols of Ancient Mesopotamia: An Illustrated Dictionary*. Austin: U of Texas P, 1992. Print.

Brundage, Burr Cartwright. *Empire of the Inca*. Norman: U of Oklahoma P, 1985. Print.

Budge, Ernest A. Wallis. *The Egyptian Book of the Dead*. New York: Dover, 1967. Print.

---. *Egyptian Tales and Romances*. 1931. New York: Arno, 1980. Print.

Carrasco, Davíd. *City of Sacrifice: The Aztec Empire and the Role of Violence in Civilization*. Boston: Beacon, 1999. Print.

---. *Religions of Mesoamerica: Cosmovision and Ceremonial Centers*. Long Grove: Waveland, 1998. Print.

Carrasco, Davíd, and Scott Sessions. *Daily Life of the Aztecs*. 2nd ed. Santa Barbara: ABC-CLIO, 2011. Print.

Clendennin, Inga. *Aztecs: An Interpretation*. Cambridge: Cambridge UP, 1991. Print.

Colum, Pádraic. *Orpheus: Myths of the World*. New York: Macmillan, 1930. Print.

Dalley, Stephanie, trans. and ed. *Myths from Mesopotamia: Creation, the Flood, Gilgamesh, and Others*. Rev. ed. Oxford: Oxford UP, 2000. Print.

Davies, Bronwyn. *Frogs and Snails and Feminist Tales: Preschool Children and Gender*. London: Allen, 1989. Print.

Des Bouvrie, Synnøve. *Women in Greek Tragedy: An Anthropological Approach*. Oslo: Norwegian UP, 1990. Print.

Dimmit, Cornelia, and J. A. B. van Buitenen, eds. and trans. *Classical Hindu Mythology: A Reader in the Sanskrit Purānas*. Philadelphia: Temple UP, 1978. Print.

Doniger, Wendy. *Splitting the Difference: Gender and Myth in Ancient Greece and India*. Chicago: U of Chicago, 1999. Print.

Dowden, Ken. *The Uses of Greek Mythology*. London: Routledge, 1992. Print.

Ebbutt, M. I. *Hero-Myths & Legends of the British Race*. London: Harrap, 1920. Print.

Evelyn-White, Hugh G., trans. *Hesiod, the Homeric Hymns, and Homerica*. Cambridge: Harvard UP, 1954. Print.

Fee, Christopher R. *Mythology in the Middle Ages: Heroic Tales of Monsters, Magic, and Might*. Santa Barbara: Praeger, 2011. Print.

Garry, Jane, and Hasan El-Shamy, eds. *Archetypes and Motifs in Folklore and Literature: A Handbook*. Armonk: Sharp, 2005. Print.

Greenhill, Pauline, and Sidney Eve Matrix. *Fairy Tale Films: Visions of Ambiguity*. Logan: Utah State UP. 2010. Print.

Griffith, Mari. *Myths and Legends*. New Haven: Yale UP, 2006. Print.

Haase, Donald. "Yours, Mine, or Ours? Perrault, the Brothers Grimm, and the Ownership of Fairy Tales." *Once upon a Folktale: Capturing the Folktale Process with Children*. Ed. Gloria T. Blatt. New York: Teachers College P, 1993. 63–79. Print.

Harries, Elizabeth Wanning. *Twice Upon a Time: Women Writers and the History of the Fairy Tale*. Princeton: Princeton UP, 2001. Print.

Herrera-Sobek, Maria. *Chicano Folklore: A Handbook.* Westport: Greenwood, 2006. Print.

Homer. *The Iliad.* Trans. A. T. Murray. Cambridge: Harvard UP, 1924. Print.

Jacobs, Joseph. *English Fairy Tales.* London: Nutt, 1890. Print.

Jacobsen, Thorkild. *The Treasures of Darkness: A History of Mesopotamian Religion.* New Haven: Yale UP, 1976. Print.

Johnson, W. J. *A Dictionary of Hinduism.* Oxford: Oxford UP, 2009. Print.

Jones, Gwyn, and Thomas Jones, trans. *The Mabinogion.* Rev. ed. London: Dent, 1974. Print.

Jung, Emma, and Marie-Louise von Franz. *The Grail Legend.* Princeton: Princeton UP, 1998. Print.

Kramer, Samuel Noah. *Sumerian Mythology: A Study of Spiritual and Literary Achievement in the Third Millenium B.C.* Rev. ed. Philadelphia: U of Pennsylvania P, 1972. Print.

Lang, Andrew. *The Complete "Fairy Book" Series: Traditional Folk Tales and Fairy Stories from around the World.* Morden, England: Shoes and Ships and Sealing Wax, 2006. Print.

Leeming, David Adams. *Mythology: The Voyage of the Hero.* New York: Oxford UP, 1998. Print.

Lefkowitz, Mary R. *Women in Greek Myth.* Baltimore: Johns Hopkins UP, 2007. Print.

Leick, Gwendolyn. *Sex and Eroticism in Mesopotamian Literature.* London: Routledge, 1994. Print.

León-Portilla, Miguel. *Aztec Thought and Culture: A Study of the Ancient Nahuatl Mind.* Trans. Jack Emory Davis. Norman: U of Oklahoma P, 1990. Print.

Littleton, C. Scott. *Gods, Goddesses and Mythology.* Tarrytown: Cavendish, 2005. Print.

Lyons, Deborah J. *Gender and Immortality: Heroines in Ancient Greek Myth and Cult.* Princeton: Princeton UP, 1996. Print.

Mackenzie, Donald. *Egyptian Myth and Legend.* London: Gresham, 1907. Print.

---. *Myths of Babylonia and Assyria.* London: Gresham, 1915. Print.

Malory, Sir Thomas. *Le Morte Darthur.* Ed. Stephen H. A. Shepherd. New York: Norton, 2004. Print.

Malpass, Michael. *Daily Life in the Inca Empire.* 2nd ed. Westport: Greenwood, 2009. Print

Martin, Richard P. *The Language of Heroes.* Ithaca: Cornell UP, 1989. Print.

McKinnell, John. *Meeting the Other in Norse Myth and Legend.* London: Brewer, 2005. Print.

McLean, Adam. *The Triple Goddess: An Exploration of the Archetypal Feminine.* Grand Rapids: Phanes, 1989. Print.

Mudrooroo. *Aboriginal Mythology.* London: Aquarian, 1994. Print.

Murray, Margaret Alice. *Ancient Egyptian Legends.* London: Murray, 1920. Print.

Ong, Walter S., and John Hartley. *Orality and Literacy: The Technologizing of the Word.* New York: Routledge, 2012. Print.

Ovid. *Metamorphoses.* Trans. A. D. Melville. New York: Oxford UP, 1986. Print.

Penglase, Charles. *Greek Myths and Mesopotamia: Parallels and Influence in the Homeric Hymns and Hesiod.* London: Routledge, 2003. Print.

Philippi, Donald, trans. *The Kojiki.* Tokyo: U of Tokyo P, 1977. Print.

Pinch, Geraldine. *Egyptian Mythology: A Guide to the Gods, Goddesses, and Traditions of Ancient Egypt.* New York: Oxford UP, 2004. Print.

Propp, Vladimir. *Morphology of the Folktale.* 2nd ed. Trans. Laurence Scott. Austin: U of Texas P, 1990. Print.

---. *Theory and History of Folklore.* Trans. Ariadna Y. Martin and Richard P. Martin. Ed. Anatoly Liberman. Minneapolis: U of Minnesota P, 1984. Print.

Rosenberg, Donna. *Folklore, Myths, and Legends: A World Perspective.* Chicago: NTC, 1997. Print.

Rowe, Karen E. "Feminism and Fairy Tales." *Don't Bet on the Prince: Contemporary Feminist Fairy Tales in North America and England.* Ed. Jack Zipes. Aldershot: Gower, 1986. 209–26. Print.

Shattuck, Cybelle. *Hinduism.* New York: Routledge, 1999. Print.

Shaw, Ian, ed. *The Oxford History of Ancient Egypt.* New York: Oxford UP, 2004. Print.

Simpson, William Kelly, ed. *The Literature of Ancient Egypt: An Anthology of Stories, Instructions, Stelae, Autobiographies, and Poetry.* New Haven: Yale UP, 2003. Print.

Sproul, Barbara. *Primal Myths: Creation Myths around the World.* New York: HarperCollins, 1991. Print.

Stephens, James. *Irish Fairy Tales.* New York: Macmillan, 1920. Print.

Stookey, Lorena Laura. *Thematic Guide to World Mythology.* Westport: Greenwood, 2004. Print.

Sturluson, Snorri. *The Prose Edda: Tales from North Mythology.* Trans. Jean I. Young. Berkeley: U of California P, 2012. Print.

Sullivan, Bruce M. *Historical Dictionary of Hinduism.* London: Scarecrow, 1997. Print.

Tatar, Maria, ed. *The Classic Fairy Tales: Texts, Criticism.* New York: Norton, 1999. Print.

Thompson, William Irwin. *The Time Falling Bodies Take to Light: Mythology, Sexuality, and the Origins of Culture.* New York: St. Martin's Griffin, 1996. Print.

Van Buitenen, J. A. B., trans. and ed. *The Mahābhārata.* Vol. 2. Chicago: U of Chicago P, 1975. Print.

Warner, Marina. *From the Beast to the Blonde: On Fairy Tales and Their Tellers.* London: Vintage, 1994. Print.

Warner, Marina, et al. *Cinema and the Realms of Enchantment: Lectures, Seminars and Essays by Marina Warner and Others.* Ed. Duncan Petrie. London: British Film Inst., 1993. Print.

Werner, Alice. *Myths and Legends of the Bantu.* 1933. Charleston: BiblioBazaar, 2007. Print.

Werner, Edward T. C. *Myths and Legends of China.* 1922. New York: Dover, 1994. Print.

White, Richard, ed. *King Arthur in Legend and History.* New York: Routledge, 1998. Print.

Witzel, E. J. Michael. *The Origins of the World's Mythologies.* New York: Oxford UP, 2013. Print.

Wilkins, W. J. *Hindu Mythology: Vedic and Purānic.* London: Curzon, 1973. Print.

Wood, Michael. *In Search of Myths and Heroes: Exploring Four Epic Legends of the World.* Berkeley: U of California P, 2007. Print.

Wratislaw, Albert Henry, trans. *Sixty Folk-Tales from Exclusively Slavonic Sources.* London, 1889. Print.

Yang, Lihui, and Deming An. *Handbook of Chinese Mythology.* New York: Oxford UP, 2008. Print.

Zajko, Vanda, and Miriam Leonard, eds. *Laughing with Medusa: Classical Myth and Feminist Thought.* Oxford: Oxford UP, 2006. Print.

Zipes, Jack. *Breaking the Magic Spell: Radical Theories of Folk and Fairy Tales.* London: Heinemann, 1979. Print.

---. *The Great Fairy Tale Tradition: From Straparola and Basile to the Brothers Grimm.* New York: Norton, 2001. Print.

INDEXES

COUNTRY AND CULTURE INDEX

CHRONOLOGICAL INDEX

INDEX